THE SONNET IN ENGLAND AND AMERICA

THE SONNET IN ENGLAND AND AMERICA

A Bibliography of Criticism

Compiled by Herbert S. Donow

GREENWOOD PRESS
WESTPORT, CONNECTICUT • LONDON, ENGLAND

Library of Congress Cataloging in Publication Data

Donow, Herbert S.
The sonnet in England and America.

Bibliography: p.
Includes index.
1. Sonnets, English—History and criticism—Bibliography. 2. Sonnets, American—History and criticism—Bibliography. 3. Sonnet—Bibliography. I. Title.
Z2014.S6D66 [PR509.S7] 821'.042'09 82-929
ISBN 0-313-21336-4 (lib. bdg.) AACR2

Library of Congress Catalog Card Number: 82-929
ISBN: 0-313-21336-4

First published in 1982

Greenwood Press
A division of Congressional Information Service, Inc.
88 Post Road West, Westport, Connecticut 06881

Printed in the United States of America

10 9 8 7 6 5 4 3 2 1

To Carolyn

CONTENTS

PREFACE

During the four years that I have worked on this bibliography, the thought has occasionally crossed my mind that a bibliography of a literary genre is a relative rarity. If the reason for this is that most genres tend to be defined too broadly or too narrowly, the sonnet, like the last of Goldilocks's ursine porridge bowls, seems to be "just right." A dozen years ago, I noted in my Preface to *A Concordance to the Sonnet Sequences of Daniel, Drayton, Shakespeare, Sidney, and Spenser* that there exists among sonnets a "degree of homogeneity" sufficient to allow treating them as a group. I was speaking then of those Elizabethan sonnets written within a few years of each other. Although the seventeenth century saw the sonnet turned to new subjects in the hands of Donne, Herbert, Milton, and others, the form still retained a degree of homogeneity and conventionality. As a result, students of Renaissance poetry have been inclined to treat the sonnet as something apart.

Perhaps because traditionally the sonnet has been such a definable form and subject to more rigorous rules than any other kind of poetry, it is not uncommon to see critics associating one poet's sonnets with those of others, be they contemporary or otherwise. The result is a body of secondary literature that, like its subject, can be easily identified. I have no idea how many of the forty-two hundred titles that appear in this book contain some form of the word "sonnet," but the number is substantial. Also substantial are the numbers of those genre studies that seek to show some continuity in the use of the form, even to the present day. Although one might be struck by how far the sonnet has come from Shakespeare's time to Hopkins's, it is fitting that the first item to appear in the Hopkins section is an article that examines Hopkins's interest in Shakespeare's use of the sonnet form.

One ought not be surprised, however, to observe that the modern sonnet has changed a great deal from its Elizabethan ancestor. As it has changed, it has lost certain of its distinctive qualities. Sonnets still have fourteen lines, to be sure. Exceptions to that rule are probably no more plentiful in the nineteenth century (*Modern Love*, for instance), than in the seventeenth century, where we find Herbert and Milton using extra lines. What has changed materially in the sonnet is no more or less than what has happened to poetry in general. Traditional rhyme schemes are less evident; regular form has been replaced by variations, sometimes radical; form no longer seems to dictate content; and convention, where it still exists, is a pale shadow of itself. If we can identify an important moment in the history of the sonnet when this began to take place, it might have been when Milton commenced to write his two dozen sonnets. One is forced to wonder if his startling innovations, the unconventional subject matter of his poems, did not have something to do with the century-long slumber that the genre experienced following him. The whys and wherefores of all this are amply reported, so I will not repeat the story. However, I allude to this bit of literary history mainly to explain something about this bibliography.

With the passage of time, the sonnet, in losing some of its distinctive qualities, has gradually ceased to attract critics as a special topic. While my chapter on the eighteenth and nineteenth centuries have an abundance of titles that might belie this observation, a Keats scholar, for one, will undoubtedly notice some well-known books on Keats's poetry missing from the list—books that contain references to "Chapman's Homer," "Bright Star," and "On Seeing the Elgin Marbles." It would hardly do, however, in a specialized bibliography on the sonnet to include a work on poetry merely because it mentions poems that happen to be sonnets. Making a distinction between that kind of work, which I try not to include, and a work that has something to say about a poem and its "sonnetness" became very difficult as I moved into the modern epoch. What I found particularly in Hopkins and the twentieth-century poets was that much of the secondary literature contributed only marginally to the special aspects of our topic. Although there are some excellent essays on the sonnets of modern poets—Auden, Cummings, and Frost, for example—the task of winnowing out the wheat seemed to be greater than I cared to undertake. For this reason, I chose to retire from the field at the end of the Victorian period.

The modern poet is still writing sonnets, and critics are still writing about them, but we may be witnessing, in its modern incarnation, the assimilation of the sonnet. The laws against miscegenation have been rescinded, and the descendents of the patriarchal, Petrarchan sonnet may cease to be differentiable from their poetic cousins.

SCOPE

When one utters the word, "sonnet," there is a deceptive simplicity to it. Who would have suspected, when Sir Thomas Wyatt began to dabble with this charming Petrarchan lyric, that hundreds of thousands of them would, in the next four centuries, be offered as adornments to our tongue, or that within these fourteen lines we would find over fifty thousand possible rhyme schemes? In the last one hundred and fifty years, literally thousands of students of English poetry have published books, articles, notes, reviews, and even sonnets about the sonnet in dozens of languages. When several thousand people find that they have something to say about a subject, no matter how simple that subject may have seemed at the outset, simplicity is out the window.

Just as the gardeners in King Richard II's employ were bade "like an executioner" to "cut off the heads of too fast growing sprays," I have had to prune my subject here and there to create the illusion of a subject under control. While the sonnet is a brief poem, it is certainly not a brief subject. It is firmly engrafted, to force my horticultural conceit one notch further, to the lyric and to the literatures of other lands. Furthermore, the personal nature of the genre has given rise to a cottage industry among critics: discovering the poet in the poem. Works preoccupied wth biographical detail comprise a sizable proportion of the secondary literature which appears in this bibliography. And since works on the continental sonnet and lyric traditions abound, as do biographies of our major poets, I have "lopped off" almost all items about foreign literatures, poetic conventions, philosophical origins, and biographies unless they included discussion of the sonnet in England and America.

This book is essentially a bibliography of secondary materials, published prior to mid-1981, on the subject of the sonnet and the sonneteer. Covered in the text are poets of the British Isles and North America who flourished from 1530, when Wyatt introduced the sonnet to the English-speaking world, to the end of the nineteenth century. I cite anthologies of sonnets, since virtually all of these anthologies have introductions that can be considered part of the secondary literature. Even without these introductions, sonnet anthologies have an intrinsic value to the student of the sonnet that warrants their inclusion. I have selectively listed editions of sonnets or collected works of individual poets where these texts contained valuable secondary material. In a few instances, editions of poets' works appear that do not technically meet this test. Sir Robert Ayton, Richard Barnfield, E. C., George Chapman, Alexander Craig, Francis Davison, or William Fowler (several of those whom I treat in this exceptional manner) would not otherwise appear in the Contents if their *Works* were not cited. Many of these poets, particularly the Scots, made important enough contributions to the sonnet to deserve enrollment in my pantheon.

There are one or two other instances where I permitted myself to act with an unbridled lack of discipline. In one instance, though it has nothing to say about the English sonnet, I include an article on "The *Enueg*" (No. 211) because it provides important background to this little known convention and complements two related articles that appear elsewhere. Or then we have the *Index of English Literary Manuscripts* (No. 34), from which one can acquire information about sonnet manuscripts, and George Bernard Shaw's one-act play, "The Dark Lady of the Sonnets," (No. 2934), which yields nothing useful save entertainment. On the whole, however, I have tried to act with restraint.

Although this is not a select bibliography, to call it comprehensive is like speaking of a "large" size box of laundry detergent. Large is smaller than family size, and they both are dwarfed by the economy size. I have not attempted, by any means, to include everything in my "comprehensive" bibliography. Since every literary history of England and America, every school text and anthology, every handbook of literary terms, and indeed every dictionary of the English language, says something about the sonnet, I exercised a degree of selectivity when it came to works like these. Likewise, book reviews of works that qualified for inclusion were included only if the reviews themselves had something to say about the sonnet.

Whatever my editorial difficulties might have been, they would hardly be worth mentioning were it not for Shakespeare. That is a name that must strike terror into the heart of any bibliographer, for once embarked into the jungle of Shakespeareana, the explorer finds himself on a wearying trek. Not only is the literature vast, but it grows apace. In 1901 W. J. Rolfe began an article by writing, "Of books on Shakespeare's Sonnets there is no end." The eight decades that have elapsed since Rolfe made that understated declaration have only made those words seem more like absolute truth than any other nine words penned by mortal man. If every book, article, review, and privy wall that contained some reference to Shakespeare's sonnets were collected and sent by space ship into the nearest black hole, before the rocket's red glare faded from the eastern sky, fifty times as much will have found its way into print.

Managing such a volume of criticism has been a chastening experience. Of the English, French, and German literature, I believe that I have accumulated most of what is extant. The Italian, East European, Scandinavian, and Japanese materials undoubtedly have gaps. The obvious problem is that if an article is published in a foreign journal or newspaper that is unavailable in American university libraries or in the Library of Congress, it will not be cited. There are probably close to two hundred items, almost all from eastern Europe or Japan for which I have incomplete or unverifiable citations. I felt I could not include these in the bibliography. I mention this not so much by way of apology but simply to alert the user that more has been written in Bulgarian, Ukrainian, Georgian, and Japanese, for example, than I have been able to record on these pages.

Although it has been my fervent desire to examine all titles herein contained, that goal has proved, in a few instances, elusive. In only two or three cases have I seen American dissertations; I have, however, read the abstracts when they were published. Other works that I have not been able to see are marked by an asterisk. In most cases I have been able to find at least two citations for these works, so their accuracy is probable. However, I have grown rather skeptical of the work of my fellow bibliographers. It is not my intention to detract from their labors but to make clear that a reliable bibliographer should be very chary about taking his material secondhand. A single illustration should suffice to make my point.

In the *Shakespeare Quarterly* Bibliography for 1974 a citation was given for an article by Rudolf Stamm that appeared in *Neue Zurcher Zeitung* (February 19). No page was given and I had no success, after two years of trying, in obtaining that number. However, before I included the item, with an asterisk, I set about to verify the information that I had and, perhaps, to get some page numbers. In short order I located another reference to the article in the Bibliography of the Modern Humanities Research Association. The page number given for the article was sixty-seven. My pleasure was shortlived when I saw that the MHRA gave the date as October 20, 1974. What now? I hastened to the *Zeitung Index* and once again found the Stamm article. Page sixty-seven it was, but here I found that it had been published on October 19. Three bibliographies—three dates. Dare I try a fourth? No thanks. It was obvious that my ingenuity was being tested. Since two out of three said October, and two out of three said the nineteenth of the month (albeit not the same month), and two out of three agreed on page sixty-seven, and since I trust the Germans in matters such as this, my citation appears as October 19, 1974, p. 67. To conclude, I make no claims for the accuracy of asterisked items beyond offering the assurance that I exercised some care in attempting to verify the data.

ORGANIZATION

The first of the book's four chapters is devoted to general works, both anthologies and critical works not associated with a specific period or poet. The second chapter covers the sonnet in the Renaissance, from Wyatt to Milton, exclusive of Shakespeare, while the third chapter is devoted to Shakespeare. The final chapter, on eighteenth- and nineteenth-century British and American poetry, might conceivably have been broken down into three chapters. However, the eighteenth-century material comprises about two dozen items, half of those on Gray's "Sonnet on the Death of Richard West." While there would be a bit more meat in an American chapter, I could see no useful purpose in separating the British and American.

Each chapter, except that on Shakespeare, begins with sections on Anthologies and General Criticism followed by units on the individual poets, alphabetically arranged. The entries within each unit are alphabetically arranged by the first-mentioned author of the item.

There are some users who may object to this mode of organization, preferring entries arranged by date or subject. As a user myself, I can sympathize. There are many occasions when we might wish that reference works had formats more suitable to our needs. If a scholar were interested in the offerings of a particular publishing house, he would be delighted to find entries arranged by publisher. If this bibliography were part of a computerized information system, the user could query the system for keywords, dates or places of publication, or names of authors or editors. He could obtain readouts of all articles that appeared about Shakespeare's Sonnets in *The Athenaeum* from 1880 to 1900, or all those titles that contained a certain keyword. While this sort of information system is beginning to be available in our profession, for all practical purposes we scholars of literature must continue our Sisyphean struggles for perhaps another generation or two. But that is what makes us so bright and interesting: on our respective ways to finding the answers to our questions, we gather up vast quantities of irrelevant but enriching information. Automated information systems and interstate highways are marvelous ways of getting places fast, but at what cost?

Ultimately the organization of the entries makes little difference. Except for Shakespeare, the longest sections (those on Sidney, Milton, and Hopkins) would take the user scarcely an hour to peruse thoroughly—hardly a prohibitive exertion for a diligent scholar. Shakespeare, of course, is a different matter, and on that I shall have more to say in my discussion of the index.

While the authors of the entries are listed alphabetically, items are arranged chronologically where an author has multiple entries within a unit. Though it is usual practice not to repeat printing an author's name in such cases, it is often the case that an author's name appears differently from publication to publication. In an effort to provide the reader with exact information, I chose not to follow this convention. The one exception is where the author of the work is the poet—in the case of editions. Editions are also treated differently, in that they are arranged alphabetically by editor.

Joint authorship is treated in one of two ways. If a work is truly the result of joint authorship, the item will appear following the last entry for the first-named author. However, most of the jointly authored items are, in reality, two or more notes or letters, independently written, which are printed together on the pages of a periodical. Such items are placed chronologically in the list of entries for the first-named author.

There are certain occasions where it proves difficult to distinguish between a critical work that contains some or all of a poet's sonnets and an edition that contains an abundance of scholarly apparatus. Where the *raison d'etre* of the volume appears to be to provide a text of the poems, I treat it as an edition; where, as in Alfred Dodd's *The Personal Poems of Francis Bacon . . . Arranged in Chronological Order*, the principal rationale is to argue a thesis, the book is treated as a critical work.

Brief annotations accompany most of the items. Where a title is self-explanatory, such as "Calendar Symbolism in the 'Amoretti'," I provide no note on the contents. Likewise, where the work is a general survey, a brief note can do little more than state the obvious, which I try to avoid. My notes employ the orthographic practices of the text being described. Thus if the work cited spells Sidney's hero "Astrophel," my practice is to follow that spelling. In the next note his name may appear as "Astophil." While one might find some inconsistencies in my work, that particular one has some logic.

At the end of some entries, one may find a number:

Russell, Matthew, S. J. *Sonnets on the Sonnet: An Anthology.* London: Longmans, Green, 1898.

Each sonnet in the anthology has something to say about the sonnet. Following the text is an Afterword on "Sonnet Principles."
66

This is a cross-reference number, directing the reader to the item bearing that number. Where items are closely related, as in the case of notes or letters in response to an earlier publication, or in some other way intimately connected, I use the cross-referencing system. Cross-referencing is not used merely where items treat the same subject.

Reviews are treated as separate publications and are not listed in the same entry with the book about which they comment. Since my interest is to bring to your attention all publications commenting on the sonnet, a review deserves the same status as a note or article. Information given in the review is sufficient to direct the reader to the book being reviewed. Furthermore, by consulting the index under the name of the book's author, one may find all included reviews of that book. I do not use the cross-referencing system to direct the reader from review to book to other reviews. The Contributor Index provides that service.

INDEXES

Indexing consists of four parts (or five if you count the cross-referencing system). The Contents is an index to the work about each poet or general area. Following each section title (that is, Anthologies, General Criticism, or poet's name) are the inclusive citation numbers for the section and the number of the page on which the section begins. For example:

NAME	CITATION NUMBERS	PAGE NUMBER
John Donne	423-557	47

The citation numbers run continuously throughout the book.

The Contributor index lists alphabetically all the authors, editors, and translators, with citation numbers following their names. The system is similar to that used by the MLA Bibliography. In cases where scholars wrote under more than one name (for example, women who have used both their maiden and married names), the index will contain both names, and each index entry will refer the user to all items by that individual.

Up to now, everything about the indexes is quite straightforward. The Poet and Subject indexes, however, must be used warily. Although they promise shortcuts through the forest, neither index is thorough. Where an item is principally about one poet but discusses another, the Poet Index will direct you to the item. Item 654, for example, an article by Richard Greene on Griffin's *Fidessa*, also touches on Shakespeare. This index will identify all items about Shakespeare, including 654, that do not appear in the Shakespeare chapter. The caveat here is that this index is highly selective. For one thing, I rarely tried to index items listed in the sections entitled "General Criticism." Books and articles in these sections are presumed to be about many sonneteers and an attempt to index them would have been redundant. Indeed, any book or essay, broad in scope and regardless of where it may be listed, will have far fewer index references than its contents might justify.

It is likewise true of the Subject Index that the larger and richer the item being referenced, the less likely will the index do justice to its contents. Ironically, the shorter and more specialized the note or article, the more attention it gets from this index. If the item is on an easily characterized subject, like Rhetoric, Imagery, or the Identity of Mr. W. H., the index is more useful than if the item is an article about the ebb and flow of Spenser's emotions in the *Amoretti*. Were it not for the great number of citations in the Shakespeare chapter, I would have been tempted to omit a subject index. However, given the number of hours needed to work through Chapter 3, the user is bound to welcome any small assistance. This index is strongest in its references to explicative items on individual poems or on certain easily defined topics. A brief perusal of the index itself should reveal its virtues and defects making further comment here unnecessary.

In most instances, the Subject Index contains few references to poets whose sections are relatively brief. Where a poet does appear in the Subject Index, his entry begins with a section on his relations with other poets or persons (for example, Shakespeare and Apollinaire or Wordsworth and Daniel). Following this is a section on translation, another on special topics, and finally the poet's works.

In the Subject Index the names are frequently abbreviated (and in a few cases, truncated) to confine them to thirty-three characters. Some subjects are linked to a poet's name (for example, Shake.—Punctuation). Other subjects are not so linked (for example, Psychoanalysis). However, in the case of the latter subject, users familiar with the citation numbers for each of the four chapters can immediately isolate those that relate to Shakespeare or to the poets of one of the other chapters.

There may be two or three places to look in the indexes to find all references to a particular subject. For example, William Herbert (Lord Pembroke) is mentioned in the following references: Mr. W. H.—Herbert; Shake. and Herbert; and Shake.—Friend (Herbert). Each of these subject heads suggests a different emphasis. The reader will note that I make a distinction in the index between those items that identify some other person as the author of Shakespeare's works and those that merely suggest some other poet for certain of the sonnets. The former items are listed under the heading, Anti-Strat. (Anti-Stratfordian material). The latter focus on far narrower concerns.

Those books and articles that treat the relationship between Shakespeare's plays and sonnets are listed under his play titles. These titles are not placed under Shakespeare but appear scattered throughout the entire Subject Index. Certain other common Shakespearean topics, such as Mr. W. H., the Rival Poet, and the Dark Lady, are likewise not indexed under Shakespeare.

ABBREVIATIONS

I have always grown testy with bibliographies that forced me to turn from section to section to obtain all the infomation related to a single citation. I have, therefore, included complete information with each citation, even though it results in repetitions of certain titles throughout the book. I have also chosen to use virtually no abbreviations for periodicals. The only exceptions are *TLS* for *Times Literary Supplement* and *DA* and *DAI* for *Dissertations Abstracts* and *Dissertation Abstracts International*, respectively. There are a few instances where the official name of the journal is an abbreviation, as in *PMLA* or *ELH*. In those cases, I follow accepted practice and use the initials. *Modern Language Notes*, in 1962, changed its format and also its name. Therefore, I use both the new name, *MLN*, and the former name, as appropriate. Aside from saving the reader from the inconvenience of frequent reference to a table of abbreviations, this practice enhances the readability of the text. Abbreviations tend to make bibliographical entries very dense and difficult to read over sustained periods, particularly for those of us whose eyes have grown weak toiling in dimly-lit library stacks.

MANUSCRIPT PREPARATION

Material for this bibliography, as it was gathered, was stored on disk and accessed by computer. The material is now permanently stored and is periodically edited as new material comes in. The disk files were formatted and typed out under SCRIPT, a word-processing language. This procedure has made editing the text considerably easier and more consistent. However, there are some peculiarities that have crept into the finished manuscript. Although I have been able to override some of the foolishness of my electronic coauthor, you will note, here and there, ellipses that are divided between two lines, or perhaps a dash that is hyphenated (leaving one word at the end of a line with two hyphens, and another at the beginning of the next preceded by a single hyphen). Some words, foreign ones in particular, may be hyphenated incorrectly. While I think I have caught most of these irregularities, undoubtedly a few have escaped me.

The odd spacing that occurs occasionally in the index is attributable to the right justification command in SCRIPT. Had I suppressed right justification, the spacing would have been normal, with a ragged right margin in each column. However, right justification achieves two desirable results: leaving more white space in an index and thus relieving some of the tedium of reading it, and printing numbers in large entries in columns, another feature that contributes to readability.

One limitation that I have not been able to overcome is the handling of diacritical marks. Our terminals are not designed to produce most diacriticals. While I could have contrived to produce some (backspacing and striking quotation marks above a vowel for the umlaut, for example), such contrivances looked sloppy. Had I opted to use ersatz diacritical marks, there was still no way that I could have produced many of them. I asked a German friend what he thought about leaving off the umlauts and others, and he replied: "To someone who knows German and recognizes German names, the absence of the umlaut will create no problem; to someone who does not know German, all the umlauts in the world won't make his way any easier." Hence my typescript was prepared with no diacritical marks.

ACKNOWLEDGMENTS

I want to express my gratitude to the Office of Research Development and Adminstration and the Graduate School of Southern Illinois University at Carbondale for a budget that allowed me to employ several research assistants and to travel to other libraries. Thanks are also due to the Department of English, which funded one of my trips to the Library of Congress.

It would be difficult to measure the debt that I owe to members of the Morris Library staff, who, by virtue of their knowledge and helpfulness, transformed a facility with a good collection, into a first-rate research library. I wish particularly to acknowledge Alan Cohn, Humanities Librarian and himself a bibliographer of Joyce and Dickens, who kept a keen eye out for new materials coming into the library and who helped in innumerable other ways. Kathleen Eads and Angela Ruben obtained countless books for me through interlibrary loan for which I am most grateful.

Although I am an old hand around computers, I needed a great deal of help and instruction in learning and using SCRIPT. Two of my research assistants, Dennis Neumayer and Thomas Pasch, were invaluable in getting that part of my undertaking started. Members of the Academic Computing staff, particularly Al Allen and Dan Seaman, have given freely of their time when I have needed it. The Computer Science Department generously allowed me to use their facilities in producing this manuscript, for which I am indebted.

For the profitable weeks that I have spent in Urbana, at the University of Illinois Library, and in Washington, at the Library of Congress and the Folger Shakespeare Library, I wish to thank those who made that possible.

When one labors on a project with the aid of others, the product sometimes takes on a life of its own. Sometimes I discovered things in my text for which I could offer no explanation. One day as I was reading through my Sidney material, I came across an interesting item. I found in *Sir Philip Sidney: A Study of His Life and Works*, that the author, A. C. Hamilton, had a chapter in which he discussed "Sidney's 'Undetected Vacation'." I was fascinated. Had Hamilton turned up some information that proved that Sidney had spent a week with Penelope Devereux in some secluded corner of England? As it turned out, the answer proved to be far less sensational. One of my assistants, in typing my cards into the computer had misread what was, to her, an unfamiliar phrase: "Sidney's 'Unelected Vocation'." Not unreasonably she sent Sidney on an illicit retreat. Now that this book is done, I think I will join him.

THE SONNET IN ENGLAND AND AMERICA

1
THE SONNET: A GENERAL OVERVIEW

Anthologies

1. Barnes, R.G. Episodes in Five Poetic Traditions: The Sonnet, The Pastoral Elegy, The Ballad, The Ode, Masks and Voices. Scranton, Pa.: Chandler-Intext, 1972.

   Sonnet selections are from poets from the sixteenth to the twentieth centuries.

2. Baym, Max I. Let These Symbols Speak: A Book of Sonnets With an Essay on the Sonnet. St. Paul, Minn.: North Central Publishing Co., 1974.

   This collection of 50 sonnets is introduced by an essay on "The Psychodynamics of the Sonnet," in which Baym explores the reasons that psychoanalysts find the sonnet so interesting.

3. Bender, R.M., and Charles L. Squier. The Sonnet: A Comprehensive Anthology of British and American Sonnets from the Renaissance to the Present. New York: Washington Square Press, 1965.

4. Busch, Karl Theodor. Sonette Der Volker: Siebenhundert Sonette aus sieben Jahrhunderten. Heidelberg: Drei Brucken Verlag, 1954.

   Includes translations from about 80 English and American poets.

5. Caine, T. Hall. Sonnets of Three Centuries. London: Elliot Stock, 1882.

6. Carpenter, Frederic Ives. English Lyric Poetry 1500-1700. London: Blackie and Son, 1897. rpt. Freeport, N.Y.: Books for Libraries Press, 1969.

7. Clarence, Luce. Sonnets d'Angleterre de Thomas Wyatt (1503-1542) a Francis Thompson (1859-1907): Traduction avec texte original en regard. Paris: C. Balland, 1931.

8. Dennis, John. English Sonnets. London: Henry S. King, 1873.

9. Dyce, Alexander. Specimens of English Sonnets. London: William Pickering, 1833.

10. Hamer, Enid Hope. The English Sonnet: An Anthology. London: Methuen, 1936. rpt. Folcroft, Pa.: Folcroft Press, 1969.

This anthology of 150 sonnets covers material from Wyatt to the early 20th-century and includes an introduction.

11. Herrick, S.B. A Century of Sonnets. New York: R.H. Russell, 1902.

A selection of sonnets from America, England and Europe (in translation) with an introduction.

12. Housman, Robert Fletcher. A Collection of English Sonnets. London: Simpkin, Marshall, 1835. 1841.

Includes sonnets from Surrey (but not Wyatt) to the 1830's, with a Preface.

13. Hunt, Leigh, and Samuel Adams Lee. The Book of the Sonnet. 2 vol. London: Sampson, Low, Son and Marston; Boston: Roberts Brothers, 1867.

Begins with "An Essay on the Cultivation, History, and Varieties of the Species of Poem Called the Sonnet" by Hunt (pp. 3-91) followed by another essay by Lee on "American Sonnets and Sonneteers" (pp. 95-131). Contents include selections of American and English sonnets up to the date of publication.

14. Lockwood, Laura Emma. Sonnets Selected from English and American Authors. Boston: Houghton Mifflin, 1916.

The anthology contains selections from Wyatt to poets of the early 20th century, with a brief introduction on the form.

15. Lofft, Capel. Laura, or An Anthology of Sonnets and Elegiac Quatuorzains (on the Petrarcan Model). 5 vol. London: B. and R. Crosby, 1814.

The first volume contains a long introduction with samples of sonnets from different languages.

16. Lynd, Robert. The Silver Book of English Sonnets: A Selection of Less-known Sonnets. London: Pleiad, 1927.

Forty-five sonnets from most of the famous and some now obscure poets from Spenser to Rossetti.

17. Main, David M. A Treasury of English Sonnets. New York: R. Worthington, 1881.

    Extensive notes to these 463 sonnets.

18. Main, David M. Three Hundred English Sonnets. Edinburgh and London: William Blackwood, 1884.

    A selection drawn from Main's A Treasury of English Sonnets.

19. Michelagnoli, Alfredo. Il Sonetto nella letteratura inglese: con cento Sonetti dal Wyatt allo Swinburne. Padua: CEDAM, 1938.

20. Nichols, Bowyer. A Little Book of English Sonnets. London: Methuen, 1903.

21. Nicoll, Henry J. C Sonnets by C Authors. Edinburgh: MacNiven and Wallace, 1883.

22. Nye, Robert. A Book of Sonnets. New York: Oxford University Press, 1976.

    Contains 372 sonnets from Wyatt to the present.

23. Peterson, Houston. The Book of Sonnet Sequences. London and New York: Longmans, Green, 1929.

    Sonnets by 21 poets: Sidney, Shakespeare, Donne, Wordsworth, Keats, Elizabeth Barrett Browning, David Gray, Meredith, Longfellow, Hardy, Rossetti, Christina Rossetti, Blunt, etc.

24. Quiller-Couch, A.T. English Sonnets. London: Chapman and Hall, 1897. rpt. Freeport, N.Y.: Books for Libraries Press, 1968.

    A small anthology from Wyatt to Elizabeth Barrett Browning.

25. Robertson, William. The Golden Book of English Sonnets. Philadelphia: J.B. Lippincott; London: George C. Harrap, 1913.

26. Russell, Matthew, S.J. Sonnets on the Sonnet: An Anthology. London: Longmans, Green, 1898.

    Each sonnet in the anthology has something to say about the sonnet. Following the text is an Afterword on "Sonnet Principles." 66

27. *Taylor, Walt. English Sonnets. London: Longmans, Green, 1947.

28. *Turpin, Edna Henry Lee. English and American Sonnets. New York: Maynard, [c.1897].

29. Waddington, Samuel. English Sonnets by Poets of the Past. London: George Bell and Sons, 1882.

30. Waddington, Samuel. *The Sonnets of Europe: A Volume of Translations*. London: Walter Scott, 1886.

An anthology of sonnets from nine different countries in English translations.

31. Woodford, A. Montagu. *The Book of Sonnets*. London: Saunders and Otley, 1841.

From Wyatt to Wordsworth, Southey, Brydges, including sections on continental poets as well.

General Criticism

32. Alden, Raymond Macdonald. *English Verse: Specimens Illustrating Its Principles and History*. New York: Henry Holt, 1903. rpt. New York: AMS Press, 1970.

A chapter is devoted to "The Sonnet" (pp. 267-97).

33. Baum, Paull Franklin. *The Principles of English Versification*. Cambridge, Mass.: Harvard University Press, 1929.

Discusses the Sonnet--both the Italian and the English forms (pp. 118-31).

34. Beal, Peter. *Index of English Literary Manuscripts*. London: Mansell; New York: R.R. Bowker, 1980.

The first volume (in two parts) covers manuscripts from 1450 to 1625: Part I includes Andrewes to Donne and Part II Douglas to Wyatt. (Four other volumes, bringing coverage to 1900, are proposed.) Many of the writers included are sonneteers and the text includes information about sonnet manuscripts.

35. Belden, H.M. "On the Form of the Sonnet." *Modern Language Notes*, 25 (1910), 231.

In response to Weeks's article on rhyme patterns in English sonnets.
115

36. Bennett, Josephine Waters. Review of Robert M. Bender and Charles L. Squier, *The Sonnet: A Comprehensive Anthology of British and American Sonnets from the Renaissance to the Present*. *Shakespeare Quarterly*, 19 (1968), 177-78.

37. Blench, J.W. Review of John Fuller, *The Sonnet*. *Durham University Journal*, 66 (1974), 221-22.

38. Brewer, Wilmon. *Sonnets and Sestinas*. Boston: Cornhill Publishing Co., 1937.

The book is divided into two parts: the first is a collection of Brewer's sonnets and sestinas that "illustrate almost every important form" and the second is "a comprehensive account of the sonnet" over its 700 year history.

39. Burgess, W.V. *One Hundred Sonnets Prefaced by an Essay on the Sonnet's History and Place in English Verse*. Manchester: Sherrat and Hughes, 1901.

The sonnets are all by Burgess, but the Preface covers the history of the genre.

40. Cecchini, Antonio. *Serafino Aquilano e la Lirica inglese del '500*. Aquila: Vecchioni, 1935.

Cecchini includes a discussion of the development of the sonnet in England from Wyatt to Keats (pp. 117-24) and chapters on the poetry of Wyatt and Surrey.

41. Closs, August. Review of Walter Monch, *Das Sonett: Gestalt und Geschichte*. *Deutsche Literaturzeitung*, 77 (1956), 421-22.

42. Corson, Hiram. *A Primer of English Verse: Chiefly in Its Aesthetic and Organic Character*. Boston: Ginn, 1893.

Devotes a long chapter to the sonnet (pp. 143-85).

43. Crosland, Thomas W.H. *The English Sonnet*. London: Martin Secker, 1917. rpt. Norwood, Pa.: Norwood Editions, 1975.

A lengthy discussion of the form and its major practitioners: Wyatt, Surrey, the Elizabethans, Milton and Wordsworth.

44. Cruttwell, Patrick. *The English Sonnet*. Writers and Their Work, 191. London: Longmans, Green, 1966.

45. Cygan, Jan. "English Sonnet Structure." *Germanica Wratislaviensia* (Wroclaw), 14 (1971), 103-18.

Examines the development of the form from Wyatt to the Rossettis.

46. [Davies, William]. "The Sonnet." *Quarterly Review*, 134 (1873), 186-204.

A review article based principally on *The Book of the Sonnet*, ed. by Leigh Hunt and S. Adams Lee, covering Wyatt to Wordsworth and including an observation about a verbal correspondence between the song in *The Merchant of Venice* ("Tell me where is fancy bred") and a sonnet by Jacopo da Lentino ("Amore e un desio . . .").
653

47. [Dennis, John.] "The English Sonnet." *Cornhill Magazine*, 25 (May, 1872), 581-98.

A survey of the major sonneteers from Wyatt to Wordsworth, whom the writer considers to be "the greatest of all English sonnet-writers."

48. Dennis, John. "The English Sonnet." Studies in English Literature. London: Edward Stanford, 1876; rev. ed. 1883, pp. 392-444.

A survey of the sonnet from Wyatt and Surrey to Elizabeth Barrett Browning, including some of the latter's lesser known contemporaries. (Pagination refers to 1883 edition.)

49. Deshler, Charles D. Afternoons With the Poets. New York: Harper, 1879.

Although not exclusively about the sonnet, most of this book focuses on the sonnets from Wyatt through the 19th-century, including those by minor poets not usually discussed in critical essays.

50. Dowsing, William. Sonnets, Personal and Pastoral. London: Kegan Paul, Trench, Trubner, 1909.

This collection of Dowsing sonnets is accompanied by a long essay entitled "The Construction of the Sonnet."

51. Editors of The Early Modern English Dictionary. "Sonnet." PMLA, 47 (1932), 893-97.

52. *Ehrentreich, Alfred. "Das 'Englische' Sonett und die Deutsche Lyrik." Neuphilologische Zeitschrift (Hannover), 2 (1950), 38-44.
107

53. Forseth, Roger. "Sonnet and Couplet: A Note on the Elegance of English Verse." Wisconsin Studies in Literature, No. 3 (1966), 67-73.

54. Frankenberg, Lloyd. Invitation to Poetry. New York: Doubleday, 1950.

Brief comments on over 200 poems including Matthew Arnold's sonnet, "Shakespeare" (pp. 93-94), Shakespeare's Sonnet 18 (pp. 51-52), G.M. Hopkins's "To R.B." (pp. 65-66), John Clare's "Schoolboys in Winter" (p. 235); Henry Wadsworth Longfellow's "Chaucer" (pp. 83-85); William Wordsworth's "London, 1802" (pp. 91-92); John Milton's "On Shakespeare" (p. 92), etc.

55. Fuller, John. The Sonnet. The Critical Idiom Series, 26. London: Methuen, 1972.

A survey of the form in English including a chapter on "Variants and Curiosities."

56. Fussell, Paul, Jr. Poetic Meter and Poetic Form. New York: Random House, 1965.

Chapter 6, "Structural Principles: The Example of the Sonnet" (pp. 113-33), discusses sonnets from all periods.

57. Goller, Karl Heinz, ed. Die Englische Lyrik: Von der Renaissance bis zur Gegenwart. 2 vol. Dusseldorf: August Bagel, 1968.

A collection of explications and translations into German, including ones on sonnets by Wyatt, Surrey, Sidney, Shakespeare, Drayton, and Wordsworth in Volume 1 and Elizabeth Barrett Browning, D.G. Rossetti, and Hopkins in Volume 2.

58. Goodwin, K.L. Review of Robert Nye, The Faber Book of Sonnets. AUMLA, No. 47 (1977), 69.

59. Greene, Thomas M. Review of Jack D'Amico, Petrarch in England: An Anthology of Parallel Texts. Yearbook of English Studies, 11 (1981), 231-32.

60. Hall, William C. "The Sonnet." Manchester Quarterly, 48 (1929), 263-83.

A history of the sonnet, a discussion of its form and remarks about some of its chief exponents.

61. Hamer, Enid. The Metres of English Poetry. New York: Macmillan, 1930.

Chapter 9 (pp. 186-217) deals with "The Sonnets."

62. [Hasell, Elizabeth J.] "A Talk About Sonnets." Blackwood's Edinburgh Magazine, 128 (1880), 159-74.

Basil, Geoffrey and Henry share appreciations of the sonnets of Shakespeare, Milton and Wordsworth.

63. Heuer, Hermann. "Shakespeares Sonette." Shakespeare Jahrbuch, 91 (1955), 326-28.

Reviews of Walter Monch, Das Sonett, Gestalt und Geschichte, and William Shakespeare: Sonetti, ed. and tr. Alberto Rossi.

64. Highet, Gilbert. "Scorn Not the Sonnet." The Powers of Poetry. New York: Oxford University Press, 1960, pp. 190-96.

A brief appreciation of the form with primary attention to Shakespeare, Wordsworth and Keats.

65. Hornsby, Sam, and James R. Bennett. "The Sonnet: An Annotated Bibliography from 1940 to the Present." Style, 13 (1979), 162-77.

66. Jacobs, Elijah L. "The Sonnet on the Sonnet." South Atlantic Quarterly, 42 (1943), 282-88.

A survey of sonnets celebrating the sonnet as a verse-form, in which Jacobs mentions poems by Wordsworth, D.G. Rossetti, Richard Watson Gilder, Theodore Watts-Dunton, et al.
26

67. Johnson, Charles F. "The Sonnet." Forms of English Poetry. New York: American Book Co., 1904, pp. 107-45.

In this essay on the history of the form, Johnson discusses some of the representative figures from the 16th-century to Rossetti.

68. Jost, Francois. "Le Contexte europeen du sonnet." Zagadienia rodzajow literackich, 13, i (1970), 5-28.

One section is devoted to the Sonnet in England (pp. 18-20).

69. Kleinschmidt, Oswald. "Die Kunst des Sonettes: Regel und Rhythmus im Gedicht." Zeitschrift fur Deutschkunde, 53 (1939), 241-46.

70. Lentzner, K.A. Uber das sonett und seine gestaltung in der englischen dichtung bis Milton. Leipzig: Metzger und Wittig, 1886.

The third chapter, "Regeln fur den Inhalt des englischen Sonettes" (pp. 11-33) refers to Wordsworth, Arnold, Browning and other post-Miltonic poets.

71. Levy, Jiri. "On the Relations of Language and Stanza Pattern in the English Sonnet." Worte und Werte: Bruno Markwardt zum 60. Geburtstag. Ed. Gustav Erdmann and Alfons Eichstaedt. Berlin: Walter de Gruyter, 1961, pp. 214-31.

Levy speaks of "the complex relations into which a prosodic form enters if transferred into a foreign literature" (i.e. from Italian into English).

72. Long, Mason. Poetry and Its Forms. New York: G.P. Putnam's Sons, 1938.

Chapter 11 ("Sonnet"), in addition to a history of the form, gives a select list of English and American sonneteers with titles of some of their important sonnets (pp. 292-313).

73. Matthews, G.M. "Sex and the Sonnet." Essays in Criticism, 2 (1952), 119-37.

An attempt to discover the nature of the social "milieu in which the sonnet was born."
102

74. Monch, Walter. Das Sonett: Gestalt und Geschichte. Heidelberg: F.H. Kerle, 1955.

The text deals with the sonnet in France and England, covering particularly Spenser, Sidney and Shakespeare (pp. 135-39); later sections on the sonnet cover the English Romantic Period and D.G. Rossetti.

75. Moore, John. Review of Robert Nye, A Book of Sonnets. Seventeenth Century News, 35, i-ii (1977), 13-14.

76. Morton, David. The Sonnet Today--and Yesterday. New York and London: G.P. Putnam's Sons, 1926.

This essay on the sonnet discusses the changing fashions in the genre.

77. Mroczkowski, Przemyslaw. Review of Jerzy Strzetelski, The English Sonnet: Syntax and Style. Kwartalnik neofilologiczny, 17 (1970), 446-52.

In Polish.

78. Murray, Patrick. Literary Criticism: A Glossary of Major Terms. London: Longman, 1978.

Contains a chapter (pp. 147-55) on the sonnet.

79. Noble, James Ashcroft. The Sonnet in England and Other Essays. London: E. Mathews and John Lane, 1893. London: John Lane; Chicago: Way and Williams, 1896. First published in Contemporary Review, 38 (1880), 446-71.

80. Nocon, Peter. The English Sonnet: an Introduction to the Study of Poetry. Texts for English and American Studies, 5. Paderborn: Ferdinand Schoningh, 1979.

A collection of sonnets with notes and comments about the genre and about the particular poems, plus a Teachers' book.

81. Oliphant, E.H.C. "The Sonnet Form: A Determination of the Rules." Poetry Review, 21 (1930), 337-51.

82. Oliphant, E.H.C. "Sonnet Structure: An Analysis." Philological Quarterly, 11 (1932), 135-48.

83. Ordeman, D. Thomas. "How Many Rhyme Schemes has the Sonnet?" College English, 1 (1939), 171-73.

The sonnet, as we commonly recognize the form, may have over 50,000 possible rhyme schemes.

84. O[tis], J.F. "Something on Sonnets." Southern Literary Messenger, 4 (1838), 130-32.

An appreciation of the Sonnet, mentioning Wordsworth, Shakespeare, Milton, et al.

85. Palmer, Herbert. "The English Sonnet." Poetry Review, 48 (1957), 215-18; 49 (1958), 26-28, 84-87.

This three-part article concentrates on the form of the sonnet.

86. Raymond, George Lansing. _Rhythm and Harmony in Poetry and Music Together With Music as a Representative Art: Two Essays in Comparative Aesthetics_. New York: G.P. Putnam's Sons, 1895. 1909.

Some brief comments on the sonnet form (pp. 70-73) in a chapter in which he discusses "the rhythmic possibilities of different forms of stanzas."

87. Reed, Edward Bliss. _English Lyrical Poetry From Its Origins to the Present Time_. New Haven: Yale University Press, 1912.

Chapter 3, "The Tudor Lyric" (pp. 99-137) and Chapter 4, "The Elizabethan Lyric" (pp. 138-222) discuss the sonnet at great length. To a somewhat lesser extent, the sonnet is discussed in Chapter 5, "Jacobean and Caroline Lyric" (pp. 223-301), which includes discussion of Donne's _Holy Sonnets_, Chapter 7, "Lyric of the Transition" (on the 18th-century), and Chapter 8, "Nineteenth Century Lyric."

88. Rich, Morton David. "The Dynamics of Tonal Shift in The Sonnet." Ph.D. Dissertation, New York University, 1975. _DAI_, 36 (1975), 2179A.

This is a linguistic study comparing syntactic analysis with recorded reading of sonnets.

89. Rinaker, Clarissa. "Some Unconscious Factors in the Sonnet as a Poetic Form." _International Journal of Psycho-Analysis_, 12 (1931), 167-87.

Sonnets express those incest fantasies of the poet for his "first love." The Shakespearean form is more masculine than the Petrarchan form, suggesting more "the rival father than the desired mother." The poet's selection of this form to write about love is rooted in the unconscious.

90. Ruiz Gaitan, Alberto. "Algo acerca del soneto." _Abside_, 39 (1975), 215-23.

A brief survey of the sonnet's history in Europe and England.

91. [Russell, C.W.] "Critical History of the Sonnet." _Dublin Review_, 79 (1876), 400-30; 80 (1877), 141-80.

A review article covering Charles Tomlinson, _The Sonnet: Its Origin, Structure, and Place in Poetry_; _English Sonnets: A Selection_, ed. John Dennis; and a number of other English, French and German sonnet collections. Part I discusses the sonnet in Europe as well as England, from its inception; Part II deals with the sonnet in the 19th-century.

92. Ruthven, K.K. _The Conceit_. London: Methuen, 1969.

Contains, as part of Chapter 3, a discussion of the "Sonneteering Conceits" (pp. 18-31).

93. Salomon, L.B. The Devil Take Her! A Study of the Rebellious Lover in English Poetry. Philadelphia: University of Pennsylvania Press, 1931. rpt. New York: A.S. Barnes, 1961.

Frequent references to 16th-century sonnets throughout.

94. Schelling, Felix E. The English Lyric. Boston and New York: Houghton Mifflin, 1913.

Chapters on the Tudor, Stuart, Romantic, and Victorian lyric.

95. Schipper, Jakob. Englische Metrik in historischer und systematischer entwickelung dargestellt. 2 vol. in 3. Bonn: E. Strauss, 1881-88.

96. Schipper, Jakob. Grundriss der Englischen Metrik. Wiener Beitrage zur Englischen Philologie, 2. Wien und Leipzig: Wilhelm Braumuller, 1895.

97. Schipper, Jakob. A History of English Versification. Oxford: Clarendon Press, 1910. rpt. New York: AMS Press, 1971.

A translated, partially revised version of Grundriss der Englischen Metrik. Contains a chapter on "The Sonnet" (pp. 371-79).

98. Schirmer, Walter F. "Das Sonett in der Englischen Literatur." Anglia, 49 (1925), 1-31.

A survey from Tottel's Miscellany to the Rossettis.

99. Scott, Clive. "The Limits of the Sonnet: Towards a Proper Contemporary Approach." Revue de Litterature Comparee, 50 (1976), 237-50.

Considers whether the sonnet is a fixed form or one which is in constant state of evolution.

100. Scott, David H.T. Sonnet Theory and Practice in Nineteenth-century France: Sonnets on the Sonnet. Hull: University of Hull Publications, 1977.

Makes a brief distinction between the English sonnet and its Franco-Italian counterpart (pp. 12-13) and compares French to English writers (pp. 18-19).

101. Sharp, William. "The Sonnet, Its Characteristics and History." Studies and Appreciations. London: William Heinemann; New York: Duffield, 1912, pp. 1-70.

102. Siegel, Paul N. "Sex and the Sonnet." Essays in Criticism, 2 (1952), 465-68.

A response to G.M. Matthews.
73

103. Smith, Barbara Herrnstein. *Poetic Closure: A Study of How Poems End*. Chicago and London: University of Chicago Press, 1968.

Contains a section of a chapter, "Closure and Formal Conventions: The English Sonnet" (pp. 50-56).

104. Stageberg, Norman C. "The Aesthetic of the Petrarchan Sonnet." *Journal of Aesthetics and Art Criticism*, 7 (1948), 132-37.

In commenting on the sonnet form, Stageberg refers to Keats's "Sonnet on the Sonnet" and a sonnet by Spenser.

105. Stoddard, Richard Henry. "The Sonnet in English Poetry." *Scribner's Monthly*, 22 (1881), 905-21.

A survey from Wyatt to Elizabeth Barrett Browning.

106. Strzetelski, Jerzy. *The English Sonnet: Syntax and Style*. Zeszyty Naukowe, Uniwersytetu Jagiellonskiego, 213. Prace Jezykoznawcze, Zeszyt, 27. Krakow: Uniwersytetu Jagiellonskiego, 1970.

Applying modern linguistic and stylistic analysis, the author's study includes 278 14-line sonnets that were found in the *Oxford Book of English Verse*.

107. Taube, Otto v. "Noch einmal das 'Englische Sonett'." *Neuphilologische Zeitschrift* (Hannover), 2 (1950), 403-04.
52

108. Thompson, John. *The Founding of English Metre*. London: Routledge and Kegan Paul; New York: Columbia University Press, 1961.

Finds the metrical practice of Sir Philip Sidney's *Astrophel and Stella* to be the basis for English poetry for the next three centuries.

109. Timrod, Henry. "The Character and Scope of the Sonnet." *Essays of Henry Timrod*. Ed. Edd Winfield Parks. Athens: University of Georgia Press, 1942, pp. 61-68. First published in *Russell's Magazine*, 1 (May, 1857), 156-59.

Alluding to several of the general criticisms of the form, Timrod defends the sonnet because of the unity its briefness enforces on the expression.

110. Tomlinson, Charles. *The Sonnet: Its Origin, Structure, and Place in Poetry*. London: John Murray, 1874. rpt. Folcroft, Pa.: Folcroft Press, 1970.

Although the book is primarily about the development of the sonnet before it reached England, there are sections that deal with translation of Italian sonnets into English (Petrarch and Michelangelo) and that discuss most of the major English sonneteers.

111. Voisine, J. Review of Walter Monch, Das Sonett: Gestalt und Geschichte. Revue de Litterature Comparee, 34 (1960), 324-30.

112. Wassermann, F.M. Review of Walter Monch, Das Sonett: Gestalt und Geschichte and Karl Theodor Busch, Sonette der Volker: 700 Sonette aus sieben Jahrhunderten. Journal of English and Germanic Philology, 55 (1956), 318-21.

113. W[atts]-D[unton], T[heodore]. "Sonnet." Encyclopaedia Britannica, 11th ed. Cambridge: University Press, 1911, vol. 25, pp. 414-16.

114. Watts-Dunton, Theodore. "The Sonnet." Poetry and the Renascence of Wonder. London: Herbert Jenkins, 1916, pp. 171-88.

This essay originally appeared in the 1891 edition of Chambers Encyclopedia.

115. Weeks, L.T. "The Order of Rimes of the English Sonnet." Modern Language Notes, 25 (1910), 176-80.

Includes a table showing "all the octaves and sestets used by the entire body of English sonnet writers, together with all the various individual combinations of octave with sestet . . . ." 35

116. Wilder, Charlotte F. "Sonnet-Hunting." Methodist Review, 91 (1909), 372-85.

A survey of the major sonneteers--Shakespeare, Milton, Wordsworth, Elizabeth Barrett Browning, and Dante Gabriel Rossetti.

117. Winch, Gordon Clappison. "The Effects of Different Post-Reading Instructional Procedures on Comprehension Responses to Three Sonnets." Ph.D. Dissertation, Wisconsin, 1971. DAI, 32 (1972), 4584A.

118. Wood, Clement. The Craft of Poetry. New York: E.P. Dutton, 1929.

A brief reference to George Sterling's Sonnets to Craig. (p.144), with more general discussion of the sonnets (pp. 208-19.)

119. Y. "Sonnettomania." New Monthly Magazine, 1 (1821), 652-56.

A whimsical piece on the recent outburst of sonnet writing.

120. Z[illman], L[awrence] J. "Sonnet" and "Sonnet Cycle." Encyclopedia of Poetry and Poetics. Ed. Alex Preminger. Princeton, N.J.: Princeton University Press, 1965. Enl. ed., 1974, pp. 781-84.

121. "On the Sonnet." Christian Remembrancer, NS 2 (1841), 321-29, 401-13.

Discusses the Italian sonnet form and the degree to which various English poets have adhered to it. Comments on some early 19th-century poets as well as Shakespeare, Milton, *et al*.

122. Review of *The Book of the Sonnet*, ed. Leigh Hunt and S. Adams Lee. *Athenaeum*, February 16, 1867, p. 217.

One of the reviewer's cavils is that Lee, in his essay on American sonneteers, "errs amiably on the side of over-appreciation."

123. "The Sonnet in English Poetry." *Scribner's Monthly Magazine*, 22 (1881), 905-21.

Reviews the major poets from Wyatt to Elizabeth Barrett Browning.

124. "The Sonnet." *Academy*, 64 (1903), 180-81.

A superficial overview of the sonnet in English literature.

125. "A History of the Sonnet." *TLS*, September 2, 1955, p. 506.

Review of Walter Monch, *Das Sonett: Gestalt und Geschichte*.

126. Review of John Fuller, *The Sonnet*. *Modern Languages*, 54 (1973), 94-95.

127. "Sonnet Analyzed." *Literary Half-Yearly*, 22, i (1981), 137-38.

Review of John Fuller, *The Sonnet*.

2
THE SONNET IN THE RENAISSANCE

Anthologies

128. B.,B. A Garland of Elizabethan Sonnets. London: Leonard Parsons, 1923.

A selection of 64 sonnets.

129. Bender, Robert M. Five Courtier Poets of the English Renaissance. New York: Washington Square Press, 1967.

Includes sonnets by Wyatt, Surrey, Sidney, Greville, and Raleigh.

130. Black, Matthew W. Elizabethan and Seventeenth Century Lyrics. Philadelphia: J.B. Lippincott, 1938.

Contains a commentary and section on "The Sonneteers."

131. Bullett, Gerald. Silver Poets of the Sixteenth Century. London: J.P. Dent, 1947.

Includes sonnets by a number of the principal sonneteers.

132. Crow, Martha Foote. Elizabethan Sonnet Cycles. 4 vol. London: Kegan Paul, Trench, Trubner, 1896-98. rpt. New York: AMS Press, 1969.

Volume 1: "Phillis" by Thomas Lodge; "Licia" by Giles Fletcher. Volume 2: "Delia" by Samuel Daniel; "Diana" by Henry Constable. Volume 3: "Idea" by Michael Drayton; "Fidessa" by Bartholomew Griffin; "Chloris" by William Smith. Volume 4: "Caelica" by Fulke Greville.

133. D'Amico, Jack. Petrarch in England: An Anthology of Parallel Texts from Wyatt to Milton. Ravenna: Longo Editore, 1979.

Following an introduction in which he discusses the various English versions of Petrarch, D'Amico prints the text of the Petrarchan canzoniere and the English translations or imitations.

134. Evans, Maurice. Elizabethan Sonnets. London: J.M. Dent; Totowa, N.J.: Rowman and Littlefield, 1977

135. Grabes, Herbert. Elizabethan Sonnet Sequences. Tubingen: Max Niemeyer, 1970.

Contains Astrophel and Stella, Daniel's Delia, Drayton's Idea's Mirrour, Spenser's Amoretti.

136. Hiller, Geoffrey G. Poems of the Elizabethan Age: An Anthology. London: Methuen, 1977.

Contains a section of sonnets with 80 poems by 11 poets.

137. Lee, Sir Sidney. Elizabethan Sonnets. 2 vol. Westminster: Constable; New York: E.P. Dutton, 1904.

Long introduction; vol. 1: Sidney (Astrophel and Stella), Daniel (Delia), Watson (Tears of Fancy), Barnes (Parthenophil); Vol. 2: Lodge (Phillis), G. Fletcher (Licia), Constable (Diana), Percy (Coelia), Anon. (Zepheria), Drayton (Idea), Spenser (Amoretti), Griffin (Fidessa), Linche (Diella), Smith (Chloris) Tofte (Laura).

138. Lever, J.W. Sonnets of the English Renaissance. London: Athlone Press, 1974.

Contains an introduction with selections from the major poets.

139. Marshall, Murray Linwood. English Sonnets of Long Ago. Landover, Maryland: Dreamland Press, 1929.

Sonnets by Thomas Wyatt, Earl of Surrey and others.

140. McClure, Norman E. Sixteenth Century English Poetry. New York: Harper, 1954.

This anthology contains a chapter on the minor "Sonnet Sequences" (pp. 341-62) as well as selections of the sonnets of the major poets.

141. Muir, Kenneth. Elizabethan Lyrics: A Critical Anthology. London: George C. Harrap, 1952.

Parts of the introduction (pp. 14-28) and text are devoted to the sonnet.

142. Padelford, Frederick M. Early Sixteenth Century Lyrics. Boston and London: D.C. Heath, 1907.

A long introduction which, among other things, compares Wyatt's sonnets to Petrarch. Contains Wyatt, Surrey, miscellaneous minor poets.

143. Rollins, Hyder Edward, ed. Tottel's Miscellany (1557-1587). 2 vol. Cambridge, Mass.: Harvard University Press, 1928-29. 1965.

144. Saintsbury, George. Minor Poets of the Caroline Period. 3 vol. Oxford: Clarendon Press, 1905-21.

Contains sonnets of Patrick Hannay, Thomas Stanley (7 rhymed couplets), Philip Ayres.

145. Schelling, Felix E. A Book of Elizabethan Lyrics. Boston: Ginn, 1903.

Introduction discusses sonnets and is followed by a selection.

146. Sylvester, Richard S. The Anchor Anthology of Sixteenth-Century Verse. Garden City, N.Y.: Anchor Books, 1974.

147. Thomson, Patricia. Elizabethan Lyrical Poets. London: Routledge and Kegan Paul, 1967.

Introduction includes sections on Sidney's Astrophel and Stella and Shakespeare's Sonnets.

148. Ward, Thomas H. The English Poets. London and New York: Macmillan, 1881, vol. 1.

Volume 1 covers the 16th-century with critical introductions to each poet.

General Criticism

149. Allen, Don Cameron. The Star-Crossed Renaissance: The Quarrel about Astrology and Its Influence in England. Durham, N.C.: Duke University Press, 1941. London: Cass, 1967.

In brief portions of a chapter on "Astrology and English Literature," Allen discusses specific astrologic allusions in different sequences (pp. 158-59, 165-66).

150. Alpers, Paul J. Elizabethan Poetry: Modern Essays in Criticism. New York: Oxford University Press, 1967.

Contains essays on sonnets by Yvor Winters, Neil Rudenstine, David Kalstone, L.C. Knights, and C.L. Barber.

151. Altieri, Charles. "Rhetorics, Rhetoricity and the Sonnet as Performance." Tennessee Studies in Literature, 25 (1980), 1-23.

Most of this essay, which deals with the theoretical aspects of rhetoric in the sonnet, focuses on Elizabethan poets.

152. Arnold, Aerol. Review of J.W. Lever, The Elizabethan Love Sonnet. Personalist, 39 (1958), 311-12.

153. Ashley, Leonard R.N. Review of J.W. Lever, Sonnets of the English Renaissance. Bibliotheque d'Humanisme et Renaissance, 37 (1975), 519-20.

154. Bachrach, A.G.H. Review of J.W. Lever, The Elizabethan Love Sonnet. English Studies, 41 (1960), 206-09.

155. Baldi, Sergio. "Il petrarchismo e la lirica elisabettiana." Cultura e scuola, 1, iii (1962), 56-64.

156. Berdan, John. "A Definition of Petrarchismo." PMLA, 24 (1909), 699-710.

Pays particular attention to the Elizabethan sonnet sequences.

157. Berdan, John M. Early Tudor Poetry: 1485-1547. New York: Macmillan, 1920.

158. Black, L.G. Review of J.W. Lever, Sonnets of the English Renaissance. Notes and Queries, 221 (1976), 267-68.

159. Blissett, William. Review of Claes Schaar, An Elizabethan Sonnet Problem: Shakespeare's Sonnets, Daniel's Delia, and Their Literary Background. English Studies, 42 (1961), 61.

160. Borghesi, Peter. Petrarch and his Influence on English Literature. Bologna: Nicholas Zanichelli, 1906.

161. Bradner, Leicester. "From Petrarch to Shakespeare." The Renaissance: Six Essays. New York: Harper and Row, 1962, pp. 97-119. Originally published as The Renaissance: A Symposium by The Metropoitan Museum of Art (1953).

An essay dealing with the major genres in Renaissance literature and containing a brief discussion on the sonnet (pp. 103-04).

162. Brainerd, Mary Bowen. "The Influence of Petrarch Upon the Elizabethan Sonnet." Ph.D. Dissertation, Chicago, 1897.

163. Broadbent, J.B. Poetic Love. London: Chatto and Windus, 1964.

Chapter 6 is partially devoted to Spenser's sonnets, chapter 8 partially to Sidney's and chapter 9 entirely to Shakespeare's sonnets. Includes also some discussion of Wyatt, Surrey, et al.

164. Brooke, C.F. Tucker. "The Renaissance (1500-1660)." A Literary History of England. Ed. Albert C. Baugh. New York: Appleton-Century-Crofts, 1948.

The sonnet is discussed in part 2, chapter 8, "Sidney and the Sonneteers," as well as in portions of other chapters.

165. Brown, John Russell, and Bernard Harris, ed. Elizabethan Poetry. Stratford-upon-Avon Series, 2. London: Edward Arnold, 1960.

Contains essays related to the sonnet by F.T. Prince, Franklin Dickey, D.G. Rees, and Jean Robertson.

166. Burgess, Robert M. "The Sonnet--a Cosmopolitan Literary Form--in the Renaissance." Actes du IVe Congres de l'Association Internationale de Litterature Comparee, Fribourg, 1964. Ed. Francois Jost. The Hague: Mouton, 1966, pp. 169-84.

A survey of the sonnet's vogue in Europe. The sonnet in England is covered briefly (pp. 176-79).

167. Bush, Douglas. English Poetry: The Main Currents from Chaucer to the Present. New York: Oxford University Press, 1952. London: Methuen, 1965.

Comments about the sonnet may be found throughout, with the most extended discussion in the chapter on "The Renaissance."

168. Buxton, John. A Tradition of Poetry. London: Macmillan; New York: St. Martin's, 1967.

Includes chapters on Wyatt, Surrey, Gascoigne, and Drayton, with references to sonnets throughout.

169. Carey, John. Review of J.B. Broadbent, Poetic Love. Essays in Criticism, 15 (1965), 334-37.

Discusses Spenser, Donne, and Shakespeare.

170. Child, Harold H. "The New English Poetry." The Cambridge History of English Literature. Ed. A.W. Wood and A.R. Waller. Cambridge: University Press, 1911, vol. 3, pp. 187-215.

171. Cluett, Robert. Review of Herbert S. Donow, A Concordance to the Sonnet Sequences of Daniel, Drayton, Shakespeare, Sidney, and Spenser. Computers and the Humanities, 6 (1972), 161-62.

172. Colie, Rosalie. The Resources of Kind: Genre-Theory in The Renaissance. Berkeley: University of California Press, 1973.

In Chapter 2, "Small Forms: Multo in Parvo," (in particular pp. 69 ff.), Colie associates the sonnet and the epigram. Chapter 4, "Kindness and Literary Imagination," begins by speaking of the sonnet's "aspirations" as a form.

173. Cook, Albert S. "The Elizabethan Invocations to Sleep." Modern Language Notes, 4 (1889), 229-31.

Sources of the invocations to sleep found in sonnets by Sidney, Daniel, Griffin, and Drummond.

174. Courthope, William John. History of English Poetry. London: Macmillan, 1920-24, vol. 2-3.

Volume 2 includes the English sonneteers from Wyatt to Spenser, and Volume 3 from Daniel to Milton.

175. Craig, Hardin. "The Literature of the English Renaissance 1485-1660." A History of English Literature. New York: Oxford University Press, 1950.

This literary history contains a section on "The Elizabethan Sonnet" (pp. 240-45).

176. Dedeyan, Charles. Review of J.W. Lever, The Elizabethan Love Sonnet. Erasmus, 20 (1968), 287-88.

177. DeMarchi, Luigi. "L'influenza della lirica italiana sulla lirica inglese del secolo XVI (Sir Tommaso Wyatt)." Nuova Antologia, 141 (1895), 136-55.

Latter half of article focuses on sonnet rhyme schemes. In addition to Wyatt the author refers to the sonnets of Shakespeare and others.

178. Dickey, Franklin. "Collections of Songs and Sonnets." Elizabethan Poetry. Ed. John Russell Brown and Bernard Harris. Stratford-upon-Avon Studies, 2. London: Edward Arnold, 1960, pp. 30-51.

Surveys Elizabethan anthologies from Tottel on.

179. Dickinson, John Wesley. "The Elizabethan Religious Sonnet." Ph.D. Dissertation, University of California at Los Angeles, 1960.

180. Dodge, R.E.N. "An Obsolete Elizabethan Mode of Rhyming." Shakespeare Studies by Members of the Department of English of the University of Wisconsin. Madison: University of Wisconsin, 1916, pp. 174-200.

Discusses rhyming in a number of poems (including sonnets) from Wyatt to Spenser.

181. Donow, Herbert S. "Concordance and Stylistic Analysis of Six Elizabethan Sonnet Sequences." Computers and the Humanities, 3 (1969), 205-08.

Report on computer-assisted work on Daniel, Drayton, Shakespeare, Sidney, and Spenser.

182. Donow, Herbert S. Concordance to the Sonnet Sequences of Daniel, Drayton, Shakespeare, Sidney, and Spenser. Carbondale, Il.: Southern Illinois University Press, 1969.

183. Dunn, Esther C. The Literature of Shakespeare's England. New York: Charles Scribner's Sons, 1936.

A survey touching on the major poets: Sidney, Spenser, Shakespeare, Daniel, Drayton. Chapter 3 includes a section on the "Sonnet Cycles."

184. Earl, A.J. "Romeo and Juliet and the Elizabethan Sonnets." English, 27 (1978), 99-119.

The Petrarchism of the sonnets of the 1580's and 1590's found its way into Shakespeare's Romeo and Juliet.

185. Einstein, Lewis. The Italian Renaissance in England. New York: Columbia University Press, 1902. New York: Burt Franklin, 1962.

Chapter 8, "The Italian Influence in English Poetry" (pp. 316-72), discusses sonnets.

186. Ellrodt, Robert. Review of J.W. Lever, The Elizabethan Love Sonnet. Etudes Anglaises, 14 (1961), 235-37.

187. *Enzensberger, Christian. Sonett und Poetik: Die Aussagen der Elisabethanischen Sonettzyklen uber das Dichten im Vergleich mit der Zeitgenossischen Dichtungslehre. Munchen: n.p., 1962.

188. Erskine, John. The Elizabethan Lyric: A Study. New York: Columbia University Press, 1903. rpt. New York: Gordian Press, 1967.

189. Evans, Maurice. "Metaphor and Symbol in the Sixteenth Century." Essays in Criticism, 3 (1953), 267-84.

Evans illustrates his discussion of biblical and mythical metaphor with references to sonnets by Greville, Donne, Spenser, Drayton, and Drummond.

190. Evans, Maurice. English Poetry in the Sixteenth Century. London: Hutchinson's University Library, 1955. 1967.

Chapters 5, "Wyatt and Surrey," and 6, "Shorter Forms of Elizabethan Poetry," deal at length with the sonnet.

191. Ewbank, Inga-Stina. "Sincerity and the Sonnet." Essays and Studies 1981 (English Association, NS 34). Ed. Anne Barton. London: John Murray, 1981, pp. 19-44.

Paying special attention to Sidney and Shakespeare, Ewbank attempts to separate the principle of sincerity from autobiographical fact or speculation.

192. Finn, Sister Dorothy Mercedes. "Love and Marriage in Renaissance Literature." Ph.D. Dissertation, Columbia University, 1955. DA, 15 (1955), 2188-89.

193. Fisher, John H. "The Myth of Petrarch." Jean Misrahi Memorial Volume: Studies in Medieval Literature. Ed. Hans R. Runte, Henri Niedzielski, and William L. Hendrickson. Columbia, S.C.: French Literature Publications, 1977, pp. 359-73.

Discusses what lay behind the English fascination with Petrarchanism.

194. Forster, L.W. The Icy Fire: Five Studies in European Petrarchism. Cambridge: University Press, 1969.

The first two studies in particular, "The Petrarchan Manner" and "Petrarchism as Training," touch on the English sonneteers.

195. Fowler, Alastair. Triumphal Forms: Structural Patterns in Elizabethan Poetry. Cambridge: University Press, 1970.

In chapter 9, "Sonnet Sequences" (pp. 174-97), he discusses Sidney's Astrophil and Stella, Spenser's Amoretti, and Shakespeare's Sonnets.

196. Fowler, Alastair. Conceitful Thought: The Interpretation of English Renaissance Poems. Edinburgh: University Press, 1975.

References to Astrophil and Stella, Amoretti, and several other sonnet sequences.

197. Fraser, Russell. "A Classic of Literary Criticism." Shakespeare Quarterly, 27 (1976), 508-11.

Review of J.W. Lever, The Elizabethan Love Sonnet.

198. Frye, Prosser Hall. "The Elizabethan Sonnet." Literary Reviews and Criticisms. New York: Putnam, 1908. Freeport, N.Y.: Books for Libraries Press, 1968, pp. 1-18.

In this general study on the sonnet, Frye estimates that more than 300,000 sonnets were written in Europe in the 16th-century.

199. Fuzier, Jean. Review of Maurice Evans, Elizabethan Sonnets. Etudes Anglaises, 31 (1978), 377.

200. Going, W.T. "Gascoigne and the Term 'Sonnet Sequence'." Notes and Queries, 199 (1954), 189-91.

201. Goldman, Lloyd Nathaniel. "Attitudes toward the Mistress in Five Elizabethan Sonnet Sequences." Ph.D. Dissertation, Illinois, 1964. DA, 25 (1965), 6590-91.

On Sidney, Drayton, Shakespeare, Daniel, and Spenser.

202. Gourvitch, I. Review of Janet G. Scott, Les Sonnets elisabethains: les sources et l'apport personnel. Modern Language Review, 25 (1930), 345-46.

203. Grabau, Carl. "Zeitschriftenschau." Shakespeare Jahrbuch, 45 (1909), 281-317.

In a section entitled "Elisabethanische Sonettendichtung" (p. 287), Grabau comments on Kastner's article on "The Elizabethan Sonneteers and the French Poets."

204. Griem, Eberhard. "Die Elisabethanische Epoche." Epochen der englischen Lyrik. Ed. Karl Heinz Goller. Dusseldorf: August Bagel, 1970, pp. 79-99.

Discusses the sonnet and sonnet sequence (pp. 89-99).

205. Hannay, David. The Later Renaissance. New York: Charles Scribner's Sons, 1898. rpt. New York: Burt Franklin, 1964.

Chapter 7, "Elizabethan Poetry" (pp. 185-222), includes sections on the sonnet.

206. Harris, William O. "Early Elizabethan Sonnets in Sequence." Studies in Philology, 68 (1971), 451-69.

Covers some minor poets: Bernard Garter, George Gascoigne, James Yates, and Arthur Broke.

207. Harrison, G.B. Review of Janet G. Scott, Les Sonnets elisabethains: les sources et l'apport personnel. Modern Philology, 27 (1929), 241-42.

208. Harrison, John Smith. Platonism in English Poetry of the Sixteenth and Seventeenth Centuries. New York: Columbia University Press, 1903.

The teachings of Platonism found a place in the sonnets of Sidney, Spenser, Shakespeare, et al. (pp. 126-39).

209. Hasselkuss, Hermann Karl. Der Petrarkismus in der Sprache der englischen Sonettdichter der Renaissance. Munster: Westfalischen Wilhelms-Universitat, 1927.

A doctoral dissertation.

210. Heuer, Hermann. Review of J.W. Lever, The Elizabethan Love Sonnet. Shakespeare Jahrbuch, 92 (1956), 379-81.

211. Hill, Raymond T. "The Enueg." PMLA, 27 (1912), 265-96.

Although the article does not treat English poetry, the "Enueg" is found in some major Elizabethan sonnet sequences. "Enueg" means vexation--a poem which treats the annoyances of life. "Plazer" is the opposite.

212. Hinely, Jan Lawson. "The Sonnet Sequence in Elizabethan Poetry." Ph.D. Dissertation, Ohio State, 1966. DA, 27 (1967), 3011A.

The main emphasis is on Sidney, Spenser, and Shakespeare.

213. Hoffmeister, Gerhart. Petrarkistische Lyrik. Sammlung Metzler, Bd. 119. Stuttgart: J.B. Metzler, 1973.

In his section on English Petrarchism, Hoffmeister includes several pages on Wyatt and Surrey and the Elizabethan sonnet cycles (pp. 46-50).

214. Hudson, Hoyt H. "The Transition in Poetry." Huntington Library Quarterly, 5 (1942), 188-90.

Abstract of an address to The Renaissance Conference at the Huntington Library with references to Sidney, Daniel and Greville.

215. Inglis, Fred. The Elizabethan Poets: The Making of English Poetry from Wyatt to Ben Jonson. London: Evans Brothers, 1969.

Sections of the text deal with the sonnets of Wyatt, Sidney, Greville, Shakespeare, et al.

216. Jack, Ronald D.S. "Imitation in the Scottish Sonnet." Comparative Literature, 20 (1968), 313-28.

217. Jack, R.D.S. "Petrarch in English and Scottish Renaissance Literature." Modern Language Review, 71 (1976), 801-11.

The article speaks more of Petrarchism in general than in relation to sonnets, but at the end of the article, Jack comments about William Alexander's sonnet sequence, Aurora (pp. 809-10).

218. Jameson, Anna Brownell (Murphy). Memoirs of the Loves of the Poets: Biographical Sketches of Women Celebrated in Ancient and Modern Poetry. Boston: Ticknor and Fields, 1857. rpt. Freeport, N.Y.: Books for Libraries Press, 1972. [First published under the title Loves of the Poets. London, 1829.]

Includes sketches of the seven "mistresses" of Spenser, Shakespeare, Sidney, Drayton, Daniel, Drummond, and Habington.

219. Jayne, Sears. "Ficino and the Platonism of the English Renaissance." Comparative Literature, 4 (1952), 214-38.

In the section on "The Period of Platonic Poetry" (pp. 225-36) sonnets and sonnet sequences are used to illustrate his thesis.

220. John, Lisle Cecil. "The Elizabethan Sonnet Sequences: Studies in Conventional Conceits." Ph.D. Dissertation, Columbia University, 1939.

221. John, L.C. The Elizabethan Sonnet Sequence, Studies in Conventional Conceits. Columbia University Studies in English and Comparative Literature, 133. New York: Columbia University Press, 1938. New York: Russell and Russell, 1964.

222. John, Lisle Cecil. Review of J.W. Lever, The Elizabethan Love Sonnet. Renaissance News, 9 (1956), 201-06.

223. Jones, G.P. "You, Thou, He or She? The Master-Mistress in Shakespearian and Elizabethan Sonnet Sequences." Cahiers Elisabethains, No. 19 (April, 1981), 73-84.

Examines the distributions of "thou," "you" and "she" in 16 Elizabethan sonnet sequences.

224. Jusserand, Jean Jules. The Literary History of the English People. 3rd ed. New York: G.P. Putnam, 1926, vol. 2-3.

Several chapters in volume 2 cover the 16th-century sonneteers. Shakespeare's sonnets are discussed in volume 3, chapter 6.

225. Kastner, L.E. "The Scottish Sonneteers and the French Poets." Modern Language Review, 3 (1907), 1-15.

226. Kastner, L.E. "The Elizabethan Sonneteers and the French Poets." Modern Language Review, 3 (1908), 268-77.

Illustrates the indebtedness of the English sonneteers to the French poets.

227. Kaun, Ernst. Konventionelles in den Elisabethanischen Sonetten mit Berucksichtigung der franzosischen und italienischen Quellen. Greifswald: E. Panzig, 1915.

Doctoral dissertation at the University of Greifswald.

228. Keller, Luzius, ed. Ubersetzung und Nachahmung im europaischen Petrarkismus: Studien und Texte. Stuttgart: J.B. Metzler, 1974.

In addition to the essays, the text of Petrarchan poems and their various translations are included.

229. Keller, Wolfgang. "Sammelreferat." Shakespeare Jahrbuch, 65 (1929), 189-209.

Includes a review of Herman K. Hasselkuss, Der Petrarkismus in der Sprache der englischen Sonettdichter der Renaissance (p. 196).

230. Kelley, Tracy Randall. "Studies in the Development of the Prosody of the Elizabethan Sonnet." Ph.D. Dissertation, University of California, Berkeley, 1937.

231. Koeppel, E. "Studien zur Geschichte des englischen Petrarchismus im sechzehnten Jahrhundert." Romanische Forschungen, 5 (1890), 65-97.

Discussion covers Tottel's Miscellany (Wyatt, Surrey and the uncertain authors) and Sidney's Astrophel and Stella.

232. Lanier, Sidney. Shakespere and His Forerunners: Studies in Elizabethan Poetry and its Development from Early English. New York: Doubleday, Page, 1902. rpt. New York: AMS Press, 1966, vol. 1.

Volume 1 contains 4 chapters (7-10) on the Elizabethan sonnet.

233. Lee, Sidney. "Ben Jonson on the Sonnet." Athenaeum, July 9, 1904, p. 49.

Notes that Jonson's simile comparing the sonnet to the bed of Procrustes came from Stefano Guazzo.

234. Lee, Sidney. "The Elizabethan Sonnet." The Cambridge History of English Literature. Ed. A.W. Ward and A.R. Waller. Cambridge: University Press, 1911. 1949, vol. 3, pp. 281-310.

235. Lee, Sidney. The French Renaissance in England. New York: Charles Scribner's Sons, 1910.

Book II, chapter 8 discusses Wyatt and Surrey; Book IV, chapters 12 and 13 examine "The Assimilation of the French Sonnet" and "Shakespeare and the French Sonnet," respectively.

236. Legouis, Emile. Review of Janet G. Scott, Les Sonnets elisabethains: les sources et l'apport personnel. Revue Anglo-americaine, 7 (1929), 66-67.

237. Legouis, Emile H. A Short History of English Literature. Tr. V.F. Boyson and J. Coulson. Oxford: Clarendon Press, 1965.

238. Leishman, J.B. Review of J.W. Lever, The Elizabethan Love Sonnet. Modern Language Review, 52 (1957), 251-55.

239. Leishman, J.B. Review of Janet G. Scott, Les Sonnets elisabethains: les sources et l'apport personnel. Review of English Studies, 7 (1931), 343-45.

240. Lentzner, Karl August. Uber das Sonett und seine Gestaltung in der englischen Dichtung bis Milton. Leipzig: Metzger und Wittig, 1886.

Dissertation from the University of Leipzig.

241. Lever, J.W. The Elizabethan Love Sonnet. London: Methuen, 1956.

242. Levin, Richard. "A Second English Enueg." Philological Quarterly, 53 (1974), 428-30.

In addition to Shakespeare's Sonnet 66, another English enueg is an anonymous sonnet in the Harrington manuscript (p. 92).

243. Levy, Jiri. "The Development of Rhyme-Scheme and of Syntactic Pattern in the English Renaissance Sonnet." Philologica (Acta Universitatis Palackianae Olumucensis), 4 (1961), 167-85.

244. Lewis, C.S. English Literature in the Sixteenth Century, Excluding Drama. Oxford History of English Literature, vol. 3. Oxford: Clarendon Press, 1954.

Although Lewis discusses sonnets in a number of places, the most notable passages are in connection wth Sidney (pp. 327-30) and Shakespeare (pp. 502-08).

245. Macintire, Elizabeth Jelliffe. "French Influence on the Beginnings of English Classicism." PMLA, 26 (1911), 496-527.

Includes a discussion of the French influence on Watson's Passionate Century of Sonnets (1582) and Spenser's sonnets (both in the Amoretti and elsewhere).

246. Maiberger, Max. Studien uber den Einfluss Frankreichs auf die elisabethanische Literatur, Ersterteil: Die Lyrik in der zweiten halfte des XVI. Jahrhunderts. Frankfurt a.M.: Gebruder Knauer, 1903.

Doctoral dissertation. The major part of the text deals with the sonnet.

247. Marcum, Patricia Johnson. "The English Sonnet as a Renaissance Form: Development and Disintegration." Ph.D. Dissertation, Illinois, 1973. DAI, 34 (1973), 732A.

248. Martz, Louis L. "The Action of the Self: Devotional Poetry in the Seventeenth Century." Metaphysical Poetry. Ed. Malcolm Bradbury and David Palmer. Stratford-upon-Avon Studies, 11. London: Edward Arnold, 1970, pp. 100-21.

The devotional sonnets of Alabaster and Donne are discussed along with poetry of others.

249. Mason, H.A. Humanism and Poetry in the Early Tudor Period. London: Routledge and Kegan Paul, 1959.

Comments on sonnets of Wyatt and Surrey (Pt. II).

250. Maynard, Winifred. Review of Douglas L. Peterson, The English Lyric from Wyatt to Donne: A History of the Plain and Eloquent Styles. Review of English Studies, NS 19 (1968), 427-30.

251. Mazzaro, Jerome. Transformations in the Renaissance English Lyric. Ithaca, N.Y.: Cornell University Press, 1970.

Talks about the "utilization of predicaments" in Astrophel and Stella (pp. 101-07) and also offers some general remarks about the nature of sonnet sequences (pp. 141-44).

252. Michel, Laurence. Review of Claes Schaar, An Elizabethan Sonnet Problem: Shakespeare's Sonnets, Daniel's Delia and Their Literary Background. Journal of English and Germanic Philology, 60 (1961), 583-84.

253. Minta, Stephen. Petrarch and Petrarchism: The English and French Traditions. Manchester: Manchester University Press; New York: Barnes and Noble, 1980.

254. Minto, William. Characteristics of English Poets From Chaucer to Shirley. Edinburgh and London: William Blackwood and Sons, 1874; Boston: Ginn, 1891.

Chapter 5 (pp. 182-223) is devoted to the "Elizabethan Sonneteers." In Appendix B (pp. 371-82), "An Unrecognized Sonnet by Shakespeare?", Minto identifies Shakespeare as the poet of a dedicatory sonnet, "Phaeton to his Friend Florio," prefixed to John Florio's Second Frutes.
701, 1477

255. Moore, Donald Lee. "(1) The Religious Sonnet Cycle in England, 1585-1600. (2) Limitations in the Fiction of Flannery O'Connor? (3) W.H. Auden's Twentieth-Century Pattern for Elegy." Ph.D. Dissertation, Rutgers, 1977. DAI, 38 (1978), 6745A.

Discusses Lok, Alabaster, Barnes, Greville, and Constable.

256. More, Paul Elmer. "Elizabethan Sonnets." Shelburne Essays, Second Series. Boston and New York: Houghton Mifflin, 1905, pp. 1-19.

257. Morris, Helen. Elizabethan Literature. London: Oxford University Press, 1958.

Chapters on "Spenser and Sidney" and "Non-Dramatic Poetry" cover the sonnet.

258. Mortimer, Anthony, ed. Petrarch's Canzoniere in the English Renaissance. Bergamo: Minerva Italica, 1975.

Discusses in an introduction the relationship between Petrarch and an array of English sonneteers, including Wyatt, Surrey, John Harrington the Elder, Sidney, Watson, Nicholas Yonge.

259. Muir, Kenneth. "Sonnets in the Hill Manuscript." Proceedings of the Leeds Philosophical and Literary Society, 6 (1950), 464-71.

Discusses the 12 anonymous sonnets found in this manuscript and reprinted in the article.

260. Mumford, Ivy L. "The Canzone in Sixteenth Century English Verse with Particular Reference to Wyatt's Renderings from Petrarch's Canzoniere." English Miscellany, 11 (1960), 21-32.

Although the canzone was not a sonnet, Spenser adapted it in The Visions of Petrarch so that it had 14 lines with the rhyme scheme introduced by Surrey (pp. 27-29).

261. Mumford, Ivy L. "Petrarchism in Early Tudor England." Italian Studies, 19 (1964), 56-63.

262. Neely, Carol Thomas. "The Structure of English Renaissance Sonnet Sequences." ELH, 45 (1978), 359-89.

263. Nicholson, F.C. "Minnesong and the Elizabethan Sonnets." Modern Language Quarterly (London), 4 (1901), 180-84.

A comparison between the German medieval love lyric and the Elizabethan sonnets.

264. Nixon, W.D. "The Tudor Petrarchans: A Study of the Influence of Petrarch's Canzoniere on Sixteenth-Century English Poets." Ph.D. Dissertation, Leeds, 1977.

265. Ogle, M.B. "The 'White Hand' as a Literary Conceit." Sewanee Review, 20 (1912), 459-69.

Comments on the use of the conceit in Shakespeare's and others' sonnets (pp. 462-63).

266. Ogle, M.B. "The Classical Origin and Tradition of Literary Conceits." American Journal of Philology, 34 (1913), 125-52.

Many of the illustrations of common conceits on feminine charms are drawn from Elizabethan sonnets.

267. Osgood, Charles G. Review of Janet G. Scott, Les Sonnets elisabethains: les sources et l'apport personnel. Modern Language Notes, 45 (1930), 328-29.

268. Owen, Daniel E. The Relations of the Elizabethan Sonnet Sequences to Earlier English Verse. Philadelphia: Chilton Printing, 1903.

Owen's comparison focuses on Chaucer and the Elizabethans.

269. Parker, William R. "The Sonnets in Tottel's Miscellany." PMLA, 54 (1939), 669-77.

270. Parsons, Roger Loren. "Renaissance and Baroque: Multiple Unity and Unified Unity in the Treatment of Verse, Ornament and Structure." Ph.D. Dissertation, Wisconsin, 1959. DA, 19 (1959), 2958.

Includes a comparison of Spenser's sonnet verse with Donne's and Milton's.

271. Pearson, Lu Emily. Elizabethan Love Conventions. Berkeley: University of California Press, 1933. New York: Barnes and Noble, 1967.

Pearson's book opens with a discussion of "Love Conventions and the Sonnet" and goes on to cover Wyatt, the sonneteering craze, Sidney, Spenser, Shakespeare and most of the other important figures in the genre.

272. Peter, John. Complaint and Satire in Early English Literature. Oxford: Clarendon Press, 1956.

Discusses the influence of satire on the sonnet (pp. 295-98).

273. Peterson, Douglas L. The English Lyric from Wyatt to Donne: A History of the Plain and Eloquent Styles. Princeton, N.J.: Princeton University Press, 1967.

Contains chapters on "Tottel's Miscellany," "Shakespeare's Sonnets," and "Fulke Greville's Caelica."

274. Poirier, Michel. Review of J.W. Lever, The Elizabethan Love Sonnet. Etudes Anglaises, 20 (1967), 73-74.

275. Policardi, S. Lyrical Poetry in Renaissance England. Biblioteca di Saggi e Lezioni Accademiche, 9. Milano: Montuoro Editore, 1943.

In one part (pp. 41-53) where he talks of Wyatt and Surrey, Policardi underscores the former's importance in introducing the sonnet in England.

276. Potter, James Lain. "The Development of Sonnet Patterns in the Sixteenth Century." Ph.D. Dissertation, Harvard University, 1954.

277. Potter, James L. The Development of Sonnet Patterns in the Sixteenth Century. Washington, D.C.: Howard University, 1954.

278. Praz, Mario. The Flaming Heart: Essays on Crashaw, Machiavelli and other studies in the Relation between Italian and English Literature from Chaucer to T.S. Eliot. New York: Doubleday, 1958. New York: W.W. Norton, 1973.

His essay "Petrarch in England" (pp. 264-86) is largely concerned with the sonnet and its more important English exponents.

279. Praz, Mario. Review of Janet G. Scott, Les Sonnets elisabethains: les sources et l'apport personnel. English Studies, 11 (1929), 227-31.

280. Prescott, Anne Lake. French Poets and the English Renaissance: Studies in Fame and Transformation. New Haven and London: Yale University Press, 1978.

Brief and occasional discussion of English sonnets but mainly useful as a background on Marot, DuBellay, Ronsard, Desportes, DuBartas.

281. Prince, F.T. "The Sonnet from Wyatt to Shakespeare." Elizabethan Poetry. Ed. J.R. Brown and Bernard Harris. Stratford-Upon-Avon Studies, 2. London: Edward Arnold, 1960, pp. 10-29. Reprinted in Shakespeare: The Sonnets: A Casebook, ed. Peter Jones. London: Macmillan, 1977, pp. 164-84.

282. Reed, Edward Bliss. "Shakespeare's Sonnets." English Lyrical Poetry From Its Origins to the Present Time. New Haven: Yale University Press, 1912.

In addition to remarks on Wyatt and Surrey in chapter on "The Tudor Lyric," Reed reserves one section from the chapter on "The Elizabethan Lyric" for the sonnet sequences (pp. 145-76).

283. Rees, D.G. "Italian and Italianate Poetry." Elizabethan Poetry. Ed. J.R. Brown and Bernard Harris. Stratford-Upon-Avon Studies, 2. London: Edward Arnold, 1960, pp. 52-69.

284. Rees, Joan. Review of J.W. Lever, Sonnets of the English Renaissance. Yearbook of English Studies, 7 (1977), 214-15.

285. Reichert, John Frederick. "Formal Logic and English Renaissance Poetry." Ph.D. Dissertation, Stanford, 1963. DA, 24 (1963), 1174.

Importance of logical structure in the sonnets and lyrics.

286. Rhys, Ernest. Lyric Poetry. New York: E.P. Dutton, 1913.

In the chapters on Wyatt and Surrey, Spenser, and Sidney the subject of sonnets is of prime importance.

287. Richmond, H.M. The School of Love: The Evolution of the Stuart Love Lyric. Princeton: Princeton University Press, 1964.

While the treatment is of love poetry in general, certain passages in the first two chapters and throughout refer to the sonnets, with greatest attention to Shakespeare and Sidney.

288. Ricks, Christopher. English Poetry and Prose, 1540-1674. London: Barrie and Jenkins, 1970.

This volume, which is the second in the series History of Literature in the English Language, contains essays on Wyatt and Surrey, Sidney, Spenser, Shakespeare, and Milton.

289. Robertson, Jean. Review of J.W. Lever, The Elizabethan Love Sonnet. Review of English Studies, NS 8 (1957), 429-32.

290. Robertson, John M. Elizabethan Literature. London: Williams and Norgate, 1914.

This survey includes the sonnet sequences.

291. R[oot], R[obert] K. Review of Daniel E. Owen, Relations of the Elizabethan Sonnet Sequences to Earlier English Verse, especially that of Chaucer. Journal of English and Germanic Philology, 5 (1904), 371-72.

292. Ross, Ian. "Sonneteering in Sixteenth-Century Scotland." Texas Studies in Literature and Language, 6 (1964), 255-68.

Contains a number of references to Alexander Montgomerie.

293. Rubel, Vere. *Poetic Diction in the English Renaissance from Skelton through Spenser*. MLA Revolving Fund Series, 12. New York: Modern Language Association of America, 1941.

294. Ruthven, K.K. "The Composite Mistress." *AUMLA*, No. 26 (1966), 198-214.

The merging of various gifts belonging to gods and goddesses in a single mistress became a popular convention in the Renaissance, and one which the sonneteers exploited.

295. Saintsbury, George. *History of Elizabethan Literature*. London and New York: Macmillan, 1887.

296. Saintsbury, George. *History of English Prosody from the Twelfth Century to the Present Day*. London: Macmillan, 1923, vol. 1-2.

Vol. 1: Book 4, Ch. 1 (Wyatt and Surrey); Ch. 5 (Spenser); Vol. 2: Book 5, Ch. 3 (contemporaries and followers of Spenser); Ch. 4 (Donne); Book 6, Ch. 1 (Milton).

297. *Sakurai, Shoichiro. "The Concluding Couplets in English Sonnets from Wyatt to Shakespeare." *Eibungaku Hyoron* (Kyoto University), 38 (1977), 1-84.

In Japanese.

298. *Sakurai, Shoichiro. *What the Last Two Lines Express. On the Sonnets of the English Renaissance*. Kyoto: Yamaguchi Shoten, 1979.

Examines the closing couplet from Wyatt on. In Japanese.

299. Schaar, Claes. *On the Motif of Death in 16th-Century Sonnet Poetry*. Lund: C.W.K. Gleerup, 1960.

300. Schelling, Felix E. *English Literature During the Lifetime of Shakespeare*. New York: Henry Holt, 1910.

Chapter 8 deals with "The Pastoral Lyric and the Sonnet."

301. Scott, Janet G. "The Names of the Heroines of Elizabethan Sonnet-Sequences." *Review of English Studies*, 2 (1926), 159-62.

302. Scott, Janet G. "Minor Elizabethan Sonneteers and their Greater Predecessors." *Review of English Studies*, 2 (1926), 423-27.

303. Scott, Janet Girvan. *Les Sonnets Elisabethains: Les Sources et l'Apport Personnel*. Paris: Honore Champion, 1929.

304. [Scott], Janet G. Espiner. "Les Sonnets Elisabethains." *Revue de Litterature Comparee*, 15 (1935), 107-09.

The author comments on a review of her book, Les Sonnet Elisabethains by Hugues Vaganay in Revue (1934).
321

305. Scott, Janet Espiner-. "Les Sonnets elisabethains: Cupidon et l'influence d'Ovide." Revue de Litterature Comparee, 31 (1957), 421-26.

306. Seccombe, Thomas, and J.W. Allen. "Sidney and the Sonneteers." The Age of Shakespeare (1579-1631). London: George Bell, 1904, vol. 1, pp. 8-29.

307. Sells, A. Lytton. The Italian Influence in English Poetry from Chaucer to Southwell. London: Allen and Unwin, 1955.

A substantial part of his work deals with the major poets and their sonnets with a chapter devoted to the minor sonneteers.

308. Shawcross, John T. "The Poet as Orator: One Phase of His Judicial Pose." The Rhetoric of Renaissance Poetry from Wyatt to Milton. Ed. Thomas O. Sloan and Raymond B. Waddington. Berkeley: University of California Press, 1974, pp. 5-36.

Discusses poetry of the early and late Renaissance, commenting in detail on Daniel's Sonnet 11 from Delia (pp. 17-18), Sonnet 16 from Greville's Caelica (pp. 19-21), Sonnet 1 from Spenser's Amoretti (pp. 21-22), and Gascoigne's "The Constancy of a Lover Hath Thus Sometimes Been Briefly Declared" (pp. 13-14).

309. Siegel, Paul N. "The Petrarchan Sonneteers and Neo-Platonic Love." Studies in Philology, 42 (1945), 164-82.

310. Smith, Hallett. Elizabethan Poetry: A Study in Conventions, Meaning, and Expression. Cambridge, Mass.: Harvard University Press, 1952. Rev. ed. 1968.

311. Southall, Raymond. "Love Poetry in the Sixteenth Century." Essays in Criticism, 22 (1972), 362-80.

312. Southall, Raymond. Literature and the Rise of Capitalism: Critical Essays Mainly on the Sixteenth and Seventeenth Centuries. London: Lawrence and Wishart, 1973.

Chapter 2, "Love Poetry in the Sixteenth Century," discusses sonnets of Wyatt, Sidney, Spenser, Shakespeare et al. with reference to their economic allusions.

313. Stein, David Neill. "On the Basis of English Iambic Pentameter." Ph.D. Dissertation, Illinois, 1975. DAI, 36 (1976), 6652A-53A.

Contains discussion of sonnets, including those of Shakespeare and Milton.

314. Stevenson, David Lloyd. The Love-Game Comedy. New York: Columbia University Press, 1946. rpt. New York: AMS Press, 1966.

Chapter 8 (pp. 123-47) examines sonnets of Wyatt, Sidney, Greville, et al. Chapter 10 (pp. 174-84) deals with "Conflict in Shakespeare's Sonnets."

315. Stull, William L. "Elizabethan Precursors of Donne's 'Divine Meditations'." Comitatus, 6 (1975), 29-44.

Includes discussion of many of the 16th-century sonneteers.

316. Stull, William L. "The English Religious Sonnet from Wyatt to Milton." Ph.D. Dissertation, UCLA, 1978. DAI, 39 (1978), 2961A.

317. Thomson, Patricia. "Petrarch and the Elizabethans." English, 10 (1955), 177-80.

Compares Petrarchan sonnets with some by major Elizabethans. Deals particularly with Shakespeare's Sonnet 116 and Spenser's Amoretti 61.

318. Thomson, Patricia. Review of Claes Schaar, An Elizabethan Sonnet Problem: Shakespeare's Sonnets, Daniel's Delia and their Literary Background. Modern Language Review, 56 (1961), 101.

319. Tuve, Rosemond. Elizabethan and Metaphysical Imagery: Renaissance Poetic and Twentieth-Century Critics. Chicago: University of Chicago Press, 1947.

Contains discussions of sonnets by Sidney, Spenser, Daniel, Donne, et al.

320. Upham, Alfred Horatio. The French Influence in English Literature, from the Accession of Elizabeth to the Restoration. New York: Columbia University Press, 1908. rpt. New York: Octagon Books, 1965.

Chapter 3 (pp. 91-144) treats "The Elizabethan Sonnet."

321. Vaganay, Hugues. "Les sonnets elisabethains." Revue de Litterature Comparee, 14 (1934), 333-37.

Review of Janet G. Espiner Scott, Les sonnets elisabethains.

322. Vallette, Jacques. Review of J.W. Lever, The Elizabethan Love Sonnet. Mercure de France, 327 (1956), 528-30.

323. Vivarelli, Ann West. Review of Jack D'Amico, Petrarch in England: An Anthology of Parallel Texts from Wyatt to Milton. MLN, 96 (1981), 159-70.

Discusses most of the Renaissance sonneteers.

324. Warkentin, Germaine. "'Love's sweetest part, variety': Petrarch and the Curious Frame of the Renaissance Sonnet Sequence." Renaissance and Reformation, 11 (1975), 14-23.

Comments about Shakespeare predominate, but other English sonneteers are included.

325. Warton, Thomas. History of English Poetry from the Twelfth to the Close of the Sixteenth Century. Ed. W. Carew Hazlitt. London: Reeves and Turner, 1871. Hildesheim: Georg Olms, 1968, vol. 4.

Warton writes on the early sonneteers--Constable, Watson, Barnfield (pp. 430-40).

326. Watson, George. The English Petrarchans: A Critical Bibliography of the Canzoniere. Warburg Institute Surveys, 3. London: Warburg Institute, University of London, 1967.

Lists the English versions of Petrarch's 366 Canzoniere.

327. Watson, George. "Petrarch and the English." Yale Review, 68, iii (1979), 383-93.

References to Sidney's Astrophil and Stella, Wyatt, Shakespeare, et al.

328. Weiss, Wolfgang. Die elisabethanische Lyrik. Ertrage der Forschung, 55. Darmstadt: Wissenschaftliche Buchgesellschaft, 1976.

Chapter 4, "Sonette und Sonettsequenzen," discusses Wyatt, Surrey, Sidney, Spenser, and Shakespeare.

329. West, Bill C. "Anti-Petrarchism. A Study of the Reaction against the Courtly Tradition in English Love-Poetry from Wyatt to Donne." Ph.D. Dissertation, Northwestern, 1950.

330. White, Harold Ogden. Plagiarism and Imitation During the English Renaissance: A Study in Critical Distinctions. Cambridge, Mass.: Harvard University Press, 1935.

Sidney's anti-Petrarchism is expressed in Astrophel and Stella (1,3,15,74,90) (pp. 63-64). White refers to several other sonnet sequences.

331. Wilcox, Helen. Review of Elizabethan Sonnets, ed. Maurice Evans. Notes and Queries, 223 (1978), 465-66.

332. Wilkins, E.H. "A General Survey of Renaissance Petrarchism." Comparative Literature, 2 (1950), 327-42. Reprinted in Studies in the Life and Works of Petrarch. Cambridge, Mass.: Harvard University Press, 1955, pp. 280-99.

Discusses Petrarchism in every country where it occurred, including England and Scotland.

333. Wilson, Katharine M. "Shakespeare's Sonnets: The First Interpretation." Calcutta Review, 3rd Series, 37 (1930), 179-97; 38 (1931), 46-70.

The first part of this two-part article is an assessment of the Elizabethan sonnet's conventions; the second part is an examination of Shakespeare's particular treatment of the sonnet.

334. Winters, Yvor. "The Sixteenth Century Lyric in England: A Critical and Historical Reinterpretation." Poetry, 53 (1939), 258-72, 320-35; 54 (1939), 35-51. Reprinted in Elizabethan Poetry: Modern Essays in Criticism. Ed. Paul J. Alpers. New York: Oxford University Press, Galaxy Book, 1967, pp. 93-125. Reprinted and revised as "Aspects of the Short Poem in the English Renaissance" in Forms of Discovery.

335. Winters, Yvor. Forms of Discovery. Denver: Alan Swallow, 1967.

The first essay, "Aspects of the Short Poem in the English Renaissance," includes sections on the sonneteers of the Petrarchan movement (pp. 29-36), on Shakespeare's Sonnets (pp. 52-63), and on Donne's "Holy Sonnets" (pp. 74-75, 78-79).

336. Wolff, Max J. Review of Janet G. Scott, Les sonnets elisabethains. Englische Studien, 66 (1931), 265-68.

337. Yates, Frances A. "The Emblematic Conceit in Giordano Bruno's De Gli Eroici Furori and in the Elizabethan Sonnet Sequences." Journal of the Warburg and Courtauld Institutes, 6 (1943), 101-21.

338. Zocco, Irene. Petrarchismo e Petrarchisti in Inghilterra. Palermo: G. Pedone Lauriel, 1906.

A survey of Petrarchism in 16th-century England with frequent reference to the sonnet throughout.

339. "Italian Influence on English Poetry." Edinburgh Review, 183 (1896), 28-54.

Review of David Main, A Treasury of English Sonnets (1880).

340. "Elizabethan Sonnets." TLS, June 17, 1904, pp. 185-86.

Review of Sidney Lee, Elizabethan Sonnets.

341. "The Pleiade and the Elizabethans." Edinburgh Review, 205 (1907), 353-79.

A review article covering nine books, eight on French literature and the ninth, Sidney Lee's Elizabethan Sonnets. The principal focus of this discussion is on Elizabethan poetry, and the sonnets in particular.

342. Review of Janet G. Scott, Les Sonnets elisabethains: les sources et l'apport personnel. Notes and Queries, 158 (1930), 126.

343. "Elizabethan Sonneteers." TLS, April 6, 1956, p. 206.

Review of J.W. Lever, <u>The Elizabethan Love Sonnet</u>.

William Alabaster

344. Alabaster, William. <u>The Sonnets of William Alabaster</u>. Ed. G.M. Story and Helen Gardner. London and New York: Oxford University Press, 1959.

345. Caro, Robert Vincent. "Rhetoric and Meditation in the Sonnets of William Alabaster." Ph.D. Dissertation, University of Washington, 1977. <u>DAI</u>, 38 (1977), 1404A.

346. Coutts, Eleanor Jean. "The Life and Works of William Alabaster, 1568-1640." Ph.D. Dissertation, Wisconsin, 1957. <u>DA</u>, 17 (1957), 620.

347. Dobell, Bertram. "The Sonnets of William Alabaster." <u>Athenaeum</u>, December 26, 1903, pp. 856-58.

348. Guiney, Louise Imogen. <u>Recusant Poets: With a Selection from their Work</u>. New York: Sheed and Ward, 1939, vol. 1 (St. Thomas More to Ben Jonson).

This selection includes sonnets by Surrey and Alabaster.

349. Martz, Louis L. Review of <u>The Sonnets of William Alabaster</u>, ed. G.M. Story and Helen Gardner. <u>Modern Language Notes</u>, 76 (1961), 348-53.

350. Pollen, J.H. "William Alabaster, a newly discovered Catholic Poet of the Elizabethan Age." <u>Month</u>, 103 (April, 1904), 426-30.

Biographical sketch with three of his sonnets.

351. *Sakamoto, Yoshiharu. "W. Alabaster's Sonnets and the Counter Reformation." <u>Daigaku (Kyoto) Jimbun Kagaku Kenkyujo</u> [Doshisha University Studies in Humanities], No. 108, 1-27.

In Japanese.

Sir William Alexander, Earl of Stirling

352. Alexander, William. <u>The Poetical Works of Sir William Alexander, Earl of Stirling</u>. Ed. L.E. Kastner and H.B. Charlton. Edinburgh and London: Scottish Text Society, W. Blackwood and Sons, 1929, vol. 2.

Contains the poetry: a commendatory sonnet by Drummond and <u>Aurora</u>, a sequence of 105 sonnets with songs and other lyrics interspersed.

353. McDiarmid, Matthew P. "Scots Versions of Poems by Sir Robert Aytoun and Sir William Alexander." Notes and Queries, NS 4 (1957), 32-35.

The poems being discussed, which are ascribed to Alexander, are apparently from his sonnet sequence Aurora (1604).

Sir Robert Ayton

354. Ayton, Sir Robert. The English and Latin Poems of Sir Robert Ayton. Ed. Charles B. Gullans. Edinburgh and London: Scottish Text Society, 1963.

Includes a number of sonnets.

Sir Francis Bacon

355. Ingleby, C.M. "Bacon's Essex-sonnet, and Thomson's Essay 'On Renascence Drama, or History Made Visible,' 1881." Notes and Queries, 6th Series, 5 (1882), 62-63.

Rejects Thomson's contention that Bacon's sonnet entitled "Apology concerning the Earl of Essex" can in any way support the theory that Bacon wrote Shakespeare's Sonnets.

Barnabe Barnes

356. Barnes, Barnabe. Ten Poems from 'Parthenophil and Parthenophe'. Ed. Madeleine Hope Dodds. Tynemouth: Priory Press, 1929.

357. ______________. Parthenophil and Parthenophe. Ed. Victor A. Doyno. Carbondale, Ill.: Southern Illinois University Press, 1971.

358. Blank, Phillip Everett, Jr. "Lyric Forms in the Sonnet Sequences of Barnabe Barnes." Ph.D. Dissertation, North Carolina, 1965. DA, 26 (1966), 3944-45.

359. Blank, Phillip E., Jr. Lyric Forms in the Sonnet Sequences of Barnabe Barnes. The Hague: Mouton, 1974.

360. Davidson, Clifford. "Barnabe Barnes' A Divine Centurie of Spirituall Sonnets." Lock Haven Review, No. 11 (1969), 3-16.

361. Doyno, Victor A. "An Edition of Barnes's Parthenophil and Parthenophe." Ph.D. Dissertation, Indiana, 1966. DA, 28 (1968), 2644A.
357

362. Eccles, Mark. "Barnabe Barnes." Thomas Lodge and Other Elizabethans. Ed. C.J. Sisson. Cambridge, Mass.: Harvard University Press, 1933, pp. 165-241.

References to "Parthenophil" throughout this biographical essay.

Richard Barnfield

363. Barnfield, Richard. Poems 1594-1598. Ed. Edward Arber. The English Scholar's Library of Old and Modern Works, vol. 14. Birmingham: n.p., 1882. Westminster: Archibald Constable, 1895.

Contains Cynthia with Certaine Sonnets (1595).

364. ________. The Poems of Richard Barnfield. Ed. Montague Summers. London: The Fortune Press, 1936.

Mark Alexander Boyd

365. Fergusson, James. "The Text of Boyd's 'Sonet'." TLS, May 12, 1950, p. 293.

A description of the earliest extant text of Boyd's sonnet, "Fra banc to banc."

366. Speirs, John. The Scots Literary Tradition: An Essay in Criticism. London: Chatto and Windus, 1940.

Discusses Alexander Boyd's Sonet (pp. 86-87).

E. C.

367. Edmonds, Charles, ed. A Lamport Garland, from the Library of Sir Charles Edmund Isham, Bart. Comprising Four Unique Works Hitherto Unknown. London: Roxburghe Club, 1881.

Includes Emaricdulfe by E.C. (1595) and Celestial Elegies by Thomas Rogers (1598).

George Chapman

368. Chapman, George. Poems. Ed. Phyllis Brooks Bartlett. New York: Modern Language Association of America, 1941. 1962.

Contains over 2 dozen sonnets.

Henry Constable

369. Andrews, Michael Cameron. "Constable's 'To Sir Philip Sydneyes Soule'." Explicator, 36, iii (1978), 34-35.

370. Constable, Henry. The Poems. Ed. Joan Grundy. Liverpool: Liverpool University Press, 1960.

The introductory essay treats Diana and the Spiritual Sonnets at length.

371. Fleissner, Robert F., ed. Resolved to Love: the 1592 Edition of Henry Constable's Diana. Salzburg Studies in English Literature, Elizabethan and Renaissance Studies, 93. Salzburg: Institut fur Anglistik und Amerikanistik, Universitat Salzburg, 1980.

In his Foreword to Diana Fleissner explains the textual problems associated with its previous editions. His Afterword, on much the same subject, is more specific and technical.

372. Muir, Kenneth. "The Order of Constable's Sonnets." Notes and Queries, 199 (1954), 424-25.

373. Scott, Janet G. "A Latin Version of a Sonnet of Constable's." Modern Language Review, 20 (1925), 462.

374. Sledd, Hassell Brantley. "The Text of Henry Constable's Sonnets to Penelope Devereux." Ph.D. Dissertation, Boston University, 1965. DA, 26 (1965), 2761-62.

375. Taylor, Estelle W. Review of Robert F. Fleissner, Resolved to Love: The 1592 Edition of Henry Constable's Diana. CLA Journal, 24 (1980), 233-35.

376. Wickes, George. "Henry Constable: Courtier Poet." Renaissance Papers 1956. Southeastern Renaissance Conference, 1956, pp. 102-07.

Discusses Constable's reputation as a sonneteer and some of the influences apparent in the sonnets.

377. Wickes, George. "Henry Constable's Spiritual Sonnets." Month, 18 (1957), 30-40.

Alexander Craig of Rosecraig

378. Craig, Alexander. The Poetical Works of Alexander Craig of Rosecraig. Ed. D. Laing. Glasgow: R. Anderson, Hunterian Club, 1873.

Contains a number of sonnets in The Amorose Songes, Sonets and Elegies of M. Alexander Craige (1606).

Samuel Daniel

379. Adamany, R.G. "Daniel's Debt to Foreign Literatures and *Delia* Edited." Ph.D. Dissertation, Wisconsin, 1963. *DA*, 23 (1963), 4350-51.

380. Beeching, H.C., and C.C.B. "Daniel's 'Sonnets to Delia'." *Notes and Queries*, 100 (1899), 170-71.

A reply to W.F. Prideaux.
401

381. Bludau, Diethild. "Sonnetstruktur bei Samuel Daniel." *Shakespeare Jahrbuch*, 94 (1958), 63-89.

382. Brady, George K. *Samuel Daniel: A Critical Study*. Urbana: University of Illinois Press, 1926.

383. Callanan, Philip W. "Samuel Daniel's Delia, A Critical Edition." Ph.D. Dissertation, Cornell, 1948.

384. Daniel, Samuel. *Poems and A Defence of Ryme*. Ed. Arthur Colby Sprague. Cambridge, Mass.: Harvard University Press, 1930. 1950.

385. Daniel, Samuel, and Michael Drayton. *Daniel's Delia and Drayton's Idea*. Ed. Arundell Esdaile. London: Chatto and Windus, 1908.

The first part of his introduction is a history of the sonnet in England up to the time of Drayton and Daniel.

386. Eccles, Mark. "Samuel Daniel in France and Italy." *Studies in Philology*, 34 (1937), 148-67.

Some of the sonnets provide evidence of his visit to Italy before the publication of *Delia* (1592).

387. Fleay, F.G. "On the Career of Samuel Daniel." *Anglia*, 11 (1889), 619-30.

Discusses briefly some links between Daniel's life and some of the *Delia* sonnets.

388. Goldman, Lloyd. "Samuel Daniel's *Delia* and the Emblem Tradition." *Journal of English and Germanic Philology*, 67 (1968), 49-63.

389. Guggenheim, Josef. *Quellenstudien zu Samuel Daniels Sonettencyklus "Delia."* Berlin: E. Ebering, 1898.

390. Hild, Harold N. "'The Speaking Picture of the Mind': The Poetic Style of Samuel Daniel." Ph.D. Dissertation, Loyola (Chicago), 1974. *DAI*, 35 (1974), 2224A-25A.

Includes a discussion of the sonnet sequence (*Delia*).

391. Hoepfner, Theodore. "Daniel's Delia, Sonnet XL." Explicator, 10 (1952), Item 38.

392. Johnson, Marsue McFaddin. "The Well-Rimed Daniel: An Examination of 'Delia' and 'A Defence of Rhyme'." Ph.D. Dissertation, Arkansas, 1965. DA, 26 (1966), 4661.

Also includes discussion of Sidney's Astrophel and Stella.

393. Kastner, L.E. "The Italian Sources of Daniel's Delia." Modern Language Review, 7 (1912), 153-56.

394. Kau, Joseph Leong Choo. "Art That Conceals Art: Samuel Daniel's Delia." Ph.D. Dissertation, Tufts, 1968. DA, 31 (1970), 1762A.

395. Kau, Joseph. "Daniel's Delia and the Imprese of Bishop Paolo Giovio: Some Iconological Influences." Journal of the Warburg and Courtauld Institute, 33 (1970), 325-28.

396. Kau, Joseph. "Delia's Gentle Lover and the Eternizing Conceit in Elizabethan Sonnets." Anglia, 92 (1974), 334-48.

397. LaBranche, Anthony. "Imitation: Getting in Touch." Modern Language Quarterly, 31 (1970), 308-29.

Includes an examination of some sonnets from Daniel's Delia in an attempt to explain what is meant by a "Petrarchan imitation."

398. Miller, Edward H. "Samuel Daniel's Revisions in Delia." Journal of English and Germanic Philology, 53 (1954), 58-68.

399. Mitchell, Dennis S. "Samuel Daniel's Sonnets 'To Delia'--A Critical Edition." Ph.D. Dissertation, Princeton, 1969. DAI, 31 (1970), 1235A.

400. Murchison, Margaret Lynne. "A Study of Imagery in Samuel Daniel's Delia. Ph.D. Dissertation, Mississippi, 1978. DAI, 39 (1978), 1597A.

401. Prideaux, W.F. "Daniel's 'Sonnets to Delia'." Notes and Queries, 100 (1899), 101-03, 209-10.

Review of H.C. Beeching, A Selection from the Poetry of Samuel Daniel and Michael Drayton, ed. H.C. Beeching (1899).

402. Rees, Joan. Samuel Daniel: A Critical and Biographical Study. Liverpool English Texts and Studies, 9. Liverpool: Liverpool University Press, 1964.

403. Ruutz-Rees, C. "Some Debts of Samuel Daniel to du Bellay." Modern Language Notes, 24 (1909), 134-37.

Discusses Sonnets 11 and 14 of Delia.

404. Schaar, Claes. "A Textual Puzzle in Daniel's Delia." English Studies, 40 (1959), 382-85.

Discusses Sonnet 37.

405. Seronsy, Cecil C. Samuel Daniel. Twayne's English Authors Series, 49. New York: Twayne, 1967.

406. Seronsy, Cecil C. "Well-Languaged Daniel: A Reconsideration." Modern Language Review, 52 (1957), 481-97.

407. Spriet, Pierre. Samuel Daniel, Sa Vie--Son Oeuvre. Etudes Anglaises, 29. Paris: Didier, 1968.

Part II, Chapter 2 is on sonnets and other lyrics.

408. Svensson, Lars-Hakan. Silent Art: Rhetorical and Thematic Patterns in Samuel Daniel's "Delia." Lund Studies in English, 57. Lund: C.W.K. Gleerup, 1980.

The body of the work consists of a detailed study of each sonnet.

409. Thiselton, Alfred E. "Daniel's 'Sonnets to Delia'." Notes and Queries, 100 (1899), 293.

Reply to Prideaux and Beeching.
380, 401

410. Thomson, Patricia. "Sonnet 15 of Samuel Daniel's Delia: A Petrarchan Imitation." Comparative Literature, 17 (1965), 151-57. Reprinted in Ubersetzung und Nachahmung im europaischen Petrarkismus: Studien und Texte. Ed. Luzius Keller. Stuttgart: J.B. Metzler, 1974, pp. 210-17.

411. Ure, Peter. "Two Elizabethan Poets: Daniel and Raleigh." The Age of Shakespeare. Ed. Boris Ford. Harmondsworth, Penguin Books, 1955, pp. 131-46.

One of his observations about Daniel's Delia is that in these lyrics, the poet does not reveal much about his private passions and thoughts (pp. 134-37, 139-40).

412. Williamson, C.F. "The Design of Daniel's Delia." Review of English Studies, NS 19 (1968), 251-60.

413. "Daniel's Poems." Retrospective Review, 8 (1823), 227-46.

This review article discusses The Poetical Works of Mr. Samuel Daniel, Author of the English History to which is prefixed, Memoirs of his Life and Writings. 2 vol. London, 1718. Includes comments about and extracts of Delia.

Sir John Davies

414. Davies, Sir John. The Complete Poems of Sir John Davies. Ed. Alexander B. Grosart. 2 vol. London: Chatto and Windus, 1876.

415. ______________. Poems. Ed. Clare Howard. New York: Columbia University Press, 1941.

416. ______________. The Poems of Sir John Davies. Ed. Robert Krueger. Oxford: Clarendon Press, 1975.

417. Rogers, P. Burwell. "Sir John Davies' Gulling Sonnets." Bucknell University Studies, 4 (1954), 193-204.

418. Sanderson, James L. Sir John Davies. Twayne English Author Series, 175. Boston: Twayne, 1975.

Chapter 2 (pp. 38-59) "'Our English Martial'" treats the epigrams and the sonnets.

419. Wilkes, G.A. "The Poetry of Sir John Davies." Huntington Library Quarterly, 25 (1962), 283-98.

Discusses "Gulling Sonnets."

John Davies of Hereford

420. Davies, John, of Hereford. The Complete Works of John Davies of Hereford (15??-1618). Ed. Alexander B. Grosart. 2 vol. Edinburgh: privately printed, 1878.

The Scourge of Folly contains Epigrams (30,31,55,56, etc.) that are sonnets. Wittes Pilgrimage is a collection of sonnets. He wrote a number of other sonnets as well.

421. Rope, H.E.G. "John Davies of Hereford, Catholic and Rhymer." Anglo-Welsh Review, 11, no. 28 (1961), 20-36.

Reviews briefly (p. 24) Davies's work, Microcosmos (1603), which contains sonnets to great people.

Francis Davison

422. Davison, Francis. Davison's Poetical Rhapsody. Ed. A.H. Bullen. 2 vol. London: George Bell, 1890.

Contains sonnets by Davison, Watson et al.

John Donne

423. Adams, Judith Porter. "John Donne's 'Holy Sonnets': The Paradox of 'This Intermitting Aguish Pietie?'" Ph.D. Dissertation, Miami University, 1975. DAI, 36 (1975), 3722A-23A.

424. Archer, Stanley. "Meditation and the Structure of Donne's 'Holy Sonnets.'" ELH, 28 (1961), 137-47.

425. Archer, Stanley. "Donne's 'Holy Sonnets IX.'" Explicator, 30 (1971), Item 4.

426. Archer, Stanley. "The Archetypal Journey Motif in Donne's Divine Poems." New Essays on Donne. Ed. Gary A. Stringer. Salzburg Studies in English Literature, Elizabethan and Renaissance Studies, 57. Salzburg: Institut fur Englische Sprache und Literatur, Universitat Salzburg, 1977, pp. 173-91.

427. Bald, R.C. John Donne, A Life. New York: Oxford University Press, 1970.

Touches on the years when he wrote the Holy Sonnets and La Corona (pp. 233-36).

428. Bell, Arthur Henry. "Donne's Atonement Conceit in the Holy Sonnets." Cresset, 32, vii (1969), 15-17.

429. Bellette, Antony F. "'Little Worlds Made Cunningly': Significant Form in Donne's Holy Sonnets and 'Goodfriday, 1613.'" Studies in Philology, 72 (1975), 322-47.

430. Black, Lynette. "Principles of Medieval Exegesis in John Donne's 'Oh my black soul!'" [Abstract of a paper read at the Tennessee Philological Association at the University of Tennessee, Martin, February 27, 1981.] Tennessee Philological Bulletin, 18 (July, 1981), 21-22.

431. Blanch, Robert J. "Fear and Despair in Donne's Holy Sonnets." American Benedictine Review, 25 (1974), 476-84.

432. Bond, Ronald B. "John Donne and the Problem of 'Knowing Faith'." Mosaic, 14 (1981), 25-35.

An attempt to "unwrap the unusual doctrinal richness" of Holy Sonnet 1.

433. Brooks, Cleanth. "Three Revolutions in Poetry: II. Wit and High Seriousness." Southern Review, 1 (1935), 328-38.

Brief comment on "Batter my heart" (pp. 330-31).

434. Brower, Reuben A. The Fields of Light. New York: Oxford University Press, 1951.

Discusses Donne's "Show me deare Christ thy spouse, so bright and clear" and Hopkins's "Thou art indeed just, Lord, if I contend" (pp. 24-27), Donne's "At the round earth's imagined corners . . ." (pp. 60-70), and Wordsworth's "Surprised by joy . . ." (pp. 75, 89-92).

435. Carlson, Norman E. "Donne's Holy Sonnets, XIX." Explicator, 32 (1973), Item 19.

436. Cayward, Margaret. "Donne's 'Batter My Heart, Three-Personed God'." Explicator, 38, iii (1980), 5.

An anagram in line 6, "no end," spells Donne.

437. Chambers, A.B. "The Meaning of the 'Temple' in Donne's La Corona." Journal of English and Germanic Philology, 59 (1960), 212-17. Reprinted in Essential Articles for the Study of John Donne's Poetry, ed. John R. Roberts. Hamden, Conn.: Archon, 1975, pp. 349-52.

438. Chambers, A.B. "Christmas: The Liturgy of the Church and English Verse of the Renaissance." Literary Monographs, volume 6. Ed. Eric Rothstein and Joseph Anthony Wittreich, Jr. Madison: University of Wisconsin Press, 1975, pp. 109-53.

Discusses Donne's third sonnet of La Corona on the "Nativitie" (pp. 118-20) and briefly comments on Herbert's sonnet, "Christmas" (p. 127).

439. Chambers, A.B. "La Corona: Philosophic, Sacred, and Poetic Uses of Time." New Essays on Donne. Ed. Gary A Stringer. Salzburg Studies in English Literature, Elizabethan and Renaissance Studies, 57. Salzburg: Institut fur Englische Sprache und Literatur, Universitat Salzburg, 1977, pp. 140-72.

440. Chanoff, David R. "The Conversion of John Donne." Ph.D. Dissertation, Brandeis, 1974. DAI, 35 (1974), 1041A.

In his second chapter Chanoff discusses "the despair evident in the Holy Sonnets ."

441. Clements, Arthur L. "Donne's Holy Sonnet XIV." Modern Language Notes, 76 (1961), 484-89.

442. Clements, Arthur L. John Donne's Poetry: Authoritative Texts: Criticism. New York: W.W. Norton, 1966.

In addition to the textual selections, there are reprints of general essays on the Holy Sonnets by Stanley Archer, Helen Gardner, Louis Martz, and readings of Sonnet 14 by Clements, Herman, Knox, Levenson, and Parish.

443. Combecher, Hans. "John Donnes 'Annunciation': Eine Interpretation." Neueren Sprachen, NS 9 (1960), 488-92.

444. Conlon, Sister Mary Samuel, O.P. "John Donne's <u>Divine Poems</u>: Another Dimension." Ph.D. Dissertation, Stanford, 1963. <u>DA</u>, 24 (1964), 2890.

445. Cornelius, David K. "Donne's 'Holy Sonnet XIV.'" <u>Explicator</u>, 24 (1965), Item 25.

446. Daniels, Edgar. "Donne's 'Crucyfying,' 8." <u>Explicator</u>, 30 (1971), Item 25.

On the fifth sonnet of <u>La Corona</u>.

447. Daniels, Edgar F., and J. Max Patrick. "Donne's 'Holy Sonnets VI.'" <u>Explicator</u>, 31 (1972), Item 12.

448. Delany, Paul. "Donne's Holy Sonnet V, Lines 13-14." <u>American Notes and Queries</u>, 9 (1970), 6-7.

Offers some Scriptural basis for the paradox of the last two lines--the "fiery zeale . . . which doth in eating heale."

449. Denonain, Jean-Jacques. <u>Themes et formes de la Poesie "Metaphysique": Etude d'un aspect de la Litterature Anglaise au Dix-Septieme Siecle</u>. Publications de la Faculte des Lettres d'Alger, 28. Paris: Presses Universitaires de France, 1956.

He discusses Donne's religious poems (pp. 146-59); he also has a chapter on George Herbert in which some of the sonnets are discussed (pp. 185-220).

450. Divver, Albert John. "Seventeenth Century French and English Devotional Poetry and the Ignatian Paradigm." Ph.D. Dissertation, Michigan, 1972. <u>DAI</u>, 33 (1972), 2368A.

Considers the sonnets of Donne and Alabaster.

451. Donne, John. <u>The Complete Poems</u>. Ed. Roger Bennett. Chicago: Packard, 1942. New York: Hendricks House, 1958.

452. __________. <u>The Complete Poetry of John Donne</u>. Ed. John T. Shawcross. Garden City, N.Y.: Anchor Books, 1967.

453. __________. <u>The Divine Poems</u>. Ed. Helen Gardner. Oxford: Clarendon Press, 1952. 1978.

The <u>Holy Sonnets</u> and other "divine poems" with full introduction and apparatus. Includes in Appendix C, "The Interpretation of Donne's Sonnet on the Church."

454. __________. <u>The Poems</u>. Ed. H.J.C. Grierson. London: Oxford University Press, 1912. 1966.

455. Ellrodt, Robert. <u>L'Inspiration personnelle et l'esprit du temps chez les poetes metaphysique anglais</u>. Paris: Jose Corti, 1960, vol. 1.

Part 1 contains comments on the Holy Sonnets throughout.

456. Esch, Arno. Englische Religiose Lyrik des 17. Jahrhunderts: Studien zu Donne, Herbert, Crashaw, Vaughan. Tubingen: Max Niemeyer, 1955.

Compares La Corona with Holy Sonnets in Chapter 2.

457. Faerber, Hansruedi. Das Paradoxe in der Dichtung von John Donne. Zurich: A.G. Ruschlikon, 1950.

Chapter I treats the paradoxes in Donne's religious poetry.

458. Faulkner, Eleanor, and Edgar F. Daniels. "Donne's 'Holy Sonnets XVII' (Since she whome I lovd), 1-2." Explicator, 34 (1976), Item 68.

459. Fausset, Hugh I'Anson. "Donne's Holy Sonnets." Poets and Pundits: Essays and Addresses. London: Jonathan Cape, 1947, pp. 130-34.

460. Fizdale, Tay N. "Patterns of Preception in the Religious Verse of Donne, Herbert and Crashaw." Ph.D. Dissertation, UCLA, 1972. DAI, 33 (1973), 3643A.

461. French, A.L. "The Psychopathology of Donne's Holy Sonnets." Critical Review, 13 (1970), 111-24.

462. Fuzier, Jean. "Donne sonnettiste: Les Holy Sonnets et la tradition europeene." De Shakespeare a T.S. Eliot: Melanges offerts a Henri Fluchere. Paris: Didier, 1976, pp. 153-71.

463. Gardner, Helen. "Donne's 'Divine Poems.'" TLS, January 30, 1953, p. 73.

On La Corona, No. 6 and Holy Sonnet 4, l. 6.

464. Gardner, Helen. "Another Note on Donne: 'Since She Whome I Lov'd'." Modern Language Review, 52 (1957), 564-65.

In response to A.J. Smith's note on Holy Sonnet 17.
535

465. Gardner, Helen. "The Religious Poetry of John Donne." John Donne: A Collection of Critical Essays. Englewood Cliffs, N.J.: Prentice-Hall, 1962, pp. 123-36.

This essay is from Part I of the General Introduction to The Divine Poems, ed. Helen Gardner.
453

466. Grant, Patrick. "Augustinian Spirituality and the Holy Sonnets of John Donne." ELH, 38 (1971), 542-61. Appears as chapter 2 of The Transformation of Sin: Studies in Donne, Herbert, Vaughan, and Traherne. Montreal and London: McGill-Queens University Press; Amherst, Mass.: University of Massachusetts Press, 1974, pp. 40-72.

467. Grant, Patrick. "Donne, Pico, and Holy Sonnet XII." Humanities Association Bulletin, 24 (1973), 39-42.

468. Gregory, Michael. "A Theory for Stylistics--Exemplified: Donne's 'Holy Sonnet XIV.'" Language and Style, 7 (1974), 108-18.

469. Grenander, M.E. "Donne's 'Holy Sonnets,' XII." Explicator, 13 (1955), Item 42.

470. Grenander, M.E. "Holy Sonnets VIII and XVII: John Donne." Boston University Studies in English, 4 (1960), 95-105. Reprinted in Essential Articles for the Study of John Donne's Poetry, ed. John R. Roberts. Hamden, Conn.: Archon, 1975, pp. 324-32.

471. Guss, Donald L. John Donne, Petrarchist: Italianate Conceits and Love Theory in the Songs and Sonets. Detroit: Wayne State University Press, 1966.

Does not discuss sonnets, but its treatment of Petrarchism makes it a useful resource.

472. Hagopian, John V. "Some Cruxes in Donne's Poetry." Notes and Queries, 202 (1957), 500-02.

On Holy Sonnet 11, l. 1. [Author's name appearing at end of note is printed "Hagspian."]

473. Hahn, Thomas. "The Antecedents of Donne's Holy Sonnet XI." American Benedictine Review, 30 (1979), 69-79.

474. Halewood, William H. The Poetry of Grace: Reformation Themes and Structures in English Seventeenth-Century Poetry. New Haven and London: Yale University Press, 1970.

Examines Donne's Holy Sonnets (pp. 80-85); Herbert's "The Holdfast" (p. 108).

475. Handscombe, Richard. "Donne's Holy Sonnet VI: A Problem of Plainness." Language and Style, 13 (1980), 98-108.

476. Heist, William W. "Donne on Divine Grace: Holy Sonnet XIV." Papers of the Michigan Academy of Science, Arts and Letters, 53 (1968), 311-20.

477. Herbert, Rembert Bryce, Jr. "An Analysis of Nine Holy Sonnets of John Donne Set to Music by Benjamin Britten." Ph.D. Dissertation, American University, 1974. DAI, 35 (1974), 2224A.

478. Herman, George. "Donne's 'Holy Sonnets' XIV." Explicator, 12 (1953), Item 18.

479. Holtgen, Karl Josef. "Eine Emblemfolge in Donnes Holy Sonnet XIV. Archiv fur das Studium der neueren Sprachen und Literaturen, 200 (1963), 347-52.

480. Hughes, Richard E. The Progress of the Soul: The Interior Career of John Donne. New York: William Morrow, 1968.

The chapter on "The Middle Years, 1605-1609" (particularly pp. 175-95) covers the Holy Sonnets. La Corona is discussed briefly (pp. 144-45).

481. Hunt, Clay. Donne's Poetry: Essays in Literary Analysis. New Haven: Yale University Press, 1954.

482. Jackson, Robert S. John Donne's Christian Vocation. Evanston, Ill.: Northwestern University Press, 1970.

Final chapter, "Donne's Sonnet on Christ's Spouse," discusses "Show me deare Christ . . ." (Sonnet 18).

483. Kermode, Frank, Stephen Fender, and Kenneth Palmer. English Renaissance Literature: Introductory Lectures. London: Gray-Mills, 1974.

Part of Lecture VII by Kermode deals with some of the Holy Sonnets.

484. Kerrigan, William. "The Fearful Accommodations of John Donne." English Literary Renaissance, 4 (1974), 337-63.

Although he refers to the Holy Sonnets throughout, in one section of the paper Kerrigan focuses on the paradoxes of two--"Batter my heart" and "Show me deare Christ" (pp. 351-60).

485. Knox, George. "Donne's 'Holy Sonnets, XIV.'" Explicator, 15 (1956), Item 2.

486. Kremen, Kathryn R. The Imagination of the Resurrection: The Poetic Continuity of a Religious Motif in Donne, Blake, and Yeats. Lewisburg, Pa.: Bucknell University Press, 1972.

In her chapter, "The First Resurrection in Donne's Religious Prose and Poetry: The Whole 'World's Contracted Thus'," Kremen discusses Holy Sonnets 7, 14, 18.

487. Leishman, J.B. The Monarch of Wit: An Analytical and Comparative Study of the Poetry of John Donne. London: Hutchinson, 1951. 5th ed., rev. 1962.

"The Divine Poems" are discussed in Chapter 5 (particularly pp. 256 ff.).

488. Leishman, J.B. Review of Helen Gardner, John Donne: The Divine Poems. Review of English Studies, NS 5 (1954), 74-83.

489. Levenson, J.C. "Donne's 'Holy Sonnets, XIV.'" Explicator, 11 (1953), Item 31.

490. Levenson, J.C. "Donne's 'Holy Sonnets, XIV.'" Explicator, 12 (1954), Item 36.

491. Linguanti, Elsa. "Una Crisi di Identita: Il 19th degli 'Holy Sonnets' di John Donne." Critical Dimensions, Volume III (English, German and Comparative Literature Essays in Honour of Aurelio Zanco). Ed. Mario Curreli and Alberto Martino. Cuneo, Italy: SASTE, 1978, pp. 201-19.

492. Linville, Susan. "Donne's 'Holy Sonnets IX.'" Explicator, 36, iv (1978), 21-22.

493. Louthan, Doniphan. The Poetry of John Donne, a Study in Explication. New York: Bookman Associates, 1951.

Discusses Holy Sonnets 13, 14, 17, 18 (pp. 118-28).

494. Low, Anthony. Love's Architecture: Devotional Modes in Seventeenth-Century English Poetry. New York: New York University Press, 1978.

Chapter 3 ("John Donne: Liturgy, Meditation, and Song") includes sections on La Corona and the Holy Sonnets. Chapter 4 ("George Herbert: Varieties of Devotion") includes discussions of "Sinner" and "Redemption" (pp. 97-99).

495. Mahood, Molly M. Poetry and Humanism. New Haven: Yale University Press, 1950. New York: Norton, 1970.

In the chapter "Donne: The Progress of the Soul," Mahood briefly discusses his otherworldliness in the Holy Sonnets (pp. 122-25).

496. Martz, Louis L. The Poetry of Meditation: A Study in English Religious Literature. New Haven and London: Yale University Press, 1954.

Chapter 1 contains a section entitled "Donne's 'Holy Sonnets' and 'Good Friday, 1613'," and Chapter 2 a section entitled "Donne's 'La Corona'." The index makes numerous references to sonnets by Donne and Herbert.

497. Martz, Louis L. "John Donne: The Meditative Voice." Massachusetts Review, 1 (1960), 326-42. Reprinted in The Poetry of the Mind. New York: Oxford University Press, 1966, pp. 3-20.

Includes illustrations from Holy Sonnets.

498. Masson, David I. "Thematic Analysis of Sounds in Poetry." Essays on the Language of Literature. Ed. Seymour Chatman and Samuel R. Levin. Boston: Houghton Mifflin, 1967, pp. 54-68.

Includes a phonological examination of Holy Sonnet 7 (pp. 60-61).

499. McCanles, Michael. Dialectical Criticism and Renaissance Literature. Berkeley and Los Angeles: University of California Press, 1975.

Discusses Holy Sonnet 19 (pp. 70-71).

500. McGuire, Philip C. "Private Prayer and English Poetry in the Early Seventeenth Century." Studies in English Literature, 1500-1900, 14 (1974), 63-77.

Donne's Holy Sonnet 1 conforms to the rules for the "prayer of petition" (pp. 67-68).

501. Messenger, Ruth Lester. "John Donne's Twelve 'Holy Sonnets': Concupiscence of Wit." Ph.D. Dissertation, Case Western Reserve, 1976. DAI, 39 (1978), 1596A-97A.

502. *Milward, Peter, and Shonosuke Ishii. "John Donne no 'Seinaru Sonnet' Hyoshaku." Eigo Seinen (Tokyo), 122 (1976), 17-19, 138-40, 222-24, 413-15, 541-44; 123 (1977), 21-23.

503. Morris, Harry. "John Donne's Terrifying Pun." Papers on Language and Literature, 9 (1973), 128-37.

Donne puns both on his name and his late wife's (Ann More); an example of the latter is given in line 9 of "Since she whome I loved, hath payd her last debt" (pp. 133-35).

504. Moseley, C.W.R.D. "A Reading of Donne's Holy Sonnet XIV." Archiv fur das Studium der neueren Sprachen und Literaturen, 217 (1980), 103-08.

505. Mueller, William R. "Donne's Adulterous Female Town." Modern Language Notes, 76 (1961), 312-14.

On Sonnet 14 ("Batter my heart").

506. *Muraoka, Isamu. "Donne no Holy Sonnet: 'Death, be not proud.'" Eigo Seinen, 116 (1970), 246-48.

On Holy Sonnet 10.

507. Nania, John, and P.J. Klemp. "John Donne's La Corona: A Second Structure." Renaissance and Reformation, NS 2 (1978), 49-54.

508. Nelson, T.G.A. "Death, Dung, the Devil and Worldly Delights: A Metaphysical Conceit in Harrington, Donne, and Herbert." Studies in Philology, 76 (1979), 272-87.

Begins by discussing the 52nd sonnet of Astrophel and Stella and Donne's Holy Sonnet 6.

509. Newton, Willoughby. "A Study of John Donne's Sonnet XIV." Anglican Theological Review, 41 (1959), 10-12.

510. Novarr, David. "The Dating of Donne's 'La Corona.'" Philological Quarterly, 36 (1957), 259-65.

511. Novarr, David. The Disinterred Muse: Donne's Texts and Contexts. Ithaca, N.Y.: Cornell University Press, 1980.

Includes a chapter on "The Dating of Donne's La Corona" (pp. 85-93) and sections of the following chapter in which he discusses "The Dating of the Sonnets in the Westmoreland Manuscript" (pp. 115-20) and several of the Holy Sonnets.

512. Parini, Jay. "The Progress of the Soul: Donne and Hopkins in Meditation." Forum for Modern Language Studies, 13 (1977), 303-12.

Discusses the Holy Sonnets of Donne and the "Terrible Sonnets" of Hopkins.

513. Parish, John E. "Donne's 'Holy Sonnets,' XIII." Explicator, 22 (1963), Item 19.

514. Parish, John E. "No. 14 of Donne's Holy Sonnets." College English, 24 (1963), 299-302.

515. Partridge, A. C. John Donne: Language and Style. London: Andre Deutsch, 1978.

Chapter 5 (pp. 127-54), "The Divine Poems," gives commentary on many of the Holy Sonnets and on La Corona.

516. Peterson, Douglas L. "John Donne's Holy Sonnets and the Anglican Doctrine of Contrition." Studies in Philology, 56 (1959), 504-18. Reprinted in Essential Articles for the Study of John Donne's Poetry. Ed. John R. Roberts. Hamden, Conn.: Archon, 1975, pp. 313-23.

517. Pitts, Arthur W., Jr. "Donne's Holy Sonnets VI." Explicator, 29 (1971), Item 39.

518. Praz, Mario. "Donne and the Poetry of His Time." A Garland for John Donne. Ed. Theodore Spencer. Cambridge, Mass.: Harvard University Press, 1931.

Compares Donne's Holy Sonnets to sonnets by Michelangelo (pp. 69-72).

519. Richmond, H.M. "Ronsard and the English Renaissance." Comparative Literature Studies, 7 (1970), 141-59.

In part of this essay which discusses Ronsard's influence on several major English writers, the author examines the influence of the French poet on Holy Sonnet 14 (pp. 143-45).

520. Ricks, Don M. "The Westmoreland Manuscript and the Order of Donne's 'Holy Sonnets.'" Studies in Philology, 63 (1966), 187-95.

521. Roberts, John R., ed. *Essential Articles for the Study of John Donne.* Hamden, Conn.: Archon, 1975.

See A.B. Chambers, M.E. Grenander, and Douglas L. Peterson. 437, 470, 516

522. Roston, Murray. *The Soul of Wit: A Study of John Donne.* Oxford: Clarendon Press, 1974.

Chapter 5, "The Paradox of Faith," discusses the *Holy Sonnets.*

523. Ruffo-Fiore, Silvia. *Donne's Petrarchism: A Comparative View.* Firenze: Grafica Toscana, 1976.

Although there is no discussion of the *Holy Sonnets*, the subject is highly relevant to the influence of Petrarchan conventions in the English lyric--including the sonnet.

524. Rugoff, Milton Allan. *Donne's Imagery: A Study in Creative Sources.* New York: Corporate Press, 1939. rpt. New York: Russell and Russell, 1962.

In a brief passage on the *Holy Sonnets*, he discusses the fusion of the holy and the erotic (pp. 86-87).

525. Ruotolo, Lucio P. "The Trinitarian Framework of Donne's Holy Sonnet XIV." *Journal of the History of Ideas*, 27 (1966), 445-46.

526. Sanders, Wilbur. *John Donne's Poetry.* Cambridge: University Press, 1971.

Considers the *Holy Sonnets* in Chapter 6, "Divinity, Love and Wonder" (particularly pp. 120-32).

527. *Sayama, Eitaro. "John Donne no 'Holy Sonnets': Seinaru Mokuso." *Keijijoshi to Meisoshi.* Ed. Peter Milward and Shonosuke Ishii. Tokyo: Aratake, 1977, pp. 39-81.

528. Schwartz, Elias. "Donne's Holy Sonnets, XIV." *Explicator*, 26 (1967), Item 27.

529. Schwartz, Elias. "*Mimesis* and the Theory of Signs." *College English*, 29 (1968), 343-54.

The essay includes an examination of Holy Sonnet 1 as an imitation of human action (pp. 350-52).

530. Scodel, Joshua. "Holy Sonnet VII and the Ethics of Imagination." *Princeton Journal of the Arts and Sciences*, 2, ii (1978), 5-19.

531. Simon, Irene. "Some Problems of Donne Criticism." *Revue des Langues Vivantes* (Bruxelles), 18 (1952), 317-24, 393-414; 19 (1953), 14-39, 114-32, 201-02. Reprinted in *Some Problems of Donne Criticism.* Langues Vivantes, 40. Bruxelles: Marcel Didier, 1952.

The discussion of La Corona and Holy Sonnets are in vol. 19 (pp. 30-39 and 114-26, respectively).

532. Simpson, Arthur L. "Donne's Holy Sonnets XII." Explicator, 27 (1969), Item 75.

533. Simpson, Evelyn M. "The Text of Donne's 'Divine Poems'." Essays and Studies by Members of the English Association, 26 (1940), pp. 88-105.

534. Simpson, Evelyn M. A Study of the Prose Works of John Donne. Oxford: Clarendon Press, 1924. 1948.

References to Holy Sonnets and La Corona throughout.

535. Smith, A.J. "'Since she whom I lov'd': A Note on Punctuation." Modern Language Review, 51 (1956), 406-07.

Supports Grierson's punctuation of line 10. See Helen Gardner for another view.
464

536. Sparrow, John. "George Herbert and John Donne among the Moravians." Bulletin of the New York Public Library, 68 (1964), 625-53. Reprinted in Martha Winburn England and John Sparrow, Hymns Unbidden: Donne, Herbert, Blake, Emily Dickinson and the Hymnographers. New York: New York Public Library, 1964, pp. 1-28.

Some adaptations of Donne's Holy Sonnets into hymns (pp. 644-45, 651).

537. Steele, Thomas J., S.J. "Donne's Holy Sonnets XIV." Explicator, 29 (1971), Item 74.

538. Steig, Michael. "Donne's Divine Rapist: Unconscious Fantasy in Holy Sonnet XIV." Hartford Studies in Literature, 4 (1972), 52-58.

539. Stephenson, A.A. "G.M. Hopkins and John Donne." Downside Review, 77 (1959), 300-20.

Illustrates Hopkins's dependence on Donne in the beginning of the article by comparing Holy Sonnet 1 with The Wreck of the Deutschland.

540. Stewart, Stanley. The Enclosed Garden: The Tradition and the Image in Seventeenth-Century Poetry. Madison: University of Wisconsin Press, 1966.

Examines "Show me deare Christ" (pp. 19-22).

541. Stringer, Gary. "Donne's Religious Personae: A Response." Southern Quarterly, 14 (1976), 191-94.
542

542. Thomas, Helen. "The Concept of the Persona in John Donne's Religious Poetry." Southern Quarterly, 14 (1976), 183-90.

See Stringer's response.
541

543. Turnell, Martin. "Donne's Quest for Unity." Commonweal, 57 (1952), 15-18.

On Holy Sonnet 18 ("Show me deare Christ").

544. Untermeyer, Louis. "Wit and Sensibility: Metaphor into Metaphysics." Play in Poetry. New York: Harcourt, Brace, 1938, pp. 3-24.

The Henry Ward Beecher Lectures Delivered at Amherst College, October, 1937 on "Batter my Heart" (pp. 16-18).

545. Vernon, John. Poetry and the Body. Urbana, Illinois: University of Illinois Press, 1979.

"On Donne's Holy Sonnet 14" (pp. 73-84).

546. Wagner, Linda Welshimer. "Donne's Secular and Religious Poetry." Lock Haven Review, 7 (1965), 13-22.

Includes a close reading of Holy Sonnet 2.

547. Wall, John N., Jr. "Donne's Wit of Redemption: The Drama of Prayer in the Holy Sonnets." Studies in Philology, 73 (1976), 189-203.

548. Walter, James. "Donne's 'Holy Sonnet XVIII' and the Bride of Christ." Innisfree, 2 (1975), 4-7.

549. Wanninger, Mary Tenney. "Donne's 'Holy Sonnets,' XIV." Explicator, 28 (1969), Item 37.

550. Ward, Elizabeth. "Holy Sonnet X." English "A" Analyst, 12 (1949), 1-4.

551. Wennerstrom, Mary H. "Sonnets and Sound: Benjamin Britten's Settings of Shakespeare, Donne, and Keats." Yearbook of Comparative and General Literature, No. 27 (1978), 59-61.

On Donne's Sonnet 7 ("At the round earths imagin'd corners") and Shakespeare's Sonnet 43 ("When most I wink, then do mine eyes best see").

552. White, Helen C. The Metaphysical Poets: A Study in Religious Experience. New York: Macmillan, 1936.

Chapter 5 (pp. 121-49) is on Donne's Holy Sonnets. Passing reference to George Herbert's sonnets in Chapters 6 and 7.

553. Williamson, George. "Textual Difficulties in the Interpretation of Donne's Poetry." *Modern Philology*, 38 (1940), 37-72.

Discusses *Holy Sonnets* 3, 13, and 16 (pp. 60-64).

554. Wilson, Edward M. "Spanish and English Religious Poetry of the Seventeenth Century." *Journal of Ecclesiastical History*, 9 (1958), 38-53.

Concerns Donne's *Holy Sonnets* (pp. 48-51).

555. Wolfe, Ralph Haven, and Edgar F. Daniels. "Rime and Idea in Donne's Holy Sonnet X." *American Notes and Queries*, 5 (1967), 116-17.

556. Zimmerman, Donald E. *The Nature of Man: John Donne's Songs and Holy Sonnets*. Emporia State Research Studies, vol. 8, no. 3. Emporia, Kans.: Kansas State Teachers College, 1960.

Discusses *Holy Sonnets* (pp. 25-30).

557. Zitner, S.P. "Rhetoric and Doctrine in Donne's Holy Sonnet IV." *Renaissance and Reformation*, NS 3 (1979), 66-76.

Michael Drayton

558. Beeching, H.C. "The Sonnets of Michael Drayton." *Literature*, 5 (1899), 181-83.

Takes issue with Sidney Lee, who believed Shakespeare's Sonnets were influenced by Drayton. Beeching argues that it was Drayton who was influenced by Shakespeare.
2341

559. Behr, Eugene Thomas. "Structure and Meaning in the Sonnet Sequences of Michael Drayton, 1594-1619." Ph.D. Dissertation, Princeton, 1976. *DAI*, 37 (1977), 5135A.

560. Berthelot, Joseph A. *Michael Drayton*. Twayne's English Authors Series, 52. New York: Twayne, 1967.

The first chapter, "The Sonnet Sequence" (pp. 17-44) traces the editorial history of *Ideas Mirrour*, later changed to *Idea* in subsequent editions.

561. Bolieu, Louis Sherman, Jr. "Michael Drayton, Transitional Sonneteer: The Place of Drayton in English Renaissance Sonnet Development." Ph.D. Dissertation, Texas A and M, 1972. *DAI*, 33 (1973), 6301A-02A.

Includes discussion of Sidney and Donne.

562. Broich, Ulrich. "Michael Drayton: 'The Paradox'." *Die Englische Lyrik: Von der Renaissance bis zur Gegenwart*. Ed. Karl Heinz Goller. Dusseldorf: August Bagel, 1968, vol. 1, pp. 65-75.

In one part of this explication of Amour 50 of *Idea's Mirror* the poem is briefly compared to Barnes's Sonnet 31 of *Parthenophil and Parthenophe*, a poem similar to Drayton's in its use of paradox.

563. Clark, Paul O. "Other Visits to Love's Deathbed." *CEA Critic*, 37,i (1974), 30-31.

In response to Higdon, on Sonnet 61 ("Love's Farewell").
576

564. Clary, Frank Nicholas, Jr. "Drayton, Greville, and Shakespeare: Sonneteers in an Age of Satire." Ph.D. Dissertation, Notre Dame, 1971. *DAI*, 32 (1971), 2634A.

565. Collier, J. Payne. "Michael Drayton and his 'Idea's Mirror'." *Gentleman's Magazine*, NS 34 (1850), 262-65.

566. Collier, J.P. "The Registers of the Stationers' Company." *Notes and Queries*, 26 (1862), 421-23.

Contains an entry from Stationers' Register for "Ideas Myrrour, &c . . ." with note.

567. Davis, Walter R. "'Fantastickly I sing': Drayton's *Idea* of 1619." *Studies in Philology*, 66 (1969), 204-16.

Compares Drayton's sonnets with those of Sidney and Greville.

568. Drayton, Michael. *Minor Poems of Michael Drayton*. Ed. Cyril Brett. Oxford: Clarendon Press, 1907.

569. Drayton, Michael. *Poems*. Ed. John Buxton. 2 vol. London: Routledge and Kegan Paul; Cambridge, Mass.: Harvard University Press, 1953.

570. Drayton, Michael. *The Works of Michael Drayton*. Ed. J.W. Hebel, K. Tillotson, B.H. Newdigate. 5 vol. Oxford: Shakespeare Head Press, 1931-41. 1961.

Includes in volume 5 (pp. 302-04), a valuable "Finding-List For Drayton's Sonnets" which places the location of each sonnet in the six versions published in Drayton's lifetime.

571. Elton, Oliver. *An Introduction to Michael Drayton*. Manchester: Spenser Society, 1895.

572. Elton, Oliver. *Michael Drayton: A Critical Study*. London: A. Constable, 1905. rpt. New York: Russell and Russell, 1966.

Enlarged and revised edition of Elton's An Introduction. An appendix contains an index to various editions of his sonnets.

573. Ewell, Barbara C., S.S.N.D. "Art and Experience in the Poetry of Michael Drayton." Ph.D. Dissertation, Notre Dame, 1974. DAI, 35 (1974), 2264A-65A.

"Ideas Mirrour" (1594) and "Idea" (1619) occupy an important place in the study.

574. Greg, W.W. "Drayton's Sonnets." Modern Language Review, 2 (1906), 164-65.

On a variant reading in "Since there's no help, come let us kiss and part" (Sonnet 61).

575. Hardin, Richard F. Michael Drayton and the Passing of Elizabethan England. Lawrence, Kansas: University Press of Kansas, 1973.

Discussion of Sonnets (pp. 18-25).

576. Higdon, David Leon. "Love's Deathbed Revisited." CEA Critic, 36, i (1973), 35.

On Sonnet 61 ("Love's Farewell")--a monologue or a dialogue? For responses see Reamer, Clark and Stringer.
563, 584, 589

577. Hillyer, Robert. "The Drayton Sonnets." Freeman, 6 (1923), 488-89.

578. Love, John Michael. "'To Varietie Inclin'd': A Study of Michael Drayton's Idea." Ph.D. Dissertation, North Carolina, 1975. DAI, 36 (1975), 3732A-33A.

579. Newdigate, B.H. "Michael Drayton and his 'Idea'." Dublin Review, 200 (1937), 79-92.

580. Newdigate, Bernard H. Michael Drayton and his Circle. Oxford: Shakespeare Head Press, 1941. 1961.

Ch. 4 ("Anne Goodere") deals in part with "Ideas Mirrour." Another section dealing with sonnets (pp. 141-45) examines Drayton as Shakespeare's rival poet.

581. Phillipson, John S. "A Drayton Sonnet." CEA Critic, 25, vii (1963), 3.

On Sonnet 61, "Love's Farewell."

582. Perrine, Laurence. "A Drayton Sonnet." CEA Critic, 25, ix (1963), 8.

On "Love's Farewell."

583. Praz, Mario. "Michael Drayton." English Studies, 28 (1947), 97-107.

584. Reamer, Owen J. "Come Back to Love's Deathbed." CEA Critic, 37, i (1974), 28-29.

A response to Higdon, on Sonnet 61 ("Love's Farewell"). 576

585. Robertson, Jean. "Drayton and the Countess of Pembroke." Review of English Studies, NS 16 (1965), 49.

Refers to a passage in 'Amour 51' in Idea's Mirrour.

586. Schonert, Jorg. "Draytons Sonett-Revisionen: Zum Problem, des 'Ubergangsdichters'." Anglia, 85 (1967), 161-83.

587. Schroder, William Thomas. "Michael Drayton: A Study of the Idea Sonnet Revisions." Ph.D. Dissertation, Northwestern, 1959. DA 20 (1959), 2277-78.

588. St. Clair, F.Y. "Drayton's First Revision of his Sonnets." Studies in Philology, 36 (1939), 40-59.

589. Stringer, Gary. "Love's Deathbed One More Time: A Reply to Mr. Leon Higdon." CEA Critic, 37, i (1974), 27-28.

A response to Higdon, on Sonnet 61 ("Love's Farewell"). 576

590. Sweeney, Kevin McConnell. "The Structural Importance of the First Quatrain in the Sequence Sonnets of Michael Drayton: A Study of the 4-10 Sonnet." Ph.D. Dissertation, Catholic University of America, 1977. DAI, 38 (1977), 2147A.

591. Westling, Louise Hutchings. The Evolution of Michael Drayton's "Idea." Salzburg Studies in English Literature, Elizabethan and Renaissance Studies, 37. Salzburg: Institut fur Englische Sprache und Literature, Universitat Salzburg, 1974.

592. Westling, Louise Hutchings. "The Pose of the Libertine in Michael Drayton's Idea." Ph.D. Dissertation, Oregon, 1974. DAI, 35 (1974), 3706A.

593. Whitaker, Lemuel. "The Sonnets of Michael Drayton." Modern Philology, 1 (1904), 563-67.

594. Williams, Franklin B., Jr. "A Sonnet by Drayton?" TLS, December 11, 1937, p. 947.

Attributes to Michael Drayton a commendatory sonnet that accompanied John Weever's "Faunus and Melliflora."

William Drummond of Hawthornden

595. Arens, J.C. "Twee Sonnetten bij Revius en Drummond." Neophilologus, 47 (1963), 151-53.

596. Baldensperger, Fernand. "Un Sonnet de William Drummond et son point de depart dans 'La Semaine' de du Bartas." Modern Language Notes, 55 (1940), 493-95.

597. Drummond, William. The Poetical Works of William Drummond of Hawthornden. Ed. Leon Emile Kastner. 2 vol. London: W. Blackwood and Sons, 1913.

598. ________________. Poems. Ed. William C. Ward. London: Lawrence and Bullen; New York: Charles Scribner's, 1894.

599. Kastner, L.E. "Drummond of Hawthornden and the Poets of the Pleiade." Modern Language Review, 4 (1909), 329-41.

600. Kastner, L.E. "Drummond of Hawthornden and the French Poets of the Sixteenth Century." Modern Language Review, 5 (1910), 40-53.

Speaks, in part, of several of Drummond's sonnets and their relationship to French sources (p. 44).

601. Kastner, L.E. "Drummond's Indebtedness to Sidney." Modern Language Review, 6 (1911), 157-64.

602. Kastner, L.E. "Some Unpublished Poems of Drummond from the Hawthornden MSS." Modern Language Review, 6 (1911), 324-34.

603. Kastner, L.E. "On the Italian and French Sources of Drummond of Hawthornden." Modern Language Review, 6 (1911), 462-70.

604. Kastner, L.E. "The Italian and Spanish Sources of William Drummond of Hawthornden." Miscellanea di studi critici in onore di Vincenzo Crescini. Cividale: Fratelli Stagni, 1927, pp. 150-82. Torino: Bottega d'Erasmo, 1957, pp. 151-82.

Most of the poems discussed are Drummond's sonnets.

605. Masson, David. Drummond of Hawthornden: The Story of His Life and Writings. London: Macmillan, 1873.

Chapter 5 contains some critical remarks on his poetry. Refers to the high reputation of his sonnets among the 19th-century critics.

606. Severance, Sibyl Lutz. "'Some Other Figure': The Vision of Change in Flowres of Sion, 1623." Spenser Studies: A Renaissance Poetry Annual, II. Ed. Patrick Cullen and Thomas P. Roche, Jr. Pittsburgh: University of Pittsburgh Press, 1981, pp. 217-25.

The first sonnet notes that "constant Change" is the only constant, and he resolves in this poem and in the sequence to fix his mind on Christ's permanence.

Giles Fletcher the Elder

607. Fletcher, Giles, the Elder. The English Works of Giles Fletcher, the Elder. Ed. Lloyd E. Berry. Madison: University of Wisconsin Press, 1964.

608. Scott, Janet G. "The Sources of Giles Fletcher's Licia." Modern Language Review, 20 (1925), 187-88.

William Fowler

609. Fowler, William. The Works of William Fowler. Ed. Henry W. Meikle. Edinburgh: Scottish Text Society, 1914, vol. 1 (verse).

Includes over 130 sonnets.

George Gascoigne

610. Gascoigne, George. The Posies. Ed. J.W. Cunliffe. Cambridge: University Press, 1907.

This is volume 1 of the two volume Works.

611. Gascoigne, George. A Hundreth Sundrie Flowres. Ed. C.T. Prouty. Columbia: University of Missouri, 1942.

Contains a number of sonnets by Gascoigne scattered through the work.

612. Hull, Mary Lou. "Invention in George Gascoigne's Poetry: A Hundreth Sundrie Flowres and The Posies." Ph.D. Dissertation, Colorado, 1964. DA, 25 (1965), 5907-08.

613. Johnson, Ronald C. George Gascoigne. Twayne English Authors Series, 133. New York: Twayne, 1972.

Of relevance to the sonnet are Chapter 2 on "Gascoigne and Petrarch" and Chapter 3 on "The Love Lyrics."

614. Prouty, Charles Tyler. George Gascoigne, Elizabethan Courtier, Soldier, and Poet. New York: Columbia University Press, 1942.

Last part of chapter 5 is concerned with sonnets. Includes also discussion of Wyatt.

615. Sasek, Lawrence A. "Gascoigne and the Elizabethan Sonnet Sequences." Notes and Queries, 201 (1956), 143-44.

616. Schelling, Felix E. The Life and Writings of George Gascoigne. University of Pennsylvania Series in Philology, Literature and Archaeology, Vol. II, No. 4. Philadelphia: University of Pennsylvania, 1893. rpt. New York: Russell and Russell, 1967.

Contains 2 pages on his sonnets (pp. 34-35).

Barnabe Googe

617. Googe, Barnabe. Eglogs, Epytaphes, and Sonettes (1563). Ed. Edward Arber. Westminster: A. Constable, 1895.

618. Harting, P.N.U. "The 'Sonnettes' of Barnabe Googe." English Studies, 11 (1929), 100-02.

Googe's two sonnets were printed in 28 short lines but when reprinted in decasyllabic lines are obviously sonnets.

619. Hudson, Hoyt H. Review of Hyder E. Rollins, Tottel's Miscellany. Modern Language Notes, 45 (1930), 541-42.

He briefly makes the same point that appeared later in his PMLA article on Googe; i.e. Googe wrote two real sonnets, which went unrecognized because of the manner in which they were printed.

620. Hudson, Hoyt H. "Sonnets by Barnabe Googe." PMLA, 48 (1933), 293-94.

Hudson notes that he first published the observation that Googe had two bona fide sonnets in Hebel and Hudson, Poetry of the English Renaissance (1929) and later in the above review of Tottel's Miscellany. It would appear that Hudson was unaware or chose to ignore the fact that Harting had published on the same point in 1929.

Robert Greene

621. Greene, Robert. The Poetry of Robert Greene. Ed. Tetsumaro Hayashi. Ball State Monographs, 27. Muncie, Ind.: Ball State University, 1977.

Contains some sonnets.

622. Jordan, John Clark. Robert Greene. New York: Columbia University Press, 1915.

Chapter 5 discusses Greene's poetry including a brief reference to his sonnets (pp. 149-50).

Fulke Greville

623. Bernat, Paula. "Images of Life: A Study of Theme and Convention in Fulke Greville's Caelica." Ph.D. Dissertation, Columbia, 1970. DAI, 33 (1973), 5669A.

624. Chaudhuri, Sukanta. Infirm Glory: Shakespeare and the Renaissance Image of Man. Oxford: Clarendon Press, 1981.

His chapter on "The English Renaissance" contains a section entitled "Greville and Donne: the Experience of Love." Donne's ideal of love is able to absorb "the imperfections of the human state"; in Greville's Caelica the problem remains unresolved (pp. 96-99).

625. Croll, Morris W. The Works of Fulke Greville. Philadelphia: J.B. Lippincott, 1903.

The first chapter of this monograph deals with Caelica.

626. De Mourgues, Odette. Metaphysical Baroque and Precieux Poetry. Oxford: Clarendon Press, 1953.

Discusses Greville's Sonnet 87 from Caelica (pp. 24-25).

627. Devereux, James A., S.J. "Love Human and Divine in Fulke Greville's Caelica." Christianity and Literature, 29, iv (1980), 19-31.

628. Farmer, Norman K., Jr. "Fulke Greville's Caelica: A Study in Meaning and Style." Ph.D. Dissertation, Pennsylvania, 1966. DA, 27 (1966), 1335A.

629. Farmer, Norman K., Jr. "Fulke Greville and the Poetic of the Plain Style." Texas Studies in Literature and Language, 11 (1969), 657-70.

A brief but significant application of his thesis to Caelica (p. 669).

630. Frost, William. Fulke Greville's "Caelica": An Evaluation. Brattleboro, Vt.: privately printed, 1942.

631. Gilman, Ernest B. The Curious Perspective: Literary and Pictorial Wit in the Seventeenth Century. New Haven: Yale University Press, 1978.

In his chapter "The Pauline Perspectives of the Mind," Gilman discusses Caelica, Sonnet 100 (pp. 197-201).

632. Glowe, Anthony George. "The Search for a Permanent and Satisfying Love in Fulke Greville's Caelica." Ph.D. Dissertation, Case Western Reserve, 1973. DAI, 34 (1974), 7191A.

633. Greville, Fulke. _Poems and Dramas of Fulke Greville_. Ed. Geoffrey Bullough. 2 vol. Edinburgh: Oliver and Boyd, 1939. New York: Oxford University Press, 1945.

634. Greville, Fulke. _Caelica_. Ed. Una Ellis-Fermor. Newtown, Montgomeryshire: n.p., 1936.

635. Greville, Fulke. _Selected Poems of Fulke Greville_. Ed. Thom Gunn. London: Faber and Faber; Chicago: University of Chicago Press, 1968.

636. Greville, Fulke. _Selected Writings of Fulke Greville_. Ed. Joan Rees. London: Athlone Press, 1973.

637. Heidtmann, Peter. "The Lyrics of Fulke Greville." _Ohio University Review_, 10 (1968), 28-41.

On _Caelica_.

638. Korach, Alice Florence. "The Dialectic Structure of English Renaissance Literature." Ph.D. Dissertation, Texas, 1980. _DAI_, 41 (1980), 1612A.

Includes a discussion of _Caelica_.

639. Kristal, Peter L. "Greville's Well Framed Art: Essays on the Poetry of Fulke Greville, with Special Reference to _Caelica_." Ph.D. Dissertation, Brandeis, 1975. _DAI_, 36 (1975), 2848A.

640. Larson, Charles. _Fulke Greville_. Twayne's English Authors Series, 302. Boston: Twayne, 1980.

Chapter 2, "The Love Poet" (pp. 25-42), examines Greville's _Caelica_. Only 41 of its 109 lyrics are sonnets.

641. Litt, Gary L. "'Images of Life': A Study of Narrative and Structure in Fulke Greville's _Caelica_. _Studies in Philology_, 69 (1972), 217-30.

642. Meehan, Brian J. "Fulke Greville's _Caelica_: A Study in Sources and Meaning." Ph.D. Dissertation, UCLA, 1972. _DAI_, 33 (1973), 5687A-88A.

643. Mostysser, Toby. "Fulke Greville's _Caelica_: The Lyrics of a Courtier and a Calvinist." Ph.D. Dissertation, City University of New York, 1974. _DAI_, 35 (1974), 2287A.

644. Rebholz, Ronald A. _The Life of Fulke Greville, First Lord Brooke_. Oxford: Clarendon Press, 1971.

In the chapter "Limits as Poet and Lover" (pp. 50-67), Rebholz discusses Sidney's influence on _Caelica_. An appendix considers some of the problems of its dating (pp. 325-28, 338-40, _et passim_).

645. Rees, Joan. *Fulke Greville, Lord Brooke, 1554-1628: A Critical Biography*. Berkeley: University of California Press, 1971.

Chapter 5 (pp. 78-118) discusses *Caelica*.

646. Roberts, David A. "Fulke Greville's *Caelica* and the Language of Convention." Ph.D. Dissertation, Connecticut, 1972. *DAI*, 33 (1972), 2949A.

647. *Shikoda, Mitsuo. "Fulke Greville as a Calvinist (II)--Aspects of Love in *Caelica*." *Essays and Studies in English Language and Literature*, 51-52 (1967), 127-44.

In Japanese.

648. Waswo, Richard. *The Fatal Mirror: Themes and Techniques in the Poetry of Fulke Greville*. Charlottesville: University Press of Virginia, 1972.

Extensive discussion of *Caelica* and the individual sonnets throughout.

649. Waswo, Richard. "The Petrarchan Tradition as a Dialectic of Limits." *Studies in the Literary Imagination*, 11 (1978), 1-16.

Greville is considered to be the epitome of Petrarchanism among English poets; *Caelica* shows the Petrarchan influence that was typical among the Elizabethan sonnet sequences.

650. Wilkes, G.A. "The Sequence of Writings of Fulke Greville, Lord Brooke." *Studies in Philology*, 56 (1959), 489-503.

651. Williamson, George. "The Convention of *The Extasie*." *Seventeenth Century Contexts*. Chicago: University of Chicago Press, 1960, pp. 63-77.

Includes discussion of *Caelica*, no. 75.

652. Williamson, George. *The Proper Wit of Poetry*. London: Faber and Faber, 1961.

In his chapter on "Jacobean Wit" he discusses Sonnets 22, 69, and 87 from *Caelica* (pp. 28-30).

Bartholomew Griffin

653. Dowden, Edward. "The Date of *The Merchant of Venice*." *Academy*, 29 (1886), 44-45.

A sonnet in *Fidessa* is similar to the song in *The Merchant of Venice* ("Tell me where is fancy bred").

654. Greene, Richard. "Griffin's 'Fidessa'." Notes and Queries, 1st Series, 10 (1854), 367-69.

Greene believes that a sonnet (No. 3) that appeared in Fidessa and later in The Passionate Pilgrim did not belong in Fidessa. 1979

655. Lanier, Sidney. "A Forgotten English Poet." Music and Poetry: Essays Upon Some Aspects and Inter-relations of the Two Arts. New York: Charles Scribner's Sons, 1898. rpt. New York: Haskell House, 1969, pp. 115-35.

Principally about Griffin's sonnets with reference to Sidney and Daniel.

Nicholas Grimald

656. Arens, J.C. "DuBellay's Sonnet Face le Ciel Adapted by Nicholas Grimald." Papers on English Language and Literature, 1 (1965), 77-78.

657. Grimald, Nicholas. The Life and Poems of Nicholas Grimald. Ed. LeRoy R. Merrill. Yale Studies in English, No. 69. New Haven: Yale University Press, 1925.

William Habington

658. Combs, Homer C. "Habington's Castara and the Date of His Marriage." Modern Language Notes, 63 (1948), 182-83.

Henry VIII of England

659. Brooks, Sarah W. "Some Predecessors of Spenser." Poet-Lore, 1 (1890), 214-23.

Mentions a book of sonnets by Henry VIII (a manuscript edition) in the possession of the "late" Lord of Eglinton.

George Herbert

660. Bell, Ilona. "'Setting Foot into Divinity': George Herbert and the English Reformation." Modern Language Quarterly, 38 (1977), 219-41.

Makes some pointed comparisons between Herbert's work and Alabaster's devotional sonnets before turning to an examination of Herbert's poems, including the sonnet "Redemption" (pp. 237-38).

661. Dundas, Judith. "Levity and Grace: The Poetry of Sacred Wit." Yearbook of English Studies, 2 (1972), 93-102.

In illustrating her thesis she briefly discusses Herbert's sonnet "Prayer" (I) (pp. 96-97).

662. Dyson, A.E. and Julian Lovelock. Masterful Images: English Poetry from Metaphysicals to Romantics. London: Macmillan, 1976.

The second chapter is an explication of Herbert's sonnet "Redemption" (pp. 29-35).

663. Edgecombe, Rodney. "Sweetnesse Readie Penn'd": Imagery, Syntax and Metrics in the Poetry of George Herbert. Salzburg Studies in English Literature, 84:2. Salzburg: Institut fur Anglistik und Amerikanistik, 1980.

The monograph contains an appendix devoted exclusively to a discussion of the sonnets in The Temple (pp. 164-75).

664. El-Gabalawy, Saad. "The Pilgrimage: George Herbert's Favourite Allegorical Technique." CLA Journal, 13 (1970), 408-19.

Includes discussions of "Redemption" and "Christmas" (pp. 414-16).

665. Fish, Stanley E. "Letting Go: The Reader in Herbert's Poetry." ELH, 37 (1970), 475-94.

"The Holdfast" is discussed (pp. 480-85).

666. Fish, Stanley. Self-Consuming Artifacts: The Experience of Seventeenth-Century Literature. Berkeley: University of California Press, 1972.

Discusses "The Holdfast" (pp. 173-76), Sonnets from Walton's Lives (pp. 191-92), Love (I) and (II) (pp. 192-93).

667. Greenwood, E.B. "George Herbert's Sonnet 'Prayer': A Stylistic Study." Essays in Criticism, 15 (1965), 27-45.

668. Hammond, Gerald. "Herbert's Prayer I." Explicator, 39 (1980), 41-43.

669. Herbert, George. The Works of George Herbert. Ed. F.E. Hutchinson. Oxford: Clarendon Press, 1941.

670. Hilberry, Conrad. "Two Cruxes in George Herbert's 'Redemption'." Notes and Queries, 201 (1956), 514.

671. Hughes, R.E. "George Herbert's Rhetorical World." Criticism, 3 (1961), 86-94.

Includes discussions of three sonnets--"Prayer," "Redemption," and "Christmas."

672. Knieger, Bernard. "Herbert's 'Redemption'." Explicator, 11 (1953), Item 24.

673. Lapidus, Lawrence A. "'Lean Not Unto Thine Own Understanding': Grammar as Theme in George Herbert's 'Good Friday' and 'Prayer (1)'." Quarterly Journal of Speech, 62 (1976), 167-78.

674. Mollenkott, Virginia R. "Experimental Freedom in Herbert's Sonnets." Christian Scholar's Review, 1 (1971), 109-16.

675. Mollenkott, Virginia R. "George Herbert's Epithet-Sonnets." Genre, 5 (1972), 131-37.

Discusses "Holy Scriptures (I)" and "Prayer (I)."

676. Mollenkott, Virginia R. "George Herbert's 'Redemption'." English Language Notes, 10 (1973), 262-67.

677. Ottenhoff, John H. "Herbert's Sonnets." George Herbert Journal, 2, ii (1979), 1-14.

678. Rickey, Mary Ellen. Utmost Art: Complexity in the Verse of George Herbert. Lexington: University of Kentucky Press, 1966.

Numerous references to most of the sonnets.

679. Schwartz, Helen J. "Herbert's 'Grief'." Explicator, 31 (1973), Item 43.

The poet's grief overflowing the form of the sonnet requires an additional 4 lines to what otherwise is a sonnet.

680. Stanwood, P.G. "The Liveliness of Flesh and Blood: Herbert's 'Prayer I' and 'Love III'." Seventeenth Century News, 31 (1973), 52-53.

681. Stein, Arnold. George Herbert's Lyrics. Baltimore: Johns Hopkins Press, 1968.

Includes discussions of most of Herbert's sonnets (plus "Grief"--an 18-line "sonnet").

682. Summers, Joseph. "From 'Josephs coat' to 'A true Hymne'." George Herbert Journal, 2 (1978), 1-11.

Includes discussion of two sonnets, "Josephs coat" and "Grief" (the latter an 18-line sonnet).

683. Summers, Joseph H. George Herbert: His Religion and Art. Cambridge, Mass.: Harvard University Press; London: Chatto and Windus, 1954.

Chapter 9, "Allegory and Sonnet: A Traditional Mode and a Traditional Form" (pp. 171-84).

684. Tuve, Rosemond. "George Herbert and Caritas." Journal of the Warburg and Courtauld Institute, 22 (1959), 303-31.

Refers to Herbert's sonnets throughout.

685. Unrau, John. "Three Notes on George Herbert." Notes and Queries, 213 (1968), 94-95.

The first note discusses "Holy Scriptures I," ll. 8-9.

686. Vendler, Helen. The Poetry of George Herbert. Cambridge, Mass.: Harvard University Press, 1975.

References throughout to most of the sonnets.

687. Vendler, Helen. "The Re-invented Poem: George Herbert's Alternatives." Forms of Lyric: Selected Papers from the English Institute. Ed. Reuben A. Brower. New York: Columbia University Press, 1970, pp. 19-45.

Discusses the sonnet "Prayer (I)" (pp. 28-31).

688. Von Ende, Frederick. "George Herbert's 'The Sonne': In Defense of the English Language." Studies in English Literature, 1500-1900, 12 (1972), 173-82.

This sonnet is built upon the conventional "son-sun" pun.

689. Wilson, Edward M. "Spanish and English Religious Poetry of the Seventeenth Century." Spanish and English Literature of the 16th and 17th Centuries. Cambridge: Cambridge University Press, 1980, pp. 234-49. First published in Journal of Ecclesiastical History, 9 (1958), 38-53.

This essay makes some comparisons between Donne's Holy Sonnets, Herbert's "Redemption" and the work of Spanish poets.

Hugh Holland

690. Withington, Eleanor. "Hugh Holland's Acrostic Sonnet." Notes and Queries, 203 (1958), 424-25.

Since Holland once wrote that he had "sung acrosticke sonets sweetely," it is not unreasonable to assume that this sonnet by H.H. (with an acrostic to a Fraunces Parker) was probably by Holland.

Thomas Hudson

691. Hudson, Thomas. Thomas Hudson's Historie of Judith. Ed. James Craigie. Edinburgh: Scottish Text Society, 1941.

Contains 3 sonnets by Hudson, 1 by King James VI, and 1 by William Fowler. Craigie also discusses "The Sonnet at the Court of King James VI of Scotland" (xcii-ci).

James I of England

692. James VI of Scotland. The Basilicon Doron of King James VI. Ed. J. Craigie. 2 vol. Edinburgh: Scottish Text Society, 1944.

Includes 2 sonnets.

693. ______. New Poems by James I of England. Ed. Allen F. Westcott. New York: Columbia University Press, 1911.

Contains list of occasional sonnets by other poets (p. li).

694. ______. The Poems of James VI of Scotland. Ed. James Craigie. 2 vol. Edinburgh and London: Scottish Text Society, 1955-58.

Volume 2 contains a great number of sonnets--his "Unpublished and Uncollected Poems."

Thomas Lodge

695. Kastner, L.E. "Thomas Lodge as an Imitator of the French Poets." Athenaeum, October 22, 1904, pp. 552-53; October 29, 1904, p. 591.

Kastner mentions a number of other Elizabethan sonneteers who were also indebted to Desportes.

696. Kastner, L.E. "Thomas Lodge as an Imitator of the Italian Poets." Modern Language Review, 2 (1907), 155-61.

Examines several of the sonnets in Lodge's cycle, Phillis.

697. Walker, Alice. "Italian Sources of the Lyrics of Thomas Lodge." Modern Language Review, 22 (1927), 75-79.

In part deals with the source of "Midst lasting griefes, to have but short repose," which was one of Lodge's contributions to The Phoenix Nest.

Henry Lok

698. Campbell, Lily B. Divine Poetry and Drama in Sixteenth-Century England. Cambridge: University Press; Berkeley and Los Angeles: University of California Press, 1959.

Contains a chapter on "Divine Sonnets" (pp. 130-38) in which she discusses Lok, Constable, and Barnes.

699. Collins, Joseph B. Christian Mysticism in the Elizabethan Age: With its Background in Mystical Methodology. Baltimore: Johns Hopkins Press, 1940.

Part III, Chapt. 1. "The Mystical Sonneteers" (pp. 137-43), includes discussions of Constable and Barnes.

Christopher Marlowe

700. Kocher, Paul H. "A Marlowe Sonnet." Philological Quarterly, 24 (1945), 39-45.

Finds a blank verse sonnet imbedded in a speech in I Tamburlaine (V.ii.97-110).

701. Ranson, D. Nicholas. "A Marlowe Sonnet?" Publications of the Arkansas Philological Association, 5 (Fall, 1979), 1-8.

Ascribes a sonnet prefacing John Florio's Second Frutes (1591) to Marlowe. The sonnet was signed by "Phaeton," a name which can be linked to the Tamburlaine plays.
254

John Milton

702. Abercrombie, Lascelles. "Milton Sonnet XVII." TLS, April 11, 1936, p. 316.

703. *Arai, Akira. "Milton's Heroism in His Sonnet XIX." Research Bulletin, Department of General Education, Nagoya University (Japan), 12 (1968), 1-13.

704. Baldi, Sergio. "Poesie italiane di Milton." Biblioteca dell' "Archivum Romanicum," vol. 90. Studi Secenteschi, 7 (1966), 103-30.

The first part of the article discusses the Italian Sonnets and Canzone. Part 2 contains the text and variorum commentary of these poems.

705. Baumgartner, P.R. "Milton and Patience." Studies in Philology, 60 (1963), 203-13.

Discusses Sonnet 19 in the context of Milton's writings and sees it as a turning point after which patience becomes an important theme for him.

706. Bayne, Thomas, Jonathan Bouchier, C.C.B., E. Yardley, and H.T. "Milton's Sonnet on Shakespeare." Notes and Queries, 8th Series, 9 (1896), 114-15.

With sixteen lines (eight rhymed couplets) "On Shakespear" is not a sonnet.

707. Belloc, Hillaire. "The Sonnets." Milton. Philadelphia and London: J.B. Lippincott, 1935, pp. 211-33.

Milton's sonnets are for the most part without a "waist"--i.e. they do not have a break between the octave and sestet. Belloc praises Sonnets 18, 23 and 8 finding the rest full of "shocks of the prosaic."

708. Berkeley, David S. "Milton's 'On the Late Massacre in Piedmont'." Explicator, 15 (1957), Item 58.

709. Bhattacharya, Sakuntala. "Milton and Love Poetry." Bulletin of the Department of English (University of Calcutta), 11, ii (1975-76), 42-50.

Includes comment on early sonnets.

710. Blanchard, Sheila. "Milton's Foothill: Pattern in the Piedmont Sonnet." Genre, 4 (1971), 39-44.

711. Boas, George. "The Problem of Meaning in the Arts." Meaning and Interpretation: Lectures Delivered Before the Philosophical Union of the University of California, 1948-1949. University of California Publications in Philosophy, 25. Berkeley and Los Angeles: University of California Press, 1950, pp. 301-25.

Contrasts the timeless universality of Shakespeare's sonnets with Milton's (23 in particular) which without knowledge of his life would be "as opaque as wood."

712. *Boas, George. "Understanding Spitzer." Hopkins Review, 4, iv (1951), 28-30.

On Sonnet 23, a rejoinder to Spitzer.
876

713. Brisman, Leslie. Milton's Poetry of Choice and Its Romantic Heirs. Ithaca, N.Y.: Cornell University Press, 1973.

Discusses Milton's sonnets in the first chapter (pp. 34-54). In the final chapter, Brisman examines Milton's influence on Wordsworth's sonnets.

714. Bromley, Laura Ann. "1. Continuity in Milton's Sonnets. 2. Attitudes Toward Love in 'Venus and Adonis.' 3. The Victorian 'Good Woman' and the Fiction of Charlotte Bronte." Ph.D. Dissertation, Rutgers, 1973. DAI, 34 (1973), 3336A.

715. Brooks, Cleanth, and John Edward Hardy, eds. Poems of Mr. John Milton: The 1645 Edition with Essays in Analysis. New York: Harcourt Brace, 1951. New York: Gordian Press, 1968.

Contains ten sonnets (five in Italian) with accompanying essays.

716. Brown, Eleanor Gertrude. Milton's Blindness. New York: Columbia University Press, 1934. New York: Octagon Books, 1968.

Chapter 7, "The Sonnets" (pp. 51-58), discusses references to Milton's blindness in his sonnets, in particular 19, 22, and 23.

717. Budick, Sanford. Poetry of Civilization: Mythopoeic Displacement in the Verse of Milton, Dryden, Pope, and Johnson. New Haven and London: Yale University Press, 1974.

In Chapter 3, "Milton's Epic Reclamations," he discusses "On the Late Massacre in Piedmont" as one of those poems influential in the myth-making of Augustan verse (pp. 42-45).

718. Buxton, John. Review of Milton's Sonnets, ed. E.A.J. Honigmann. Review of English Studies, NS 19 (1968), 73-74.

719. Came, J.-F. Review of Anna K. Nardo, Milton's Sonnets and the Ideal Community. Cahiers Elisabethains, No. 19 (April, 1981), 111-13.

720. Carey, John. "The Date of Milton's Italian Poems." Review of English Studies, NS 14 (1963), 383-86.

Argues that the Italian sonnets and Canzone were done "in or before" December, 1629.

721. Carpenter, Nan Cooke. "Milton and Music: Henry Lawes, Dante, and Casella." English Literary Renaissance, 2 (1972), 237-42.

She finds allusions to Dante and the Florentine composer, Casella, in Milton's Sonnet 13, "To H. Lawes, on his Aires."

722. Cheek, Macon. "Of Two Sonnets of Milton." Renaissance Papers, 1956. Southeastern Renaissance Conference, 1956, pp. 82-91. Reprinted in Milton: Modern Essays in Criticism. Ed. A.E. Barker. New York: Oxford University Press, 1965, pp. 125-35.

The two sonnets discussed are "On Having Arrived at the Age of Twenty-three" and "On His Blindness."

723. Colaccio, John J. "'A Death Like Sleep': The Christology of Milton's Twenty-Third Sonnet." Milton Studies, 6 (1974), 181-97.

724. Combecher, Hans. "Drei Sonette-drei Epochen: Eine Vergleichende Interpretation." Neueren Sprachen, 4 (1959), 178-89.

On Shakespeare's Sonnet 29, Milton's 19, and Wordsworth's "Composed upon Westminster Bridge."

725. Condee, Ralph W. "Milton's Gaudy-Day with Lawrence." Directions in Literary Criticism: Contemporary Approaches to Literature. Ed. Stanley Weintraub and Philip Young. University Park: Pennsylvania State University Press, 1973, pp. 86-92.

On Sonnet 20.

726. Cox, Lee Sheridan. "Milton's 'I Did But Prompt,' ll. 13-14." English Language Notes, 3 (1965), 102-04.

727. Dahlberg, Charles R. "Milton's Sonnet 23 on His 'Late Espoused Saint'." Notes and Queries, 194 (1949), 321.

728. Daiches, David. Milton. Rev. ed. London: Hutchinson University Library, 1959.

Surveys Milton's sonnets (pp. 130-43).

729. D[ale], J[ames]. "Sonnets, Milton's." A Milton Encyclopedia. Ed. William B. Hunter, Jr. Lewisburg, Pa.: Bucknell University Press, 1980, vol. 8, pp. 17-28.

Following some general comments, Dale touches on each of the twenty-three sonnets.
774

730. Daniels, Earl. The Art of Reading Poetry. New York: Farrar and Rinehart, 1941.

Dismisses blindness as an important theme in Sonnet 19 and emphasizes the parable of the talents (Math. 25:14-30), pp. 34-36.

731. Davies, William. "Milton's Sonnets." Athenaeum, September 29, 1888, pp. 418-19.

Sonnets 20 ("To Mr. Lawrence") and 21 ("To Cyriak Skinner") and 14 ("To the Memory of Mrs Catherine Thompson") show the influence of some 16th-century Italian sonnets by Mantova.

732. Diekhoff, John S. "The Milder Shades of Purgatory." Modern Language Notes, 52 (1937), 409-10.

Discusses what it is the shades are "milder" than in Sonnet 13 ("To My Friend Mr. Henry Lawes").

733. Dixon, J. "Milton Queries (2)--Sonnet xxii." Notes and Queries, 4th Series, 9 (1872), 445; 10 (1872), 153.

Suggests an emendation for the first line of 22--"Three years this day" for "this three years day." Responds to Oakley in defense of his emendation.
828

734. Dorian, Donald C. "'On the New Forcers of Conscience,' line 17." Modern Language Notes, 56 (1941), 62-64.

735. Dorian, Donald C. "Milton's 'On His Having Arrived at the Age of Twenty-Three'." Explicator, 8 (1949), Item 10.

736. Dorian, Donald C. "Milton's 'On his Blindness'." Explicator, 10 (1951), Item 16.

737. Fabian, David R. "Milton's 'Sonnet 23' and Leviticus XVIII.19." Xavier University Studies, 5 (1966), 83-88.

738. Fallon, Robert Thomas. "Milton's 'defenseless doors': The Limits of Irony." Milton Quarterly, 13 (1979), 146-51.

On Sonnet 8, Milton's first work on a military theme.

739. Finley, John H., Jr. "Milton and Horace: A Study of Milton's Sonnets." Harvard Studies in Classical Philology, 48 (1937), 29-73.

The Horatian influence in many of Milton's sonnets adds an important dimension to their meaning.

740. Fischer, Walther. Review of John S. Smart, The Sonnets of Milton. Beiblatt zur Anglia, 34 (1923), 84-86.

741. Fiske, Dixon. "Milton in the Middle of Life: Sonnet XIX." ELH, 41 (1974), 37-49.

742. Fiske, Dixon Davis. "Milton's Sonnets." Ph.D. Dissertation, Princeton, 1969. DAI, 31 (1970), 756A.

743. Fiske, Dixon Davis. "The Theme of Purification in Milton's Sonnet XXIII." Milton Studies, 8 (1975), 149-63.

744. Fletcher, Harris Francis. The Intellectual Development of John Milton. 2 vol. Urbana: University of Illinois Press, 1956-61.

Frequent references to sonnets throughout.

745. Forker, Charles R. "Milton and Shakespeare: The First Sonnet on Blindness in Relation to a Speech from Troilus and Cressida." English Language Notes, 11 (1974), 188-92.

On Sonnet 19 and a portion of Ulysses's speech on degree (I.iii.85-94).

746. Foxell, Nigel. Ten Poems Analysed. Oxford: Pergamon, 1966.

On Sonnet 19, "On His Blindness," pp. 13-22.

747. Franks, Jesse. "Linguistic Awareness in the Teaching of Poetry." Ball State University Forum, 9, i (1968), 51-56.

Uses "On the Late Massacre in Piedmont" to show that a knowledge of sentence structure is an important part of understanding a poem.

748. French, Roberts W. "Reading a Poem: Two Sonnets by Milton." *Concerning Poetry*, 2, ii (1969), 11-16.

He compares the earlier Sonnet 7 ("How soon hath Time, the subtle thief of youth") with Sonnet 19 ("When I consider how my light is spent").

749. French, Roberts W. "Spenser and Sonnet XVIII." *Milton Quarterly*, 5 (1971), 51-52.

Compares the sonnet to a passage from *The Faerie Queen* (I. viii. 36-37).

750. French, Roberts W. "Satan's Sonnet." *Milton Quarterly*, 11 (1977), 113-14.

Satan's speech to Beelzebub (PL, I, 178-91) is a blank verse sonnet not mentioned in Lee M. Johnson's article on "Milton's Blank Verse Sonnets."
781

751. Frye, Roland Mushat. "Milton's Sonnet 23 on his 'Late Espoused Saint'." *Notes and Queries*, 194 (1949), 321.

752. Goldstein, Charles E. "The Hebrew Element in Milton's Sonnet XVIII." *Milton Quarterly*, 9 (1975), 111-14.

753. Goodman, Paul. *The Structure of Literature*. Chicago: University of Chicago Press, 1954.

Discusses Sonnet 19 with respect to diction, verse form, syntax, and a number of other subjects (pp. 192-215).

754. Gorecki, J.E. "Milton's Sonnet XXIII and Aeschylus' 'Agamemnon'." *Notes and Queries*, NS 25 (1978), 17.

755. Gossman, Ann, and George W. Whiting. "Milton's First Sonnet on His Blindness." *Review of English Studies*, NS 12 (1961), 364-70.

On Sonnet 19. Article is followed by a rejoinder by Pyle (pp. 370-72).

756. Greenbaum, Sidney. "The Poem, the Poet, and the Reader: An Analysis of Milton's Sonnet 19." *Language and Style*, 11 (1978), 116-28.

757. Grierson, H.J.C. "The Text of Milton." *TLS*, January 15, 1925, p. 40.

Suggests a new reading of the word "themes" in Sonnet 14, l. 12.

758. Griffith, Benjamin W. "Milton's Meditations and Sonnet XIX." American Notes and Queries, 10 (1971), 7-8.

759. Grossman, Allen. "Milton's Sonnet 'On the Late Massacre in Piemont': A Note on the Vulnerability of Persons in a Revolutionary Situation." Tri-Quarterly, 23-24 (1972), 283-301.

On Sonnet 18.

760. Hanford, James H. "The Arrangement and Dates of Milton's Sonnets." Modern Philology, 18 (1921), 475-83.

761. Hanford, James Holly, and James G. Taafe. A Milton Handbook. 5th ed. New York: Appleton-Century-Crofts, 1970.

Brief section on the sonnets (pp. 140-43).

762. Harrington, David V. "Feeling and Form in Milton's Sonnets." Western Humanities Review, 20 (1966), 317-28.

763. Haug, Ralph A. "They also serve . . . ." Notes and Queries, 183 (1942), 224-25.

Connects the final line of Sonnet 19 to a biblical passage (I Sam.30:24).

764. Haviland, Thomas P. "Hugh Henry Brackenridge and Milton's 'Piedmontese' Sonnet." Notes and Queries, 176 (1939), 243-44.

On Milton's influence on an American writer.

765. Hazlitt, William. "On Milton's Sonnets." The Complete Works of William Hazlitt in Twenty-One Volumes. Ed. P.P. Howe. London and Toronto: J.M. Dent, 1931, vol. 8, pp. 174-81.

Originally published in the second volume of Table-Talk (1822).

766. Heinzelman, Kurt. "'Cold Consolation': The Art of Milton's Last Sonnet." Milton Studies, 10 (1977), 111-25.

On Sonnet 23.

767. Hellings, Peter. "A Note on the Sonnets of Milton." Life and Letters, 64 (1950), 165-69.

Discusses the style of language in Milton's sonnets.

768. Henry, Nathaniel H. "Who Meant Licence When They Cried Liberty?" Modern Language Notes, 66 (1951), 509-13.

On Sonnets 11 and 12, Milton's "divorce sonnets."

769. Herron, Dale. "Poetic Vision in Two Sonnets of Milton." Milton Newsletter, 2, ii (1968), 23-28.

Discusses biblical echoes in Sonnets 18 and 19.

770. Hill, John Spencer. "'Alcestis from the Grave': Image and Structure in Sonnet XXIII." Milton Studies, 10 (1977), 127-39.

771. Hill, John Spencer. John Milton: Poet, Priest and Prophet: A Study of Divine Vocation in Milton's Poetry and Prose. London: Macmillan, 1979.

Passing references to Sonnets 16, 19, 23 with a somewhat longer comment on the evidence that Sonnet 7 gives for his vocation (pp. 34-36).

772. Hinz, Evelyn J. "New Light 'On His Blindness'." Massachusetts Studies in English, 2 (1969), 1-10.

On Sonnet 19.

773. Hunter, William B., Jr. "The Date of Milton's Sonnet 7." English Language Notes, 13 (1975), 10-14.

This sonnet, which refers to Milton's twenty-third year, must have been written in 1631 rather than in 1632, as William R. Parker argues.

830

774. Hunter, William B., Jr., ed. A Milton Encyclopedia. 8 vol. Lewisburg, Pa.: Bucknell University Press; London: Associated University Presses, 1978-81.

A ninth volume with bibliographies and additional apparatus is forthcoming. There are, in all eight volumes, a number of entries relating to the Sonnets (e.g. on Henry Lawes or Edward Lawrence or Cyriak Skinner); however, there is a signed article by James Dale discussing all of the numbered sonnets in volume 8, and by Michael Lieb covering "On the New Forcers of Conscience" in volume 6.

729, 793

775. Huntley, John F. "The Ecology and Anatomy of Criticism: Milton's Sonnet 19 and the Bee Simile in Paradise Lost, I, 768-776." Journal of Aesthetics and Art Criticism, 24 (1966), 383-91.

776. Huntley, John. "Milton's 23rd Sonnet." ELH, 34 (1967), 468-81.

777. Hutchinson, Francis E. Milton and the English Mind. New York: Macmillan, 1948.

Discussion of sonnets scattered throughout.

778. Hyman, Lawrence W. "Milton's 'On the Late Massacre in Piedmont'." English Language Notes, 3 (1965), 26-29.

779. Jackson, Elizabeth. "Milton's Sonnet XX." PMLA, 65 (1950), 328-29.

A note responding to Fraser Neiman's article.
825

780. Jackson, James L., and Walter E. Weese. "'. . . Who Only Stand and Wait': Milton's Sonnet 'On His Blindness'." Modern Language Notes, 72 (1957), 91-93.

781. Johnson, Lee M. "Milton's Blank Verse Sonnets." Milton Studies, 5 (1973), 129-53.

There are several dozen "14-line units" in Paradise Lost, Paradise Regained, and Samson Agonistes that the author calls blank verse sonnets.

782. Jones, Nicholas R. "The Education of the Faithful in Milton's Piedmontese Sonnet." Milton Studies, 10 (1977), 167-76.

783. Keightley, Thomas. An Account of the Life, Opinions, and Writings of John Milton. London: Chapman and Hall, 1855.

Discusses the sonnets (pp. 307-15).

784. Kelley, Maurice. "Milton's Later Sonnets and the Cambridge Manuscript." Modern Philology, 54 (1956), 20-25.

785. *Kemp, Lysander. "On a Sonnet by Milton." Hopkins Review, 6 (1952), 80-83.

Loss of poetic inspiration not blindness is the theme of Sonnet 19.

786. Kendall, Lyle H., Jr. "Sonnet XIX and Wither's Emblem III.xlvii." Milton Newsletter, 3 (1969), 57.

787. Knowles, David, and Helen Gardner. "Milton's 'Talent'." TLS, February 1, 1974, p. 108.

On the Biblical background of Sonnet 19.

788. Komori, Teiji. "Milton's Recreation in Sonnets XX and XXI." Milton Center of Japan News, 3 (December, 1979), 6-7. Abstracted in Milton Quarterly, 14 (1980), 107.

"Sonnets XX and XXI show that Milton had 'grown mellow, kindly, sweet-tempered, and lovable' as a result of his earlier hardships, which prompted an inner growth and maturity."

789. Kuhl, Ernest P. Review of The Sonnets of Milton, ed. John S. Smart. Modern Language Notes, 39 (1924), 45-50.

790. Le Comte, Edward S. "The Veiled Face of Milton's Wife." Notes and Queries, 199 (1954), 245-46.

On Sonnet 23.

791. Le Comte, Edward S. A Milton Dictionary. New York: Philosophical Library, 1961.

Contains a substantial entry under "Sonnets" (pp. 299-312).

792. Leishman, James B. Milton's Minor Poems. Ed. Geoffrey Tillotson. London: Hutchinson, 1969.

793. Lieb, Michael. "On the New Forcers of Conscience Under the Long Parliament." A Milton Encyclopedia. Ed. William B. Hunter, Jr. Lewisburg, Pa.: Bucknell University Press; London: Associated University Presses, 1979. vol. 6, pp. 34-35.
774

794. Lien, Dennis. "Milton's Fourteenth Sonnet: A Textual Study." Graduate English Papers, 3, ii (1968), 5-9.

An examination of the evolution of the poem based on the evidence of the text in the Trinity Manuscript.

795. Lievsay, John Leon. "Milton Among Nightingales." Renaissance Papers 1958, 1959, 1960. Southeastern Renaissance Conference, 1958-60, pp. 36-45.

Discussion of Milton's special interest in the nightingale, which includes his sonnet "O Nightingale, that on yon bloomy Spray" (Sonnet 1).

796. Lievsay, John Leon. Review of Anna K. Nardo, Milton's Sonnets and the Ideal Community. South Atlantic Review, 46 (1981), 124-27.

Lievsay disagrees with Nardo that the sonnets constitute a sequence.

797. Lockwood, Laura E. "Milton's Corrections to the Minor Poems." Modern Language Notes, 25 (1910), 201-05.

Briefly discusses changes made to the fifteen sonnets in the Cambridge MS.

798. Low, Anthony. "Milton's Last Sonnet." Milton Quarterly, 9 (1975), 80-82.

Argues that Sonnet 23 is probably about Katherine Woodcock.

799. Mabbott, T.O. "Milton's Sonnet on 'His Late Espoused Saint'." Notes and Queries, 189 (1945), 239.

800. Maresca, Thomas E. "The Latona Myth in Milton's Sonnet XII." Modern Language Notes, 76 (1961), 491-94.

801. Martz, Louis L. "The Rising Poet, 1645." The Lyric and Dramatic Milton. Ed. Joseph Holmes Summers. New York: Columbia University Press, 1965, pp. 3-33.

Martz discusses, among other of Milton's early poetry, the Italian sonnets and the first four English sonnets.

802. Masson, David. The Life of John Milton: Narrated in Connexion with the Political, Ecclesiastical, and Literary History of His Time. 7 vol. and index. Cambridge and London: Macmillan, 1859-94. rpt. Gloucester, Mass.: P. Smith, 1965.

A vast work which includes comments about Milton's sonnets throughout.

803. McCarthy, William Paul. "Part I. The Lives of the Poets: Johnson's Essay on Man. Part II. Stories from The Secret Rose by W.B. Yeats: A Critical Variorum Text. Part III. The Continuity of Milton's Sonnets." Ph.D. Dissertation, Rutgers, 1974. DAI, 35 (1974), 3692A.

804. McCarthy, William. "The Continuity of Milton's Sonnets." PMLA, 92 (1977), 96-109.

Although the sonnets were written from about 1628 to 1658, the unity in their arrangement in the 1673 edition of his works justifies their being called a sequence.

805. McCutcheon, Elizabeth. Review of Anna K. Nardo, Milton's Sonnets and the Ideal Community. Rocky Mountain Review of Language and Literature, 35 (1981), 171-72.

806. Mengert, James G. "The Resistance of Milton's Sonnets." English Literary Renaissance, 11 (1981), 81-95.

The last words of Milton's sonnets "turn back," evoking earlier ideas, thereby giving a strong sense of unity to the poems.

807. *Milner, George. "A Note on Two Sonnets by Milton and Tennyson." Manchester Quarterly, 11 (1892), 356-59.

On Milton's sonnet "On the Late Massacre in Piedmont" (Sonnet 18).

808. Milton, John. The Shorter Poems of John Milton. Ed. Dennis Burden. New York: Barnes and Noble, 1970.

Contains the texts of the sonnets (pp. 47-58) and a commentary (pp. 132-43).

809. __________. The Poems of John Milton. Ed. John Carey and Alastair Fowler. London: Longmans, Green, 1968.

810. __________. The Poems of John Milton: English, Latin, Greek and Italian, Arranged in Chronological Order. Ed. H.J.C. Grierson. London: Chatto and Windus, 1925, vol. 1.

In the Preface of this volume Grierson discusses the order and dating of the sonnets.

811. __________. Milton's Sonnets. Ed. E.A.J. Honigmann. London: Macmillan; New York: St. Martin's, 1966.

812. __________. Complete Poems and Major Prose. Ed. Merritt Y. Hughes. New York: Odyssey Press, 1957.

813. __________. The Poetical Works of John Milton. Ed. David Masson. London and New York: Macmillan, 1883, vol. 1.

Volume 1 includes an introduction to the sonnets.

814. __________. The Works of John Milton: The Minor Poems. Ed. Frank A. Patterson. New York: Columbia University Press, 1931.

Volume 1, Part 1 of the Columbia University Edition of the Works of John Milton.

815. __________. The Sonnets of John Milton. Ed. Mark Pattison. London: Kegan Paul, Trench, 1883. 1892.

A general introduction with a comment and notes attached to each poem.

816. __________. The Sonnets of Milton. Ed. John S. Smart. Glasgow: Maclehose, Jackson, 1921. Oxford: Clarendon Press, 1966.

817. __________. The Poetical Works of John Milton. Ed. Henry J. Todd. 7 vols. London: n.p., 1809. rpt. New York: AMS Press, 1970.

In volume 6 Todd has an essay, "Preliminary Observations on the Sonnets" (pp. 437-43) followed by the sonnets and notes (pp. 445-503). The sonnets are also discussed in Volume 1, "Some Account of the Life and Writings of Milton."

818. __________. Milton's Sonnets. Ed. A. Wilson Verity. Cambridge: University Press, 1895.

Contains a brief introductory essay to the sonnets (pp. xxiv-xxvii) plus notes and commentary for each sonnet.

819. Monteiro, George. "Milton's 'On His Blindness (Sonnet XIX)'." Explicator, 24 (1966), Item 67.

On Matthew 25:14-30 and the conclusion of the poem.

820. Morse, C.J. "The Dating of Milton's Sonnet XIX." TLS, September 15, 1961, p. 620.
854

821. Mueller, Martin. "The Theme and Imagery of Milton's Last Sonnet." Archiv fur das Studium der neueren Sprachen und Literaturen, 201 (1964), 267-71.

822. Nardo, Anna Karen. "Milton's Sonnets and the Crisis of Community." Ph.D. Dissertation, Emory, 1974. DAI, 35 (1975), 4444A.
824

823. Nardo, A.K. "The Submerged Sonnet as Lyric Moment In Miltonic Epic." Genre, 9 (1976), 21-35.

An examination of sonnet-like passages in Paradise Lost.

824. Nardo, Anna K. Milton's Sonnets and the Ideal Community. Lincoln, Nebr.: University of Nebraska Press, 1979.

An attempt to discover what unifies Milton's "sonnet sequence."

825. Neiman, Fraser. "Milton's Sonnet XX." PMLA, 64 (1949), 480-83.

826. Nelson, James G. The Sublime Puritan: Milton and the Victorians. Madison: University of Wisconsin Press, 1963.

Chapter 3, "The Miltonic Sonnet" (pp. 20-38), discusses the important influence of Miltonic sonnets on Victorian poets.

827. Nicolson, Marjorie. John Milton: A Reader's Guide to his Poetry. New York: Farrar, Strauss, 1963.

The second part of Chapter 2 takes up such subjects as the sonnet tradition, Milton's conventional sonnets, his personal sonnets, and his political sonnets (pp. 140-74).

828. Oakley, J.H.I. "Milton Queries (2): Sonnet XXII." Notes and Queries, 4th Series, 10 (1872), 76-77.

Refutes Dixon's emendation and offers possible readings for the first line.
733

829. Parker, David. "The Love Poems of 'Paradise Lost' and the Petrarchan Tradition." ARIEL, 3, i (1972), 34-43.

Compares some passages in Paradise Lost with sonnets by Constable, Shakespeare (98), Sidney (Astrophel and Stella, 35) and Spenser (Amoretti, 61).

830. Parker, William Riley. "Some Problems in the Chronology of Milton's Early Poems." Review of English Studies, 11 (1935), 276-83.

The first problem he takes up concerns the dating of Sonnet 7, "How soon hath time."

831. Parker, William Riley. "Milton's Last Sonnet." Review of English Studies, 21 (1945), 235-38.

Advances the argument that Mary Powell was the "late espoused saint" (Sonnet 23).

832. Parker, William Riley. "Milton's Sonnet: 'I did but prompt,' 6." Explicator, 8 (1949), Item 3.

833. Parker, William Riley. "Milton's Last Sonnet Again." Review of English Studies, NS 2 (1951), 147-52.

Parker's article is a reply to Fitzroy Pyle's earlier article with a further comment by Pyle (pp. 152-54).
841

834. Parker, William Riley. "The Dates of Milton's Sonnets on Blindness." PMLA, 73 (1958), 196-200.

On Sonnets 19 and 22.

835. Parker, William Riley. Milton: A Biography. 2 vol. Oxford: Clarendon Press, 1968.

Abundant references (some lengthy) to the sonnets.

836. Pattison, Mark. Milton. English Men of Letters Series. London: Macmillan, 1909.

A literary biography which contains a number of passing references to the sonnets.

837. Pequigney, Joseph. "Milton's Sonnet XIX Reconsidered." Texas Studies in Literature and Language, 8 (1967), 485-98.

838. Pironon, J. "The Images of Woman in the Sonnets and Some Minor Poems of John Milton." Cahiers Elisabethains, No. 18 (October, 1980), 43-52.

839. Potter, James L. "Milton's 'Talent' Sonnet and Barnabe Barnes." Notes and Queries, 202 (1957), 447.

Two sonnets by Barnabe Barnes preceded Milton's Sonnet 19 in using the parable of the talents as a conceit.

840. Prince, F.T. The Italian Element in Milton's Verse. Oxford: Clarendon Press, 1954.

Chapter 6 deals with his sonnets.

841. Pyle, Fitzroy. "Milton's Sonnet on his 'Late Espoused Saint'." Review of English Studies, 25 (1949), 57-60.

842. Pyle, Fitzroy. "Milton's First Sonnet on his Blindness." Review of English Studies, NS 9 (1958), 376-87.

On Sonnet 19.

843. Radzinowicz, Mary Ann. Toward Samson Agonistes: The Growth of Milton's Mind. Princeton, N.J.: Princeton University Press, 1978.

She sees the sonnets falling into five clusters--"primarily chronological, thematic units"--throughout which Milton champions "the causes of liberty and truth" (pp. 128-44).

844. Raizada, Harish. "Milton's 'Soul-Animating Strains': A Study of his Sonnets." Essays on John Milton: A Tercentenary Tribute. Ed. Asloob Ahmad Ansari. Aligarh: Aligarh Muslim University, 1976, pp. 48-66.

845. Ramsay, Robert L. "Morality Themes in Milton's Poetry." Studies in Philology, 15 (1918), 123-58.

Discusses Milton's use of medieval allegory in Sonnet 14 (pp. 142-43).

846. Rapin, Rene. "Milton's Sonnet XIX." Notes and Queries, 218 (1973), 380-81.

847. Rauber, D.F. "Milton's Sonnet XI--'I Did But Prompt . . . '." Philological Quarterly, 49 (1970), 561-64.

848. Reader, Willie D. "Dramatic Structure and Prosodic Form in Milton's Sonnet 'On His Deceased Wife'." Language Quarterly, 11, i-ii (1972), 21-25, 28.

849. Rinehart, Keith. "A Note on the First Fourteen Lines of Milton's 'Lycidas'." Notes and Queries, 198 (1953), 103.

Milton deliberately approximates the sonnet form in these lines.

850. Robins, Harry F. "Milton's First Sonnet on his Blindness." Review of English Studies, NS 7 (1956), 360-66.

On Sonnet 19.

851. Rooney, William J.J. "Discrimination Among Values." Journal of General Education, 13 (1961), 40-52.

Discusses "On His Blindness" and its implications for general education.

852. Rosen, Alan D. "Milton's 'War Sonnets': A Comparative Analysis of Theme and Form." (Abstract) Milton Quarterly, 13 (1979), 161.

Paper was presented at the Lycidas Symposium in Kyoto, Japan and reported in Milton Center of Japan News, 2 (October, 1978), 14-15.

853. Rudrum, Alan. A Critical Commentary on Milton's "Comus" and Shorter Poems. Macmillan Critical Commentaries. London: Macmillan, 1967.

Contains commentary on Milton's English sonnets (pp. 79-109).

854. Saillens, Emile. "The Dating of Milton's Sonnet XIX." TLS, October 6, 1961, p. 672.

A response to C.J. Morse.
820

855. Sampson, Alden. Milton's Sonnets. New York: DeVinne Press, 1886. rpt. Folcroft, Pa.: Folcroft Press, 1969.

This is an earlier version of his essay "From Lycidas to Paradise Lost" in Studies in Milton.

856. Sampson, Alden. Studies in Milton and an Essay on Poetry. New York: Moffat, Yard, 1913.

Throughout his first chapter, "From Lycidas to Paradise Lost" (pp. 3-163), he discusses the Sonnets which he calls the "brief record of Milton's poetic life."

857. Sanderlin, George. "The Influence of Milton and Wordsworth on the Early Victorian Sonnet." ELH, 5 (1938), 225-51.

858. Sasek, Lawrence A. "'Ere half my days': A Note on Milton's Sonnet 19." Milton Quarterly, 15 (1981), 16-18.

Offers an explanation of the first two lines where "half my days" refers not to his entire life but only to his life in blindness.

859. Schultz, Howard. "A Book Was Writ of Late." Modern Language Notes, 69 (1954), 495-97.

On the Tetrachordon sonnet (12).

860. Serrell, George. "Milton as Seen in his Sonnets." Temple Bar, 121 (September, 1900), 27-42.

Examines the English sonnets for their autobiographical content.

861. Shaw, J.E., and A. Bartlett Giamatti. "The Italian Poems of John Milton." A Variorum Commentary on the Poems of John Milton. Ed. Merritt Y. Hughes. New York: Columbia University Press, 1970, vol. 1, pp. 363-88.

Discusses the 5 Italian sonnets and the canzone.

862. Shawcross, John T. "Milton's Fairfax Sonnet." Notes and Queries, 200 (1955), 195-96.

On some possible textual errors in Sonnet 15.

863. Shawcross, John T. "Milton's Sonnet 23." Notes and Queries, 201 (1956), 202-04.

864. Shawcross, John T. "Milton's Sonnet 19: Its Date of Authorship and Its Interpretation." *Notes and Queries*, 202 (1957), 442-46.

865. Shawcross, John T. "Two Milton Notes: 'Clio' and Sonnet 11." *Notes and Queries*, 206 (1961), 178-80.

866. Shawcross, John T. "Of Chronology and the Dates of Milton's Translation from Horace and the *New Forcers of Conscience*." *Studies in English Literature, 1500-1900*, 3 (1963), 77-84.

Deals with the dating of, among others, Milton's sonnets and the *New Forcers*.

867. Shawcross, John T. "Milton's Italian Sonnets: An Interpretation." *University of Windsor Review*, 3 (1967), 27-33.

On Sonnets 2-6 and the accompanying canzone.

868. Shawcross, John T. "Milton and Diodati: An Essay in Psychodynamic Meaning." *Milton Studies*, 7 (1975), 127-63.

Discusses the Italian sonnets (pp. 142-45).

869. Sirluck, Ernest. "Milton's Idle Right Hand." *Journal of English and Germanic Philology*, 60 (1961), 749-85.

In an appendix to this article exploring Milton's quarter century of slight poetic activity, the author discusses the dating of Sonnet 7 (pp. 781-84).

870. Slakey, Roger L. "Milton's Sonnet 'On His Blindness'." *ELH*, 27 (1960), 122-30.

871. Smart, Alastair. "Milton's 'Talent'." *TLS*, January 25, 1974, p. 81; February 8, 1974, p. 134.

On Sparrow's note on Sonnet 19.
875

872. Smart, John S. "The Italian Singer in Milton's Sonnets." *Musical Antiquary*, 4 (January, 1913), 91-97.

Attempts to establish the identity of the lady addressed in Milton's Italian sonnets. Her name, Smart says, was Emilia.

873. Smith, Roland M. "Spenser and Milton: An Early Analogue." *Modern Language Notes*, 60 (1945), 394-98.

Cites parallels between a verse-letter from Spenser to Harvey and Milton's sonnet "How soon hath Time" (Sonnet 7).

874. Smith, W.F. "Milton's Sonnet on Tetrachordon." *Notes and Queries*, 12th Series, 2 (1916), 7.

On Sonnet 12.

875. Sparrow, John. "Milton's 'Talent which is death to hide'." *TLS*, January 18, 1974, p. 54.

Discusses "On his Blindness" (Sonnet 19).

876. Spitzer, Leo. "Understanding Milton." *Hopkins Review*, 4, iv (1951), 16-27. Reprinted in *Essays on English and American Literature*. Ed. Anna Hatcher. Princeton: Princeton University Press, 1962, pp. 116-31.

On Milton's Sonnet 23 (in opposition to Boas).
712

877. Stevens, David Harrison. "The Order of Milton's Sonnets." *Modern Philology*, 17 (1919), 25-33.

878. Stevens, David H. Review of *The Sonnets of Milton*, ed. John S. Smart. *Modern Philology*, 20 (1922), 219-20.

879. Stoehr, Taylor. "Syntax and Poetic Form in Milton's Sonnets." *English Studies*, 45 (1964), 289-301.

In noting that Milton's sonnets link form and meaning more rigorously than his predecessors, Stoehr talks in some detail about 7, 16, 18, 19, 23 with a comment on Herbert's "Holdfast."

880. Stringer, Gary A. "Milton's 'Thorne in the Flesh': Pauline Didacticism in *Sonnet XIX*." *Milton Studies*, 10 (1977), 141-54.

881. Stringer, Gary. "A Jot and Tittle More on Milton's 'How soon hath Time' and the 'Letter To A Friend'." *Seventeenth Century News*, 36, i (1978), 9-10.

Finds a biblical allusion in the 'letter' bearing on Sonnet 7.

882. Stroup, Thomas B. "Aeneas' Vision of Creusa and Milton's Twenty-Third Sonnet." *Philological Quarterly*, 39 (1960), 125-26.

883. Stroup, Thomas B. "Dido, the Phoenix, and Milton's Sonnet XVIII." *Milton Newsletter*, 4 (1970), 57-60.

884. Stroup, Thomas B. "'When I Consider': Milton's Sonnet XIX." *Studies in Philology*, 69 (1972), 242-58.

885. Svendsen, Kester. "Milton's Sonnet on the Massacre in Piedmont." *Shakespeare Association Bulletin*, 20 (1945), 147-55.

On the rhetoric of Sonnet 18.

886. Svendsen, Kester. "Milton's 'On His Having Arrived at the Age of Twenty-Three." *Explicator*, 7 (1949), Item 53.

887. *Thomas, Walter. "Les sonnets de Milton et sa vie intime." Revue de l'enseignment des langues vivantes, 41 (1924), 252-58, 289-96.

Relates composition of sonnets to Milton's life; translates some of the better known sonnets.

888. Thompson, Elbert N.S. Essay on Milton. New Haven: Yale University Press, 1914.

Brief portion of the first essay "Milton, the 'Last of the Elizabethans'," examines the relationship between Milton's sonnets and those of his precursors (pp.30-31).

889. Tillyard, E.M.W. The Metaphysicals and Milton. London: Chatto and Windus, 1956.

Compares Milton's Sonnet 23 with Donne's "Since she whom I lov'd hath payd her last debt" (pp. 2-11, 77-78).

890. Tillyard, E.M.W. Milton. London: Chatto and Windus, 1930.

References throughout to his sonnets. Appendix G (p. 388), "On the Dating of the Sonnet 'When I Consider . . '." (19).

891. Treip, Mindele. Milton's Punctuation and Changing English Usage, 1582-1676. London: Methuen, 1970.

The punctuational practices of Paradise Lost "are illustrated, if anything more clearly, in the final drafts of the mature Sonnets punctuated by Milton's hand" (pp. 64-68).

892. Ulreich, John C. "Typological Symbolism in Milton's Sonnet XXIII." Milton Quarterly, 8 (1974), 7-10.

893. Vance, John A. "God's Advocate and His Pupils: Milton's Sonnets to Lawrence and Skinner." South Atlantic Bulletin, 42, iv (1977), 31-40.

On Sonnets 20 ("Lawrence of Virtuous Father . . ."), 21 ("Cyriak, whose Grandsire . . ."), and 22 ("To Mr. Cyriak Skinner upon His Blindness").

894. Van Doren, Mark. Introduction to Poetry: Commentaries on Thirty Poems. New York: Dryden Press, 1951. New York: Hill and Wang, 1968.

a) Contrasts Milton's Sonnet 20 with Sonnet 18 (pp. 120-25; b) Contrasts Shakespeare's Sonnet 71 and 64 (pp. 116-20); c) Discusses Wordsworth's "Composed upon Westminster Bridge" (pp. 55-58).

895. Weitzman, Arthur J. "The 'Babylonian Wo' of Milton's Piedmontese Sonnet." Milton Newsletter, 3 (1969), 55-57.

On Sonnet 18.

896. Wentersdorf, Karl P. "Images of 'Licence' in Milton's Sonnet XII." Milton Quarterly, 13 (1979), 36-42.

897. Wheeler, Thomas. "Milton's Twenty-third Sonnet." Studies in Philology, 58 (1961), 510-15. Reprinted in Milton: Modern Essays in Criticism. Ed. Arthur E. Barker. New York: Oxford University Press, 1965, pp. 136-41.

The "late espoused saint" refers to neither of his wives but to an ideal.

898. Wigler, Stephen. "Outrageous Noise and the Sovereign Voice: Satan, Sin, and Syntax in Sonnet XIX and Book VI of Paradise Lost." Milton Studies, 10 (1977), 155-65.

899. Wilde, Hans-Oskar. "Miltons Sonett 'On His Blindness' (im Problemkreis der neueren Miltonforschung)." Beitrage zur Englischen Literaturgeschichte des 17. Jahrhunderts. Sprache und Kultur der Germanischen und Romanischen Volker, 10. Breslau: Priebatsch, 1932, pp. 36-49.

Sees this sonnet as a turning point for Milton.

900. Willcock, J. "Milton and Fairfax." Notes and Queries, 11th Series, 9 (1914), 147.

Line 2 of Sonnet 18 is from Fairfax's Tasso.

901. Williamson, Marilyn L. "A Reading of Milton's Twenty-Third Sonnet." Milton Studies, 4 (1972), 141-49.

902. Withim, Philip M. "A Prosodic Analysis of Milton's Seventh Sonnet." Bucknell Review, 6, iv (1957), 29-34.

903. Wittreich, Joseph Anthony, Jr., ed. The Romantics on Milton. Cleveland: Press of Case Western Reserve University, 1970.

Includes a number of comments by Romantic writers on Milton's sonnets.

904. Woodhouse, A.S.P. "Notes on Milton's Early Development." University of Toronto Quarterly, 13 (1943), 66-101.

Opens by reviewing the dates of the Italian poems and Sonnet 7. He prefers a later dating for these poems.

905. Woodhouse, A.S.P. Milton the Poet. Toronto: J.M.Dent, 1955.

Discusses Sonnets 7 and 19 as illustrations of "the poem as realization of an experience" (pp. 7-8).

906. Woodhouse, A.S.P. The Heavenly Muse: A Preface to Milton. Ed. Hugh MacCallum. Department of English Studies and Texts, 21. Toronto: University of Toronto Press, 1972.

References to sonnets throughout, most frequently to Sonnet 7.

907. Woodhouse, A.S.P., and Douglas Bush. *The Minor English Poems* (Part II). *A Variorum Commentary on the Poems of John Milton*. Ed. Merritt Y. Hughes. New York: Columbia University Press, 1972, Vol. 2, pp. 339-501, 508-18.

Provides commentary on the 18 English sonnets and "On the New Forcers of Conscience."

908. "English Sonnets." Review of David Main, *A Treasury of English Sonnets* and Samuel Waddington, *English Sonnets by Living Writers*. *Nation*, 32 (April 14, 1881), 262-63.

Some extensive comments on Milton's Sonnet 18 and on the relative merits of Shakespeare, Milton, and Wordsworth as sonneteers.

909. *"On the Sonnets of Milton, with a Translation of One of His Italian Sonnets." *Censura literaria*, 6 (1908), 414-17.

Translation of the 4th sonnet, "Diodati, io te'l diro . . . ."

Alexander Montgomerie

910. Brotanek, Rudolf. *Untersuchungen uber das Leben und die Dichtungen Alexander Montgomeries*. Wien und Leipzig: W. Braumuller, 1896.

911. Hoffmann, Oscar. *Studien zu Alexander Montgomerie*. *Englische Studien*, 20 (1895), 24-69.

Two sections (pp. 35-36 and 45-54) deal directly with Montgomerie's sonnets.

912. Jack, Ronald D.S. "The Lyrics of Alexander Montgomerie." *Review of English Studies*, 20 (1969), 168-81.

Concerns his sonnets *inter alia*.

913. Montgomerie, Alexander. *The Poems of Alexander Montgomerie*. Ed. James Cranstoun. Edinburgh and London: Scottish Text Society, 1887.

Contains 70 sonnets.

914. ____________________. *Alexander Montgomerie: A Selection from his Songs and Poems*. Ed. Helena M. Shire. Edinburgh: Saltire Society, 1960.

Includes 13 sonnets.

915. ____________________. *Poems of Alexander Montgomerie And Other Pieces from Laing MS. No. 447: Supplementary Volume*. Ed. George Stevenson. Edinburgh and London: Scottish Text Society, 1910.

Introduction lists sonnets written by Scottish poets contemporary with Montgomerie (pp. xliii-xlv).

Sir William Mure

916. Jack, Ronald D.S. "Scottish Sonneteer and Welsh Metaphysical: A Study of the Religious Poetry of Sir William Mure and Henry Vaughn." Studies in Scottish Literature, 3 (1966), 240-47.

Sir David Murray of Gorthy

917. Murray, Sir David, of Gorthy. Poems by Sir David Murray of Gorthy. Ed. T. Kinnear. Edinburgh: Bannatyne Club, 1823.

Contains Caelia, a sequence of 22 sonnets, plus some miscellaneous others.

Sir Walter Raleigh

918. Brooke, C.F. Tucker. "Sir Walter Ralegh as Poet and Philosopher." ELH, 5 (1938), 93-112.

In this essay Brooke touches upon "A vision upon this conceit of the Fairy Queen," which he calls "one of the great sonnets of the language."

919. Oakeshott, Walter. The Queen and the Poet. London: Faber and Faber, 1960.

Includes some sonnets and annotations.

920. Ralegh, Sir Walter. The Poems of Sir Walter Ralegh. Ed. Agnes M.C. Latham. Boston and New York: Houghton Mifflin, 1929. London: Routledge and Kegan Paul, 1951. 1962.

Includes his sonnets.

Thomas Rogers

921. Williams, Franklin B., Jr. "Thomas Rogers of Bryanston, An Elizabethan Gentleman-of-Letters." Harvard Studies and Notes in Philology and Literature, 16 (1934), pp. 253-67.

An attempt to identify Thomas Rogers, who wrote the volume of sonnets entitled Celestial Elegies (1598), as the author of the anonymous Leicester's Ghost, a rime-royal "tragedy."

Thomas Sackville

922. Flugel, Ewald. "Verschollene Sonette." Anglia, 13 (1891), 72-76.

Two "lost" sonnets--one which he attributes to Henry Parker, the other to Sackville.

923. Orrick, Allan H. "Sackville's Sonnets." Notes and Queries, 201 (1956), 7-9.

Argues that Jasper Heywood's reference to "Sackvyldes Sonnets" meant only his contribution to the Mirror for Magistrates and not to any lyrics that we traditionally call sonnets.

Sir Philip Sidney

924. Adams, Robert M. Strains of Discord: Studies in Literary Openness. Ithaca, N.Y.: Cornell University Press, 1958.

Provides an explication of Astrophel and Stella, Sonnet 1 (pp. 4-6).

925. Addleshaw, Percy. Sir Philip Sidney. London: Methuen; New York: G.P. Putnam's Sons, 1909.

Chapter 17 concerns "Penelope Devereux and the Sonnets" (pp. 321-35).

926. Ahrends, Gunter. Liebe, Schonheit und Tugend als Strukturelemente in Sidneys "Astrophel and Stella" und in Spensers "Amoretti." Bonn: Rheinische Friederich-Wilhelms-Universitat, 1966.

927. Alden, Raymond Macdonald. "The Lyrical Conceit of the Elizabethans." Studies in Philology, 14 (1917), 129-52.

Uses the sonnets of Sidney and Shakespeare to illustrate the several types of conceit.

928. Banks, Theodore H. "Sidney's Astrophel and Stella Reconsidered." PMLA, 50 (1935), 403-12.

929. Barkan, Leonard. Nature's Work of Art: The Human Body as Image of the World. New Haven and London: Yale University Press, 1975.

Chapter 4, "Astrophil and Stella: The Human Body as Setting for the Petrarchan Drama" (pp. 175-200).

930. Baughan, Denver Ewing. "Sir Philip Sidney and the Matchmakers." Modern Language Review, 33 (1938), 506-19.

931. Baughan, Denver E. "The Question of Sidney's Love for his Wife." Notes and Queries, 177 (1939), 383-85.

Considers whether Lady Frances might have been 'Stella' or if Penelope Devereux might, in any case, not have been his true love.

932. Beal, Peter. "Poems by Sir Philip Sidney: The Ottley Manuscript." Library, 33 (1978), 284-95.

Describes a manuscript that contains, inter alia, 17 of the Certain Sonnets.

933. Bernard, John Dana. "Studies in the Love Poetry of Wyatt, Sidney, and Shakespeare." Ph.D. Dissertation, Minnesota, 1970. DAI, 31 (1971), 3538A.

934. Bernt, Joseph Philip. "Sir Philip Sidney and the Politics of Astrophil and Stella."" Ph.D. Dissertation, Nebraska, 1979. DAI, 40 (1980), 5449A.

Thesis suggests that Astrophil and Stella contains a political allegory commenting on the proposed marriage between Queen Elizabeth and Francis, Duke of Alencon.

935. Berry, J. Wilkes. "Unnamed Lady in Astrophil and Stella 97." American Notes and Queries, 12 (1974), 135-37.

936. Bevan, Bryan. "Sir Philip Sidney." Contemporary Review, 186 (1954), 346-49.

A biographical sketch with a paragraph on Astrophel and Stella.

937. Bill, Alfred H. Astrophel or The Life and Death of the Renowned Sir Philip Sidney. New York: Farrar and Rinehart, 1937.

Chapter 10, "Orlando Innamorato" (pp. 203-33), focuses on Astrophel and Stella and Penelope Devereux.

938. Blum, Irving D. "The Paradox of Money Imagery in English Renaissance Poetry." Studies in the Renaissance, 8 (1961), 144-54.

Includes discussions of money imagery in Sidney's Astrophel and Stella, Daniel's Delia, and in "Avarice" by George Herbert.

939. Boas, Frederick S. Sir Philip Sidney, Representative Elizabethan: His Life and Writings. London: Staples Press, 1955.

Chapters 21 and 22 (pp. 131-53) on Astrophel and Stella.

940. Bond, William H. "Sidney and Cupid's Dart." Modern Language Notes, 63 (1948), 258.

An image in Sonnet 5 refers to Sidney's coat of arms.

941. Bourne, H.R. Fox. A Memoir of Sir Philip Sidney. London: Chapman and Hall, 1862.

Chapter 10 (pp. 280-320) deals with his relationship with Penelope Rich and Astrophel and Stella.

942. Bourne, H.R. Fox. Sir Philip Sidney: Type of English Chivalry in the Elizabethan Age. New York and London: G.P. Putnam's Sons, 1891.

Discusses Astrophel and Stella in the context of Sidney's biography.

943. Bowen, Mary. "Some New Notes on Sidney's Poems." Modern Language Notes, 10 (1895), 118-23.

On the contents of the Rawlinson MS., Poetic 85, including some of Sidney's sonnets.

944. Bradbrook, M.C. Review of Richard B. Young, et al. Three Studies in the Renaissance: Sidney, Jonson, and Milton. Modern Language Review, 54 (1959), 584-85.

945. Brannin, James. "Astrophel, the Puritan." Sewanee Review, 16 (1908), 452-57.

Speaks of the divergence between his poems of "moral conflict" and those of "courtly playing."

946. Brodwin, Leonora Leet. "The Structure of Sidney's Astrophel and Stella." Modern Philology, 67 (1969), 25-40.

947. Brown, Russell M. "Sidney's Astrophel and Stella, Fourth Song." Explicator, 29 (1970), Item 48.

This song creates a transition in the sequence: the sonnets preceding deal with the physical side of love, the sonnets following with separation.

948. Brown, Russell M., Jr. "'Through All Maskes My Wo': Poet and Persona in Astrophil and Stella." Ph.D. Dissertation, SUNY at Binghamton, 1972. DAI, 33 (1972), 2317A.

949. Brown, Russell M. "Sidney's Astrophel and Stella, I." Explicator, 32 (1973), Item 21.

950. Brownbill, J. "Philip Sidney and Penelope Rich." TLS, September 20, 1928, p. 667.

951. Buchloh, Paul Gerhard, und Reimer Jehmlich. "Astrophel and Stella." Die Englische Lyrik: Von der Renaissance bis zur Gegenwart. Ed. Karl Heinz Goller. Dusseldorf: August Bagel, 1968, vol. 1, pp. 55-64.

Although commenting on several sonnets, the authors are principally concerned with Sonnet 76.

952. Bullitt, John M. "The Use of Rhyme Links in the Sonnets of Sidney, Drayton and Spenser." Journal of English and Germanic Philology, 49 (1950), 14-32.

953. Burhans, Clinton S., Jr. "Sidney's 'With How Sad Steps, O Moon'." Explicator, 18 (1960), Item 26.

On Sonnet 31 (Astrophel and Stella).

954. Buxton, John. Review of Richard B. Young, et al. Three Studies in the Renaissance: Sidney, Jonson, and Milton. Review of English Studies, NS 11 (1960), 202-03.

955. Buxton, John. "On the Date of Syr P.S. his Astrophel and Stella . . . . Printed for Matthew Lownes." Bodleian Library Record, 6 (1960), 614-16.

Suggests 1597-98 as the date of printing.

956. Buxton, John. Review of R.L. Montgomery, Symmetry and Sense: The Poetry of Sir Philip Sidney. Review of English Studies, NS 14 (1963), 99-100.

957. Buxton, John. Elizabethan Taste. New York: St. Martin's Press, 1964.

Chapter 6 contains a section on Astrophel and Stella (pp. 269-94).

958. Carr, John Wayne. "'That Love and Honor Might Agree': An Ethical Study of Astrophil and Stella." Ph.D. Dissertation, Stanford, 1974. DAI, 35 (1975), 6090A-91A.

959. *Castley, J.P., S.J. "Astrophel and Stella -- 'High Sidnaean Love' or Courtly Compliment?" Melbourne Critical Review, 5 (1962), 54-65.

960. Cherubini, William. The 'Goldenness' of Sidney's Astrophel and Stella: Test of a Quantitative-Stylistics Routine." Language and Style, 8 (1975), 47-59.

961. Colie, Rosalie L. Paradoxia Epidemica: The Renaissance Tradition of Paradox. Princeton: Princeton University Press, 1966.

Chapter 2 (pp. 89-95) deals with Sidney's Astrophel and Stella.

962. Collins, Michael J. "Comedy in the Love Poetry of Sidney, Drayton, Shakespeare and Donne." Ph.D. Dissertation, New York University, 1973. DAI, 34 (1974), 7743A.

963. Combellack, C.R.B., and E.H. Essig. "Sidney's 'With how sad steps, o Moon'." Explicator, 20 (1961), Item 25.

On Sonnet 31 (Astrophel and Stella).

964. Connell, Dorothy. Sir Philip Sidney: The Maker's Mind. Oxford: Clarendon Press, 1977.

965. Cooper, Sherod Monroe, Jr. "A Stylistic Study of The Sonnets of Astrophel and Stella." Ph.D. Dissertation, Pennsylvania, 1963. DA, 24 (1963), 1612-13.

966. Cooper, Sherod M., Jr. The Sonnets of Astrophil and Stella: A Stylistic Study. The Hague: Mouton Press, 1968.

967. Cotter, James Finn. "A Glasse of Reason: The Art of Poetry in Sidney's Astrophil and Stella." Ph.D. Dissertation, Fordham, 1963. DA, 24 (1964), 5382.

968. Cotter, James F. "Sidney's Astrophel and Stella, Sonnet 40." Explicator, 27 (1969), Item 51.

969. Cotter, James F. "Sidney's Astrophel and Stella, Sonnet 75." Explicator, 27 (1969), Item 70.

970. Cotter, James Finn. "The Songs in Astrophil and Stella." Studies in Philology, 67 (1970), 178-200.

Discusses the relationship between the songs and the sonnets.

971. Cotter, James Finn. "The 'Baiser' Group in Sidney's Astrophil and Stella." Texas Studies in Literature and Language, 12 (1970), 381-403.

Principally covers the 2nd Song and Sonnets 73-83, all of which deal with the theme of the kiss.

972. Cowan, Stanley A., and Fred A. Dudley. "Sidney's 'Astrophel and Stella, IX, 12-14'." Explicator, 20 (1962), Item 76.

973. Cunningham, James V. "Tragic Effect and Tragic Process in Some Plays of Shakespeare and Their Background in the Literary and Ethical Theory of Classical Antiquity and the Middle Ages." Ph.D. Dissertation, Stanford, 1945.

Notes the importance of Scholastic doctrine for Astrophel and Stella (p. 302).

974. Dahl, Curtis. "Sidney's Astrophel and Stella, LXXXIV." Explicator, 6 (1948), Item 46.

975. Davie, Donald. Articulate Energy: An Enquiry into the Syntax of English Poetry. London: Routledge and Kegan Paul, 1955.

Chapter 5 deals with sonnets by Sidney, Daniel and Shakespeare.

976. Davis, Sarah M. The Life and Times of Sir Philip Sidney. Boston: Ticknor and Fields, 1859. Rev. ed. New York: J.B. Ford, 1875.

Chapter 9 (pp. 224-38) focuses on *Astrophel and Stella* and Sidney's relationship with Penelope Devereux.

977. De Grazia, Margreta. "Lost Potential in Grammar and Nature: Sidney's *Astrophil and Stella*." *Studies in English Literature, 1500-1900*, 21 (1981), 21-35,

Sidney's use of "the potential mood" (i.e. his choice of certain auxiliary verbs expressing the mood of possibility) is an important element in understanding Astrophil's problem.

978. Deming, Robert H. "Love and Knowledge in the Renaissance Lyric." *Texas Studies in Literature and Language*, 16 (1974), 389-410.

In this discussion of the relationship between loving and knowing, Deming notes the development of the theme in *Astrophel and Stella* (pp. 398 ff.), with particular attention to Sonnet 1.

979. Dempsey, Paul K. "Sidney's 'And Have I Heard Her Say? O Cruell Paine!'" *Explicator*, 25 (1967), Item 51.

On Sonnet 11 (*Certain Sonnets*).

980. Denkinger, Emma Marshall. *Immortal Sidney*. New York: Brentano's, 1931.

Chapter 13, "Astrophel and Stella" (pp. 167-96).

981. Devereux, E.J. "A Possible Source for 'Pindare's Apes' in Sonnet 3 of 'Astrophil and Stella'." *Notes and Queries*, 222 (1977), 521.

982. Dickson, Arthur. "Sidney's *Astrophel and Stella*, Sonnet I." *Explicator*, 3 (1944), Item 3.

983. Donow, Herbert S. *A Concordance to the Poems of Sir Philip Sidney*. Ithaca, N.Y.: Cornell University Press, 1975.

984. Duncan-Jones, Katherine. Review of Sherod M. Cooper, *The Sonnets of "Astrophel and Stella": A Stylistic Study*. *Notes and Queries*, 214 (1969), 475.

985. Endicott, Annabel. "Pip, Philip and Astrophil: Dicken's Debt to Sidney?" *Dickensian*, 63 (1967), 158-62.

986. Fabry, Frank J. "Sidney's Poetry and Italian Song-Form." *English Literary Renaissance*, 3 (1973), 232-48.

Sidney made a distinction between the song lyric and the literary lyric. Apparently he considered some of the sonnets in the *Arcadia* to be in the former group.

987. Falls, Cyril. "Penelope Rich and the Poets: Philip Sidney to John Ford." *Essays by Divers Hands, Being the Transactions of the Royal Society of Literature*, 28 (1956), 123-37.

988. Finnegan, Robert Emmett. "Sidney's 'Astrophel and Stella' #14." Explicator, 35, ii (1976), 22-23.

989. Fletcher, Jefferson B. "Did Astrophel Love Stella?" Modern Philology, 5 (1907), 253-64. Reprinted in The Religion of Beauty in Women, and Other Essays on Platonic Love in Poetry and Society. New York: Macmillan, 1911. rpt. New York: Haskell House, 1966, pp. 147-65.

990. Flower, Timothy Frank. "1. Forms of Recreation in Nabokov's 'Pale Fire': 2. Charles Dickens and Gothic Fiction. 3. Making It New: Problems of Meaningful Form in the Sonnets of Sidney and Keats." Ph.D. Dissertation, Rutgers, 1972. DAI, 32 (1972), 6927A.

991. Fogel, Ephim G. "The Personal References in the Fiction and Poetry of Sir Philip Sidney." Ph.D. Dissertation, Ohio State, 1958. DA, 19 (1958), 809.

Includes discussion of Astrophel and Stella and Arcadia.

992. Fogel, Ephim G. "The Mythical Sorrows of Astrophil." Studies in Language and Literature in Honor of Margaret Schlauch. Ed. Mieczyslaw Brahmer, Stanislaw Helsztynski, and Julian Krzyzanowski. New York: Russell and Russell, 1971, pp. 133-52.

An attempt to dispose of the "phantom story" underlying Astrophil and Stella, i.e. the biographical readings of the poems which, the author claims, are unsupported by the "non-literary records." He pays special attention to Sonnets 2 and 33.

993. Fowler, Alastair. Triumphal Forms: Structural Patterns in Elizabethan Poetry. Cambridge: University Press, 1970.

Chapter 9 (pp. 174-97) discusses the numerological patterns in the sonnet sequences of Sidney, Spenser and Shakespeare.

994. Friedrich, Walter G. "The 'Stella' of 'Astrophel'." ELH, 3 (1936), 114-39.

995. Fucilla, Joseph G. "Parole Identiche in the Sonnet and Other Verse Forms." PMLA, 50 (1935), 372-402.

Mostly about continental poetry, but a brief passage deals with Drummond and Sidney (pp. 394-95).

996. *Gentili, Vanna. "La 'Tragicomedy' dell' Astrophil and Stella." Annali dell'Universita di Lecce, 1 (1963-64), 57-92.

997. Giles, Mary Dooley. "The Elizabethan Sonnet Sequence: Segmented Form in Its Earliest Appearances, Astrophil and Stella, Hekatompathia and Delia." Ph.D. Dissertation, Virginia, 1977. DAI, 39 (1978), 872A-73A.

998. Godshalk, William L. Review of Neil L. Rudenstine, Sidney's Poetic Development. Comparative Literature, 22 (1970), 90-91.

999. Godshalk, William L. "Sidney's Astrophel." American Notes and Queries, 17 (1978), 19-20.

Argues for "Astrophel" as correct spelling.

1000. Godshalk, W.L. "Cicero, Sidney, and the 'Sunne-Burn'd Braine'." Notes and Queries, 225 (1980), 139-40.

Considers the ambiguities and possible sources for the phrase "sunne-burn'd braine" from Astrophel and Stella, 1.

1001. Gosse, Edmund. "Sir Philip Sidney." Contemporary Review, 50 (1886), 632-46.

1002. Gottfried, Rudolf. "Autobiography and Art: An Elizabethan Borderland." Literary Criticism and Historical Understanding: Selected Papers from the English Institute. Ed. Philip Damon. New York: Columbia University Press, 1967, pp. 109-34.

Discusses the autobiographical aspects of the sonnet sequences of Sidney, Daniel and Spenser.

1003. Goulston, Wendy. "The 'Figuring Forth' of Astrophil: Sidney's Use of Language." Southern Review (Adelaide), 11 (1978), 228-46.

Explores how the use of language reveals the corruption of Astrophil's passion.

1004. Grundy, Joan. Review of The Poems of Sir Philip Sidney, ed. William A. Ringler, Jr. Modern Language Review, 58 (1963), 551-52.

1005. Grundy, Joan. Review of Neil L. Rudenstine, Sidney's Poetic Development. Modern Language Review, 64 (1969), 631-32.

1006. Hamilton, A.C. "The Modern Study of Renaissance English Literature: A Critical Survey." Modern Language Quarterly, 26 (1965), 150-83.

Talks about Sidney and the "sonneteering craze" (pp. 174-83).

1007. Hamilton, A.C. "Et in Arcadia Ego." Modern Language Quarterly, 27 (1966), 332-50.

This article includes a review of David Kalstone, Sidney's Poetry: Contexts and Interpretations (pp. 346-50).

1008. Hamilton, A.C. "Sidney's Astrophel and Stella as a Sonnet Sequence." ELH, 36 (1969), 59-87.

1009. Hamilton, A.C. Sir Philip Sidney: A Study of His Life and Works. New York and London: Cambridge University Press, 1977.

Discusses Astrophel and Stella (pp. 79-106) in chapter 3, "Sidney's 'Unelected Vocation'."

1010. Hamilton, A.C. "The 'mine of time': Time and Love in Sidney's Astrophel and Stella." Mosaic, 13, i (1979), 81-91.

Unlike Petrarch, Dante and Shakespeare, in whose poetry time is an explicit theme, Sidney deals with time "as an actual presence, the medium within which the poet writes."

1011. Hanford, James Holly. Review of James M. Purcell, Sidney's Stella. Modern Philology, 32 (1934), 207-09.

1012. Harfst, B.P. "Astrophil and Stella: Precept and Example." Papers on Language and Literature, 5 (1969), 397-414.

1013. Haublein, Ernst. Strophe und Struktur in der Lyrik Sir Philip Sidneys. Frankfurt: Peter Lang; Bern: Herbert Lang, 1971.

1014. Helgerson, Richard. The Elizabethan Prodigals. Berkeley: University of California Press, 1976.

Discusses Sidney's Astrophel and Stella (pp. 144-46). See also p. 171 where he argues for "Astrophel" as correct spelling.

1015. Helm, K. "Zur Entstehung von Ph. Sidney's Sonetten." Anglia, 19 (1897), 549-53.

1016. Henderson, Katherine Usher. "A Study of the Dramatic Mode in the English Renaissance Love Lyric: Sidney's Astrophil and Stella and Donne's Songs and Sonnets." Ph.D. Dissertation, Columbia, 1969. DA, 30 (1970), 4413A-14A.

1017. Hoffman, Dan G. "Sidney's 'Thou blind man's mark'." Explicator, 8 (1950), Item 29.

On Sonnet 31 (Certain Sonnets).

1018. Hough, Gordon. "A Quiet Image of Disquiet: The Persona in the Lyrics of Wyatt, Sidney and Donne." Ph.D. Dissertation, SUNY at Buffalo, 1975.

1019. Howe, Anne Romayne. "A Critical Edition of Sir Philip Sidney's Astrophel and Stella, with an introduction." Ph.D. Dissertation, Boston University, 1962. DA, 23 (1963), 1686.

1020. Howe, Ann Romayne. "Astrophel and Stella: 'Why and How'." Studies in Philology, 61 (1964), 150-69.

In this analysis of rhetorical devices, Howe appears to have found evidence to suggest that many of the first 27 sonnets were composed earlier than the rest. Contains also an appendix of rhetorical devices.

1021. Howell, Roger. *Sir Philip Sidney, the Shepherd Knight*. London: Hutchinson, 1968.

Devotes a chapter to "Astrophel and Stella" (pp. 178-204).

1022. Hudson, Hoyt H. "Penelope Devereux as Sidney's Stella." *Huntington Library Bulletin*, 7 (1935), 89-129.

Supports Penelope as Stella in refutation of James Purcell's thesis in *Sidney's Stella*.
1085

1023. *Imanishi, Masaaki. "Sir Philip Sidney no *Astrophel and Stella* no Hyogen to Giho--Elizabeth-cho Love-sonnet Shiron." [Expression and Technique in *Astrophel and Stella:* An Essay on the Elizabethan Love-sonnet.] *Gengo to Buntai: Higashida Chiaki Kyoju Kanreki Kinen Ronbunshu*. Osaka: Osaka Kyoiku Tosho, 1975, pp. 30-42.

1024. Jackson, MacD. P. "The Printer of the First Quarto of *Astrophil and Stella* (1591)." *Studies in Bibliography*, 31 (1978), 201-03.

Identifies the printer as John Charlewood.

1025. Jakobson, Roman. "The Grammatical Texture of a Sonnet from Sir Philip Sidney's *Arcadia*." Ed. Mieczyslaw Brahmer, Stanislaw Helsztynski, and Julian Krzyzanowski. *Studies in Language and Literature in Honour of Margaret Schlauch*. New York: Russell and Russell, 1971, pp. 165-73.

On a sonnet from the *Old Arcadia*, "Loved I am, and yet complaine of Love."

1026. Jehmlich, Reimer. "Feurige Liebesdampfe: Zu drei Sonetten Sir Philip Sidneys." *Literatur in Wissenschaft und Unterricht*, 4 (1971), 147-57.

On sonnets 16, 42, 76 from *Astrophel and Stella*.

1027. Jenkins, Annibel. "A Second Astrophel and Stella Cycle." *Renaissance Papers 1970*. Southeastern Renaissance Conference, 1970, pp. 73-80.

About the 11 songs that were interspersed among the 14-line sonnets.

1028. John, L.C. "The Date of the Marriage of Penelope Devereux." *PMLA*, 49 (1934), 961-62.

1029. Juel-Jensen, Bent. "Some Uncollected Authors XXXIV: Sir Philip Sidney, 1554-1586." *Book Collector*, 12 (1963), 196-201.

A bibliographical description of several rare editions of *Astrophel and Stella*.

1030. Kalstone, David. "Sir Philip Sidney and 'Poore Petrarchs Long Deceased Woes'." Journal of English and Germanic Philology, 63 (1964), 21-32.

On Astrophel and Stella.

1031. Kalstone, David. Sidney's Poetry: Contexts and Interpretations. Cambridge, Mass.: Harvard University Press, 1965. New York: Norton, 1970.

Second half of the book deals with Astrophel and Stella (pp. 103-81).

1032. Kalstone, David. "Sir Philip Sidney: The Petrarchan Vision." Elizabethan Poetry: Modern Essays in Criticism. Ed. Paul J. Alpers. New York: Oxford University Press, Galaxy Books, 1967, pp. 187-209.

An excerpt from Sidney's Poetry: Contexts and Interpretations.

1033. Kalstone, David. "Sir Philip Sidney." English Poetry and Prose 1540-1674. Ed. Christopher Ricks. London: Barrie and Jenkins, 1970, pp. 41-59.

Last section of the essay is on Astrophel and Stella.

1034. Kennedy, William J. Rhetorical Norms in Renaissance Literature. New Haven and London: Yale University Press, 1978.

A portion of chapter 1 (pp. 57-78) is entitled "Sidney's Astrophil and Stella."

1035. Kimbrough, Robert. Sir Philip Sidney. Twayne's English Author Series, 114. New York: Twayne, 1971.

1036. Kinsman, Robert. "Sidney's Astrophel and Stella, Sonnet XII, 1-2." Explicator, 8 (1950), Item 56.

1037. Koeppel, E. "Sidneiana. I. Zur textkritik von Sir Philip Sidney's gedichten. II. Zur Willy-frage." Anglia, 10 (1887), 522-32.

The first of the notes makes some textual comparison between Abraham Fraunce's edition of Sidney's Arcadia and Astrophel and Stella and Grosart's 19th-century edition.

1038. Koeppel, E. "Zur 'Astrophel and Stella'." Anglia, 13 (1891), 467-68.

1039. Krieger, Murray. "The Continuing Need for Criticism." Concerning Poetry, 1, i (1968), 7-21.

Discussion of the broad need for criticism includes an explication of Wyatt's "Divers doth use as I have heard and know" (pp. 14-17) and Sidney's Astrophel and Stella 35 (pp. 18-21).

1040. Krieger, Murray. "Poetic Presence and Illusion: Renaissance Theory and the Duplicity of Metaphor." Critical Inquiry, 5 (1979), 597-619. Reprinted as "Poetic Presence and Illusion I: Renaissance Theory and the Duplicity of Metaphor" in Poetic Presence and Illusion: Essays in Critical History and Theory. Baltimore: Johns Hopkins University Press, 1979, pp. 3-27.

In this discussion of the Renaissance view of language, Krieger focuses on a number of sonnets from Astrophil and Stella and from Shakespeare.

1041. Kuin, R.J.P. "Scholars, Critics, and Sir Philip Sidney, 1945-1970." British Studies Monitor, 2, iii (1972), 3-22.

Includes a survey of scholarship on Astrophel and Stella (pp. 9-13).

1042. Lamb, Charles. "Some Sonnets of Sir Philip Sidney." Last Essays of Elia. New York: John B. Alden, 1885, pp. 91-99. From The Works of Charles and Mary Lamb. Ed. E.V. Lucas. New York: Macmillan, 1913, vol. 2.

1043. Lanham, Richard. "Astrophil and Stella: Pure and Impure Persuasion." English Literary Renaissance, 2 (1972), 100-15.

1044. Latham, Jacqueline E.M. "Sidney's Astrophil and Stella, Sonnet 30." Explicator, 33 (1975), Item 47.

1045. Lavin, J.A. "The First Two Printers of Sidney's Astrophil and Stella." Library, 26 (1971), 249-55.

1046. Lemmi, C.W. "Italian Borrowings in Sidney." Modern Language Notes, 42 (1927), 77-79.

Includes some Italian parallels to the last line of "With how sad steps, O Moone . . ." (Astrophel and Stella, 31).

1047. Long, Percy W. "Spenser and Sidney." Anglia, 38 (1914), 173-92.

A discussion of the possibility of mutual indebtedness of the two writers with some reference to their sonnets.

1048. Luther, Susan M. "Sidney's Astrophil and Stella, Sonnet 29." Explicator, 33 (1975), Item 40.

1049. Lyles, Albert M. "A Note on Sidney's Use of Chaucer." Notes and Queries, 198 (1953), 99-100.

A parallel between Astrophel and Stella, Sonnet 39 and lines 242-64 of Book of the Duchess.

1050. Mahoney, John F. "The Philosophical Coherence and Literary Motive of 'Astrophel and Stella'." Essays and Studies in Language and Literature, (Duquesne Studies, Philological Series) 5 (1964), 24-37.

1051. *Marenco, Franco. "Astrophel and Stella." Filologia e Letteratura, 13 (1967), 72-91, 162-91.

1052. Mazzaro, Jerome. Transformation in the Renaissance English Lyric. Ithaca, N.Y.: Cornell University Press, 1970.

Discusses the creation of the persona in Astrophel and Stella (pp. 101-07).

1053. Miller, Jacqueline T. "'Love doth hold my hand': Writing and Wooing in the Sonnets of Sidney and Spenser." ELH, 46 (1979), 541-58.

1054. Montgomery, Robert L., Jr. "Structure, Theme, and Style in Sidney's Astrophel and Stella." Ph.D. Dissertation, Harvard, 1956.

1055. Montgomery, Robert L., Jr. "Reason, Passion, and Introspection in Astrophel and Stella." University of Texas Studies in English, 36 (1957), 127-40.

1056. Montgomery, Robert L., Jr. Symmetry and Sense: The Poetry of Sir Philip Sidney. Austin: University of Texas Press, 1961.

The final chapter, "Astrophel and Stella: 'Reasons Audite'" (pp. 100-20) is a revised version of "Reason, Passion, etc." 1055

1057. Montgomery, Robert L., Jr. Review of David Kalstone, Sidney's Poetry: Context and Interpretations. Journal of English and Germanic Philology, 65 (1966), 167-68.

1058. Montgomery, Robert L., Jr. Review of Neil L. Rudenstine, Sidney's Poetic Development. Journal of English and Germanic Philology, 67 (1968), 695-97.

1059. Montgomery, Robert L., Jr. Review of A.C. Hamilton, Sir Philip Sidney: A Study of His Life and Works. Modern Language Quarterly, 39 (1978), 73-76.

1060. *Morley, Edith J. The Works of Sir Philip Sidney. The Quain Essay, University College, 1901. London: H. Rees, 1901.

1061. Morrissey, Thomas J. "1. The Self Versus the Meditative Tradition in Donne's Devotions. 2. 'Intimate and Unidentifiable': The Voices of Fragmented Reality in the Poetry of T.S. Eliot. 3. Sir Philip Sidney's Poetic Theory and Practice." Ph.D. Dissertation, Rutgers, 1977. DAI, 38 (1977), 2754A-55A.

Analysis of Defense, Arcadia and Astrophel and Stella.

1062. Mourgues, Odette de. Metaphysical, Baroque, and Precieux Poetry. Oxford: Clarendon Press, 1953.

Chapter 2 deals with sonnets of Sidney and Greville.

1063. Muir, Kenneth. "'Astrophel and Stella', XXXI." Notes and Queries, 205 (1960), 51-52.

1064. Muir, Kenneth. Sir Philip Sidney. Writers and Their Work, 120. London: Longmans, Green, 1960. Reprinted in British Writers. Ed. Ian Scott-Kilvert. New York: Charles Scribner's Sons, 1979, vol. 1, pp. 160-75.

1065. Murphy, Karl M. "Studies in Astrophel and Stella." Ph.D. Dissertation, Harvard, 1949.

1066. Murphy, Karl M. "The 109th and 110th Sonnets of Astrophel and Stella." Philological Quarterly, 34 (1955), 349-52.

"Thou blind man's mark" and "Leave me, o love" were thought by some (Grosart for one) to be part of Astrophel and Stella, a notion rejected by Murphy.

1067. Murray, Howard. "The Trend of Shakespeare's Thought." TLS, January 5, 1951, p. 7.

Letter comparing Sidney's Sonnet 84 and Shakespeare's Sonnet 50.

1068. Myrick, Kenneth O. Review of Robert L. Montgomery, Jr., Symmetry and Sense: The Poetry of Sir Philip Sidney. Renaissance News, 15 (1962), 240-42.

1069. Nelson, T.G.A. "'Astrophel and Stella': A Note on Sonnet LXXV." AUMLA, 27 (1967), 79-80.

1070. Nelson, Thomas Edward. "The Syntax of Sidney's Poetry." Ph.D. Dissertation, Ohio, 1975. DAI, 36 (1976), 6710A-11A.

Deals with Astrophel and Stella.

1071. Nichols, J.G. The Poetry of Sir Philip Sidney: An Interpretation in the Context of his Life and Times. Liverpool: Liverpool University Press, 1974.

Includes a chapter, "When I say Stella" (pp. 52-79) on Astrophil and Stella, et passim.

1072. Ogden, James. "Hazlitt, Lamb and Astrophel and Stella." Trivium, 2 (1967), 141-42.

1073. Paganelli, Eloisa. Review of Philip Sidney: Astrophil and Stella. Ed. Vanna Gentili. Annali della Facolta di Lingue e Letterature Straniere di Ca' Foscari, 6 (1967), 162-64.

1074. Pellegrini, Angelo Mario. "Bruno, Sidney, and Spenser." Studies in Philology, 40 (1943), 128-44.

Connection between Sidney and Spenser and Giordano Bruno with references to Astrophel and Stella.

1075. Pettet, E.C. "Sidney and the Cult of Romantic Love." English, 6 (1947), 232-40.

Sidney's direct and spontaneous style in Astrophel and Stella makes it stand out from the sonnets of his contemporaries.

1076. Pettit, Henry, and Gerald Sanders. "Sidney's Astrophel and Stella." Explicator, 1 (1942), Item 26.

On Sonnet 1.

1077. Poirier, Michel. "Quelques Sources des Poemes de Sidney." Etudes Anglaises, 11 (1958), 150-54.

Two of the poems mentioned are from Astrophel and Stella (92) and the Certain Sonnets (18).

1078. Poirier, Michel. Review of William A. Ringler, Jr. The Poems of Sir Philip Sidney. Etudes Anglaises, 17 (1964), 69-71.

1079. Poirier, Michel. Sir Philip Sidney: Le Chevalier Poete Elisabethain. Lille: Bibliotheque Universitaire, 1948.

Discusses Astrophel and Stella in Livre 2, Chapitre 3 (pp. 180-97) et passim.

1080. Purcell, J.M. "Sonnet CV of Astrophel and Stella and Love's Labour's Lost." Philological Quarterly, 10 (1931), 399.

Compares the sonnet with Love's Labour's Lost (IV.ii.26-41).

1081. Purcell, J.M. [no title]. PMLA, 46 (1931), 945-46.

On the marriage of Penelope Devereux.

1082. Purcell, J.M. Review of several works including Astrophel and Stella, ed. Mona Wilson. Philological Quarterly, 11 (1932), 218-20.

1083. Purcell, J.M. "A Note on Sonnet II of Astrophel and Stella." Philological Quarterly, 11 (1932), 402-03.

1084. Purcell, J.M. "The Date of the Marriage of Penelope Devereux." PMLA, 49 (1934), 961-62.

1085. Purcell, James M. Sidney's Stella. New York and London: Oxford University Press, 1934.

Argues against Penelope Devereux as Stella.

1086. Purcell, James M. "The Contemporary References in Sir Philip Sidney's Astrophel and Stella." Ph.D. Dissertation, New York University, 1935.

1087. Purcell, J.M. "Sidney's 'Astrophel and Stella' and Greville's 'Caelica'." PMLA, 50 (1935), 413-22.

1088. Putzel, Max. "Sidney's Astrophel and Stella, IX." Explicator, 19 (1961), Item 25.

1089. Rawson, Maude S. Penelope Rich and Her Circle. London: Hutchinson, 1911.

Much of the first half of the book deals with Sidney's relationship with Penelope and with Astrophel and Stella.

1090. Rees, Joan. "Four Hundred Years On: Sidney Today." Cahiers Elisabethains, No. 15 (1979), 87-95.

The first part of this review article includes a discussion of Astrophil and Stella.

1091. Regan, Mariann S. "Astrophel: Full of Desire, Emptie of Wit." English Language Notes, 14 (1977), 251-56.

Discusses Sidney's use of the "foolish poet" convention in Astrophel and Stella.

1092. Richmond, H.M. "Tradition and the Lyric: An Historical Approach to Value." Comparative Literature Studies, 1 (1964), 119-32.

Sidney's Astrophel and Stella, Sonnet 54, demonstrates how, by the speaker publicly arguing his case, the poem achieves greater "immediacy and dramatic verve" (pp. 129-30).

1093. Ringler, William, Jr. "Poems Attributed to Sir Philip Sidney." Studies in Philology, 47 (1950), 126-51.

The last or 30th poem he discusses is a sonnet.

1094. Robertson, Jean. Review of Sir Philip Sidney: Astrophel and Stella, ed. Michel Poirier. Etudes Anglaises, 11 (1958), 346-49.

1095. Robertson, Jean. "Sir Philip Sidney and his Poetry." Elizabethan Poetry. Ed. John Russell Brown and Bernard Harris. Stratford-upon-Avon Studies, 2. London: Edward Arnold, 1960, pp. 110-29.

Discusses Astrophel and Stella and Certain Sonnets (pp. 117-22, 125-29).

1096. Robertson, Jean. "Sir Philip Sidney and Lady Penelope Rich." Review of English Studies, NS 15 (1964), 296-97.

1097. Robertson, Jean. "Macbeth on Sleep: 'Sore Labour's Bath' and Sidney's 'Astrophil and Stella,' XXXIX." Notes and Queries, 212 (1967), 139-41.

Discusses the relationship among several texts on sleep--including Griffin's sonnet from _Fidessa_, "Care-charmer sleep, sweet ease in restless misery."

1098. Robertson, Jean. Review of Neil L. Rudenstine, _Sidney's Poetic Development_. _Review of English Studies_, NS 19 (1968), 307-10.

1099. Rogers, Donald O. "Nature and Art in Sidney's _Astrophel and Stella_." _South Central Bulletin_, 31 (1971), 211-14.

1100. Rudenstine, Neil. _Sidney's Poetic Development_. Cambridge, Mass.: Harvard University Press, 1967.

Both Chapter 8, "'A Courtier's _Certain Sonnets_" (pp. 115-30), and Appendix I are on _Certain Sonnets_. Chapter 11, "The Styles of _Astrophel_," and much of the rest of the book discusses _Astrophel and Stella_.

1101. Rudenstine, Neil. "Sidney and Energia." _Elizabethan Poetry_. Ed. Paul Alpers. New York: Oxford University Press, 1967, pp. 210-34.

An excerpt from _Sidney's Poetic Development_ by Rudenstine.

1102. Ryken, Leland. "Sidney's 'Leave Me, O Love Which Reachest But to Dust'." _Explicator_, 26 (1967), Item 9.

On Sonnet 32 (_Certain Sonnets_).

1103. Ryken, Leland. "The Drama of Choice in Sidney's _Astrophil and Stella_." _Journal of English and Germanic Philology_, 68 (1969), 648-54.

1104. Ryken, Leland. "Sidney's 'Leave Me, O Love': An Interpretation." _Christian Scholar's Review_, 1 (1971), 19-26.

On Sonnet 32 (_Certain Sonnets_).

1105. Salesses, John Joseph. "The Lyric Voice From Wyatt to Donne: An Essay in the Poetic Process." Ph.D. Dissertation, Rhode Island, 1979. _DAI_, 40 (1980), 2702A.

One part of the dissertation deals with Sidney's _Astrophil and Stella_. His discussion of Wyatt also includes commentary on the sonnets.

1106. Scanlon, James J. "Sidney's _Astrophil and Stella_: 'See what it is to Love' Sensually!" _Studies in English Literature, 1500-1900_, 16 (1976), 65-74.

Explores the "ethical implications" of Sidney's "representation of Astrophil's emotional states."

1107. Scott, Janet G. "Parallels to Three Elizabethan Sonnets." _Modern Language Review_, 21 (1926), 190-92.

On Astrophel and Stella 25 and 17 and a poem from Lodge's Phillis.

1108. Sherman, Stuart P. "Stella and The Broken Heart." PMLA, 24 (1909), 274-85.

The story of Ford's play was based on Sidney's love for "Stella"--Lady Rich.

1109. Shirreff, A.G. "A Suggested Emendation in Sidney's Sonnets." Notes and Queries, 194 (1949), 129.

Response to Paul Siegel's note on Sonnet 3.
1128

1110. Sidney, Sir Philip. Sir Philip Sidney: Selected Poetry and Prose. Ed. T.W. Craik. London: Methuen, 1965.

Introduction includes essay on Astrophel and Stella (pp. 7-12) plus an annotated selection of poems from Astrophel and Stella.

1111. ________________. Selected Poems. Ed. Katherine Duncan-Jones. Oxford: Clarendon Press, 1973.

1112. ________________. The Last Part of The Countess of Pembroke's Arcadia, Astrophel and Stella and Other Poems, The Lady of May. Ed. Albert Feuillerat. Cambridge: University Press, 1922. Volume 2 of The Complete Works of Sir Philip Sidney.

1113. ________________. Sir Philip Sidney's Astrophel and Stella und Defence of Poesie nach den altesten Ausgaben mit einer Einleitung uber Sidney's Leben und Werke. Ed. Ewald Flugel. Halle: Max Niemeyer, 1889.

1114. ________________. Astrophel et Stella. Traduit et preface par Charles M. Garnier. Paris: Aubier Editions Montaigne, 1943.

1115. ________________. Sir Philip Sidney: Astrophel and Stella. Ed. Vanna Gentili. Biblioteca italiana di testi inglesi, 10. Bari: Adriatica, 1965.

1116. ________________. The Miscellaneous Works of Sir Philip Sidney, knt. With a Life of the Author and Illustrative Notes. Ed. William Gray. London: William Gibbings, 1893. rpt. New York: AMS Press, 1966.

Discusses Penelope Devereux and Astrophel and Stella (pp. 34-37). Also contains 4 sonnets "by Henry Constable to Sir Philip Sidney's Soul."

1117. ________________. The Complete Poems of Sir Philip Sidney. Ed. A.B. Grosart. 2 vol. London: Robson and Sons, 1873.

Contains a prefatory "Essay on the Poetry of Sir Philip Sidney" (xvii-lx) and Astrophel and Stella, both in volume 1.

1118. ________. Astrophel and Stella. Ed. Kingsley Hart. London: Folio Society, 1959.

1119. ________. Selected Poetry and Prose. Ed. David Kalstone. New York: New American Library, 1970.

1120. ________. Sir Philip Sidney: Selected Prose and Poetry. Ed. Robert Kimbrough. New York: Holt, Rinehart and Winston, 1969.

1121. ________. Astrophel and Stella, 1591. Menston, England: Scolar Press, 1970. Facsimile of 1591 edition by Thomas Newman.

1122. ________. Sir Philip Sidney: Astrophel and Stella. Ed. and tr. Michel Poirier. Paris: Aubier, 1957.

1123. ________. Sir Philip Sidney's Astrophel and Stella. Ed. Alfred W. Pollard. London: David Stott, 1888.

1124. ________. Astrophil and Stella. Ed. Max Putzel. Garden City, N.Y.: Anchor Books, 1967.

1125. ________. The Poems of Sir Philip Sidney. Ed. William A. Ringler, Jr. Oxford: Clarendon Press, 1962.

1126. ________. Astrophel and Stella. Ed. Mona Wilson. London: Nonesuch Press, 1931. New York: Oxford University Press, 1932.

1127. Siebeck, Berta. Das Bild Sir Philip Sidneys in der Englischen Renaissance. Schriften der Deutschen Shakespeare-Gesellschaft, Neue Folge, 3. Weimar: Hermann Bohlaus Nachfolger, 1939.

Discussion of Astrophel and Stella (pp. 35-38).

1128. Siegel, Paul N. "A Suggested Emendation for One of Sidney's Sonnets." Notes and Queries, 194 (1949), 75-76.

On Sonnet 3 (Astrophel and Stella).
1109

1129. Sinfield, Alan. "Sexual Puns in Astrophil and Stella." Essays in Criticism, 24 (1974), 341-55.

1130. Sinfield, Alan. "Astrophil's Self-Deception." Essays in Criticism, 28 (1978), 1-18.

An attempt to balance the psychological aspects of Astrophil's emotional experience with the ethical principles implicit in Sidney's view of the world.

1131. Sloan, Thomas O. "The Crossing of Rhetoric and Poetry in the English Renaissance." The Rhetoric of Renaissance Poetry from Wyatt to Milton. Ed. Thomas O. Sloan and Raymond B. Waddington. Berkeley: University of California Press, 1954, pp. 212-42.

Discusses the rhetoric in Sonnet 1 (Astrophel and Stella).

1132. Smith, G.C. Moore. "Astrophel and Stella." TLS, September 18, 1930, p. 735.

Letter on Sonnet 105 replying to an earlier letter by Mona Wilson (p. 716).
1170

1133. Spencer, Theodore. "The Poetry of Sir Philip Sidney." ELH, 12 (1945), 251-78.

1134. Stevenson, Ruth. "The Influence of Astrophil's Star." Tennessee Studies in Literature, 17 (1972), 45-57.

Although most critics agree "that Astrophil's personality dominates the sequence," it is Stella who directs it through Astrophil's reaction to her and to her changes.

1135. Stignant, William. "Sir Philip Sidney." Cambridge Essays. London: John W. Parker, 1858, pp. 81-126.

A brief treatment (p. 99) of Sidney's passion for Penelope with a comment on "Leave me, oh Love . . ." (Sonnet 32, Certain Sonnets).

1136. Stillinger, Jack. "The Biographical Problem of Astrophel and Stella." Journal of English and Germanic Philology, 59 (1960), 617-39.

1137. Stillinger, Jack. Review of The Poems of Sir Philip Sidney, ed. William A. Ringler, Jr. Journal of English and Germanic Philology, 62 (1963), 372-78.

1138. Stroup, Thomas B. "The 'Speaking Picture' Realized: Sidney's 45th Sonnet." Philological Quarterly, 29 (1950), 440-42.

1139. Suddard, S.J. Mary. "'Astrophel and Stella'." Keats, Shelly and Shakespear: Studies and Essays in English Literature. Cambridge: University Press, 1912, pp. 162-76.

1140. Symonds, J.A. Sir Philip Sidney. London: Macmillan, 1886.

Chapter 6, "Astrophel and Stella" (pp. 115-54).

1141. Taylor, Arvilla Kerns. "The Manege of Love and Authority: Studies in Sidney and Shakespeare." Ph.D. Dissertation, Texas, 1969. DA, 30 (1969), 3025A-26A.

Includes Astrophel and Stella.

1142. Thaler, Alwin. Shakespeare and Sir Philip Sidney: The Influence of "The Defense of Poesy." Cambridge, Mass.: Harvard University Press, 1947. rpt. New York: Russell and Russell, 1967.

Numerous brief references to Shakespeare's and Sidney's sonnets.

1143. Thomas, Dylan. "Sir Philip Sidney." Quite Early One Morning. New York: New Directions, 1954, pp. 112-21.

A brief biographical essay which touches on the sonnets (pp. 142-44).

1144. Thomas, W.K. "Sidney's 'Leave Me, O Love, Which Reachest but to Dust." Explicator, 28 (1970), Item 45. Reprinted and revised as "Bouncing off the Board: Progression through Sidney's Famous Sonnet" in The Fizz Inside: Critical Essays of a Lighter Kind. Waterloo, Canada: University of Waterloo Press, 1980, pp. 165-69.

On Sonnet 32 (Certain Sonnets).

1145. Thompson, John. "The Iambic Line from Wyatt to Sidney." Ph.D. Dissertation, Columbia, 1957. DA, 18 (1958), 1040.

Discusses, among other works, Sidney's Astrophel and Stella.

1146. Thompson, John. "Sir Philip And the Forsaken Iamb." Kenyon Review, 20 (1958), 90-115.

Thompson's discussion of Sidney's great metrical variety includes Astrophel and Stella (pp. 104 ff.), which he calls "a new kind of poetry" depending on "a new kind of metrical practice."

1147. Thompson, John. The Founding of English Metre. New York: Columbia University Press; London: Routledge and Kegan Paul, 1961.

Chapter 6 (pp. 139-55) on Sidney's poetry including Astrophel and Stella.

1148. Thomson, Patricia. Review of David Kalstone, Sidney's Poetry: Contexts and Interpretations. Modern Language Review, 61 (1966), 486-87.

1149. Traister, Daniel H. "'Pity the Tale of Me': A Reading of Sidney's Astrophil and Stella." Ph.D. Dissertation, New York University, 1973. DAI, 34 (1974), 7724A.

1150. Tucker, Virginia A. "'Directing Threds . . . Through the Labyrinth': The Moral Use of Platonic Conventions and Patterns of Imagery in Sidney's Astrophil and Stella." Ph.D. Dissertation, North Carolina at Greensboro, 1973. DAI, 34 (1973), 2583A.

1151. Van Dorsten, J.A. Poets, Patrons, and Professors: Sir Philip Sidney, Daniel Rogers, and the Leiden Humanists. Leiden: University Press, 1962.

Part II, "Sir Philip Sidney," begins with a chapter ("Leiden Visits England") dealing with the translation of Constable's sonnets by Dutch poets and the connection between these poets and "Stella."

1152. Voss, Anthony E. "The Search for Words: The Theme of Language in Four Renaissance Poems." Ph.D. Dissertation, University of Washington, 1967. DA, 28 (1968), 3690A-91A.

Astrophel and Stella is one of the four.

1153. Wallace, Malcolm W. The Life of Sir Philip Sidney. Cambridge: University Press, 1915.

Chapter 13, "Astrophel and Stella" (pp. 241-59).

1154. Waller, Gary F. "Acts of Reading: Explicit and Implicit Readings in Astrophil and Stella." Abstract of a paper read at Modern Language Association, Houston, December, 1980: Writers of the English Renaissance. Sidney Newsletter, 2, i (1981), 26.

1155. Waller, G.F. "'This Matching of Contraries': Bruno, Calvin and the Sidney Circle." Neophilologus, 56 (1972), 331-43.

Briefly comments about Astrophel and Stella (p. 338).

1156. Walter, J.H. "Astrophel and Stella and The Romaunt of the Rose." Review of English Studies, 15 (1939), 265-73.

1157. Walton, Eda Lou. "The Stella of Sydney's Famous Sonnets." New York Times Book Review, September 16, 1934, p. 3.

Review of James M. Purcell, Sidney's Stella.

1158. Warkentin, Germaine T. "Astrophil and Stella in the Setting of Its Tradition." Ph.D. Dissertation, Toronto, 1972. DAI, 34 (1974), 5211A.

1159. Warkentin, Germaine. "Sidney's Certain Sonnets: Speculations on the Evolution of the Text." Library, 6th Series, 2 (1980), 430-44.

Includes some comments about the relationship between these poems and the "much more exciting" Astrophil and Stella.

1160. Warren, C. Henry. Sir Philip Sidney: a Study in Conflict. London: Thomas Nelson and Sons, 1936. rpt. New York: Haskell House, 1967.

Chapter 6 is a biographical treatment of Astrophel and Stella.

1161. Weiner, Andrew D. "'In a grove most rich of shade': A Figurative Reading of the Eighth Song of *Astrophil and Stella*." *Texas Studies in Literature and Language*, 18 (1976), 341-61.

Commentary applies to the whole sonnet sequence and contains comments on individual sonnets as well.

1162. Weiner, Andrew D. "Structure and 'Fore Conceit' in *Astrophil and Stella*." *Texas Studies in Literature and Language*, 16 (1974), 1-25.

The division of *Astrophil and Stella* into five major movements is determined in large part by how we feel about Astrophil as the sequence progresses.

1163. Wentworth, Michael Douglas. "Studies on Selected Elizabethan Sonnet Sequences: *Astrophel and Stella*, *Delia*, *Amoretti*, *Idea*." Ph.D. Dissertation, Bowling Green State, 1979. *DAI*, 40 (1980), 5458A.

1164. Whigam, R.G., and O.F. Emerson. "Sonnet Structure in Sidney's 'Astrophel and Stella'." *Studies in Philology*, 18 (1921), 347-52.

1165. Wickes, George. "A Portrait of Penelope Rich." *Renaissance Papers 1957*. Southeastern Renaissance Conference, 1957, pp. 9-14.

Poetic descriptions of Penelope Rich after Sidney.

1166. Williamson, Colin. "Structure and Syntax in *Astrophil and Stella*." *Review of English Studies*, NS 31 (1980), 271-84.

1167. Wilson, Christopher R. "*Astrophil and Stella*: A Tangled Editorial Web." *Library*, 6th Series, 1 (1979), 336-46.

At the end of the first printed edition of *Astrophil and Stella* (1591) was appended "The Poems and Sonets of Sundrie Other Noblemen and Gentlemen," which is the subject of this article.

1168. Wilson, Harold S. "Sidney's *Astrophel and Stella*, Sonnet 78." *Explicator*, 2 (1943), Item 17.

1169. Wilson, Harold S. "Sidney's Leave Me, O Love, Which Reachest But to Dust." *Explicator*, 2 (1944), Item 47.

On Sonnet 32 (*Certain Sonnets*).

1170. Wilson, Mona. "Astrophel and Stella." *TLS*, September 11, 1930, p. 716.

See G.C. Moore Smith's reply.
1132

1171. Wilson, Mona. Sir Philip Sidney. New York: Oxford University Press, 1932.

Chapter 10 "Astrophel and Stella" (pp. 167-206).

1172. Woods, Susanne. "Aesthetic and Mimetic Rhythms in the Versification of Gascoigne, Sidney, and Spenser." Studies in the Literary Imagination, 11 (1978), 31-44.

Her illustrations are drawn from Astrophel and Stella and the Amoretti.

1173. Yates, Frances A. A Study of Love's Labour's Lost. Cambridge: University Press, 1936.

In her chapter on, "Bruno and 'Stella'" (pp. 102-36), Yates has much to say about Giordano Bruno's influence on Sidney's Astrophel and Stella.

1174. Yoch, James J. "Brian Twyne's Commentary on Astrophel and Stella." Allegorica, 2, ii (1977), 114-16.

1175. Young, Richard B. "English Petrarke: A Study of Sidney's Astrophel and Stella." Richard B. Young, W. Todd Furniss, and William G. Madsen, Three Studies in the Renaissance: Sidney, Jonson, Milton. Yale Studies in English, 138. New Haven: Yale University Press, 1958.

1176. *Yuasa, Nobuyuki. "Rhetoric in the Sonnets of Sidney, Spenser and Shakespeare: A Morphology of Metaphor, Antanaclasis, and Oxymoron." Studies in English Literature (Japan), English Number (1977), 33-52.

1177. "Astrophel Without Stella." TLS, November 29, 1934, p. 853.

Review of James M. Purcell, Sidney's Stella.

1178. "High Erected Thoughts." TLS, January 6, 1966, p. 5.

Review of several books: Selected Poetry and Prose, ed. T.W. Craik; Walter Davis and Richard Lanham, Sidney's Arcadia; David Kalstone, Sidney's Poetry.

1179. Review of Neil L. Rudenstine, Sidney's Poetic Development. TLS, December 14, 1967, p. 1206.

Robert Sidney

1180. Duncan-Jones, Katherine. "'Rosis & Lysa': Selections from the Poems of Sir Robert Sidney." English Literary Renaissance, 9 (1979), 240-63.

The introduction is followed by a number of poems including four sonnets.

1181. Kelliher, Hilton, and Katherine Duncan-Jones. "A Manuscript of Poems by Robert Sidney: Some Early Impressions." British Library Journal, 1 (1975), 107-44.

The manuscript contains 35 sonnets, some of which the article discusses and reprints.

1182. Waller, G.F. "'My wants and your perfections': Elizabethan England's Newest Poet." ARIEL: A Review of International English Literature, 8, ii (1977), 3-14.

Several pages are devoted to discussing a few of Robert Sidney's sonnets, Sonnet 25 at some length.

1183. Wright, Deborah Kempf. "The Poetry of Robert Sidney: A Critical Study of His Autograph Manuscript." Ph.D. Dissertation, Miami University, 1980. DAI, 41 (1980), 1621A.

Includes a discussion of the structure of the sonnet sequence included in the manuscript.

Edmund Spenser

1184. Austin, Warren B. "Spenser's Sonnet to Harvey." Modern Language Notes, 62 (1947), 20-23.

Attempts to explain the occasion for Spenser writing a sonnet to Gabriel Harvey.

1185. Bahr, Howard. "Spenser and the 'Painted Female Beauty of Conventional Sonneteers'." Southern Quarterly, 9 (1970), 1-5.

Using illustrations from Spenser's and Shakespeare's sonnets, he suggests that Florimell's description in Book III, Canto 8 of The Faerie Queene is a satire on the Petrarchan glorification of the mistress.

1186. Baroway, Israel. "The Imagery of Spenser and the Song of Songs." Journal of English and Germanic Philology, 33 (1934), 23-45.

Spenser used imagery from the Canticum Canticorum in the Amoretti as well as in several other poems.

1187. Beall, Chandler B. "A Tasso Imitation in Spenser." Modern Language Quarterly, 3 (1942), 559-60.

Sonnet 30 of the Amoretti may have come from Tasso.

1188. Bennett, Josephine Waters. "Spenser's Amoretti LXII and the Date of the New Year." Renaissance Quarterly, 26 (1973), 433-36.

Believes the new year referred to was January 1 and not March 25, and that the sonnet sequence extends through an eighteen month period.

1189. Benson, Robert G. "Elizabeth as Beatrice: A Reading of Spenser's 'Amoretti'." South Central Bulletin, 32 (1972), 184-88.

1190. Bernard, John D. "Spenserian Pastoral and the Amoretti." ELH, 47 (1980), 419-32.

Speaks of the use of the refuge or the pastoral oasis in the Amoretti and his other major poems.

1191. Bizzarri, Edoardo. "L'Influenza italiana sugli 'Amoretti' di E. Spenser." Romana, 6 (1942), 626-37.

1192. Bludau, Diethild. "Humanismus und Allegorie in Spensers Sonetten." Anglia, 74 (1956), 292-332.

1193. Bondanella, Julia Conaway. Petrarch's Visions and Their Renaissance Analogues. Madrid: Jose Porrua Turanzas, 1978.

Chapter 5 deals with "Spenser's Meditations on the World's Vanity,"--covering "Visions of the World's Vanity," "Visions of Bellay," and "Visions of Petrarch" (pp. 73-98).

1194. Brown, James Neil. "'Lyke Phoebe': Lunar Numerical and Calendrical Patterns in Spenser's Amoretti." Gypsy Scholar, 1, i (1973), 5-15.

1195. Bullen, A.H., ed. Lyrics from The Song-Books of the Elizabethan Age. London: Lawrence and Bullen, 1896.

A note on p. 222 compares one of the songs with Amoretti 15 and a sonnet by E.C.

1196. Casady, Edwin. "The Neo-Platonic Ladder in Spenser's Amoretti." Philological Quarterly, 20 (1941), 284-95. Reprinted in Renaissance Studies in Honor of Hardin Craig. Ed. Baldwin Maxwell, et al. Stanford, Cal.: Stanford University Press, 1941.

1197. Catz, Justin Enoch. "Edmund Spenser's Amoretti and Epithalamion." Ph.D. Dissertation, Wisconsin, 1969. DA, 29 (1969), 4451A.

Attempts to show the sonnet sequence and the marriage ode as a single artistic structure.

1198. Cory, Herbert E. Edmund Spenser: a Critical Study. University of California Publications in Modern Philology, 5. Berkeley: University of California Press, 1917.

Chapter 4 (pp. 226-53) is on Amoretti and Epithalamion.

1199. Cummings, L. "Spenser's Amoretti VIII: New Manuscript Versions." Studies in English Literature, 1500-1900, 4 (1964), 125-35.

1200. Cummings, Peter M. "Spenser's Amoretti as an Allegory of Love." Texas Studies in Literature and Language, 12 (1970), 163-79.

1201. Dunlop, Alexander. "Calendar Symbolism in the 'Amoretti'." Notes and Queries, 214 (1969), 24-26.

Revised and reprinted as "The Unity of Spenser's Amoretti."
1204

1202. Dunlop, Alexander. "The Concept of Structure in Three Renaissance Sonnet Sequences." Ph.D. Dissertation, North Carolina, 1976. DAI 38 (1977), 774A.

In addition to the Amoretti, Dunlop also discusses Ronsard and Shakespeare.

1203. Dunlop, Alexander. "The Drama of Amoretti." Spenser Studies: A Renaissance Poetry Annual I. Ed. Patrick Cullen and Thomas P. Roche, Jr. Pittsburgh: University of Pittsburgh Press, 1980, pp. 107-20.

In "an attempt to synthesize the insights of traditionalists and numerologists" Dunlop reads the Amoretti as a dramatization of the process of learning to love.

1204. Dunlop, Alexander. "The Unity of Spenser's Amoretti." Silent Poetry. Ed. Alastair Fowler. London: Routledge and Kegan Paul; New York: Barnes and Noble, 1970, pp. 153-69.

Calendar symbolism is the key to the unity of the sonnet sequence.

1205. Ellrodt, Robert. Neoplatonism in the Poetry of Spenser. Travaux d'Humanisme et Renaissance, 35. Geneva: E. Droz, 1960.

Touches on the Amoretti throughout.

1206. Emerson, Oliver Farrar. "Spenser, Lady Carey, and the Complaints Volume." PMLA, 32 (1917), 306-22.

Includes discussion of the sonnets in the Visions.
1245

1207. Fitzmaurice, James. "Spenser at Kalamazoo." Spenser Newsletter, 9 (1978), 34-41.

One of the papers abstracted is "The Drama of Amoretti" presented by Alexander Dunlop. Another is "Amoretti: A Comic Monodrama?" by Carol Barthel.

1208. Fitzmaurice-Kelly, James. "Note on Three Sonnets." Revue Hispanique, 12 (1905), 259-60; 13 (1905), 257-60.

Shows a connection between Spenser's Amoretti 81 and sonnets by Francisco de la Torre and Torquato Tasso.

1209. Fletcher, Jefferson B. "Spenser and The Theatre of Worldlings." Modern Language Notes, 13 (1898), 205-08.

Applies metrical tests that prove Spenser to be the "one possible poet of the Visions of Bellay of '91 and the Shepheard's Calendar." The article includes comments on Koeppel's work.
1238

1210. Fletcher, J.B. "Mr. Sidney Lee and Spenser's Amoretti." Modern Language Notes, 18 (1903), 111-13.

Objects to Lee's inclination to see Spenser's lady as an "ideal," rather than the real woman, Elizabeth Boyle.

1211. Fletcher, J.B. "Spenser's Earliest Translations." Journal of English and Germanic Philology, 13 (1914), 305-08.

Adds some comments to Friedland's conclusions about the authenticity of the translations of Bellay and Petrarch in Vander Noodt's "Theatre of Worldlings."
1213

1212. Fowler, Earle B. Spenser and the System of Courtly Love. Louisville: Standard Printing Co., 1934.

Discusses Amoretti throughout the text.

1213. Friedland, Louis Sigmund. "Spenser's Earliest Translations." Journal of English and Germanic Philology, 12 (1913), 449-70.

Strengthens the case for Spenser's authorship of the Visions.
1211

1214. Garrod, H.W. "Spenser and Elizabeth Boyle." TLS, May 10, 1923, p. 321; May 24, 1923, p. 355.

Elizabeth Boyle was a widow at the time of her courtship by Spenser, having been married to a man named Peace.

1215. Gollancz, I. "Spenseriana." Proceedings of the British Academy, 1907-08. London: Henry Frowde, 1908.

"Happy ye leaves . . ." (Amoretti 1) was originally attached to The Faerie Queene and referred to that poem.

1216. Hamer, Douglas. "Spenser's Marriage." Review of English Studies, 7 (1931), 271-90.

Discusses the "Peace" references in the Amoretti (pp. 289-90) thought by Garrod to be clues to Elizabeth's earlier marriage.
1214

1217. Hardison, O.B., Jr. "Amoretti and the Dolce Stil Nuovo." English Literary Renaissance, 2 (1972), 208-16.

1218. Harman, Edward George. Edmund Spenser and the Impersonations of Francis Bacon. London: Constable, 1914.

The book deals with the Amoretti (pp. 374-86) and Visions of Bellay and Visions of Petrarch (pp. 201-11) in his effort to show points of similarity between Spenser's and Bacon's work.

1219. Harrison, Thomas P. They Tell of Birds: Chaucer, Spenser, Milton, Drayton. Austin: University of Texas, 1956.

Discusses birds in the Amoretti (pp. 83-84) and in Milton's sonnets (pp. 85-87).

1220. Hickman, Dixie Elise. "The Development of Love: Structure and Narrative in Edmund Spenser's Amoretti." Ph.D. Dissertation, Iowa, 1977. DAI, 38 (1978), 4181A.

1221. Hieatt, A. Kent. "A Numerical Key for Spenser's Amoretti and Guyon in the House of Mammon." Yearbook of English Studies, 3 (1973), 14-27.

A modification of Dunlop's thesis on the Amoretti.
1204

1222. Hunter, G.K. "Spenser's Amoretti and the English Sonnet Tradition." A Theatre for Spenserians: Papers of the International Spenser Colloquium, Fredericton, New Brunswick, October 1969. Ed. Judith M. Kennedy and James A. Reither. Toronto and Buffalo: University of Toronto Press; Manchester: Manchester University Press, 1973, pp. 124-44.

1223. Hunter, G.K. "'Unity' and Numbers in Spenser's Amoretti." Yearbook of English Studies, 5 (1975), 39-45.

Evaluates Dunlop's and other's findings regarding the "calendrical unity" of the Amoretti.
1201,1204,1217,1221

1224. Jessee, Jack Willard. "Spenser and the Emblem Books." Ph.D. Dissertation, Kentucky, 1955. DA, 20 (1960), 3729.

Includes discussion of Amoretti.

1225. Johnson, William Clarence. "'Vowd to Eternity': A Study of Spenser's Amoretti." Ph.D. Dissertation, Iowa, 1969. DAI, 30 (1970), 3909A.

1226. Johnson, William C. "Rhyme and Repetition in Spenser's Amoretti." Xavier University Studies, 9,ii (1970), 15-25.

1227. Johnson, William C. "Spenser's Sonnet Diction." Neuphilologische Mitteilungen, 71 (1970), 157-67.

1228. Johnson, William C. "Spenser's Amoretti VI. Explicator, 29 (1971), Item 38.

1229. Johnson, William C. "Amor and Spenser's Amoretti." English Studies, 54 (1973), 217-26.

1230. Johnson, William C. "Spenser's Amoretti and the Art of the Liturgy." Studies in English Literature, 1500-1900, 14 (1974), 47-61.

1231. Jones, H.S.V. A Spenser Handbook. New York: F.S. Crofts, 1930.

Contains chapters on "Visions of the Worlds Vanitie" (pp. 118-19), "The Visions of Bellay . . ." (pp. 120-25) and the "Amoretti" (pp. 335-47).

1232. Judson, A.C. "Amoretti, Sonnet I." Modern Language Notes, 58 (1943), 548-50.

Disagrees with Gollancz's contention that this sonnet belongs with The Faerie Queene and not the Amoretti.
1215

1233. Jusserand, J.J. "Spenser's 'Visions of Petrarch'." Athenaeum, May 10, 1902, pp. 595-96.

Spenser seems, in these early poems, to be working from Marot rather than the originals by Petrarch.

1234. Kalil, Judith. "'Mask in Myrth Lyke to a Comedy': Spenser's Persona in the Amoretti." Thoth, 13, ii (1973), 19-26.

1235. Kaske, Carol V. "Another Liturgical Dimension of 'Amoretti' 68." Notes and Queries, 222 (1977), 518-19.

1236. Kastner, L.E. "Spenser's 'Amoretti' and Desportes." Modern Language Review, 4 (1909), 65-69.

1237. Kellogg, Robert. "Thought's Astonishment and the Dark Conceit of Spenser's Amoretti." Renaissance Papers 1965. Ed. George Walton Williams. Southeastern Renaissance Conference, 1966, pp. 3-13. Reprinted in The Prince of Poets: Essays on Edmund Spenser. Ed. John R. Elliott. New York: New York University Press; London: University of London Press, 1968, pp. 139-51.

1238. Koeppel, Emil. "Uber die Echtheit der Edmund Spenser zugeschriebenen 'Visions of Petrarch' und 'Visions of Bellay'." Englische Studien, 15 (1891), 53-81; 27 (1903), 100-11.

1239. Kostic, V. "Spenser's Amoretti and Tasso's Lyrical Poetry." Renaissance and Modern Studies, 3 (1959), 51-77.

1240. Legouis, Emile Hyacinthe. Spenser. London: J.M. Dent; New York: E.P. Dutton, 1926.

Chapter 4 is entitled "His Personal Poetry: The 'Amoretti' and 'Epithalamion'" (pp. 75-95).

1241. Legouis, Emile. Edmond Spenser. (Nouvelle edition revisee et mise a jour par P. Legouis) Paris: Didier, 1956.

Chapter 9 (pp. 176-86) deals with the Amoretti and the poet's courtship of Elizabeth Boyle.

1242. Lievsay, John L. "Spenser's Other Sonnets." South Atlantic Bulletin, 43, iii (1978), 42.

Abstract of paper read at the 1978 Southeastern Renaissance Conference.

1243. Littledale, H. "A Note on Spenser's Amoretti." Modern Language Review, 6 (1911), 203.

1244. Locatelli, Carla. "Prolegomena alla decodifica di un canzoniere petrarchesco e lettura strutturale de 'Sonnet I' degli Amoretti di E. Spenser." Annali (Feltre, Italy)(1974), 345-51.

1245. Long, Percy W. "Spenser and Lady Carey." Modern Language Review, 3 (1908), 257-67.

Lady Carey is discussed as a candidate for the mistress in the Amoretti.

1246. Long, Percy W. "Spenser's Sonnets 'As Published'." Modern Language Review, 6 (1911), 390-97.

Response to J.C. Smith on the subject of Spenser and Lady Carey.
1272

1247. Markland, Murray F. "A Note on Spenser and the Scottish Sonneteers." Studies in Scottish Literature, 1 (1963), 136-40.

Spenser had little apparent influence on the Scottish sonneteers, James VI and Alexander Montgomerie, despite the fact that they used the same sonnet form as he.

1248. Martz, Louis L. "The Amoretti: 'Most Goodly Temperature'." Form and Convention in the Poetry of Edmund Spenser: Selected Papers from the English Institute. Ed. William Nelson. New York and London: Columbia University Press, 1961, pp. 146-68. Reprinted in The Prince of Poets: Essays on Edmund Spenser. Ed. John R. Elliott. New York: New York University Press; London: University of London Press, 1968, pp. 120-38.

Refutes the thesis that the Amoretti is fraught with inconsistencies and disproportions.

1249. Mayr, Roswitha. The Concept of Love in Sidney and Spenser. Salzburg Studies in English Literature, Elizabethan and Renaissance Studies, 70. Salzburg: Institut fur Englische Sprache und Literatur, Universitat Salzburg, 1978.

1250. McNeir, Waldo F. "An Apology for Spenser's Amoretti." Neueren Sprachen, NF 14 (1965), 1-9. Reprinted in Essential Articles for the Study of Edmund Spenser. Ed. A.C. Hamilton. Hamden, Conn.: Archon Books, 1972, pp. 524-33.

1251. McPeek, James A.S. Catullus in Strange and Distant Britain. Harvard Studies in Comparative Literature, 15. Cambridge, Mass.: Harvard University Press, 1939.

Brief discussions of Spenser's use in the Amoretti of some Catullan themes (pp. 64-65, 107-08).

1252. Moore, John. Review of Roswitha Mayr, The Concept of Love in Sidney and Spenser. Seventeenth-Century News, 37 (1979), 15-16.

1253. Nelson, William. The Poetry of Edmund Spenser. New York: Columbia University Press, 1963.

A discussion that includes some comment on Spenser's sonnet in praise of Gabriel Harvey as well as of the Amoretti (chapter 4, "Love Creating").

1254. Nicholson, Br[insley]. "Spenser's 1569 'Visions of Bellay,' Sonets viii. ix." Notes and Queries, 7th series, 2 (1886), 443-44.

1255. Nicholson, Br[insley]. "Spenser's 'Visions of Petrarch'." Notes and Queries, 7th series, 3 (1887), 262-63.

The poems were probably translated from French rather than the original Italian.

1256. Nicholson, Br[insley]. "Spenser the Translator of the 'Revelation Sonnets', 1569." Notes and Queries, 7th series, 3 (1887), 344.

1257. Orange, Linwood E. "Spenser's Word-Play." Notes and Queries, 203 (1958), 387-89.

On Amoretti, The Faerie Queene, et al.

1258. Palgrave, F.T. "Essays on the Minor Poems of Spenser." The Complete Works in Verse and Prose of Edmund Spenser. Ed. Alexander B. Grosart. Manchester: Hazell, Watson and Viney, 1882-84, vol. 4, pp. ix-cvii.

In his discussion of the Amoretti (pp. lxxxvii-xcii) Palgrave notes similarities with Petrarch and Sanazzaro, particularly the latter.

1259. Pienaar, W.J.B. "Edmund Spenser and Jonker Jan van der Noot." English Studies, 8 (1926), 33-44; 67-76.

Spenser's Visions of Bellay and Visions of Petrarch are revised versions of poems that first appeared in English in The Theatre for Worldlings. This two-part article considers The Theatre's importance and the evidence for the authorship of this work.

1260. Quitslund, Jon A. "Spenser's Amoretti VIII and Platonic Commentaries on Petrarch." Journal of the Warburg and Courtauld Institutes, 36 (1973), 256-76.

1261. Rasmussen, Carl J. "'Quietnesse of Minde': A Theatre for Worldlings as a Protestant Poetics." Spenser Studies: A Renaissance Poetry Annual I. Ed. Patrick Cullen and Thomas P. Roche, Jr. Pittsburgh: University of Pittsburgh Press, 1980, pp. 3-27.

These sonnets by Jan Van Der Noot, translated by a youthful Spenser, are "dramatic monologues which explore spiritual states." Rasmussen calls The Theatre England's first sonnet sequence.

1262. Renwick, W.L. Edmund Spenser: An Essay on Renaissance Poetry. London: Edward Arnold, 1925. London: Methuen, 1964.

Brief discussion of Amoretti and The Complaints (chapter 5, pp. 125-30).

1263. Ricks, Don M. "Conventions and Structure in Edmund Spenser's 'Amoretti'." Proceedings of the Utah Academy of Sciences, Arts and Letters, 44 (1967), 438-50.

1264. Ricks, Don M. "Persona and Process in Spenser's 'Amoretti'." ARIEL: A Review of International English Literature, 3, iv (1972), 5-15.

1265. Righetti, Angelo. "Le due versioni spenseriane della canzone CCCXXIII del Petrarca." Annali della Facolta di Lingue e Letterature Straniere di Ca' Foscari, 5 (1966), 115-22.

One version of this Petrarchan canzone is in the 1569 Epigrams, the second in the 1591 Visions of Petrarch.

1266. Rogers, William Elford. "Narcissus in Amoretti. XXXV." American Notes and Queries, 15 (1976), 18-20.

1267. Rosenbach, Abraham Simon Wolf. Books and Bidders: The Adventures of a Bibliophile. Boston: Little, Brown, 1927.

Speaks of a signed presentation copy of The Faerie Queene dated 1590 to Elizabeth Boyle with the complete text of "Happy ye leaves" inscribed in his hand (pp. 148-50).

1268. Satterthwaite, Alfred W. "Moral Vision in Spenser, DuBellay, and Ronsard." Comparative Literature, 9 (1957), 136-49.

An examination of Spenser's Visions of the Worldes Vanitie --a sequence of twelve "dull and colorless sonnets." Pays particular attention to similarities between these poems and those by du Bellay and Ronsard.

1269. Satterthwaite, Alfred W. "A Re-examination of Spenser's Translations of the 'Sonets' from A Theatre for Worldlings." Philological Quarterly, 38 (1959), 509-15.

1270. Satterthwaite, Alfred W. Spenser, Ronsard, and du Bellay: A Renaissance Comparison. Princeton, N.J.: Princeton University Press, 1960.

Discusses Visions of the World, Bellay, Petrarch.

1271. Scott, Janet G. "The Sources of Spenser's Amoretti." Modern Language Review, 22 (1927), 189-95.

Three sonnets--72, 73 and 81--are translations from Tasso. Other Italian influence is also evident.

1272. Smith, J.C. "The Problem of Spenser's Sonnets." Modern Language Review, 5 (1910), 273-81.

Discusses Percy Long's theory about the relationship between the Amoretti and Epithalamion. Smith partially agrees that the two may not at first have been addressed to the same woman, that the Amoretti had probably been addressed to Lady Carey but later reshaped to apply to Elizabeth Boyle.
1245

1273. Spenser, Edmund. Spenser's Minor Poems. Ed. Ernest de Selincourt. London: Oxford University Press, 1910.

Volume 1 of the 3 volume The Poetical Works of Edmund Spenser.

1274. ______________. The Complete Poetical Works of Edmund Spenser. Ed. R.E. Neil Dodge. Boston and New York: Houghton Mifflin, 1908.

1275. ______________. The Works of Edmund Spenser: A Variorum Edition: The Minor Poems. Ed. Edwin Greenlaw, Charles Grosvenor Osgood, Frederick Morgan Padelford, and Ray Heffner. Baltimore: Johns Hopkins, 1943, vol. 2.

1276. ______________. Books I and II of The Faerie Queene, The Mutability Cantos and Selections from The Minor Poetry. Ed. Robert Kellogg and Oliver Steele. New York: Odyssey Press, 1965.

Includes 26 of the sonnets and an introduction to the Amoretti.

1277. ______________. Spenser's Minor Poems: A Selection Ed. R.P.C. Mutter. London: Methuen, 1957.

Contains critical notes on the *Amoretti* (pp. 121-25).

1278. ——————. *Complaints*. Ed. W.L. Renwick. London: Scholartis Press, 1928.

Contains *Ruins of Rome*, *Visions of the Worlds Vanitie*, *Visions of Bellay* --all series of sonnets.

1279. ——————. *Daphnaida and Other Poems*. Ed. W.L. Renwick. London: Scholartis Press, 1929.

Contains *Amoretti*.

1280. ——————. *The Poetical Works*. Ed. J.C. Smith and Ernest de Selincourt. London: Oxford University Press, 1912.

1281. Stein, Harold. *Studies in Spenser's Complaints*. New York: Oxford University Press, 1934.

Contains discussion of *Visions of the Worlds Vanitie*, *Visions of Bellay*, and *Visions of Petrarch*.

1282. Stewart, Jack F. Spenser's *Amoretti*, LXXIX, 10." *Explicator*, 27 (1968), Item 74.

1283. Strathmann, Ernest A. "Lady Carey and Spenser." *ELH*, 2 (1935), 33-57.

In part Lady Carey's importance to Spenser rests in the fact that he addressed *The Faerie Queene* dedicatory sonnet and several others to her and because some (P.W. Long, e.g.) think her the mistress of the *Amoretti*.

1284. Viglione, Francesco. *La Poesia Lirica di Edmondo Spenser*. Genoa: Emiliano degli Orfini, 1937.

Chapter 5 deals with the love poetry, including *Amoretti*.

1285. Welply, W.H. "Spenser and Elizabeth Boyle." *TLS*, May 24, 1923, pp. 355-56.

Refutes Garrod's notion that Elizabeth Boyle had been previously married.
1214

1286. *Yuasa, Nobuyuki. "A Study of Metaphor in Spenser's 'Amoretti'." *Studies in English Literature* (Tokyo), 37 (1961), 163-86.

1287. "Spenser's Sonnets of Petrarch." *Athenaeum*, February 8, 1845, p. 150.

Believes Spenser's *Visions of Petrarch* were translated directly from Italian and not from French.

John Stewart of Baldynneis

1288. McDiarmid, M.P. "Notes on the Poems of John Stewart of Baldynneis." Review of English Studies, 24 (1948), 12-18.

Includes some brief comments on some of his sonnets.

1289. Stewart, John of Baldynneis. Poems of John Stewart of Baldynneis. Ed. Thomas Crockett. Edinburgh: Scottish Text Society, 1913.

Contains a number of his sonnets.

Henry Howard, Earl of Surrey

1290. Bapst, Edmond. Deux Gentilhommes-Poetes de la Cour de Henry VIII. Paris: E. Plon, Nourrit, 1891.

Deals with George Boleyn and Henry Howard. Final chapter is concerned with Surrey's relationship to Eizabeth Fitzgerald and his sonnets.

1291. Casady, Edwin. Henry Howard Earl of Surrey. MLA Revolving Fund Series, 8. New York: Modern Language Association of America, 1938.

1292. Coogan, Robert. "Surrey's Petrarchism and Tudor Concepts of Translation and Imitation." English Miscellany, 25 (1975-76), 46-83.

Includes discussion of sonnets translated or imitated from originals by Petrarch.

1293. Daniels, Edgar F. "Surrey's 'In the Rude Age,' 5-6." Explicator, 36, iv (1978), 14-15.

1294. Davis, Walter R. "Contexts in Surrey's Poetry." English Literary Renaissance, 4 (1974), 40-55.

Includes comments on some sonnets--"Norfolk sprang thee" and "Divers thy death."

1295. Edwards, A.S.G. "Henry Howard, Earl of Surrey." British Writers. Ed. Ian Scott-Kilvert. New York: Charles Scribner's Sons, 1979, vol. 1, pp. 113-20.

1296. Fehse, H. Henry Howard, Earl of Surrey. Ein Beitrag zur Geschichte des Petrarchismus in England. Chemnitz: J.C.F. Pickenhahn, 1883.

1297. Foley, Stephen Merriam. "The Honorable Style of Henry Howard, Earl of Surrey: A Critical Reading of Surrey's Poetry." Ph.D. Dissertation, Yale, 1979. DAI, 40 (1980), 2693A-94A.

"The Sonnets, like the rest of Surrey's poetry . . . fall into two major thematic groups: love poems and poems on public themes."

1298. Harris, William O. "Love that doth raine': Surrey's Creative Imitation." Modern Philology, 66 (1969), 298-305.

1299. Howard, Henry, Earl of Surrey. Henry Howard, Earl of Surrey: Poems. Ed. Emrys Jones. Oxford: Clarendon Press, 1964.

1300. ______________. The Works of Henry Howard Earl of Surrey, and of Sir Thomas Wyatt the Elder. Ed. George F. Nott. 2 vol. London: n.p., 1816. rpt. New York: AMS Press, 1965.

1301. ______________. The Poems of Henry Howard, Earl of Surrey. Ed. F.M. Padelford. Rev. ed. Seattle: University of Washington Publications, 1928. rpt. New York: Haskell House, 1966.

1302. ______________. The Poems of Henry Howard, Earl of Surrey. Aldine Edition, revised. London: Bell and Daldy, 1866.

Contains a lengthy Memoir on his life and work.

1303. *Hurst, Carl B. "An Analysis of the Sonnets of Henry Howard Earl of Surrey." Ph.D. Dissertation, Tuebingen, 1895.

1304. Jentoft, Clyde W. "Rhetoric and Structure in the Poetry of Henry Howard, Earl of Surrey." Ph.D. Dissertation, Ohio State, 1969. DAI, 30 (1970), 4415A-16A.

Includes discussion of Petrarchan "translations."

1305. Jentoft, C.W. "Surrey's Five Elegies: Rhetoric, Structure, and the Poetry of Praise." PMLA, 91 (1976), 23-32.

Three of these elegies are sonnets, one on Thomas Clere ("Norfolk sprang thee") and two on Wyatt ("Dyvers thy death" and "In the rude age").

1306. Low, Anthony. "Surrey's Five Elegies." PMLA, 91 (1976), 914-15.

A reply to Jentoft ("Surrey's Five Elegies"). This note is followed by a brief response by Jentoft.
1305

1307. Mumford, Ivy L. "Italian Aspects of Surrey's Lyrics." English Miscellany, 16 (1965), 19-36.

Part of the article compares Surrey's sonnet form to Wyatt's.

1308. Nathan, Leonard. "The Course of the Particular: Surrey's Epitaph on Thomas Clere and the Fifteenth-Century Lyric Tradition." Studies in English Literature, 1500-1900, 17 (1977), 3-12.

This sonnet, "Norfolk sprang thee," is a "revolutionary" departure from courtly themes.

1309. Padelford, Frederick Morgan. "The Manuscript Poems of Henry Howard, Earl of Surrey." Anglia, 29 (1906), 273-338.

The seven manuscripts in the British Museum containing Surrey's poetry include a number of his sonnets.

1310. Pratt, Samuel M. "Surrey and the Fair Geraldine: A Review and a Discovery." Cornell Library Journal, 10 (1970), 35-39.

Some background to the sonnet, "From Tuskane came my Ladies Worthy Race."

1311. Schelp, Hanspeter. "Henry Howard, Earl of Surrey: 'Love that Doth Raine and Live within my Thought'; 'The Soote Season, that Bud and Blome furth Bringes'." Die Englische Lyrik: Von der Renaissance bis zur Gegenwart. Ed. Karl Heinz Goller. Dusseldorf: August Bagel, 1968, vol. 1, pp. 43-54.

Joshua Sylvester

1312. Potter, James L. "Sylvester's Shaped Sonnets." Notes and Queries, 202 (1957), 405-06.

Discusses the eleven sonnets, ten of which are in a "corona" and printed in the shape of altars and short columns.

G. W.

1313. Carpenter, Frederic Ives. "G.W. Senior and G.W.I." Modern Philology, 22 (1924), 67-68.

On the authorship of the two sonnets "To the Author" prefixed to the Amoretti in 1595.

1314. Gottfried, Rudolf. "The 'G.W. Senior' and 'G.W.I.' of Spenser's Amoretti." Modern Language Quarterly, 3 (1942), 543-46.

On the authorship of the two sonnets which precede the Amoretti.

Thomas Watson

1315. Cecioni, Cesare G. "Frances Walsingham ispiratrice dell' Hecatompathia." Rivista di letterature moderne e comparate, 20 (1967), 26-29.

1316. *Cecione, Cesare G. "Introduzione all' 'Hecatompathia di Thomas Watson." Siculorum Gymnasium, 17 (1964), 8-22.

1317. Cecioni, Cesare G. Primi Studi su Thomas Watson. Catania: Universita degli Studi, 1964.

1318. Cecioni, Cesare G. Thomas Watson e la tradizione petrarchista. Milano: Giuseppe Principato, 1969.

1319. Murphy, William M. "Thomas Watson's Hecatompathia (1582) and the Elizabethan Sonnet Sequence." Journal of English and Germanic Philology, 56 (1957), 418-28.

1320. Nicholson, Brinsley. "Thomas Watson and Nicholas Breton." Athenaeum, October 13, 1877, pp. 468-69.

Much of Watson's Sonnets 56 and 57 from "The Tears of Fancie" are incorporated into the first 13 stanzas of "The Countesse of Penbroke's Passion" believed to be by Nicholas Breton.

1321. Palgrave, F.T. Review article of Thomas Watson: Poems. Ed. Edward Arber. North American Review, 114 (1872), 87-110.

1322. Scott, Janet. "The Sources of Watson's 'Tears of Fancy'." Modern Language Review, 21 (1926), 303-06, 435.

Watson borrowed from Gascoigne's Posies, from the Earl of Oxford and from foreign poets also.

1323. Thomson, Patricia. "Firenzuola, Surrey and Watson." Renaissance News, 18 (1965), 295-98.

Watson's Passion XXXIV (Hekatompathia) is based on sonnets by Surrey ("Give place, ye lovers") and Firenzuola.

1324. Watson, Thomas. Hecatompathia. Ed. Cesare G. Cecioni. Catania: Universita di Catania, 1964.

1325. ____________. The Hecatompathia or Passionate Centurie of Love (1582). Ed. S.K. Heninger. Gainesville, Fla.: Scholars Facsimiles and Reprints, 1964.

1326. ____________. The Hecatompathia or Passionate Centurie of Love. Manchester: Spenser Society, 1869.

John Webster

1327. Howarth, R.G. "A Commendatory Sonnet by John Webster." English Studies in Africa, 9 (1966), 109-16.

The First of four commendatory poems, signed by I.W., prefixed to "Mirrha The Mother of Adonis . . . by William Barksted" is ascribed to John Webster.

Lady Mary Wroth

1328. Hargreaves, H.A. Review of Lady Mary Wroth, Pamphilia to Amphilanthus, ed. G.F. Waller. English Studies in Canada, 5 (1979), 491-94.

1329. Paulissen, May Nelson. "The Love Sonnets of Lady Mary Wroth: A Critical Introduction." Ph.D. Dissertation, Houston, 1976. DAI, 38 (1977), 286A.

1330. Paulissen, May Nelson. "Forgotten Love Sonnets of the Court of King James: The Sonnets of Lady Mary Wroth." Publications of the Missouri Philological Association, 3 (1978), 24-31.

1331. Roberts, Josephine A. "Renaissance Discovery: A New Sonnet Sequence." South Central Bulletin, 37 (Fall, 1977), 96.

This sonnet sequence of Lady Mary Wroth attempts to explore the mind of the woman. An abstract of a paper delivered to the South Central MLA, October 28, 1977.

1332. Roberts, Josephine A. "Lady Mary Wroth's Sonnets: A Labyrinth of the Mind." Journal of Women's Studies in Literature, 1 (1979), 319-29.

Discusses the sonnet sequence Pamphilia to Amphilanthus.

1333. Wroth, Lady Mary. Pamphilia to Amphilanthus. Ed. G.F. Waller. Salzburg Studies in English Literature, Elizabethan and Renaissance Studies, 64. Salzburg: Institut fur Englische Sprache und Literatur, Universitat Salzburg, 1977.

This edition contains an introduction and notes to the 1621 text of the sonnet sequence.

Sir Thomas Wyatt

1334. Alscher, Rudolf. Sir Thomas Wyatt und seine Stellung in der Entwickelungsgeschichte der englischen Literatur und Verkunst. Wiener Beitrage zur deutschen und englischen Philologie, No. 1. Wien: Wilhelm Braumuller, 1886.

Discusses Wyatt's life and works, including the sonnets (pp. 21-23).

1335. Baldi, Sergio. La Poesia di Sir Thomas Wyatt. Florence: Le Monnier, 1953.

1336. Baldi, Sergio. "Una fonte petrarchesca di Sir Thomas Wyatt." Friendship's Garland: Essays Presented to Mario Praz on his Seventieth Birthday. Ed. Vittorio Gabrieli. Rome: Edizioni di Storia e Letteratura, 1966, vol. 1, pp. 87-93.

1337. Baldi, Sergio. *Sir Thomas Wyatt*. Tr. F.T. Prince. Writers and their Work, 139. London: Longmans, Green, 1961. Reprinted in *British Writers*. Ed. Ian Scott-Kilvert. New York: Charles Scribner's Sons, 1979, vol. 1, pp. 97-112.

1338. Bateson, F.W. *English Poetry: A Critical Introduction*. New York: Barnes and Noble, 1950. 1966.

Bateson's chapter on "Sir Thomas Wyatt and the Renaissance" (pp. 99-104) includes a discussion of "Whoso list to hunt."

1339. Berdan, John M. "Migrations of a Sonnet." *Modern Language Notes*, 23 (1908), 33-36.

Discusses the relationship between Wyatt's "Like unto these unmeasurable mountains" and poems by Sannazaro and St. Gelais.

1340. Berdan, John M. "Wyatt and the French Sonneteers." *Modern Language Review*, 4 (1909), 240-49.

Argues that Saint-Gelais used Wyatt's "Like unto these unmeasurable mountains" as a source for one of his sonnets.

1341. Berdan, John M. "Professor Kastner's Hypothesis." *Modern Language Notes*, 25 (1910), 1-4.

A reply to Kastner on the connection between Saint-Gelais and Wyatt.
1379

1342. Bernard, John D. "Studies in the Love Poetry of Wyatt, Sidney and Shakespeare." Ph.D. Dissertation, Minnesota, 1970. *DAI*, 31 (1971), 3538A.

1343. Birenbaum, Harvey. "Convention and Self: A Study in the Poetry of Sir Thomas Wyatt." Ph.D. Dissertation, Yale, 1963.

1344. Bonheim, Helmut. "Notes on a Sonnet by Sir Thomas Wyatt." *Literatur in Wissenschaft und Unterricht*, 5 (1972), 1-5.

Notes on the persona and imagery in "Whoso list to hunt."

1345. Brodie, Philip T. "So Kindly Served: Wyatt's Egerton MS. As Narrative Sequence." Ph.D. Dissertation, Pittsburgh, 1973. *DAI*, 34 (1974), 4188A.

Sees the Egerton MS. as a work that "presents a consistently developed persona, a coherent theme, and a plot with a definite sense of chronology" similar to *Astrophil and Stella*, the *Amoretti*, and Shakespeare's Sonnets.

1346. Brownlow, E.B. "Sir Thomas Wyatt." *Nation*, 51 (1890), 211.

Asks about possible sources for "Like unto these unmeasurable mountains," and identifies the source of "Avising the bright beams of those fair eyes."

1347. Brownlow, E.B. "Sonnets of Sir Thomas Wyatt." Poet-Lore, 3 (1891), 44-45.

Identifies the sources of two Wyatt sonnets--"Avising the bright beams of those fair eyes" and "I abide, and abide; and better abide"--as Petrarch and Marot, respectively.
1354

1348. Brownlow, E.B. "Wyatt's Sonnets and Their Sources." Poet-Lore, 3 (1891), 127-34.

1349. Bullock, W.L. "The Genesis of the English Sonnet Form." PMLA, 38 (1923), 729-44.

Wyatt was the originator of the three quatrain and couplet form, and Surrey "gave it its final permanent shape by relaxing and simplifying the type which Wyatt had adopted."

1350. Candelaria, Frederick H. "The Necklace of Wyatt's 'Diere'." English Language Notes, 1 (1963), 4-5.

On "Who so list to hunt . . . ."

1351. Cermak, Mary M. "Terminal Structures in the Sonnets of Wyatt and Surrey." Ph.D. Dissertation, Catholic University of America, 1969. DAI, 30 (1969), 2522A-23A.

1352. Chambers, E.K. Sir Thomas Wyatt and Some Collected Studies. London: Sidgwick and Jackson, 1933. rpt. New York: Russell and Russell, 1965.

1353. Clinard, Turner Norman. "A Critical History of the Pre-Elizabethan English Sonnet." Ph.D. Dissertation, Vanderbilt, 1956. DA, 16 (1956), 1139.

Discusses Wyatt, Surrey, and Grimald.

1354. Cook, Albert S. "The Original of Wyatt's 'Unmeasurable Mountains'." Poet-Lore, 3 (1891), 97-98.
1347

1355. Curley, Stephen Joseph. "Of Man and the Wheel: Poetic Attitudes Toward Fortune in the Verse of Sir Thomas Wyatt." Ph.D. Dissertation, Rice, 1974. DAI, 35 (1974), 2217A.

The credit he has received for his "introduction of the sonnet form and Petrarchism to England" has "diverted attention from his intrinsic poetic merit."

1356. Daalder, Joost. "Wyatt and 'Liberty'." Essays in Criticism, 23 (1973), 63-67.

Discusses what Wyatt means in his sonnets and other love poems when he speaks of "liberty."

1357. Evans, Robert O. "Some Aspects of Wyatt's Metrical Technique." Journal of English and Germanic Philology, 53 (1954), 197-213.

Reply to Swallow on Sonnets 3, 8, 9, 22 [Foxwell numbering]. 1406

1358. Evans, Robert O. "Some Autobiographical Aspects of Wyatt's Verse." Notes and Queries, 203 (1958), 48-52.

Includes some comment on lines from "Whoso list to hunt."

1359. Felheim, Marvin. "The Elizabethan Lyric." Papers of the Michigan Acadamy of Science, Arts, and Letters, 43 (1957), 345-51.

Focuses on a comparison of Wyatt's "The longe love" and Surrey's "Love that doth reign . . . ."

1360. Fiero, John Wesley. "The Bright Transparent Glass: A Critical Study of the Poetry of Sir Thomas Wyatt." Ph.D. Dissertation, Florida State, 1968. DAI, 30 (1969), 683A-84A.

1361. Flugel, Ewald. "Die handschriftliche uberlieferung der gedichte von Sir Thomas Wyatt." Anglia, 18 (1896), 263-90, 455-516; 19 (1897), 175-210, 413-50.

The 4-part article includes discussion of sonnets.

1362. Foxwell, A.K. A Study of Sir Thomas Wyatt's Poems. London: University of London Press, 1911. rpt. New York: Russell and Russell, 1964.

1363. Friedman, Donald M. "The 'Thing' in Wyatt's Mind." Essays in Criticism, 16 (1966), 375-81.

Brief comment on "Farewell Love and all thy laws forever" (pp.376-77).

1364. Friedman, Donald M. "Wyatt's Amoris Personae." Modern Language Quarterly, 27 (1966), 136-46.

1365. Fuller, Jean Overton. "Wyatt and Petrarch." Essays in Criticism, 14 (1964), 324-26.

This note on "Whoso list to hunt" has appended to it a response by Raymond Southall (pp. 326-27).

1366. Greenblatt, Stephen. "Power, Sexuality, and Inwardness in Wyatt's Poetry." Renaissance Self-Fashioning, From More to Shakespeare. Chicago: University of Chicago Press, 1980, pp. 115-56.

A portion of this chapter (pp. 145-50) is devoted to a discussion of the sonnet, "Whoso list to hunt."

1367. Guss, Donald L. "Wyatt's Petrarchism: An Instance of Creative Imitation in the Renaissance." Huntington Library Quarterly, 29 (1965), 1-15. Reprinted in Ubersetzung und Nachahmung im europaischen Petrarkismus: Studien und Texte. Ed. Luzius Keller. Stuttgart: J.B. Metzler, 1974.

1368. Hangen, Eva Catherine. A Concordance to the Complete Poetical Works of Sir Thomas Wyatt. Chicago: University of Chicago Press, 1941.

1369. Hanscom, Elizabeth Deering. "The Sonnet Forms of Wyatt and Surrey." Modern Language Notes, 16 (1901), 137-40.

1370. Harding, D.W. "The Rhythmical Intention in Wyatt's Poetry." Scrutiny, 14 (1946), 90-102.

1371. Harding, D.W. "The Poetry of Wyatt." The Age of Chaucer. Ed. Boris Ford. Harmondsworth: Penguin, 1954. London: Cassell, 1961, pp. 197-212.

1372. Harrier, Richard C. "A New Biographical Criticism of Wyatt." Notes and Queries, 204 (1959), 189.

Discusses "Whoso list to hunt" and the biographical background to Wyatt's relationship with Anne Boleyn.

1373. Harrier, Richard. The Canon of Sir Thomas Wyatt's Poetry. Cambridge, Mass.: Harvard University Press, 1975.

1374. *Hashiguchi, Minoru. "Wyatt to Surrey--Eishi no Rhythm" [Wyatt and Surrey: Rhythm in English Poetry]. Eigo Seinen, 119 (1974), 62-64.

Scans Wyatt's "The longe love" and Surrey's "Love that doth raine."

1375. Heine, Ingeborg. "The Metrical Intentions of Wyatt's Sonnets: 'Who so list to hount,' 'I fynde no peace,' and 'The longe love'." Kwartalnik Neofilologiczny, 25 (1978), 407-20.

1376. Hietsch, Otto. Die Petrarcaubersetzungen Sir Thomas Wyatts: Eine Sprachvergleichende Studie. Wiener Beitrage zur Englischen Philologie, 67. Wien und Stuttgart: Wilhelm Braumuller, 1960.

1377. Hough, Gordon Richard. "A Quiet Image of Disquiet: The Persona in the Lyrics of Wyatt, Sidney, and Donne. Ph.D. Dissertation, SUNY at Buffalo, 1975. DAI, 36 (1976), 6705A.

1378. Johnson, S.F., and William R. Orwen. "Wyatt's 'The Lover Compareth His State'." Explicator, 5 (1947), Item 40.

1379. Kastner, L.E. "Wyatt and the French Sonneteers." Modern Language Review, 4 (1909), 249-53.

A refutation of Berdan's thesis regarding Wyatt and Saint-Gelais.
1340

1380. Koeppel, E. "Sir Thomas Wyatt und Melin de Saint-Gelais." Anglia, 13 (1891), 77-78.

Compares a sonnet by Saint-Gelais with "Lyke unto these unmesurable mountaines" by Wyatt.

1381. Krieger, Murray. "The Continuing Need for Criticism." Concerning Poetry, 1, i (1968), 7-21. Reprinted in Sense and Sensibility in Twentieth-Century Writing: A Gathering in Memory of William Van O'Connor. Carbondale: Southern Illinois University Press, 1970, pp. 1-15.

This discussion of the need for criticism includes an explication of Wyatt's "Divers doth use as I have heard and know" (pp. 14-17), and of Sidney's Astrophel and Stella, 35 (pp. 18-21).

1382. Larbaud, Valery. "Sir Thomas Wyatt." Commerce, 4 (1925), 129-45.

Discusses the relationship of Wyatt to continental sonneteers of the period.

1383. Lathrop, H.B. "The Sonnet Forms of Wyatt and Surrey." Modern Philology, 2 (1905), 463-70.

An analysis of rhyme schemes and other formal elements of all of the sonnets of Wyatt and Surrey.

1384. Leonard, Nancy S. "The Speaker in Wyatt's Lyric Poetry." Huntington Library Quarterly, 41 (1977), 1-18.

Among the poems discussed are the sonnets, "My galley charged with forgetfulness" and "Whoso list to hunt."

1385. Luria, Maxwell S. "Wyatt's 'The Lover Compareth His State' and the Petrarchan Commentators." Texas Studies in Literature and Language, 12 (1971), 531-35.

1386. Mason, H.A. Editing Wyatt: An Examination of Collected Poems of Sir Thomas Wyatt together with suggestions for an improved edition. Cambridge: Cambridge Quarterly Publications, 1972.

1387. Merrill, Rodney H. "Formal Elements in the Late Medieval Courtly Love Lyric." Ph.D. Dissertation, Stanford, 1970. DAI, 31 (1971), 4172A.

Mostly background, but some discussion of Wyatt's sonnets.

1388. Muir, Kenneth. Sir Thomas Wyatt and his Circle: Unpublished Poems. Liverpool: Liverpool University Press, 1961.

1389. Muir, Kenneth. The Life and Letters of Sir Thomas Wyatt. Liverpool: Liverpool University Press, 1963.

1390. Mumford, Ivy L. "Sir Thomas Wyatt's Verse and Italian Musical Sources." English Miscellany, 14 (1963), 9-26.

Includes discussion of some of the sonnets.

1391. Ogle, Robert B. "Wyatt and Petrarch: A Puzzle in Prosody." Journal of English and Germanic Philology, 73 (1974), 189-208.

In particular comparing "The longe love" to "Amor che nel penser mio vive e regna."

1392. Ostriker, Alicia. "Thomas Wyatt and Henry Surrey: Dissonance and Harmony in Lyric Form." New Literary History, 1 (1970), 387-405.

Compares, among other things, the sonnets "The longe love" by Wyatt and "Love that doth reign and live within my thought" by Surrey.

1393. Padelford, F.M. "The Scansion of Wyatt's Early Sonnets." Studies in Philology, 20 (1923), 137-52.

1394. Parker, William R. "The Sonnets in Tottel's Miscellany." PMLA, 54 (1939), 669-77.

1395. Pecoraro, Marco. "Un nuovo contributo sulla prima esperienza petrarchesca in Inghilterra." Italica, 38 (1961), 91-97.

Background on the influence of Petrarch in Wyatt's poetry--including his sonnets.

1396. Rees, D.G. "Sir Thomas Wyatt's Translations from Petrarch." Comparative Literature, 7 (1955), 15-24.

1397. Rees, D.G. "Wyatt and Petrarch." Modern Language Review, 52 (1957), 389-91.

On "Was I never yet of your love greved."

1398. Schelp, Hanspeter. "Sir Thomas Wyatt: 'The Long Love, that in My Thought Doeth Harbar'." Die Englische Lyrik: Von der Renaissance bis zur Gegenwart. Ed. Karl Heinz Goller. Dusseldorf: August Bagel, 1968, vol. 1, pp. 33-42.

1399. Schwartz, Elias. "The Meter of Some Poems of Wyatt." Studies in Philology, 60 (1963), 155-65.

Discusses two sonnets, "Brittle beauty that nature made so frail" (authorship disputed) and "Whoso list to hunt."

1400. Segre, Carlo. "Due petrarchisti inglesi del secolo XVI." Relazioni Letterarie fra Italia e Inghilterra. Firenze: Le Monnier, 1911, pp. 53-159.

1401. Setamanit, Sudah S. "The Place of Sir Thomas Wyatt's Lyrics in the Provencal-Italian Tradition of Amorous Poems." Ph.D. Dissertation, Michigan, 1970. DAI, 31 (1971), 4135A.

1402. Simonds, William E. Sir Thomas Wyatt and his Poems. Boston: D.C. Heath, 1889.

Dividing the love poems into four groups, Simonds discusses formal aspects of the sonnets in connection with three of those groups.

1403. Smith, Hallett. "The Art of Sir Thomas Wyatt." Huntington Library Quarterly, 9 (1946), 323-55.

1404. Southall, Raymond. The Courtly Maker: An Essay on the Poetry of Wyatt and his Contemporaries. Oxford: Blackwell; New York: Barnes and Noble, 1964.

1405. Southall, Raymond. "The Personality of Sir Thomas Wyatt." Essays in Criticism, 14 (1964), 43-64.

Last half of the article explores the sonnets.

1406. Swallow, Alan. "The Pentameter Lines in Skelton and Wyatt." Modern Philology, 48 (1950), 1-11.

The Wyatt illustrations are largely from the sonnets.

1407. Thomson, Patricia. "The First English Petrarchans." Huntington Library Quarterly, 22 (1959), 85-105.

Explores the connection between Petrarchan poems and those of Wyatt and Surrey.

1408. Thomson, Patricia. "Wyatt and the Petrarchan Commentators." Review of English Studies, NS 10 (1959), 225-33.

1409. Thomson, Patricia. "Wyatt and the School of Serafino." Comparative Literature, 13 (1961), 289-315.

The Petrarchanism evident in Wyatt's sonnets was filtered through this school of Italian poets.

1410. Thomson, Patricia. Sir Thomas Wyatt and his Background. Stanford, Cal.: Stanford University Press, 1964.

1411. Thomson, Patricia. "Wyatt and Surrey." English Poetry and Prose, 1540-1674. Ed. Christopher Ricks. London: Barrie and Jenkins, 1970, pp. 19-40.

1412. Thomson, Patricia. Wyatt: The Critical Heritage. London and Boston: Routledge and Kegan Paul, 1974.

1413. Tilley, Arthur. "Wyatt and Sannazaro." Modern Language Quarterly (London), 5 (1902), 149.

Wyatt ("Like unto these unmeasurable Mountains") and Saint Gelais ("Voyant ces monts de veue ainsi lointaine") are both indebted to a sonnet by Sannazaro. Tilley is in agreement with Waddington (Athenaeum, July 11, 1891).
1418

1414. Tilley, Edmond Allen, Jr. "Phonemic Differentiation Analyses of Poems by Sir Thomas Wyatt and Others." Ph.D. Dissertation, Iowa, 1972. DAI, 33 (1972), 1697A.

Uses 14 of Wyatt's sonnets plus other poetry in the study.

1415. Tillyard, E.M.W. The Poetry of Sir Thomas Wyatt: A Selection and a Study. London: Scholartis Press, 1929. Rev. ed. London: Chatto and Windus, 1949.

1416. Tottel, Richard. Tottel's Miscellany. Ed. Hyder Edward Rollins. 2 vol. Cambridge, Mass.: Harvard University Press, 1928. Rev. ed. 1965.

Volume 2 contains abundant commentary and notes on the sonnet material in the text.

1417. Waddington, Samuel. "The Sonnets of Sir Thomas Wyatt." Athenaeum, May 23, 1891, p. 667.

A sonnet by Mellin de Saint-Gelais, compared with Wyatt's version ("Like unto these unmeasurable mountains") and an 1886 translation by Austin Dobson.

1418. Waddington, Samuel. "Mellin de St. Gelais and the Introduction of the Sonnet into France." Athenaeum, July 11, 1891, p. 64.

Raises the possibility that Wyatt's poem "Like unto these unmeasurable mountains" was not a translation from St. Gelais but that both poets were translating Sannazaro.
1413

1419. Wiatt, William H. "Sir Thomas Wyatt and 'Sephame'." Notes and Queries, 197 (1952), 244.

In the sonnet that begins "You that in love . . ." the "sephame" referred to in line 9 may have been Edward Sepham.

1420. Wiatt, William H. "Sir Thomas Wyatt's Wordplay." Annuale Mediaevale, 1 (1960), 96-101.

Sonnets are used as illustrations of Wyatt's use of paranomasia.

1421. Wintermantel, Egon. Biographisches in den Gedichten von Sir Thomas Wyatt und Henry Howard, Earl of Surrey. Furtwangen: Wilhelm Kirchberg's Buchdruckerei, 1903.

Doctoral dissertation from Albert-Ludwigs-Universitat zu Freiburg. Includes an examination of sources for their sonnets.

1422. Wyatt, Sir Thomas. The Poems of Sir Thomas Wiat. Ed. A.K. Foxwell. 2 vol. London: University of London Press, 1913. rpt. New York: Russell and Russell, 1964.

1423. ______________. Sir Thomas Wyatt, the Collected Poems. Ed. Kenneth Muir. Cambridge, Mass.: Harvard University Press, 1950.

1424. ______________. Collected Poems of Sir Thomas Wyatt. Ed. Kenneth Muir and Patricia Thomson. Liverpool: Liverpool University Press, 1969.

1425. ______________. The Poetical Works of Sir Thomas Wyatt. Ed. with a memoir by Nicholas Harris Nicholas. London: William Pickering, 1831.

Contains a prefatory "Memoir of Sir Thomas Wyatt" by Sir Harris Nicholas. Memoir is reprinted in a number of later editions of the Poetical Works.

1426. ______________. Sir Thomas Wyatt: The Complete Poems. Ed. R.A. Rebholz. Harmondsworth: Penguin Books, 1978.

In his front matter, Rebholz has a section on Wyatt's meters which he devotes largely to the sonnets.

1427. "Three Modes in Poetry." TLS, September 12, 1958, p. 512.

This review of Josephine Miles, Eras and Modes in English Poetry illustrates her thesis by reference to sonnets by Wyatt, Spenser, and Shakespeare.

ADDENDUM

1427a. Pivato, Joseph. "Wyatt, Tudor Translator of Petrarca: Italian Plain Style." Canadian Review of Comparative Literature, 8 (1981), 239-55.

Compares two sonnets by Wyatt ("Whoso list to hunt" and "Was I never, yet, of your love greeved") with their Petrarchan sources.

3
WILLIAM SHAKESPEARE

1428. Abend, Murray. "Two Unique Gender Forms in the Shakespeare Sonnets." Notes and Queries, 195 (1950), 325.

Both April (Sonnet 98) and summer (Sonnet 5) are personified as male.

1429. Acheson, Arthur. Shakespeare and the Rival Poet: Displaying Shakespeare as a Satirist and Proving the Identity of the Patron and the Rival of the Sonnets: With a Reprint of Sundry Poetical Pieces by George Chapman, Bearing on the Subject. London and New York: John Lane, 1903. rpt. New York: AMS Press, 1970.

1430. Acheson, Arthur. Mistress Davenant: The Dark Lady of Shakespeare's Sonnets. London: B. Quaritch, 1913.

Includes a sixteen-page supplement called "A Woman Coloured Ill."

1431. Acheson Arthur. "Trailing the Dark Lady of the Sonnets." New York Times Book Review, March 20, 1921, pp. 4, 27.

1432. Acheson, Arthur. "Shakespeare and the Davenants." TLS, July 28, 1921, p. 484.

Adds his voice to an exchange of letters between Poel and Newbon.

2559, 2654

1433. Acheson, Arthur. Shakespeare's Sonnet Story 1592-1598: Restoring the Sonnets written to the Earl of Southampton to their original books and correlating them with personal phases of the Plays of the Sonnet period; with documentary evidence identifying Mistress Davenant as the Dark Lady. London and New York: B. Quaritch, 1922. rpt. New York: Haskell House, 1971.

1434. Adams, Hazard. Review of Murray Krieger, A Window to Criticism: Shakespeare's Sonnets and Modern Poetics. Criticism, 7 (1965), 190-93.

1435. Adams, Joseph Quincy. "Two Notes on Hamlet." Modern Language Notes 29 (1914), 1-3.

Second note deals with the phrase "potions of eisel" (Sonnet 111) to explain a reading in Hamlet (V.i. 299).
1682

1436. Adams, Joseph Quincy. A Life of William Shakespeare. Boston: Houghton Mifflin, 1923.

Main passage dealing with the sonnets (pp. 160-83) is in the chapter on "Period of Non-Dramatic Composition." Adams believes the Sonnets to be artificial and conventional, without true emotion.

1437. Adnes, Andre. Shakespeare et la Folie: Etude Medico-Psychologique. Paris: Librairie Maloine, 1936.

The book contains an "Addenda.--Shakespeare et les Sonnets" (pp. 281-89) in which Adnes considers, among other things, the possibility that Shakespeare suffered from an "anomalie sexuelle."

1438. Aggeler, Geoffrey D. "A Prophetic Acrostic in Anthony Burgess's 'Nothing Like the Sun'." Notes and Queries, 219 (1974), 136.

In Burgess's novel, the young Shakespeare composes a Sonnet with the name Fatimah as an acrostic; a woman of this name is later to play a fateful part in his life.

1439. Aiken, Ralph. "A Note on Shakespeare's Sonnet 30." Shakespeare Quarterly, 14 (1963), 93-94.

Discusses possible sources of the phrase "remembrance of things past."

1440. Ainger, Alfred. "'The Only Begetter' of Shakspeare's Sonnets." Athenaeum, Jan. 14, 1899, pp. 59-60; Jan. 28, 1899, pp. 121-22.

Disputes Samuel Butler's interpretation of the word "begetter."
1656

1441. Akrigg, G.P.V. "The Shakespeare of the Sonnets." Queen's Quarterly, 72 (1965), 78-90.

1442. Akrigg, G.P.V. Shakespeare and the Earl of Southhampton. Cambridge, Mass.: Harvard University Press, 1968.

Two chapters deal specifically with the Sonnets--"The First Sonnets" (pp. 201-206) and "The Unfaithful Friend and the Sonnets" (pp. 228-39).

1443. Alden, Raymond M. "The Sonnet." An Introduction to Poetry For Students of English Literature. New York: Henry Holt, 1909, pp. 325-32.

1444. Alden, Raymond M. "The Quarto Arrangement of the Sonnets." Anniversary Papers by Colleagues and Pupils of George Lyman Kittredge. Presented on the Completion of his Twenty-Fifth Year of Teaching in Harvard University. Boston: Ginn, 1913, pp. 279-88.

1445. Alden, R.M. Review of Arthur Acheson, Mistress Davenant: The Dark Lady of Shakespeare's Sonnets and Countess de Chambrun, The Sonnets of William Shakespeare: New Light and Old Evidence. Journal of English and Germanic Philology, 14 (1915), 449-60.

Alden finds little merit in the theory that Mistress Davenant was Shakespeare's dark lady--a theory, he points out, which was first advanced by F.G. Fleay some thirty years earlier.

1446. Alden, Raymond M. "The 1640 Text of Shakespeare's Sonnets." Modern Philology, 14 (1916), 17-30.

1447. Alden, Raymond M. "The 1710 and 1714 Texts of Shakespeare's Poems." Modern Language Notes. 31 (1916), 268-74.

1448. Alden, Raymond M. "The Lyrical Conceit of the Elizabethans." Studies in Philology, 14 (1917), 129-52.

Principally illustrated from Astrophel and Stella and Shakespeare's Sonnets.

1449. *Alden, Raymond M. "J. Strong's Note upon The Dark Lady." Literary Review, July 23, 1921.

1450. Alden, Raymond M. "The Poems." Shakespeare. New York: Duffield, 1922. rpt. New York: AMS Press, 1971, pp. 105-46.

1451. Alexander, P. Review of J.A. Fort, A Time Scheme for Shakespeare's Sonnets. Review of English Studies, 6 (1930), 467-69.

1452. *Alexeyev, M.P. "Derzhavin and Shakespeare's Sonnets." XVIII Century. Russian Literature of the Eighteenth Century and Its International Connections. Leningrad: "Nauka," 1975, vol. 10, pp. 226-35.

Derzhavin's poem "Hot Spring" has common Greek sources with Sonnets 153 and 154.

1453. [Alger, William R.] "Shakespeare and Friendship." Christian Examiner, 73 (1862), 209-26.

This review of Richard Grant White's edition of The Works of William Shakespeare, which focuses on the theme of friendship, deals in part with the Sonnets (pp. 210-13).

1454. [Alger William R.] "Shakespeare's Sonnets and Friendship." Christian Examiner, 73 (1862), 403-35.

After reviewing a number of the theories, the writer declares that Pembroke is the friend to whom some of the sonnets are directed.

1455. Allen, Michael J.B. "Shakespeare's Man Descending a Staircase: Sonnets 126 to 154." Shakespeare Survey, 31 (1978), 127-38.

1456. A[llen], P[ercy]. "Rhyme-Linked Order of Shakespeare's Sonnets." Christian Science Monitor, January 18, 1929, p. 9.

1457. Allen, Percy. The Case for Edward de Vere, 17th Earl of Oxford as "William Shakespeare." London: Cecil Palmer, 1930.

Finds some evidence for this attribution among the sonnets.

1458. Allen, Percy. Anne Cecil, Elizabeth and Oxford. London: Denis Archer, 1934.

Finds in the relationship between Oxford and Elizabeth the key to a number of Shakespearean enigmas-not the least of which were the identities of the Dark Lady and fair youth of the sonnets.

1459. Allen, Percy. "The 'Mortal Moon'." TLS, March 8, 1934, p. 162.

On Sonnet 107.
2082

1460. Allen, Percy, and B.M. Ward. An Inquiry into the Relations Between Lord Oxford as Shakespeare, Queen Elizabeth and the Fair Youth of Shakespeare's Sonnets. London: Percy Allen, 1936.

1461. Almansi, Guido. "L'affaire mysterieuse de l'abominable tongue-in cheek." Tr. from the English by Claude Beguin. Poetique, No. 36 (November, 1978), 413-26.

Includes a discussion of ambivalent meanings in Sonnet 76 (pp. 423-26).

1462. Alter, Jean V. "Apollinaire and Two Shakespearean Sonnets." Comparative Literature, 14 (1962), 377-85.

Discusses Apollinaire's "covert adaptation of Shakespeare's Sonnets 147 and 148."

1463. Anders, H.R.D. Shakespeare's Books: A Dissertation on Shakespeare's Reading and the Immediate Sources of his Works. 2 vol. Berlin: Georg Reimer, 1904.

References throughout covering the sonnets. See, in particular, Chapter 3 on "English Non-Dramatic Polite Literature."

1464. Andreasjan, Bjurakn. "Die Sonette Shakespeares in Armenischer Ubersetzung." Shakespeare Jahrbuch, 114 (1978), 142-49.

Summary of a Russian thesis from Yerevan: Institute of Literature, 1975.

1465. Angell, Pauline K. "Light on the Dark Lady: A Study of Some Elizabethan Libels." PMLA, 52 (1937), 652-74.

1466. Anspacher, Louis. Shakespeare as Poet and Lover and the Enigma of the Sonnets. New York: Island Press, 1944. rpt. New York: Haskell House, 1973.

1467. *Antipova, A.M. "Rhythm and Intonation in the Structure of Shakespeare's Sonnets." A Collection of Scholarly Essays. Moscow "M. Thorez" Institute of Foreign Languages, 75. Moscow: "M. Thorez" Institute of Foreign Languages, 1974, pp. 5-14.

In Russian.

1468. Archer, C. "'Thou' and 'You' in the Sonnets." TLS. June 27, 1936, p. 544.

1469. Archer, William. "Shakespeare's Sonnets: The Case Against Southampton." Fortnightly Review, 68 (1897), 817-34.

Limiting himself to the autobiographical aspects of the Sonnets, Archer presents his arguments against Southampton as the friend of the Sonnets.

1470. Archer, William. "The Sonnets of Shakespeare." Living Age, 244 (1905), 313-16.

A review of H.C. Beeching's edition of The Sonnets of Shakespeare.

1471. Aring, Charles D. "Perception As a Moral Test." Journal of Nervous and Mental Diseases, 144 (1967), 539-45.

Aring's thesis, that perception of beauty is a measure of moral sense, is demonstrated by Shakespeare whose sonnets are remarkable pieces of perception.

1472. Arns, Karl. Review of Shakespeares Sonette, Ubertragung von Karl Hauer. Deutsche Literaturzeitung, 51 (1930), 2469-70.

1473. Aronstein, Ph. Review of Shakespeares Sonette, Ubersetzt von Max J. Wolff. Deutsche Literaturzeitung, 25 (1904), 1370-71.

1474. Askew, Melvin W. "Form and Process in Lyric Poetry." Sewanee Review, 72 (1964), 281-99.

Uses Sonnet 73 as an illustration of his thesis.

1475. Auden, W.H. "Shakespeare's Sonnets." Listener, 72 (1964), 7-9, 45-47.

Published in 2 parts from a talk on BBC's Third Programme.

1476. Auden, W.H. "Shakespeare's Sonnets." Forewords and Afterwords. Selected by Edward Mendelson. New York: Random House, 1973, pp. 88-108.

Despite the fact that he deprecates the vain efforts of scholars to discover the identity of the "fair friend" or the "dark lady", Auden spends a fair amount of time on such speculations.

1477. Austin, Warren B. "Thomas Nashe's Authorship of a Sonnet Attributed to Shakespeare." Shakespeare in the Southwest: Some New Directions. Ed. T.J. Stafford. Literature Series, 1. El Paso: Texas Western Press, 1969, pp. 94-105.

Austin disagrees with William Minto that the commendatory sonnet to John Florio's Second Frutes (1591), entitled "Phaeton to his Friend Florio," was written by Shakespeare.
254

1478. Avtonomova, N., and M. Gasparov. "Sonety Shekspira-perevody Marshaka." [Shakespeare's Sonnets--Marshaka's translation]. Voprosy Literatury, 13, ii (1969), 100-12.

1479. Axelrad, A. Jose. Review of Edward Hubler, The Sense of Shakespeare's Sonnets. Revue de Litterature Comparee, 28 (1954), 496-97.

1480. Axon, William E.A. "Mrs. Mary Fitton." Academy, 26 (July 26, 1884), 62.

A few more facts on Mary Fitton, a dark lady candidate.

1481. Aycock, John L., Bennett Weaver, Samuel B. Hemingway, Sarah Wingate Taylor, Martin Erlich, and Roy B. Clark. "Atlantic Repartee." Atlantic, 185 (February, 1950), 17-19.

A series of letters in response to Leslie Hotson's "When Shakespeare Wrote the Sonnets."

1482. B., A. Review of Thomas Tyler, The Herbert-Fitton Theory of Shakespeare's Sonnets. A Reply. Shakespeare Jahrbuch, 35 (1899), 336.

1483. B., C.C. "Sonnet CXLVI. 1, 2." Notes and Queries, 7th Series, 12 (1891), 423.

Expresses reservation about Nicholson's emendation of line 2.
2570

1484. B., C.C. "Sonnet CXXVI." Notes and Queries, 8th series, 3 (1893), 285.

Responding to Brownlow's note on line 2.
1639

1485. B., C.C. "Sonnet C., 1, 9." Notes and Queries, 8th Series, 4 (1893), 444.

More on "Rise, resty muse."
2571, 3118.

1486. B., C.C. "The Sonnets: The Two Obeli in the Globe Edition." Notes and Queries, 8th Series, 11 (1897), 223.

Rejects two speculative readings on Sonnets 60 and 146 by R.M. Spence.
2987

1487. B., C.C. "Shakespeare's Sonnets: The Rival Poet." Notes and Queries, 11th Series, 5 (1912), 190.

Offers Marlowe as the candidate for rival poet.

1488. B., C.C., and Tom Jones. "The Text of Shakespeare's Sonnets CXXV. and CXXVI." Notes and Queries, 11th Series, 7 (1913), 32.

Both correspondents disagree with W.B. Brown's earlier reading of these poems.
1632

1489. B., C.C. "The Text of Shakespeare's Sonnets CXXV. and CXXVI." Notes and Queries, 11th Series, 7 (1913), 153.
1632

1490. B., C.C. "'Buds of Marjoram'." Notes and Queries, 11th Series, 8 (1913), 237-38.

On a phrase from Sonnet 99, in response to comments by W.B. Brown and A.R. Bayley.
1530, 1633

1491. B., J. "To What Person the Sonnets of Shakespeare Were Actually Addressed." Gentleman's Magazine, 102 (1832), 217-21; 308-13.

After rejecting a whole list of candidates in Part I, the author reveals in Part II that W.H. was the Earl of Pembroke.

1492. B., J.G. "'Looks' or 'Books' in Sonnet XXIII." Shakespeariana, 2 (1885), 495-97.

On the reading of the first line.

1493. B., J.G. "Sonnet LVIII." Shakespeariana, 3 (1886), 176-77.

Suggests an emendation proposed originally by Malone changing "To what you will" to "Do what you will."

1494. B., S.J.C. "Vondel en het Shakespeare-Sonnet." Tijdschrift voor nederlandsche Taal- en Letterkunde, 13 (1894), 179-84.

Discusses the influence of Shakespeare's Sonnets on Vondel, the Dutch poet and dramatist.

1495. B., S.J.C. "Shakespeare-Sonnetten bij Vondel." Tijdschrift voor nederlandsche Taal- en Letterkunde, 13 (1894), 306-12.

1496. *Bacigalupo, Massimo. "I sonetti di Shakespeare: Struttura come metodo." Verri, 7 (1974), 76-92.

Relates his discussion to Melchiori's L'uomo e il potere.

1497. Bacon, Wallace A. Review of G. Wilson Knight, The Mutual Flame. Quarterly Journal of Speech, 42 (1956), 201-02.

1498. Bagg, Robert. "Some Versions of Lyric Impasse in Shakespeare and Catullus." Arion, 4 (1965), 65-95.

Comparisons between Catullus's lyrics and the Sonnets.

1499. Bailey, John. Shakespeare. London and New York: Longmans, Green, 1929. rpt. Folcroft, Pa.: Folcroft Library Editions, 1973.

Bailey rejects the autobiographical interpretation in his discussion of the Sonnets (pp. 58-65).

1500. Baker, Herschel. Review of Edward Hubler, The Sense of Shakespeare's Sonnets. Shakespeare Quarterly, 3 (1952), 374-75.

1501. Baldi, Sergio. "Shakespeare's Sonnets as Literature." Shakespeare Celebrated: Anniversary Lectures Delivered at the Folger Library. Ed. Louis B. Wright. Ithaca, N.Y.: Cornell University Press, 1966, pp. 133-54.

Among other things, he discusses the imagery in the Sonnets.

1502. Baldi, Sergio. Review of John Dover Wilson, An Introduction to the Sonnets of Shakespeare for the Use of Historians and Others. Shakespeare Quarterly, 19 (1968), 175-77.

Evaluates Wilson's theories about the identity of Mr. W.H., Shakespeare's role in organizing the sonnets, etc.

1503. Baldwin, T.W. On the Literary Genetics of Shakspere's Poems and Sonnets. Urbana: University of Illinois Press, 1951.

Part III, "The Literary Genetics of Shakspere's Sugred Sonnets" (pp. 157-360).

1504. *Balota, Nicolae. "Adevar si poezie in Sonetele lui Shakespeare." Romania Literara, May 24, 1979, p. 20.

1505. Baltzer, A. Die schonsten Sonette von W. Shakespeare. Wismar: Hans Bartholdi, 1910.

An essay which includes translations of over 30 sonnets.

1506. Banerjee, Srikumar. "The Sonnets of Shakespeare." Shakespeare Commemoration Volume. Ed. Taraknath Sen. Calcutta: Presidency College, 1966, pp. 1-10.

Essentially an appreciation of the poems both as an excellent example of a traditional form and as a record of personal feeling.

1507. Banks, Theodore. "Shakespeare's Sonnet No. 8." Modern Language Notes, 63 (1948), 541-42.

1508. Barber, C.L. "Introduction." The Sonnets by William Shakespeare. Ed. Charles Jasper Sisson. New York: Dell, 1960. Reprinted as "An Essay on the Sonnets " in Elizabethan Poetry: Modern Essays in Criticism. Ed. Paul Alpers. New York: Oxford University Press, Galaxy Book, 1967, pp. 299-320. Excerpted and reprinted as "The Sonnets as an Action" in Discussions of Shakespeare's Sonnets. Ed. Barbara Herrnstein. Boston: D.C. Heath, 1964, pp. 159-64.

1509. Barber, C.L. "Shakespeare in His Sonnets." Massachusetts Review, 1 (1960), 648-72.

A shortened version of his essay in the Laurel Shakespeare.
1508

1510. Barber, C.L. "Full to Overflowing." Review of Shakespeare's Sonnets, ed. Stephen Booth. New York Review of Books, 25 (April 6, 1978), 32-38.

1511. Barnard, Finch. "The Shakespeare Sonnets: The Psychology of Shakespeare as Revealed in the Sonnets." Science and the Soul. London: Selwyn and Blount, 1918, pp. 9-34.

An attempt to ascribe authorship of the sonnets to a Barnard, one of the author's ancestors.

1512. Barnet, Sylvan. Review of Giorgio Melchiori, Shakespeare's Dramatic Meditations. Renaissance Quarterly, 30 (1977), 404-07.

1513. Barnstorff, D. Schlussel zu Shakspeares Sonnetten. Bremen: J. Kuhtmann, 1860. Published in English as A Key to Shakespeare's Sonnets. Translated by T.J. Graham. London: Trubner, 1862. rpt. New York: AMS, 1975.

1514. *Barrell, Charles Wisner. "The Wayward Water-Bearer Who Wrote Shakespeare's Sonnet 109." Shakespeare Fellowship Quarterly, 6 (1945), 37-39.

1515. [Barrett, H.W.] "Shakespeare's Sonnets." American [Whig] Review, 6 (1847), 304-09.

Believes that Shakespeare wrote the Sonnets to express his remorse for being unfaithful to his wife.

1516. Barroll, J. Leeds. Review of J. Dover Wilson, An Introduction to the Sonnets of Shakespeare for the Use of Historians and Others. College English, 26 (1964), 61.

1517. Barry, Jackson G. "'Had, Having, and in Quest to Have, Extreme': Shakespeare's Rhetoric of Time in Sonnet 129." Language and Style, 14 (1981), 1-12.

In his conclusion of this reading of the sonnet, Barry draws some analogies to the way Shakespeare refers to time in Macbeth.

1518. Bartlett, Henrietta C. "First Editions of Shakespeare's Quartos." Library, 16 (1935), 166-72.

Includes reference to the Quartos, the number extant, and their location.

1519. Barton, Sir Dunbar Plunket. Links Between Shakespeare and the Law. London: Faber and Gwyer, 1929.

Mentions several legal allusions in Sonnets 30, 35, 46, 134, and 137.

1520. Basdekis, Demetrius. "Death in the Sonnets of Shakespeare and Camoes." Hispania, 46 (1963), 102-05.

1521. Bates, Ernest Sutherland. "The Sincerity of Shakespeare's Sonnets." Modern Philology, 8 (1910), 87-106.

The fact that scholars have failed to identify the friend, rival and dark lady does not mean they did not exist. But even if they did not, the poems are still sincere expressions of Shakespeare's emotions.

1522. Bates, Paul A. "Virgil and Shakespeare: A New Key to Shakespeare's Sonnets." Shakespeare Newsletter, 11 (1961), 2.

Abstract of a paper delivered at the Modern Language Association Meeting, December 27-29, 1960, Philadelphia, Pa. Followed by a critique by T.M. Pearce and a rejoinder by Bates entitled "Once More on Pastoral in Shakespeare's Sonnets."

1523. Bates, Paul A. "Shakespeare's Sonnets and Pastoral Poetry." Shakespeare Jahrbuch, 103 (1967), 81-96.

Believes that Shakespeare's sequence was influenced by the pastoral tradition and, particularly, the poems of Richard Barnfield.

1524. Bates, Paul A. "Shakespeare's Sonnets and the Growth of his Dramatic Art." Shakespeare Jahrbuch, 114 (1978), 70-74.

1525. Bateson, F.W. "Elementary My Dear Hotson: A Caveat for Literary Detectives." Essays in Criticism, 1 (1951), 81-88. Reprinted in F.W. Bateson, Essays in Critical Dissent. Totowa, N.J.: Rowman and Littlefield, 1972, pp. 49-56. Also reprinted in Discussions of Shakespeare's Sonnets. Ed. Barbara Herrnstein. Boston: D.C. Heath, 1964, pp. 22-27.

Focusing on the dating of Sonnet 107, this essay is a reply to Hotson's Shakespeare's Sonnets Dated.
2158

1526. Bateson, F.W. "The Function of Criticism at the Present Time." Essays in Criticism, 3 (1953), 1-27.

Discusses Empson's analysis of Sonnet 73 in Seven Types of Ambiguity (pp. 7-9). For additional comments see next item.
1878

1527. Bateson, F.W., and William Empson. "Bare Ruined Choirs." Essays in Criticism, 3 (1953), 357-63.

A 3-part exchange between Empson and Bateson and finally Empson on this famous line from Sonnet 73. See Wheeler and Bateson for the "final" word on this line.
3186

1528. Bathurst, Charles. Remarks on the Differences in Shakespeare's Versification in Different Periods of His Life. London: John W. Parker and Son, 1857. rpt. New York: AMS Press, 1970.

Includes a discussion of the sonnets (pp. 110-15).

1529. Baxter, James Phinney. The Greatest of Literary Problems: The Authorship of the Shakespeare Works: An Exposition of All Points at Issue, From Their Inception to the Present Moment. Boston and New York: Houghton Mifflin, 1915.

Baxter, in a chapter on "The Sonnets," finds that a study of Bacon's life followed by a reading of the Sonnets make the latter comprehensible (pp. 378-91).

1530. Bayley, A.R. "'Buds of Marjoram'." Notes and Queries, 11th Series, 8 (1913), 213.

Cites various authorities on the meaning of this phrase in Sonnet 99. See also W.B. Brown and C.C.B.
1490, 1633

1531. Bayley, John. "Who Was the 'Man Right Fair' of the Sonnets?" TLS, January 4, 1974, p. 15; February 1, 1974, p. 108; February 15, 1974, p. 158; March 8, 1974, p. 238.

Bayley follows his article with several letters responding to his critics.
1886, 2030, 2984

1532. Bayley, John. "Marriage of Whose Minds?" Review of S.C. Campbell, Only Begotten Sonnets, and Shakespeare's Sonnets, ed. S.C. Campbell. Listener, March 22, 1979, pp. 433-34.

1533. Baym, Max I. "Recurrent Poetic Themes." Shakespeare Association Bulletin, 12 (1937), 155-58.

A theme from Ronsard finds its way into modern poetry (e.g. that of Dowson and Yeats) via Shakespeare's Sonnets 12 and 32 and Richard II.

1534. Bayne, Thomas. "Sonnet LXVI." Notes and Queries, 7th Series, 4 (1887), 304; 5 (1888), 62.

Bayne proposes an emendation--"dishabited" for "disabled" in line 8. For additional comments see Robert F. Gardiner, D.C.T., C.B.M., and B. Nicholson.
1980, 2566

1535. Beach, Elizabeth. Shakespeare and the Tenth Muse. Hamburg, N.J.: Willoughby Books, 1969.

Mary Browne Wriothesley (mother of the 3rd Earl of Southampton) was the "onlie begetter" of the Sonnets; Mr. W.H. was William Harvey (her third husband). [Ivor Brown proposed this theory some years earlier.] The book also discusses The Lover's Complaint and The Phoenix and the Turtle.

1536. Beatty, Arthur. "Shakespeare's Sonnets and Plays." Shakespeare Studies by Members of the Department of English of the University of Wisconsin. Madison: University of Wisconsin Press, 1916, pp. 201-14.

Includes a list of "sonnet-like" passages in sixteen plays.

1537. Beaugrande, Robert-Alain de. "Toward a General Theory of Creativity." Poetics, 8 (1979), 269-306.

Uses linguistics as a basis for establishing a general theory of creativity in language, and then considers the creativity of Shakespeare's Sonnet 33 with the help of network representation (pp. 280-86).

1538. Beckwith, Elizabeth. "On the Chronology of Shakespeare's Sonnets." Journal of English and Germanic Philology, 25 (1926), 227-42.

1539. Beeching, H.C. "The Sonnets of Shakespeare." Cornhill Magazine, NS 12 (1902), 244-63.

Essentially a response to Sidney Lee's conclusions in the Life of Shakespeare. Beeching concludes that the mysteries surrounding the identities of the rival and the friend are still "as dark as ever." This much can be said: Chapman is not the rival and Southampton is not the friend.
2341

1540. Beeching, H.C. "The Sonnets." The Works of William Shakespeare. Ed. A.H. Bullen. Stratford-on-Avon: The Shakespeare Head Press; New York: Duffield, 1907, vol. 10, pp. 363-72.

Bullen, in his notes (pp. 448-50), disagrees with Beeching on the latter's belief that the Quarto was full of errors. Most of Beeching's essay, however, is addressed to the usual problems. He assumes the friendship was with a real person and reviews the various theories on the subject.

1541. Beese, Henriette. Nachdichtung als Erinnerung: Allegorische Lekture einiger Gedichte von Paul Celan. Darmstadt: Agora-Verlag, 1976.

Contains two pertinent chapters: "Zu Celans Nachdichtungen von Shakespeare Sonetten (I-V, XLIII, LX, LXV, CXXXVII)" (pp. 93-150) and "Zu den Shakespeare Sonetten CVI und CVII ihrer Um-, Vor- und Nachdichtung (George, Rang, Celan)" (pp. 151-94).

1542. [Begley, Walter E.] Is It Shakespeare? The Great Question of Elizabethan Literature. Answered in the Light of New Revelations and Important Contemporary Evidence Hitherto Unnoticed. London: John Murray, 1903.

This Baconian, who wrote this book anonymously as "A Cambridge Graduate," has several sections devoted to the sonnets (pp. 129-42, 190-250 et passim).

1543. Bejblik, Alois. "K Vrchlickeho prekladu Shakespearovych sonetu." Casopis pro Moderni Filologii, 38 (1956), 157-66.

Review of Jaroslav Vrchlicky's translation of the Sonnets. (Vrchlicky was the pseudonym for Emil Bohuslav Frida.)

1544. Bell, Robert. "Shakespeare's Sonnets." Fortnightly Review, 5 (1866), 734-41.

Review of Gerald Massey, Shakespeare's Sonnets Never Before Interpreted.

1545. *Benedetti, Anna. "L'Ordine originale dei sonetti di Guglielmo Shakespeare." Rivista d'Italia, 31, i (1928), 120-29.

1546. Benezet, Louis P. The Six Loves of "Shake-speare." New York: Pageant, 1958.

Anti-Stratfordian (in favor of de Vere).

1547. Bennett, J.A.W. "Remembrance of Things Past." Notes and Queries, 207 (1962), 151-52.

Finds the most likely source of this line, which appears in Sonnet 30, to be from the Apocrypha (Wisdom xi, 12).

1548. Bennett, Josephine A.W. "Benson's Alleged Piracy of Shake-speares Sonnets and of Some of Jonson's Works." Studies in Bibliography, 21 (1968), 235-48.

1549. Benzon, William. "Cognitive Networks and Literary Semantics." Modern Language Notes, 91 (1976), 952-82.

Applies cognitive network theory to Shakespeare's Sonnet 129 (pp. 969-80).

1550. Bercovitch, Sacvan. "Shakespeare's 'Sonnet CXXIV'." Explicator, 27 (1968), Item 22.

1551. Berkelman, Robert G. "The Drama in Shakespeare's Sonnets." College English, 10 (1948), 138-41.

Discusses the dramatic conflicts that vitalize Sonnets 129, 144, 73, and, most importantly, 146.

1552. Bermann, Sandra Lekas. "Perspectives on the Sonnet: Poetic Structure in Petrarch, Shakespeare, Baudelaire." Ph.D. Dissertation, Columbia University, 1976. DAI, 39 (1978), 2233A.

Sees Shakespeare's sonnets with their strong metaphoric tendencies as being, in many ways, the opposite of Petrarch's.

1553. Bernard, John D. "'To Constancie Confin'de': The Poetics of Shakespeare's Sonnets." PMLA, 94 (1979), 77-90.

1554. Berry, Francis. "'Thou' and 'You' in Shakespeare's Sonnets." Essays in Criticism, 8 (1958), 138-46. An expanded version appeared as "'Thou' and 'You' in the Sonnets in Relation to Tense" in Poets' Grammar: Person, Time and Mood in Poetry. London: Routledge and Kegan Paul, 1958, pp. 36-48.

Thomas Finkenstaedt has a note in response to Berry in a later number of this volume of Essays in Criticism (pp. 456-57).

1555. Berry, Francis. Poetry and the Physical Voice. London: Routledge and Kegan Paul, 1962.

In Chapter 7, "Shakespeare's Voice and the Voices of His Instruments," he begins by looking at the "I" poet of the Sonnets before proceeding to a consideration of the plays.

1556. Berry, Francis. Review of S.C. Campbell, Only Begotten Sonnets and Shakespeare's Sonnets, ed. S.C. Campbell. Tablet, 233 (March 24, 1979), 298.

1557. Berry, J. Wilkes. "Shakespeare's Sonnet XII." Explicator, 27 (1968), Item 13.

1558. Berry, Ralph. "Shakespeare's Sonnets and his Life." Queen's Quarterly, 85 (1978), 469-74.

Review article on Shakespeare's Sonnets, ed. Stephen Booth, and two books on other subjects.

1559. Berryman, John. "Shakespeare at Thirty." Hudson Review, 6 (1953), 175-203. Reprinted in The Freedom of the Poet. London and New York: Farrar, Straus, and Giroux, 1976, pp. 29-55.

Some comment about Sonnets 110-112 (pp. 182-84) and 107 and 124 (pp. 193-97) within the context of a biographical sketch.

1560. Berzeviczy, Albert von. "Die Sonette Michelangelos und Shakespeares." Ungarische Rundschau, 3 (1914), 398-412.

1561. Bibliothecary. "The Crux of Sonnet CXVI." Notes and Queries, 5th Series, 12 (1879), 24.

Proposes a change in the eighth line from "higth" to "hight," the latter meaning "promise or vow." Thus the line would read "Whose worths unknowne, although his hight [vow] be taken."

1562. Biese, Alfred. The Development of the Feeling for Nature In the Middle Ages and Modern Times. London: G. Routledge and Sons, 1905. rpt. New York: Burt Franklin, [1963].

In a chapter on "Shakespeare's Sympathy for Nature," Biese cites a number of passages from sonnets in which some image drawn from Nature is employed (pp. 168-70).

1563. Biggs, Alan J. "Carew and Shakespeare." Notes and Queries, 201 (1956), 225.

Identifies a similarity in both image and wording between Sonnet 116 and Carew's poem to his absent mistress, subtitled "A Ship."

1564. Birchenough, Josephine, and Edward B. Goodacre. "Fair Youth and Dark Lady." TLS, September 17, 1964, p. 868.

Remarks on William Hatcliff, Hotson's "fair youth" in Mr. W.H.
2162

1565. Birdwood, George. "Canker-blooms and Canker." Athenaeum, August 13, 1904, pp. 219-20.

Challenges Towndrow's contention about the canker-blooms in Sonnet 54.
3098

1566. Blackmur, R.P. "A Poetics for Infatuation." Kenyon Review, 23 (1961), 647-70. Reprinted in The Riddle of Shakespeare's Sonnets. Ed. Edward Hubler. New York: Basic Books, 1962, pp. 129-61.

A reading of the poems in support of "the accidentally established order [of the Sonnets] we possess." The theme of the poems throughout is "infatuation: its initiation, cultivation, and history . . . ."

1567. Blatt, William M. "A New Light on the Sonnets." Modern Philology, 11 (1913), 135-40.

A rereading of the poems using "internal evidence" to support the idea that the Sonnets were written by Shakespeare for a lame and aging man (Mr. W.H.). The poems are not, therefore, about Shakespeare's life at all.

1568. Blissett, William. Review of Claes Schaar, Elizabethan Sonnet Themes and the Dating of Shakespeare's Sonnets. English Studies, 46 (1965), 262-63.

Pays particular attention to Sonnet 106.

1569. B[oaden], J[ames]. "To What Person the Sonnets of Shakspeare Were Actually Addressed." Gentleman's Magazine, 102 (1832), 217-21; 308-14.

Boaden's two-part article declares Herbert as his candidate for Mr. W.H.

1570. Boaden, James. "Letter." Gentleman's Magazine, 102 (1832), 407.

Boaden responds to letters by Hunter and Bright, which were prompted by his own earlier article in Gentleman's Magazine.
2188

1571. Boaden, James. On the Sonnets of Shakespeare Identifying the Person to Whom They Are Addressed and Elucidating Several Points in the Poet's History. London: Thomas Rodd, 1837. rpt. New York: AMS Press, 1970.

Specifically rejects Southampton and embraces William Herbert as Mr. W.H.

1572. *Boas, Coenraad van Emde. Shakespeare's Sonnetten en Hun Verband met de Travesti-Double Spelen. Een Medisch-Psychologische Studie. Amsterdam and Antwerp: Wereld-Bibliotheek, 1951.

Doctoral dissertation at the University of Amsterdam.

1573. Boas, Frederick S. Shakspere and his Predecessors. London: John Murray, 1896. rpt. New York: Gordian Press, 1968.

Chapter 7 (pp. 107-129), "Shakspere in London--The Sonnets."

1574. Boas, F.S. "Dr. Hotson's Arguments." TLS, July 7, 1950, p. 421.

Differs with Hotson on dating of Sonnet 107 and suggests 1603 as the year.

1575. Boas, Frederick S. Review of Leslie Hotson, Shakespeare's Sonnets Dated and Other Essays. English, 8 (1950), 32-33.

1576. Bodden, H[orst], and H. Kaussen. Modellanalysen englischer Lyrik: Shakespeare, Marvell, Milton, Blake, Keats, Shelley, Hopkins, Yeats, Hughes. Stuttgart: Ernst Klett, 1974.

Presents an interpretation and analysis of Shakespeare's Sonnet 29, Milton's sonnet "On His Blindness," and Hopkins's "The Windhover."

1577. Boerner, Oskar. "Zur Frage der Politischen Sonette Shakespeares." Archiv fur das Studium der neueren Sprachen, 180 (1942), 9-18.

Sonnets 107, 124 and 125 form a group of political sonnets.

1578. Booth, Stephen Walter. "The Structures of Shakespeare's Sonnets." Ph.D. Dissertation, Harvard, 1964.

1579. Booth, Stephen. An Essay on Shakespeare's Sonnets. New Haven and London: Yale University Press, 1969.

1580. Booth, Stephen. Review of Philip Martin, Shakespeare's Sonnets: Self, Love and Art. Modern Language Quarterly, 35 (1974), 82-85.

1581. Booth, Wayne C. A Rhetoric of Irony. Chicago and London: University of Chicago Press, 1974.

In his discussion on the "Intentions of Parody" he uses Sonnet 130 (pp. 123-29) as his principal illustration.

1582. Booth, William Stone. "The Sonnets." Some Acrostic Signatures of Francis Bacon, Baron Verulam of Verulam, Viscount St. Alban, Together with Some Others, All of Which are Now the First Time Deciphered and Published. Boston: Houghton Mifflin, 1907 (1909), pp. 149-75.

Discovers acrostics of Bacon's name in a number of the sonnets.

1583. Borgmeier, Raimund. Shakespeare's Sonett "When forty winters" und die deutschen Ubersetzer: Untersuchungen zu den Problemen der Shakespeare-Ubertragung. Munchen: Wilhelm Fink, 1970.

1584. Borgmeier, Raimund. "'This powerful rhyme'--An Analysis of the Importance of Rhyme in the German Translation of Shakespeare's Sonnets." Shakespeare Translation, 2 (1975), 101-15.

1585. Borgmeier, Raimund. "Shakespeare." *Sonett mit Beitragen von Raimund Borgmeier und Heinz Willi Wittschier*. Ed. Hans-Jurgen Schlutter. Stuttgart: J.B. Metzler, 1979, pp. 63-73.

Except for the Borgmeier essay, the book deals with the sonnet's continental appearances.

1586. Bose, Kalidas. "The New Problem of the Shakespeare Sonnets." *Essays on Shakespeare*. Ed. Bhabatosh Chatterjee. Bombay: Orient Longmans, 1965, pp. 128-44.

A review of most of the important critical views from the 19th-century on.

1587. Boston, Richard. "Mr. W.H." *TLS*, June 17, 1965, p. 519.

A spoof of L.M. Turner's earlier letter. Boston finds, in a half-dozen places, anagrams of the name of Harold Wilson (Labor Prime Minister of the mid-1960's).

1588. Bowen, Gwynneth. "Oxford's Letter to Bedingfield and 'Shakespeares Sonnets'." *Shakespearean Authorship Review*, No. 17 (1967), 6-12.

Ideas in Oxford's 1571 letter are echoed in a number of the sonnets adding evidence to Oxford's claim as the author of Shakespeare's work.

1589. Bowen, Gwynneth. "The Mysterious Mr. W.H." *Shakespearean Authorship Review*, No. 21 (1969), 1-4.

Is inclined toward B.R. Ward's hypothesis that Mr. W.H. is William Hall of Hackney.
3163

1590. B[owen], G[wynneth] M. "Oxfordian Views on the Sonnets." *Shakespearean Authorship Review*, No. 21 (1969), 16-18.

A report of a March 20, 1969, lecture in which Ruth Wainewright surveyed the scholarship from J.T. Looney onward.

1591. Bowman, William. "A Poem Turned in Process." *ELH*, 43 (1976), 444-60.

On Sonnet 104 *et al*.

1592. Boyette, Purvis E. "Shakespeare's Sonnets: Homosexuality and the Critics." *Tulane Studies in English*, 21 (1974), 35-46.

1593. Bradbrook, Muriel C. *Shakespeare and Elizabethan Poetry*. London: Chatto and Windus, 1951. New York: Oxford University Press, 1952.

In her chapter on "The Fashioning of a Courtier" Bradbrook discusses the Sonnets (pp. 141-46), *Two Gentlemen of Verona* and *Midsummer Night's Dream*. The image of the "interchange of hearts" is an important and innovative conceit in Shakespeare's hands. The chapter contains several references to Sidney's Astrophel and Stella.

1594. Bradbrook, M.C. "A New Reading of Sonnets 85 and 86." Filoski Pregled, 2 (1964), 155-57.

Doubts Rowse's reading of these two Sonnets, on which he based his conclusion that Marlowe had been the Rival Poet and that the date of the poems had corresponded with Marlowe's death in 1593.

1595. Bradbrook, M.C. Shakespeare: The Poet in His World. London: Weidenfeld and Nicolson, 1978.

A somewhat biographical treatment of the Sonnets (pp. 78-85 et passim).

1596. Bradby, Godfrey Fox. Short Studies in Shakespeare. London: J. Murray; New York: Macmillan, 1929. rpt. New York: Haskell House, 1977.

First essay (pp. 1-26) is on the Sonnets.

1597. Braddy, Haldeen. "Shakespeare's Sonnet Plan and the Effect of Folk Belief." Midwest Folklore, 12 (1962), 235-40.

The author observes that over 20 "varieties of love comprise the structural plan of the sonnets." He gives special attention to one of these varieties, the love of the white man for the black woman.

1598. Bradford, Alan T. "Mirrors of Mutability: Winter Landscapes in Tudor Poetry." English Literary Renaissance, 4 (1974), 3-39.

Discusses Sonnet 73 relative to the imagery of winter.

1599. Bradford, Alan Taylor. "A Note on Sonnet 73, Line 12." Shakespeare Quarterly, 26 (1975), 48-49.

Orthodox interpretation tends to read "Consumed with that which it was nourished by," as if it were "Consumed by." The author takes an opposing view.

1600. Bradley, A.C. "Shakespeare the Man." Oxford Lectures on Poetry. London: Macmillan, 1909. New York: St. Martin's Press, 1965, pp. 311-57.

His comments about the Sonnets are woven throughout the lecture.

1601. Brae, A.E. "Shakespeare's Sonnets CXVI." Lippincott's, 19 (1877), 761.

Argues for an emendation--"width's" for "worth's" in line 8 of Sonnet 116.

1602. Brainerd, Barron. "Graphs, Topology and Text." Poetics, 6 (1977), 1-14.

Using Sonnet 57 as an example, the author employs mathematical models to define the concept of textual coherence.

1603. Brandes, Georg. William Shakespeare: A Critical Study. Tr. from Danish by William Archer, Diana White, and Mary Morison. New York: Macmillan, 1898. 1935.

Book 2 (pp. 265-301) is on the sonnets.

1604. Brandl, A. Review of The Sonnets of Shakespeare, ed. H.C. Beeching. Shakespeare Jahrbuch, 42 (1906), 292.

1605. B[randl], A. Review of A. Baltzer, Die schonsten Sonette von W. Shakespeare. Archiv fur das Studium der neueren Sprachen und Literaturen, 124 (1910), 217.

1606. Brandl, Alois, and Ludwig Fulda. Shakespeares Sonette. Stuttgart und Berlin: J.G. Cotta, 1913.

1607. Branscomb, Ernest Jackson. "Attitudes Toward Time In Spenser, Shakespeare's Sonnets, and Donne." Ph.D. Dissertation, North Carolina, 1972. DAI, 34 (1973), 306A.

1608. Bray Sir Denys. The Original Order of Shakespeare's Sonnets. London: Methuen, 1925.

Contains an extensive introductory essay explaining his rearrangement of the sonnets. The first sonnet of his rearranged text is Sonnet 20, the "master-mistress" sonnet, and the last is Sonnet 146, "Poor Soul, the center of my sinful earth."

1609. Bray, Sir Denys. "The Art-form of the Elizabethan Sonnet Sequence and Shakespeare's Sonnets." Shakespeare Jahrbuch, 63 (1927), 159-82.

1610. Bray, Denys. Shakespeare's Sonnet Sequence. London: M. Secker, 1938.

A rewritten and enlarged edition of The Original Order of Shakespeare's Sonnets (1925).

1611. Bray, Denys. "Sonnet CXLIX." TLS, July 4, 1942, p. 331.

Suggests that "I love thee not" should be in quotation marks as if from the woman's mouth.

1612. Bray, Sir Denys. "Difficult Passages in the Sonnets Re-examined." Notes and Queries, 190 (1946), 200-02; 191 (1946), 92-95.

1613. Breuer, Hans-Peter. "A Reconsideration of Samuel Butler's Shakespeare's Sonnets Reconsidered." Dalhousie Review, 57 (1977), 507-24.

1614. Brewer, Leighton. Shakespeare and the Dark Lady. Boston: Christopher, 1966.

In his chapter on "The Sonnets" (pp. 13-29) Brewer finds similarities between the dark lady sonnets and Hamlet and Troilus and Cressida suggesting that they were all written between 1599-1601.

1615. Bridgeman, C.G.O. "The Fitton Portraits at Arbury." Academy, 41 (January 9, 1892), 40.

Suggests that Tyler's observations of the Arbury portraits were biased in favor of his theory.
3117

1616. Bridges, Horace James. Our Fellow Shakespeare. Chicago: A.C. McClurg, 1916. Chicago: Pascal Covici, 1925.

Final chapter (pp. 270-88) on "The Sonnets."

1617. Brien, Alan. "Afterthought." Spectator, April 17, 1964, pp. 529-30.

Some comments on Hotson's Mr. W.H. and on several sexual puns (spirit and will).

1618. Bright, James W. "Two Notelets on Shakespeare." Modern Language Notes, 14 (1899), 186-87.

The second of the two notes is a reading of "Sonnet i, 13-14."

1619. Brockbank, Philip. "Sonnet 146." TLS, October 7, 1977, p. 1150.

Suggests "Braved by" as an emendation for the beginning of line 2.

1620. Brockbank, Philip. "The Semantics of the Sonnet." TLS, June 23, 1978, pp. 686-87.

Review of Shakespeare's Sonnets, ed. Stephen Booth.

1621. Brockbank, Philip. "The Sonnets." TLS, July 7, 1978, p. 777.

Corrects his earlier review of Booth's edition of the Sonnets, in which he wrote "uvula" but meant "vulva."
1620

1622. *Broido, Ephrayim. "On Translating the Sonnets in Hebrew." Moznayim (Tel Aviv), 46, iv (1978), 298-303.

Responds to Zemorah's review of his work in a previous number. 3246

1623. Brooks, Alden. Will Shakspere, Factotum and Agent. New York: Round Table Press, 1937.

An attempt to uncover information about Shakespeare's life. Deals with the sonnets in his final chapter (pp. 294-354) ascribing authorship of the sonnets to various hands.

1624. Brophy, James. "Shakespeare's 'Saucy Jacks'." English Language Notes, 1 (1963), 11-13.

An explanation of Shakespeare's use of the word "jacks" in Sonnet 128.

1625. Brown, Charles Armitage. Shakespeare's Autobiographical Poems: Being his Sonnets Clearly Developed With His Character Drawn Chiefly From His Works. London: James Bohn, 1838. rpt. New York: AMS Press, 1972.

In his discussion of the Sonnets Brown divides the sequence into six groups.

1626. Brown, Henry. The Sonnets of Shakespeare Solved, and the Mystery of his Friendship, Love, and Rivalry Revealed: Illustrated by Numerous Extracts from the Poet's Works, Contemporary Writers, and Other Authors. London: John Russell Smith, 1870. rpt. New York: AMS Press, 1970.

A poem by poem reading in which he treats the sonnets as a kind of poetic diary. The "friend" is William Herbert whom he allegorically marries to his Muse.

1627. Brown, Henry. Shakespeare's Patrons and Other Essays. London: J.M. Dent, 1912.

Includes "The Singing of the Sonnets" (pp. 107-11), which discusses those sonnets which appeared as songs in Shakespeare's plays; "Love Confessions of Shakespeare" (pp. 115-24), which considers the identity of the Dark Lady and W.H.; and "Shakespeare's Choice" (pp. 127-44) which uses the sonnets as evidence for Shakespeare's preference in women.

1628. Brown, Ivor. Shakespeare. Garden City, N.Y.: Doubleday, 1949.

Has some lengthy passages on the dark lady (pp. 166-99) and W.H. (pp. 154-61). His "own guess" as to the identity of the latter is William Harvey, Southampton's stepfather.

1629. Brown, Ivor. Dark Ladies. London: Collins, 1957.

In his chapter, "Shakespeare's Dark Lady" (pp. 253-309), Brown explores the various theories about this "sister" of Helen of Troy, Sappho of Lesbos and Cleopatra.

1630. Brown, I. "Problem Children." _Drama_, 107 (1972), 72-73.

Includes a review of R.J.C. Wait, _The Background to Shakespeare's Sonnets_.

1631. Brown, Joseph. "The Begetter of the Sonnets." _Baconiana_, 3rd Series, 3 (1905), 68.

Bacon (Shakespeare) may have been referring to Cavendish as the fair youth.

1632. Brown, W.B. "The Text of Shakespeare's Sonnets CXXV. and CXXVI. _Notes and Queries_, 11th Series, 6 (1912), 446-47; 7 (1913), 76, 236.

a) These two poems refer to _Venus and Adonis_ (ll. 649-60) and speak of jealousy; b) answers C.C.B. and Tom Jones.
1488

1633. Brown, W.B. "'Buds of Marjoram'." _Notes and Queries_, 11th Series, 8 (1913), 169.

Reference to marjoram in Sonnet 99 may suggest that his friend had dark hair. For additional comments on the subject, see C.C.B. and A.R. Bayley.
1490

1634. Brown, W.B. "The W.H. of Shakespeare's Sonnets." _Notes and Queries_, 11th Series, 7 (1913), 241-43; 262-63.

An examination of the text of the poems in support of the Will Hews theory.

1635. Browne, C. Elliot. "Shakespeare's Sonnets: an old Theory." _Athenaeum_, Aug. 30, 1873, p. 277.

Some speculation about the identity of "A man in hew all Hewes in his controlling" (Sonnet 20).

1636. Browne, C. Elliot. "A Shakespearean Discovery." _Athenaeum_, November 1, 1873, p. 563.

Disagrees with Edmonds's revelation about W.H.
1865

1637. Browne, C. Elliot. "The Play upon 'You' and 'Hews' in the Sonnets, and Its Relation to the Herberts." _Notes and Queries_, 6th Series, 1 (1880), 210.

William Herbert was also Lord Fitzhugh--hence the punning on the word "hews" could easily refer to him.

1638. Browne, Junius Henri. "Shakespeare's Sonnets in a New Light." _Manhattan_, 3 (1884), 145-55.

Argues for Southampton as the friend and an early date for authorship. Has brief comments about most of the sonnets.

1639. Brownlow, E.B. "Sonnet CXXVI." *Notes and Queries*, 8th Series, 3 (1893), 102.

On the reading of line 2--"Dost hold time's fickle glass, his sickle hour."
1484

1640. Brugaletta, John J. "Sonnet CXXX Revisited." *Scholia Satyrica*, 4, ii-iii (1978), 34.

A sonnet parodying Shakespeare's Sonnet 130.

1641. Bryant, E.P. Review of Philip Martin, *Shakespeare's Sonnets: Self, Love and Art*. *Unisa English Studies* 11, ii (1973), 58.

1642. Buchloh, Paul G. "Shakespeares Sonnet XXX in deutschen Ubertragungen." *Literatur in Wissenschaft und Unterricht*, 1 (1968), 274-81.

Examines three translations--those of Stefan George, Otto Gildemeister, and Karl Kraus.

1643. Bucke, Richard Maurice. *Cosmic Consciousness*. New York: Dutton, 1923.

Part IV, chapter 9 (pp. 153-80) expounds his theory that Bacon wrote the plays and sonnets.

1644. Budd, Thomas D. *Shakespeare's Sonnets, with Commentaries*. Philadelphia: John Campbell, 1868.

In the two brief papers preceding the sonnets, the author argues that the poems refer not to a contemporary (Southampton, e.g.) but to mankind in general.

1645. Bullough, G. Review of Edward Hubler, *The Sense of Shakespeare's Sonnets*. *Modern Language Notes*, 69 (1954), 514-16.

1646. Bullough, Geoffrey. Review of J.B. Leishman, *Themes and Variations in Shakespeare's Sonnets*. *Review of English Studies*, NS 14 (1963), 194-95.

1647. Bunselmeyer, J. "Appearances and Verbal Paradox: Sonnets 129 and 138." *Shakespeare Quarterly*, 25 (1974), 103-08.

1648. Burckhardt, Sigurd. "The Poet as Fool and Priest." *ELH*, 23 (1956), 279-98. Reprinted in *Shakespearean Meanings*. Princeton, N.J.: Princeton University Press, 1968, pp. 22-46.

A discussion of poetic devices which touches briefly on Shakespeare's Sonnets 94 and 138 and at greater length on Sonnet 116.

1649. Burgersdijk, L.A.J. "Zu Sonett 121." _Shakespeare Jahrbuch_, 14 (1879), 363-64.

1650. [Burr, William Henry]. Antiquary. _The Sonnets of Shakespeare. When, to Whom, and by Whom, Written_. New York: np, 1883.

Bacon wrote the Sonnets in 1590 and addressed them to Essex.

1651. Burr, W[illia]m Henry. _Bacon and Shakspere. Proof that William Shakspere Could Not Write. The Sonnets Written by Francis Bacon to the Earl of Essex and his Bride, A.D. 1590. Bacon Identified as the Concealed Poet Ignoto, A.D. 1589-1600._ Washington and New York: Brentano Bros., 1886.

This pamphlet is made up of the three essays mentioned in the title.

1652. *Burr, William Henry. "Bacon the Author of the Sonnets." _Baconiana_, NS 1 (November, 1893), 139 ff.

1653. Butler, James D. "World Without End." _Notes and Queries_, 9th Series, 11 (1903), 448-49.

Discusses the religious implications of Shakespeare's use of this phrase in Sonnet 57.

1654. Butler, Samuel. "Shakspeare's Sonnets." _Athenaeum_, July 30, 1898, p. 161.

Indicates why he believes the dates of Sonnets 2, 104, and 107 fall between 1585 and 1588.

1655. Butler, Samuel. "Shakespeare's Sonnets and the Ireland Forgeries." _Athenaeum_, December 24, 1898, pp. 907-08.

Rejects the notion that Mr. W.H. was only the "procurer" of and not the inspiration for the Sonnets.

1656. Butler, Samuel. "The 'Only Begetter' of Shakspeare's Sonnets." _Athenaeum_, January 21, 1899, p. 92.

Response to Alfred Ainger on the meaning of "begetter."
1440

1657. Butler, Samuel. _Shakespeare's Sonnets Reconsidered, and in part rearranged with introductory chapters, notes, and a reprint of the original 1609 edition_. London: Jonathan Cape, 1899. Reprinted as _Shakespeare's Sonnets_. London: Jonathan Cape; New York: E.P. Dutton, 1925. The Shrewsbury Edition of _The Works of Samuel Butler_. Ed. Henry Festing Jones and A.T. Bartholomew, vol. 14.

1658. Buxton, John. Review of Claes Schaar, _An Elizabethan Sonnet Problem_. _Studia Neophilologica_, 33 (1961), 337-40.

1659. Buxton, John. "Shakespeare's Sonnets." TLS, January 2, 1964, p. 9.

Notes that Thomas Thorpe's dedication contains an example of polyptoton--a favorite figure in Shakespeare's Sonnets.

1660. Buyal's'ky, Boleslav. "Tayemnytsya Shekspirovykh sonetiv." Vil'yam Shekspir: Sonety, Tr. Dmytro Palamarchuk. Kiev: Dnipro, 1966, pp. 5-28.

An introduction to Palamarchuk's Russian translation of the Sonnets.

1661. Byars, William Vincent. "The Dark Lady." Reedy's Mirror, 22, v (March 28, 1913), 4-6.

Attempts to explain how the conditions of Elizabethan life resulted in the complexity of Shakespeare's language and the genius of his Sonnets.

1662. Byvanck, W.G.C. "Reading Shakespeare's Sonnets." A Book of Homage to Shakespeare to Commemorate the Three Hundredth Anniversary of Shakespeare's Death MCMXVI. Ed. Israel Gollancz. London: Humphrey Milford, 1916, pp. 468-72.

Discovers a different sonnet form in those "sonnets" that are found in the plays--leading him to suggest that Shakespeare added "superabundant lines"--i.e. changing two quatrain sonnets to three.

1663. Cabaniss, Allen. "Shakespeare and the Holy Rosary." University of Mississippi Studies in English, 1 (1960), 118-28.

Notes a similarity between the structure of the Sonnets and the Holy Rosary and concludes they were a parody of the Rosary.

1664. Cadain, F. Review of Germaine Lafeuille, William Shakespeare: Essai d'une Traduction en vers francais. Bibliotheque d'Humanisme et Renaissance (Geneve), 39 (1977), 212-13.

1665. Cain, Tom. Review of S.C. Campbell, Only Begotten Sonnets: A Reconstruction of Shakespeare's Sonnet Sequence. British Book News, July, 1979, p. 602.

1666. Caldwell, George S. Is Sir Walter Raleigh the Author of Shakespere's Plays and Sonnets? Melbourne: Stillwell and Knight, 1877.

1667. Caldwell, James R. "States of Mind: States of Consciousness." Essays in Criticism, 4 (1954), 168-79.

Uses Sonnet 64 to develop his ideas about the kinds of mental experience involved in poetry.

1668. Calvert, George Henry. Shakespeare: A Biographic Aesthetic Study. Boston: Lee and Shepard; New York: Charles T. Dillingham, 1879.

Part of Chapter 2, "Ripeness," contains a discussion of the Sonnets as a biographical statement (pp. 69-84).

1669. Campbell, Oscar James. "A Review of Recent Shakespeare Scholarship." Shakespeare Quarterly, 2 (1951), 103-10.

Includes a review of Hotson's Shakespeare's Sonnets Dated and Other Essays (pp. 104-05) in which he takes sharp exception to Hotson's early dating of the poems.

1670. Campbell, S.C. "Only Begotten Sonnets." TLS, September 4, 1970, p. 976.

Suggests some changes in the order of the Sonnets.

1671. Campbell, S.C. Only Begotten Sonnets: a Reconstruction of Shakespeare's Sonnet Sequence, Which integrates the Dark Lady sonnets into an earlier position in the sequence and discerns a single tenor throughout and a single addressee. London: Bell and Hyman, 1978.

1672. C[ampbell], T[homas]. "The Sonnets of Shakespeare." New Monthly Magazine (London), 2nd Series, 26 (1829), 577-83.

Campbell has little use for A.W. Schlegel's notion that the Sonnets are a "mine" of biographical information.

1673. *Caraion, Ion. "Doamna bruna din Sonete." Luceafarul (Bucharest), February 10, 1979, p.6

On the dark lady.

1674. Carey, John. "Detective Story." Spectator, April 24, 1964, p. 555.

Review of J. Dover Wilson, 1) Shakespeare's Sonnets: An Introduction for the Use of Historians and Others, 2) Shakespeare's Sonnets, ed. A.L. Rowse, 3) Leslie Hotson, Mr. W. H.

1675. Cargill, Alexander. Shakespeare the Player. London: Constable, 1916.

Contains a chapter, "The Sonnets and What They Reveal" (pp. 101-18).

1676. Carlisle, Carol. "Shakespeare's Sonnet 127." Explicator, 38, i (1979), 33-35.

1677. Carpenter, B. Frank. "Shakespeare's Sonnets: To Whom Dedicated?" Catholic World, 106 (1918), 496-507.

Agrees with Appleton Morgan's original thesis (before his apostasy) that the dedication to Mr. W.H. was not Shakespeare's but Thomas Thorpe's dedication to a personal friend.
2506

1678. Carter, Albert Howard. "The Punctuation of Shakespeare's Sonnets of 1609." Joseph Quincy Adams Memorial Studies. Ed. J.G. McManaway, et al. Washington, D.C.: Folger Shakespeare Library, 1948, pp. 409-428.

1679. *Carter, Albert Howard. "The Punctuation of Shakespeare's Sonnets of 1609." Gaya College Journal, 2 (1961), 10-16.

1680. Carter, Thomas. Shakespeare and Holy Scripture, with the Version He Used. New York: Dutton, 1905. rpt. New York: AMS Press, 1970.

Indicates probable biblical influences in the Sonnets (pp. 221-24).

1681. Castrop, Helmut. "Die nicht-dramatischen Dichtungen." Shakespeare-Handbuch: Die Zeit, Der Mensch, Das Werk, Die Nachwelt. Ed. Ina Schabert. Stuttgart: Alfred Kroner, 1972, pp. 589-624.

Most of this section (pp. 589-616) deals with the Sonnets.

1682. Causton, H.K. Staple. An Essay on Mr. Singer's "Wormwood," Embracing a Restoration of the Author's Reply, Mutilated in "Notes and Queries," No. 72; with a Note on the Monk of Bury; and a Reading of Shakspere's Sonnet, CXI. "Supplementary to All the Commentators." London: Henry Kent Causton, [185-].
1435

1683. Cellini, Benvenuto. Vita e Arte nei Sonetti di Shakespeare: Col testo dei Sonetti riordinati e commentati. Rome: Tumminelli, 1943.

Cellini regroups both the dark lady sonnets and the fair youth sonnets by themes: e.g. promise of immortality, marriage, jealousy, etc.

1684. Cellini, Benvenuto. "Significato e valore dei sonetti di Shakespeare." Nuova Antologia, 94 (June, 1959), 223-32.

Reviews many of the earlier authorities and their theories, but finally concludes that Shakespeare's value lies in the universality of his sentiments and his ability to reveal the human heart.

1685. Chakravorty, Jagannath. "Shakespeare's 'Civil War' Sonnets in Bengali Translation." Jadavpur Journal of Comparative Literature (Calcutta), 6 (1966), 86-106.

On the difficulties of translating Sonnets 33, 34, 35 into Bengali.

1686. Chamaillard, Pierre. Review of Edward Hubler, The Sense of Shakespeare's Sonnets. Etudes Anglaises, 5 (1952), 243-44.

1687. Chambers, E.K. "Shakespeare's Sonnets." Academy, 52 (July 31, 1897), 98; (August 14, 1897), 138-39.

Chambers rejects Pembroke as W.H. and Mary Fitton as the dark lady.
3121

1688. Chambers, E.K. "The Sonnets." William Shakespeare, a Study of Facts and Problems. Oxford: Oxford University Press, 1930, vol. 1, pp. 555-76.

Examines the various theories regarding the friend, the dark lady, etc.

1689. Chambers, E.K. "The 'Mortal Moon' Sonnet." TLS, January 25, 1934, p. 60.

In response to remarks by G.B. Harrison made some years earlier (TLS, November 29, 1928).
2082

1690. Chambers, E.K. Shakespearean Gleanings. London: Oxford University Press, 1944.

Contains three essays on the sonnets: "The Order of the Sonnets," "The 'Youth' of the Sonnets," and "The 'Mortal Moon' Sonnet."

1691. Chambers, Sir Edmund K. "The 'Youth' of Shakespeare's Sonnets." Review of English Studies, 21 (1945), 331.

In this answer to Leishman's review of Shakespearean Gleanings, Chambers considers whether line 7 of Sonnet 20 ("A man in hew all Hews in his controwling,") refers to the mysterious William Hughes, another candidate for Mr. W.H.

1692. C[hambers], E.K. "Shakespeare: The Poems." Encyclopaedia Britannica. Chicago: William Benton, 1970, vol. 20, pp. 328-31.

1693. Chambrun, Clara Longworth de. "The Inspirers of Shakespeare's Sonnets." North American Review, 198 (1913), 131-34.

Discussion of some of the candidates for Mr. W.H.

1694. Chambrun, Countess de. The Sonnets of William Shakespeare: New Light and Old Evidence. New York and London: G.P. Putnam's Sons, 1913.

Argues for Southampton as Mr. W.H., provides a rearrangement of the sonnets and addresses the other problems in the course of her book.

1695. Chambrun, Clara Longworth de. Two Loves I Have, The Romance of William Shakespeare. Philadelphia and London: J.B. Lippincott, 1934.

This fictionalized narrative biography contains a chapter on "'Sugred Sonnets'" (pp. 152-64) and "The Dark Lady of Shakespeare's Sonnets" (pp. 206-09) whom she identifies as Nan Davenant.

1696. Chambrun, Clara Longworth de. "Who Mr. W.H. Really Was." Essential Documents Never Yet Presented in the Shakespeare Case. Bordeaux: Delmas, 1934. rpt. Folcroft, Pa.: Folcroft Library Editions, 1972, pp. 33-46.

Finds evidence that W.H. was William Hervey, third husband of Lady Southampton.

1697. Chambrun, Clara Longworth de. Shakespeare Rediscovered by Means of Public Records, Secret Reports and Private Correspondence Newly Set Forth as Evidence on His Life and Work. New York and London: Scribner's Sons, 1938.

In her chapter on "The Sonnet Sequence" (pp. 133-63) Chambrun has some things to say about the sonnet order. When read correctly the sonnets will "reveal a sentimental monodrama, composed between Shakespeare's thirtieth and forty-third years." In another chapter (pp. 164-87), she identifies Mr. W.H. as William Hervey.

1698. Chambrun, C. Longworth. "Dr. Hotson's Arguments." TLS, March 31, 1950, p. 201.

Chambrun, disagreeing that Sonnet 107 is about the defeat of the Spanish Armada, puts the date at 1603.

1699. Chambrun, Countess Clara Longworth de. An Explanatory Introduction to Thorpe's Edition of Shakespeare's Sonnets, 1609, with Text Transcription. Aldington, Kent: Hand and Flower Press, 1950.

1700. Chambrun, Longworth. "The Rival Poet." TLS, February 2, 1951, p. 69.

Marlowe is "the better spirit" referred to in several sonnets.

1701. Chambrun, Longworth. "Une Critique de la Critique: Mr. Leslie Hotson et la Date des 'Sonnets' de Shakespeare." Etudes Anglaises, 5 (1952), 44-49.

Disagrees with Hotson on the early date of the Sonnets and on the identity of Mr. W.H.
2158

1702. Chapman, J.A. "Marching Song." Essays and Studies by Members of the English Association, 28 (1942), 13-21.

Shakespeare's Sonnets are without peer as "marching song"--poetry that is committed to memory and "read" while tramping country roads.

1703. Chapman, John Jay. A Glance toward Shakespeare. Boston: Atlantic Monthly Press, 1922.

Chapter 13, "The Sonnets" (pp. 90-107).

1704. Charlton, William. "Living and Dead Metaphors." British Journal of Aesthetics, 15 (1975), 172-78.

His argument is illustrated with references to several metaphors from Shakespeare's Sonnets.

1705. Charney, Maurice. Review of Stephen Booth, An Essay on Shakespeare's Sonnets. Journal of English and Germanic Philology, 70 (1971), 296-97.

1706. Chasles, Philarete. "Hints for the Elucidation of Shakespeare's Sonnets." Athenaeum, January 25, 1862, pp. 116-17.

Subscribes to William Herbert as Mr. W.H., a position that he abandons in later statements.

1707. Chasles, Philarete. "Shakespeare's Sonnets." Athenaeum, February 16, 1867, pp. 223-24; March 9, 1867, p. 323; April 13, 1867, pp. 486-87; May 18, 1867, pp. 662-63.

1) Identifies the various actors in the dedication: the "onlie begetter" is Southampton but Southampton is not W.H. 2) Disagrees with Samuel Neil on the identity of W.H. 3) Expresses disagreement with Gerald Massey. 4) Some concluding remarks on the word "begetter."

2451, 2452, 2548, 2549

1708. Chatman, Seymour. "Paraphrase." An Introduction to the Language of Poetry. Boston: Houghton Mifflin, 1968, pp. 38-44.

Chatman illustrates the use of paraphrase in a reading of Sonnet 1.

1709. Chiarini, G. "Il Matrimonio e gli Amori di Guglielmo Shakespeare." Nuova Antologia, 110 (1890), 5-33, 438-62; 111 (1890), 112-39.

A three-part review of Thomas Tyler's edition of the Sonnets, Angelo Olivieri's translation of I Sonetti di William Shakespeare, and James Walter, Shakespeare's True Life.

1710. *Chkhenkeli, T. "Shakespeare's Sonnets in Georgian." Literaturnaya Gruzia (Tbilisi), 6 (1978), 149-51.

On Rezo Tabukashvili's translation of one hundred sonnets. Sonnet 45 is given special attention. In Russian.

1711. Chute, Marchette. Shakespeare of London. New York: E.P. Dutton, 1949.

Appendix 1 (pp. 339-44) deals with the sonnets.

1712. *Ciummo, Candido. "Dualismo e funzionalita nei Sonnets di William Shakespeare." Cenobio (Lugano), 14 (1965), 254-60.

1713. Ciummo, Candido. Dualismo e funzionalita nei "Sonnets" di William Shakespeare. Lugano, Switzerland: Cenobio, 1966.

1714. Clark, Cumberland. Shakespeare and Psychology. London: Williams and Norgate, 1936. rpt. Folcroft, Pa.: Folcroft Library Editions, 1976.

Chapter 16, "Psychology of the Sonnets" (pp. 140-47)

1715. Clark, William Ross. "Poems for Study: Sonnet CXVI." Clearing House, 34 (1960), 316.

An elementary reading of the poem for young readers.

1716. Clarke, Robert F. "An Emendation of Sonnet 146." Shakespeare Newsletter, 8 (1958), 11.

Suggests "Rob'd by" as an emendation for line 2. The pun on "robbed" and "robed" is pivotal.

1717. Clarkson, Paul Stephen. "Mr. W. H.?" Saturday Review of Literature, 12 (May 4, 1935), 13.

Suggests a new candidate as Mr. W.H.--William Hughes of Gray's Inn, a legal scholar.

1718. Clarkson, Paul S., and Clyde T. Warren. "Pleading and Practice in Shakespeare's Sonnet XLVI." Modern Language Notes, 62 (1947), 102-10.

On Shakespeare's use of legal terms.

1719. Cliff's Notes Editors. Shakespeare's Sonnets Notes. Lincoln, Nebraska: Cliff's Notes, 1970.

1720. Clutton-Brock, Arthur. "Shakespeare's Sonnets." Essays on Books. London: Methuen, 1920, pp. 15-26.

1721. Coleridge, Samuel Taylor. Miscellaneous Criticism. Ed. T.M. Raysor. Cambridge, Mass.: Harvard University Press, 1930. London: Constable, 1936.

Contains a harsh indictment of Shakespeare's sonnets by Wordsworth and a defense by Coleridge (pp. 454-55).

1722. Colie, Rosalie L. Shakespeare's Living Art. Princeton, N.J.: Princeton University Press, 1974.

In her first chapter, "Criticism and the Analysis of Craft: Love's Labour's Lost and the Sonnets," Colie suggests that the Sonnets dramatize literary criticism (pp. 50-67); the second chapter, "Mel and Sal: Some Problems in Sonnet-Theory" (pp. 68-134) focuses on the couplets, the relationship between the sonnet and the epigram, and the connection between the Friend and the Mistress.

1723. Collier, J. Payne. "The Passionate Pilgrim and Shakespeare's Sonnets." Notes and Queries, 201 (1957), 468-69.

The sonnet beginning "If music and sweet poetry agree" appeared both in The Passionate Pilgrim and in Richard Barnfield's The Encomium of Lady Pecunia (1598); Collier believes the poem to be Shakespeare's.

1724. Collins, John Churton. "Shakespeare's Sonnets." Saturday Review (London), 85 (1898), 285.

1725. Collins, John Churton. "Shakespeare's Sonnets." Ephemera Critica: or Plain Truths About Current Literature. Westminster: Archibald Constable; New York: E.P. Dutton, 1901, pp. 219-35.

A review of the recent work, much of which he regards as "preposterous." Collins himself believes the Sonnets to be conventional pieces after the fashion of the time.

1726. Colvin, Ian. "'Shakespeare Unlocked His Heart'." Atlantic Monthly, 144 (1929), 56-62.

Discusses Sir Denys Bray's theory about the order of Shakespeare's sonnets based upon rhyme links between the Sonnets. Colvin refers to other Elizabethan sonneteers who presumably used this device.

1727. *Combecher, Hans. "Drei Sonette--drei Epochen. Eine vergleichende Interpretation." Neueren Sprachen, No. 4 (1959), 178-89.

On Shakespeare's Sonnet 29 and sonnets by Milton and Wordsworth.

1728. Combecher, Hans. "Shakespeares Sonett CXVI: Eine Interpretation." Neueren Sprachen, 1961, pp. 519-24.

1729. Combellack, C.R.B. "Shakespeare's Sonnet XXXIV, 13-14." Explicator, 29 (1970), Item 30.

1730. Combellack, C.R.B. "Shakespeare's Sonnet CXXXVIII'." Explicator, 30 (1971), Item 33.

1731. Combellack, C.R.B. "Shakespeare's Sonnet 137.6." Explicator, 37, i (1978), 34-35.

1732. Combellack, C.R.B. "Shakespeare's 'Sonnet 125'." Explicator, 37, ii (1979), 25-26.

1733. Conrad, Hermann. "Shakspere und die Essex-Familie." Preussiche Jahrbucher, 79 (1895), 183-229.

Possibility of Essex as the friend is explored in the first half of the article.

1734. Conrad, Hermann. "Der Freund der Shaksperesche Sonette. Preussiche Jahrbucher, 177 (1919), 220-32.

1735. Conway, Eustace. The Supernatural in Shakespeare. Yellow Springs, Ohio: Antioch Press, 1932, pp. 27-35.

The last few pages of this brief monograph have nothing to do with the supernatural but offer speculations of one kind or another about the Sonnets.

1736. Cook, I.R.W. "William Hervey and Shakespeare's Sonnets." Shakespeare Survey, 21 (1968), 97-106.

Another candidate for Mr. W.H.

1737. Corney, Bolton. "M. Philarete Chasles." Notes and Queries, 3rd Series, 1 (1862), 87-88.

Discusses the dedication to the 1609 Quarto (by whom, to whom, etc.)

1738. Corney, Bolton. "The Sonnets of Shakspere." Notes and Queries, 3rd Series, 1 (1862), 162-64.

Gives an editorial history of the sonnets and answers some questions about them: date, the "begetter," autobiographical content.

1739. Corney, Bolton. The Sonnets of William Shakspere: A Critical Disquisition Suggested by a Recent Discovery. London: F. Shoberl, 1862.

Some of his conclusions are that the Sonnets were written soon after 1594, that they were written in fulfillment of a promise to Southampton, that the Sonnets are mere poetical exercises.

1740. Corney, Bolton. "A Writer in Notes and Queries." Notes and Queries, 3rd Series, 8 (1865), 482.

A reply to Hazlitt's note of the preceding number on Thomas Thorpe and the 1609 Quarto.
2101

1741. Cowart, David. "Ramifications of Metaphor in Shakespeare's Sonnet 151." Massachusetts Studies in English, 5, ii (1975), 1-9.

1742. Cowling, G.H. A Preface to Shakespeare. London: Methuen, 1925.

Contains a portion of a chapter on the sonnets (pp. 76-82).

1743. Craig, Edward Gordon. "The Sonnets of Shakespeare." Books and Theatres. London and Toronto: J.M. Dent, 1925, pp. 151-58.

A fanciful account of how Shakespeare came to write his sonnets.

1744. Craig, Hardin. "A Woman Colour'd Ill." Shakespeare Newsletter, 15 (1965), 24.

Proposes Elizabeth Vernon, who became Southampton's wife in 1598, as the Dark Lady.

1745. Crane, Milton. Review of Stephen Booth, An Essay on Shakespeare's Sonnets. Modern Philology, 68 (1971), 383-84.

1746. [Creighton, C.]. "Shakespeare and the Earl of Pembroke." Blackwood's Edinburgh Magazine, 169 (1901), 668-83, 829-45.

In Part I, subtitled "The Key to the Sonnets Enigma," he defends the 1609 Quarto as having been authorized by Shakespeare and proceeds to answer a number of the popularly debated questions. In Part II, "Mistress Fitton," he considers the connection between Mary Fitton and the dark lady.

1747. Creighton, C. "Shakespeare's Sonnets: A Reading." TLS, January 23, 1919, p. 46.

Supports reading "Reserve" in Sonnet 85, 1. 3.

1748. Crosby, Joseph. "The 'Crux' in Sonnet 126." Literary World (Boston), 14 (1883), 64.

Suggests "his fickle hour" as a reading for line 2.

1749. Cruttwell, Patrick. "A Reading of the Sonnets." Hudson Review, 5 (1953), 554-70.

1750. Cruttwell, Patrick. "Shakespeare's Sonnets and the 1590's." The Shakespearean Moment and its Place in the Poetry of the Seventeenth Century. New York: Random House, 1954. 1960, pp. 1-38. Reprinted in Modern Shakespearean Criticism. Ed. Alvin B. Kernan. New York: Harcourt, Brace and World, 1970, pp. 110-40. and Discussions of Shakespeare's Sonnets. Ed. Barbara Herrnstein. Boston: D.C. Heath, 1964, pp. 46-55.

1751. Cuadrado, Beatriz P. de. "Los sonetos de Shakespeare." Humanitas (Tucuman University), 13 (1965), 141-55.

Readings of Sonnets 19, 71, 73, 141, 116, 146.

1752. Culler, Jonathan. "Jakobson and the Linguistic Analysis of Literary Texts." Language and Style, 5 (1971), 53-66.

Acknowledging Jackobson's contribution to literary studies, the author points out how Jackobson has gone astray in several texts, including Sonnet 129 (pp. 62-64).
2220

1753. Cuningham, Henry. "Shakespeare's Sonnets: A Reading." TLS, January 9, 1919, p. 21.

On Sonnet 85, 1.3, in response to Richmond and Sergeaunt.
2730, 2841

1754. Cutts, John P. "Two Hitherto Unpublished Settings of Sonnets from The Passionate Pilgrime." Shakespeare Quarterly, 9 (1958), 588-94.

"Veanus, and young Adonis sitting by hir" and "Faire Citherea sitting by a Brooke" are the two sonnets found in musical settings.

1755. Cutts, John P. "Two Seventeenth-Century Versions of Shakespeare's Sonnet 116." Shakespeare Studies, 10 (1977), 9-15.

1756. Cyr, Gordon C. "The Case of the 'Alias' Earl!" Shakespeare Newsletter, 31 (1981), 20.

An argument for Oxford as author of the Sonnets.

1757. Daiches, David. "Shakespeare's Poetry." The Living Shakespeare. Ed. Robert Gittings. London: Heinemann; New York: Barnes and Noble, 1960, pp. 44-53.

Discusses Sonnet 71 (pp. 44-48).

1758. Daly, Peter M. "A Note on Sonnet 116: A Case of Emblematic Association." Shakespeare Quarterly, 28 (1977), 515-16.

Argues that Doebler's thesis on the "compass" emblem fails to take into account other senses of the word.
1810

1759. Danckelman, Eberhard von. Shakespeare in seinen Sonetten: ein Sendschreiben an Herrn Lic. Dr. Schaumkell. Leipzig: Hermann Haacke, 1897.

An evaluation of the various theories about the identity of the friend. Danckelman believes that some of the sonnets are a poetic correspondence between Shakespeare and Southampton.

1760. Dannenberg, Friedrich. "Shakespeares Sonette: Herkunft, Wesen, Deutung." Shakespeare Jahrbuch, 70 (1934), 37-64.

1761. Darby, Robert H. "The Date of Some Shakespeare Sonnets." *Shakespeare Jahrbuch*, 75 (1939) 135-38.

A number of sonnets seem to allude to eclipses and climatic changes suggesting May, 1594, as an approximate date for these poems.

1762. Darlow, Biddy. *Shakespeare's Lady of the Sonnets, with Wood Engravings by the Author*. Oxford: R.F. Haslam, 1974.

A biographical reading of the sonnets in which Elizabeth Vernon is the object of his love and Southampton, his friend, a rival for her love.

1763. Daugherty, Leo. "Sir John Davies and the Question of Topical Reference in Shakespeare's Sonnet 107." *Shakespeare Quarterly*, 30 (1979), 93-95.

1764. Davenport, A. "The Seed of a Shakespeare Sonnet?" *Notes and Queries*, 182 (1942), 242-44.

Certain images that Shakespeare uses in Sonnet 2 might have been drawn from Drayton's "The Shepheards Garland"(1593).

1765. D[avenport], A. "Shakespeare's Sonnets." *Notes and Queries*, 196 (1951), 5-6.

Compares Shakespeare's Sonnet 29 with Sidney's *Astrophel and Stella* 64 and 108. Notes also some echoes of commonplaces in Shakespeare's Sonnets from Lily's Latin grammar.

1766. Davenport, A. "Shakespeare's Sonnet 51 Again." *Notes and Queries*, 198 (1953), 15-16.

1767. Davenport, William H. Review of Edward Hubler, *The Sense of Shakespeare's Sonnets*. *Personalist*, 34 (1953), 203.

1768. "David Diary." "The Day." *Port Folio*, NS 1 (1806), 385-89.

Reprints the first 17 sonnets with some simple-minded commentary; e.g. the writer explains that the first sonnet was addressed to a lady name "Rose."

1769. Davies, Charles Llewelyn. "Shakespeare's Sonnets." *TLS*, December 25, 1924, p. 885.

Raises half-dozen questions about notes and emendations in T.G. Tucker's edition of the Sonnets.
2917

1770. Davies, H. Neville. "Shakespeare's Sonnet LXVI Echoed in 'All for Love'." *Notes and Queries*, 213 (1968), 262-63.

1771. Davies, Randall. *Notes upon Some of Shakespeare's Sonnets*. Kensington, England: Cayme Press, 1927.

Notes on some of the first 126 sonnets based on the assumption that Francis Bacon wrote them to Southampton.

1772. Davis, Horace. "Shakespeare's Sonnets." Overland Monthly, 2nd Series, 11 (1888), 248-59. Reprinted as The Story of Shakespeare's Life, as It May be Gleaned From his Sonnets. San Francisco: C.A. Murdock, 1888.

A reading of the Sonnets as autobiography describing a time of "temptation and trial."

1773. Davis, Jack M., and J.E. Grant. "A Critical Dialogue on Shakespeare's Sonnet 71." Texas Studies in Literature and Language, 1 (1959), 214-32.

A discussion among three critics: a Neo-Aristotelian, an Archetypal and an Eclectic.

1774. Davis, Latham. Shake-speare England's Ulysses, The Masque of Love's Labor's Won or The Enacted Will, Dramatized from the Sonnets of 1609. Seaford, Del.: M.N. Willey, 1905.

The Sonnets, rearranged, are used as the text for this masque.

1775. Dawson, George. "Sonnets of Shakespeare." Shakespeare and Other Lectures. Ed. George St. Clair. London: Kegan Paul, Trench, 1888, pp. 34-41.

An introductory lecture touching superficially on the main critical problems.

1776. *Debeljak, Anton. "Shakespearov Sonet 97 Pojasnjen." [Shakespeare's Sonnet 97 Explained.] Novi Svet (Ljubljana), 6 (1951), 382-84.

1777. Deckner, Elise. Review of J.A. Fort, The Two Dated Sonnets of Shakespeare. Beiblatt zur Anglia, 36 (1925), 367-72.

1778. Deckner, Elise. Review of Shakespeares Sonette. Erlautert von Alois Brandl, Ubersetzt von Ludwig Fulda. Beiblatt zur Anglia, 37 (1926), 271-86.

1779. Deckner, Elise. Review of H. McClure Young, The Sonnets of Shakespeare: A Psycho-Sexual Analysis. Beiblatt zur Anglia, 49 (1938), 116.

1780. De Grazia, Margreta. "Shakespeare's View of Language: An Historical Perspective." Shakespeare Quarterly, 29 (1978), 374-88.

"Will," the speaker in Sonnets 127-154, is surrounded by linguistic confusion--as much as are the characters in the plays (pp. 386-88).

1781. De Grazia, Margreta. "Babbling Will in _Shake-speares Sonnets_ 127 to 154." _Spenser Studies: A Renaissance Poetry Annual I_. Ed. Patrick Cullen and Thomas P. Roche, Jr. Pittsburgh: University of Pittsburgh Press, 1980, pp. 121-34.

The poet's devotion to blackness and to flesh in these 28 sonnets has radical linguistic implications.

1782. Deleanu, Andrei Ion. "Translating Shakespeare's Sonnets into Romanian." _Shakespeare Translation_, 4 (1977), 11-23.

Translation of Sonnet 135 included.

1783. Delius, N. "Uber Shakespeare's Sonette. Ein Sendschreiben an Friedrich Bodenstedt." _Shakespeare Jahrbuch_, 1 (1865), 18-56.

Considers the identity of Mr. W.H. and shows a developing autobiographical theme through the sonnets. There are frequent references to Charles Armitage Brown's sonnet grouping.

1784. Dellinger, J. Howard. "An 1899 Identification of Shakespeare." _Shakespeare Authorship Review_, No. 5 (1961), 1-2.

Dellinger, an Oxfordian, summarizes and comments on Jesse Johnson's thesis about the identity of the Sonnet poet.
2230

1785. De Montmorency, J.E.G. "The Mystery of Shakespeare's Sonnets." _Contemporary Review_, 101 (1912), 737-42.

Examines the Sonnets as allegory.

1786. De Montmorency, J.E.G. "The 'Other Poet' of Shakespeare's Sonnets." _Contemporary Review_, 101 (1912), 885-89.

Prefers Spenser to Barnabe Barnes as the Rival Poet.

1787. Denning, W.H. "Who Wrote the Shakespeare Sonnets?" _English Review_, 40 (1925), 766-68.

Denning concludes from Sonnets 37, 66, and 89 that the poet was lame; Sonnet 113 indicates blindness. This all points to Anthony Bacon, elder brother of Francis, as the poet of the Sonnets.

1788. Deurbergue, Jean. "Les Sonnets." _Bulletin de la faculte des lettres de Strasbourg_, 43 (1965), 1043-44.

Review of John Dover Wilson, _An Introduction to the Sonnets of Shakespeare for the Use of Historians and Others_.

1789. Deurbergue, Jean. Review of _Shakespeare's Sonnets_, ed. Martin Seymour-Smith. _Bulletin de la faculte des lettres de Strasbourg_, 43 (1965), 1069-70.

1790. Deutschbein, Max. "Die politischen Sonette Shakespeares." Shakespeare Jahrbuch, 76 (1940), 161-88.

The "political sonnets" examined are 107, 124, 125.

1791. Deutschbein, Max. "Shakespeares personliche und literarische Sonette." Shakespeare Jahrbuch, 77 (1941), 151-88; 78-79 (1943), 105-27.

1792. Devereux, James A., S.J. "Shakespeare's Sonnets of Participation." Shakespeare Newsletter, 26 (1976), 49.

An abstract of a paper read at MLA meeting (1975). Discusses the notion of Platonic "participation."

1793. *Devereux, James A., S.J. "Shakespeare's Sonnets of Participation." Upstart Crow, 2 (Fall, 1979), 18-25.

Discusses the Platonic idea of the relationship of sensible things to ideal forms in connection with the sonnets to the friend.

1794. Devereux, James A., S.J. "The Last Temptation of Shakespeare: The Sonnets and Despair." Renaissance Papers 1979. Ed. A. Leigh Deneef and M. Thomas Hester. Southeastern Renaissance Conference, 1980.

Examines the role played by despair in the Sonnets, which he sees as a "dramatic tableau."

1795. Devlin, C. Review of G. Wilson Knight, The Mutual Flame. Month, NS 14 (1955), 372-74.

1796. De Vries, Hendrik. "Shakespeare's Homoerotiek." Critisch Bulletin, 18 (1951), 449-57.

Review of Coenraad van Emde Boas, Shakespeare's Sonnetten en hun verband met de travesti-double spelen.

1797. Dibelius, Wilhelm. "Zeitschriftenschau." Shakespeare Jahrbuch, 35 (1899), 349-61.

This review of the literature contains a section on "Shakespeares Sonette" (pp. 354-57).

1798. Dibelius, Wilhelm. "Zeitschriftenschau." Shakespeare Jahrbuch, 37 (1901), 270-305.

Two sections, "Zur Datierung der Sonette" and "William Harvey und die Widmung von Shakespeares Sonetten (pp. 285-87), review studies on the Sonnets.

1799. Dibelius, Wilhelm. Review of Samuel Butler, Shakespeare's Sonnets, Reconsidered. Shakespeare Jahrbuch, 38 (1902), 266-67.

1800. Dibelius, Wilhelm. "Zeitschriftenschau." Shakespeare Jahrbuch, 38 (1902), 296-338.

A section on the Sonnets (pp. 315-18).

1801. Dillon, Janette. Shakespeare and the Solitary Man. London: Macmillan, 1981.

In this book discussing the theme of solitude, Dillon, in her chapter "'Walls of glass': The Sonnets" (pp. 77-91), calls the sonnet "a perfect form . . . for expressing the withdrawal of the individual into the inescapable and autonomous solitude of the mind."

1802. Disher, M. Willson. "The Trend of Shakespeare's Thought." TLS, October 20, 1950, p. 668; October 27, 1950, p. 684; November 3, 1950, p. 700.

This three-part article examines Sidneian echoes in Shakespeare. Part of the article involves their sonnets.

1803. Dobell, Bertram. "An Early Variant of a Shakespeare Sonnet." Athenaeum, August 2, 1913, p. 112.

On Sonnet 2.

1804. Dodd, Alfred. The Personal Poems of Francis Bacon (our Shakespeare), The Son of Queen Elizabeth, Arranged in Chronological Order. 3rd. ed. Liverpool: Daily Post, 1936.

The Sonnets, which were by Bacon, prove that Bacon believed himself to be Elizabeth's son. Furthermore, the Sonnets were published in 1625 not in 1609, as commonly believed. The book contains the text of the poems with notes explaining their relationship to Bacon's ideas and to events in his life.

1805. Dodd, Alfred. Shakespeare, Creator of Freemasonry, Being a Remarkable Examination of the Plays and Poems, Which proves incontestably that these works were saturated in Masonry, that Shakespeare was a Freemason and the Founder of the Fraternity. London: Rider, 1937.

Chapter 8, "The Diary of William Shakespeare: 'Shakespeare's Sonnets'" (pp. 174-92) examines the sonnets both as a diary and as a document of Freemasonry.

1806. Dodd, Alfred. The Marriage of Elizabeth Tudor Being an exhaustive inquiry into her alleged Marriage with the Earl of Leicester and the alleged Births of her Two Sons, Francis Bacon and the Earl of Essex: an historical research based on one of the themes in "Shakespeare's Sonnets." London: Rider, 1940.

Involves a rearrangement of the Sonnets.

1807. *Dodd, Alfred. The Secret History of Francis Bacon (our Shake-speare) the Son of Queen Elizabeth, as revealed by Sonnets arranged in the correct numerical and chronolgical order. 7th ed. London: C.W. Daniel, 1941.

1808. Dodd, Alfred. The Secret Shake-speare: Being the missing chapter from "Shakespeare, Creator of Freemasonry" in which the identity of Shakespeare is plainly declared together with Many Curious Secret Messages of profound interest to all lovers of literature, to Elizabethan Students and Freemasons in particular. London: Rider and Co., 1941.

1809. *Dodd, Alfred. The Mystery of Shakespeare's Sonnets: the Riddle Solved. London: George Lapworth, 1947.

Above title is the cover title. On the title page appears Francis Bacon's Diary. Shake-speare's Sonnets. Who wrote them? When were they written? Why were they written? Were they a diary from youth to old age? Proof that the sonnets were written after Shaksper's death.

1810. Doebler, John. "A Submerged Emblem in Sonnet 116." Shakespeare Quarterly, 15, i (1964), 109-10.

The emblem is the "spread compass held by a hand coming out of a cloud," similar to the metaphor of Donne's "A Valediction Forbidding Mourning."

1811. Donald, Roslyn Lander. "'Rhetoricall Courtings': The Blazon in Elizabethan and Stuart Poetry, Its Conventional Patterns and Contexts." Ph.D Dissertation, Texas, 1974. DAI, 35 (1975), 5340A.

Sonnet 130 is one of the principal works considered.

1812. Donnelly, Ignatius. The Sonnets of Shakespeare: An Essay. St. Paul, Minn.: Geo. W. Moore, 1859.

Donnelly evaluates the various claimants for male friend, but finally concludes that the greatness of the Sonnets is owing to the fact that they reveal something of Shakespeare's passions and human weaknesses.

1813. Donoghue, Denis. "Shakespeare at Sonnets." Sewanee Review, 88 (1980), 463-73.

A review of some old and some recent books on Shakespeare's Sonnets, including Booth's edition of the Sonnets, Paul Ramsey, The Fickle Glass, Katharine Wilson, Shakespeare's Sugared Sonnets, and a number of others.

1814. Donow, Herbert S. "Linear Word Count as a Function of Rhythm: An Analysis of Shakespeare's Sonnets." Hephaistos, 1 (1970), 1-27.

Metrical analysis employing the computer. The greater part of this paper is a listing of the Sonnet lines by the number of words per line and by the number of function words per line.

1815. Doran, Madeleine. "The Idea of Excellence in Shakespeare." Shakespeare Quarterly, 27 (1976), 133-49.

In discussing the convention of praise, she devotes several pages (pp. 134-36) to the sonnets (Nos. 130, 21, 53, 94).

1816. Douglas, Lord Alfred. The True History of Shakespeare's Sonnets. London: M. Secker, 1933. Port Washington, N.Y.: Kennikat, 1970.

After an introductory chapter on the history of the text and review of various theories about the sonnets, Douglas reprints each sonnet with explanatory notes.

1817. Douglas, Lord Alfred. "Lord A. Douglas, Shakespeare and Will Hughes." TLS, May 21, 1938, p. 353.

In this response to an article on "The Problem of the Sonnets" (TLS, May 14, 1938, p. 334), Douglas reiterates his position that W.H. is Will Hughes.
3303

1818. Douglas, Alfred, and A.R. Cripps. "Shakespeare and Will Hughes." TLS, May 28, 1938, p. 370.

Douglas adds evidence that Hughes and Shakespeare would have known each other; Cripps rejects the Hughes theory.

1819. Douglas, Lt. Col. Montagu W. The Earl of Oxford as Shakespeare: an Outline of the Case. London: Palmer, 1931.

The book contains a chapter, "The Evidence of the Sonnets" (pp. 107-32) in which Douglas supports Edward de Vere as the poet of the Sonnets. Subsequent editions of this book are retitled Lord Oxford was Shakespeare and Lord Oxford and the Shakespeare Group, respectively.

1820. Douse, T. Le Marchant. "Shakespeare's Sonnet XXVI." Notes and Queries, 10th Series, 2 (1904), 133.

Response to a Query by Ne Quid Nimis.
2555

1821. Douse, T. Le Marchant. "Shakespeare's Sonnets." Literature, 6 (1900), 229.

Comments on two earlier letters by R. Garnett (on dating) and A. Hall (on W.H.).
1982, 2064

1822. Dowden, Edward. "Shakspere's Sonnets." Academy, 29 (January 30, 1886), 67-68.

A generally favorable critique of Thomas Tyler's theories about W.H. (Pembroke) and the dark lady (Mistress Fitton).

1823. Dowden, Edward, Samuel Butler, and C. Trice Martin. "'Beget and 'Begetter' in Elizabethan English." Athenaeum, March 10, 1900, pp. 315-16.

These three letters respond critically to Sidney Lee's theories stated two weeks earlier.
2346

1824. Dowden, Edward, and Samuel Butler. "'Beget' and 'Begetter' in Elizabethan English." Athenaeum, March 24, 1900, pp. 379-80.
2347

On the use of the word "begetter" in the dedication to the 1609 Quarto.

1825. Downing, Charles (Clelia). God in Shakespeare: The Course of the Poet's Spiritual Life with his Reflections thereon and his Resultant Conception of his World-Personality Inductively Established from his Text. London: T.F. Unwin, 1890. London: Greening, 1901.

Book III ("Friendship") refers frequently to the Sonnets in his attempt to describe Shakespeare's spiritual growth.

1826. [Downing, Charles]. Clelia. Great Pan Lives: Shakespeare's Sonnets, 20-126. London: Luzac, 1892.

A paraphrase and commentary designed to show that the "friend" is Beauty.

1827. [Downing, Charles]. Clelia. The Messiahship of Shakespeare, Sung and Expounded. London: Greening, 1901. rpt. New York: Haskell House, 1977.

Downing has two chapters "On the Sonnets" (pp. 16-37) and "The Method of the Symbolism of The Sonnets Displayed" (pp. 92-101) in which he argues that the poems are really about "the poet's communings with his ideas of Beauty, Truth, Virtue, Art and his own genius . . . and with his ideas of Love."

1828. Drakakis, John. Review of Giorgio Melchiori, Shakespeare's Dramatic Meditations. Notes and Queries, 223 (1978), 171-72.

1829. Drake, Nathan. Shakespeare and his Times. Including The Biography of the Poet, Criticisms on his Genius and Writings, A New Chronology of His Plays, A Disquisition on the Object of His Sonnets and A History of the Manners, Customs, Amusements, Superstitions, Poetry, and Elegant Literature of His Age. London: T. Cadell and W. Davies, 1817. rpt. New York: Burt Franklin, 1969.

Contains a discussion of the Sonnets and their literary background (pp. 372-88).

1830. Draper, R.P. Review of J.B. Leishman, Themes and Variations in Shakespeare's Sonnets. English Studies, 49 (1968), 250-52.

1831. Dubrow, Heather. Review of Shakespeare's Sonnets, ed. Stephen Booth. Durham University Journal, 72 (1979), 115-16.

1832. Dubrow, Heather. "Shakespeare's Undramatic Monologues: Toward a Reading of the Sonnets." Shakespeare Quarterly, 32 (1981), 55-68.

Rejects that critically popular view of the Sonnets that sees the poems as dramatic and narrative.

1833. [Duggan, John]. Julius, Jr. Fair, Kind and True. Scranton, Pa.: Scranton Republican, 1896.

A running commentary, which assumes Bacon to have been the poet, accompanies the Sonnets.

1834. Dulek, Ron. "A Device for Teaching Shakespeare's Sonnets." CEA Forum, 9, iv (April, 1979), 7-9.

The strategy of observing the "floating pronoun" with its multiple antecedents may direct students to better understanding of the text.

1835. Dulek, Ronald Ervin. "Modes of Disclosure in the Sonnet." Ph.D. Dissertation, Purdue University, 1977. DAI, 39 (1978), 859A-60A.

Emphasizes four of Shakespeare's sonnets (18, 60, 73, 94) and three of Keats's ("When I have fears," "On first looking into Chapman's Homer," and "Bright Star").

1836. Duncan-Jones, Katherine. Review of New Essays on Shakespeare's Sonnets, ed. Hilton Landry. Notes and Queries, 223 (1978), 173-74.

1837. Duncan-Jones, Katherine. Review of Shakespeare: The Sonnets, A Casebook, ed. Peter Jones. Notes and Queries, 224 (1979), 168-69.

1838. Duncan-Jones, Katherine. Review of Shakespeare's Sonnets, ed. W. G. Ingram and Theodore Redpath. Notes and Queries, 224 (1979), 569-70.

The book, first published in 1964, is being reviewed on the occasion of its reissue in paperback.

1839. Duncan-Jones, Katherine. "In Sequence to Sublimation." TLS, May 9, 1980, p. 518.

Review of Shakespeare's Sonnets, ed. by S.C. Campbell, and S.C. Campbell, Only Begotten Sonnets.

1840. Duncan-Jones, Katherine. "So long more or less lives this." TLS, July 25, 1980, p. 843.

Duncan-Jones reviews, not too favorably, Simon Callow's reading of the Sonnets in the National Theatre performance on July 9, 1980.

1841. Duncan-Jones, Katherine. Review of Gerald Hammond, The Reader and Shakespeare's Young Man. TLS, April 17, 1981, p. 442.

1842. Dunning, Edwin James. The Genesis of Shakespeare's Art, a Study of his Sonnets and Poems. Boston: Lee and Shepard, 1897.

Assumes the Sonnets form a continuous narrative. An appendix examines the use of "you" and "thou" in the Sonnets.

1843. Durrell, Lawrence. "The Rival Poet." TLS, January 5, 1951, p. 7.

Urges reconsideration of Marlowe's claim.

1844. Durrell, Lawrence. "L'amour, clef du mystere?" Marcel Pagnol, et al. Shakespeare. Paris: Hachette, 1962, pp. 173-92.

Focuses on the significance of Mr. W.H. and the "dark lady."

1845. Dyboski, Roman. O sonetach i poematach Szekspira. Warszawa: Gebethner and Wolff, 1914.

Dyboski's discussion of the Sonnets in Chapter 3 (pp. 27-80) is basically a review of scholarship to date.

1846. E[agle], R.L. "'The Master Mistress' Identified." Baconiana, 3rd Series, 12 (1914), 159-64.

Interprets Sonnet 20 allegorically, freeing it from the "troubling" sexual connotations.

1847. Eagle, R.L. "'The Dark Lady' (Sonnets 127-142)." Baconiana, 3rd Series, 12 (1914), 218-26.

Eagle believes the dark lady is not a fleshly "mistress" but is the personification of Fortune.

1848. Eagle, R. "The Rival Poet." Baconiana, 3rd Series, 12 (1914), 227-30.

Suggests Drayton for the post.

1849. Eagle, R.L. "Shakespeare and his Patron." TLS, July 20, 1916, p. 346.

A reply to Skipwith.
2951

1850. Eagle, Roderick L. New Light on the Enigmas of Shakespeare's Sonnets. London: J. Long, 1916. London: Mitre Press, 1965.

1851. Eagle, R.L. "Sonnets, 153-154." Baconiana, 3rd Series, 16 (1920), 60-66.

Finds evidence that these poems, based on a Greek epigram, were most likely by Bacon.

1852. Eagle, R.L. "Shakespeare's Sonnets." Saturday Review, 136 (August 25, 1923), 218.

Notes that the "sugred Sonnets" referred to by Meres were written in sugared ink so that the writing would shine.

1853. Eagle, R.L. "The Problem of Shakespeare's Sonnets." Quest, 16 (1925), 508-16.

Shakespeare did not speak to or of individuals; his poems were allegorical.

1854. Eagle, Roderick. Shakespeare: New Views for Old. London: Palmer, 1930; Rider, 1943.

The book contains four chapters on the Sonnets. "The Problem of Shakespeare's Sonnets," "The 'Rival Poet'," "The 'Dark Lady'," and "A Lover's Complaint" (pp. 45-66).

1855. Eagle, R. L. "The Headpiece on Shakespeare's Sonnets, 1609." Notes and Queries, 192 (1947), 38.

He has traced this device, the chief features of which are a light and dark "A", to a number of other books.

1856. Eagle, Roderick L. The Secrets of the Shakespeare's Sonnets. London: Mitre Press, 1965.

With a facsimile of the 1609 Quarto. In his chapters on the dedication, the friend, dark lady, rival poet, etc., Eagle finds frequent opportunities to note parallels between passages in the Sonnets and Bacon's writing.

1857. Eagle, Roderick, and R.J.C. Wait. "Shakespeare's Sonnets." TLS, August 17, 1973, pp. 955-56.

Both letters speak of the Ovidian influence in the Sonnets.

1858. Eagle, Roderick, and R.R. Henshaw. "Dark Lady's Clavichord." TLS, September 7, 1973, p. 1029.

Both letters, which comment on the use of the word "Jacks" in Sonnet 128, are in response to Madeau Stewart.
3016

1859. Eastman, Arthur M. A Short History of Shakespearean Criticism. New York: Random House, 1968.

A summary of Edward Hubler's The Sense of Shakespeare's Sonnets (pp. 314-22).

1860. Eccles, C.M. "Shakespeare and Jacques Amyot: Sonnet LV and 'Coriolanus'." Notes and Queries, 210 (1965), 100-02.

Phrases of Amyot from Amiot to the Readers may be found in Sonnet 55 and in Coriolanus.

1861. Eccles, Mark, and J.A. Fort. "The 'Mortal Moon' Sonnet." TLS, February 15, 1934, p. 108.
2082

1862. Eckhardt, Eduard. Review of Karl Wanshura, Die Sonette Shakespeares von Franz Bacon geschrieben. Deutsche Literaturzeitung, 52 (1931), 649-51.

The review of Wanshura (p. 651) is one of four reviews.

1863. Eckhoff, Lorentz. "Shakespeare's Sonnets in a New Light." Studia Neophilologica, 39 (1967), 3-14.

The sonnets are about a single subject: the description of a "perfect love."

1864. Edmond, Mary, and Peter Grant. "Shakespeare's Sonnets." TLS, May 10, 1974, p. 502.

Edmond corrects Rowse on the year of Emilia Lanier's death (1645); Grant raises a question about Richard Jacob's thesis about the Benson 1640 Quarto.
2216

1865. Edmonds, Charles. "A Shakespearean Discovery." Athenaeum, October 25, 1873, pp. 528-29; November 22, 1873, pp. 661-62.

1) A work by Robert Southwell contains a dedication signed by W.H.--the same person, Edmonds believes, that was named in the 1609 Quarto of the Sonnets. 2) A response to Browne's letter in an earlier issue (p. 563).
1636

1866. Edwards, H.L.R. "A Shakespeare Emendation." TLS, October 25, 1934, p.735.

Argues against John Kenyon's view that line 12 of Sonnet 111 should be emended.
2266

1867. Edwards, Philip. "The Sonnets to the Dark Woman." Shakespeare and the Confines of Art. London: Methuen; New York: Barnes and Noble, 1968, pp. 17-31.

1868. Eichhoff, Theodor. Unser Shakespeare. Beitrage zu einer wissenschaftlichen Shakespeare-Kritik. 2 vol. Halle: Max Niemeyer, 1903-1904.

Volume 2 contains two parts: "Shakespeare's Sonette und ihr Wert" and "Die Sonettensatire." The latter talks about sonnet satire in a number of the early plays and the work of some of Shakespeare's contemporaries--Sidney, Sir John Davies and Drayton.

1869. Ellis, Charles. Shakspeare and the Bible: Fifty Sonnets with Their Scriptural Harmonies. London: Bagster, 1896.

Also appears under the title The Christ in Shakspeare accompanied by a supplement (in typescript) containing Meditations on 24 sonnets. Each of the Sonnets appears with a headnote explaining the Christian allegory.

1870. Elmen, Paul. "Shakespeare's Gentle Hours." Shakespeare Quarterly, 4 (1953), 301-09.

The word "hours" in Sonnet 5 refers not only to time but to the Greek goddesses, "the gracious Horae."

1871. Elson, Louis C. Shakespeare in Music. Boston: L.C. Page, 1901.

A brief observation about a puzzling allusion in Sonnet 128, the playing of a virginal (pp. 37-40).

1872. Elton, Charles Isaac. William Shakespeare, His Family and Friends. Ed. A. Hamilton Thompson. London: John Murray; New York: E.P. Dutton, 1904.

Numerous brief references to the Sonnets in a biographical context.

1873. Elton, Oliver. Modern Studies. London: E. Arnold, 1907. rpt. Freeport, N.Y.: Books for Libraries Press, 1967.

On fame and its achievement through literature. A brief discussion of Shakespeare's Sonnets (pp. 59-62) with passing references elsewhere to Shakespeare, Spenser, et al.

1874. Emanuele, Pietro. "Mikroasthetische Analyse von zwei Shakespeare-Versen mit Hilfe der 'Grossen Matrix'." Semiosis 20, 5, iv (1980), 14-22.

A semiotic study of the first two lines of Sonnet 40.

1875. *Emerson, John M. Anagram from the Shakespeare Sonnets Discovered by J.M. Emerson. Liverpool: 1908.

Purporting to show that Bacon was their author.

1876. *Emerson, John M. *Two Anagrams from the Shakespeare Sonnets and Francis Bacon's Will*. Liverpool: 1912.

1877. Emerson, Oliver Farrar. "Shakespeare's Sonneteering." *Studies in Philology*, 20 (1923), 111-36.

Includes also discussion of Sidney, Watson, and Spenser.

1878. Empson, William. *Seven Types of Ambiguity*. London: Chatto and Windus, 1930. Rev. and reset, New York: New Directions, 1947.

Discusses Gerard Manley Hopkins's "The Windhover" (pp. 224-26) and Shakespeare Sonnets (pp. 50-56, 133-38). An excerpt, entitled "Some Types of Ambiguity in Shakespeare's Sonnets," appears in *Discussions of Shakespeare's Sonnets*. Ed. Barbara Herrnstein. Boston: D.C. Heath, 1964, pp. 124-36.

1879. Empson, William. "They That Have Power." *Some Versions of Pastoral*. London: Chatto and Windus, 1935. Norfolk, Conn.: New Directions, 1960, pp. 89-115.

The first part of the essay is devoted to an examination of the irony in Sonnet 94.

1880. Empson, William, and F.W. Bateson. "'Bare Ruined Choirs'." *Essays in Criticism*, 3 (1953), 357-63.

Empson and Bateson go at it on Empson's suggestion of a reading of this line from Sonnet 73--originally proposed in *Seven Types of Ambiguity*.

1881. Empson, William. "Shakespeare's Angel." *New Statesman*, 66 (1963), 447-48.

Review of *Shakespeare's Sonnets*, ed. Martin Seymour-Smith; A.L. Rowse, *William Shakespeare*; and Peter Quennell, *Shakespeare*. Focuses mainly on Shakespeare's alleged relationship with Southampton.

1882. Empson, William. "Shakespearean Indelicacies." *New Statesman*, 66 (1963), 612.

An exchange with Seymour-Smith on the subject of the dark lady. 2846

1883. Empson, William. "Evidence for Herbert." *New Statesman*, 67 (February 7, 1964), 216-17.

Review of J. Dover Wilson's Preface (published separately) to *Shakespeare's Sonnets*. Empson finds Wilson's arguments on behalf of Herbert as W.H. unconvincing.

1884. Empson, William. "Mr. W. H." *New Statesman*, 67 (April 24, 1964), 642.

Review of Leslie Hotson's Mr. W.H.

1885. Empson, William, A.L. Rowse, Ivor R.W. Cook. "The Dark Lady." TLS, May 18, 1973, p. 536.

These three letters are mostly in response to G. Wilson Knight (TLS, May 11, 1973, p. 528).
2292

1886. Empson, William. "Shakespeare's Friend'." TLS, March 8, 1974, pp. 238-39.

1887. *Engel, Werner. "Veranderlichkeit-verganglichkeit-Tod in Shakespeares Sonetten." Ph.D. Dissertation, Marburg, 1949.

1888. Estermann, Barbara. "Shakespeare's 'Sonnet 73'." Explicator, 38, iii (1980), 11.

1889. Evans, E.C. "Shakespeare's Sonnet 97." Review of English Studies, NS 14 (1963), 379-80.

1890. Evans, Judge. "'Venus and Adonis' and the Earlier Sonnets of Shakespeare." Saturday Review, 118 (1914), 647-48.

There exists a common feature in Venus and Adonis and the first seventeen sonnets--the importunate pleading of both Venus and the poet of the Sonnets.

1891. Evans, Willa McC. "Lawes' Version of Shakespeare's Sonnet 116." PMLA, 51 (1936), 120-22.

1892. Evans, Willa McClung. Henry Lawes: Musician and Friend of Poets. Revolving Fund Series, 11. New York: MLA of America; London: Oxford University Press, 1941.

Discusses Lawes's musical setting of two sonnets--Shakespeare's Sonnet 116 (pp. 41-45) and Spenser's Amoretti, Sonnet 8 (pp. 67-69).

1893. Ewart, Gavin. "Sonnet: Shakespeare's Universality." Literary Half-Yearly, 22, i (1981), 1.

This sonnet expresses an unfavorable critical view of Shakespeare's Sonnets.

1894. Ewbank, Inga-Stina. "Shakespeare's Poetry." A New Companion to Shakespeare Studies. Ed. Kenneth Muir and Samuel Schoenbaum. Cambridge: University Press, 1971, pp. 99-115.

In the first half of the essay, Ewbank examines the Sonnets for indications of how Shakespeare was developing as a poetic dramatist.

1895. F., H.C. "Essex and the Sonnets." Baconiana, 3rd Series, 4 (1906), 92-97.

Finds unconvincing the theory of R.J.D.S. that Essex was the fair youth.
2791

1896. Farmer, Norman K., Jr. Review of William Bowman Piper, Evaluating Shakespeare's Sonnets. South Central Bulletin, 40, i (1980), 24-25.

1897. Farnell, Frederic J. "Erotism as Portrayed In Literature." International Journal of Psycho-analysis, 1 (1920), 396-413.

Infers information about Shakespeare's love life from Sonnets 127, 142, 147, 152, 119 and from some of the plays (pp. 408-413).

1898. Farr, Harry. "Notes on Shakespeare's Printers and Publishers with Special Reference to the Poems and Hamlet." Library, 4th series, 3 (1923), 225-60.

A brief paragraph on p. 251 deals with Thomas Thorp and the Sonnets.

1899. Farrell, Kirby Charles. "Shakespeare's Creation: Art and the Artist's Role as Structural Principles in the Sonnets and Plays." Ph.D. Dissertation, Rutgers, 1972. DAI, 32 (1972), 6926A.

1900. Farrell, Ralph. Stefan Georges Beziehungen zur englischen Dichtung. Germanische Studien, 192. Berlin: Ebering, 1937. Nendeln/Liechtenstein: Kraus Reprint, 1967.

Discusses Shakespeare's Sonnets and George's translations of them (pp. 200-18).

1901. Feldman, A. Bronson. "The Confessions of William Shakespeare." American Imago, 10 (1953), 113-66.

Using psychoanalysis, Feldman adds evidence to support Oxford as the author of the plays and poems. A substantial portion of the article is devoted to the Sonnets.

1902. Ferguson, W.A. "The Sonnets of Shakespeare: The 'Oxfordian' Solution." Shakespearean Authorship Review, 13 (1965), 9-12.

In support of Gerald Rendall's "Oxfordian" thesis described in Shakespeare Sonnets and Edward de Vere (1930).
2719

1903. *Ferrara, Fernando. "Sesso e potere. Le truffe di Cleopatra." Annali-Anglistica, 22 (1977), 27-80.

There are echoes, particularly from Enobarbus, of themes and situations reminiscent of the Sonnets.

1904. Ferry, Anne. All in War with Time: Love Poetry of Shakespeare, Donne, Jonson, Marvell. Cambridge, Mass.: Harvard University Press, 1975.

In her discussion of the first 126 sonnets, Ferry examines their preoccupation with Time (pp. 3-63). She also comments on some of Sidney's sonnets from Astrophel and Stella in the section on Jonson (pp. 129-82).

1905. Fetrow, Fred M. "Strata and Structure: A Reading of Shakespeare's Sonnet 73. Concerning Poetry, 9, ii (1976), 23-25.

1906. Fiedler, Leslie. "Some Contexts of Shakespeare's Sonnets." The Riddle of Shakespeare's Sonnets. Ed. Edward Hubler. New York: Basic Books, 1962, pp. 55-90.

1907. Fiedler, Leslie. The Stranger in Shakespeare. New York: Stein and Day, 1972.

"Introduction: The Passionate Pilgrim" deals directly with sonnets, with references to them throughout the rest of the book.

1908. Figgis, Darrell. Shakespeare, A Study. London: J.M. Dent, 1911.

A discussion of the biographical implications of the sonnets (pp. 304-08, 321-28). Includes an attempt to fix the date of Sonnet 29 (pp. 306-08).

1909. Filon, Augustin. Les Sonnets de Shakespeare." Revue des deux mondes, 5th series, 2 (1901), 795-830.

1910. Findheisen, Helmut. Review of Raimund Borgmeier, Shakespeares Sonett "When forty winters" und die deutschen Ubersetzer. Untersuchungen zu den Problemen der Shakespeare-Ubertragung. Shakespeare Jahrbuch, 108 (1972), 229-30.

1911. Fischer, Kuno. Shakespeare und die Bacon-Mythen. Festvortrag gehalten auf der General-Versammlung der Deutschen Shakespeare-Gesellschaft zu Weimar am 23. April 1895. Heidelberg: Carl Winter, 1895.

Third chapter deals in part with "Bacon als geheimnissvoller Dichter, Das Sonett" (pp. 26-28).

1912. Fischer, Rudolf. Shakespeares Sonette (Gruppierung, Kunstform). Ed. Karl Brunner. Wiener Beitrage zur englischen Philologie, 53. Wien und Leipzig: Wilhelm Braumuller, 1925.

This monograph, edited by Brunner from Fischer's literary remains, discusses in the first part the grouping of the sonnets into three periods. The second part of the work deals with formal aspects of the sonnets.

1913. Fischer, W. Review of Shakespeares Sonette, ubertragung von Richard Flatter. Beiblatt zur Anglia, 46 (1935), 117-18.

1914. Fisher, Edward. Shakespeare and Son. London: Abelard-Schuman, 1962.

In this novel, Fisher suggests some answers to those perplexing questions: who was the Dark Lady? an invention; and who was Mr. W.H.? William Honyng.

1915. Fisher, Edward. *Love's Labour's Won: A Novel About Shakespeare's Lost Years.* London: Abelard-Schuman, 1963.

In his preface (pp. 9-15), Fisher suggests William Honyng, Clerk Controller of Her Majesty's Revels, as Mr. W.H.

1916. Fisher, Edward. "Shakespeare's Sonnets." *TLS*, March 12, 1964, p. 215.

Notes that he preceded Somervell in suggesting William Honyng as Mr. W.H.
2980

1917. Flatter, Richard. "Zur Frage der Shakespeare-Sonette." *Antiquariat*, 7, No. 21-24 (1951), 86-87.

Examines different German translations with particular attention to Sonnets 30 and 105.

1918. Fleay, F.G. "On the Motive of Shakespere's Sonnets (1-125): A Defence of His Morality." *Macmillan's Magazine*, 31 (1875), 433-45.

Sees the Sonnets as 125 14-line stanzas, not to be read individually or in small groups.

1919. Fleissner, Robert F. "A Plausible Mr. W. H." *Notes and Queries*, 214 (1969), 129.

Presents some evidence for William Houghton.

1920. Fleissner, Robert F. "That 'Cheek of Night': Toward the Dark Lady." *CLA Journal*, 16 (1973), 312-23.

Argues that the dark lady was a black woman.

1921. Fleissner, Robert F. "Herbert's Aethiopesa and Dark Lady: A Mannerist Parallel." *CLA Journal*, 19 (1976), 458-67.

1922. Fleissner, Robert F. "Shakespeare's Sonnet 137." *Explicator*, 35, iii (1977), 21-22.

1923. F[lugel], E[wald]. "The W.H. of Shakspere's Sonnets." *Beiblatt zur Anglia*, 2 (1892), 276-77.

Reprints a notice in the November 20, 1891 *Pall Mall Gazette* regarding an early portrait of William Herbert.

1924. Foakes, R.A. "Much Ado About the Sonnets." *English*, 15 (1964), 50-52.

A well-deserved, though perhaps too moderate, attack on A.L. Rowse's proclamation that he has solved "all the major problems of the sonnets."

1925. Forbis, John F. The Shakespearean Enigma and an Elizabethan Mania. New York: American Library Service, 1924. rpt. New York: AMS Press, 1970.

In addition to a lengthy commentary, the Sonnets are printed with their "secret message" revealed: the person addressed is Shakespeare himself; the marriage proposed is "the espousal of, surrender to, Wine" from which his inspiration came; etc.

1926. *Forker, Charles R. "A Response to James Devereux." Upstart Crow, 2 (Fall, 1979), 26-33.

The Sonnets are "too dramatic, too full of psychic conflict . . . to fit without considerable strain into the discursive, abstract, and finely spun formularies of Ficino . . . ."
1793

1927. Forrest, H.T.S. The Five Authors of "Shake-speares Sonnets." London: Chapman and Dodd, 1923.

The five poets are Shakespeare, "the minor poet" (Barnabe Barnes), "the lawyer" (William Warner), "the humorist" (John Donne), "the newcomer" (Samuel Daniel).

1928. Forrest-Thomson, Veronica. Poetic Artifice: A Theory of Twentieth-Century Poetry. Manchester: Manchester University Press, 1978.

Discusses Sonnet 94 (pp. 1-17).

1929. Forster, Max. "Sonstige Shakespeare-Literatur." Shakespeare-Jahrbuch, 50 (1914), 179-248.

Review of current publications which includes a section on the sonnets (pp. 180-84).

1930. Fort, J.A. The Two Dated Sonnets of Shakespeare. London: Oxford University Press, 1924.

Believes that the order of the first 126 Sonnets as printed by Thorpe was authentic, that Southampton (or a close friend) authorized their publication, and that Sonnets 104 and 107 can be precisely dated.

1931. Fort, J.A. "The Time-Scheme of the First Series of Shakespeare's Sonnets." Nineteenth Century and After, 100 (1926), 272-79.

Most of the first 126 sonnets were written between 1593 and 1598.

1932. Fort, James A. "Thorpe's Text of Shakespeare's Sonnets." Review of English Studies, 2 (1926), 439-45.

1933. Fort, J.A. "The Story Contained in the Second Series of Shakespeare's Sonnets." Review of English Studies, 3 (1927), 406-14.

Believes that the incidents in the dark lady Sonnets are real and that Thorpe's order of the sonnets is approximately correct.

1934. Fort, J.A. "Further Notes on Shakespeare's Sonnets." Library, 4th series, 9 (1928), 305-25.

A progress report on the author's efforts to establish dates for the "Fair Youth" Sonnets (1-126) and to answer several related questions.

1935. Fort, James A. A Time Scheme for Shakespeare's Sonnets with a Text and Short Notes. London: Mitre Press, 1929. New York: AMS Press, 1970.

Attempts to assign groups of sonnets to specific time periods.

1936. Fort, J.A. "The Date of Shakespeare's 107th Sonnet." Library, 4th series, 9 (1929), 381-84.

Agrees with G.B. Harrison that Sonnets 107 to 126 were written between April, 1596 and February, 1598.
2082

1937. Fort, J.A. "The Order and Chronology of Shakespeare's Sonnets." Review of English Studies, 9 (1933), 19-23.

1938. Fort, J.A. "The 'Mortal Moon' Sonnet." TLS, February 22, 1934, p. 126; March 22, 1934, p. 214.

On Sonnet 107.
2082

1939. Fort, J.B. Review of Biddy Darlow, Shakespeare's Lady of the Sonnets. Etudes Anglaises, 27 (1974), 358.

1940. Fowler, Alastair. Conceitful Thought: The Interpretation of English Renaissance Poems. Edingurgh: University Press, 1975.

One essay 'The Shakespearean Conceit' (pp. 87-113) deals with the conceits in the Amoretti, and in several of Sidney's and Shakespeare's sonnets.

1941. Fowler, Clayton V. "Shakespeare's 'Sonnet 24' in the Light of Contemporary Art Theory." Ph.D. Dissertation, Iowa, 1952.

1942. Fowler, Roger. "Language and the Reader: Shakespeare's Sonnet 73." Style and Structure in Literature: Essays in the New Stylistics. Ed. Roger Fowler. Oxford: Basil Blackwell, 1975, pp.79-122.

Refers to a number of critics--Booth, Ransom, Mizener, Jakobson, et al.--in his reading of the poem.

1943. Fox, Charles Overbury. "Shakespearean Allusion." Notes and Queries, 196 (1951), 412.

Notes a resemblance between Sonnet 66 and a passage from Sir Thomas Overbury's "Wife."

1944. Fox, Charles Overbury. "Shakespeare's Sonnet 126, Lines 1 and 2." Notes and Queries, 197 (1952), 134-35.

Comments on possible origin of Time's "sickle hour."

1945. Fox, Charles O. "Early Echoes of Shakespeare's 'Sonnets' and 'The Passionate Pilgrim'." Notes and Queries, 198 (1953), 370.

Some verses by John Davies of Hereford echo Shakespeare's lines.

1946. Fox, Charles A. O. "Shakespeare's Sonnet 146." Notes and Queries, 199 (1954), 83.

Offers the phrase "Mocked by" to correct the obvious error beginning line 2.

1947. Fox, Charles A. O. "Thomas Lodge and Shakespeare." Notes and Queries, 201 (1956), 190.

Points out the similarity between Sonnet 129 and some lines spoken by Corydon in Thomas Lodge's Rosalynde.

1948. Franklyn, Cecil W. "William Shakespeare, Gentleman." Westminster Review, 132 (1889), 348-61.

Imagines what circumstances might have existed when Shakespeare wrote some of the Sonnets.

1949. Fraser, G.S. "Baffled Power." New Statesman, 76 (December 27, 1968), 908-09.

Review of James Winny, The Master-Mistress: A Study of Shakespeare's Sonnets, Philip Edwards, Shakespeare and the Confines of Art, and Ivor Brown, The Women in Shakespeare's Life.

1950. Fraser, Ian Forbes. Review of The Sonnets of Shakespeare Translated into French "Regular" Sonnets, by Dikran Garabedian. Shakespeare Quarterly, 17 (1966), 181-83.

1951. Frazer, Robert. The Silent Shakespeare. Philadelphia: William J. Campbell, 1915.

In his discussion of the Sonnets (pp. 93-109) Frazer argues that William Stanley, 6th Earl of Derby, was their author.

1952. Friedman, Donald M. Review of Anne Ferry, All in War with Time: Love Poetry of Shakespeare, Donne, Jonson, Marvell. Modern Language Quarterly, 38 (1977), 310-14.

1953. Friedman, Martin B. "Shakespeare's 'Master Mistris': Image and Tone in Sonnet 20." Shakespeare Quarterly, 22 (1971), 189-91.

Rejects the notion that the poem expresses sexual frustration; rather it is "sportive" in tone.

1954. Friesen, H. Freiherrn v. "Ueber Shakespeare's Sonette." Shakespeare Jahrbuch, 4 (1869), 94-120.

Main emphasis is on the possible relationships between the Sonnets and Southampton and William Herbert.

1955. Friesen, Herm. Freih. von. Altengland und William Shakspere. Shakspere Studien, 1. Wien: Wilhelm Braumuller, 1874.

Contains a chapter dealing with "Shakspere's episch-lyrische Gedichte und Sonette" (pp. 308-48).

1956. Fripp, Edgar Innes. Master Richard Quyny, Bailiff of Stratford-Upon-Avon and Friend of William Shakespeare. London: Oxford University Press, 1924.

A section (pp. 64-75) deals with "Shakespeare's Sonnets, 1590-3."

1957. Fripp, Edgar I. Shakespeare, Man and Artist. London: Oxford University Press, 1938, vol.2.

In a chapter entitled "A Century of Sonnets" (pp. 322-31), Fripp notes that Sonnets 27-126 constitute a "Century," written during 1592-93.

1958. Frye, Northrop. "How True a Twain." The Riddle of Shakespeare's Sonnets. Ed. Edward Hubler. New York: Basic Books, 1962, pp. 23-53.

1959. *Fujita, Kiyomi. "The Sonnets--The World of Homosexuality." Mimesis (Tezukayama Gakuin University), 11 (1979), 44-68.

In Japanese.

1960. Furnivall, F.J. "Shakspereana.--Sonnet CXLVI. L. 2." Academy, 8 (1875), 282.

Proposes "Hemm'd with" to begin line 2 because Shakespeare uses the phrase in a similar context in Venus and Adonis (l. 1022).

1961. F[urnivall], F.J. "The W.H. or Will of Shakspere's Sonnets." Notes and Queries, 5th Series, 5 (1876), 443-44.

Furnivall reprints a letter by Colonel Joseph Chester listing the various people named Hughes, who might conceivably have been the "hues" or "Hews" referred to in the Sonnets.

1962. Furnivall, F.J. Review of The Sonnets of William Shakespeare, ed. Edward Dowden. Academy, 20 (1881), 154.

1963. Furnivall, F.J. "Mary Fitton Again." Academy, 39 (March 21, 1891), 282-83.

Finds an abundance of evidence--portraits, letters, etc.--to argue against Mary Fitton as the dark lady.

1964. Furnivall, F.J. "Shakspere and Mary Fitton." Theatre, 42 (December, 1897), 293-98.

William Herbert and Mary Fitton are the best guess for fair youth and dark lady, but there is no proof for it.

1965. Fuzier, Jean. "Amour et Sincerite dans les sonnets de Shakespeare." Langues Modernes, 59 (1965), 63-72.

1966. Fuzier, Jean. "Une Belle Trop Fidele." Langues Modernes, 59 (1965), 201-03.

Review of The Sonnets of Shakespeare Translated into French "Regular" Sonnets by Dikran Garabedian.

1967. Fuzier, Jean. "L'Affaire W.H." Langues Modernes, 59 (1965), 207-13.

Reviews of 1) John Dover Wilson, An Introduction to the Sonnets of Shakespeare for the Use of Historians and Others, 2) Shakespeare's Sonnets, ed. A.L. Rowse, and 3) Leslie Hotson, Mr. W.H.

1968. Fuzier, Jean. "Poesie et perplexite: reflexions sur un sonnet de Shakespeare." Langues Modernes, 61 (January-February, 1967), 38-45.

Finds in Sonnet 1 some complexities often overlooked.

1969. Fuzier, Jean. "'Mine is thy good report': A Note on Shakespeare's Sonnets 36 and 96." Cahiers Elisabethains, 9 (1976), 55-58.

Believes that the appearance of the same couplet in Sonnets 36 and 96 was intentional.

1970. F[uzier], J[ean]. Review of 1) Giorgio Melchiori, Shakespeare's Dramatic Meditations, and 2) New Essays on Shakespeare's Sonnets, ed. Hilton Landry. Cahiers Elisabethains, 11 (1977), 98-102.

1971. Fuzier, Jean. Review of Giorgio Melchiori, Shakespeare's Dramatic Meditations: An Experiment in Criticism. Etudes Anglaises, 30 (1977), 479-80.

1972. F[uzier], J[ean]. Review of Shakespeare's Sonnets, ed. Stephen Booth. Cahiers Elisabethains, 13 (1978), 109-12.

1973. Fuzier, Jean. Review of New Essays on Shakespeare's Sonnets, ed. Hilton Landry. Etudes Anglaises, 31 (1978), 223-24.

1974. Fuzier, Jean. Review of Shakespeare's Sonnets, ed. Stephen Booth. Etudes Anglaises, 31 (1978), 377-79.

1975. Fuzier, Jean. Review of Emilia Lanier, The Poems of Shakespeare's Dark Lady. Cahiers Elisabethains, No. 15 (1979), 105-06.

1976. Fuzier, Jean. "Le Banquet de Shakespeare: Les Sonnets et le Platonisme Authentique." Etudes Anglaises, 34 (1981), 1-15.

A comparison of some sonnets with Plato's Symposium.

1977. Fuzier, Jean. Review of Shakespeare's Sonnets, ed. Stephen Booth; S.C. Campbell, Only Begotten Sonnets: A Reconstruction of Shakespeare's Sonnet Sequence; Shakespeare's Sonnets, edited as a continuous sequence by S.C. Campbell; Shakespeare Sonnets, ed. Kenneth Muir; Paul Ramsey, The Fickle Glass: A Study of Shakespeare's Sonnets. Etudes Anglaises, 34 (1981), 215-17.

1978. G. Review of Edmond L'Hommede, Le Secret de Shakespeare: Les Sonnets. Revue Anglo-Americaine, 10 (1933), 436-37.

1979. G., J.M. "Griffin's 'Fidessa,' and Shakspeare's 'Passionate Pilgrim'." Notes and Queries, 1st Series, 9 (1854), 27.

Concerning the insertion of a sonnet from Fidessa in The Passionate Pilgrim.
654

1980. Gardiner, Robert F., D.C.T., and C.B.M. "Sonnet LXVI." Notes and Queries, 7th Series, 4 (1887), 405.

These three notes reject Bayne's emendation "disabled" in line 8.

1981. Gardner, C.O. Some Reflections on Shakespeare's Sonnets Nos. 33, 34, and 35. Theoria, 42 (June, 1974), 43-55.

Sonnets 33, 34, 35 belong together and probably in that order.

1982. Garnett, R. "The Date of the Sonnets." Literature, 6 (1900), 211-12.

Believes that a phrase in Sonnet 66 ("Art made tongue-tied by authority") may refer to an event in Summer, 1597.

1983. Garnier, Charles. Review of The Sonnets of Shakespeare, ed T.G. Tucker. Revue Anglo-Americaine, 2 (1925), 542-45.

1984. Garrigues, Gertrude. "Shakespeare's 'Sonnets'." Journal of Speculative Philosophy, 21 (1887), 241-58.

After dismissing the debate about the Dedication as being irrelevant, Garrigues focuses upon the themes of the Sonnets 1 - 126, the arrangement of which shows "unmistakable evidence of design."

1985. Gascht, Andre. "Marcel Thiry: Attouchements des Sonnets de Shakespeare. Revue generale, No. 6 (1971), 100-02.

A review.

1986. Gent, Lucy. "At the Health Farm." English, 27 (1978), 185-91.

Review of Giorgio Melchiori, Shakespeare's Dramatic Meditations: An Experiment in Criticism.

1987. Gerard, Albert S. "The Stone as Lily: A Discussion of Shakespeare's Sonnet XCIV." Shakespeare Jahrbuch, 96 (1960), 155-60.

1988. Gerard, Albert S. "Iconic Organization in Shakespeare's Sonnet CXLVI." English Studies, 42 (1961), 157-59. Reprinted in A Casebook on Shakespeare's Sonnets. Ed. Gerald Willen and Victor B. Reed. New York: Thomas Y. Crowell, 1964, pp. 279-82.

1989. Gerlach, Lee. "A Lecture on Meter as Meaning." Spectrum, 5 (1961), 79-89.

Sonnet 29 is used to illustrate the manner in which meter is used to strengthen the content.

1990. Germer, Rudolf. "Shakespeares Sonette als Sprachkunstwerke." Shakespeare Jahrbuch West, 1965, 248-63.

After reviewing the changing styles in the criticism of Shakespeare's Sonnets, Germer examines the Shakespearean sonnet structure.

1991. Gervinus, Georg Gottfried. "Shakespeare's Sonnette." Shakespeare. Leipzig: Wilhelm Engelmann, 1872, vol. 1, pp. 560-602. Translated as Shakespeare Commentaries by F.E. Bunnett. London: Smith, Elder, 1883.

1992. Giannetti, Robert Michael. "Amor Razionale and Amor Sensuale: An Approach to Shakespeare's Sonnets." Ph.D. Dissertation, Duquesne, 1979. DAI, 40 (1980), 6271A.

Examines Shakespeare's Sonnets in relation to the Italian Cinquecento poets and the Renaissance Neo-Platonists.

1993. Giannetti, Robert M. "Cooperation in the Study of the Continental Backgrounds of Shakespeare's Sonnets--A Model for Cooperation." Spenser Newsletter, 10 (Winter, 1979), 21-23.

1994. *Gilbank, P.E. "'Shakespeare's' Sonnets: A New Interpretation." Culture, 24 (1963), 107-15.

1995. Gilbert, A.J. "Philosophical Conceits in Shakespeare and Chapman." English Studies, 54 (1973), 118-21.

A comparison between Sonnet 24 and George Chapman's Ovid's Banquet of Sence (1595).

1996. Gilbert, A.J. "Techniques of Focus in Shakespeare's Sonnets." Language and Style, 12 (1979), 245-67.

1997. Gilman, Sander L. Review of Raimund Borgmeier, Shakespeares Sonett "When forty winters" und die deutschen Ubersetzer: Untersuchungen zu den Problemen der Shakespeare-Ubertragung. Arcadia, 8 (1973), 201-05.

1998. Gittings, Robert. Shakespeare's Rival: A Study in Three Parts. London: Heinemann, 1960.

The third part of this book, which seeks to argue a case for Gervase Markham as Shakespeare's rival, includes chapters on "The Sonnets," "The Rival Poet" and Markham's poem "Devoreux and the Sonnets." He stops short, however, of claiming Markham was the rival poet.

1999. Gleeson, James F. "Introducing Shakespeare." English Journal, 56 (1967), 1293-94.

On teaching Shakespeare's Sonnets to high school students.

2000. Godshalk, W.L. Review of Shakespeare's Sonnets, ed. by Stephen Booth; and Giorgio Melchiori, Shakespeare's Dramatic Meditations. Journal of English and Germanic Philology, 77 (1978), 428-33.

2001. Godshalk, W.L. "The Semantics of the Sonnets." TLS, August 11, 1978, p. 912.

Referring to Brockbank's review (June 23, 1978), Godshalk says that Shakespeare was addressing a man in Sonnet 80 and related sonnets.

1620

2002. Godshalk, W.L. "Puns in Shakespeare's Sonnet 1, Line 4." English Language Notes, 16 (1979), 200-02.

2003. Godwin, Parke. A New Study of the Sonnets of Shakespeare. New York: G.P. Putnam's Sons, 1900. rpt. New York: AMS Press, 1970.

After a history of the sonnets and a review of the literature about them, Godwin expounds his own view and concludes with a new arrangement of the sonnets.

2004. Goedeke, Karl. "Ueber Sonette Shakespeare's." Deutsche Rundschau, 10 (1877), 386-409.

2005. Goldsmith, Robert Hillis. "Shakespeare's Christian Sonnet, Number 146." Studies in the Literary Imagination, 11 (1978), 99-106.

2006. Goldsmith, Ulrich K. "Words Out of a Hat? Alliteration and Assonance in Shakespeare's Sonnets." Journal of English and Germanic Philology, 49 (1950), 33-48.

2007. Goldsmith, Ulrich K. "Shakespeare and Stefan George: The Sonnets." Theorie und Kritik. Zur Vergleichenden und neueren deutschen Literatur: Festschrift fur Gerhard Loose zum 65. Geburtstag. Ed. Stefan Grunwald and Bruce A. Beatie. Bern und Munchen: Francke, 1974, pp. 67-86.

On George's German translation of the Sonnets.

2008. Goldstien, Neal L. "Money and Love in Shakespeare's Sonnets." Bucknell Review, 17, iii (1969), 91-106.

Examines the use of money imagery in the Sonnets, with special attention to "sacred money imagery."

2009. Goodlet, I. "A New Word on Shakespeare's Sonnets." Poet-Lore, 3 (1891), 505-18.

A review of theories about when the poems were written, what they mean, and to whom they were addressed.

2010. Goodwin, M.A. "On Shake-speare's Sonnets." Baconiana, NS (2nd Series) 5 (1897), 186-200; NS (2nd Series) 6 (1898), 15-21.

The author's "mistress" is the Fame of his poetical works, but Shakespeare, who received the Fame, is not the author.

2011. Gordon, George. [Baldwin, Charles Crittenton.] Airy Nothings or What You Will. New York: Sturgis and Walton, 1917.

A supporter of Pembroke as Mr. W.H. (pp. 69-87), the author writes a play in one-act, "Mary, Mary," about Mary Fitton, the putative dark lady.

2012. Gothein, Marie. Review of Shakespeare-Sonnette, umdichtung von Stephan [sic] George; and Shakespeares Sonette, ubertragen von Eduard Sanger. Shakespeare Jahrbuch, 46 (1910), 266-68.

2013. Grabau, Carl, mit Beitragen von F.W. Moorman und W. Dibelius. "Zeitschriftenschau." Shakespeare Jahrbuch, 40 (1904), 315-50.

Contains a section on "Die Sonette" (pp. 331-32) and "Die Sonette von William Alabaster." (p. 345).

2014. Grabau, Carl, mit Beitragen von F.W. Moorman. "Zeitschriftenschau." Shakespeare Jahrbuch, 41 (1905), 273-95.

Contains a brief note on "Shakespeares Sonette" (p. 282) and another on Michael Drayton's sonnets (p. 289).

2015. Grabau, Carl. "Zeitschriftenschau." Shakespeare Jahrbuch, 44 (1908), 273-311.

Section on "Shakespeares Gedichte: Die Sonette" (p. 292).

2016. Grabau, Carl. "Zeitschriftenschau." Shakespeare Jahrbuch, 46 (1910), 195-251.

The section entitled "Die Gedichte Shakespeares: Zu den Sonetten" (pp. 214-15) considers Sidney Lee's article on "Ovid and Shakespeare's Sonnets."
2348

2017. Grabau, Carl. "Zeitschriftenschau 1914." Shakespeare Jahrbuch, 51 (1915), 218-44.

In the section on "Die Gedichte Shakespeares: Die Sonette," Grabau discusses an article by Gregor Sarrazin in the Internationale Monatsschrift (pp. 225-26).
2811

2018. Grabau, Carl. "Zeitschriftenschau 1915/16." Shakespeare Jahrbuch, 53 (1917), 188-228.

Reviews Wolff's article on "Petrarkismus und Antipetrarkismus in Shakespeares Sonetten," Morsbach's article "Sonette Shakespeares im Lichte der Uberlieferung" and Henry David Gray's paper on "The Arrangement and the Date of Shakespeare's Sonnets" (pp. 202-04).
2024, 2511, 3226

2019. Grabau, Carl. "Zeitschriftenschau 1916/17." Shakespeare Jahrbuch, 54 (1918), 109-40.

Reviews Arthur Beatty's paper on "Shakespeare's Sonnets and Plays" and R.M. Alden's "The 1640 Text of Shakespeare's Sonnets" (p. 121).
1446, 1536

2020. Grant, Peter. "Shakespeare's Sonnets." TLS, May 24, 1974, pp. 558-59.

Responds to Richard Jacobs (May 17, 1974) on the 1640 Quarto. 2217

2021. Grant, Robert. "Shakespeare's Sonnets: The Various Theories That Have Been Given to Account for Them." Ph.D. Dissertation, Harvard, 1876.

2022. Graves, Robert, and Laura Riding. "A Study in Original Punctuation and Spelling: Sonnet 129." _The Common Asphodel: Collected Essays on Poetry 1922-1949_. London: Hamish Hamilton, 1949, pp. 84-95. Reprinted in _Discussions of Shakespeare's Sonnets_. Ed. Barbara Herrnstein. Boston: D.C. Heath, 1964, pp. 116-23. Also reprinted in _A Casebook on Shakespeare's Sonnets_. Ed. Gerald Willen and Victor B. Reed. New York: Thomas Y. Crowell, 1964, pp. 161-72.

2023. Gray, Arthur. "The Sonnets." _A Chapter in the Early Life of Shakespeare_. Cambridge: University Press, 1926, pp. 97-101.

Believes that the first sonnets could not have been written before 1594.

2024. Gray, Henry David. "The Arrangement and the Date of Shakespeare's Sonnets." _PMLA_, 30 (1915), 629-44.

2025. Gray, Henry David. "Shakespeare's Last Sonnets." _Modern Language Notes_, 32 (1917), 17-21.

Since a handful of the later sonnets express a bitterness of tone, Gray argues that they were contemporary with the plays of similar tone--_Hamlet_ to _Timon_.

2026. Gray, Henry David. "Shakespeare's Rival Poet." _Journal of English and Germanic Philology_, 47 (1948), 365-73.

Adds evidence in support of Spenser as the "rival poet."

2027. Green, A. Wigfall. "Significant Words in Shakespeare's Sonnets." _University of Mississippi Studies in English_, 3 (1962), 95-113.

A selective concordance.

2028. Green, A. Wigfall. "Echoes of Shakespeare's Sonnets, Epitaph, and Elegiac Poems of The First Folio in Milton's 'On Shakespear. 1630'." _University of Mississippi Studies in English_, 4 (1963), 41-47.

Lists lines from the Sonnets and other texts that contain words appearing in Milton's poem "On Shakespear."

2029. Green, Martin B. _The Labyrinth of Shakespeare's Sonnets: An Examination of Sexual Elements In Shakespeare's Language_. London: Charles Skilton, 1974.

2030. Green, Martin. "The 'Man right fair'." TLS, January 18, 1974, p. 54.

2031. Green, Rosemary." "The Treasure Chest of the Mind: Uses of Memory in Sidney, Shakespeare, and Renaissance Lyric Poetry. Ph.D. Dissertation, Boston University, 1976. DAI, 37 (1976), 1563A.

"The Sonnets suggest that man's memory can recreate ideal love and beauty in a way that resembles the procreative powers of Nature."

2032. Greenfield, Stanley B. "Grammar and Meaning in Poetry." PMLA, 82 (1967), 377-87.

Greenfield writes about Shakespeare's Sonnet 30 and S.R. Levin's work with that poem in Linguistic Structures in Poetry. 2384

2033. Greenwood, Sir Granville George. The Shakespeare Problem Restated. London: John Lane, 1908. rpt. Westport, Conn.: Greenwood Press, 1970.

Although he skirts the "tremendous question" of the Sonnets, Greenwood appends a note to chapter 3 in which he states that the idea that Shakespeare wrote the poems is "preposterous" (pp. 82-83).

2034. Greenwood, G.G. Is There a Shakespeare Problem? With a Reply to Mr. J.M. Robertson and Mr. Andrew Lang. London: John Lane, 1916.

Greenwood, a moderate Baconian, examines the authorship question with references to the Sonnets throughout. The work is, in large part a response to critics of his earlier book, The Shakespeare Problem Restated.

2035. *Greenwood, G.G. "The Dark Lady." Observer, February 1, 1920, p. 18.

2036. Greenwood, G.G. "Mary Fitton." TLS, Jan. 12, 1922, p. 29.

Disputes the idea that Mary Fitton, whom he says was fair, was the dark lady.

2037. Grimshaw, James. "Amphibology in Shakespeare's Sonnet 64." Shakespeare Quarterly, 25 (1974), 127-29.

An ambiguity of meaning in the couplet stems from the fact that the pronoun in "which cannot choose" may refer to "thought" or to "death."

2038. Grivelet, Michel. Review of The Sonnets of Shakespeare, translated into French "Regular" Sonnets by Dikran Garabedian. Modern Language Review, 60 (1965), 249-50.

2039. Grivelet, Michel. "Shakespeare's 'War with Time': the Sonnets and 'Richard II'." Shakespeare Survey, 23 (1970), 69-78.

Following the lead of Mahood ("Love's Confined Doom"), Grivelet looks for parallels of imagery and theme between the Sonnets and Richard II.

2040. Groos, Karl, and Ilse Netto. "Psychologisch-Statistische Untersuchungen uber die Visuellen Sinneseindrucke in Shakespeares Lyrischen und Epischen Dichtungen." Englische Studien, 43 (1910), 27-51.

The Sonnets are discussed on pp. 32-38.

2041. Groth, Ernst. Review of Shakespeares Sonette, ubertragung und hrsg. von Karl Hauer. Beiblatt zur Anglia, 41 (1930), 136-40.

2042. Groth, Ernst. Review of Karl Wanschura, Die Sonette Shakespeares, von Franz Bacon geschrieben. Beiblatt zur Anglia, 42 (1931), 108-12.

2043. Grundlehner, Philip. "Kraus vs. George: Shakespeare's Sonnets." Shakespeare Jahrbuch West, 1977, 109-28.

Two German translators compared.

2044. Grundy, Joan. Review of Edward Hubler, et al. The Riddle of Shakespeare's Sonnets. Review of English Studies, NS 15 (1964), 73-75.

2045. Grundy, Joan. "Shakespeare's Sonnets and the Elizabethan Sonneteers." Shakespeare Survey, 15 (1962), 41-49. Reprinted in Shakespeare: The Sonnets: A Casebook, ed. Peter Jones. London: Macmillan, 1977, pp. 185-99.

2046. Guenther, Ralph R. "A Commentary on Norman Lowrey's Music to Selected Sonnets of William Shakespeare, For Soprano and Orchestra." Shakespeare 1964. Ed. Jim W. Corder. Fort Worth: Texas Christian University Press, 1965, pp. 81-87.

The selected sonnets are 8, 146, and 60.

2047. Guidi, Augusto. "Una Traduzione Italiana dei 'Sonetti' di Shakespeare." Lettere italiane, 10 (1958), 363-66.

Some critical comments on a translation of the Sonnets by Luigi De Marchi.

2048. Guiney, L.I. "Shakespeare and 'Warray': Sonnet CXLVI." Notes and Queries, 11th Series, 4 (1911), 84-85.

Comments on the various suggestions for the missing words in line 2. Also sugests, speculatively, "sentry" for "centre" in line 1, as being in keeping with the military metaphor in the poem.

2049. Gundolf, Friedrich. "Shakespeare's Sonnets and Poems." Shakespeare, 1 (1928), 163-80, 450-67.

2050. Gundry, W.G.C. "The Shake-speare Sonnets Interpreted." Baconiana, 3rd Series, 20 (1929), 48-51.

In paraphrases of Sonnet 48 and 49, Gundry claims 1) that Bacon addresses Shakespeare, whose name he uses, and 2) that Bacon may never get credit for the plays because he must remain a "concealed poet."

2051. Gurney, L.S. "Shakespeare's Sonnet 82." Explicator, 37, i (1978), 8-9.

2052. Gurr, Andrew. "Shakespeare's First Poem: Sonnet 145." Essays in Criticism, 21 (1971), 221-26.

Suggests Sonnet 145 was written in 1582 to Ann Hathaway eventually finding its way into his later sonnet collection.

2053. Guttmann, Bernhard. "Shakespeare im Selbstgesprach." Das alte Ohr. Frankfurt am Main: Societats-Verlag, 1955, pp. 123-39.

In the first part of the essay Guttmann considers what of significance is revealed by the Sonnets about Shakespeare's personality and his view of the world.

2054. H., C.E. "Shakespeare's 'Sonnets,' Print 1609." Notes and Queries, 9th Series, 6 (1900), 435-36.

Refutes A. Hall's reading of Sonnet 126.
2065

2055. Haefner, Gerhard. "William Shakespeare Sonnet 130: Skizzen zu einer Interpretation." Neusprachliche Mitteilungen aus Wissenschaft und Praxis, 23 (1970), 48-49.

2056. Hafker, H. Was sagt Shake-speare? Die Selbstbekenntnisse des Dichters in seinen Sonetten. Ein Beitrag zur Shakspere-Bacon-Frage. Berlin: Schuster and Loeffler, 1896.

2057. Hales, J.W. "From Stratford to London." Cornhill Magazine, 35 (1877), 69-83.

In Part I of the article, Hales notes those sonnets in which Shakespeare speaks of journeys and absences.

2058. *Halikowska, Teresa. "Czarna dama z 'Sonetow' Szekspira." [The Dark Lady in Shakespeare's Sonnets.] Zycie literackie (Krakow), May 15, 1973, 14-15.

2059. *Halkin, Simon. "Shakespeare's Sonnets." Yedioth Aharonoth, August 12, 1977.

In Hebrew, a review of Broido's translation of the Sonnets.

2060. Hall, A. "A Literary Craze." Notes and Queries, 6th Series, 10 (1884), 21-22; 61-62; 101-02; 181-82.

This four-part article explores the subject of the rival poet, dismissing Dante and Spenser and supporting Drayton as the likely candidate.

2061. Hall, A. "A Literary Craze." Notes and Queries, 6th Series, 10 (1884), 389-90.

Disagreeing with Ingleby, Hall does not believe that Shakespeare wrote a number of the sonnets in the The Passionate Pilgrim.
2201

2062. H[all], A. "A Literary Hoax." Notes and Queries, 6th Series, 12 (1885), 126-27.

As in his series of notes, "A Literary Craze," Hall has some sharp things to say about the efforts by some to make a unified whole of the first 126 sonnets. He refers specifically to a series of articles in Blackwood's Magazine.
2412

2063. Hall, A. "Shakespeare's Sonnets." Academy, 52 (September 11, 1897), 207.

Proposes Penelope Devereux (Lady Rich) as the dark lady.

2064. Hall, A. "Mr. 'W.H.'" Literature, 6 (1900), 212, 248.

In response to Sidney Lee's discussion of the term "begetter," Hall identifies the "begetter" as Southampton.
2346

2065. Hall, A. "Shakespeare's 'Sonnets.' Print 1609." Notes and Queries, 9th Series, 6 (1900), 348.

Suggests that Sonnet 126 was a supplement added at the time of publication as an envoi.

2066. Hall, Willine. "The Living Record: Aesthetic Structure in Shakespeare's Sonnets." Ph.D. Dissertation, Vanderbilt, 1976. DAI, 37 (1976), 2196A-97A.

2067. Halliday, F.E. "Dr. Hotson's Arguments." TLS, February 24, 1950, p. 121.

Notes that Samuel Butler had, 50 years before Hotson, dated Sonnet 107 in 1588.

2068. Halliday, F.E. Shakespeare and his Critics. London: Gerald Duckworth, 1949. Rev. ed. 1958.

In a brief section on the Sonnets (pp. 502-06), Halliday summarizes some of the facts and theories about the poems.

2069. Hamer, Douglas. "Shakespeare: Sonnet 143." _Notes and Queries_, 214 (1969), 129-30.

The image of the mother pursuing a hen and being herself pursued by her bawling infant has its origin in the English translation of Pasqualigo's comedy, _Il Fedele_.

2070. Hamer, Douglas. Review of R.J.C. Wait, _The Background to Shakespeare's Sonnets_, and Philip Martin, _Shakespeare's Sonnets: Self, Love and Art_. _Review of English Studies_, NS 25 (1974), 76-80.

2071. Hamer, Douglas. Review of _Shakespeare's Sonnets_, ed. Stephen Booth. _Review of English Studies_, 29 (1978), 476-79.

2072. Hamilton, A.C. "Recent Studies in the English Renaissance." _Studies in English Literature 1500-1900_, 9 (1969), 169-97.

Includes a review of Brents Stirling, _The Shakespeare Sonnet Order: Poems and Groups_ (pp. 181-82).

2073. Hammond, Gerald. Review of _Shakespeare's Sonnets_, ed. Kenneth Muir. _Critical Quarterly_, 22, ii (1980), 85.

A very negative review of Muir's 1979 edition.

2074. Hammond, Gerald. _The Reader and Shakespeare's Young Man Sonnets_. London: Macmillan, 1981.

Argues for 1) the order of the poems in the 1609 Quarto, 2) the same young man as the subject throughout, and 3) a reading that is not "circumscribed by the ideas and ideologies of the sixteenth and seventeenth centuries."

2075. Hancher, Michael. "Understanding Poetic Speech Acts." _College English_, 36 (1975), 632-39.

Examines Sonnet 19 with respect to what the speaker is doing while uttering the lines.

2076. Hankins, John Erskine. _Shakespeare's Derived Imagery_. Lawrence: University of Kansas Press, 1953.

Although he examines a number of parallels between imagery in the Sonnets and Renaissance and classical texts, Hankins focuses in particular upon the _Zodiake_ of Palingenius (pp. 245-56).

2077. Hannah, Donald. Review of J. Dover Wilson, _An Introduction to the Sonnets of Shakespeare For the Use of Historians and Others_, and William Shakespeare, _The Sonnets_, ed. J. Dover Wilson. _Archiv fur das Studium der neueren Sprachen und Literaturen_, 205 (1968), 320-22.

2078. Harbage, Alfred. "Dating Shakespeare's Sonnets." Shakespeare Quarterly, 1 (1950), 57-63.

Comments on Leslie Hotson's book, Shakespeare's Sonnets Dated, and Other Essays.

2079. Harries, Frederick J. Shakespeare and the Welsh. London: T. Fisher Unwin, 1919.

In a chapter "Shakespeare's Sonnets and 'Mr. W.H.'" (pp. 186-94), Harries summarizes the various theories and mentions some Welsh connections.

2080. Harris, Frank. The Man Shakespeare and His Tragic Life Story. London: Frank Palmer, 1909. rpt. New York: Horizon Press, 1969.

Three chapters (pp. 202-53) are devoted to "The Sonnets"--a highly biographical and not at all scholarly reading of the poems. [Pagination refers to the London edition.]

2081. Harris, Frank. The Women of Shakespeare. London: Methuen, 1911.

Contains a chapter on "The Sonnets: The Lover's Complaint: Shakespeare's Dark Mistress" (pp. 104-19) in which he makes a connection between the "Dark Lady" and the "Rosalines" of Love's Labour's Lost and Romeo and Juliet.

2082. Harrison, G.B. "The Mortal Moon." TLS, November 29, 1928, p. 938.

Eventually gives rise to a series of letters on Sonnet 107 initiated by E.K. Chambers (TLS, January 25, 1934, p. 60).
1459, 1689, 1861, 1938, 2084, 2540, 2723

2083. Harrison, G.B. Review of J.A. Fort, A Time Scheme for Shakespeare's Sonnets. Modern Language Review, 25 (1930), 488.

In this review, Harrison notes a parallel between the relationship of Shakespeare and Southampton and Falstaff and Hal.

2084. Harrison, G.B. "The 'Mortal Moon' Sonnet." TLS, February 1, 1934, p. 76.
2082

2085. Harrison, G.B. Review of Edward Hubler, The Sense of Shakespeare's Sonnets. Saturday Review of Literature, 35 (June 14, 1952), 29.

2086. Harrison, T.P., Jr. "Shakespeare and Montemayor's 'Diana'." University of Texas Studies in English, No. 6 (1926), 72-120.

In the last few pages of the article, Harrison notes that the Sonnets resemble passages in the Diana, e.g. in the reference to the eternizing powers of marriage and verse.

2087. Harrison, W.A. "The Dark Lady of Shakspere's Sonnets and Mistress Mary Fitton." *Academy*, 26 (July 5, 1884), 9-10. Translated and printed as "Die 'dunkle Dame' in Shakespeare's Sonetten und Mrs. Mary Fitton." *Shakespeare Jahrbuch*, 20 (1885), 327-29.

2088. Harrison, W.A. "Mistress Mary Fitton." *Academy*, 26 (July 12, 1884), 30.

Some corrections to his earlier letter (July 5) about Mary Fitton, the possible dark lady.

2089. Hart, John S. "Shakespeare's Sonnets." *Sartain's Union Magazine*, 5 (1849), 153-57, 217-23.

Discusses the dedication to the 1609 edition, the order of the Sonnets and some of the other usual concerns.

2090. Harwood, Henry H. *Two of the Most Remarkable and Interesting of the Sonnets of Francis Bacon, the True Shakespeare: A Compilation, Arrangement, and Composition*. Richmond, Va.: Ware and Duke, 1908.

Sonnets 26 and 66 are the two poems he uses to press his argument that Bacon wrote the Sonnets, plays, and poems.

2091. Haskin, Dayton, S.J. "Pardon as a Weapon Against Time in Shakespeare's *Sonnets*." *Xavier University Studies*, 11, iii (1972), 27-37.

2092. Hasler, Jorg. Review of Edward Hubler, *et al*. *The Riddle of Shakespeare's Sonnets*. *English Studies*, 48 (1967), 238-40.

2093. Hasler, Jorg. Review of Brents Stirling, *The Shakespeare Sonnet Order: Poems and Groups*. *English Studies*, 54 (1973), 70-71.

2094. Hasler, Jorg. Review of Philip Martin, *Shakespeare's Sonnets: Self, Love and Art*. *English Studies*, 55 (1974), 391-93.

2095. *Hattori, Yukiko. "'Show' and 'Seem' in Shakespeare's Sonnets." *English and American Literature* (Rikkyo University), No. 28 (1967), 57-75.

In Japanese. Discusses Shakespeare's quest for eternal love.

2096. Hausermann, H.W. "Hat Goethe Shakespeares 64. Sonett gekannt?" *Archiv fur das Studium der neueren Sprachen und Literaturen*, 201 (1964), 161-68.

2097. Hawkins, Harriet. Review of Anne Ferry, *All in War With Time: Love Poetry of Shakespeare, Donne, Jonson, Marvell*. *Modern Philology*, 76 (1979), 291-93.

Deals with Shakespeare's sonnets.

2098. Hayashi, Tetsumaro. "The Sonnet Mystery." Shakespeare Newsletter, 13 (1963), 42.

This is an abstract of Hayashi's series in The Times (London), September 18-20, 1963, on A.L. Rowse's findings.

2099. Hayashi, Tetsumaro. Shakespeare's Sonnets: A Record of 20th Century Criticism. Metuchen, N.J.: Scarecrow Press, 1972.

2100. Hayes, Ann L. "The Sonnets." "Starre of Poets": Discussions of Shakespeare. Carnegie Series in English, 10. Pittsburgh: Carnegie Institute of Technology, 1966, pp. 1-15.

The essay looks at sonnet structure, imagery and tone.

2101. Hazlitt, W. Carew. "Shakespeare's Sonnets: 'Mr. W.H.'." Notes and Queries, 3rd Series, 8 (1865), 449-50.

Rejects all of the popular theories about Mr. W.H. believing that William Hammond is "the only sensible proposal . . . yet broached."

2102. Hazlitt, William Carew. Shakespeare. London: B. Quaritch, 1902. Later published as Shakespear Himself and His Work: A Biographical Study. 4th ed. London: Bernard Quaritch, 1912.

Chapters 10-12 (pp. 208-67) deal with the Sonnets.

2103. Heath-Stubbs, John. Review of G. Wilson Knight, The Mutual Flame. Time and Tide, 36 (1955), 534.

2104. Hedberg, Johannes. "Enjoying a Shakespearian Sonnet in Class." Moderna sprak, 59 (1965), 5-10.

A reading of Sonnet 60.

2105. Hegedus, Stephan V. "Die griechische Quelle zu Shakespeares zwei letzten Sonetten. Ungarische Rundschau, 2 (1913), 586-96. Reprinted and translated from the Hungarian "Shakespeare ket utolso szonettjenek gorog forrasa." Magyar Shakespeare-tar (1912), 219-29.

On Sonnets 153-154.

2106. Helgerson, Richard. "Shakespeare's 'Sonnet CXXXVIII'." Explicator, 28 (1970), Item 48.

2107. *Helton, Tinsley. "Contemporary Trends in Shakespeare Sonnet Scholarship." Wisconsin English Journal, 8, ii (1965), 13-16.

2108. Hemingway, Samuel B. "Sonnet 8, and Mr. William Hughes, Musician." Modern Language Notes, 25 (1910), 210.

Mr. W.H. was equal to Shakespeare in rank and probably a musician or at least a lover of music.

2109. Henderson, W.A. "Shakespeare in the Sonnets." Notes and Queries, 9th Series, 10 (1902), 343-44.

Suggests that Edmund, Shakespeare's youngest sibling, was the person whom Shakespeare was urging to marry.

2110. Henrion, Pierre. Shakespeare: Supreme Masterpiece and Proof (Chef d'oeuvre et Preuve) Definitive. Lycee Hoche, Versailles: np, 1964.

In this 20-page pamphlet (in both English and French), the author tries to show that in Sonnet 76 the names of Shakespeare and Bacon are linked.

2111. Henry, Fernand. "Mr. William Hall." Literature, 6 (1900), 321.

Challenges Sidney Lee's theory that W.H. was a printer named William Hall.

2112. Heraud, John A. Shakspere: His Inner Life as Intimated in His Works. London: John Maxwell, 1865.

Heraud believes the Sonnets were actually a single poem revealing Shakespeare to be a man of religion with a great and profound mind.

2113. Herbert, T. Walter. "Shakespeare's Word-Play on Tombe." Modern Language Notes, 64 (1949), 235-41.

Principally concerned with Sonnet 83 although he discusses the four other sonnets in which the word appears (3,17,86,101).

2114. Herbert, T.W. "Shakespeare's Sonnet CXLII." Explicator, 13 (1955), 38.

2115. Herbert, T. Walter. "Sound and Sense in Two Shakespeare Sonnets." Tennessee Studies in Literature, 3 (1958), 43-52.

On Sonnets 12 and 30.

2116. Herbert, T. Walter. "Dramatic Personae in Shakespeare's Sonnets." Shakespeare's "More Than Words Can Witness": Essays on Visual and Nonverbal Enactment in the Plays. Ed. Sidney Homan. Lewisburg, Pa.: Bucknell University Press, 1980, pp. 77-91.

Finds contexts in various plays to explain by whom and to whom a number of sonnets might have been directed.

2117. Herford, C.H. A Sketch of Recent Shakespearean Investigation 1893-1923. London: Blackie, 1923.

Discusses work done on the Sonnets by Sidney Lee, Raymond Alden, and Arthur Acheson (pp. 56-58).

2118. Herrnstein, Barbara, ed. Discussions of Shakespeare's Sonnets. Boston: D.C. Heath, 1964.

Contains parts or all of essays by Hotson, Bateson, Hubler, Cruttwell, Knight, Lever, Ransom, Winters, Graves and Riding, Empson, Mizener, Nowottny, and Barber.

2119. Hertzberg, W. "Eine griechische Quelle zu Shakespeare's Sonetten." Shakespeare Jahrbuch, 13 (1878), 158-62.

Discusss a Greek epigram as a possible source of Sonnet 154.

2120. *Heshiki, Hirokuni. "Lights and Shadows in the Imagery of Shakespeare's Sonnets." Kiyo (Okinawa Kokusai University), 5 (1978), 1-28.

Discusses Sonnets 127-154, analyzing the character of the dark lady. In Japanese.

2121. Hettich, Blaise. Review of Paul Ramsey, The Fickle Glass: A Study of Shakespeare's Sonnets. Christianity and Literature, 29, iv (1980), 67-68.

2122. Heuer, Hermann. Review of G. Wilson Knight, The Mutual Flame. Shakespeare Jahrbuch, 92 (1956), 381-83.

2123. Heuer, Hermann. Review of Florens Christian Rang, Shakespeare der Christ, eine Deutung der Sonette. Shakespeare Jahrbuch, 92 (1956), 383-84.

2124. Heuer, Hermann. Review of Shakespeares Sonette, tr. Richard Flatter. Shakespeare Jahrbuch, 93 (1957), 277-79.

2125. Heuer, Hermann. Review of J.B. Leishman, Themes and Variations in Shakespeare's Sonnets. Shakespeare Jahrbuch, 99 (1963), 268-73.

2126. Heuer, Hermann. Review of Shakespeare's Sonnets, ed. Martin Seymour-Smith. Shakespeare Jahrbuch, 100 (1964), 328.

2127. Heuer, Hermann. "Zu Shakespeares Sonetten." Shakespeare Jahrbuch West, 1965, 382-83.

A review of Leslie Hotson, Mr. W.H.

2128. Heuer, Hermann. "Bucherschau." Shakespeare Jahrbuch West, 1967, pp. 283-306.

Includes reviews of 1) The Sonnets, ed. John Dover Wilson; 2) Shakespeare's Sonnets, ed. W.G. Ingram and Theodore Redpath; 3) A Casebook on Shakespeare's Sonnets, ed., Gerald Willen and Victor B. Reed; and 4) Shakespeares Sonette, nachdichtung Karl Kraus (pp. 302-06).

2129. Heuer, Hermann. Review of Theodor Wolpers, "William Shakespeare, Die Sonette," from Die englische Lyrik: Von der Renaissance bis zur Gegenwart. Ed. Karl Heinz Goller. Shakespeare Jahrbuch West, 1969, 299-300.

2130. Heuer, Hermann. Review of Raimund Borgmeier, Shakespeare's Sonett "When forty winters" und die deutschen Ubersetzer: Untersuchungen zu den Problemen der Shakespeare-Ubertragung. Shakespeare Jahrbuch West, 1971, 220-23.

2131. Heuer, Hermann. Review of 154 Sonette, ed. Hugo Goke. Shakespeare Jahrbuch West, 1972, 219-20.

2132. Heuer, Hermann. Review of Philip Martin, Shakespeare's Sonnets: Self, Love and Art; R.J.C. Wait, The Background to Shakespeare's Sonnets; and Eduard Eugen Schmid, Shakespeare und die Schwarze Dame. Shakespeare Jahrbuch West, 1973, 219-23.

2133. Heuer, Hermann. Review of William Shakespeare, The Sonnets/ Die Sonette, ed. Raimund Borgmeier. Shakespeare Jahrbuch West, 1975, 227-29.

2134. Heuer, Hermann. Review of Barbara Puschmann-Nalenz, "Loves of Comfort and Despair": Konzeptionen von Freundschaft und Liebe in Shakespeares Sonetten. Shakespeare Jahrbuch West, 1977, 180-83.

2135. Heuer, Hermann. Review of Hilton Landry, New Essays on Shakespeare's Sonnets. Shakespeare Jahrbuch West, 1978/79, 344-47.

2136. Highet, Gilbert. "The Autobiography of Shakespeare." People, Places, and Books. New York: Oxford University Press, 1953, pp.86-93.

He considers the Sonnets to be interesting yet inferior to Shakespeare's other work because they were a description of the poet's private world.

2137. Highet, Gilbert. "Shakespeare in Love." The Powers of Poetry. New York: Oxford University Press, 1960, pp. 39-46.

Believes the Sonnets to be very early--"a preparation for something better."

2138. Hillard, Kate. "On the Study of Shakespeare's Sonnets." Lippincott's, 15 (1875), 497-506.

A discussion of the autobiographical aspects of the poem with liberal references to the principal commentators of the time.

2139. Hinman, Charlton. "The Pronunciation of 'Wriothesley'." TLS, October 2, 1937, p. 715.

There is the possibility that the first syllable of the name gives rise to a pun on the word "rose" in Sonnets 1-126. Refuted by A.F. Pollard, TLS, October 9, 1937, p. 735.

2140. Hinman, Charlton. Review of Barbara Mackenzie, _Shakespeare's Sonnets: Their Relation to his Life_. _Modern Language Notes_, 63 (1948), 213-14.

2141. [Hitchcock, Gen. Ethan Allen]. _Remarks on the Sonnets of Shakespeare: With the Sonnets. Showing That They Belong to the Hermetic Class of Writings, and Explaining Their General Meaning and Purpose._ New York: James Miller, 1865.

What or whom Shakespeare is addressing in his Sonnets is what Sidney had called Immortal Beauty and Immortal Goodness.

2142. Hobbs, Mary. "Shakespeare's Sonnet II--'A Sugred Sonnet'?" _Notes and Queries_, 224 (1979), 112-13.

2143. Hobday, C.H. "Dr. Hotson's Argument." _TLS_, March 24, 1950, p. 185.

Reference in Sonnet 104 to "three hot Junes" may date this Sonnet after the hot summers of 1591-93.

2144. Hobday, C.H. "Shakespeare's Venus and Adonis Sonnets." _Shakespeare Survey_, 26 (1973), 103-09.

Argues for Shakespeare's authorship of three sonnets about Venus and Adonis in _The Passionate Pilgrim_.

2145. Hoffmann, Banesh. "Sherlock, Shakespeare and the Bomb." _Baker Street Journal_, 10 (1960), 69-79.

Holmes demonstrates ingeniously from references to Sonnets 12 and 64 that Shakespeare was familiar with the theory of relativity and the atomic bomb.

2146. Hoffmann, Friedrich. "Stefan Georges Ubertragung der Shakespeare-Sonette." _Shakespeare Jahrbuch_, 92 (1956), 146-56.

2147. Holland, Bernard. "The 'Dark Lady' to Mr. William Shakespeare: About 1605." _National Review_ (London), 56 (1910), 260-65.

Holland, in the persona of the Dark Lady, writes some sonnets to Shakespeare which include a number of allusions to the latter's Sonnets.

2148. Holland, Norman N. _Psychoanalysis and Shakespeare_. New York: McGraw-Hill, 1964. 1966.

Holland discusses Freud's theories on the authorship of the Sonnets (pp. 56-59) and summarizes psychoanalytical readings of the Sonnets by Clarissa Rinaker and Gordon Smith (pp. 267-69). [Page references to 1966 edition.]
88, 2965

2149. Hollander, John. "Past Reason Hunted." _Kenyon Review_, 18 (1956), 659-63.

A review of G. Wilson Knight, The Mutual Flame, in which Hollander calls most of the book "either nonsense or beside the point," because of its urge to discover the poet in his poems.

2150. Hollander, John. The Untuning of the Sky: Ideas of Music in English Poetry, 1500-1700. Princeton, N.J.: Princeton University Press, 1961.

Hollander discusses musical conceits in some of the sonnets of Shakespeare, Daniel, Drayton, John Davies of Hereford, and Percy (pp. 131-39).

2151. [Holzapfel], Rudolf Melander. New Shakespearean Notes. np: privately printed, 1947.

A group of lectures in which he conjectures that William Herbert was Shakespeare's son. He offers readings of a number of sonnets to support this thesis.

2152. Holzapfel, Rudolf Melander. Shakespeare's Secret: A New and Correct Interpretation of Shakespeare's Sonnets, which are now for the first time Fully Explained, with a word-for-word interpretation of each Sonnet and a running Commentary proving the Continuity of the first 126 Sonnets and a re-arrangement of the Dark Lady Sonnets. Dublin: Dolmen Press for Melander Shakespeare Society, 1961.

2153. Holzer, Gust. "The Grave's Tiring-Room and Sonnet 68." Baconiana, 3rd Series, 5 (1907), 201-09.

This Baconian links ideas in The Tempest to several sonnets.

2154. Honigmann, E.A.J. Review of Claes Schaar, An Elizabethan Sonnet Problem. Shakespeare Quarterly, 13 (1962), 351-53.

2155. Hoover, Sister Mary Frederic, S.N.D. "A Study of Imagery in Shakespeare's Sonnets, Troilus and Cressida, Macbeth, Antony and Cleopatra, and The Winter's Tale." Ph.D. Dissertation, Case Western Reserve, 1973. DAI, 34 (1974), 5103A-04A.

2156. Horvath, Laszlo. "Variaciok az elmulas temajara. (Negy Shakespeare-szonett uj forditasa ele)." [Variations on the Theme of Evanescence. Plans for a New Translation of Shakespeare's Sonnets.] Filologiai kozlony (Budapest), 20 (1974), 220-23.

2157. Hosmer, H.L. Bacon and Shakespeare in the Sonnets. San Francisco: Bancroft, 1887.

Hosmer reads the poems as if Bacon were the poet and Shakespeare a mere "front." He finds in them references to the other "Bacon-Shakespeare" works.

2158. Hotson, Leslie. Shakespeare's Sonnets Dated, and Other Essays. New York: Oxford University Press; London: Rupert Hart-Davis, 1949. Reprinted in Discussions of Shakespeare's Sonnets, ed. Barbara Herrnstein. Boston: D.C. Heath, 1964, pp. 8-21.

In the title essay (pp. 1-36) Hotson explains that the key to dating the Sonnets is Sonnet 107. Those that have believed "the mortall Moone hath her eclipse indur'de" refers to Elizabeth's death in 1603 have been led down a false trail. Hotson speaks of Sonnets 123 and 124 also in establishing 1589 as a completion date for the Sonnets.

2159. Hotson, Leslie. "When Shakespeare Wrote the Sonnets." Atlantic, 184 (December, 1949), 61-67.

A review of some of the "topical allusions" in the Sonnets used to provide dating evidence--particularly in Sonnets 107, 123, 124.

2160. Hotson, Leslie. "The Date of Shakespeare's Sonnets." TLS, June 2, 1950, p. 348.

Hotson recapitulates his thesis that the date of the Sonnets is before 1590; he specifically responds to I.A. Shapiro's views expressed in a previous issue of TLS (p. 245).
2930

2161. Hotson, Leslie. "More Light on Shakespeare's Sonnets." Shakespeare Quarterly, 2 (1951), 111-18.

Argues for an early date (c. 1589) for the Sonnets.

2162. Hotson, Leslie. Mr. W.H. London: Hart-Davis; New York: Alfred A. Knopf, 1964.

Shakespeare's friend, Mr. W.H., is William Hatcliffe.

2163. Hotson, Leslie. "The Shakespeare Mystery Solved." Sunday Times Magazine (London), April 12, 1964, pp. 6-24.

A recapitulation of Hotson's theories about Mr. W.H., the dark lady, etc.

2164. Hotson, Leslie. "Taking Shakespeare at His Word." Shakespeare Studies, 1 (1965), 137-41.

The Sonnets are a work of his youth completed about 1589.

2165. Hotson, Leslie. Shakespeare by Hilliard. London: Chatto and Windus; Berkeley and Los Angeles: University of California Press, 1977.

Hotson concludes that Nicholas Hilliard's miniature of an "Unknown Man" is Shakespeare's friend, Master William Hatcliffe, a "fact" which throws some light on the Sonnets.

2166. Hovey, Richard B., James Schroeter, and Robert Berkelman. "Sonnet 73." College English, 23 (1962), 672-75.

A series of four letters prompted by Schroeter's original article about Sonnet 73 in College English.
2832

2167. Howard-Hill, T.H. Review of Brents Stirling, The Shakespeare Sonnet Order: Poems and Groups and James Winny, The Master-Mistress: A Study of Shakespeare's Sonnets. Review of English Studies, NS 20 (1969), 489-91.

2168. Howell, Anthony. "A Question of Form." Poetry Review, 60 (1969), 41-49.

Discusses the Baroque influence on poetry, including comments on Shakespeare's Sonnets and Meredith's Modern Love.

2169. Hoy, Cyrus. "Shakespeare and the Revenge of Art." Renaissance Studies in Honor of Carroll Camden. Ed. J.A. Ward. Rice University Studies (Special Festschrift Number), 60, ii, (1974), pp. 71-94.

Where the plays give us an oblique view of Shakespeare's feelings, the Sonnets are a direct and intimate expression of those feelings. Hoy looks at such feelings in the two media.

2170. Hubler, Edward. "Three Shakespearean Myths: Mutability, Plenitude, and Reputation." English Institute Essays 1948. Ed. D.A. Robertson. New York: Columbia University Press, 1949, pp. 95-119.

In his comments he refers to the plays but predominantly to Shakespeare's Sonnets.

2171. Hubler, Edward. "Shakespeare's Sonnets Dated." Shakespeare Quarterly, 1 (1950), 78-83.

Review of Leslie Hotson's Shakespeare's Sonnets Dated, and Other Essays.

2172. Hubler, Edward. The Sense of Shakespeare's Sonnets. Princeton University Studies in English, 33. Princeton, N.J.: Princeton University Press, 1952.

2173. Hubler, Edward. "Shakespeare's Sonnets and the Commentators." The Riddle of Shakespeare's Sonnets. New York: Basic Books, 1962, pp. 1-21.

In addition to this essay by Hubler, the book contains the text of the sonnets with essays by Northrop Frye, Leslie Fiedler, Stephen Spender, R.P. Blackmur, and Oscar Wilde's short story, "The Portrait of Mr. W.H."

2174. Hubler, Edward. "The Secret of Shakespeare's Sonnet?" Shakespeare Newsletter, 12 (1962), 21.

Review of Rudolf Melander Holzapfel, Shakespeare's Secret.

2175. Hubler, Edward. "Shakespeare and the Unromantic Lady." Discussions of Shakespeare's Sonnets. Ed. Barbara Herrnstein. Boston: D.C. Heath, 1964, pp. 28-45. Reprinted from The Sense of Shakespeare's Sonnets (pp. 38-63).

Discusses Shakespeare's dark lady who, because she was not idealized, was unique in Renaissance sonnet literature.
2172

2176. Hubler, Edward. "Form and Matter." A Casebook on Shakespeare's Sonnets. Ed. Gerald Willen and Victor B. Reed. New York: Thomas Y. Crowell, 1964, pp. 236-56. Reprinted from Edward Hubler, The Sense of Shakespeare's Sonnets. Appears also in Discussions of Poetry: Form and Structure. Ed. Francis Murphy. Boston: D.C. Heath, 1964, pp. 160-78.

Hubler considers Shakespeare's poetic practice: his use of the sonnet form, puns, the couplet, etc.
2172

2177. Hubler, Edward. "The Range of Shakespeare's Comedy." Shakespeare 400: Essays by American Scholars on the Anniversary of the Poet's Birth. Ed. James G. McManaway. New York: Holt, Rinehart and Winston, 1964, pp. 57-66.

Discusses sonnet 130 as high comedy (p. 61).

2178. Hubler, Edward. "The Economy of the Closed Heart." Shakespeare: Modern Essays in Criticism. Ed. Leonard Dean. New York: Oxford University Press, Galaxy Books, 1967, pp. 467-76. Reprinted from The Sense of Shakespeare's Sonnets.

The Sonnets give a sketch of a troubled friendship.
2172

2179. Hulme, Hilda. "Sonnet 145: 'I Hate, From Hathaway She Threw'." Essays in Criticism, 21 (1971), 427-29.

Hulme finds no evidence for Andrew Gurr's hypothesis on the early dating of Sonnet 145.
2052

2180. Hunt, F.C. "Cupid in the Sonnets." Baconiana, 2nd Series, 10 (1902), 66-75.

Cites an abundance of allusions to Cupid to prove that the poems did not refer to real people.

2181. Hunt, F.C. "'The Unspeakable Sonnets': Two Hundred and Ninety-Four Years of Their Criticism." New Shakespeareana, 2 (1903), 9-22.

Hunt, reviewing approximately twenty books published during the previous forty years, comments on the various theories.

2182. Hunt, F.C., et al. "Eclipse Endured." Baconiana, 3rd Series, 4 (1906), 134-37.

2183. Hunt, F.C. "Bacon's 'Inquisitions' and The Sonnets." Baconiana, 3rd Series, 5 (1907), 48-53.

Systematic allusions to the four elements are further evidence that Bacon wrote the Sonnets.

2184. Hunt, Fred C. "'The Grave's Tiring Room': A Criticism." Baconiana, 3rd Series, 6 (1908), 238-43.

Offers a somewhat different reading of the Sonnets from J.E. Roe but reaches the same conclusion: Bacon was the poet.
2745

2185. Hunt, Theodore W. "The English Sonnet--The Sonnets of Shakespeare." Bibliotheca Sacra, 67 (1910), 611-24.

Opens with a general discussion of the sonnet before reviewing some of the prominent theories about Shakespeare's.

2186. Hunter, G.K. "The Dramatic Technique of Shakespeare's Sonnets." Essays in Criticism, 3 (1953), 152-64. Reprinted in Shakespeare: The Sonnets: A Casebook. Ed. Peter Jones. London: Macmillan, 1977, pp. 120-33.

2187. Hunter, George K. "The Critics' Use of Shakespeare." Yale Review, 68 (1978), 118-23.

Review of Shakespeare's Sonnets, ed. Stephen Booth.

2188. Hunter, Joseph, and B. Heywood Bright. "Sonnets of Shakespeare to Lord Pembroke." Gentleman's Magazine, 102 (1832), 296.

Both Hunter and Bright, in respective letters, claim that the latter had, some years before, discovered that Pembroke was Mr. W.H. See James Boaden on the same subject.
1570

2189. *Husain, Rizwan, S.M. Review of Giorgio Melchiori, Shakespeare's Dramatic Meditations: An Experiment in Criticism. Aligarh Journal of English Studies, 4 (1979), 201-07.

2190. Hussey, Richard. "Shakespeare and Gower." Notes and Queries, 180 (1941), 386.

Notes a similarity between Sonnet 64 and two passages in Gower's Vox Clamantis.

2191. Hutchins, Virginia. "A Humanist's Personal Infatuation: A Brief Study of Shakespeare's Sonnets to the Dark Lady." The Humanist in His World: Essays in Honor of Fielding Dillard Russell. Ed.

Barbara W. Bitter and Frederick K. Sanders. Greenwood, S.C.: Attic Press, 1976, pp. 70-78.

Examines some puns and themes in the Sonnets.

2192. Hutchinson, John. "The Sonnets of 'Shakespeare.' (A New View)." Baconiana, 3rd Series, 10 (1912), 82-94.

Believes that the poet (Bacon) was addressing himself throughout the sequence, and the characters are personifications of virtues and vices.

2193. Hutchinson, John. "The 'Shakespeare' Sonnets." Baconiana, 3rd Series, 10 (1912), 221-30.

A rejoinder to Waddington and Theobald.
3148

2194. Huttar, Charles A. "The Christian Basis of Shakespeare's Sonnet 146." Shakespeare Quarterly, 19 (1968), 355-65.

2195. Hutton, James. "Analogues of Shakespeare's Sonnets 153-54: Contributions to the History of a Theme." Modern Philology, 38 (1941), 385-403. Reprinted in James Hutton, Essays on Renaissance Poetry. Ed. Rita Guerlac. Ithaca, N.Y.: Cornell University Press, 1980, pp. 149-68.

2196. Hux, Samuel. "Shakespeare's Sonnet CXXXVIII." Explicator, 25 (1967), Item 45.

2197. *Iinuma, Mariko. "On Shakespeare's Farewell Sonnets." Kiyo (Heian Jogakuin Junior College), 9 (1979), 16-22.

Discusses the changing relationship between the poet and his lover. In Japanese.

2198. Inge, William Ralph. "Did Shakespeare Unlock His Heart?" A Pacifist in Trouble. London: Putnam, 1939, pp. 275-79.

Believes the Sonnets to be conventional and hence devoid of biographical statements.

2199. Ingleby, C.M. The Soule Arayed: A Letter to Howard Staunton, Esq., Concerning Shakespeare's Sonnet CXLVI. London: R. Barrett and Sons, 1872.

Explores the various emendations for the second line of Sonnet 146 and finally concludes that "Leagu'd with these rebel powers . . ." is most satisfying.

2200. Ingleby, C.M., and C. Elliot Browne. "A Shakespearean Discovery." Athenaeum, December 13, 1873, p. 771.

More on Edmonds's theory about the "W.H." who signed the dedication to a work by Robert Southwell.
1865

2201. Ingleby, C.M. "A Literary Craze." Notes and Queries, 6th Series, 10 (1884), 274.

Earlier in this volume, A. Hall wrote that Shakespeare never referred to Spenser in his writing; Ingleby finds a reference to Spenser in a sonnet in The Passionate Pilgrim, one which most editors ascribe to Shakespeare.
2060

2202. Ingleby, Holcombe, and Ne Quid Nimis. "Shakespeare's Sonnet: 'A New Theory'." Notes and Queries, 9th Series, 12 (1903), 210-11.

Rejects Stronach's theory that Barnes wrote Sonnet 86.
3047

2203. Ingram, W.G. "The Shakespearean Quality." New Essays on Shakespeare's Sonnets. Ed. Hilton Landry. New York: AMS Press, 1976, pp. 41-63.

2204. Ingram, W.G., and Theodore Redpath, ed. Sixty-five Sonnets of Shakespeare. London: University of London Press, 1967.

In addition to the text of the poems, the editors provide a number of essays covering such topics as Shakespeare's diction, Elizabethan vocabulary and idiom, Shakespeare's rhetoric, his imagery, the editions, etc.

2205. Isaac, Hermann. "Zu den Sonetten Shakspere's." Archiv fur das Studium der neueren Sprachen und Literaturen, 59 (1878), 155-204, 241-72; 60 (1878), 33-64; 61 (1879), 177-200, 393-426; 62 (1879), 1-30, 129-72.

Part I is a survey of the criticism and the subsequent parts deal with those specific sonnets (including poems from The Passionate Pilgrim) that Isaac believes are concerned with love.

2206. Isaac, Hermann. "Wie weit geht die Abhangigkeit Shakespeare's von Daniel als Lyriker?" Shakespeare Jahrbuch, 17 (1882), 165-200.

Indicates parallels between the sonnets of the two poets.

2207. Isaac, Hermann. "Shakespeare's Selbstbekenntnisse." Preussiche Jahrbucher, 54 (1884), 237-69; 313-29.

Sees the Sonnets as a spiritual biography.

2208. Isaac, Hermann. "Die Sonett-Periode in Shakespeare's Leben." Shakespeare Jahrbuch, 19 (1884), 176-264.

Discusses the principal themes in the sonnets: procreation, praise of beauty in a friend, immortality, love, jealousy, etc.

2209. *Izzo, Carlo. "I Sonetti." Civilta Brittanica. Roma: Edizioni di Storia e Letteratura, 1970, vol. 1, pp. 70-77.

2210. J., D. "Shakespeare's Sonnets: Their Dedication." Notes and Queries, 10th Series, 12 (1909), 265.

Notes a similarity between the dedication of the 1609 Quarto and a dedication to a translation of St. Augustine's De Civitate Dei by J.H. The latter was dedicated to "Lord William, Earl of Pembroke."

2211. Jabez. "A Shakespeare Myth Exploded." Notes and Queries, 5th Series, 1 (1874), 81-82.

Dismisses the idea that Shakespeare was lame (a notion derived from lines in Sonnets 37 and 89).

2212. Jabez. "Sonnet LXXXVI." Notes and Queries, 5th Series, 7 (1877), 283, 465.

Jabez disputes Legis's reading of "fild" in line 13 (pp. 244-45).
2355

2213. *Jackson, Edith A. A Consideration of Shakespeare's Sonnets. np: 1904.

2214. Jackson, MacD. P. "Punctuation and the Compositors of Shakespeare's Sonnets, 1609." Library, 5th series, 30 (1975), 1-24.

Punctuational differences correlating with other differences in the Quarto may point to the possibility of two compositors.

2215. Jackson, MacD. P. "Shakespeare's 'Sonnets', 'Parthenophil and Parthenophe', and 'A Lover's Complaint'." Notes and Queries, 217 (1972), 125-26.

2216. Jacobs, Richard. "Shakespeare's Sonnets." TLS, May 3, 1974, p. 477.

Makes some points about why the 1609 quarto was replaced by the inferior text of the Benson 1640 quarto. Also adds some observations to those made by A.L. Rowse in "Shakespeare and Emilia" (TLS, April 26, 1974, p. 447).
2772

2217. Jacobs, Richard. "Shakespeare's Sonnets." TLS, May 17, 1974, p. 527.

Comments on Josephine Waters Bennett's work on Benson's 1640 edition of the Sonnets.
1548

2218. Jaeger, Ronald W. "A Biblical Allusion in Shakespeare's Sonnet 154." Notes and Queries, 217 (1972), 125.

The closing line of the poem is very similar to Song of Solomon 8:7.

2219. Jahn, Jerald D. "Shakespeare's Aristotelian Memory." Shakespeare Newsletter, 27 (1977), 24.

Abstract of a paper given at the 1977 meeting of the Shakespeare and Renaissance Association of West Virginia. Mentions 22,24,46,53, and 77 in speaking of the phenomenon of visual perception.

2220. Jakobson, Roman, and Lawrence G. Jones. Shakespeare's Verbal Art in th'Expence of Spirit. De Proprietatibus Litterarum, Series Practica, 35. The Hague: Mouton, 1970. Translated into French by Andre Jarry in "L'art verbal dans 'Th'expence of spirit' de Shakespeare," in Roman Jakobson, Questions de Poetique. Paris: Editions du Seuil, 1973, pp. 356-77.

2221. James, George. Francis Bacon in the Sonnets. Bacon-Shakespeare Pamphlets, 5. Birmingham: Midland Educational Co., 1900.

By recognizing Bacon's authorship of the Sonnets, the difficulties of the poems are elucidated and "order [is brought] out of chaos."

2222. Jane-Mansfield, Cecil. "Mr. W.H." Saturday Review of Literature, 12 (June 1, 1935), 9.

Replies to Paul Clarkson, suggesting several names with the initials of W.H. who might be possible candidates.
1717

2223. Jenkins, Harold. Review of Barbara A. Mackenzie, Shakespeare's Sonnets: Their Relation to His Life. Modern Language Review, 42 (1947), 261-62.

He speaks of "one brilliant conjecture" in Mackenzie's book--on the word "ore-greene" in Sonnet 112.

2224. Jiriczek, O. Review of Samuel Butler, Shakespeare's Sonnets, Reconsidered. Beiblatt zur Anglia, 13 (1902), 100-04.

2225. *Johannes, J.G. The Mysteries about Shakespeare's Sonnets Solved? Batavia: G. Kolff, 1928.

2226. *Johannes, J.G. Shakespeare's Mysterious W.H. and Dark Mistress Revealed (as William Harvey and Elizabeth, Countess of Derby)? Batavia: Kolff, 1928.

2227. Johnson, A.L. Review of R.R. Quintavalle, Saggi sulla connotazione: tre sonetti di Shakespeare. Lingua e Stile, 12 (1977), 739-41.

2228. Johnson, B.S. "No Lady?" Spectator, September 28, 1962, p. 444.

Review of Edward Hubler et al. The Riddle of Shakespeare's Sonnets.

2229. Johnson, C.M.W. "Shakespeare's Sonnet 129." The Explicator, 7 (1949), Item 41. Also in A Casebook on Shakespeare's Sonnets. Ed. Gerald Willen and Victor B. Reed. New York: Thomas Y. Crowell, 1964, pp. 274-75.

2230. Johnson, Jesse. Testimony of the Sonnets as to the Authorship of the Shakespearean Plays and Poems. New York and London: G.P. Putnam's Sons, 1899.

Sonnets were not written by Shakespeare but by a great "unknown" poet who was probably responsible for many of the plays.

2231. Johnson, S.F. Review of Edward Hubler, The Sense of Shakespeare's Sonnets. Shakespeare Newsletter, 2 (1952), 39.

2232. Jones, Charles V. "'One Is Not a Number': The Literal Meaning of a Figure of Speech." Notes and Queries, 225 (1980), 312-14.

This note on Aristotelian mathematics and the character of the number 'one' sheds some light on lines in Sonnets 136 and 8.

2233. Jones, Henry Festing. Samuel Butler, Author of Erewhon (1835-1902): A Memoir. 2 vol. London: Macmillan, 1919.

In volume 2, chapter 38, there are passages from Butler's writings about his thoughts on Shakespeare's Sonnets (pp. 307-19).

2234. Jones, John. "Fair Youth or Dark Lady?" New Statesman and Nation, 49 (1955), 478-79.

Review of G. Wilson Knight, The Mutual Flame.

2235. Jones, Peter, ed. Shakespeare: The Sonnets: A Casebook. London: Macmillan, 1977.

Contains a number of notes and brief excerpts from books and articles on Shakespeare's Sonnets.

2236. Jonson, G.C. Ashton. "Shakespeare's Sonnets." Poetry Review, 22 (1931), 274-92.

2237. Jorgensen, Virginia. "Of Love and Hate." English Journal, 53 (1964), 459-61.

A reading of Sonnet 90.

2238. Jouve, Pierre Jean. "Sonnets de Shakespeare." Mercure de France, 324 (1955), 5-16.

Contains a French prose translation of eleven sonnets with some introductory remarks.

2239. Jouve, Pierre Jean. "Sur les Sonnets de W.S." Revue de Paris, 62 (Avril, 1955), 112-19.

Following his comments, he includes prose translations of nine sonnets.

2240. Kahn, Ludwig W. "Ludwig Tieck als Ubersetzer von Shakespeares Sonetten." Germanic Review, 9 (1934), 140-42.

2241. Kahn, Ludwig W. Shakespeares Sonette in Deutschland: Versuch einer Literarischen Typologie. Bern und Leipzig: Gotthelf, 1935.

A discussion of the reception of Shakespeare's Sonnets in Germany and a review of the various German translations.

2242. Kahn, Ludwig W. "Burgerlicher Stil und burgerliche Ubersetzungen." Das Problem des Ubersetzens. Ed. Hans Joachim Storig. Darmstadt: Wissenschaftliche Buchgesellschaft, 1963, pp. 299-321.

This selection originally appeared as the fourth chapter of Kahn's book, Shakespeares Sonette in Deutschland (1935).

2243. Kallsen, T.J. "Shakespeare's Sonnet XXXIV, 13." Explicator, 27 (1969), Item 63.

2244. Kaplan, Milton. "Retarding Shakespeare." Harper's Magazine, 212 (January, 1956), 37-38.

Satiric proposal to rewrite Sonnet 73 for the slow reader.

2245. Kardos, Laszlo. "A 73. szonett magyar utja." [The Hungarian Career of Sonnet 73.] Shakespeare Tanulmanyok [Studies in Shakespeare]. Ed. Laslo Kery, Laslo Orszagh, and Miklos Szenczi. Budapest: Akademiai Kiado, 1965, pp. 56-79.

2246. Karpf, Carl. TO TI HN EINAI. Die Idee Shakespeare's und deren Verwirklichung, Sonettenerklarung und Analyse des Dramas Hamlet, (indirecter Beitrag zur Zeitfrage "Glauben und Wissenschaft)." Hamburg: W. Mauke Sohne, 1869.

Karpf sees a thematic movement from "Die Selbstliebe (Moment des Schonen)" to "Die Negation (Moment des Hasslichen)." His discussion concludes with his chapter "Die Moglichkeit und Wirklichkeit" (pp. 28-124).

2247. Kau, Joseph. "Daniel's Influence on an Image in Pericles and Sonnet 73: An 'Impresa' of Destruction." Shakespeare Quarterly, 26 (1975), 51-53.

2248. Kaufmann, U. Milo. Review of Murray Krieger, A Window to Criticism: Shakespeare's Sonnets and Modern Poetics. Journal of English and Germanic Philology, 65 (1966), 592-95.

2249. Kaula, David. "'In War with Time': Temporal Perspectives in Shakespeare's Sonnets." Studies in English Literature, 1500-1900, 3 (1963), 45-57.

2250. Kawanishi, Susumu. "The Use of Translation: A Note on Sonnet 73." Shakespeare Translation, 3 (1976), 61-65.

Japanese translators seem to have some difficulty in rendering the couplet in Sonnet 73.

2251. *Kawanishi, Susumu. "The Conflict of Time and Love in Shakespeare's Sonnets." Literature and Thought in the Renaissance, Dedicated to Professor Masao Hirai. Tokyo: Chikuma Press, 1977, pp. 39-55.

In Japanese.

2252. Keller, Wolfgang. "Sprache und Metrik." Shakespeare Jahrbuch, 55 (1919), 159-65.

First part of this review (pp. 159-61) discusses the work of Albert Wietfeld, Die Bildersprache in Shakespeares Sonetten.

2253. Keller, Wolfgang. "Sammelreferat." Shakespeare Jahrbuch, 58 (1922), 120-44.

Reviews Shakespeare Sonette, translated into German by Friedrich Huch (p. 126).

2254. Keller, Wolfgang, und Clare Hunekuhl. "Zeitschriftenschau." Shakespeare Jahrbuch, 59-60 (1924), 221-39.

Keller reviews Mats Redin's article, "The Friend in Shakespeare's Sonnets" (p. 232).

2255. Keller, Wolfgang. "Sammelreferat." Shakespeare Jahrbuch, 62 (1926), 165-72.

Includes a review of Rudolf Fischer, Shakespeares Sonette (Gruppierung, Kunstform) (pp. 167-68).

2256. Keller, Wolfgang. "Sammelreferat." Shakespeare Jahrbuch, 64 (1928), 188-202.

Includes a review of J.M. Robertson, The Problems of the Shakespeare Sonnets (pp. 197-98).

2257. Keller, Wolfgang. Review of Ludwig W. Kahn, Shakespeares Sonette in Deutschland. Shakespeare Jahrbuch, 71 (1935), 122-23.

2258. Keller, Wolfgang. Review of Shakespeare's Sonnets, ed. C.F. Tucker Brooke. Shakespeare Jahrbuch, 73 (1937), 153.

2259. Keller, Wolfgang. Review of Denys Bray, Shakespeare's Sonnet-Sequence. Shakespeare Jahrbuch, 75 (1939), 162-63

2260. Keller, Wolfgang. Review of The Sonnets of William Shakespeare and Henry Wriothesley, Third Earl of Southampton, ed. Walter Thomson. Shakespeare Jahrbuch, 77 (1941), 195-96.

2261. Kellner, Leon. "Shakespeares Sonette." Englische Studien, 68 (1933), 57-80.

Believes the sonnets form a coherent "Herzengeschichte."

2262. Kemeny, Tomaso. "L'espunzione del referente in un canzoniere." Strumenti Critici, 10 (1976), 275-80.

This piece of criticism is based mainly on Alessandro Serpieri's I Sonetti dell'imortalita.

2263. Kenchoshvili, Irakli. "New Translations of Shakespeare's Sonnets." Georgian Shakespeariana 3. Ed. Nico Kiasashvili. Tbilisi: Xelovneba, 1972, pp. 107-24.

In Georgian. Summaries in English (p. 337) and in Russian (p. 330). Discusses the translation of the Sonnets by Revaz Tabukashvili, and notes the similarity of the friendship theme in the Sonnets with the 12th century Georgian epic, "The Knight in the Panther's Skin" by Shota Rustaveli.

2264. Kenchoshvili, I. "Concept of Friendship in Rustaveli's Poem and Shakespeare's Sonnets." Georgian Shakespeareana 4. Ed. Nico Kiasashvili. Tbilisi: Tbilisi University Press, 1975, pp. 179-86.

In Russian.

2265. Kent, Sydney. The People in Shakespeare's Sonnets. London: John Long, 1915. New York: Longmans and Green, 1917.

2266. Kenyon, John S. "A Shakespeare Emendation." TLS, October 18, 1934, p. 715.

Line 12 of Sonnet 111 ("Nor double penance to correct correction") reads better as "too correct correction."

2267. Kenyon, John. "Shakespeare, Sonnet CXI. 12." Modern Language Notes, 60 (1945), 357-58.

2268. Keogh, J.G. "Shakespeare's Sonnet LXXIII." Explicator, 28 (1969), Item 6.

2269. Kerckhove, Michael van de. Review of J. Decroos, Shakespeare's Sonnetten, met Inleiding en Aanteekeningen. Shakespeare Jahrbuch, 70 (1934), 146-48.

2270. Kermode, Frank. "A New Era in Shakespeare Criticism?" New York Review of Books, 15, viii (November 5, 1970), 33-38.

A review covering 13 books, including Stephen Booth, An Essay on Shakespeare's Sonnets and Roman Jakobson and Lawrence Jones, Shakespeare's Verbal Art in Th'Expense of Spirit (pp. 36-38).

2271. Kernan, Alvin. "Shakespeare's Essays on Dramatic Poesy: The Nature and Function of Theater within the Sonnets and the Plays." The Author in His Work: Essays on a Problem in Criticism. Ed. Louis L. Martz and Aubrey Williams. New Haven and London: Yale University Press, 1978, pp. 175-96.

2272. Keys, A.C. "Shakespeare en francais: Les 'Sonnets' aux antipodes." Revue de Litterature Comparee, 30 (1956), 98-102.

Talks about the 19th-century translation of Shakespeare's Sonnets by Louis Direy--a scholar who left France and settled in New Zealand.

2273. *Kikuchi, Wataru. "Shakespeare's Sonnets and Time." Gengo Bunka (Hitosubashi University), 15 (1978), 3-18.

In Japanese.

2274. Kiraly, Gyorgy. "Shakespeare szonettjei." Fuggetlen Szemle, 1921, p. 267.

On Lorinc Szabo's "revolutionary" 1921 translation of the Sonnets into Hungarian.

2275. Kirov, Todor T. "The First Step of a Giant." Shakespeare Jahrbuch, 104 (1968), 109-140.

Kirov includes a discussion of the Sonnets in attempting to find a unifying principle in Shakespeare's early imagery,

2276. *Kishi, Hidero. "Sheikusupia no sonetto." Metropolita (Tokyo Metropolitan University), 8 (1960), 39-51.

Discusses the first 17 sonnets.

2277. *Kiss, Katalin E. "Adalekok a Shakespeare-szonnetek magyarorszagi tortenetehez." [New Materials on Shakespeare's Sonnets in Hungarian Literary History.] Studia Litteraria (University of Debrecen), 12 (1974), 119-33.

2278. Kiss, Katalin E. Shakespeares szonettjei Magyarorszagon. [Shakespeare's Sonnets in Hungary.] Modern Filologiai Fuzetek, 22. Budapest: Akademiai Kiado, 1975.

Contains an extensive bibliography of translations and editions.

2279. Kiss, Katalin E. "Shakespeare's Sonnets in Hungary." Shakespeare Translation, 5 (1978), 31-46.

2280. Klay, Andor. Review of The Sonnets of Shakespeare-- Shakespeare Szonettjei, tr. into Hungarian by Pal Justus. Shakespeare Quarterly, 9 (1958), 189-92.

2281. Klein, David. "Foreign Influence on Shakespeare's Sonnets." *Sewanee Review*, 13 (1905), 454-74.

Notes the presence of a number of Platonic conceits and themes. Finds connections with Ronsard, DuBellay, Petrarch *et al*.

2282. Kliem, Hans. *Sentimentale Freundschaft in der Shakespeare-Epoche*. Jena: Bernhard Vopelius, 1915.

Kliem justifies the man-friendship of the Sonnets (pp. 38-40).

2283. Klotz, Gunther. Review of William Shakespeare, *Sonette*, Ubertragen von Gottlob Regis (1836), Nachwort von Anselm Schlosser. *Shakespeare Jahrbuch*, 103 (1967), 260-61.

2284. Knight, G. Wilson. "The Theme of Romantic Friendship in Shakespeare." *Holborn Review*, 71 (1929), 450-60.

Knight examines the theme in several plays in an effort to establish a context for Shakespeare's friendship for the "fair boy" of the Sonnets.

2285. Knight, G. Wilson. *The Shakespearian Tempest*. London: Humphrey Milford, Oxford University Press, 1932.

In the second chapter, "The Histories, Early Tragedies, and Poems," he comments on the use of the tempest and related images in a number of the sonnets.

2286. Knight, G. Wilson. *The Mutual Flame: On Shakespeare's Sonnets and The Phoenix and the Turtle*. London: Methuen, 1955. New York: Barnes and Noble, 1962.

After considering the facts and problems, Knight looks into some important themes (time, death, eternity), the symbolism of the sonnets, Shakespeare's language, etc.

2287. Knight, G. Wilson. "Shakespeare's Sonnets." *TLS*, December 26, 1963, p. 1072. Reprinted in *Shakespeare and Religion: Essays of Forty Years*. London: Routledge and Kegan Paul; New York: Barnes and Noble, 1967, pp. 329-32.

An explanation of Thorpe's dedication and a comment on the Rival Poet.

2288. Knight, G. Wilson. "Shakespeare's Sonnets." *TLS*, January 30, 1964, p. 93; March 12, 1964, p. 215. Reprinted in *Shakespeare and Religion: Essays of Forty Years*, pp. 332-35.

Adds further observations about the dedication of the 1609 Quarto.

2287

2289. Knight, G. Wilson. "Symbolism." A Casebook on Shakespeare's Sonnets. Ed. Gerald Willen and Victor B. Reed. New York: Thomas Y. Crowell, 1964, pp. 257-66. Reprinted from The Mutual Flame (pp. 58-68).

An examination of some important symbols in the Sonnets.

2290. Knight, G. Wilson. "Time and Eternity." Discussions of Shakespeare's Sonnets. Ed. Barbara Herrnstein. Boston: D.C. Heath, 1964, pp. 56-72. Reprinted from The Mutual Flame (Part I, chapter 4).

2291. Knight, G. Wilson. "New Light on Shakespeare's Sonnets." Listener, 71 (1964), 715-17. An expanded version of this appears in Shakespeare and Religion: Essays of Forty Years, pp. 253-65.

Examines some of the popular issues of the day: identity of Mr. W.H., dating of the sonnets, interpreting the dedication, Shakespeare's sexual preferences.
2287

2292. Knight, G. Wilson. "The Dark Lady." TLS, May 11, 1973, p. 528; May 25, 1973, p. 587.

1) Comments on Thorpe's dedication to the Sonnets and some of Rowse's theories; 2) Responds to letters by Empson and Cook (TLS, May 18, 1973, p. 536).
1885

2293. Knights, L.C. "Shakespeare's Sonnets." Scrutiny, 3 (1934), 133-60. Reprinted in 1) Explorations: Essays in Criticism, Mainly on the Literature of the Seventeenth Century. London: Chatto and Windus, 1946. New York: George W. Stewart, 1947, pp. 55-81. 2) Elizabethan Poetry: Modern Essays in Criticism. Ed. Paul Alpers. New York: Oxford University Press, 1967, pp. 274-98. 3) Shakespeare: The Sonnets: A Casebook. Ed. Peter Jones. London: Macmillan, 1977, pp. 74-102. 4) A Casebook on Shakespeare's Sonnets. Ed. Gerald Willen and Victor B. Reed. New York: Thomas Y. Crowell, 1964, pp. 173-97.

Knights believes that "the Sonnets yield their significance only when seen in the context of Shakespeare's development as a dramatist."

2294. Knights, L.C. Review of G. Wilson Knight, The Mutual Flame. Review of English Studies, NS 8 (1957), 302-04.

Objects to the fact that Knight offers no more than "stabs of insight" and that he fails to make distinctions between good and bad sonnets.

2295. Knights, L.C. "Time's Subjects: The Sonnets and King Henry IV, Part II." Some Shakespearean Themes. London: Chatto and Windus, 1959, pp. 45-64.

Both the Sonnets and King Henry IV, Part II express similar attitudes toward time.

2296. Kobayashi, Minoru. "A Note on 'The Inverted Platonism' of Shakespeare's Sonnets." Shakespeare Studies (Shakespeare Society of Japan), 2 (1963), 31-48.

Refers to Wyndham and Leishman in their earlier observations that Sonnets 14, 53, and 98 contained examples of "inverted Platonism" where the abstractions of love and beauty receive their ultimate expression in the "friend." Kobayashi considers other Renaissance texts for additional examples of this phenomenon.

2297. Koch, Max. Review of Shakespeare's Sonnets, ed. Thomas Tyler. Englische Studien, 15 (1891), 433-38.

2298. Kock, Ernst A. "Three Shaksperian Passages Explained." Anglia, 31 (1908), 132-34.

The third, on Sonnet 30 (lines 1-4), offers a new reading that hinges on reading "times" as plural, not possessive, and "old woes" as possessive.

2299. *Kogan, Pauline. "A Materialist Analysis of Shakespeare's Sonnets." Literature and Ideology, 1 (1969), 8-21.

2300. Konig, Wilhelm. "Shakespeare und Giordano Bruno." Shakespeare Jahrbuch, 11 (1876), 97-139.

Touches on the Sonnets principally in two places (p. 114 and pp. 135 ff.).

2301. Koskimies, Rafael. "The Question of Platonism in Shakespeare's Sonnets." Neuphilologische Mitteilungen, 71 (1970), 260-70.

2302. Koszul, A. "L'eternel probleme de la traduction: A propos d'une nouvelle version des Sonnets de Shakespeare." Etudes Anglaises, 9 (1956), 1-9.

A review article of a French translation of the Sonnets de Shakespeare by P.-J. Jouve.

2303. *Kotani, Yoichi. "Shakespeare's Dark Lady Sonnets--With Reference to His Drama." Bungakubu Kiyo (Hosei University), 24 (1979), 135-52.

In Japanese.

2304. Kott, Jan. Szkice o Szekspirze. Warsaw: Panstwowe Wydawnictwo Naukowe, 1964.
2305

2305. Kott, Jan. Shakespeare Our Contemporary. Tr. Boleslaw Taborski. Garden City, N.Y.: Doubleday, 1966.

An English translation of Szkice o Szekspirze. In the first half of his chapter, "Shakespeare's Bitter Arcadia," Kott interprets the Sonnets as a drama with action, heroes, and an antagonist--Time (pp. 287-305).

2306. *Kott, Ian. "Arcadia Amara." Arcadia Amara. La Tempesta e altri saggi shakespeariani. Ed. and tr. into Italian by Ettore Capriolo. Milan: Edizioni Il Formichiere, 1978, pp. 7-56.

Sexual disguise in the Sonnets, Twelfth Night and As You Like It. The master-mistress figure reflects the court-country theme.

2307. [Kraus, Karl.] "Sakrileg an George oder Suhne an Shakespeare." Die Fackel, 34, Nos. 885-87 (1932), 45-64.

Discusses his translations of Shakespeare's Sonnets and those of Stefan George.

2308. Krause, Florence Phyfer. "Negative Capability and Objective Correlative in Shakespeare's Sonnets." Tennessee Studies in Literature, 20 (1975), 17-25.

Shows how Shakespeare's narrator in the Sonnets possesses the qualities that Keats called negative capability.

2309. Krauss, Fritz. "Shakespeare und seine Sonette." Nord und Sud, 8 (1879), 226-43.

2310. Krauss, Fritz. "Die schwarze Schone der Shakespeare-Sonette." Shakespeare Jahrbuch, 16 (1881), 144-212.

Takes an extensive look at Sidney's Astrophel and Stella and its influence on Shakespeare.

2311. Krauss, Fritz. Shakespeare's Selbstbekenntnisse: nach zum Theil noch unbenutzen Quellen. Weimar: A. Huschke, 1882.

2312. Kreyssig, F. "Shakespeare's lyrische Gedichte und ihre neuesten deutschen Bearbeiter." Preussiche Jahrbucher, 13 (1864), 484-504; 14 (1864), 91-114.

A review of the Jordan and Bodenstedt translations with comments on the autobiographical elements in the Sonnets.

2313. Krieger, Murray. A Window to Criticism: Shakespeare's Sonnets and Modern Poetics. Princeton: Princeton University Press, 1964.

2314. Krieger, Murray. "The Strategy of Language in Shakespeare's Sonnets." Shakespeare Newsletter, 14 (1964), 80.

An abstract of a paper, which he calls a postscript to his Window to Criticism, delivered at the Shakespeare Symposium, University of Notre Dame, November 17, 1964.

2315. Krieger, Murray. "The Innocent Insinuations of Wit: The Strategy of Language in Shakespeare's Sonnets." The Play and Place of Criticism. Baltimore: Johns Hopkins, 1967, pp. 19-36.

2316. *Kroll, Josef. "Die Briefe Philstrats in Shakespeares Sonetten." Philologus, 106, iii-iv (Festheft fur Kurt Latte, 1962), 246-66.

The "letters" of Philostratus influenced the form and content of the Sonnets.

2317. *Kurihara, Toshiko. "On Shakespeare's Sonnets." Tokiwa Gakuen Junior College Kenkyu Kiyo, 5 (1977), 99-103.

In Japanese.

2318. *Kushnerivich, R. "An Untranslated Shakespeare Sonnet." The Art of Translation. Moscow: Sovetskii pisatel, 1977, vol. 2, pp. 318-24.

On various Russian translations of Sonnet 130. In Russian.

2319. *Kuz'mina, R.I. "Sonety Shekspira i ich perevody na russkij jazyk S. Marshakom." Trudy Kirgizskogo Universiteta, (Filologicheskie nauki), 17 (1972), 125-31.

Discusses Marshak's role in translating Shakespeare's Sonnets into Russian, with particular attention to Sonnet 12.

2320. Lambin, G. Review of Leslie Hotson, Shakespeare's Sonnets Dated, and Other Essays. Langues Modernes, 44 (1950), 123.

2321. Landau, E. Das Shakespeare-Mysterium: Eine Characterologische Untersuchung. Berlin: Pan-Verlag, 1930.

A study of the various theories on Shakespeare's identity as they bear upon several of his works--including a chapter on the sonnet (pp. 122-33).

2322. Landauer, Gustav. "Die Sonette." Shakespeare: Dargestellt in Bortragen. Frankfurt am Main: Rutten und Loening, 1920, vol. 2, pp. 318-70.

Includes a section comparing various German translations of the Sonnets.

2323. Landry, Hilton James. "Readings in Shakespeare's Sonnets." Ph.D. Dissertation, Harvard, 1958.

2324. Landry, Hilton. Interpretations in Shakespeare's Sonnets. Perspectives in Criticism, 14. Berkeley and Los Angeles: University of California Press, 1963. London: Cambridge University Press, 1964.

2325. Landry, Hilton. "Malone as Editor of Shakespeare's Sonnets." Bulletin of the New York Public Library, 67 (1963), 435-42.

2326. Landry, Hilton. "A Slave to Slavery: Shakespeare's Sonnet 57 and 58." A Casebook on Shakespeare's Sonnets. Ed. Gerald Willen and Victor B. Reed. New York: Thomas Y. Crowell, 1964, pp. 282-88.

2327. Landry, Hilton. "The Sonnets." Shakespeare Newsletter, 14 (1964), 41.

A bibliographic overview of editions and criticism.

2328. Landry, Hilton. "The Use and Abuse of Poetry: John Crowe Ransom on Shakespeare's Sonnets." Paunch, No. 23 (1965), 18-35.

Takes issue with Ransom's essay "Shakespeare at Sonnets." 2696

2329. Landry, Hilton. Review of Murray Krieger, A Window to Criticism: Shakespeare's Sonnets and Modern Poetics. Shakespeare Studies, 1 (1965), 328-32.

2330. Landry, Hilton. "The Marriage of True Minds: Truth and Error in Sonnet 116." Shakespeare Studies, 3 (1967), 98-110.

2331. Landry, Hilton. Review of Brents Stirling, The Shakespeare Sonnet Order: Poems and Groups. English Language Notes, 7 (1970), 300-04.

2332. Landry, Hilton. "In Defense of Shakespeare's Sonnets." New Essays on Shakespeare's Sonnets. Ed. Hilton Landry. New York: AMS Press, 1976, pp. 129-55.

Contains essays by Rodney Poisson, Martin Seymour-Smith, W.G. Ingram, Winifred Nowottny, Anton Pirkhofer, Hilton Landry, Marshall Lindsay, Paul Ramsey and Theodore Redpath.

2333. Lanham, Richard. The Motives of Eloquence: Literary Rhetoric in the Renaissance. New Haven and London: Yale University Press, 1976.

His chapter, "Superposed Poetics: The Sonnets," discusses Shakespeare's rhetorical style, which he says "works best when most rhetorical, most opaque, most outrageous" (pp. 111-28).

2334. Lanier, Emilia. The Poems of Shakespeare's Dark Lady: "Salve Deus Rex Judaeorum." Intro. A.L. Rowse. London: Jonathan Cape, 1978.

Rowse's introduction to these poems expands on his theory that Emilia Lanier nee Bassano was the dark lady.

2335. Larbaud, Valery. "'Motley'." TLS, June 24, 1926, p. 432.

Proposes an explanation of the word "motley" which appears in Sonnet 110.

2336. Latham, Jacqueline E. M. "Shakespeare's Sonnet 21." Notes and Queries, 223 (1978), 110-12.

2337. Laurent, C.-P. "Les sonnets de Shakespeare: etude d'une desillusion." Les langues modernes, 61 (January-February, 1967), 46-52.

Discusses the sexual conflict in the poet's attraction to the "fair youth" and the dark lady.

2338. Law, Robert Adger. "Two Notes on Shakespearian Parallels." University of Texas Studies in English, No. 9 (1929), 82-85.

The first of the two notes observes a parallel between Sonnets 18 and 33 and Arthur Brooke's Romeus and Juliet.

2339. Lawrence, Basil E. Notes on the Authorship of the Shakespeare Plays and Poems. London: Gay and Hancock, 1925.

This Baconian does not think that Bacon was the author of the Sonnets (pp. 333-48).

2340. Lee, Gabrielle. "Sonnet CXXVIII." Poet Lore, 5 (1893), 433-34.

An imaginative evocation of the scene from Sonnet 128.

2341. Lee, Sir Sidney. A Life of William Shakespeare. London: Smith, Elder, 1898; rev. and enl., 1915.

Lee has three chapters dealing with the Sonnets: "The Sonnets and their Literary History" (pp. 153-76), "The Conceits of the Sonnets" (pp. pp. 177-95), and "The Patronage of the Earl of Southampton" (pp. 196-230).

2342. Lee, Sir Sidney. "Shakespeare and the Earl of Pembroke." Fortnightly Review, 69 (1898), 210-23.

Rejects Pembroke and supports Southampton as the friend to whom the Sonnets were addressed.

2343. Lee, Sidney. "Shakespeare and the Earl of Southampton." Cornhill Magazine, NS 4 (1898), 482-95.

2344. L[ee], S[idney]. "Thomas Thorpe (1570?-1635?)." Dictionary of National Biography, London: Oxford University Press, 1949-50, vol. 19, pp. 803-04. Originally published as vol. 55-57 in 1898-99.

Mr. W.H., "The onlie begetter," is held to be the stationer, William Hall.

2345. L[ee], S[idney]. "Henry Wriothesley, Third Earl of Southampton (1573-1624)." Dictionary of National Biography. London: Oxford University Press, 1949-50, vol. 21, pp. 1055-61. Originally published as vol. 61-63 in 1900.

Lee includes material about Southampton's association with Shakespeare and his Sonnets.

2346. Lee, Sidney. "'Beget' and 'Begetter' in Elizabethan English." Athenaeum, February 24, 1900, pp. 250-51.

Explores the meaning of these words to better understand what Thorpe's dedication meant.

2347. Lee, Sidney, and Alfred Ainger. "'Beget' and 'Begetter' in Elizabethan English." Athenaeum, March 17, 1900, pp. 345-46.
1823, 1824, 2064, 2346

2348. Lee, Sir Sidney. "Ovid and Shakespeare's Sonnets." Quarterly Review, 210 (1909), 455-76. Reprinted in Elizabethan and Other Essays. Oxford: Clarendon Press, 1929, pp. 116-39.

2349. Lee, Sidney. "Shakespeare and the Italian Renaissance." Proceedings of the British Academy, 7 (1915-16), 121-43.

Lee cites the sonnets "as consummating evidence of the genuine strength of Shakespeare's affinities with Italian Platonism" (p. 142).

2350. Leech, Clifford. "Introduction." The Two Gentlemen of Verona. The Arden Edition. London: Methuen, 1969.

Briefly discusses the links between the sonnets and the play (lxix-lxx).

2351. Leeper, Alex. "Shakespeare's Seventy-Sixth Sonnet." Notes and Queries, 9th Series, 10 (1902), 517-18.
2608, 3046, 3131

2352. Legis, R.H. "Identification of Michael Drayton With the Rival Poet of Shakespeare's Sonnets." Notes and Queries, 5th Series, 6 (1876), 163-64.

Suggests also that the date of the Sonnets may be from between 1599 to as late as 1608.

2353. Legis, R.H. "Thorpe's Prefix to Shakespeare's Sonnets." Notes and Queries, 5th Series, 6 (1876), 421-22.

Offers a number of interpretations of the dedication.

2354. Legis, R.H. "The One Hundred and Twenty-sixth of Shakspeare's Sonnets." Notes and Queries, 5th Series, 7 (1877), 261-62.

He refers to a number of other sonnets to elucidate Sonnet 126. He regards the first 125 sonnets as a connected whole. (See R.M. Spence for a reply.)
2986

2355. Legis, R.H. "Sonnet LXXXVI." Notes and Queries, 5th Series, 7 (1877), 244-45, 384.

The first part concerns Drayton as the rival poet; the second involves a reading of the word "fild" in line 13.
2212

2356. Leigh, G.A. "The Rival Poet in Shakespeare's Sonnets." Westminster Review, 147 (1897), 173-87.

Identifies Tasso as the rival poet.

2357. Leimberg, Inge. "'To Hear with Eyes': Eine Interpretation von Shakespeare's 30 Sonett." Miscellanea Anglo-Americana: Festschrift fur Helmut Viebrock. Ed. Kuno Schuhmann, Wilhelm Hortmann, and Armin Paul Frank. Munchen: Karl Pressler, 1974, pp. 335-50.

2358. Leishman, J.B. Review of E.K. Chambers, Shakespearean Gleanings. Review of English Studies, 21 (1945), 148-51.

Half of the review is devoted to Chambers's three essays on the sonnets: "The Order of the Sonnets," "The 'Youth' of the Sonnets," and "The 'Mortal Moon' Sonnet."

2359. Leishman, J.B. "Variations on a Theme in Shakespeare's Sonnets." Elizabethan and Jacobean Studies Presented to Frank Percy Wilson in honour of his seventieth birthday. Ed. Herbert Davis and Helen Gardner. Oxford: Clarendon Press, 1959, pp. 112-49.

2360. Leishman, J.B. Themes and Variations in Shakespeare's Sonnets. London: Hutchinson; New York: Hillary House, 1961. New York: Harper and Row, 1966.

2361. Leisi, Ernst. "A Possible Emendation of Shakespeare's Sonnet 146." English Studies, 47 (1966), 271-85.

Argues that "array" cannot have a military sense and there is no idea of a siege in the poem.

2362. Leith, Alicia Amy. "Sonnet CXLIV." Baconiana, 3rd Series, 13 (1915), 85-87.

Identifies the "two loves" that the poet has as the Augustinian heavenly and earthly cities.

2363. Lengefeld, Kleinschmit von. "Der Manierismus in der Dichtung Shakespeares." Shakespeare-Jahrbuch, 97 (1961), 63-99.

Brief section on the Sonnets (p. 93) in which Lengefeld comments on Patrick Cruttwell's The Shakespearean Moment.
1750

2364. Leo, F.A. "Hilfsmittel bei Untersuchungen uber Shakespeare's Sonette." Shakespeare Jahrbuch, 23 (1886), 304-17.

Classifies the Sonnets into groups and gives a brief statement on the contents of each sonnet.

2365. *Leporace, Pasquale. Il petrarchismo e i sonetti de Shakespeare. Cosenza: R. Riccio, 1907.

2366. Lerner, Laurence. Review of Murray Krieger, A Window to Criticism: Shakespeare's Sonnets and Modern Poetics. Modern Language Review, 60 (1965), 430-32.

2367. Lerner, Laurence. The Truest Poetry: An Essay on the Question, What is Literature? London: Hamish Hamilton, 1960.

The book illustrates how two poets (Shakespeare in Sonnet 138 and Hopkins in "I wake and feel the fell of dark, not day") write about loss of faith (pp. 94-96). Lerner also writes about the unity of Shakespeare's Sonnets (pp. 97-99).

2368. Leslie, Shane. "Mr. W.H." Saturday Review of Literature, 12 (May 25, 1935), 9.

Answers Paul Clarkson and even throws another name into the hopper, William Heygate, albeit with no conviction.
1717

2369. Lever, J.W. "Shakespeare's French Fruits." Shakespeare Survey, 6 (1953), 79-90.

"Shakespeare's Sonnet 130 might almost be a versified reply to [John] Eliot," whose Ortho-epia uses very similar images in the inventory of the lady (pp. 83-84).

2370. Lever, J.W. "Chapman and Shakespeare." Notes and Queries, 203 (1958), 99-100.

Notes a similarity between Shakespeare's Sonnet 55 and a passage from Chapman's Homer.

2371. Lever, J.W. Review of Edward Hubler et al. The Riddle of Shakespeare's Sonnets. Modern Language Review, 58 (1963), 406-07.

2372. Lever, J.W. "The Poet in Absence" and "The Poet and His Rivals." Discussions of Shakespeare's Sonnets. Ed. Barbara Herrnstein. Boston: D.C. Heath, 1964, pp. 73-86. Reprinted from The Elizabethan Love Sonnet (pp. 202-08, 227-35).

The first selection is principally concerned with the "eyes-heart" conceit and Sonnets 24,46,47. The second selection deals mainly with Sonnets 78-80 and 82-86.

2373. Lever, J.W. Review of Stephen Booth, An Essay on Shakespeare's Sonnets. Studia Neophilologica, 42 (1970), 463-65.

2374. Levin, Harry. Review of Murray Krieger, A Window to Criticism: Shakespeare's Sonnets and Modern Poetics. Yale Review, 54 (1964), 263-64.

2375. Levin, Richard. "Correspondence." Review of English Studies, NS 15 (1964), 408-09.

Replies to E.C. Evans's article on Sonnet 97.
1889

2376. Levin, Richard. "Shakespeare's 'Sonnet LXVI'." Explicator, 22 (1964), Item 36.

2377. Levin, Richard. "Sonnet CXXIX as a 'Dramatic' Poem." Shakespeare Quarterly, 16 (1965), 175-81.

2378. Levin, Richard. "Shakespeare's 'Sonnet LXIV'." Explicator, 24 (1965), Item 39.

2379. Levin, Richard. "Shakespeare's 'Sonnet XXXIV'." Explicator, 29 (1971), Item 49.

2380. Levin, Richard. "Shakespeare's Sonnet 138." Explicator, 36, iii (1978), 28-29.

2381. Levin, Richard. "'The Expense of Spirit'." Studies in English and American Literature. American Notes and Queries Supplement, vol. 1. Ed. John L. Cutler and Lawrence S. Thompson. Troy, N.Y.: Whitston, 1978, pp. 53-54.

Offers evidence that "spirit" means "semen" in Sonnet 129.

2382. Levin, Richard. "Shakespeare's Sonnet 127." Explicator, 38, i (1979), 31-33.

2383. Levin, Richard. "The Sonnets and Shakespeare's Personality." Shakespeare Newsletter, 29 (1979), 5.

Summarizes papers given at MLA Seminar in 1977, which includes Carol Thomas Neely ("The Structure of Shakespeare's Sonnets") and Richard P. Wheeler ("Towards Tragedy: The Sonnets"). See also Rebholz.
2705

2384. Levin, Samuel R. Linguistic Structures in Poetry. Janua Linguarum, 23. The Hague: Mouton, 1962.

One chapter of this monograph is devoted to a linguistic analysis of Sonnet 30 (pp. 51-58).

2385. Lewis, Michael, and Catherine W. Scotland. "Dr. Hotson's Arguments." TLS, June 23, 1950, p. 389.

In commenting on Hotson's theories about Sonnet 107, Lewis offers some information regarding the alleged crescent-shaped formation of the Armada. Scotland suggests that the "mortal moon" might refer to the dark lady.

2386. L'Hommede, Edmond. "Le Secret de Shakespeare." Revue de Paris, 2 (1923), 171-92.

Takes up the usual problems of the Sonnets.

2387. L'Hommede, Edmond. Le Secret de Shakespeare: Les Sonnets. Paris: Didier, 1932.

Comments on most of the usual issues and provides a rearranged text.

2388. Liddel, Mark H. An Introduction to the Scientific Study of Poetry. New York: Doubleday, Page, 1902.

Examines what he calls "thought-moments" (pp. 147-52) and other prosodic concerns (pp. 169-79) in Sonnet 146.

2389. L[iddel], M.H. "Shakspere Sonnets in MS." Nation, 75 (1902), 10-11.

Describes a folio miscellany with a MS. containing Sonnets 60, 65 and 107.

2390. Liggins, E.M., and H.W. Piper. "Sound and Sense in a Shakespeare Sonnet." Langue et Litterature: Actes du VIII Congres de la Federation Internationale des Langues et Litteratures Modernes. Bibliotheque de la Faculte de Philosophie et Lettres de l'Universite de Liege, Fasc. CLXI. Paris: Societe d'Edition "Les Belles Lettres," 1961, p. 417.

On Shakespeare's Sonnet 2.

2391. Lindsay, Marshall. "French Translations of the Sonnets." New Essays on Shakespeare's Sonnets. Ed. Hilton Landry. New York: AMS Press, 1976, pp. 157-92.

2392. Lloyd, J.D.K. "Shakespeare's Sonnets." TLS, November 15, 1974, p. 1288.

Ridicules John Sparrow's suggestion that the name Lanier evokes la nera.
2985

2393. Loane, George G. "Shakespeare's Sonnets." TLS, March 19, 1925, p. 200.

Some explicative remarks about Sonnets 77, 105, and 140.

2394. Loane, George G., and Alfred Douglas. "Chapman, the Rival Poet." TLS, June 11, 1938, p. 402.

Responds to J.M. Murray's earlier letter on this subject. 2535

2395. Loewenberg, J. "The Idea of Mutability in Literature." University of California Chronicle, 24 (1922), 129-51.

Comments on the theme of change in Sonnet 64 (pp. 133-34).

2396. Looney, J. Thomas. "Shakespeare" Identified In Edward De Vere the Seventeenth Earl of Oxford. London: C. Palmer, 1920. New York: Duell, Sloan and Pearce, 1949.

Looney devotes a chapter to the Sonnets ("Poetic Self-Revelation: The Sonnets") fitting Oxford into the picture (pp. 369-89).

2397. Louthan, Doniphan. "Sonnet 113." TLS, July 6, 1951, p. 421.

Concerns a reading of the final line depending on the phonological similarity of "minde" and "mine."

2398. Lowers, James K. Shakespeare's Sonnets: Notes. Lincoln, Neb.: Cliff's Notes, 1965.

Gives a brief background to the Elizabethan sonnet and then proceeds to examine the major problems and themes of Shakespeare's Sonnets. Includes comments on several of the major sonnets.

2399. Luce, Morton. A Handbook to the Works of Shakespeare. London: George Bell, 1906. 2nd ed. rev., 1907. rpt. New York: AMS, 1972.

Contains a general introduction to the Sonnets (pp. 82-97).

2400. Luce, Morton. "Some New Facts About the Sonnets." Shakespeare: The Man and His Work: Seven Essays. Bristol: J.W. Arrowsmith, 1913, pp. 11-66.

Luce takes issue with conclusions drawn by some contemporary critics about the dark lady, the date of the Sonnets, etc.

2401. Ludeke, H. Review of Edward Hubler, The Sense of Shakespeare's Sonnets. English Studies, 38 (1957), 79-82.

2402. Lukas, Mykola. "Ukrajins'kyj sonetarij Shekspira." Zovten', No. 1 (1967), 149-51.

On Ukrainian translations of the Sonnets.

2403. Lumiansky, R.M. "Shakespeare's Sonnet LXXIII." Explicator, 6 (1948), Item 55. Reprinted in A Casebook on Shakespeare's Sonnets. Ed. Gerald Willen and Victor B. Reed. New York: Thomas Y. Crowell, 1964, p. 269.

2404. *Lundquist, Carole. "Sonnet 66." LIT, No. 5 (1964), 22-23.

2405. Lynch, Arthur. "Shakespeare Found Out! The Name of His Mysterious Patron of the 'Sonnets' Wrapped in a Line." Book Monthly, 14 (1919), 543-46.

Henry Wriothesley's name appears in Sonnet 76, line 7.

2406. Lynch, Arthur. "The 'Onlie Begetter' of Shakespeare's Sonnets: A Fresh Clue." Review of Reviews (London), 80 (1930), 307-12.

Argues his theory that "Hery Wrothsley" is written in Sonnet 76, line 7.

2407. Lynskey, Winifred. "A Critic in Action: Mr. Ransom." College English, 5 (1944), 239-49.

Includes an attack on Ransom's essay, "Shakespeare at Sonnets," in which Lynskey responds to his criticism of Shakespeare's imagination and the structure of the sonnets (pp. 243-49). She also discusses Spenser's sonnets as well.

2408. M., J. Shakespeare Self-Revealed in his Sonnets and Phoenix and Turtle. London and Manchester: Sherratt and Hughes, 1904.

His "two loves, figured by a man and a woman, are respectively Love of Beauty and Love of Fame." Following a lengthy introduction expanding on this idea, the Sonnets are printed with explicative headnotes.

2409. M., J. A Recantation. (Being a Supplement to a Book entitled Shakespeare Self-Revealed). [London: np. 1909].

A 3-page pamphlet which finds a cryptogram in the italicized words of the Sonnets.

2410. *Maanen, W. van. "Zeven vertalingen van Shakespeares Sonnet I." De Gids, 127, v (1964), 413-19.

On seven Dutch translations of Sonnet 1.

2411. Mabie, Hamilton Wright. "Sonnets of Shakespeare." Outlook, 92 (1909), 1025-30.

An introduction of a general character followed by five sonnets.

2412. [Macaulay, George C.] "New Views of Shakespeare's Sonnets: The 'Other Poet' Identified." Blackwood's Edinburgh Magazine, 135 (1884), 727-61; 137 (1885), 774-800; 139 (1886), 327-50.

In this three-part article the "rival poet," referred to in Sonnets 78-86, is identified as Dante.

2413. MacCracken, H.N., F.E. Pierce and W.H. Durham. An Introduction to Shakespeare. New York: Macmillan, 1910.

Contains a section on the Sonnets (pp. 63-70).

2414. Mackail, J. W. "Shakespeare's Sonnets." Lectures on Poetry. London and New York: Longmans, Green, 1911. rpt. Freeport, N.Y.: Books for Libraries Press, 1967, pp. 179-207.

A general review of the publication history of the sonnets and of the various unanswered questions about them.

2415. Mackail, J.W. The Approach to Shakespeare. Oxford: Clarendon Press, 1930. rpt. New York: AMS Press, 1970.

In discussing the Sonnets in the chapter, "The Romances and Fragments, and the Sonnets," Mackail notes that recognition of the Sonnets was long delayed, but these poems now eclipse the work of his contemporaries (pp. 110-19).

2416. Mackay, Charles. "A Tangled Skein Unravelled. Or the Mystery of Shakespeare's Sonnets." Nineteenth Century, 16 (1884), 238-62.

Believes the sonnets belong in six distinct groups: a series addressed to a rich, noble youth; a series to a dark lady; a series vindicating the poet's character and addressed to a powerful friend; love sonnets addressed to various women; miscellaneous sonnets; sonnets predicting the poet's immortality.

2417. Mackenzie, Agnes Mure. The Women in Shakespeare's Plays. London: William Heinemann, 1924. rpt. Folcroft, Pa.: Folcroft Library Editions, 1973.

An appendix is devoted to the dark lady Sonnets (pp. 461-68) in which Mackenzie notes themes common to those in the plays.

2418. Mackenzie, Barbara A. Shakespeare's Sonnets: Their Relation to His Life. Cape Town: Maskew Miller, 1946. rpt. New York: AMS Press, 1978.

Some of Mackenzie's conclusions are that Southampton is the "fair friend," the Sonnets are related more to Southampton's life than to Shakespeare's, the order of the Sonnets in the 1609 Quarto is incorrect, and the Sonnets were written between 1592 and 1596.

2419. MacLeish, Archibald. "The Proper Pose of Poetry." Saturday Review, 38 (March 5, 1955), 11-12, 47-49.

Uses Sonnet 116 to explore the nature of poetry.

2420. MacMahan, Anna B. Shakespeare's Love Story, 1580-1609. Chicago: A.C. McClurg, 1909.

Into this romantic and fanciful treatment of Shakespeare's life are inserted several "relevant" sonnets.

2421. Madden, D.H. Shakespeare and His Fellows: An Attempt to Decipher the Man and His Nature. London: Smith, Elder, 1916.

Briefly surveys the principal opinions about the amount of autobiography in the Sonnets (pp. 9-11).

2422. Mahony, Patrick. "Shakespeare's Sonnet Number 20: Its Symbolic Gestalt." American Imago, 36 (1979), 69-79.

2423. Mahood, M.M. Shakespeare's Wordplay. London: Methuen, 1957.

In Chapter 4, entitled "The Sonnets" (pp. 89-110), Mahood considers Shakespeare's imagery and punning in the Sonnets, poems which she considers to be "a very mixed lot."

2424. Mahood, Molly M. "Love's Confined Doom." Shakespeare Survey, 15 (1962), 50-61. Reprinted in Shakespeare: The Sonnets: A Casebook. Ed. Peter Jones. London: Macmillan, 1977, pp. 200-18.

Looks for parallels in language, imagery and theme between the plays and the Sonnets.

2425. M[alone], K[emp]. Review of J.A. Fort, The Two Dated Sonnets of Shakespeare. Modern Language Notes, 40 (1925), 384.

Malone call's Fort's study "ingenious."

2426. [Marder, Louis]. "Computer Used to Study Sonnet Rhythm." Shakespeare Newsletter, 21 (1971), 18.

Review of article by Herbert S. Donow, "Linear Word Count as a Function of Rhythm: An Analysis of Shakespeare's Sonnets."
1814

2427. [Marder, Louis]. "The New Shakespeare Discoveries and Attributions." Shakespeare Newsletter, 23 (1973), 1-2.

Regarding Rowse's "solution" of the riddle of the dark lady's identity.

2428. M[arder], L[ouis]. "The 'Dark Lady': Demise of a Theory." Shakespeare Newsletter, 23 (1973), 24.

Discusses A.L. Rowse's theory that Emilia Lanier was Shakespeare's dark lady.

2429. M[arder], L[ouis]. "The Dark Lady, Rowse and His Critics." Shakespeare Newsletter, 23 (1973), 35.

A continuation of his earlier review of Rowse's theory on the dark lady.
2428

2430. M[arder], L[ouis]. "Shakespeare's CVL 'To A.L. Rowse . . . '." Shakespeare Newsletter, 23 (1973), 53.

A spoof on Rowse's "discoveries" including Shakespeare's Sonnet "CVL" which contains an anagram of "A.L. Rowse" in each line.

2431. M[arder], L[ouis]. "Shakespeare's Passionate Code." Shakespeare Newsletter, 25 (1975), 26.

Summarizes an article by Roger Prior that appeared in The Times (London), May 12, 1973. In it Prior discusses the theory that Emilia Bassano Lanier was the dark lady.

2432. *Mares, Alexandru. "Sonetele lui Shakespeare." Studii de literatura universala (Societatea de stiinte istorice si filologice din Republica Socialista Romania (Bucaresti)), 8 (1966), 51-70.

2433. *Marlowe, Arthur. Shakespeare, Digging for the Truth. Transcription by Brian Paine. Market Harborough: Green, 1978.

Discusses Shakespeare-Fitton-Herbert triangle and various candidates for the dark lady and Mr. W.H. Evidence offered includes actual excavations of graves.

2434. *Marlowe, Phil. "Mr. Wh--. A Contribution to Shakespearian Scholarship." Cambridge Review, 85 (1964), 357-59.

A parody suggesting George Whetstone as Mr. W.H.

2435. Marotta, Kathleen Frances. "Two Readings in Shakespeare's Sonnet Sequence." Ph.D. Dissertation, Iowa, 1972. DAI, 33 (1973), 6877A.

2436. Marotti, Arthur F. Review of Shakespeare's Sonnets, ed. Stephen Booth. Criticism, 20 (1978), 346-47.

2437. Marrapodi, Michele. "Sul Sonetto 94 di Shakespeare." Blue Guitar (Rivista annuale di Letteratura inglese e americana), 2 (1976), 259-70.

2438. *Marrapodi, Michele. "A New Approach to Shakespeare's Sonnets: A Note on 'Pluralist Criticism'." Blue Guitar, 3-4 (1977-78).

As of this moment (mid-1981), this volume, though announced by the publishers (Herder Editrice e Libreria), has apparently not been published.

2439. Marrian, F.J.M. Shakespeare's Sonnet Friend as Pioneer of the New World: (a fresh interpretation of Sonnet 122). London: Villiers, 1977.

On Sonnet 122, identifying the friend as Sir Robert Dudley.

2440. Marschall, Wilhelm. Aus Shakespeares poetischem Briefwechsel. Heidelberg: Herbert Grossberger, 1926.

Marschall suggests that the Sonnets were a correspondence between two friends covering several subjects and phases of their relationship.

2441. Marschall, Wilhelm. "Das Zentralproblem der Shakespeare-Sonette." Anglia, 51 (1927), 31-38.

An examination of the use of "thou" and "you" in the Sonnets.

2442. Marschall, Wilhelm. "Problematisches in Shakespeares Sonetten." Englische Studien, 63 (1928), 334-35.

A response to Max Wolff's review of Marschall's Aus Shakespeares poetischem Briefwechsel in Englische Studien, 63 (1928), 110-114.
3229

2443. Martin, C.G. "Shakespeare or His Poems." Essays in Criticism, 5 (1955), 398-404.

Review of G. Wilson Knight, The Mutual Flame.

2444. Martin, Philip. "Shakespeare's Sonnet 94." Critical Survey, 4 (1969), 84-89.

An attempt to advance our understanding of "They that have powre to hurt . . ." (Sonnet 94) beyond Empson's "brilliant" discussion of it in Some Versions of Pastoral.
1879

2445. Martin, Philip J. Shakespeare's Sonnets: Self, Love and Art. Cambridge: University Press, 1972.

In this examination of the role of self in the Sonnets, Martin has occasion to compare Shakespeare with contemporary sonneteers and with John Donne as well.

2446. Martinet, Marie-Madeleine. Review of New Essays on Shakespeare's Sonnets, ed. Hilton Landry. Etudes Anglaises, 31 (1978), 379-80.

2447. *Marucci, Franco. "I sonetti shakespeariani al microscopio dello strutturalismo." Nuova Corrente, 70 (1976), 155-70.

2448. Marx, Olga. Stephan George in seinen Ubertragungen englischer Dichtung. Castrum Peregrini, 77. Amsterdam: Castrum Peregrini Presse, 1967.

Treats George's German translation of Shakespeare's Sonnets (pp. 14-35).

2449. [Massey, Gerald]. "Shakespeare and his Sonnets." Quarterly Review, 115 (April, 1864), 430-81.

An overview of the 19th century concerns--the dedication, Southampton, the poems as autobiography, etc.

2450. Massey, Gerald. Shakespeare's Sonnets Never Before Interpreted: His Private Friends Identified: Together With A Recorded Likeness of Himself. London: Longmans, Green, 1866. rpt. New York: AMS Press, 1973. Later published as The Secret Drama of Shakespeare's Sonnets Unfolded, with the Characters Identified. London: R. Clay, Sons, and Taylor, 1872. rpt. New York: AMS Press, 1973.

This large book begins with a review of critical judgments on and theories about the sonnets including a chapter attacking the theories of Charles Armitage Brown (a supporter of Herbert as the fair youth). This is an enlarged version of his article in Quarterly Review (1864).

2451. Massey, Gerald. "Shakespeare's Sonnets." Athenaeum, March 16, 1867, pp. 355-56.

2452. Massey, Gerald, and Samuel Neil. "Shakespeare's Sonnets." Athenaeum, April 27, 1867, pp. 551-52.

Both letters by Massey and Neil are addressed to issues raised by Philarete Chasles about Thorpe's dedication.
1707

2453. Masson, David. Autobiography of Shakespeare from His Thirty-fourth to his thirty-ninth year, derived from His Sonnets Together with the Sonnets themselves arranged and elucidated. Two manuscript volumes (c. 1846) now in the Folger Shakespeare Library.

Part I consists of biographic information both from outside sources and from the Sonnets. Part II is an elucidation of the individual sonnets. Part III is an historical supplement in which Masson discusses the identity of Mr. W.H., dwelling at length on Pembroke.

2454. Masson, David. Shakespeare Personally. New York: E.P. Dutton, 1914.

In his final chapter, "The Sonnets" (pp. 191-238), Masson discusses the value of these poems for their autobiographical insights into the poet.

2455. Masson, David I. "Free Phonetic Patterns in Shakespeare's Sonnets." Neophilologus, 38 (1954), 277-89.

2456. *Masui, Michio. "Shakespeare no Sonnets no Eigo." Eigo Seinen, 114 (1968), 366-67.

2457. Matheson, T.P. Review of Shakespeare's Sonnets, ed. Kenneth Muir. TLS, January 9, 1981, p. 38.

2458. Mathew, Frank. An Image of Shakespeare. London: Jonathan Cape, 1922. rpt. New York: Haskell House, 1972.

In his chapter, "The Poems of Love" (pp. 81-115), Mathew takes up the subject of Southampton, the dedication, the rival poet, etc.

2459. Matthews, Charles, and Margaret M. Blum. "To the Student of Poetry: An Essay on Essays." CEA Critic, 35, ii (1973), 24-27.

On Sonnet 116.

2460. Mattingly, Garrett. "The Date of Shakespeare's Sonnet CVII." PMLA, 48 (1933), 705-21.

Prefers a late date (1603) for the "mortal moon" sonnet.

2461. Mauntz, Alfred von. "Shakespeare's lyrische Gedichte." Shakespeare Jahrbuch, 28 (1893), 274-331.

Discusses the grouping and order of the Sonnets and "The Passionate Pilgrim."

2462. Mauntz, Alfred von. "Einige Glossen zu Shakespeare's Sonett 121." Anglia, 19 (1897), 291-96.

2463. Maxwell, J.C. Review of Shakespeare's Sonnets, ed. Martin Seymour-Smith. Durham University Journal, 56 (1963), 49-50.

2464. Maxwell, J.C. "'Rebel Powers': Shakespeare and Daniel." Notes and Queries, 212 (1967), 139.

This phrase from Sonnet 146 (line 2) occurs in Daniel's Cleopatra (1594).

2465. May, Louis F., Jr. "The Figura in Sonnet 106." Shakespeare Quarterly, 11 (1960), 93-94.

2466. McAuley, James. Review of Philip Martin, Shakespeare's Sonnets: Self, Love and Art. AUMLA, No. 39 (1973), 115.

2467. McCanles, Michael. "'Increasing Store with Loss': Some Themes of Shakespeare's Sonnets." Texas Studies in Literature and Language, 13 (1971), 391-406.

2468. McClumpha, C.F. "Parallels Between Shakespere's Sonnets and Love's Labour's Lost." Modern Language Notes, 15 (1900), 168-74.

2469. McClumpha, C.F. Review of Parke Godwin, A New Study of the Sonnets of Shakespeare. Modern Language Notes, 16 (1901), 53-56.

2470. McClumpha, C.F. "Parallels Between Shakespere's Sonnets and A Midsummer Night's Dream." Modern Language Notes, 16 (1901), 164-68.

2471. McClumpha, C.F. "Shakespeare's Sonnets and Romeo and Juliet." Shakespeare Jahrbuch, 40 (1904), 187-203.

Examines parallels between the play and the poems.

2472. McGrane, Moira Joan. "A Survey of Shakespeare Sonnet Criticism: 1943-1974." Ph.D. Dissertation, Columbia, 1980. DAI, 41 (1980), 1614A.

2473. McGuinness, Kevin. "Shakespeare and the Sonnets." Revue des Langues Vivantes, 31 (1965), 287-301.

Talks about some of the recent attempts to solve the problems of dating, arrangement, etc.

2474. McKernan, John Joseph. "An Investigation of the Epistolary Nature of Shakespeare's Sonnets 1-126." Ph.D. Dissertation, Boston University, 1980. DAI, 41 (1980), 2125A.

2475. McLeod, Randall. "A Technique of Headline Analysis, With Application to Shakespeare's Sonnets, 1609." Studies in Bibliography, 2 (1979), 197-210.

This is a technique for "photographic collation."

2476. McLeod, Randall. "Unemending Shakespeare's Sonnet 111." Studies in English Literature, 1500-1900, 21 (1981), 75-96.

McLeod dismisses the emendation "with" in line 1 and argues that "wish" is correct.

2477. M[cManaway], J.G. Review of C. Longworth de Chambrun, An Explanatory Introduction to Thorpe's Edition of Shakespeare's Sonnets. Shakespeare Quarterly, 2 (1951), 366.

2478. McManaway, James G. "Textual Studies." Shakespeare Survey, 4 (1951), 153-56.

McManaway, after reviewing Leslie Hotson's arguments for the early dating of the Sonnets, leans toward a more conservative later dating.

2479. McNaughton, Duncan William. "Love Triumphant: Meditations on William Shakespeare's Sonnets." Ph.D. Dissertation, SUNY at Buffalo, 1972. DAI, 33 (1973), 4355A-56A.

2480. McNeal, Thomas H. "Studies in the Greene-Shakspere Relationship." Shakespeare Association Bulletin, 15 (1940), 210-18.

Believes that Sonnet 130 may have been an attack aimed at Robert Greene's poem "A Most Rare and Excellent Dreame."

2481. McNeal, Thomas H. "'Every Man Out of His Humour' and Shakespeare's 'Sonnets'." Notes and Queries, 197 (1952), 376.

Believes that Jonson borrowed ideas from Shakespeare's Sonnets (29 and 128) and incorporated them into "Every Man Out of His Humour."

2482. McPeek, James A.S. Catullus in Strange and Distant Britain. Harvard Studies in Comparative Literature, 15. Cambridge, Mass.: Harvard University Press, 1939.

Shows parallelism of thought between Sonnet 30 and Catullus's "Elegy on Quintilia," and Sonnet 27 and some lines from the Carmina (xxi, 7-10) (pp. 135-37).

2483. Meeks, Leslie H. "The Human Shakespeare of the Sonnets." Teachers College Journal, 2 (1931), 71-72, 86.

The Sonnets are autobiographical in only the most general sense. Shakespeare did not "unlock his heart" and lay bare the secret facts of his life.

2484. Meier, H.H. "Sonnet 146." TLS, October 28, 1977, p. 1268.

Another attempt, following Brockbank's and Padel's, to correct the obvious error in line 2.
1619, 2617

2485. Melchiori, Giorgio. Review of Shakespeare's Sonnets, ed. by W.G. Ingram and Theodore Redpath. Notes and Queries, 211 (1966), 150-52.

2486. Melchiori, Giorgio. "Love's Use and Man's Hues in Shakespeare's Sonnet 20." English Miscellany, 23 (1972), 21-38.

This essay, in which Melchiori discusses the various structural layers of the poem, was later incorporated into his book, Shakespeare's Dramatic Meditations.
2489

2487. Melchiori, Giorgio. "Shakespeare and the New Economics of His Time." Review of National Literatures, 3 (1972), 123-37.

Includes a section on the Sonnets (pp. 126-29) in which he comments on some of the references to commerce.

2488. Melchiori, Giorgio. L'uomo e il potere: Indagine sulle strutture profonde dei Sonetti di Shakespeare. Torino: Einaudi, 1973.

Shakespeare's Dramatic Meditations is a revised, English version.

2489. Melchiori, Giorgio. Shakespeare's Dramatic Meditations: An Experiment in Criticism. Oxford: Clarendon Press, 1976.

Close examination of sonnets 94,121,20,129, and 146.

2490. Meller, Horst. "An Emblematic Background for Shakespeare's Sonnet No. 116--And More Light on Mr. W.H." Archiv fur das Studium der neueren Sprachen und Literaturen, 217 (1980), 39-61.

2491. *Menasce, Esther. "Jodelle e Shakespeare: i 'Contr' Amours' e i 'vituperative sonnets'." Annali dell' Universita di Padova, 4 (1969), 1-23.

2492. Meyerfeld, Max. Review of Die Sonette von William Shakespeare, tr. by Alexander Neidhardt, and Shakespeares Sonette, tr. by Max J. Wolff. Shakespeare Jahrbuch, 40 (1904), 295-98.

2493. *Mezenin, S.M. "Zvuk i znacenie v sonetach Shekspira." [Sound and Meaning in Shakespeare's Sonnets.] Ucenye zapiski Moskovskogo pedagogicheskogo instituta imeni Lenina, 473 (1971), 82-87.

Author's translation of Sonnet 66 is included.

2494. Michel, Laurence. "Shakespeare's Sonnet 107." Journal of English and Germanic Philology, 54 (1955), 301-05.

2495. Middlebrook, Douglas. Sweet My Love: A Study of Shakespeare's Sonnets. North Adelaide: Chamber Theatre of Adelaide, 1973.

The book gives a running commentary of each sonnet (rearranged in what the author believes is the order of composition) urging the thesis that Shakespeare was a homosexual.

2496. Miles, Josephine. Eras and Modes in English Poetry. Berkeley and Los Angeles: University of California Press, 1957. Rev. and enl. 1964. rpt. Westport, Conn.: Greenwood Press, 1976.

In defining "modes," "styles," and "eras," Miles uses sonnets by Wyatt ("Against his tongue"), Shakespeare (Sonnet 1) and Spenser (Amoretti 1) (pp. 13-19).

2497. Mills, Laurens J. One Soul in Bodies Twain: Friendships in Tudor Literature and Stuart Drama. Bloomington, Ind.: Principia Press, 1937.

Chapter 4 (pp. 238-44) treats the theme of friendship in Shakespeare's Sonnets, with references to Barnfield's and Drayton's sonnets.

2498. Mincoff, M. Review of Robert Gittings, Shakespeare's Rival. English Studies, 45 (1964), 472-74.

2499. Mincoff, M. Review of John Dover Wilson, An Introduction to the Sonnets of Shakespeare for the Use of Historians and Others. Etudes Anglaises, 45 (1964), 401-03.

2500. *Mirek, R. "Problematyka psychiatryczna sonetow Szekspira." [Psychiatric problems in Shakespeare's Sonnets.] Przeglad Lekarski, 12 (1968), 885-88.

2501. Mizener, Arthur. "The Structure of Figurative Language in Shakespeare's Sonnets." Southern Review, 5 (1940), 730-47. Reprinted in 1) Discussions of Shakespeare's Sonnets. Ed. Barbara Herrnstein. Boston: D.C. Heath, 1964, pp. 137-51. 2) A Casebook on Shakespeare's Sonnets. Ed. Gerald Willen and Victor B. Reed. New York: Thomas Y. Crowell, 1964, pp. 219-35. 3) Essays in Shakespearean Criticism. Ed. James L. Calderwood and Harold E. Toliver. Englewood Cliffs, N.J.: Prentice-Hall, 1970, pp. 85-100.

Focuses principally on Sonnet 124.

2502. *Moeller, Kristian Langdal. "Shakespeare og den morke Dame." [Shakespeare and the Dark Lady.] Aarhus Stiftstidende, May 22, 1954.

2503. Moore, Carlisle. "Shakespeare's Sonnets LXXI-LXXIV." Explicator, 8 (1949), Item 2. Reprinted in A Casebook on Shakespeare's Sonnets. Ed. Gerald Willen and Victor B. Reed. New York: Thomas Y. Crowell, 1964, pp. 271-72.

2504. *Moore, H. "G. Harvey, the Rival Poet." Saturday Review, 23 (1926), 337-57.

2505. More, Paul Elmer. "Shakespeare's Sonnets." Shelburne Essays, Second Series. Boston and New York: Houghton Mifflin, 1905, pp. 20-45.

2506. Morgan, Appleton. The Shakespearean Myth: William Shakespeare and Circumstantial Evidence. Cincinnati: Robert Clarke, 1881.

In his final chapter, "The New Theory," Morgan poses the theory that the sonnets were of composite authorship--by noblemen who used Shakespeare as a front.

2507. Morgan, Appleton. "Whose Sonnets?" Manhattan, 3 (1884), 441-51.

Raises a number of questions about whether Shakespeare wrote the Sonnets but ultimately finds the questions irrelevant to the literature that we have. This essay becomes a chapter in his book mentioned below.

2509

2508. Morgan, Appleton. "Much Ado About Sonnets." Catholic World, 42 (1885), 212-22.

Opposes the autobiographical reading. This essay becomes a chapter in his book, mentioned below.

2509

2509. Morgan, Appleton. Shakespeare In Fact and In Criticism. New York: William Evarts Benjamin, 1888.

In one chapter, "Much Ado about Sonnets" (pp. 27-43), he comments on the futility of efforts to unearth biographical details from the poems. He takes a similar approach in the next chapter "Whose Sonnets" (pp. 44-89) on the question of authorship.

2510. Morgan, Appleton. "What Meres Knew about Shakespeare's Sonnets." Catholic World, 107 (1918), 235-46.

Focuses mainly on the identity of Mr. W.H.

2511. Morsbach, Lorenz. "Die Sonette Shakespeare's im Lichte der Uberlieferung." Nachrichten von der Koniglichen Gesellschaft der Wissenschaften zu Gottingen. Philologisch-historische Klasse (1915), pp. 137-66.

Morsbach gives a rather close reading of Thorpe's dedication and examines matters relating to Mr. W.H.

2512. Moser, F. de Mello. "Shakespeare in Portugal: Selected Facts and Problems." Shakespeare Translation, 4 (1977), 25-31.

Translating a sonnet without sacrificing the rhyme scheme can be something of a tour de force. Moser includes two Portuguese translations of Sonnet 116.

2513. Mueller, Martin. "Shakespeare and Virgil." TLS. August 31, 1973, p. 1003.

Finds a possible link between Virgil and line 9 in Sonnet 60.

2514. Muir, Kenneth. "Blundeville, Wyatt and Shakespeare." Notes and Queries, 206 (1961), 293-94.

Blundeville and Wyatt both use the same phrase--"pleasant remembraunce of thinges past"--which Shakespeare was later to use in Sonnet 30.

2515. Muir, Kenneth. "Biographical Red Herrings and Shakespeare's Sonnets." Literary Half Yearly, 6,i (1965), 61-69.

Muir believes the most fruitful approach to the Sonnets is as a series of individual poems.

2516. Muir, Kenneth. "Shakespeare: Prose and Verse." Modern Language Quarterly, 29 (1968), 467-75.

Includes a review of Brents Stirling's The Shakespeare Sonnet Order: Poems and Groups (pp. 471-75).

2517. Muir, Kenneth. "The Dark Lady of the Sonnets." Kanina (San Jose, Costa Rica), 1, ii (1977), 67-73.

Sharply differs with Rowse on the autobiographical nature of the Sonnets. Athough Muir does not call the sonnets "pure fiction," he denies that they are "straightforward autobiography."

2518. Muir, Kenneth. "The Order of Shakespeare's Sonnets." College Literature, 4 (1977), 190-96.

2519. Muir, Kenneth. Review of New Essays on Shakespeare's Sonnets, ed. Hilton Landry. Modern Language Review, 74 (1979), 163-64.

2520. Muir, Kenneth. Review of Giorgio Melchiori, Shakespeare's Dramatic Meditations: An Experiment in Criticism. Modern Language Review, 74 (1979), 164-65.

2521. Muir, Kenneth. Shakespeare's Sonnets. London: George Allen and Unwin, 1979.

Following this critical reading of the sonnets are several appendices dealing with the usual "problems"--Mr. W.H., the rival poet, the dark lady, etc.

2522. Muir, Kenneth. Review of Shakespeare's Sonnets: ed. Stephen Booth, and Shakespeare: The Sonnets: A Casebook, ed. Peter Jones. Modern Language Review, 75 (1980), 360-61.

2523. Muir, Kenneth. "The Onlie Begetter and His Family." Times Higher Education Supplement, September 11, 1981, p. 14.

Review of Gerald Hammond, The Reader and Shakespeare's Young Man Sonnets, and John Padel, New Poems by Shakespeare: Order and Meaning Restored to the Sonnets. Comments at some length on Padel's theories about the sonnet order and Shakespeare's relationship to William Herbert.

2524. Muller, Joachim. "Das zyklische Prinzip in der Lyrik." Germanisch-romanische Monatsschrift, 20 (1932), 1-20.

Uses Shakespeare's Sonnets as one of his illustrative texts.

2525. *Mullini Zanarini, Roberta. "A Comparative Analysis of Sonnets 46 and 47 by William Shakespeare." Spicilegio Moderno, 4 (1975), 221-24.

2526. Munro, John. "Dark Ladies of Literature." Contemporary Review, 185 (1954), 227-31.

The woman of white skin and black hair and eyes is a familiar figure not only in Shakespeare's Sonnets, but in ancient and modern literature as well.

2527. Murphy, Garry N. "Shakespeare's Sonnet 116." Explicator, 39 (1980), 39-41.

2528. Murray, Christopher. Review of Shakespeare's Sonnets, ed. Stephen Booth. Hibernia Weekly Review, 42 (June 8, 1978), p. 14.

2529. Murray, Howard. "The Trend of Shakespeare's Thought." TLS, January 5, 1951, p. 7.

In response to an earlier series of articles by Disher in TLS, Murray rejects any analogy between Shakespeare's Sonnet 50 and Sidney's 84.
1802

2530. Murray, John J. "Shakespeare's Sonnet XX." Explicator, 36, ii (1978), 16-17.

On the word "addition" in line 11.

2531. *Murry, John Middleton. "Problems of the Shakespeare Sonnets." Countries of the Mind. Second Series. London: Humphrey Milford, Oxford University Press, 1931, pp. 113-25.

In this review of J.M. Robertson's The Problems of the Shakespeare Sonnets, Murry defends Sonnets 20 and 69 against Robertson's "disintegrating skill."

2532. Murry, J.M. "Notes on Shakespeare: Concerning Sonnet 107." Adelphi, 2 (1929), 251-54.

Argues for 1596 as a likely date for this Sonnet.

2533. *Murry, John Middleton. "The Meaning of Sonnet 123." Wanderer, 1 (1934), 64.

2534. Murry, John Middleton. Shakespeare. London: Jonathan Cape, 1936.

His chapter on "The Sonnet Story" begins with a theory that Shakespeare's "bitterness" in Timon of Athens was occasioned by the unauthorized printing of the Sonnets. Murry goes on to date the Sonnets between 1593-95.

2535. Murry, J. Middleton. "Chapman the Rival Poet." TLS, June 4, 1938, pp. 385-86.

2536. Murry, John Middleton. "The Mortal Moon." John Clare and Other Studies. London: Peter Nevill, 1950, pp. 246-52.

Argues against Hotson's early dating (1588) of Sonnet 107.

2537. *Murzayeva, Yu. "An Attempt at the Comparative Stylistic Analysis of Sonnet 116 and Its Translation by S. Marshak." Problems of Stylistics. Issue 14: A Collection of Papers. Saratov State University, 1978, pp. 144-54.

In Russian.

2538. Mustanoja, Tauno F. "Shakespeare's Runaways Eyes and Children's Eyes." Neuphilologische Mitteilungen, 56 (1955), 250-58.

Believes that "children's eyes" in Sonnet 9 is parallel to "runaways eyes" in Romeo and Juliet (III.ii).

2539. Mutschmann, Heinrich. "Shakespeares Werke in funfzehn Teilen." Beiblatt zur Anglia, 27 (1916), 249-68.

The article contains brief notes on Sonnets 29 and 99 and a rather lengthy comment on Sonnet 107.

2540. Mutschmann, M. "The 'Mortal Moon' Sonnet." TLS, March 1, 1934, p.144.

Sonnet 107 may have been a model for Sir John Davies's poem on the death of James I and the accession of Charles I.
2082

2541. Naylor, E.W. The Poets and Music. London: J.M. Dent, 1928.

A muscian's explanation of the "jacks" referred to in Sonnet 128 (pp. 91-93) with an illustration of the instrument on p. 128.

2542. Nearing, Homer, Jr. "Shakespeare as a Nondramatic Poet: Sonnet XXIX." Shakespeare Quarterly, 13 (1962), 15-20.

A detailed analysis of "the unusual degree to which the sound reflects the sense in Sonnet XXIX. . . ."

2543. Nearing, Homer, Jr. Review of Hilton Landry, Interpretations in Shakespeare's Sonnets. Shakespeare Quarterly, 15 (1964), 234-35.

2544. Needham, Francis. "The Rival Poet." TLS, October 12, 1933, p. 691.

Sonnet 86 is the best bet for providing an identification of the rival, whom he suggests is Drayton.

2545. Neely, Carol T. "Detachment and Engagement in Shakespeare's Sonnets: 94,116 and 129." PMLA, 92 (1977), 83-95.

2546. Neely, Carol Thomas. Review of Shakespeare's Sonnets, ed. Stephen Booth. Modern Philology, 77 (1979), 210-14.

2547. Neil, Samuel. Shakespeare: A Critical Biography and An Estimate of the Facts, Fancies, Forgeries, and Fabrications, Regarding His Life and Works, Which Have Appeared in Remote and Recent Literature. London: Houlston and Wright, 1861.

Discusses the Sonnets in an Appendix (pp. 104-08) in which he suggests Shakespeare's brother-in-law, William Hathaway was Mr. W.H.

2548. N[eil], S[amuel]. "Shakspere Controversies." British Controversialist, 3rd Series (April, 1864), 241-55.

A review of some of the areas of controversy surrounding the Sonnets (pp. 251-54). Neil suggests William Hathaway as Mr. W.H.

2549. Neil, Samuel. "Shakespeare's Sonnets." Athenaeum, February 23, 1867, p. 254.

Reviews his credentials as a supporter of William Hathaway as Mr. W.H.

2550. N[eil], S[amuel]. "Mr. W.H.?" Athenaeum, August 2, 1873, p. 147.

A.E. Brae's theory (presented by C.M. Ingleby before the Royal Society of Literature on June 25, 1873) rests on the idea that W.H. was a misprint for W.S. (William Shakespeare). Neil disagrees and supports William Hathaway as Mr. W.H.

2551. Nejgebauer, A. "The Sonnets," in "Twentieth Century Studies in Shakespeare's Songs, Sonnets, and Poems." Shakespeare Survey, 15 (1962), 10-18.

2552. Nejgebauer, Aleksandar. "Tradicionalno i individualno u Shakespeareovim sonetima." [Traditional and individual elements in Shakespeare's Sonnets.] Ph.D. Dissertation, Zagreb, 1963.

2553. Nejgebauer, Aleksandar. "Smenjivanje Tacke Gledista Kao Dramski Efekat U Shekspirovim Sonetima." [Shifting the Point of View: A Dramatic Effect in Shakespeare's Sonnets.] Filoski Pregled, 2 (1964), 159-70.

Contains an English summary. The article discusses how Shakespeare created tension in his sonnets by using a shifting point of view.

2554. Ne Quid Nimis. "Replies." Notes and Queries, 9th Series, 6 (1900), 317.

He argues that the poet of Sonnet 154 must have had a knowledge of Greek that he doubts Shakespeare could have had.

2555. Ne Quid Nimis. "Shakespeare's Sonnet XXVI." Notes and Queries, 10 Series, 2 (1904), 67.

Discusses the last two lines. See A. Hall and Douse for related notes.
1820, 2556

2556. Ne Quid Nimis, and A. Hall. "Shakespeare's Sonnet XXVI." Notes and Queries, 10th Series, 2 (1904), 213-14.

See earlier notes by Douse and Ne Quid Nimis.
1820, 2555

2557. Neri, Ferdinando. "I 'Sonetti'." Saggi di Letteratura: Italiana, Francese, Inglese. Napoli: Luigi Loffredo, 1936, pp. 251-56.

Sees the Sonnets as interesting not because of the usual problems about which debates rage, but because they convey to us something of Shakespeare's unique poetic spirit.

2558. Nethercot, Arthur H. "Mrs. Davenant as the 'Dark Lady'." Sir William D'Avenant. Poet Laureate and Playwright-Manager. Chicago: University of Chicago Press, 1938, pp. 427-31.

This brief appendix summarizes Acheson's theory that Mistress Davenant was Shakespeare's "Dark Lady," which he calls "one of the most remarkable farragos of documentary fact and spun-sugar imagination ever created outside the great Bacon-Shakespeare conundrum."
1433

2559. Newbon, C.E. "Shakespeare and the Davenants." TLS, June 16, 1921, p. 389; August 4, 1921, p. 500.

Rejects William Poel's thesis about Shakespeare and Mistress Davenant.

2560. Newcomer, A.G. "Shakespeare and Herbert." Nation, 96 (1913), 55.

A note on William Herbert's coming to London.
2663, 2664

2561. Newdigate, B.H., and Kathleen M. Constable. "The Rival Poet and the Youth of the Sonnets." TLS, November 9, 1933, p. 774.

Newdigate rejects the suggestion of Francis Needham (Oct. 12) that Drayton was the rival poet and offers Walter Aston as a candidate for the fair youth. Constable comments on the letter by Needham and offers an identification of Dorus and Meridicinis in Drayton's 51st sonnet (Idea's Mirror).
2544

2562. Nicholson, Brinsley. "Shakespeare's Seventy-seventh Sonnet." Notes and Queries, 4th Series, 3 (1869), 166.

The sonnet was written in or to accompany a gift table-book, suitable for a young gallant.

2563. Nicholson, B., and B.C. "The Crux of Sonnet CXVI." Notes and Queries, 6th Series, 1 (1880), 250-51.

Two responses to Bibliothecary's reading of line 8.
1561

2564. Nicholson, Brinsley. "Shakespeare's Sonnet CXIII. and 'The Phoenix and the Turtle'." Athenaeum, February 3, 1883, p. 150.

Suggests that "mien" is the modern equivalent for "mine" in the last line of the sonnet.

2565. Nicholson, Br[insley]. "Sonnet CXIII, L. 14, 'Mine.' Notes and Queries, 6th Series, 7 (1883), 464-65.

Suggests that the word "mine" in "My most true mind thus maketh mine untrue" is from the French mine which we now spell "mien."

2566. Nicholson, Br[insley]. "Sonnets LXVI., XXV." Notes and Queries, 7th Series, 5 (1888), 61-62.

Joins those rejecting Bayne's emendation for line 8 of Sonnet 66. Also explains why lines 9 and 11 of Sonnet 25 do not rhyme (worth/quite).
1554

2567. N[icholson], Br[insley], and O. "Was Shakspeare Lame?" Notes and Queries, 7th Series, 8 (1889), 454.

On the references to lameness in Sonnets 37 and 89.

2568. Nicholson, Br[insley]. "Sonnet LXXVII., 1. 10." Notes and Queries, 7th Series, 11 (1891), 24.

Rejects an emendation suggested by Lewis Theobald which replaced "blacks" with "blanks."

2569. Nicholson, Brinsley. "Was Mr. W.H. the Earl of Pembroke?" Athenaeum, July 11, 1891, pp. 74-75.

On the basis of physical characteristics, Nicholson rejects Pembroke as W.H. and, consequently, Mary Fitton as the dark lady.

2570. Nicholson, Br[insley]. "Sonnet 146, 1. 2." Notes and Queries, 7th Series, 11 (1891), 364.

Suggests an explanation and correction for the repetition of "My sinfull earth." Response by C.C.B. later in this volume (p. 423).
1483

2571. Nicholson, Br[insley]. "Sonnet C., 1.9." Notes and Queries, 8th Series, 2 (1892), 5.

Prefers the quarto reading "resty" to Tyler's "restive."
3118

2572. Nickalls, Barbara. "The Youth of the Sonnets." TLS, September 13, 1934, p. 620.

Identifies Charles Best as a candidate for the fair youth.

2573. Nicoll, Allardyce. Review of J.M. Robertson, The Problems of the Shakespeare Sonnets. Modern Language Review, 22 (1927), 330-33.

2574. Nisbet, Ulric. The Onlie Begetter. London and New York: Longmans, Green, 1936. New York: Haskell House, 1970.

Identifies W.H. as William Herbert, a descendent of the first Earl of Pembroke and a cousin of William, the third Earl.

2575. *Nishimura, Tomiteru. "A Commentary on Shakespeare's Sonnets Nos. 27-36." Kyoiku-gakubu Kiyo (Fukui University), 28 (1978), 1-48.

2576. *Nishiyama, Masahiro. "An Observation of 'Black' in 'Dark Lady Sonnets'." Kiyo (Kogakukan University), 16 (1978), 1-27.

In Japanese.

2577. *Nishiyama, Masayasu. "Immortality and Mortality in the Man Sonnets." Kiyo (Kogakkan University) 17 (1979), 14-42.

2578. Noble, James Ashcroft. "The Punctuation of Shakspere's 129th Sonnet." Academy, 33 (June 16, 1888), 415.

2579. *Nojima, Hidekatsu. "Liaisons Dangereuses--Dark Lady Sonnets ni tsuite." Eigo Seinen, (Tokyo), 116 (1970), 244-46.

Interpretations of the dark lady sonnets.

2580. *Nojima, Hidekatsu. "'No, I am that I am'--Dark Lady Sonnets ni tsuite." Eigo Seinen, 116 (1970), 319-20.

In Japanese.

2581. Nolan, Edward F. "Shakespeare's Sonnet LXXIII." Explicator, 7 (1948), Item 13. Reprinted in A Casebook on Shakespeare's Sonnets. Ed. Gerald Willen and Victor B. Reed. New York: Thomas Y. Crowell, 1964, pp. 270-71.
2403

2582. Norman, Charles. "Shakespeares Sonette: Eine Studie." Amerikanische Rundschau, 3 (December, 1947), 32-43.

Covers the usual topics--the young friend, the dark lady, the rival poet.

2583. *Noro, Toshibumi. "Themes and Images in Shakespeare's Marriage Sonnets." Kochi University Gakujutsu Kenkyu Hokoku, 25 (1977), 143-58.

In Japanese. Discusses Ovid's influence.

2584. Norris, Christopher. "Types of Ambiguity." Essays in Criticism, 28 (1978), 245-53.

Review of Shakespeare's Sonnets, ed. Stephen Booth.

2585. North, John. The Rediscovered Masterpiece: Shakespeare's Sonnets Restored After 350 Years of Deception. The True Meaning of Willobie His Avisa, The Secret Theme of Loves Labours Lost. A Study in Literary Detection. Cambridge, Mass.: North Star Press, 1968.

North offers a "rediscovery of . . . [the Sonnets'] sequence and structure"; i.e. he arranges the Sonnets into eight "books" and shows a thematic link between Love's Labour's Lost and the central four "books."

2586. Norwood, Eugene. "Stefan George's Translation of Shakespeare's Sonnets." Monatshefte (Madison), 44 (1952), 217-24.

Includes George's translations of Sonnet 29 and 88.

2587. Nosworthy, J.M. "All too Short A Date: Internal Evidence in Shakespeare's Sonnets." Essays in Criticism, 2 (1952), 311-24.

Finds verbal links with plays from which he infers some unusually late dates for many of the sonnets.

2588. Nosworthy, J.M. "Shakespeare and Mr. W.H." Library, 5th Series, 18 (1963), 294-98.

W.H. may have been a misprint for W.S. or W.SH.

2589. Nosworthy, J.M. "The Sonnets and Other Poems." Shakespeare: Select Bibliographical Guides. Ed. Stanley Wells. London: Oxford University Press, 1973, pp. 44-53.

2590. Nowottny, Winifred M.T. "Formal Elements in Shakespeare's Sonnets I-VI." Essays in Criticism, 2 (1952), 76-84. Reprinted in 1) Discussions of Shakespeare's Sonnets. Ed. Barbara Herrnstein. Boston: D.C. Heath, 1964, pp. 152-58. 2) Shakespeare: The Sonnets: A Casebook. Ed. Peter Jones. London: Macmillan, 1977, pp. 111-19.

2591. Nowottny, Winifred. The Language Poets Use. New York: Oxford University Press, 1962.

There are a number of comments about Shakespearean Sonnets, the most extensive on Sonnet 73 (pp. 76-86). Nowottny also discusses Sidney's Astrophel and Stella 68 (pp. 130-32).

2592. Nowottny, Winifred. Review of Claes Schaar, Elizabethan Sonnet Themes and the Dating of Shakespeare's "Sonnets." Review of English Studies, NS 15 (1964), 423-29.

2593. Nowottny, Winifred. "Some Features of Form and Style in Sonnets 97-126." New Essays on Shakespeare's Sonnets. Ed. Hilton Landry. New York: AMS Press, 1976, pp. 65-107.

2594. Noyes, Alfred. "The Origin of Shakespeare's Sonnets." Bookman (London), 67 (December, 1924), 159-62. Reprinted in New Essays and American Impressions. New York: Henry Holt, 1927.

In rejecting the Sonnets as autobiography, Noyes points out a number of connections between them and Venus and Adonis.

2595. Noyes, Alfred. "The Real Secret of Shakespeare's Sonnets." New Essays and American Impressions. New York: Henry Holt, 1927, pp. 97-116. Reprinted in The Opalescent Parrot. London: Sheed and Ward, 1929, pp. 190-206.

Dismisses all the talk about Shakespeare's "lovely friend" and maintains that the sonnets are largely an outgrowth of his work on Venus and Adonis and, to a lesser extent, The Rape of Lucrece.

2596. O'Connor, William D. Hamlet's Note-Book. Boston: Houghton Mifflin, 1886.

In discussing the authorship of the Sonnets (pp. 50-56), O'Connor suggests the Sonnets were dedicated by Thomas HarioT to their author Walter RaleigH.

2597. O'Dea, Raymond. "The King of Men in Shakespeare's Early Works: Time." Discourse, 11 (1968), 141-44.

Discusses the theme of time in a half-dozen early plays and poems--the Sonnets included.

2598. O'Flanagan, Jean I. Shakespeare's Self-Revelation in His Sonnets. [Paper prepared for the Stratford-on-Avon Shakespeare Club and read Tuesday, March 11, 1902.] Stratford-on-Avon: Edward Fox, 1902.

Reviews the dominant theories about the Sonnets and summarizes the main groupings.

2599. O'Neal, Cothburn. The Dark Lady. New York: Crown, 1954.

This is a novel with the central character, Rosaline (the dark lady), as the genius behind Shakespeare. Her love affair with Southampton is the motive force for her creativity. The sonnets are a record of this relationship.

2600. Ong, Walter J. "Commonplace Rhapsody: Ravisius Textor, Zwinger and Shakespeare." Classical Influences on European Culture, A.D. 1500-1700. Ed. R.R. Bolgar. Proceedings of International Conference Held at King's College, Cambridge, April, 1974. Cambridge: Cambridge University Press, 1976, pp. 91-126. Reprinted as "Typographic Rhapsody: Ravisius Textor, Zwinger and Shakespeare." Interfaces of the Word: Studies in the Evolution of Consciousness and Culture. Ithaca, N.Y.: Cornell University Press, 1977, pp. 147-88.

In this essay on commonplace books, Ong shows correspondences between Shakespeare's Sonnet 129 and Textor's Epitheta.

2601. Oppel, Horst. Review of Raimund Borgmeier, Shakespeares Sonett "When forty winters" und die deutschen Ubersetzer. Untersuchungen zu den Problemen der Shakespeare-Ubertragung. Neueren Sprachen, 72 (1973), 449.

2602. Oppel, Horst. Review of Shakespeare's Sonnets, ed. Martin Seymour-Smith. Neueren Sprachen, (1964), 52-53.

2603. Orange, Linwood E. "Shakespeare's Sonnet 24." Southern Quarterly, 4 (1966), 409-10.

Shakespeare developed a conceit based on the theory of sight by extramission.

2604. Ord, Hubert W. "A Source of the Sonnets: A New Interpretation." London Shown by Shakespeare And Other Shakespearean Studies including A New Interpretation of the Sonnets. London: George Routledge; New York: E.P. Dutton, 1916, pp. 37-57.

Ord advances the theory that Chaucer's Roman de la Rose is a source of and distinct influence in the Sonnets.

2605. Ord, Hubert, and E.M. Nancarrow. "Chaucer and Shakespeare's Sonnets." TLS, June 22, 1916, pp. 297-98; June 29, 1916, p. 310.

Ord believes Chaucer's "Romance of the Rose" to be Shakespeare's inspiration for the Sonnets, to which Nancarrow adds an observation.

2606. Ord, Hubert. Chaucer and the Rival Poet in Shakespeare's Sonnets, a New Theory. London and Toronto: Dutton, 1921. New York: AMS Press, 1970.

Some of his observations are that Shakespeare was strongly influenced by Chaucer's Roman de la Rose, that many of his allusions are literary rather than erotic, Chaucer was his Muse, and Chaucer's editor, T. Speght, was his "rival."

2607. Ord, Hubert. "Chaucer and the Rival Poet." TLS, May 18, 1922, p. 324.

Responds to a review of his book in TLS (May 4, 1922), p. 294.
3282

2608. Ormsby, W.E. "Shakespeare's Seventy-sixth Sonnet." Notes and Queries, 9th Series, 10 (1902), 125-26.

Disputes a point in Judge Thomas Webb's book, The Mystery of William Shakespeare, regarding authorship of the Sonnets. See Stronach and W.E. Wilson for replies to this note.
3046

2609. Oshio, Toshiko. "The Sonnets: From the Poems to the Poet." Shakespeare Studies (Shakespeare Society of Japan), 12 (1973-74), 46-71.

Disregarding the "riddles," Oshio examines the poems for "their literary quality and . . . the poet's inner portrait."

2610. Osterberg, V. "The 'Countess Scenes' of '<u>Edward III</u>'." <u>Shakespeare Jahrbuch</u>, 65 (1929), 49-91.

In his attempt to establish Shakespeare's hand in this play, Osterberg shows parallels between some of the sonnets and passages in <u>Edward III</u> (pp. 73-74).

2611. Ostheeren, Klaus. "Toposforschung und Bedeutungslehre: Die Glanzvorstellung im Schonheitskatalog und die mittelenglischen Farbadjektive <u>blak</u> und <u>broun</u>." <u>Anglia</u>, 89 (1971), 1-47.

Ostheeren makes a brief application of his thesis to the dark lady of the Sonnets (pp. 37-39).

2612. Otten, Kurt. "Gedankenentwicklung und Gruppenaufbau in Shakespeares Sonetten der Freundesliebe." <u>Neueren Sprachen</u>, 13 (1964), 1-19.

2613. Otten, Kurt. Review of Claes Schaar, <u>Elizabethan Sonnet Themes and the Dating of Shakespeare's "Sonnets."</u> <u>Erasmus</u>, 18 (1966), 364-65.

2614. Ousby, Heather Dubrow. "Shakespeare's Sonnet 125, 13-14." <u>Explicator</u>, 35, iii (1977), 22-23.

2615. P., C.M. "The Sonnets." <u>Baconiana</u>, NS 1 (1893), 64-85.

Finds many forms--legal terms, metaphors, antitheses, etc. common to the Sonnets and Bacon's writing.

2616. Padel, John H. "'That the Thought of Hearts Can Mend': An Introduction to Shakespeare's Sonnets for Psychotherapists and Others." <u>TLS</u>, December 19, 1975, pp. 1519-21.

2617. Padel, J.H. "Sonnet 146." <u>TLS</u>, October 21, 1977, p. 1240.

On a reading of line 2. See Philip Brockbank and H.H. Meier on the same subject (<u>TLS</u>, Oct.7, 1977, p. 1150).
1619, 2484

2618. Padel, John. <u>New Poems by Shakespeare: Order and Meaning Restored to the Sonnets</u>. London: Herbert Press, 1981.

2619. Pagnini, M. "Lettura critica (e metacritica) del Sonetto 20 di Shakespeare." <u>Strumenti Critici</u>, 3, i (1969), 1-18. Reprinted in <u>Critica della funzionalita</u>. Torino: Giulio Einaudi, 1970, pp. 121-41.

2620. Palk, Robert. "The Puzzle of 'The Sonnets'--A Solution?" <u>TLS</u>, April 20, 1916, p. 189.

Palk believes the Sonnets contain evidence that supports Sir Walter Ralegh as the poet.

2621. Palk, Robert. "Sir Walter Ralegh and Shakespeare." TLS, October 24, 1918, p. 512.

Explains his hypothesis that Ralegh wrote the Sonnets and that Penelope Devereux was his dark lady.

2622. Palmer, George Herbert. Intimations of Immortality in the Sonnets of Shakespeare. The Ingersoll Lecture, 1912. Boston and New York: Houghton Mifflin, 1912.

Palmer's main theme is the preoccupation in the Sonnets with time, death, age and the means by which they may be bested.

2623. Paolucci, Anne. Review of Giorgio Melchiori, Shakespeare's Dramatic Meditations: An Experiment in Criticism. Shakespeare Studies, 11 (1978), 322-26.

2624. Parish, Verna N. "Shakespeare's Sonnets and The French Academie." Shakespeare Newsletter, 10 (1960), 25.

Some of the ideas, particularly those on friendship and marriage, found in Pierre de la Primaudaye's The French Academie (1577) are reflected in the Sonnets.

2625. Parker, David. "Verbal Moods in Shakespeare's Sonnets." Modern Language Quarterly, 30 (1969), 331-39.

"Nearly all the sonnets can be seen as elaborate disguises of the imperative mood . . . ."

2626. Parker, David. "A Misprint in the New Cambridge Sonnets." Shakespeare Newsletter, 20 (1970), 46.

Sonnet 3 (line 8) of the J. Dover Wilson edition reads "this self-love" and should be "His self-love."

2627. Parsons, Howard. "Shakespeare's Sonnet CXLVI." Notes and Queries, 200 (1955), 97.

Attempts to resolve the reading of the poem's second line.

2628. Partridge, A.C. The Language of Renaissance Poetry: Spenser, Shakespeare, Donne, Milton. London: Andre Deutsch, 1971.

In this examination of diction and rhetoric, Partridge examines, among other poems, Shakespeare's Sonnets 19, 21, 30, 64, 106, 130 (pp. 119-40), several of Donne's Holy Sonnets (pp. 231-36), and Milton's Sonnet 7.

2629. Partridge, A.C. A Substantive Grammar of Shakespeare's Nondramatic Texts. Charlottesville, Va.: University Press of Virginia, 1976.

Includes a grammatic analysis of the Sonnets (pp. 111-57).

2630. Pashkovska-Hoppe, C. "Basic Syntactic Models in The Sonnets of Shakespeare." Shakespeare Readings 1976. Ed. A. Anikst. Moscow: "Nauka," 1977, pp. 195-214.

In Russian with an English summary.

2631. Pattison, Mark. "Shakespeare's Sonnets." Literary World, 14 (October 6, 1883), 333.

This note, reprinted from The Sonnets of Milton, edited by Pattison, comments on the Shakespearean form.

2632. P[earce], G.M. "Shakespeare's Sonnets, National Theatre--Olivier--matinee, 9 July 1980, front stalls." Cahiers Elisabethains, No. 18 (1980), 101-03.

A review of a reading of the Sonnets by Simon Callow, according to a reorganized text by John Padel.

2633. Pemberton, Henry, Jr. "The First and Second Quartos of Hamlet, The Sonnets and the Year 1601." New Shakespeareana, 7 (1908), 102-06.

Supports Thomas Tyler's dating (1601) for many of the Sonnets.

2634. Pemberton, H., Jr. "Topical Allusions in the Sonnets." New Shakespeareana, 8 (1909), 61-67.

From his reading of Sonnets 153 and 154, Pemberton concludes that the Sonnets were addressed to the Queen and written in 1602.

2635. Pemberton, Henry, Jr. Shakspere and Sir Walter Ralegh. Philadelphia and London: Lippincott, 1914. rpt. New York: Haskell House, 1971.

The book contains a chapter on "Sonnets CLIII and CLIV" (pp. 79-80) in which Pemberton concludes that Ralegh wrote these sonnets. Several other chapters and sections of the Appendix deal also with the Sonnets.

2636. Perenyi, Erzsebet. "Shakespeare's Sonnet Sequence." Studies in English and American. Ed. Tibor Frank and Erzsebet Perenyi. Budapest: Eotvos University, 1977, vol. 3, pp. 7-21.

2637. Perrett, Arthur J. "Dr. Hotson's Arguments." TLS, June 16, 1950, p. 373.

In this letter discussing Sonnet 107, Perrett finds Hotson's argument about the dating of the Sonnets unconvincing.

2638. Perrine, Laurence. "When Form and Content Kiss/ Intention Made the Bliss: The Sonnet in Romeo and Juliet." English Journal, 55 (1966), 872-74.

Shakespeare purposely wrote the passage in Romeo and Juliet (I, v) beginning "If I profane with my unworthiest hand . . ." as a sonnet.

2639. Peterson, Douglas L. "A Probable Source for Shakespeare's Sonnet CXXIX." Shakespeare Quarterly, 5 (1954), 381-84.

The rhetorical scheme of Sonnet 129 follows closely a passage in the third book of Thomas Wilson's Arte of Rhetorique (1560).

2640. Petry, Lorenz. Review of Shakespeare Sonnette, tr. Stefan George, and Shakespeares Sonette, tr. Eduard Saenger. Beiblatt zur Anglia, 22 (1911), 242-46.

2641. Phelps, William Lyon. "Notes on Shakespeare." Proceedings of the American Philosophical Society, 81 (1939), 573-79.

Among the biographical details he infers from the Sonnets, Phelps thinks that the 1609 publication of the Sonnets may have embarrassed Shakespeare and prompted him to leave London (pp. 573-74).

2642. Phillips Gerald William. The Tragic Story of "Shakespeare." Disclosed in the Sonnets, and the Life of Edward de Vere Seventeenth Earl of Oxford, Lord of Escales and Badlesmere, Lord Great Chamberlain of England. London: Cecil Palmer, 1932.

Arranges the Sonnets by date of composition, rejects Venus and Adonis as a product of the same hand, and discovers a son to whom de Vere addressed the Sonnets.

2643. Phillips, Gerald William. Sunlight on Shakespeare's Sonnets. London: Thornton Butterworth, 1935.

Phillips re-arranges the Sonnets, which are purportedly about Shakespeare's son. The dark lady sonnets are about the poet's new wife and her relations with the poet's son.

2644. Phillips, G.W. Lord Burghley in Shakespeare: Falstaff, Sly and Others. London: Thornton Butterworth, 1936.

Phillips seeks to prove that the poet of the Sonnets did not write Venus and Adonis and Lucrece ("Discussion of the Authenticity of 'Venus' and 'Lucrece'," pp. 199-220). He also has some appendices in which he compares word usage in the Sonnets, Venus and Adonis and Lucrece (pp. 245-85).

2645. Phillips, G[erald] W[illiam]. Shake spears Sonnets: Addressed to Members of the Shakespeare Fellowship. Cambridge: W. Heffer, 1954.

Gives a sonnet chronology associated with the life of Oxford.

2646. Piper, H.W. "Shakespeare's Thirty-first Sonnet." TLS, April 13, 1951, p. 229.

This sonnet is "a variation on the theme of the Church and Religion of Love."

2647. Piper, William Bowman. "A Poem Turned in Process." ELH, 43 (1976), 444-60.

Discusses "the best of Shakespeare's attacks on time"--in Sonnets 12, 64, 73 and 104.

2648. Piper, William Bowman. Evaluating Shakespeare's Sonnets. Monograph in English. Rice University Studies, 65, ii (1979).

Piper explains why he believes Sonnets 87, 104, 121 and 129 are "of special excellence."

2649. Pirkhofer, Anton M. "'A Pretty Pleasing Pricket'--On the Use of Alliteration in Shakespeare's Sonnets." Shakespeare Quarterly, 14 (1963), 3-14.

2650. Pirkhofer, Anton M. "The Beauty of Truth: The Dramatic Character of Shakespeare's Sonnets." New Essays on Shakespeare's Sonnets. Ed. Hilton Landry. New York: AMS Press, 1976, pp. 109-28.

2651. Plard, Henri. "Traductions allemandes des sonnets de Shakespeare." Etudes Germaniques, 19 (1964), 529-32.

On the translations of Stefan George and Karl Kraus.

2652. Platt, Arthur. "Edward III and Shakespeare's Sonnets." Modern Language Review, 6 (1911), 511-13.

2653. Plumptre, E.H. "Shakespeare's Travels: Somerset and Elsewhere." Contemporary Review, 55 (1889), 584-602.

Searches for the locale referred to in Sonnets 153 and 154 (and others), which he identifies as the baths in the city of Bath. These allusions suggest that Shakespeare may have been suffering from an illness.

2654. Poel, William. "Shakespeare and the Davenants." TLS, June 2, 1921, p. 356; June 23, 1921, p. 403; June 30, 1921, p. 420.

In response to the satire of Willobie His Avisa directed at Shakespeare and Southampton, Shakespeare wrote the dark lady sonnets.

2655. Pohl, Frederick J. "Where Shakespeare Saw Mountains." Shakespeare Newsletter, 8 (1958), 37.

The evidence to be inferred from his references to mountains in the Sonnets suggests he viewed mountains from Lancashire.

2656. Pohl, Frederick J. "On the Identity of 'Mr. W.H'." Shakespeare Newsletter, 8 (1958), 43.

William Houghton of Lancashire could have been Mr. W.H. as could William Haughton, a London playwright.

2657. Poirier, Michel. Review of G. Wilson Knight, The Mutual Flame. Etudes Anglaises, 9 (1956), 255-56.

2658. Poirier, Michel. Review of J.B. Leishman, Themes and Variations in Shakespeare's Sonnets. Etudes Anglaises, 15 (1962), 75-76.

2659. Poirier, Michel. Review of Edward Hubler, et al. The Riddle of Shakespeare's Sonnets. Etudes Anglaises, 17 (1964), 664.

2660. Poirier, Michel. Reviews of The Sonnets, ed. John Dover Wilson; Shakespeare's Sonnets, ed. W.G. Ingram and Theodore Redpath; A Casebook on Shakespeare's Sonnets, ed. Gerald Willen and Victor B. Reed; Murray Krieger, A Window to Criticism: Shakespeare's Sonnets and Modern Poetics. Etudes Anglaises, 19 (1966), 294-97.

2661. Poisson, Rodney. "Unequal Friendship: Shakespeare's Sonnets 18-126." English Studies in Canada, 1 (1975), 144-59. Reprinted in New Essays on Shakespeare's Sonnets. Ed. Hilton Landry. New York: AMS Press, 1976, pp. 1-19.

2662. P[ollard], A.W. Review of J.A. Fort, The Two Dated Sonnets of Shakespeare. Library, 4th Series, 5 (1925), 375-76.

2663. Porter, Charlotte. "News for Bibliophiles." Nation, 95 (1912), 532-33.

Finds evidence that would have put William Herbert in London as early as 1597, thus making him a more likely subject for Shakespeare's Sonnets.

2664. Porter, Charlotte. "Shakespeare and Herbert Again." Nation, 96 (1913), 80.

In this response to A. G. Newcomer, Porter adds some comments regarding the date of Herbert's coming to London.
2560

2665. Poteet, Lewis J. "Romantic Aesthetics in Oscar Wilde's 'Mr. W.H.'" Studies in Short Fiction, 7 (1970), 458-64.

Although not, strictly speaking, about the Sonnets themselves, the comments about Wilde's short story are relevant.

2666. Pott, Constance M. "Francis St. Alban and his 'Fair Lady'." Baconiana, 3rd Series, 5 (1907), 178-96.

Links Bacon's idealized and allegorical "fair Lady" with the "dark Lady" of the Sonnets.

2667. Pratt, Marjory Bates. Formal Designs from Ten Shakespeare Sonnets. Brooklyn, N.Y.: Comet Press, 1940.

Sonnets and corresponding designs on facing page. The designs seek "to represent visually the basic sound-patterns of poetry . . . [and] were determined wholly by the phonetic structure of the sonnets themselves."

2668. Praz, Mario. Review of Barbara A. Mackenzie, Shakespeare's Sonnets: Their Relation to His Life; Benvenuto Cellini, Vita e Arte nei Sonetti di Shakespeare; I Sonetti di Shakespeare, ed. Piero Rebora. English Studies, 29 (1948), 53-54.

2669. Price, H.T. Review of H. McClure Young, The Sonnets of Shakespeare: A Psycho-Sexual Analysis. Journal of English and Germanic Philology, 37 (1938), 432.

2670. Price, Thos. R. "The Technic of Shakspere's Sonnets." Studies in Honor of Basil L. Gildersleeve. Baltimore: Johns Hopkins Press, 1902, pp. 363-75.

A statistical examination of Shakespeare's word usage, rhyme schemes, etc.

2671. Prince, F.T. Review of Claes Schaar, Elizabethan Sonnet Themes and the Dating of Shakespeare's Sonnets." Studia Neophilologica, 35 (1963), 307-10.

2672. Prince, F.T. Review of Leslie Hotson, Shakespeare's Sonnets Dated, and Other Essays. Review of English Studies, NS 2 (1951), 271-72.

2673. Prince, F.T. William Shakespeare: The Poems. Writers and Their Work, 165. London: Longmans Green, 1963.

Contains a chapter on the Sonnets (pp. 17-42).

2674. Prior, Roger. "Was Emilia Lanier the Dark Lady?" Shakespeare Newsletter, 25 (1975), 26.

Points out that Rosaline (Love's Labour's Lost) is an anagram of "SO LANIER" or "LANIER'S O."

2675. Prokopiw, Orysia. "A Stylistic Analysis of the Ukrainian Translations of Shakespeare's Sonnets." Ph.D. Dissertation, Ottawa, 1975.

2676. Prokopiw, Orysia. The Ukrainian Translations of Shakespeare's Sonnets: A Stylistic Analysis. Ottawa and Edmonton: University of Ottawa Press and Gateway Publishers, 1976.

2677. Proser, Matthew N. "Shakespeare of the Sonnets." Critical Survey, 5 (1971), 243-54.

A look at a number of the Sonnets for what they tell us of Shakespeare's inner life--both his philosophy and his emotions.

2678. "Pudor, Proh." "On Shakespeare's Sonnets." Blackwood's, 3 (1818), 585-88.

Perhaps by Christopher North or John Wilson. Comments on several contemporary critical judgments of Shakespeare's Sonnets including references to Hazlitt, Wordsworth and Schlegel.

2679. Pugliatti, Paola Gulli. "I Sonetti di Shakespeare." Paragone, 26, No. 310 (December, 1975), 91-99.

Notes the demise of the biographical approach to sonnet criticism, emphasizes the importance of formalist treatments, and considers recent Italian criticism a step forward in this direction, especially that of Alessandro Serpieri.

2680. Pulik, Ruth. Review of Shakespeare's Sonnets, ed. A.L. Rowse. Unisa English Studies, 11, ii (1973), 58-59.

2681. Purdum, Richard. "Shakespeare's Sonnet 128." Journal of English and Germanic Philology, 63 (1964), 235-39.

A justification for Sonnet 128 in its place--as one of the dark lady Sonnets.

2682. Puschmann-Nalenz, Barbara. "Loves of Comfort and Despair": Konzeptionen von Freundschaft und Liebe in Shakespeares Sonetten. Studien zur Anglistik. Frankfort am Main: Akademische Verlagsgesellschaft, 1974.

2683. Quennell, Peter. Shakespeare: A Biography. Cleveland and New York: World, 1963.

In Chapter 5, "'His Sugared Sonnets'" (pp. 120-40) Quennell suggests that "The Sonnets . . . may be described as a monument to homosexual love raised by an otherwise heterosexual poet." He also comments on the changing attitudes toward these poems.

2684. R. "New Theories of the Sonnets." Shakespeariana, 1 (1884), 291-97.

Reviews the theories propounded by Macaulay ("New Views of Shakespeare's Sonnets") and by Charles Mackay ("A Tangled Skein Unravelled, or the Mysteries of Shakespeare's Sonnets").
2412, 2416

2685. R., E. "Note to Wordsworth's 'Prelude,' Bk. v. 26." Notes and Queries, 12th series, 8 (1921), 106.

The quotation from Wordsworth's "weep to have" is from Shakespeare's Sonnet 64.

2686. R., J.G. "Shakespeare's Sonnets." Notes and Queries, 2nd Series, 7 (1859), 125.

Asserts that Sonnet 107 was addressed to Southampton after Elizabeth's death. He mentions also that there are several references to Ben Jonson (Sonnets 78, 80, etc.).

2687. Raby, F.J.E. "Shakespeare's Sonnets." TLS, March 26, 1964, p. 255.

Brief observation on the marriage theme of the first 17 sonnets.

2688. *Racin, John. "The Will in Renaissance Literature." Selected Papers from the West Virginia Shakespeare and Renaissance Association. Ed. Sophia Blaydes and Philip Bordinat. Morgantown: West Virginia University Foundation, 1976, pp. 65-77.

Examines the "will" as volition in Lucrece, Othello, Lear and the Sonnets.

2689. Radley, Virginia L., and David C. Redding. "Shakespeare: Sonnet 110, A New Look." Shakespeare Quarterly, 12 (1961), 462-63.

Rejects the notion that the sonnet is expressing disillusionment with the stage.

2690. Rahm, Linda Kathryn. "The Poet-Lover and Shakespeare's Sonnets." Ph.D. Dissertation, Cornell, 1971. DAI, 32 (1971), 451A.

2691. Raleigh, Sir Walter. Shakespeare. New York and London: Macmillan, 1907.

Raleigh writes that those who have tried to solve the problem of the Sonnets have left "the shrine of Shakespeare . . . thickly hung with these votive offerings, all withered and dusty." He comments on the known facts and finally offers a rather general reading of the sequence (pp. 85-93).

2692. Ramsey, Paul. Review of Tetsumaro Hayashi, Shakespeare's Sonnets: A Record of 20th Century Criticism; R.J. Wait, The Background to Shakespeare's Sonnets; Philip Martin, Shakespeare's Sonnets: Self, Love and Art. Shakespeare Quarterly, 25 (1974), 364-66.

2693. Ramsey, Paul. "The Syllables of Shakespeare's Sonnets." New Essays on Shakespeare's Sonnets. Ed. Hilton Landry. New York: AMS Press, 1976, pp. 193-215.

2694. Ramsey, Paul. The Fickle Glass: A Study of Shakespeare's Sonnets. AMS Studies in the Renaissance, 4. New York: AMS Press, 1979.

The book is divided into discussions of the "Problems," "Shakespeare's Techniques," and the "Meaning" of the Poems.

2695. Rang, Florens Christian. Shakespeare der Christ: Eine Deutung der Sonette. Ed. Bernard Rang. Deutsche Akademie fur Sprache und Dichtung. Heidelberg: Lambert Schneider, 1954.

This allegorical reading includes detailed explications of over a dozen sonnets.

2696. Ransom, John Crowe. "Shakespeare at Sonnets." Southern Review, 3 (1937-38), 531-53. Reprinted in The World's Body. New York and London: Charles Scribner's Sons, 1938. Baton Rouge: Louisianna State University Press, 1968, pp. 270-303. Also in A Casebook on Shakespeare's Sonnets. Ed. Gerald Willen and Victor B. Reed. New York: Thomas Y. Crowell, 1964, pp. 198-218. Discussions of Shakespeare's Sonnets. Ed. Barbara Herrnstein. Boston: D.C. Heath, 1964, pp. 87-105.

2697. Ransom, John Crowe. "Mr. Empson's Muddles." Southern Review, 4 (1938), 322-39.

In part of this essay, which accuses Empson of over-interpreting poetry, Ransom discusses Sonnet 94 and several others (pp. 328-31).

2698. Ransom, John Crowe. The New Criticism. Norfolk, Conn.: New Directions, 1941.

Using Empson's discussion of Sonnet 73 as a point of departure (Seven Types of Ambiguity), Ransom enlarges upon the reading of the fourth line (pp. 121-31).
1878

2699. Ransom, John Crowe. "A Postscript on Shakespeare's Sonnets." Kenyon Review, 30 (1968), 523-31.

Thirty years after he first published The World's Body (1938), Ransom offers a reappraisal of Shakespeare's Sonnets.

2700. Rapin, Rene. "Shakespeare's 'Sonnet LXXIII'." Explicator, 30 (1971), Item 3.

2701. Rappaport, Gideon. "Another Sonnet in 'Romeo and Juliet'." Notes and Queries, 223 (1978), 124.

2702. Rattray, R.F. "Will Hews." TLS, April 12, 1928, p. 272.

Hews is an anagram of the initials of Henry Wriothesley Earl of Southampton, thus explaining the dedication to the 1609 Quarto.

2703. Ray, Robert H. "Shakespeare's Sonnet 16." Explicator, 38 (1979), 24-25.

2704. Razova, V. "Sonety Shekspira v russkich perevodach." [On Shakespeare's Sonnets in Russian translation.] Shekspir v mirovoj literature. Ed. B. Reizova. Moskva and Leningrad: Izdatelbstvo "Chudozestvennaja literatura," 1964, pp. 361-81.

2705. Rebholz, Ronald. "The Sonnets and Shakespeare's Personality." Shakespeare Newsletter, 28 (1978), 4.

Abstract of a paper read at MLA, Chicago, December 29, 1977. Special attention is given to Sonnets 135-136. The speaker, identified with Shakespeare, is bisexual.

2706. *Rebora, Piero. "Il tema del matrimonio nei 'Sonetti' di Shakespeare." Studi Urbinati, Serie B (1940), pp, 47-66.

2707. "Rector." "Shakspeare's Sonnets; Hathaway the Dramatist." Notes and Queries, 2nd Series, 5 (1858), 164-65.

Purely unsupported speculation that Shakespeare's brother-in-law, who might have been an actor named "Hathaway," published the Sonnets.

2708. Redin, Mats. "The Friend in Shakespeare's Sonnets." Englische Studien, 56 (1922), 390-407.

Finds it unlikely that the Sonnets are addressed to one man.

2709. Redpath, Theodore. "The Punctuation of Shakespeare's Sonnets." New Essays on Shakespeare's Sonnets. Ed. Hilton Landry. New York: AMS Press, 1976, pp. 217-51.

2710. Redpath, Theodore. "Shakespeare's Sonnets." Archiv fur das Studium der neueren Sprachen und Literaturen, 204 (1968), 401-13.

Lecture delivered at Heidelberg University, June 27, 1967. An examination of the usual arguments used to attack and defend the greatness of Shakespeare's Sonnets.

2711. Reecer, Marcia. "Dramatic Action in Shakespeare's Sonnets." Ph.D. Dissertation, Bryn Mawr College, 1969. DAI, 31 (1970), 367A.

2712. Rees, Joan. Review of A.L. Rowse, Simon Forman: Sex and Society in Shakespeare's Age. Review of English Studies, 26 (1975), 476-78.

Comments on Rowse's thesis that Emilia Lanier is Shakespeare's 'dark lady.'

2713. Reese, M.M. Shakespeare, His World and His Work. New York: St. Martin's Press, 1953.

Devotes some space to a review of the theories about Mr. W.H., whom he regards to be unknowable (pp. 408-10), and to sonnet conventions (pp. 412-21) with a number of other passages about individual sonnets.

2714. Reeves, James. The Critical Sense: Practical Criticism of Prose and Poetry. London: Heinemann, 1956.

Gives readings of sonnets by Shelley ("Ozymandias"), Hopkins ("God's Grandeur"), and Shakespeare (Sonnet 65) (pp. 95-97, 102-07).

2715. Reichel, Eugen. "Das Portrat des Herrn W.H." Gegenwart, 62 (1902), 250-51.

2716. Reichert, John F. "Sonnet XX and Erasmus' 'Epistle to Perswade a Yong Gentleman to Mariage'." Shakespeare Quarterly, 16 (1965), 238-40.

Believes the Erasmus passage is a source for Shakespeare's sonnet.

2717. Reinecke, Otto. "Einzelreferate." Shakespeare Jahrbuch, 63 (1927), 215-17.

Includes a review of Sir Denys Bray, The Original Order of Shakespeare's Sonnets.

2718. Renault, Mary, and Martin Moynihan. "'The Background to Shakespeare's Sonnets'." TLS, May 25, 1973, p. 587.

Responding to the review of R.J.C. Wait, The Background to Shakespeare's Sonnets, Renault's letter comments on topicality in Shakespeare.
3323

2719. Rendall, Gerald H. Shakespeare's Sonnets and Edward De Vere. London: John Murray, 1930.

The book, which propounds the theory that Oxford wrote the sonnets, devotes half the text to a sonnet by sonnet explication.

2720. Rendall, Gerald H. "Shakespeare's Sonnets and Edward de Vere." TLS, May 29, 1930, p. 457.

In answer to the May 22 review of his book.
3299

2721. Rendall, Gerald H. Shake-speare: Handwriting and Spelling. London: Cecil Palmer, 1931. 1969.

Illustrated exclusively from the Sonnets.

2722. Rendall, Gerald H. Personal Clues in Shakespeare Poems and Sonnets. London: John Lane, 1934.

Takes up thematic groups of the Sonnets (youth and marriage, friendship, rival poet, etc.) and relates them to de Vere's life.

2723. Rendall, G.H. "The 'Mortal Moon' Sonnet." TLS, March 15, 1934, p. 194.
2082

2724. Rewcastle, George. "That Shakespeare Mystery: An Ingenious Anagram to Prove that Henry Wriothesley was the Poet's 'Vow-fellow'." Book Monthly, 14 (1919), 704.

Finds an anagram for Southampton's name in last line of Sonnet 26.

2725. [Rice, Sir Spring Robert]. The Story of Hamlet and Horatio. London: Selwyn and Blount, 1924.

Discovering Rosicrucian symbols in the Sonnets, the author identifies Mr. W.H. (the poet) as Mr. W. Hamlet (i.e. Bacon). His analysis of various sonnets is designed to give credence to his theory (pp. 358-476).

2726. Richards, Bernard. "Whitney's Influence on Shakespeare's Sonnets 111 and 112, and on Donne's Third Satire. Notes and Queries, 225 (1980), 160-61

Traces the phrase "the dyer's hand" (Sonnet 111) to a similar image in Geoffrey Whitney's A Choice of Emblemes (1586). Suggests that a line from Sonnet 112 ("So you ore-greene my bad, my good alow") is similar to another passage in Whitney.

2727. Richards, I.A. "Jakobson's Shakespeare: The Subliminal Structures of a Sonnet." TLS, May 28, 1970, pp. 589-90.

An examination of Jakobson's study on Sonnet 129 (Shakespeare's Verbal Art in Th' Expence of Spirit).

2728. Richardson, D.L. "On Shakspeare's Sonnets, Their Poetical Merits, and on the Question To Whom They Are Addressed." Gentleman's Magazine, 158 (1835), 250-56, 361-69.

Suggests that the Sonnets are addressed to a number of people and that the order of the poems in the Quarto is corrupt.

2729. Richmond, Hugh M. Shakespeare's Sexual Comedy: A Mirror for Lovers. Indianapolis and New York: Bobbs-Merrill, 1971.

Chapter 2, "The Sonnets: Reversal of Expectations in Love" (pp. 15-47), and that part of Chapter 4 entitled "Triangles in the Sonnets and The Merchant of Venice" (pp. 123-37) discusses the evolution of Shakespeare's "sexual ethic" in the sonnets.

2730. Richmond, Oliffe. "Shakespeare's Sonnets: A Reading." TLS, December 26, 1918, p. 657.

Suggests an emendation ("rescribe" for "reserve") in Sonnet 85, l. 3.

2731. Riding, Laura, and Robert Graves. "William Shakespeare and E.E. Cummings: A Study in Original Punctuation and Spelling." A Survey of Modernist Poetry. London: William Heinemann, 1927, pp. 59-82.

Discusses Sonnet 129 and some of the typographical changes it has undergone and how that has affected the reading of the poem.

2732. Riemer, A.P. Review of Brents Stirling, The Shakespeare Sonnet Order: Poems and Groups. AUMLA, No. 35 (1971), 91-93.

2733. Ritchie, Jane Roessner. "'Mine Own True Love:' Shakespeare's Sonnets 100-116." Ph.D. Dissertation, Boston College, 1976. DAI, 37 (1977), 4375A.

2734. [Ritchie], Jane Roessner. "Double Exposure: Shakespeare's Sonnets 100-114." ELH, 46 (1979), 357-78.

These sonnets praise the young man while revealing his corruption.

2735. Ritter, Albert, ed. Der Unbekannte Shakespeare: Eine Auswahl aus Shakespeares Werken. Berlin: Gustav Grosser, 1922.

Thirty sonnets translated into German by different translators with an introduction (pp. 262-78).

2736. Rizzardi, Alfredo. Il primo Shakespeare: il Mito, la Poesia. Pubblicazioni dell'universita di Urbino. Serie di lettere e filosofia, 22. Urbino: Argalia, 1967.

In this book about Venus and Adonis Rizzardi notes certain mythic themes related to the Venus and Adonis in the Sonnets (pp. 149-60).

2737. Rizzardi, Alfredo. "Per una lettura dei sonetti shakespeariani." Tre studi elisabettiani. Pubblicazioni dell'Universita di Urbino: Serie di lettere e filosofia, 36. Urbino: Argalia, 1975, pp. 7-45.

Among other things Rizzardi examines the new as well as the conventional in the Sonnets.

2738. Robbins, R.H.A. "A Seventeenth-Century Manuscript of Shakespeare's Sonnet 128." Notes and Queries, 212 (1967), 137-38.

2739. Robertson, John M. Shakespeare and Chapman: A Thesis of Chapman's Authorship of "A Lover's Complaint" and His Origination of "Timon of Athens," With Indications of Further Problems. London: T. Fisher Unwin, 1917.

In the opening chapter on "The Rival Poet," Robertson discusses the sonnets that refer to the rival (Chapman).

2740. Robertson, J.M. The Problems of the Shakespeare Sonnets. London: George Routledge, 1926. rpt. New York: Haskell House, 1973.

An exhaustive review of the work of all of the major critics of the Sonnets from Boswell, Boaden, Coleridge, et al. to the 1920's.

2741. Roche, Thomas P. "Shakespeare and the Sonnet Sequence." English Poetry and Prose, 1540-1674. Ed. Christopher Ricks. London: Barrie and Jenkins, 1970, pp. 101-18.

2742. Roche, Thomas P., Jr. "Five Books on Shakespeare's Sonnets." Shakespeare Quarterly, 29 (1978), 439-48.

Review of Shakespeare's Sonnets, ed. Stephen Booth; Martin Green, The Labyrinth of Shakespeare's Sonnets: An Examination of Sexual Elements in Shakespeare's Language; New Essays on Shakespeare's Sonnets, ed. Hilton Landry; Giorgio Melchiori, Shakespeare's Dramatic Meditations: An Experiment in Criticism; Katharine M. Wilson, Shakespeare's Sugared Sonnets.

2743. Rodder, Paul. Shakespeares Sonette im Lichte der Neueren Forschungen. Wissenschaftliche Beilage zum Jahresbericht des Realprogymnasiums zu Gollnow. Gollnow: H. Voigt, 1913.

More on Mr. W.H. and Thorpe's dedication.

2744. Roe, J.E. The Mortal Moon; or, Bacon and his Masks: the Defoe Period Unmasked. New York: Burr, 1891.

The Sonnets are related to the life of Sir Francis Bacon, who wrote them (pp. 150-59 et passim).

2745. Roe, J.E. "The Grave's Tiring Room." Baconiana, 3rd Series, 6 (1908), 114-21, 155-65.

In identifying the poet as Bacon, Roe finds allusion to Bacon's fall.

2746. Roe, J.E. "Bacon in the Sonnets." Baconiana, 3rd Series, 7 (1909), 36-40.

Offers evidence to support Bacon as author of the Sonnets.

2747. Roe, J.E. Sir Francis Bacon's Own Story. Rochester, N.Y.: Du Bois Press, 1918.

Bacon, the poet, reveals himself through the Sonnets.

2748. Rogers, E.G. "Sonnet CXXX: Watson to Linche to Shakespeare." Shakespeare Quarterly, 11 (1960), 232-33.

Although Sonnet 130 may have been a parody of Thomas Watson's Sonnet 7 (Hecatompathia), it seems more likely a parody of several of Richard Linche's sonnets from Diella.

2749. Rolfe, William J. "The Sonnets." Shakespeariana, 6 (1889), 97-115.

Originally read before the New York Shakespeare Society, February 25, 1887. Expresses his own theories about the usual problems: the Sonnets were expressions of his own feelings, some of the Sonnets were addressed to Ann Hathaway, the arrangement of the 1609 Quarto is faulty, etc.

2750. Rolfe, W.J. "The 'Mr. W.H.' of the Sonnets." Critic, NS 16 (December 12, 1891), 334-35.

Rolfe describes an incident where Tyler and Furnivall saw a portrait of William Herbert that makes him appear delicately girlish. This same incident is reported in Beiblatt zur Anglia, 2 (1892), 276-77.

2751. Rolfe, W.J. "The Comparison of Hair to Wires in Sonnet 130." Critic, NS 19 (June 24, 1893), 419.

This note, contributed by Horace Davis and reported by Rolfe, traces the use of "wires" as a metaphor for hair.

2752. Rolfe, W.J. "Shakespeare's Sonnets Set to Music." Critic, NS 21 (April 7, 1894), 238-39.

Mentions which sonnets have been set to music.

2753. Rolfe, W.J. "Something New on Shakespeare's Sonnets." Critic, NS 24 (September 7, 1895), 152-53.

Reports on several theories: George Paston, in A Study in Prejudices, believes that the Sonnets are addressed to a woman named Rose; another is a suggestion that some of the first 126 sonnets (99 for example) are addressed to a woman; and finally W.H. is Pembroke.

2754. Rolfe, W.J. "Shakespeariana." Critic, 35 (1899), 737-45.

The first part of this review article (pp. 737-41) focuses on Sidney Lee's theories about Shakespeare's Sonnets, which are presented in A Life of William Shakespeare.

2755. Rolfe, W.J. "Two New Studies of Shakespeare's Sonnets." Critic, 39 (1901), 26-31.

Discusses Samuel Butler's book on Shakespeare's Sonnets and A New Study of the Sonnets of Shakespeare by Parke Godwin.

2756. Rolle, Dietrich. "The Sonnets: A Long Pastoral." Shakespeare Newsletter, 17 (1967), 42.

Rolle gives an abstract of Paul Bates, "Shakespeare's Sonnets and Pastoral Poetry." Shakespeare Jahrbuch, 103 (1967), 81-96.
1523

2757. Rollins, Hyder. Review of Clara Longworth de Chambrun, Shakespeare Rediscovered. Journal of English and Germanic Philology, 37 (1938), 432-37.

In this highly negative review, Rollins calls Chambrun's findings "largely chimerical" and the inaccuracies of her work "abundant."

2758. Rollins, Hyder E. Review of G. Wilson Knight, The Mutual Flame. Shakespeare Quarterly, 7 (1956), 107-08.

2759. Root, Robert Kilburn. Classical Mythology in Shakespeare. Yale Studies in English, 19. New York: Henry Holt, 1903.

Very little on the Sonnets, but he does indicate that he finds only 10 allusions to classical mythology, and those unimportant (p. 127).

2760. Rose, Millicent. "The Dark Lady's Keyboard." TLS, September 28, 1973, p. 1133.

More on Sonnet 128 and the nature of the instrument (a virginal) described therein.

2761. Rosen, Charles. "Art Has Its Reasons." New York Review of Books, 16, xi (June 17, 1971), 32-38.

A review article on three books, one of which is Roman Jakobson and Lawrence G. Jones, Shakespeare's Verbal Art in Th'Expence of Spirit.

2762. Ross, William. The Story of Anne Whateley and William Shaxpere as Revealed by "The Sonnets to Mr. W.H." and Other Elizabethan Poetry. Glasgow: W. and R. Holmes, 1939.

The author of Shakespeare's works was Anne Whateley, and the Sonnets were addressed to Shakespeare (Mr. W.H.) and Anne Hathaway (the dark lady).

2763. Rostenberg, Leona. "Thomas Thorpe, Publisher of 'Shake-speare's Sonnets'." Papers of the Bibliographical Society of America, 54 (1960), 16-37.

2764. Rothwell, Kenneth S. "Getting at the Heart of the Mystery: Six Books in Search of Shakespeare." CEA Critic, 38, iv (1976), 36-39.

One of the books reviewed is Martin Green's The Labyrinth of Shakespeare's Sonnets (p. 39).

2765. Rowse, A.L. William Shakespeare: A Biography. New York: Harper and Row, 1963.

Rowse has a chapter on "The Story of the Sonnets" (pp. 161-200). This study precedes his "discovery" of Emilia Lanier as the dark lady.

2766. Rowse, A.L. "Shadow and Substance in Shakespeare." TLS, January 16, 1964, pp. 47; January 30, 1964, p. 87; February 13, 1964, p. 127.

Rowse, objecting to the review that appeared in TLS (December 26, 1963), pp. 1062-63, is answered by the reviewer.

2767. Rowse, A.L. Shakespeare's Southampton, Patron of Virginia. London: Macmillan, 1965.

Two chapters--"The Patron and the Poet" and "The Poet and the Patron" (pp. 58-97)--are largely about the Sonnets.

2768. Rowse, A.L. "Shakespeare and the Elizabethan Historian." Spectator, September 26, 1970, 337-40.

Much of this self-advertisement has do with Rowse's own work with the Sonnets. Following this article, the Spectator carried, from October 3 to December 5, 1970, a barrage of letters that, with one exception, attack one thing or another that Rowse had to say. These letters are not indexed.

2769. Rowse, A.L. "Revealed at Last, Shakespeare's Dark Lady." Times (London), January 29, 1973, p. 12.

2770. Rowse, A.L. Shakespeare the Man. New York: Harper and Row, 1973.

A large part of this biographical sketch turns on issues raised in the Sonnets: the dark lady, his patron, etc.

2771. Rowse, A.L., and G. Wilson Knight. "The Dark Lady." TLS, May 11, 1973, p. 528.

Two letters in reaction to the TLS review of Rowse's Shakespeare the Man (April 27, 1973, pp. 457-58).
3324

2772. Rowse, A.L. "Shakespeare and Emilia." TLS, April 26, 1974, p. 477.

Sonnets were not reprinted until 1640, a year after Emilia Lanier's death.

2773. Rowse, A.L. "Shakespeare Trade Unionists and Others." Books and Bookmen, 19, x (1974), 32-34.

Includes a testy review of Martin Green, The Labyrinth of Shakespeare's Sonnets.

2774. Rowse, A.L. Shakespeare the Elizabethan. London: Weidenfeld and Nicolson, 1977.

With references to the Sonnets, Rowse incorporates his ideas about the dark lady, the patron (Southampton), and the Rival Poet into this biography.

2775. Rowse, A.L. "Shakespeare's Dark Lady." Introduction to The Poems of Shakespeare's Dark Lady: "Salve Deus Rex Judaeorum" by Emilia Lanier. London: Jonathan Cape, 1978, pp. 1-37.

2776. Rubow, Paul V. "Shakespeare's Sonnets." Orbis Litterarum, 4 (1946), 2-44.

Mainly concerned with the identities of W.H., the dark lady and other such problems.

2777. Rubow, Paul V. Shakespeare og hans Samtidige en Raekke Kritiske Studier. Copenhagen: Gyldenalske Boghandel, 1948.

In a chapter, "Shakespeares Sonetter" (pp. 57-98), Rubow discusses the dedication to the Sonnets at length.

2778. Rubow, Paul V. Shakespeares Sonetter. Det Kongelige Danske Videnskabernes Selskab. Historisk-filosofiske Meddelelser (Copenhagen), 42, iv. Copenhagen: Munksgaard, 1967.

This 64-page monograph contains abundant references throughout to most of the contemporary scholarship on the various "problems."

2779. Rundle, James U. "The 'Source' of Shakespeare's Sonnet 30." Notes and Queries, 215 (1970), 132-33.

Shakespeare in Sonnet 30 borrows from Sackville's "Induction" to A Mirror for Magistrates.

2780. Ruoff, James E. "Shakespeare's Sonnets in Turkish." Shakespeare Newsletter, 30 (1980), 42.

In November, 1978, Bulent and Bozkurt published the first translation of Shakespeare's Sonnets under the title Soneler.

2781. Rushton, W.L. "Sonnet CXLVI." Notes and Queries, 100 (1899), 142.

2782. Russ, Jon R. "Time's Attributes in Shakespeare's Sonnet 126." English Studies, 52 (1971), 318-23.

Considers the various readings of the second line, "Dost hold Time's fickle glass, his sickle, hour . . . ."

2783. Russ, Jon R. "Shakespeare's 'Sonnet LXIV'." Explicator, 30 (1972), Item 38.

2784. Rutelli, Romana. "Connotative Systems and Their Functions in Shakespeare's Sonnet 87." A Semiotic Landscape (Proceedings of the First Congress of the International Association for Semiotic Studies, Milan, June 1974). Ed. Seymour Chatman, Umberto Eco, and Jean-Marie Klinkenberg. Approaches to Semiotics, 29. The Hague: Mouton, 1979, pp. 702-08.

One of the questions with which Rutelli attempts to come to grips is whether consideration of connotation has a place in semiotics. Analysis of Sonnet 87 appears to provide an affirmative answer.

2785. Rutelli Quintavalle, Romana. Saggi sulla Connotazione: tre sonetti di Shakespeare. Torino: Tipografia Torinese Editrice, 1975.

Applies a theory of connotations to sonnets 86, 87, 104.

2786. Rutelli, Romana. "L'uomo e il tempo nella connotazione del Sonetto 104 di Shakespeare." Lettore di Provincia, 27-28 (1976-1977), 42-60.

2787. Rylands, George. "Shakespeare the Poet." A Companion to Shakespeare Studies. Ed. Harley Granville-Barker and G.B. Harrison. Cambridge: University Press; New York: Macmillan, 1934, pp. 89-115.

In a brief section on the Sonnets (pp. 109-11), Rylands focuses on Shakespeare's use of imagery.

2788. S., G. "A New View of the 'Sonnets'." Baconiana, 9 (1901), 99-100.

An ironic review of Parke Godwin, A New Study of the Sonnets of Shakespeare.

2789. S., G.C.M. Review of J.A. Fort, The Two Dated Sonnets of Shakespeare. Modern Language Review, 20 (1925), 232.

2790. S., H.S., F.C. Hunt and R.M.T. "'Eclipse Endured'." Baconiana, 3rd Series, 4 (1906), 134-37.

In this series of letters on Sonnet 107, Hunt rejects the notion that "The mortal moon hath her eclipse endured" refers to Elizabeth's death.

2791. S., R.J.D. "Essex and the Sonnets." Baconiana, 3rd Series, 4 (1906), 43-46; 188-92.

Suggests Essex is the fair youth.

2792. *Sabantzeva, M. "Philosophical and Poetic Concept of Time in Shakespeare's Sonnets." Georgian Shakespeareana 4. Ed. Nico Kiasashvili. Tbilisi: Tbilisi University Press, 1975, pp. 65-77.

In Russian.

2793. Sabbadini, Silvano, e Lorenzo Renzi. "Grammatica e senso del Sonetto xx di Shakespeare." Strumenti Critici, 6 (1972), 330-37.

2794. Sachs, [R.] "Shakespeare's Gedichte." Shakespeare Jahrbuch, 25 (1890), 132-84.

Sachs includes a section on "Die Sonette" (pp. 148-67) in which he extensively reviews much of the scholarship of the previous forty years.

2795. St. Clair, F.Y. "The Sonnets: Personal Revelation or Technical Exercise?" North Dakota Quarterly, 32 (1964), 7-13.

Although he reviews the controversies surrounding the identity of the friend, the dark lady, and the rival poet, St. Clair finds it all irrelevant to enjoyment of the poems.

2796. Saintsbury, George. "Shakespeare: Poems." Cambridge History of English Literature. Ed. A.W. Ward and A.R. Waller. New York: G.P. Putnam's Sons, 1910, vol. 5. Cambridge: University Press, 1910, vol. 5, pp. 250-63.

2797. Saintsbury, George. Shakespeare. New York: Macmillan; Cambridge: University Press, 1934.

This book contains the two chapters that Saintsbury contributed to the Cambridge History of English Literature. The comments on the Sonnets (pp. 120-31) include some of Saintsbury's patented prosodic and structural analysis.

2798. St. Swithin, and C.C.B. "Shakespeare and 'Warray': Sonnet CXLVI." Notes and Queries, 11th Series, 4 (1911), 243-44.

2799. *Sakurai, Shoichiro. "Three Problems in Shakespeare's Sonnets." Eigo Seinen, 124 (1978), 326-29.

Discusses the couplets in the Sonnets.

2800. Sale, Roger. Modern Heroism: Essays on D.H. Lawrence, William Empson, and J.R.R. Tolkien. Berkeley: University of California Press, 1973.

In his essay on William Empson, Sale discusses Empson's interpretation of Shakespeare's Sonnet 94 (pp. 156-61).

2801. Salle, J.-C. "Shakespeare's Sonnet 27 and Keats's 'Bright Star!'" Notes and Queries, 212 (1967), 24.

Not only is the central image of Shakespeare's sonnet similar to that of Keats, but there are other similarities as well.

2802. Sampson, John. "On the Repetition of a Couplet in Shakespeare's Sonnets." TLS, October 2, 1919, p. 532.

Gives an explanation for the repeated couplets in Sonnets 36 and 96.

2803. Sanderlin, George. "The Repute of Shakespeare's Sonnets in the Early Nineteenth Century." Modern Language Notes, 54 (1939), 462-66.

2804. Sanders, Norman. Review of Robert Gittings, Shakespeare's Rival: A Study in Three Parts. Shakespeare Quarterly, 15 (1964), 233-34.

2805. *Sanfelice, Ettore. "Dei 154 Sonetti di G. Shakespeare." Rivista d'Italia, 3 (1898), 286-317. Reprinted in a monograph (Estratto dalla Rivista d'Italia, 10). Roma: Societa Editrice Dante Allighieri, 1898.

Touches on most of the usual subjects--order, Mr. W.H., dark lady, etc.

2806. Santayana, George. "Shakespeare: Made in America." The New Republic Anthology, 1915:1935. Ed. Groff Conklin. New York: Dodge, 1936, pp. 13-17. Reprinted in Literature and Liberalism: An Anthology of Sixty Years of the New Republic. Ed. Edward Zwick. Washington, D.C.: New Republic Book Company, 1976, pp. 274-77.

Explains how sonnet 29 might be rendered by a modern American poet. This essay originally appeared in The New Republic (February 27, 1915).

2807. Sarrazin, G. "Die Entstehung von Shakespeare's 'Verlorener Liebesmuhe'." Shakespeare Jahrbuch, 31 (1895), 200-30.

Notes connections between Love's Labour's Lost and the Sonnets (pp. 218-30).

2808. Sarrazin, Gregor. William Shakespeares Lehrjahre. Litterarhistorische Forschungen, 5. Weimar: Emil Felber, 1897.

This monograph contains a chapter on "Die Jugend-Sonette" (pp. 149-74). While touching on the usual issues, he also makes some comparisons between Shakespeare's sonnets and those of Sidney, Daniel and Drayton.

2809. Sarrazin, G. "Zu Sonett CIV." Shakespeare Jahrbuch, 34 (1898), 368-73.

2810. Sarrazin, Gregor. Aus Shakespeares Meisterwerkstatt: Stilgeschichtliche Studien. Berlin: Georg Reimer, 1906.

This study includes a chapter on "Die Freundschafts-sonette" (pp. 75-113).

2811. *Sarrazin, Gregor. "Shakespeares Sonette." Internationale Monatsschrift fur Wissenschaft, Kunst, und Technik, 8 (1914), 1071-95.

2812. Schaar, Claes. "Shakespeare's Sonnets L-LI and Tebaldeo's Sonnet CVII." English Studies, 38 (1957), 208-09.

2813. Schaar, Claes. An Elizabethan Sonnet Problem: Shakespeare's Sonnets, Daniel's Delia, and Their Literary Background. Lund Studies in English, 28. Lund: C.W.K. Gleerup, 1960.

2814. Schaar, Claes. Elizabethan Sonnet Themes and the Dating of Shakespeare's 'Sonnets'. Lund Studies in English, 32. Lund: C.W.K. Gleerup, 1962. New York: AMS Press, 1973.

2815. Schaar, Claes. "An Italian Analogue of Shakespeare's Sonnet LXXX." English Studies, 43 (1962), 253-55.

Finds similarities between Tasso's Libra degli Amori, 111, ii, 1-13 and Sonnet 80.

2816. Schaar, Claes. "Conventional and Unconventional in the Descriptions of Scenery in Shakespeare's Sonnets." English Studies, 45 (1964), 142-49.

2817. Schaar, Claes. Review of Shakespeare's Sonnets, ed. W.G. Ingram and Theodore Redpath. Renaissance News, 19 (1966), 154-57.

2818. Schaar, Claes. "Qui me alit me extinguit." English Studies, 49 (1968), 326-27.

The image in the twelfth line of Sonnet 73 may have been suggested by a well-known love emblem depicting a down-turned torch.

2819. Schaar, Claes. Review of James Winny, The Master-Mistress: A Study of Shakespeare's Sonnets, and Stephen Booth, An Essay on Shakespeare's Sonnets. Renaissance Quarterly, 23 (1970), 198-202.

2820. Schlosser, Anselm. Review of Stephen Booth, An Essay on Shakespeare's Sonnets. Shakespeare Jahrbuch, 107 (1971), 231-32.

2821. Schlutter, Hans-Jurgen. Sonett: Mit Beitragen von Raimund Borgmeier und Heinz Willi Wittschier. Samlung Metzler Band, 177. Stuttgart: J.B. Metzlersche Verlagsbuchhandlung, 1979.

The book, essentially on German poetry, contains an essay on Shakespeare by Raimund Borgmeier (pp. 63-73).

2822. Schmid, Eduard Eugen. Shakespeare und die schwarze Dame. Urphanomene und Metamorphose bei Shakespeare und Goethe. Munchen: Kitzinger, 1972.

The beginning of the book (pp. 1-74) focuses on the Sonnets and the significance (symbolic and otherwise) of the dark lady.

2823. Schmidt, A.V.C. Review of Stephen Booth, An Essay on Shakespeare's Sonnets. Notes and Queries, 216 (1971), 475-76.

2824. Schmidt[-Hidding], Wolfgang. "Sinnesanderung und Bildvertiefung in Shakespeares Sonetten." Anglia, 62 (1938), 286-305.

2825. Schmidt-Hidding, Wolfgang. "Shakespeares Stilkritik in den Sonetten." Shakespeare-Studien: Festschrift fur Heinrich Mutschmann zum 65. Geburtstag. Hrsg. Walther Fischer und Karl Wentersdorf. Marburg: N.G. Elwert, 1951, pp. 119-26.

2826. Schmidtchen, Paul W. "Shakespeare's Sug'red Sonnets." Hobbies, 74 (April, 1969), 104-5, 113, 92.

The author's acquisition of a 1640 edition of Shakespeare's Poems gives rise to this appreciation.

2827. Schnyder, Hans. Review of Florens Christian Rang, Shakespeare der Christ, Eine Deutung der Sonette. Archiv fur das Studium der neueren Sprachen, 193 (1957), 332.

2828. Schoenbaum, S. Shakespeare's Lives. New York: Oxford University Press; Oxford: Clarendon Press, 1970.

In addition to numerous references to the Sonnets throughout, Schoenbaum has chapters on "Boaden and the Sonnets" (pp. 275-79), "The Sonnet: Divers Theories" (pp. 439-46), and about half-dozen other chapters touching directly on subjects like Mr. W.H., the rival poet and the dark lady.

2829. Schoenbaum, S. "Shakespeare's Dark Lady: a question of identity." Shakespeare's Styles: Essays in honour of Kenneth Muir. Ed. Philip Edwards, Inga-Stina Ewbank, and G.K. Hunter. Cambridge: Cambridge University Press, 1980, pp. 220-39.

Reviews the information given about the dark lady in the sonnets and attempts to match that information with the various candidates.

2830. Schoen-Rene, Otto Eugene. "Shakespeare's 'Sonnets' in Germany, 1787-1939." Ph.D. Dissertation, Harvard, 1942.

2831. Schoff, F.G. "Shakespeare's 'Fair is Foul'." Notes and Queries, 199 (1954), 241-42.

This paradox, uttered by Macbeth's witches, occurs in the Dark Lady sonnets.

2832. Schroeter, James. "Shakespeare's Not 'To-Be-Pitied Lover'." College English, 23 (1962), 250-55.

A discussion of Sonnet 73.

2833. Schucking, L.L. "Die nueste Shakespeare-Forschung Alois Brandls." Geisteswissenschaften, 1 (1914), 787-92.

On Brandl's introduction to Fulda's translation of the Sonnets.

2834. Schwartz, Elias. "Shakespeare's Sonnet XCIV." Shakespeare Quarterly, 22 (1971), 397-99.

Takes issue with Empson, L.C. Knights, and Hubler on their views that the speaker is being ironic in expressing "un-Shakespearean" thoughts.

2835. Schwartz, Robert Barnett. "Shakespeare's Parted Eye: Approaches to Meaning in the Sonnets and Plays." Ph.D. Dissertation, Virginia, 1978. DAI, 40 (1979), 3324A.

2836. Scott, David. "Shakespeare, Essex, and the Dark Lady: Solutions to the Problems." Dalhousie Review, 49 (1969), 165-182.

Discusses the relationship between Willobie His Avisa and Shakespeare's Sonnets.

2837. Sears, Donald A. "The Translacer: A Rhetorical Thread of a Shakespearean Sonnet." CEA Critic, 35, iii (1973), 11-15.

Focuses on Sonnet 31 as an example of the use of polypton.

2838. Seib, Kenneth. "Shakespeare's 'Well': A Note on Sonnet 73." Shakespeare Newsletter, 17 (1967), 55.

Suggests that "well" in the final line be read as a noun rather than an adverb.

2839. Sen Gupta, Satyaprasad. Some Aspects of Shakespeare's Sonnets. Calcutta: Vidyodaya Library, 1966.

He covers a wide range of the usual sonnet issues, including chapters on the evolution of the sonnet, Platonism in Shakespeare's Sonnets, their form, allegory, etc.

2840. Sennhenn, Carl. "The Disintegration of the Persona in Shakespeare's Sonnets." South Central Bulletin, 37 (Fall, 1977), 97.

Abstract of a paper given at the South Central MLA, October 27-29, 1977.

2841. Sergeaunt, W.D. "Shakespeare's Sonnets: A Reading." TLS, January 2, 1919, p. 10; January 16, 1919, p. 34.

Comments on "reserve" in Sonnet 85, 1.3. See Richmond and Cuningham.
1753, 2730

2842. Serpieri, Alessandro. I sonetti dell'immortalita: Il problema dell'arte e della nominazione in Shakespeare. Milano: Bompiani, 1975.

Discusses over two dozen of Shakespeare's sonnets by groupings.

2843. Serpieri, Alessandro. "I Sonetti 33 e 29 di Shakespeare: L'Interazione di due modelli culturali." Paragone, 26, No. 306 (August, 1975), 3-20.

2844. Seymour, Henry. "The Concealed Author of Shakespeare's Sonnets: An Exercise in Inductive Psychology." Baconiana, 3rd Series, 20 (1929), 106-15.

Using cryptography, Seymour finds that W.H. stands for George Sandys.

2845. Seymour, William Kean. "Shakespeare's Sonnets: The Unsolved Puzzles." Contemporary Review, 205 (1964), 327-28.

This review of several works on the Sonnets--Shakespeare's Sonnets, ed. A.L. Rowse; John Dover Wilson, An Introduction to the Sonnets of Shakespeare for the Use of Historians and Others; Leslie Hotson, Mr. W.H.; Hilton Landry, Interpretations in Shakespeare's Sonnets comments mainly on the disagreements about dating.

2846. Seymour-Smith, Martin. "Shakespearean Indelicacies." New Statesman, 66 (1963), 526, 700.

Response to Empson's review--on the dark lady, venereal disease, etc.
1882

2847. Seymour-Smith, Martin. "Shakespeare's Sonnets." TLS, Feburary 20, 1964, p. 153.

A satiric solution to the problem of Mr. W.H. aimed principally at A.L. Rowse.

2848. Seymour-Smith, Martin. "Shakespeare's Sonnets 1-42: A Psychological Reading." New Essays on Shakespeare's Sonnets. Ed. Hilton Landry. New York: AMS Press, 1976, pp. 21-39.

2849. Shackford, Martha Hale. "Rose in Shakespeare's Sonnets." Modern Language Notes, 33 (1918), 122.

The relatively frequent use of this word may be occasioned by the similarity of its pronunciation to that of Wriothesley.

2850. Shackford, Martha Hale. The Eternitie of Poetrie. Natick, Mass.: Suburban Press, 1950.

The latter half of this monograph on the theme of the eternizing power of poetry is devoted to Shakespeare's Sonnets 1-126 (pp. 15-30).

2851. Shakespeare, William. The Sonnets of Shakespeare From the Quarto of 1609, with variorum readings and commentary. Ed. Raymond Macdonald Alden. Boston and New York: Houghton Mifflin, 1916.

Preface, Appendices, Notes, Bibliography--the full scholarly apparatus.

2852. ________. Les Sonnets de Shakespeare: Traduits en vers francais et accompagnes d'un commentaire continu. Tr. Fernand Baldensperger. Berkeley and Los Angeles: University of California Press, 1943.

2853. ________. The Sonnets of Shakespeare. Ed. H.C. Beeching. Boston and London: Ginn, 1904.

In addition to a lengthy introduction and set of explanatory notes, the book contains "A Note on the Sonnets of Michael Drayton" (pp. 132-39) in which the author disagrees with Sidney

Lee and Fleay that Shakespeare was influenced by Drayton; instead he feels that Drayton borrowed from Shakespeare.
2341

2854. ________. <u>William Shakespeare's Sonette in deutscher Nachbildung</u>. Ed. Friedrich Bodenstedt. Berlin: Koniglichen Geheimen, 1862.

In addition to an introduction, the translations are followed by a general essay on the Sonnets.

2855. ________. <u>Shakespeare's Sonnets</u>. Ed. Stephen Booth. New Haven and London: Yale University Press, 1977. 1980.

2856. ________. <u>The Sonnets/Die Sonette: Englische und in ausgewahlten deutschen versubersetzungen</u>. Ed. Raimund Borgmeier. Stuttgart: Reclam, 1974. 1978.

Contains an essay by Borgmeier, "Die deutsche Ubersetzungen von Shakespeares Sonetten" (pp. 214-24).

2857. ________. <u>Shakespeares Sonette</u>. Erlautert von Alois Brandl und ubersetzt von Ludwig Fulda. Stuttgart und Berlin: J.G. Cotta, 1913.

A lengthy introductory essay by Brandl followed by Fulda's translation.

2858. *________. <u>Sonnetoth Shakespeare</u>. Tr. Ephrayim Broido with an Introduction and Notes. Tel Aviv: Devir, 1977.

Includes a Hebrew translation of the Sonnets.

2859. ________. <u>Shakespeare's Sonnets</u>. Ed. Tucker Brooke. London and New York: Oxford University Press, 1936. rpt. Folcroft, Pa.: Folcroft Library Editions, 1974.

Contains a lengthy introduction including sections on the sonnet order, dating, the use of 'thou' and 'you,' the friend, sonnet-groups, etc.

2860. ________. <u>Shakespeare's Sonnets</u>. Ed. A.H. Bullen. Stratford-on-Avon: Shakespeare Head Press, 1905. Rev. ed. 1921.

2861. ________. <u>The Sonnets</u>. Ed. William Burto with an Introduction by W.H. Auden. New York: New American Library, 1964. Text and Introduction reprinted in <u>The Complete Signet Classic Shakespeare</u>. Ed. Sylvan Barnet. New York: Harcourt Brace Jovanovich, 1972.

The New American Library text also includes selections from Empson's <u>Some Versions of Pastoral</u> on Sonnet 94 (pp. 197-219), Hallett Smith's <u>Elizabethan Poetry</u> on Sonnet 73 (pp. 220-23) and Nowottny's "Formal Elements in Shakespeare's Sonnets: Sonnets I-VI" (pp. 224 ff.).

2862. ________. *Sonnets*. Ed. Douglas Bush and Alfred Harbage. Baltimore: Penguin, 1961. Rev.. ed. 1970.

An introduction by Bush.

2863. ________. *The Sonnets, Songs and Poems of Shakespeare*. Ed. Oscar James Campbell. New York: Schocken Books, 1964.

In his introduction, Campbell outlines the "sonnet story" entailing a reordering of the poems.

2864. ________. *Shakespeare's Sonnets, Edited as a Continuous Sequence by S.C. Campbell*. London: Bell and Hyman, 1978. Totowa, N.J.: Rowman and Littlefield, 1979.

2865. ________. *The Sonnets of William Shakspere*. Ed. Robert Cartwright. London: John Russell Smith, 1859.

In his Introduction Cartwright gives the rationale for his rearrangement of the Sonnets.

2866. ________. "Sonnets." *The Complete Works of Shakespeare*. Ed. Hardin Craig and David Bevington. Rev. ed. Glenview, Illinois: Scott, Foresman, 1973, pp. 468-96.

2867. ________. *The Sonnets of William Shakespeare*. Ed. Edward Dowden. London: Kegan Paul, Trench, 1881, 1885.

Contains an introduction.

2868. ________. *Shakespeare's Sonnets/Shakespeares Sonette*. Tr. Richard Flatter. Wien: Saturn, 1934.

English and German on facing pages following a general introduction.

2869. ________. *Les Sonnets de Shakespeare*. Ed. Jean Fuzier. Paris: Armand Colin, 1970.

The first half of the book (pp. 5-156) is an extensive introduction covering a wide range of of subjects: the text, the dedication, publishing history, the sonnet order, the Elizabethan sonnet, the various themes of Shakespeare's sonnets, etc. The second part of the book contains the sonnets (in English) with an appendix of the sources and analogues of some of the sonnets.

2870. ________. *William Shakespeare: Les Sonnets*. Tr. Charles-Marie Garnier. Paris: J.M. Dent, 1922.

The original is printed beside the French translation, with an introduction.

2871. ____________________. Shakespeare's Sonette. Tr. Otto Gildemeister. Leipzig: Leipzig Brockhaus, 1871.

In his introductory critical essay, Gildemeister discusses, among other things, how the theme of friendship in the Sonnets is evident also in the plays of the 1590's.

2872. ____________________. Shakespeare 154 Sonette. Ed. Hugo Goke. Frankfurt am Main: Kurt-Werner Hesse, 1971.

The book contains the English text with two German translations on the facing page. The introductory essay discusses aspects of translation with particular attention to Sonnet 30.

2873. ____________________. Shakespeare's Sonnets. Ed. Israel Gollancz. London: J.M. Dent, 1898.

In his introduction he reviews at length the cases for and against Southampton and Herbert as Mr. W.H.

2874. ____________________. Shakespeare's Sonnets and A Lover's Complaint. Ed. W.H. Hadow. Oxford: Clarendon Press, 1907. rpt. Folcroft, Pa.: Folcroft Library Editions, 1974.

Contains an introduction.

2875. *____________________. The Sonnets. Tr. into modern Greek by Basso Haniou. Athens: Icarus, 1970.

2876. ____________________. Shakespeares Sonetter. Tr. Adolf Hansen. Copenhagen: Gyldendalske Boghandels, 1885.

In Danish.

2877. ____________________. Shakespeares Sonette. Ed. and Tr. Karl Hauer. Graz: Ulrich Moser, 1929.

Hauer's introduction covers the usual subjects and devotes but a few paragraphs to his reordering of the Sonnets into 15 groups. Group 3, for example, "Procreation Sonnets," contains Sonnets 1-17 and Group 10 (on the Rival) contains 33-35, 87-96.

2878. ____________________. Les Sonnets de Shakespeare. Traduits en sonnets francais, avec introduction, notes et bibliographie. Par Fernand Henry. Paris: Paul Ollendorf, 1900.

Contains the English version in small type below the translation.

2879. ____________________. Shakespeare's Songs and Poems. Ed. Edward Hubler. New York: McGraw-Hill, 1959.

In addition to the Introduction, the text is accompanied by notes and a brief commentary. Hubler also includes in the text sonnets that appear in the plays.

2880. ________________. The Aldus Shakespeare: Sonnets, with copious notes and comments by Henry Norman Hudson, M.A., Israel Gollancz, M.A., C.H. Herford, Litt.D., and over one hundred other eminent Shakespearean Authorities. New York: Grosset and Dunlop, 1909. New York: Funk and Wagnalls, 1968.

A "Preface" and "Analysis" by Gollancz, an "Introduction" by Henry Norman Hudson and collection of several comments by other commentators.

2881. ________________. Shakespeare's Sonnets. Ed. W.G. Ingram and T. Redpath. London: University of London Press, 1964. New York: Barnes and Noble, 1965. Rev. ed. New York: Holmes and Meier, 1978.

2882. *________________. The Sonnets of Shakespeare-Shakespeare Szonettjei. Ed. and Tr. Pal Justus. Budapest: Corvina Publishing, 1956.

Bilingual (Hungarian and English).

2883. ________________. The Sonnets. Ed. George L. Kittredge and Irving Ribner. Rev. ed. Waltham, Mass.: Blaisdell, 1968.

2884. ________________. Shekspirovi sonety. Tr. Eaghor Kostetzky. Munich: "Logos," 1958.

Kostetzky has a prefatory essay (pp. 5-18), "Ukrayinsky perekladach Shekspirovykh sonetiv," on translating the Sonnets into Ukrainian. The text contains over 150 pages of notes and essays on special subjects--Willobie His Avisa, the dedication to the Quarto, Mr. W.H., etc.

2885. *________________. Sonette. English/Deutsch. Nachdichtung und Nachwort von Karl Kraus. Wien: Verlag "Die Fackel," 1933. Diogenes-Taschenbucher, 137. Zurich: Diogenes, 1977.

2886. ________________. Shakespeare's Southampton-Sonette. Tr. Fritz Krauss. Leipzig: Wilhelm Engelmann, 1872.

Includes a lengthy introduction and notes developing the Shakespeare-Southampton relationship.

2887. ________________. Les Sonnets de Shakespeare: Essai d'une traduction en vers francais. Ed. and tr. Germaine Lafeuille. Cambridge, Mass.: Schenkman, 1976

English and French on facing pages.

2888. *________________. Shakespeare: Les Sonnets. Ed. Emile Le Brun. Introduction by Valery Larbaud. Paris: J. Schiffrin, 1927.

2889. ________________. The Plays and Poems of William Shakespeare, with the Corrections and Illustrations of Various Commentators: Comprehending A Life of the Poet, and An Enlarged History of the Stage. Ed. Edmond Malone. London: F.C. and J. Rivington, et al., 1821, vol. 20.

This edition, edited by James Boswell, includes some preliminary remarks on the Sonnets by Boswell, the text, and some comments by George Steevens and Edmond Malone on the merits of the Sonnets. Malone defends the poems against the sharply critical attacks of Steevens (pp. 217-363).

2890. ____________________. Sonetos: Prologo, traduccion y notas por Luis Astrana Marin. Madrid: Afrodisio Aguado, 1944.

English and Spanish on facing pages following an ample general introduction.

2891. ____________________. Sonety Shekspira v perevodakh. Tr. S. Marshaka with an Afterword by M. Morozov. Moskva: Sovetskii Pisatel, 1948. 1952.

2892. ____________________. Shakespeare's Sonnets. Ed. Giorgio Melchiori. Biblioteca Italiana di Testi Inglesi, 8. 2nd ed. Bari: Adriatica Editrice, 1971.

Contains introduction, bibliography and notes.

2893. ____________________. Shakespeare's Sonnets. Ed. Kenneth Muir. London: Allen and Unwin, 1979.

Contains appendixes on "Mr. W.H."; "The Dark Lady"; "The Rival Poet"; "Lover's Complaint"; and "Passionate Pilgrim."

2894. ____________________. Die Sonette von William Shakespeare. Tr. Alexander Neidhardt. Leipzig: Eugen Diederichs, 1902.

Contains a preface discussing the problems of the translation.

2895. Shakespere, William. William Shakespeares Sonetter. Tr. Carl Rupert Nyblom. Upsala, Sweden: W. Schultz, 1871.

In Swedish with introduction and notes.

2896. ____________________. The Works of Shakespeare: Sonnets. Ed. C. Knox Pooler. Arden Shakespeare. London: Methuen, 1918.

In the course of his introduction, Pooler states the chief arguments of most of the popular theories and offers his own: that Shakespeare wrote the Sonnets; Thorpe did not print them in their proper order, no adequate support exists for any of the W.H., dark lady, or rival poet claimants.

2897. ____________________. Sonnets and Minor Poems. Ed. Charlotte Porter. New York: Thomas Y. Crowell, 1912.

The introduction begins by asking "Are the sonnets autobiographical?" Her answer is yes, but not literally. They reveal his soul.

2898. * ________________. Sonnets. Essai d'Interpretation Poetique Francaise par Andre Prudhommeau. Porrentruy, Suisse: Editions des Portes de France, 1945.

2899. ________________. I Sonetti. Testo riveduto con versione a fronte. Ed. Piero Rebora. Firenze: G.C. Sansoni, 1941.

The introduction covers such subjects as for whom the Sonnets were intended, their sincerity as expressions of Shakespeare's feelings, their proper order, etc. The Sonnets are in English and Italian on facing pages.

2900. ________________. Shakespeare's Sonnets. Ed. Edward Bliss Reed. Yale Shakespeare, vol. 38. New Haven: Yale University Press, 1923.

2901. ________________. Shakespeare-Almanach. Tr. Gottlob Regis. Berlin: Beit, 1836.

Contains the Sonnets and The Passionate Pilgrim, translated. The text includes the following excerpts from Nathan Drake, Shakespeare and His Times (London: T. Cadell and W. Davies, 1817): "Leben des Grafen von Southampton," "Shakespeare's Sonnette," and "Shakespeare's Verliebten Pilger" (pp. 251-317).

2902. ________________. Sonette. Ubertragen von Gottlob Regis (1836), Nachwort von Anselm Schlosser. Leipzig: Philipp Reclam, Jr., 1964.

2903. ________________. The Sonnets. Ed. M.R. Ridley. New Temple Shakespeare. London: J.M. Dent, 1934. 1976.

Prints the Sonnets in the "linked" order suggested by Denys Bray in The Original Order of Shakespeare's Sonnets.

2904. ________________. Shakespeare's Sonnets. Ed. William J. Rolfe. New York: American Book, 1905.

Contains introduction and notes and an Appendix which deals with the Baconian theory and a consideration of Barnabe Barnes as the rival poet.

2905. ________________. The Sonnets. Ed. H.E. Rollins. A New Variorum Edition. 2 vol. Philadelphia: J.B. Lippincott, 1944.

2906. ________________. William Shakespeare Sonnets. Ed. Hyder Edward Rollins. New York: Appleton-Century-Crofts, 1951.

In his introduction, Rollins explains why he thinks the Quarto arrangement is improbable at best. He has little use for the theories about Shakespeare's life and character derived from the Sonnets.

2907. ________________. Sonetti. Tr. Alberto Rossi. Nuova Collana di Poeti Tradotti con Testo a Fronte, 1. Turin: Giulio Einaudi, 1952.

Seventy-seven sonnets are included with a lengthy introduction of 169 pages.

2908. ____________. Shakespeare's Sonnets. Ed. A.L. Rowse. London: Macmillan; New York: Harper and Row, 1964. 2nd edition published under title Shakespeare's Sonnets: The Problem Solved. New York: Harper and Row, 1973.

2909. ____________. Shakespeare's Sonnets. Ed. Martin Seymour-Smith. London: Heinemann Educational Books, 1963. New York: Barnes and Noble, 1966.

2910. ____________. Sonnets/Sonety. Tr. Jerzy S. Sito with an Introduction by Jan Kott. Warsaw: Panstwowy Instytut Wydawniczy, 1964.

In English and Polish with an introduction, also in both languages, by Jan Kott. Kott speaks of the Sonnets as drama with three characters playing against Time.

2911. ____________. William Shakespeare--Sonnets. Ed. Barbara Herrnstein Smith. New York: New York University Press, 1969.

In addition to an introduction, Herrnstein Smith includes in her apparatus a thematic index to the Sonnets and an Index to Key Words.

2912. ____________. Shakespeare's Sonnets. Ed. Charlotte C. Stopes. London: Alexander Moring, 1904.

Contains introduction and notes.

2913. ____________. William Shakespeare, Sonetter. Tr. K.A. Svensson. Lund, Sweden: Gleerup, 1964.

In Swedish with introduction and notes.

2914. ____________. Sheikusupia no sonetto: ai no kyoko. [Shakespeare's Sonnets: An Invention of Love.] Ed. Ichiro Tamura, Osamu Rottanda, Kiminobu Sakamoto and Mikio Tabuchi. Tokyo: Bunri, 1975.

The introduction, containing articles by the editors on various aspects of the Sonnets, is followed by the Sonnets in Japanese and English with an accompanying commentary.

2915. ____________. The Sonnets of William Shakespeare and Henry Wriothesley, Third Earl of Southampton Together with "A Lover's Complaint" and "The Phoenix and Turtle." Ed. Walter Thomson. Liverpool: Basil Blackwell and Henry Young, 1938.

Ties Sonnet 20 in with A Lover's Complaint, assigns over 25 sonnets to Southampton, and declares neither Shakespeare nor Southampton wrote the dark lady sonnets.

2916. __________. *Shakspere's Sonette*. Tr. Benno Tschischwitz. Halle: Emil Barthel, 1870.

This German translation is preceded by a general introduction.

2917. __________. *The Sonnets of Shakespeare: Edited from the Quarto of 1609*. Ed. T.G. Tucker. Cambridge: University Press, 1924.

In addition to the usual concerns, Tucker examines "borrowings" from Lyly's *Euphues*.

2918. __________. *Shakespeare's Sonnets*. Ed. Thomas Tyler. London: David Nutt, 1890. 1899.

The introduction, appropriately 154 pages in length, covers the field comprehensively. The 1899 edition has bound with it Tyler's "The Herbert-Fitton Theory of Shakespeare's Sonnets: A Reply."

2919. __________. "Sonnets." Ed. A. Wilson Verity in *The Works of William Shakespeare*. Ed. Henry Irving and Frank A. Marshall, vol. 8, pp. 397-453.

Introduction summarizes the literary historical problems of the Sonnets. In addition to explaining Shakespeare's meaning, Verity also discusses Shakespeare's use of the form.

2920. __________. *Shakespeare's Complete Sonnets: A New Arrangement with an Introduction and Notes*. Ed. C.M. Walsh. London: T. Fisher Unwin, 1908.

Includes the sonnets from plays and other sources; arranges the poems by "subject."

2921. __________. *Sonette/Epen und die Kleineren Dichtungen*. Nachwort von Wolfgang Weiss. Munchen: Winkler, 1968.

2922. __________. *The Sonnets*. Ed. John Dover Wilson. Cambridge: Cambridge University Press, 1966. Rev. ed. 1967.

2923. __________. *Shakespeares Sonette*. Tr. Max J. Wolff. Berlin: B. Behr, 1903.

Contains an introduction.

2924. __________. *Shakespeare's Sonnets*. Ed. Louis B. Wright and Virginia A. LaMar. Folger Library General Reader's Shakespeare. New York: Washington Square Press, 1967.

2925. __________. *The Poems of Shakespeare*. Ed. George Wyndham. London: Methuen, 1898.

In that part of the Introduction on the Sonnets (pp. ci-cxxxii), Wyndham sings praise of the perfection of the 1609 Quarto text. In addition, he discusses the sonneteering fashion, the themes of the Sonnets, etc. The text is copiously annotated.

2926. ____________________. Shakespeare's Poems: A Facsimile of the Earliest Editions. New Haven: Yale University Press, 1964.

In a brief introduction, the editors (the Elizabethan Club) discuss the effect of modern editorial changes on spelling and punctuation in the sonnets.

2927. ____________________. Shakespeare's Sonnets and A Lover's Complaint. Harmondsworth, Eng.: Penguin Books, 1938.

With introduction and notes.

2928. Shakhidi, Munira. "Chet'ire Pozta." [Four Poets.] Narody Azii i Afriki (Moscow), 1 (1977), 98-106.

This article on Rudaki, Petrarch, Hafiz and Shakespeare includes a comparison between the 14th-century Persian Ghazals (or odes) of Hafiz and Shakespeare's Sonnets. In Russian with an English summary, pp. 252-53.

2929. Shanks, Edward. "Sonnets and Common Sense." First Essays on Literature. London: W. Collins Sons, 1923, pp. 215-21.

Suggests that "consideration of style is a better avenue by which to approach [the sonnets] than the detective method commonly employed . . . ."

2930. Shapiro, I.A. "Dr. Hotson's Arguments." TLS, April 21, 1950, p. 245.

Even if "the mortal moon" of Sonnet 107 refers to the Spanish Armada, it does not necessarily follow that it was written immediately after the event as Hotson argues.

2931. Shapiro, I.A. "Correspondence." Essays in Criticism, 1 (1951), 192.

Setting the record straight on his views, expressed earlier in TLS, on Sonnet 107.
2160

2932. Sharp, William. "Shakespeare's Sonnets." Studies and Appreciations. New York: Duffield, 1912, pp. 71-105.

Covers the usual ground--supports Pembroke as W.H., Chapman as the rival poet, and comments on the order, the "begetter," etc.

2933. Shaw, G.B. "The Dark Lady of the Sonnets." English Review, 7 (1911), 258-69.

A play in one act. Will Shakespeare has a tryst with the dark lady (one of Elizabeth's ladies-in-waiting) but meets up with

Queen Elizabeth herself. Before they finish he asks for a National Theatre.

2934. Shaw, G.B. "Preface to The Dark Lady of the Sonnets." Misalliance, The Dark Lady of the Sonnets, and Fanny's First Play, with a Treatise on Parents and Children. New York: Brentano's, 1914, pp. 109-40.

In the preface to his play, Shaw talks about Shakespeare's dark lady and the views of Shaw's contemporaries about her.

2935. Sherbo, Arthur. "A Note on 'The Prelude'." Wordsworth Circle, 4 (1973), 11-12.

Finds in The Prelude an echo of Sonnet 66.

2936. Shield, H.A. "Links with Shakespeare VI." Notes and Queries, 195 (1950), 205-06.

Links Shakespeare, during the 1580's, with a company of touring actors. Shield attempts to identify William Hughes as Mr. W.H. and names Robert Greene as a likely rival poet.

2937. Shield, H.A. "Links with Shakespeare--VII." Notes and Queries, 195 (1950), 385-86.

An attempt to identify William Hughes, a candidate for Mr. W.H.

2938. Shield, H.A. "Links With Shakespeare, IX." Notes and Queries, 197 (1952), 156-57.

Offers information about another Dark Lady candidate, Jane Spencer Harsnape, who, the author believes, dallied with young William Shakespeare in 1585.

2939. *Shikoda, Mitsuo. "Matter and Manner in Shakespeare's Sonneteering." Essays and Studies in English Language and Literature (Sendai, Japan), No. 45-46 (1964), 47-70.

2940. Shindler, Robert. "The Stolen Key." Gentleman's Magazine, 272 (1892), 70-84.

Offers a number of observations--Sonnets 153-54 were probably not by Shakespeare, Quarto arrangement is incorrect and many passages need emendation. Finally, he reads the Sonnets as being "sad."

2941. Shore, W. Teignmouth. Shakespeare's Self. London: Philip Allan, 1920.

Fulminates against the critics' endless urge to use the Sonnets for autobiography (pp. 83-89).

2942. Silverstein, Norman. "Shakespeare's Sonnets in Perspective." Ball State Teachers College Forum, 5, iii (1964), 67-71.

Mainly discusses the symbolic role of Mr. W.H.

2943. Simpson, Richard. _An Introduction to the Philosophy of Shakespeare's Sonnets_. London: N. Trubner, 1868. rpt. Folcroft, Pa.: Folcroft Library Editions, 1973.

Discusses the Shakespearean "love philosophy," suggests a "true order" for the Sonnets, and seeks to differentiate those poems that express "imaginative love," "ideal love," and "vulgar love."

2944. Simpson, Richard. "The Shakespearean Love-Philosophy (1867)." _Richard Simpson as Critic_. Ed. David Carroll. London: Routledge and Kegan Paul, 1977, pp. 190-204.

This essay is one of the chapters from Simpson's _An Introduction to the Philosophy of Shakespeare's Sonnets_. Contents had first appeared in serialized form in _The Chronicle_ (1867-68).

2945. Singh, Satyaharain. "The Theme of Immortality in Shakespeare's Sonnets." _Osmania Journal of English Studies_, 4 (1964), 125-40.

Singh believes that "the poet's genuine struggle to find ways and means of making love conquer mutability and death" is the pivotal point of the poems.

2946. Sisson, C.J. Review of H. McClure Young, _The Sonnets of Shakespeare: A Psycho-Sexual Analysis_. _Modern Language Review_, 32 (1937), 659-60.

2947. Sisson, C.J. _New Readings in Shakespeare_. Cambridge: University Press, 1956, vol. 1.

The book is a series of readings for difficult or disputed passages. The section on the Sonnets contains 21 recommended readings (pp. 209-15).

2948. Sitwell, Edith. "A Note on Sonnet XIX." _A Notebook on William Shakespeare_. London: Macmillan, 1948, pp. 226-27.

Notes that the use of double vowels creates a sense of the majestic and the terrible.

2949. Skinner, B.F. "The Alliteration in Shakespeare's Sonnets: A Study in Literary Behavior." _Psychological Record_, 3 (1939), 186-92.

Doubts Shakespeare used any "process of alliteration."

2950. Skinner, B.F. "Reflections on Meaning and Structure." _I.A. Richards: Essays in His Honor_. Ed. Reuben Brower, Helen Vendler, John Hollander. New York: Oxford University Press, 1973, pp. 199-209.

Uses Sonnet 129 to discuss verbal behavior of writers.

2951. Skipwith, Grey Hubert. "Shakespeare and His Patron." TLS, July 6, 1916, p. 321; July 27, 1916, pp. 357-58; August 24, 1916, pp. 405-06.

Among other things, Skipwith conjectures that Henry Wriothesley, Third Earl of Southampton, could write his name in a cipher to spell HEWS (as in Sonnet 20).

2952. Slater, Eliot. "Sinne of Self-Love." Notes and Queries, 221 (1976), 155-56.

On Sonnet 62 with reference to 3, 37, and 140.

2953. Slavutych, Yar. Review of Shekspirovi sonety, tr. into Ukrainian by Eaghor G. Kostetzky. Shakespeare Quarterly, 10 (1959), 108-09.

Contains a history of Ukrainian translation of Shakespeare's plays and poems. Acknowledges Kostetzky's pre-eminence.

2954. Smallwood, R.L. Review of Kenneth Muir, Shakespeare's Sonnets. Modern Language Review, 76 (1981), 667-668.

2955. Smeaton, William Henry Oliphant. Shakespeare His Life and His Work. London: J.M. Dent, 1911.

In his chapter, "Intermediate Period of the 'Sonnets'" (pp. 462-71), Smeaton comments on the identity of W.H. and the dark lady and summarizes the content of the "12 groups."

2956. Smedley, W.T. "Shakespeare's Sonnets." Baconiana, 3rd Series, 10 (1912), 9-17.

The poet (Bacon) addresses himself in the Sonnets, as if he were a youth.

2957. Smidt, Kristian. ". . . Problems Involved in Translating Shakespeare's Sonnets in the Scandinavian Languages." [Paper read at the 3rd Session of the Conference on The Writer and Semantics--Literature as Concept, Meaning and Expression--32nd International Congress of P.E.N., Oslo, June 21-27, 1964]. Arena, No. 24 (October, 1965), 28-35.

2958. Smidt, Kristian. "Skandinavisk gjendiktning av Shakespeares sonetter." Ordet (Oslo), 18 (1967), 388-98.

Discusses several Scandinavian renderings of Shakespeare's Sonnets.

2959. Smidt, Kristian. Konstfuglen og Nattergalen. Essays om diktning og kritikk. [The Imitation Bird and the Nightingale. Essays on Poetry and Criticism.] Oslo: Gyldendal, 1972.

Contains two essays, "Introduksjon til Shakespeares Sonetter" (pp. 149-79) and "Grader av Fullkommenhet: Litt om Shakespeares sonetter pa skandinaviske sprak" (pp. 180-89).

2960. Smidt, Kristian. "Translating the Sonnets: Scandinavian Problems and Solutions." Shakespeare Translation, 3 (1976), 1-12.

2961. Smith, G.C. Moore. "Shakespeare, 'Sonnets' LI, ll. 10 f." Modern Language Review, 9 (1914), 372-73.

Suggests as an emendation "weigh no dull flesh" instead of "neigh no dull flesh."

2962. Smith, G.C. Moore. "Shakespeare's Sonnet XCVI, L.1." TLS, June 22, 1922, p. 413.

Offers an emendation--changing "Some say thy fault is youth, some wantonness" to "Some say thy fault is youthsome wantonness."

2963. Smith, G.C. Moore. Review of J.A. Fort, The Two Dated Sonnets of Shakespeare. Modern Language Review, 20 (1925), 232.

2964. *Smith, G. Travers. "Shakespeare's Sonnets." Victorian Review, December, 1880, 253-58.

The Sonnets were addressed to Shakespeare's illegitimate son.

2965. Smith, Gordon Ross. "A Note on Shakespeare's Sonnet 143." American Imago, 14 (1957), 33-36. Reprinted in A Casebook on Shakespeare's Sonnets. Ed. Gerald Willen and Victor B. Reed. New York: Thomas Y. Crowell, 1964, pp. 276-79.

2966. Smith, Gordon Ross. Review of A.L. Rowse, Shakespeare's Sonnets: The Problem Solved. College Literature, 2 (1975), 80.

2967. Smith, Hallett. "'No Cloudy Stuffe to Puzzell Intellect': A Testimonial Misapplied to Shakespeare." Shakespeare Quarterly, 1 (1950), 18-21.

Attacks the authority of Benson's 1640 edition of the Sonnets.

2968. Smith, Hallett. Review of Shakespeare's Sonnets, ed. W.G. Ingram and Theodore Redpath. Shakespeare Quarterly, 16 (1965), 354-55.

2969. Smith, Hallett. Review of Hilton Landry, Interpretations in Shakespeare's Sonnets. Shakespeare Studies, 1 (1965), 332-34.

2970. Smith, Hallett. Review of The New Shakespeare, The Sonnets, ed. J. Dover Wilson. Shakespeare Studies, 4 (1968), 423.

2971. Smith, Hallett. "Bare Ruined Choirs: Shakespearean Variations on the Theme of Old Age." Huntington Library Quarterly, 39 (1976), 233-49.

Suggests that Sonnets 62-74 constitute his "De Senectute and his mutability cantos."

2972. Smith, Hallett. "The Nondramatic Poems." Shakespeare: Aspects of Influence. Ed. G.B. Evans. Harvard English Studies, 7. Cambridge, Mass.: Harvard University Press, 1976, pp. 43-53.

Talks about the critical vogue of the Sonnets and their influence (pp. 46-50).

2973. Smith, Hallett. "The Permanence of Curled Metaphors." Sewanee Review, 84 (1976), 684-95.

A review article of a number of titles including Anne Ferry, All in War with Time (pp. 684-88) and Thomas O. Sloan and Raymond B. Waddington, The Rhetoric of Renaissance Poetry (pp. 690-91). Shakespeare's Sonnets are discussed in these two sections.

2974. Smith, L.E.W. Twelve Poems Considered. London: Methuen, 1963.

Among the twelve poems reproduced and explicated are Shakespeare's Sonnet 73 (pp. 29-35) and Hopkins's "The Windhover" (pp.119-29).

2975. Smith, Marion Bodwell. Dualities in Shakespeare. Toronto: University of Toronto Press, 1966.

Chapter 3, "The Poetry of Ambivalence," deals with the sonnets.

2976. Smith, Roland M. Review of Barbara A. Mackenzie, Shakespeare's Sonnets. Journal of English and Germanic Philology, 46 (1947), 218.

2977. Snider, Denton J. "Sonnets." A Biography of William Shakespeare. St. Louis: William Harvey Miner, 1922, pp. 426-43.

The Sonnets are a "poetic diary" some of which were written as late as 1609.

2978. Snow, Edward A. "Loves of Comfort and Despair: A Reading of Shakespeare's Sonnet 138." ELH, 47 (1980), 462-83.

2979. Snyder, Susan. Review of Shakespeare's Sonnets: The Problem Solved, ed. A.L. Rowse. Shakespeare Quarterly, 25 (1974), 131-33.

Chides Rowse for his "premature certainty that slams shut doors that should be left invitingly open."

2980. Somervell, R.U. "Shakespeare's Sonnets." TLS, March 5, 1964, p. 199.

Suggests that William Honyng, clerk to the Office of the Revels, might be Mr. W.H.

2981. Southam, B.C. "Shakespeare's Christian Sonnet? Number 146." Shakespeare Quarterly, 11 (1960), 67-71.

2982. Spalding, T.A. "Shakspere's Sonnets." Gentleman's Magazine, 242 [244] (1878), 300-18.

Title page of journal incorrectly indicates volume number as 242; it should be 244. A biographical analysis of the first 126 sonnets in which Spalding breaks the sequence into groups.

2983. Sparrow, John. "Dr. Hotson's Arguments." TLS, March 3, 1950, p. 137.

Adds another reference to Hotson's five that seem to support the relationship between the "mortall moone" of Sonnet 107 and the Spanish Armada.

2984. Sparrow, John. "Viewpoint." TLS, March 1, 1974, p. 210.

Sparrow begins by making the point that his letter about Milton's Sonnet 19, in which he suggested that the "one Talent" was Milton's procreative powers (TLS, January 18, 1974), was a parody of John Bayley's article and letters on Shakespeare's Sonnets 133,134,144, etc. (TLS, January 4, February 1 and 15, 1974). The parody was an attack on Bayley's ingenius effort to read sexual meanings into Shakespeare's language.

1531, 1886, 2030

2985. Sparrow, John. "Shakespeare's Sonnets." TLS, November 1, 1974, p. 1231.

Suggests that Emilia's last name, Lanier, sounds like La nera, i.e. the dark lady.

2986. Spence, R. M. "Shakespeare's Sonnets." Notes and Queries, 5th Series, 7 (1877), 324-25.

Rejects Legis's thesis on the unity of Sonnets 1-125.

2354

2987. Spence, R.M. "The Sonnets: The Two Obeli in the Globe Edition." Notes and Queries, 8th Series, 10 (1896), 450.

Offers readings for Sonnets 60 (l. 13) and 146 (l. 2).

2988. Spencer, Terence. Review of William Shakespeare, Sonnetti, tr. Alberto Rossi. Modern Language Review, 49 (1954), 541-42.

2989. *Spencer, T.J.B. "Confusion and Doubt over the Shakespeare Sonnets: Their Interpretation and Impact Today." Birmingham Post, April 17, 1964, p. xi.

2990. Spender, Stephen. "The Alike and the Other." The Riddle of Shakespeare's Sonnets. Ed. Edward Hubler. New York: Basic Books, 1962, pp. 91-128.

2991. Speriend. "Shakespeare's Lameness." Notes and Queries, 5th Series, 3 (1875), 134.

Disagrees with Jabez; thinks it quite plausible that Sonnets 37 and 89 indicate the poet's lameness.
2211

2992. Spira, Theodor. Shakespeares Sonette im Zusammenhang seines Werkes. Schriften der Koniglichen Deutschen Gesellschaft zu Konigsberg, 1. Konigsberg: Grafe und Unzer, 1929.

2993. Spitzer, Leo. "'Runaways Eyes' and 'Children's Eyes' Again." Neuphilologische Mitteilungen, 57 (1956), 257-60.

Concerns interpretations of two possibly parallel phrases in Romeo and Juliet and Sonnet 9.

2994. Spring, Leverett W. "The Friendship of Shakespeare with Mr. 'W.H.' and the Dark Lady." Education (Boston), 14 (June, 1894), 599-602.

Sees little doubt that William Herbert is W.H. and Mary Fitton the dark lady.

2995. Spurgeon, Caroline F. E. Keats's Shakespeare. London: H. Milford, Oxford University Press, 1928.

One section (pp. 38-41) concerns Keats's comments about his favorite sonnets and about the markings that are to be found in his copy of Shakespeare's Poems.

2996. Squire, J.C. "Shakespeare's Sonnets." Life and Letters: Essays. New York: George H. Doran, 1921, pp. 182-88.

Comments approvingly of C. Knox Pooler's edition of the Sonnets and asks why Shakespeare, the greatest of poets, did not take greater care in perpetuating his texts.

2997. Stainer, C.L. "The Sonnets." TLS, April 7, 1932, p. 250.

Finds an anagram of Thomas Watson's name in Sonnet 76.

2998. Stalker, Archibald. "Shakespeare's 'Sonnet,' CXXVI." Notes and Queries, 162 (1932), 403-04.

Believes that the sonnet may be referring to Endymion.

2999. Stalker, Archibald. "Shakespeare and the Rival Poet." Notes and Queries, 163 (1932), 201-05, 221-23, 236-40, 252.

Applying tests of style, Stalker discovers the hand of another writer--the rival poet (who was not Barnes or Chapman).

3000. *Stalker, Archibald. The Sonnets of Shakespeare. Stirling: Learmonth, 1933.

Imaginary conversations between Coleridge and Lamb.

3001. *Stamm, Rudolf. "Aussere oder innere Form? Zwei neue Ubersetzungen der Sonette Shakespeares." Neue Zurcher Zeitung, October 19, 1974, p. 67.

On translations by Alfred Fields and Pierre Jean Jouve.

3002. Standen, Gilbert. Shakespeare Authorship. London: Cecil Palmer, 1930.

In one section (pp. 34-50) Standen examines "Authorship of the Sonnets" concluding that Oxford was the poet and William Hall was W.H.

3003. Stanford, Donald E. "Robert Bridges and Samuel Butler on Shakespeare's Sonnets: An Exchange of Letters." Shakespeare Quarterly, 22 (1971), 329-35.

Stanford's remarks and the Bridges-Butler letters they precede examine questions about the dating of the sequence.

3004. Starnes, D.T. "Shakespeare's Sonnet 60: Analogues." Notes and Queries, 194 (1949), 454.

Finds analogues in Ovid's Metamorphoses and in George Buchanan's Jephthes (c. 1554).

3005. Stauffer, Donald A. "Critical Principles and a Sonnet." American Scholar, 12 (1943), 52-62.

A symposium-style discussion of Shakespeare's Sonnet 146--with John Crowe Ransom as one of the participants.

3006. Staunton, H. "Unsuspected Corruptions of Shakespeare's Text." Athenaeum, December 6, 1873, pp. 731-32; January 3, 1874, pp. 20-21; January 31, 1874, pp. 160-61; March 14, 1874, pp. 357-58.

Points out some "corruptions" in and offers emendations for passages in about two dozen sonnets.

3007. Steadman, John M. "'Like Two Spirits': Shakespeare and Ficino." Shakespeare Quarterly, 10 (1959), 244-46.

Sonnet 144 was indebted to two traditions--the Platonic commonplace of two loves and the medieval concept of good and evil contending for man's soul. The author attempts to show Ficinian influence.

3008. Steadman, John M. "Shakespeare's Sonnet 130 and Aretino's 'Ragionamenti'." Notes and Queries, 211 (1966), 134-35.

Discusses the similarities of both these pieces of burlesque verse.

3009. Steiner, George. "Shakespeare: Sonnet 87." Delos, 4 (1970), 178-84.

Translations of Sonnet 87 by Stefan George and Karl Kraus with an accompanying commentary by George Steiner.

3010. Steiner, George. After Babel: Aspects of Language and Translation. London: Oxford University Press, 1975.

Discusses German translations of Sonnet 87 by Stefan George and Karl Kraus, and of Sonnet 79 by Paul Celan (pp. 382-93).

3011. Stenberg, Peter. "The Expression of Time in Minnesang and in Shakespeare." Humanities Association Bulletin, 23, iv (1972), 38-46.

The figures used to describe the flow of time in the medieval minnesang, particularly in the work of Walther von der Vogelweide, are similar to those used by Shakespeare in the Sonnets.

3012. Stengel, E. "Bilden die ersten 126 Sonette Shakespere's einen Sonettcyclus, und welches ist die Ursprungliche Reihenfolge Derselben." Englische Studien, 4 (1881), 1-34.

Article contains an analysis of the first 126 sonnets, reordered.

3013. Steuerwald, Wilhelm. Lyrisches im Shakspere. Munchen: Theodor Ackermann, 1881.

Discusses Shakespeare's Sonnets and the work of his contemporaries (pp. 13-19).

3014. Stevenson, David L. The Meditations of William Shakespeare. New York: Vantage Press, 1965.

Attempts to solve the problems of the sonnets by anagram analysis.

3015. Stewart, J.I.M. "Shaping Destinies: On Shakespeare." Encounter, 53 (July, 1979), 61-67.

Review of S.C. Campbell, Only Begotten Sonnets.

3016. Stewart, Madeau. "Dark Lady's Clavichord." TLS, August 24, 1973, p. 978.

On Sonnet 128.

3017. Stirling, Brents. "A Shakespeare Sonnet Group." PMLA, 75 (1960), 340-49.

Certain usage (the phrase "my love," for example) suggests a sonnet order: 100-101, 63-68, 19, 21, 105.

3018. Stirling, Brents. "More Shakespeare Sonnet Groups." Essays on Shakespeare and Elizabethan Drama in Honor of Hardin Craig. Ed. Richard Hosley. Columbia: University of Missouri Press, 1962, pp. 115-35.

3019. Stirling, Brents. "Sonnets 109-126." Centennial Review of Arts and Science, 8 (1964), 109-20.

Stirling suggests that Sonnets 113-116 be removed from the series 109-121 and that 115-116 be relocated within the concluding group, 122-126.

3020. Stirling, Brents. "Sonnets 127-154." Shakespeare 1564-1964: A Collection of Modern Essays by Various Hands. Ed. E.A. Bloom. Providence, R.I.: Brown University Press, 1964, pp. 134-53.

3021. Stirling, Brents. The Shakespeare Sonnet Order: Poems and Groups. Berkeley: University of California Press, 1968.

"Restored" sonnet order is based on internal evidence of style and content. Sonnets fall into small groups--a miscellany as it were--and not a single coherent narrative as some argue.

3022. Stirling, Brents. "The Shakespeare Sonnet Order." TLS, December 26, 1968, p. 1462.

Refutation of the TLS review (November 7, 1968) of Stirling's book.
3321

3023. *Stocker, A. Des Hommes Qui Racontent Leur Ame. St.-Maurice, Suisse: Editions Oeuvre St.-Augustin, 1943.

Contains a chapter entitled "La Priere du Grand Will: Etude Psychologique de Quelques Sonnets de Shakespeare" (pp. 189-284).

3024. Stocking, Fred H. "Shakespeare's Temperance." The Hues of English. NCTE Distinguished Lectures, 1969. Champaign, Ill.: National Council of Teachers of English, 1969, pp. 11-32.

A reading of Sonnet 18.

3025. Stoll, Elmer Edgar. "Poetic Alliteration." Modern Language Notes, 55 (1940), 388-90.

Objects to B.F. Skinner's work on "Alliteration in Shakespeare's Sonnets" in Psychological Record (1939).
2949

3026. Stoll, Elmer Edgar. Shakespeare Studies. New York: Macmillan, 1927.

In some brief remarks Stoll asserts that the Sonnets reveal nothing about the poet but are intentionally vague where not purely conventional (pp. 14-15).

3027. Stone, Walter B. "Shakespeare and the Sad Augurs." Journal of English and Germanic Philology, 52 (1953), 457-79.

On Sonnet 107 (the "Mortall Moone"), Hotson's dating, and the Prediction of Regiomontanus.

3028. Stookey, Lorena, and Robert Merrill. "Shakespeare's Fearful Meditation: Sonnet 94." Modern Language Quarterly, 39 (1978), 27-37.

3029. Stopes, Charlotte C. "Shakespeare's Sonnets, edited by Thomas Tyler, M.A." Shakespeare Jahrbuch, 25 (1890), 185-204. Appears also in Poet-Lore, 2 (1890), 273-78.

Review article of Tyler's 1890 edition of the Sonnets.

3030. Stopes, Charlotte. "Mary Fitton and 'The Dark Lady' of Shakspere's Sonnets." Academy, 37 (March 1, 1890), 152-53.

Disagrees with Tyler that Mary Fitton was the dark lady.
2918

3031. Stopes, Charlotte C. "Shakespeare's Sonnets, 'W.H.,' and the 'Dark Lady'." Poet-Lore, 2 (1890), 460-80.

3032. Stopes, Charlotte C. "The Date of Shakspeare's Sonnets." Athenaeum, March 19, 1898, pp. 374-75; March 26, 1898, pp. 405-06.

She dismisses Lord Herbert as Mr. W.H., and while she argues for Southampton as the "fair youth," she believes William Harvey was Mr. W.H.

3033. Stopes, Charlotte Carmichael. "Mr. W.H." Athenaeum, August 4, 1900, p. 154.

As she had earlier done (Athenaeum, March 26, 1898) she argues for Sir William Harvey as Mr. W.H.

3034. Stopes, Charlotte C. "The Friends in Shakespeare's Sonnets." Transactions of the Royal Society of Literature, 2nd Series, vol. 28, part 3. London: Asher, 1908. rpt. Nendeln/Liechtenstein: Kraus Reprint, 1970, pp. 171-200.

Ties in allusions to acquaintances in the Sonnets with historical facts known about them. She also rejects the Herbert-Fitton theory while arguing for Southampton as the friend.

3035. Stopes, C.C. "An Early Variant of a Shakespeare Sonnet." Athenaeum, July 26, 1913, p. 89.

In a manuscript book of verses that belonged to Robert Killigrew (1597-1633) is a variant form of Sonnet 2.

3036. Stopes, Charlotte Carmichael. Shakespeare's Environment. London: G. Bell and Sons, 1914.

In her chapter, "The Friends in Shakespeare's Sonnets," Stopes sets forth a number of theories about the Sonnets: she identifies W.H. as William Harvey and she asserts that the order of the Sonnets in the 1609 Quarto is not correct.

3037. Stotsenburg, John H. "The Sugared Sonnets." Baconiana, 1 (1892), 19-26.

Evidence exists to make it appear unlikely that Shakespeare was the poet of the Sonnets.

3038. Stotsenburg, John H. "Sidney's Shake-speare Sonnets." Baconiana, 1 (1892), 53-61; NS 1 (1893), 38-48.

Having, in an earlier article, dismissed Shakespeare and others as the poet of the Sonnets, he proceeds to prove that Sidney was the poet.

3039. Stotsenburg, John H. An Impartial Study of the Shakespeare Title. Louisville, Ky.: J.P. Morton, 1904. rpt. Port Washington, N.Y.: Kennikat Press, 1970.

Seeking to disprove that Shakespeare wrote the works ascribed to him, Stotstenburg argues, among other things, that Sir Philip Sidney wrote the Sonnets (pp. 212-51).

3040. Strachey, Charles, and William Poel. "Sonnet LXXXV. and Mary Fitton." TLS, January 5, 1922, p. 13.

3041. Strachey, C. "The Rival Poet and the Youth of the Sonnets." TLS, November 16, 1933, p. 795.

Finds some additional evidence in Sonnet 86 to support Newdigate's theory that Walter Aston is the fair youth.
2561

3042. Strachey, Lytton. "Shakespeare's Sonnets." Spectatorial Essays. London: Chatto and Windus, 1964, pp. 71-75.

A review of H.C. Beeching's edition of The Sonnets of Shakespeare and J.M., Shakespeare Self Revealed in his Sonnets in which he dismisses the latter for being unscholarly and speculative while praising the former.

3043. Strathmann, Ernest A. Review of Edward Hubler, The Sense of Shakespeare's Sonnets. Journal of English and Germanic Philology, 52 (1953), 577-78.

3044. Stricker, Kathe. "Deutsche Shakespeare-Ubersetzungen im letzten Jahrhundert (etwa 1860-1950)." Shakespeare Jahrbuch, 92 (1956), 45-89.

Treats the Sonnets (pp. 58-59, 83-85).

3045. Stronach, George. "Bacon in the Sonnets." Baconiana, 3rd Series, 3 (1905), 58-61.

Sonnets 57 and 58 seem to be identifiable with Bacon's life.

3046. Stronach, George. "Shakespeare's Seventy-sixth Sonnet." Notes and Queries, 9th Series, 10 (1902), 274, 495-96; 11 (1903), 96, 249-51.

Initially adds his voice in support of Bacon as the writer of the Sonnets. Subsequent items are replies to Ormsby, Q.V., Wilson, C.C.B., and Leeper.
2351, 2608, 3131, 3216, 3218

3047. Stronach, George. "Shakespeare's Sonnets: A New Theory." Notes and Queries, 9th Series, 12 (1903), 141-43; 273-75.

Suggests the Sonnets were an anthology by various hands and that Shakespeare was, himself, the rival poet and Barnes the writer of Sonnet 86.

3048. Strong, John R. Note Upon the "Dark Lady" Series of Shakespeare's Sonnets. New York and London: G.P. Putnam's, 1921.

Looks at the evidence supporting Mary Fitton as the dark lady.

3049. Stroup, Thomas B. "Biron and the 116th Sonnet." Philological Quarterly, 10 (1931), 308-10.

Compares a passage from Love's Labour's Lost to Sonnet 116.

3050. *Sturtz, S.V. "Ronsard and Sonnet 61." Observer, June 19, 1927, p. 5.

3051. Subbarao, C. "Contextualist Poetic and the Nature of Language." Literary Criterion, 9, i (1969), 54-60.

On Spenser's Amoretti 54 and Shakespeare's Sonnet 23.

3052. Suddard, Sarah Julle Mary. "Three of Shakespeare's Sonnets (59, 60, 61)." Keats, Shelley and Shakespeare: Studies and Essays in English Literature. Cambridge: Cambridge University Press, 1912, pp. 177-81.

3053. *Suzuki, Takao. "Imagery and Correspondences in Shakespeare's Sonnet 124." Academia (Nanzan University), 24 (1977), 31-48.

In Japanese.

3054. *Suzuki, Takao. "Shakespeare's Sonnet LX and What It Tells Us: His Attitude Toward the Theme of Time." Studies in English Literature (Japan), English Number (1974), 27-41.

3055. Svintila, Vladimir. "Shekspirovi sonety." Rodna rech (Sofia), No. 4 (1968), 42-44.

In Bulgarian. Discusses the dating and themes of the Sonnets.

3056. Swinburne, Algernon Charles. "Short Notes on English Poets: Chaucer; Spenser; The Sonnets of Shakespeare; Milton." Fortnightly Review, 34 (1880), 708-21.

In his brief and general comments on the Sonnets, Swinburne sides with Wordsworth and against Browning on the former's contention that Shakespeare did "unlock his heart" with his Sonnets.

3057. Symonds, J.A. Review of Shakespeare's Southampton-Sonette, ed. and tr. by Fritz Krauss. Academy, 4 (1873), 43-44.

Objects to this translation on the grounds that the translator has accepted as fact Gerald Massey's theories about the subject of the Sonnets.

3058. Symons, A.J.A. "Shakespeare and Will Hughes." TLS, June 18, 1938, p. 417.

In response to Alfred Douglas's letter, Symons finds new evidence makes the connection between Will Hughes and Shakespeare more plausible.
1817, 1818

3059. Szondi, Peter. "Poetry of Constancy--Poetik der Bestandigkeit: Celans Ubertragung von Shakespeares Sonett 105." Sprache im technischen Zeitalter, 37 (1971), 9-25. Reprinted in Peter Szondi Schriften II, Essays: Satz und Gegensatz, Lekturen und Lektionen, Celan-Studien. Ed. Wolfgang Fietkau. Frankfurt: Suhrkamp, 1978, pp. 321-44.

3060. *Takahashi, Tomoyuki. "On Shakespeare's 'Sonnet 73'." Kyoyobu Kiyo (Ibaraki University), 10 (1978), 75-83.

In Japanese.

3061. Tannenbaum, Samuel A. "The Heart of Shakespeare's Mystery." Dial, 56 (1914), 494-99.

A review of Arthur Acheson, Mistress Davenant: The Dark Lady of Shakespeare's Sonnets, and The Sonnets of William Shakespeare, ed. Clara Longworth de Chambrun.

3062. Tannenbaum, Samuel A. "The 'Copy' for Shakspere's Sonnets." Philological Quarterly, 10 (1931), 393-95.

Concludes that the Sonnets were printed from copy in the "secretary script" and rejects the possibility that the copy was written in "Italian script."

3063. T[annenbaum], S[amuel] A. "Sonnet 20." Shakespeare Association Bulletin, 13 (1938), 188.

Rejects the idea that this sonnet is a revelation of Shakespeare's homosexuality.

3064. T[annenbaum], S[amuel] A. "Sonnet Speculations." Shakespeare Association Bulletin, 13 (1938), 189.

Tannenbaum is unconvinced by the theories expressed in Walter Thomson's edition of The Sonnets of William Shakespeare and Henry Wriothesley.
2915

3065. Tate, Allen. "The Unilateral Imagination; Or, I, too, Dislike It." Southern Review, NS 1 (1965), 530-42.

Includes a reading of Sonnet 73 (pp. 536-38).

3066. Tausig, Paul. "Zu Shakespeares Sonetten 153 und 154." Shakespeare Jahrbuch, 40 (1904), 231-33.

Author's name frequently appears in bibliographies as Taussig.

3067. Taylor, Dick, Jr. "The Earl of Pembroke and the Youth of Shakespeare's Sonnets: An Essay in Rehabilitation." Studies in Philology, 56 (1959), 26-54.

A biographical study of the young Earl produces no resemblance to the "fair youth" of the Sonnets.

3068. Taylor, Gary. Review of Gerald Hammond, The Reader and Shakespeare's Young Man Sonnets. British Book News (July, 1981), 434-35.

3069. Taylor, George A. "The 'Dark Lady' of Shakespeare's Sonnets." Notes and Queries, 150 (1926), 243.

Suggests Anne Fitton as the dark lady and Will Kempe as Shakespeare's rival for her affection.

3070. Taylor, Henry Osborn. Thought and Expression in the Sixteenth Century. New York: Macmillan, 1920; 2nd ed., rev. 1930, vol.2.

The Sonnets, even more than the plays, reveal Shakespeare's sensibilities (pp. 248-56). [Pagination refers to 2nd ed.]

3071. Ter Haghe, Adolf. "Over de Sonnetten van Shakespeare." Neophilologus, 17 (1932), 289-92.

On the subject of Mr. W.H.

3072. Theobald, Bertram G. Shake-speare's Sonnets Unmasked. London: Cecil Palmer, 1929.

He attempts to establish that Francis Bacon was the author of the Sonnets.

3073. T[heobald], R.M. "The Sonnets." Baconiana, NS 1 (1894), 181-93.

Finds those theories which Gerald Massey expounds in Shakespeare's Sonnets Never Before Interpreted quite plausible if Bacon's name were substituted for Shakespeare's.

3074. *Theobald, William. On the Authorship of the Sonnets Attributed to Shakespeare: an enquiry into the respective claims of Bacon, Sir Philip Sidney and others to be their author. Budleigh Salterton: F.N. Parsons, 1896.

3075. *Thiry, Marcel. Attouchements des sonnets de Shakespeare. Precedes d'un argument. Bruxelles: A. De Rache, 1970.

Includes selected sonnets.

3076. Thomas, Henri. "Une lecture des sonnets de Shakespeare ou les sonnets et la saison." Nouvelle Revue Francaise, 12 (1964), 98-106.

Comments on the great diversity of interpretations of the Sonnets.

3077. Thomas, Wright, and Stuart Gerry Brown. Reading Poems: an Introduction to Critical Study. New York: Oxford University Press, 1941.

In a concluding essay, "On Reading Poems," the authors give a reading of Sonnet 73 (pp. 743-48).

3078. Thompson, Karl F. "Shakespeare's Sonnet 129." Explicator, 7 (1949), Item 27. Reprinted in A Casebook on Shakespeare's Sonnets. Ed. Gerald Willen and Victor B. Reed. New York: Thomas Y. Crowell, 1964, pp. 273-74.

3079. Thompson, Sharon Barbara Powers. "A Comparison of Shakespeare's 'Sonnets' With Donne's 'Songs and Sonnets' By Means of a New Method for Analyzing Metaphorical Content." Ph.D. Dissertation, Minnesota, 1973. DAI, 34 (1973), 3437A.

3080. Thomson, J.A.K. Shakespeare and the Classics. London: George Allen and Unwin, 1952.

Thomson has a note in which he shows a parallel between Sonnet 60 and Ovid by way of Golding. He expresses some doubt that Sonnets 153 and 154 are renderings from Marianus (pp. 44-46).

3081. Thomson, Patricia. "The Date Clue in Shakespeare's Sonnet 98." Neophilologus, 50 (1966), 262-69.

3082. Thonon, Robert. "'Still' or 'Skill.' A Note on Shakespeare's Sonnet CVI." Shakespeare Jahrbuch, 97 (1961), 203-07.

3083. Thornton, Gregory. Sonnets of Shakespeare's Ghost. Sydney: Angus and Robertson, 1920.

Twelve sonnets by Shakespeare's "ghost" answering all the canards about him and explaining a few things about his sonnets. For example, his "friend" was the essence of Beauty, and he did indeed "unlock" his heart.

3084. Thurston, Herbert. "The 'Mr. W.H.' of Shakespeare's Sonnets." Month, 156 (1930), 425-37.

3085. *Tieck Ludwig [und Dorothea]. "Ueber Shakspears Sonette einige Worte, nebst Proben einer Uebersetzung derselben." Penelope Taschenbuch fur das Jahr 1826. Ed. Theodore Hell [pseud. for Karl Gottfried Theodor Winkler]. Leipzig: J.C. Hinrichs. 18--, pp. 314-39.

3086. Tigerschiold, Brita. "Dodsperspektivet i en Grupp Shakespearesonetter." Ord och Bild, 63 (1954), 553-61.

3087. Tirinelli, Gustavo. "I Sonetti di Shakspeare." Nuova Antologia, 38 (1878), 228-59.

3088. *Titherley, Arthur W. Shakespeare's Sonnets as from the Pen of William Stanley, Sixth Earl of Derby. London: George Philip, 1939.

3089. Titherley, A.W. Shakespeare's Identity: William Stanley, 6th Earl of Derby. Winchester: Warren and Son, 1952.

Appendix III, "The Canonical Sonnets (Quarto 1609)," contains an introduction and a detailed reading of the Sonnets supporting Stanley as the poet (pp. 299-328).

3090. Titherley, A.W. "'Speake of my Lamenesse'." Shakespearean Authorship Review, No. 5 (1961), 7-9.

Sonnet 89 refers to the poet's lameness and is addressed to a woman, the Earl of Oxford's daughter.

3091. Toliver, Harold E. "Shakespeare and the Abyss of Time." Journal of English and Germanic Philology, 64 (1965), 234-54.

He begins his discussion of time with Sonnets 73, 60 and 129 (pp. 236-37).

3092. *Tono, Keiko. "An Interpretation of Shakespeare's Sonnets." Mimesis (Tezukayama Gakuin University), 9 (1977), 54-82.

In Japanese.

3093. Toor, David. "Shakespeare's 'Sonnet XX'." Explicator, 32 (1974), Item 38.

3094. "Touchstone." "Shakespeare's Sonnets." Saturday Review, 134 (July 8, 1922), 60.

An ironic review of some of the published conclusions about the sonnets; Stopes, Eagle, Harris are among those he attacks.

3095. "Touchstone." "Shakespeare's Sonnets." Saturday Review, 135 (January 13, 1923), 50.

Follows up his letter of July 8, 1922.

3096. "Touchstone." "Shakespeare's Sonnets and Wordsworth." Saturday Review, 136 (July 21, 1923), 81.

Further views about the famous critics of the Sonnets--and in particular Wordsworth.

3097. "Touchstone." "Shakespeare's 'Sugred Sonnets'." Saturday Review, 136 (Aug. 11, 1923), 165.

More on Wordsworth's view of the Sonnets.

3098. Towndrow, Richard F. "Canker-blooms and Canker." Athenaeum, July 23, 1904, pp. 123-24.

The canker-bloom referred to in Sonnet 54 is more likely the crimson and green gall than the wild or dog rose.

3099. Travers, S. Smith. Shakespeare's Sonnets. To Whom Were They Addressed? Hobart, Tasmania: Davies Brothers, 1881. Reprinted, with a preface, from Victorian Review, December 1, 1880.

Believes that the 126 sonnets were addressed to Shakespeare's illegitimate son.

3100. Traversi, Derek. An Approach to Shakespeare. London: Sands, 1938. 3rd ed. Garden City, N.Y.: Doubleday, Anchor Books, 1969.

In chapter 4 (pp. 97-108) on "The Sonnets" Traversi speaks of Shakespeare's use of the imagery of contradiction. (Pagination refers to 3rd edition.)

3101. Triadu, Joan. Els sonets de Shakespeare: Estudi i seleccio d'interpretacions. Barcelona: "Els cinquanta-cinc," 1958.

A critical essay precedes the 40 or so translations into Spanish.

3102. Trueman, A.W. "Sonnet 130 and The Aeneid." Shakespeare Quarterly, 25 (1974), 129-30.

3103. Truskey, Edward Lee. "The Double Genius Concept in Shakespeare's Sonnets." Ph.D. Dissertation, Wayne State, 1971.

3104. Turner, Frederick. Shakespeare and the Nature of Time: Moral and Philosophical Themes in Some Plays and Poems of William Shakespeare. Oxford: Clarendon Press, 1971.

In his second chapter, "Time the 'Destroyer' in the Sonnets," Turner says that while "replications of the flesh and the order of poetry" have some efficacy in stemming the ravages of time, Shakespeare believed that the real answer was in the relationships between human beings (pp. 7-27).

3105. Turner, L.M. "Mr. W.H." TLS, June 3, 1965, p. 460.

In commenting on Hotson's book, Mr. W.H., Turner finds an anagram of Wriothesley's name in Sonnet 55, line 14.

3106. Tyler, Thomas. "The Date of Shakespeare's Fifty-fifth Sonnet." Athenaeum, September 11, 1880, pp. 337-38. Reprinted as "Entstehungszeit von Shakespeare's 55. Sonnett." Shakespeare Jahrbuch, 16 (1881), 411-12.

Believes the Horatian allusion was picked up from Mere's Palladis Tamia and, therefore, was written after 1598, probably in 1599.

3107. Tyler, Thomas. "The Epitaph on the Countess of Pembroke." Academy, 25 (March 8, 1884), 169.

Finds parallels between several of the Sonnets and a poem Tyler believes to be by William Herbert.

3108. Tyler, Thomas. "The Imprisonment of Lord Pembroke in 1601." Academy, 25 (March 22, 1884), 204.

Discusses facts that shed light on the dating of some of Shakespeare's Sonnets.

3109. Tyler, Thomas. "Shakspere and Lords Pembroke and Southampton." Academy, 25 (April 19, 1884), 279-80.

More evidence to support Pembroke as the friend of the Sonnets.

3110. Tyler, Thomas. "Mrs. Fytton and Rosaline in Love's Labour's Lost. Academy, 26 (July 19, 1884), 47. Reprinted in German in Shakespeare Jahrbuch, 20 (1885), 329-31.

If Fytton is the dark lady, certain questions about her need to be answered.

3111. Tyler, Thomas. "Shakespeare and Lord Pembroke." Academy, 27 (June 20, 1885), 438.

Notes evidence, particularly in Sonnets 57 and 58, of the close association between Pembroke and Shakespeare.

3112. Tyler, Thomas. "Mrs. Mary Fitton and Shakspere's 152nd Sonnet." Academy, 34 (December 15, 1888), 388-89.

Since Sonnet 152 appears to refer to a married woman, could it have been Mistress Fitton? Tyler thinks yes.

3113. Tyler, Thomas. "Shakspere and Marston." Academy, 35 (May 4, 1889), 306-07.

Sonnet 32 must have been written in 1598, after Marston's Pigmalion's Image.

3114. Tyler, Thomas. "Mary Fitton and the 'Dictionary of National Biography'." Athenaeum, October 19, 1889, pp. 532-33.

Rejects Lee's theory that William Kemp (the clown in Shakespeare's company) dedicated his book Nine Days' Wonder to Anne, not Mary, Fitton.

3115. Tyler, Thomas. "Mrs. Mary Fitton and Shakspere's Sonnets." Academy, 37 (March 8, 1890), 171.

Responds to Stope's letter on the same subject printed in the previous number of The Academy.
3030

3116. Tyler, Thomas. "The Dedication of Shakspere's Sonnets." Academy, 37 (June 14, 1890), 408-09.

In response to Charlotte Stopes, Tyler adds arguments on behalf of his view that Thorpe's dedication was to William Herbert.
3029

3117. Tyler, Thomas. "The Portraits at Arbury." Academy, 41 (January 16, 1892), 66.

Takes issue with Bridgeman's criticism of his theory about the Arbury portraits.
1615

3118. Tyler, Thomas, and E.S.A. "Sonnet C., L.9. Notes and Queries, 8th Series, 2 (1892), 283-84.

Both notes respond to Brinsley Nicholson's note on the same phrase, "Rise, resty muse."
2571

3119. Tyler, Thomas. "Mary Fytton and Shakespeare's Sonnets." Literature (London), 1 (1897), 150.

Reiterates his view that Mary Fitton was the dark lady.

3120. Tyler, Thomas. "'Mr. W.H.' and the 'Dictionary of National Biography'." Academy, 52 (July 24, 1897), 78-79.

Wonders about what evidence led Sidney Lee to change his opinion about the identity of W.H., whom he had formerly believed to be Pembroke.

3121. Tyler, Thomas, and A. Hall. "Shakespeare's Sonnets." Academy, 52 (August 7, 1897), 117-18.

Responding to a letter by E.K. Chambers, Tyler differs with Chambers on several points; Hall supports Southampton as W.H.
1687

3122. Tyler, Thomas. "Shakespeare's Sonnets." Academy, 52 (August 21, 1897), 155.

Defends his views on Mary Fitton as the dark lady against E.K. Chambers.
1687

3123. Tyler, Thomas. "Dr. Brandes and Shakespeare's Sonnets. Academy, 53 (January 22, 1898), 105.

Discusses findings by Georg Brandes which agree substantially with his own.
1603

3124. Tyler, Thomas. The Herbert-Fitton Theory of Shakespeare's Sonnets, A Reply. London: David Nutt, 1898.

In support of William Herbert as Mr. W.H. written in response to Sidney Lee's assertion to the contrary. This pamphlet was bound with Tyler's 1899 edition of Shakespeare's Sonnets.
2342

3125. Tyler, Thomas. "Mr. Lee and Shakespeare's Sonnets." Saturday Review (London), 87 (January 14, 1899), 50.
2343

3126. Ulrici, H. Review (in German) of Henry Brown, The Sonnets of Shakespeare Solved, and the Mystery of his Friendship, Love, and Rivalry Revealed: Illustrated by Numerous Extracts from the Poet's Works, Contemporary Writers, and Other Authors. Shakespeare Jahrbuch, 6 (1871), 345-47.

3127. Underhill, Wm. "'Mr. W.H.': Shakspeare's Sonnets." Notes and Queries, 7th Series, 9 (1890), 227-28.

Various plays on the name Hall suggest that Mr. W.H. is William Hall.

3128. Underhill, Wm., W.T. Lynn, C.A. Ward, and A. Hall. "'Mr. W.H.': Shakspeare's Sonnets." Notes and Queries, 7th Series, 9 (1890), 302-03.

Debate on the subject of William Hall as W.H.

3129. Underhill, Wm. "'Mr. W.H.': Shakspeare's Sonnets." Notes and Queries, 9th Series, 2 (1898), 344.

Comments on some points raised by Sidney Lee in his DNB article on Thomas Thorpe.
2344

3130. Urban, Sylvanus. "Table Talk." Gentleman's Magazine, 285 (1898), 102-04, 617-20.

The first article discusses the Earl of Pembroke and the mystery of Mr. W.H., and comments on George Wyndham's edition of Shakespeare's poems. The second article suggests that W.H. was a trade friend of Thorpe and was probably William Hall.
2925

3131. V., Q., W.E. Wilson, and C.C.B. "Shakespeare's Seventy-Sixth Sonnet." Notes and Queries, 9th Series, 10 (1902), 412-13.

On the subject of Sir Francis Bacon and concealed poets.
2351, 2608, 3046

3132. *Vabalens, D. Yu. Poetical Prosody and Poetical Translation: Shakespeare's Sonnets Analyzed. Vilnius: Vilnius University, 1976.

A statistical analysis of rhythm patterns in Lithuanian translations of the Sonnets. In Russian.

3133. *Valenti, Pier Luigi. "Quesiti nell'interpretazione italiana dei sonetti shakespeariani." Studi Petrarcheschi (Bologna), 3 (1950), 171-82.

3134. Vallette, J. Review of G. Wilson Knight, The Mutual Flame. Mercure de France, 324 (1955), 531-32.

3135. Vallette, Jacques. Review of J.B. Leishman, Themes and Variations in Shakespeare's Sonnets. Mercure de France, 342 (1961), 723-24.

3136. Van Doren, Mark. Shakespeare. New York: Henry Holt, 1939.

In his reading of the Sonnets, Van Doren finds the couplet, in general, to be out of step with the rest of the poem (pp. 10-16).

3137. Vaughn, John. "An 'Ancient Market Towne'." Temple Bar, 110 (January, 1897), 109-20.

In writing about Titchfield, the site of Wriothesley's seat, Vaughn discusses Henry, the 3rd Earl, and Elizabeth Vernon, about whom he believes the Sonnets were written (pp. 111-16).

3138. Vendler, Helen H. Review of Essays on Style and Language: Linguistic and Critical Approaches to Literary Styles, ed. Roger Fowler. Essays in Criticism, 16 (1966), 457-63.

Comments on Hopkins's "The Windhover," Herbert's "Prayer," and Shakespeare's Sonnets 116 and 130.

3139. Vendler, Helen. "Jakobson, Richards, and Shakespeare's Sonnet CXXIX." I.A. Richards: Essays in His Honour. Ed. Reuben Brower, Helen Vendler, John Hollander. New York: Oxford University Press, 1973, pp. 179-98.

3140. Venton, W.B. Analyses of Shakespeare's Sonnets Using the Cipher Code with Facsimiles of the Coded Sonnets and Coded Dedication of the 1609 Edition Analysed by the Author Using the Cipher Code and Verified and Confirmed by Computer. London: Mitre, 1968.

3141. Vickers, Brian. Classical Rhetoric in English Poetry. London: Macmillan; New York: St. Martin's Press, 1970.

Chapter 5 contains a discussion of Sidney's Astrophel and Stella 44 and Shakespeare's Sonnet 129.

3142. Viebrock, Helmut. Review of Stephen Booth, An Essay on Shakespeare's Sonnets. Archiv fur das Studium der neueren Sprachen und Literaturen, 209 (1972), 161-63.

3143. Viswanathan, S. "'Time's Fickle Glass' in Shakespeare's Sonnet 126." English Studies, 57 (1976), 211-14.

Educes evidence to support the reading that the "glass" refers to Time's looking glass not hourglass.

3144. Vizetelly, Ernest Alfred. Loves of the Poets. London: Holden and Hardingham, 1915.

Reviews the theories about the dark lady (pp. 62-70).

3145. Voege, Ernst. Mittelbarkeit und Unmittelbarkeit in der Lyrik. Munchen: Max Hueber, 1932. Darmstadt: Wissenschaftliche Buchgesellschaft, 1968.

Contains a section (pp. 113-23) on Shakespeare's Sonnets, discussing Sonnets 12, 41, 66, and 138, in particular.

3146. Voss, Robert F. "Paul Celan's Translation of Shakespeare's Sonnets." Ph.D. Dissertation, Cincinatti, 1973. DAI, 34 (1973), 1941A.

Investigates all twenty-one sonnets Celan translated.

3147. Waddington, Raymond B. "Shakespeare's Sonnet 15 and the Art of Memory." The Rhetoric of Renaissance Poetry from Wyatt to Milton. Ed. Thomas O. Sloan and Raymond B. Waddington. Berkeley: University of California Press, 1974, pp. 96-122.

3148. Waddington, Samuel, and R.M. T[heobald]. "The Shakespeare Sonnets." Baconiana, 3rd Series, 10 (1912), 148-53.

Waddington, responding to Hutchinson's article in an earlier issue (pp. 82-94), argues that Queen Elizabeth was being referred to in the "mortal moon" sonnet and that Sonnet 57 was

addressed to her, probably by Bacon. R.M.T. does not believe, as Hutchinson does, that "all the Sonnets are of the nature of soliloquies."
2192

3149. W[ailly].-B., A.-L[eon de]. "Sonnets de Shakespeare." Revue des Deux Mondes, 3rd Series, 4 (1834), 679-97.

The article is signed A.-L. W.-B.; the table of contents identifies the author as Armand Morlaix, a pseudonym for Leon de Wailly. First he reads the Sonnets as a romance on les amours de Shakespeare, and then he turns to look at them for their biographical and historical clues.

3150. Wait, R.J.C. The Background to Shakespeare's Sonnets. London: Chatto and Windus; New York: Schocken Books, 1972.

3151. Wait, R.J.C. "The Background to Shakespeare's Sonnets." TLS, April 20, 1973, p. 447.

A response to a TLS review (March 30, 1973, p. 346) with an accompanying reply by the reviewer.
3323

3152. Walch, Eva. Review of Raimund Borgmeier, Shakespeares Sonett, "When forty winters" und die deutschen Ubersetzer: Untersuchungen zu den Problemen der Shakespeare-Ubertragung. Zeitschrift fur Anglistik und Amerikanistik, 24 (1976), 81-82.

3153. Walker, Roy. Review of G. Wilson Knight, The Mutual Flame. Aryan Path, 26 (1955), 317.

3154. Waller, G.F. The Strong Necessity of Time: The Philosophy of Time in Shakespeare and Elizabethan Literature. De Proprietatibus Literarum; Series Practica 90. The Hague: Mouton, 1976.

"In the sonnets, man and time," Waller writes, "become adversaries in what is at once a universal and yet highly personal context" (pp. 87-96).

3155. Waller, G.F. Review of Shakespeare's Sonnets, ed. Stephen Booth. Dalhousie Review, 57 (1977), 780-83.

3156. Walters, Cuming. "The Mystery of Shakespeare's Sonnets: Who was 'Mr. W.H.'?" New Century Magazine, 4 (1898), 440-53; 5 (1899), 89-98, 207-20.

In Part I Walters attempts to prove that W.H. was not William Herbert and that the dedication had nothing to do with Shakespeare; Part II offers an analysis of the first 99 sonnets, which fall into four groups, and Part III contains an analysis of the last two groups of sonnets, with a summary of his conclusions: the Sonnets were very early and were the expressions of his private thoughts rather than statements about events in his life.

3157. Walters, Cuming. The Mystery of Shakespeare's Sonnets: An Attempted Elucidation. London: New Century Press, 1899. rpt. New York: Haskell House, 1972.

3158. Walters, Cuming. "Shakespeare's Sonnets." Literature (London), 4 (1899), 585.

Justifies his attack against the Pembroke theory in this response to a review of his book (pp. 516-17); a rejoinder by the reviewer follows.
3271

3159. Walters, Cuming. "The Pembroke Theory in Shakespeare's Sonnets." Literature (London), 4 (1899), 642.

Further justifies his attack on the Pembroke theory. See next item.

3160. Walters, Cuming. "Shakespeare's Sonnets as Clues to the Dramas." New Century Review, 6 (1899), 261-70.

Finds verbal parallels between the Sonnets and the plays.

3161. Wanschura, Karl. Die Sonette Shakespeares von Franz Bacon Geschrieben. Leipzig: O.R. Reisland; Wien: Staatsdruckerei, 1930.

3162. Ward, B.M. "The 'Mortal Moon' Sonnet." TLS, February 8, 1934, 92.
2082

3163. Ward, B.R. The Mystery of "Mr. W.H." London: Cecil Palmer, 1923.

Compiles "evidence" to show that Oxford was the poet of the Sonnets and that William Hall was Mr. W.H.

3164. *Ward, B.R. "Shakespeare's Sonnets." Poetry and the Play, 13, no. 87 (1929-30), 19-30.

3165. Warren, Roger. "Why Does It End Well? Helena, Bertram, and the Sonnets." Shakespeare Survey, 22 (1969), 79-92.

The Sonnets provide an "illuminating commentary" on the intensity of Helena's love and Bertram's reactions in All's Well That Ends Well.

3166. Warren, Roger. "'A Lover's Complaint,' 'All's Well,' and the Sonnets." Notes and Queries, 215 (1970), 130-32.

Discusses verbal links between All's Well and the Sonnets.

3167. Warren, Roger. "'Gust' and Poisoned Cups in The Winter's Tale and Sonnet 114." Notes and Queries, 215 (1970), 134-35.

Glosses "gust," which appears in both The Winter's Tale and Sonnet 114.

3168. Warren, Roger. "Orsino and Sonnet 56." Notes and Queries, 216 (1971), 146-47.

Speaks of the sea metaphor in Twelfth Night and Sonnet 56.

3169. Watkins, W.B.C. Shakespeare and Spenser. Princeton, N.J.: Princeton University Press, 1950.

Includes brief discussions of both Shakespeare's Sonnets and Spenser's Amoretti throughout.

3170. *Watson, Wilfred. "Tarquin the Master-Mistress, and the Dark Lady: The Role of the Poet in Shakespeare's Sonnets." Humanities Association Bulletin (Canada), 15, ii (1964), 7-16.

3171. Webb, Kenneth J. Review of Stephen Booth, An Essay on Shakespeare's Sonnets. Antigonish Review, No. 9 (1972), 110-11.

3172. Webb, Kenneth J. "Shakespeare's Sonnets and Literary Conventions of Friendship in English Renaissance. Ph.D. Dissertation, Ottawa, 1974.

3173. Webb, Thomas Ebenezer. The Mystery of William Shakespeare: A Summary of Evidence. London: Longmans, Green, 1902.

Sonnets were addressed to Southampton by Bacon (pp. 157-64).

3174. Weinstock, Horst. Review of Raimund Borgmeier, Shakespeares Sonett "When forty winters" und die deutschen Ubersetzer: Untersuchungen zu den Problemen der Shakespeare-Ubertragung. English Studies, 54 (1973), 174-75.

3175. Weiser, David K. "'I' and 'Thou' in Shakespeare's Sonnets." Journal of English and Germanic Philology, 76 (1977), 506-24.

3176. Weiser, David. "Theme and Structure in Shakespeare's Sonnet 121." Studies in Philology, 75 (1978), 142-62.

3177. Weiss, Wolfgang. Review of Stephen Booth, An Essay on Shakespeare's Sonnets. Anglia, 93 (1975), 525-28.

3178. Wells, Henry W. "A New Preface to Shakspere's Sonnets." Shakespeare Association Bulletin, 12 (1937), 118-29.

Dismissing Thorpe's dedication as being irrelevant to understanding the poems, Wells addresses the question of how the biographical element is important to a reading of the poems.

3179. Wells, Stanley. Review of Shakespeare's Sonnets, ed. Stephen Booth. Notes and Queries, 224 (1979), 167-68.

3180. Wendel, Karl-Heinz. Sonettstrukturen in Shakespeares Dramen. Munster: Westfalischen Wilhelms-Universitat, 1966. Summarized in English and American Studies in German: Summaries of Theses and Monographs. Supplement to Anglia, 1968, ed. Werner Habicht, pp. 35-38.

Examines 14-line units of speech in the plays (both monologue and dialogue) which correspond formally and structurally with the sonnet.

3181. Wendell, Barrett. *William Shakespeare: A Study in Elizabethan Literature*. London: J.M. Dent, 1894.

In his chapter on "Shakespeare's Sonnets" (pp. 221-37), Wendell indicates agreement with Thomas Tyler: William Herbert is the fair youth, Mary Fitton is the dark lady, etc.

3182. Werlich, Egon. *Poetry Analysis: Great English Poems Interpreted*. Dortmund: Lambert Lensing, 1967.

After giving some literary historical information for each poem, Werlich gives readings of Shakespeare's Sonnet 18 (pp. 31-40), Milton's Sonnet 19 (pp. 41-62), and Wordsworth's "Composed Upon Westminster Bridge, September 3, 1802" (pp. 85-100).

3183. *Werlich, Egon. "Sonnet 116: An Essay in Close Text Analysis." *Der fremdsprachliche Unterricht*, 3 (1969), 39-49.

3184. West, Michael. "The Internal Dialogue of Shakespeare's Sonnet 146." *Shakespeare Quarterly*, 25 (1974), 109-22.

3185. Westfall, Alfred Van Rensselaer. *American Shakespearean Criticism, 1607-1865*. New York: H.W. Wilson, 1939.

Contains a brief chapter on 19th-century criticism of the Sonnets.

3186. Wheeler, Charles B., and F.W. Bateson. "'Bare Ruined Choirs'." *Essays in Criticism*, 4 (1954), 224-26.

Were the "bare ruined choirs" in a monastery or a parish church? Wheeler, agreeing with Empson's reading of the line (in previous volume, pp. 357-63), thinks that they were in monastery churches, and Bateson, who once had thought otherwise, is persuaded to agree.
1527

3187. Wheeler, Richard P. "Poetry and Fantasy in Shakespeare's Sonnets 88-96." *Literature and Psychology*, 22 (1972), 151-62.

A psychoanalytic examination of the poems.

3188. Wheeler, Richard P. *Shakespeare's Development and the Problem Comedies*. Berkeley: University of California Press, 1981.

Wheeler discusses the Sonnets in two sections: "'Lascivious grace' in the *Sonnets* and *All's Well*" (pp. 57-75) and "Toward Tragedy: *The Sonnets*" (pp. 179-90).

3189. White, Edward Joseph. *Commentaries on the Law in Shakespeare: With Explanations of the Legal Terms used in the Plays, Poems* and Sonnets, and Discussions of the Criminal Types Presented. St. Louis: F.H. Thomas Law Book Co., 1911.

In the final chapter of the book White discusses the legal allusions found in the Sonnets (pp. 506-12).

3190. White, F.A. "'Mr. W.H'." New Century Review, 7 (1900), 228-42.

Using passages from the plays to bolster his theory, White tells the "the story" behind the Sonnets in which William Hathaway and young William Shakespeare were friends and rivals for the hand of Susannah Hamnet.

3191. White, Robert L. "Sonnet 73 Again--A Rebuttal and New Reading." College Language Association Journal, 6 (1962), 125-32.

3192. Whorlow, H. "Shakespeare's Sonnets: A Reading." TLS, January 16, 1919, p. 34.

Suggests an emendation ("tells" for "kills" in Sonnet 44, l. 9).

3193. Widmann, R.L. "Upon Looking into Shakespeare's Sonnet 73." Library Chronicle, 39 (1973), 81-88.

3194. Wietfeld, Albert. Die Bildersprache in Shakespeare's Sonetten. Studien zu Englische Philologie, 54. Halle: Max Niemeyer, 1916. Walluf bei Wiesbaden: Sandig, 1973.

3195. [Wigston, W.F.C.] A New Study of Shakespeare: An Inquiry into the Connection of the Plays and Poems, with the Origins of the Classical Drama and with the Platonic Philosophy through the Mysteries. London: Trubner, 1884.

Wigston sees the Sonnets as being allegorical expressions of Shakespeare's creative principles. It is "preposterous" that "the carnal marriage" of a friend should be "the opening proposition of these poems." The poems obviously are intended to signify something more meaningful (pp. 40-161).

3196. Wilde, Oscar. "The Portrait of Mr. W.H." Blackwood's Edinburgh Magazine, 146 (1889), 1-21. Reprinted in Essays by Oscar Wilde. Ed. Hesketh Pearson. London: Methuen, 1950, pp. 189-226. Reprinted in The Riddle of Shakespeare's Sonnets. Ed. Edward Hubler. New York: Basic Books, 1962, pp. 163-255.

A piece of short fiction propounding the view that Mr. W.H. was Will Hughes.

3197. Wilde, Oscar. The Portrait of Mr. W.H. Ed. Vyvyan Holland. London: Methuen, 1958.

Holland's introduction gives some insight into how Wilde came to be attracted by the theory that Will Hughes was Mr. W.H. and how he came to write this story.

3198. Wildi, Max. "Shakespeares Sonette." Buch der Freunde fur J.R. von Salis zum 70. Geburtstag 12. Dezember 1971. Zurich: Orell Fussli, 1971, pp. 130-38.

Superficial survey of most of the usual Sonnet subjects.

3199. Wildi, Max. "Shakespeares Sonette Heute." Shakespeare Jahrbuch West, 1980, 73-89.

A look at some sonnet criticism during the last several decades.

3200. Wilkes, G.A. Review of Hilton Landry, Interpretations in Shakespeare's Sonnets. AUMLA, No. 25 (1966), 121.

3201. Wilkins, Ernest H. "The Enueg in Petrarch and in Shakespeare." Modern Philology, 13 (1915), 495-96.

Although Sonnet 66 is an enueg, a type of lyric common to Provencal and Italian poetry, in which the poet presents a list of annoyances, that fact does not prove that Shakespeare was acquainted with the poetry of those regions.

3202. Wilkinson, L.P. "Shakespeare and Horace." TLS, May 6, 1955, p. 237.

Discusses the influence of Horace's Epode 2 on Shakespeare's Sonnet 104.

3203. Willen, Gerald, and Victor B. Reed, ed. A Casebook on Shakespeare's Sonnets. New York: Thomas Y. Crowell, 1964.

3204. Williams, Frayne. "The Sonnets of Shakespeare." Mr. Shakespeare of the Globe. New York: E.P. Dutton, 1941, pp. 194-225.

A review of the major issues (rival poet, sonnet arrangement, the dedication, etc.) with a summary of conclusions by some of the critics.

3205. Williams, Philip. Review of Edward Hubler, The Sense of Shakespeare's Sonnets. South Atlantic Quarterly, 52 (1953), 490.

3206. Williamson, C.F. Review of Leslie Hotson, Mr. W.H. Studia Neophilologica, 37 (1965), 252-55.

3207. Williamson, C.F. "Themes and Patterns in Shakespeare's Sonnets." Essays in Criticism, 26 (1976), 191-207. Reprinted in Shakespeare: The Sonnets: A Casebook. Ed. Peter Jones. London: Macmillan, 1977, pp. 230-47.

Finds parallels between the two main groups of sonnets.

3208. Williamson, Hugh Ross, and Peter Leyland. "Dr. Hotson's Arguments." TLS, February 17, 1950, p. 105.

Both writers disagree with the TLS review of Leslie Hotson's Shakespeare's Sonnets Dated (February 10, 1950, p. 88) and with Hotson's early dating of the Sonnets.
3305

3209. Wilson, J. Dover. Review of J.A. Fort, The Two Dated Sonnets of Shakespeare and The Sonnets of Shakespeare, ed. T.G. Tucker. Review of English Studies, 1 (1925), 353-59.

3210. Wilson, J. Dover. Review of Rudolf Fischer, Shakespeare's Sonette. Review of English Studies, 2 (1926), 350-54.

3211. Wilson, John Dover. The Essential Shakespeare: A Biographical Adventure. Cambridge: University Press, 1932.

Wilson believes that the poet introduces his patron, Southampton ("the fair youth"), to his mistress (the dark lady), and they both play him false. Wilson credits J.A. Fort with solving the "mystery of the Sonnets" dating them between April 1593 and September 1596 (pp. 58-61).

3212. Wilson, John Dover. An Introduction to the Sonnets of Shakespeare for the Use of Historians and Others. Cambridge: Cambridge University Press, 1963. New York: Cambridge University Press, 1964.

3213. Wilson, J. Dover. "J.B. Leishman and Shakespeare's Sonnets." Notes and Queries, 208 (1963), 442.

A brief appreciation of Leishman's book, Themes and Variations in Shakespeare's Sonnets, on the occasion of Leishman's death.

3214. Wilson, Katharine M. Shakespeare's Sugared Sonnets. London: George Allen and Unwin, 1974.

In additon to her concern with the usual issues--the dark lady, the male friend, etc.--she has a long chapter on "The Sonnet in Shakespeare's Plays."

3215. Wilson, Noel Sydney. "Shakespeare's 'Sonnets' and 'The Winter's Tale'." Ph.D. Dissertation, State University of New York at Buffalo, 1973. DAI, 34 (1973), 744A.

3216. Wilson, W.E. "Shakespeare's Seventy-sixth Sonnet." Notes and Queries, 9th Series, 10 (1902), 412.

Objects to Stronach and others who insist on reading "personal applications" into the Sonnets.
3046

3217. Wilson, W.E. "Mr. W.H." Notes and Queries, 9th Series, 11 (1903), 125-26.

On the possible "concealment" of the name W. Hall in the dedication.

3218. Wilson, W.E., and E. Yardley. "Shakespeare's Seventy-sixth Sonnet." Notes and Queries, 9th Series, 12 (1903), 35-37.

Follows a long chain of notes from the preceding volumes (commencing with W.E. Ormsby in vol. 10, p. 125) arguing the Shakespeare-Bacon question.
2608

3219. Wimsatt, W.K. Review of Murray Krieger, A Window to Criticism: Shakespeare's Sonnets and Modern Poetics. Modern Philology, 64 (1966), 71-74.

3220. Winny, James. The Master-Mistress: A Study of Shakespeare's Sonnets. London: Chatto and Windus, 1968. New York: Barnes and Noble, 1968.

3221. Winters, Yvor. "Poetic Styles, Old and New." Four Poets on Poetry. Ed. Don Cameron Allen. Baltimore: Johns Hopkins Press, 1959, pp. 44-75. Partially reprinted in Discussions of Shakespeare's Sonnets. Ed. Barbara Herrnstein. Boston: D.C. Heath, 1964, pp. 106-15.

Part of this essay deals with Shakespeare's Sonnets (pp. 47-60). Winters finds Shakespeare's sonnet style in a state of decay. What disappoints him are traces of "servile weakness" in the poet, Shakespeare's failure to take the sonnet seriously, and his failure to recognize the need for sharp denotations.

3222. Witt, Robert W. Of Comfort and Despair: Shakespeare's Sonnet Sequence. Salzburg Studies in English Literature, Elizabethan and Renaissance Studies, 77. Salzburg: Institut fur Anglistik und Amerikanistik, Universitat Salzburg, 1979.

A reordering of the Sonnets will more clearly show the neo-Platonic progression described by Bembo in The Courtier.

3223. Wittmer, Felix. "Stefan George als Ubersetzer. Beitrag zur Kunde des modernen Sprachstils zum 60. Geburtstag des Dichters." Germanic Review (New York), 3 (1928), 361-80.

Includes a discussion of Shakespeare's Sonnet 90 (pp. 376-80).

3224. Wojcik, Manfred. Review of Giorgio Melchiori, Shakespeare's Dramatic Meditations. Shakespeare Jahrbuch, 114 (1978), 198-99.

3225. Wolff, M.J. "Zu den Sonetten." Shakespeare Jahrbuch, 47 (1911), 191-92.

Regarding a possible source of Sonnets 153-154.
2119

3226. Wolff, Max J. "Petrarkismus und Antipetrarkismus in Shakespeares Sonetten." Englische Studien, 49 (1916), 161-89.

3227. Wolff, M.J. "Neue Literatur zu Shakespeares Sonetten." Englische Studien, 50 (1916), 152-64.

Reviews a number of early twentieth-century studies and editions--among them works by Acheson, Brandl, Morsbach, Rodder, Sarrazin.

3228. Wolff, Max J. Review of Albert Wietfeld, Die Bildersprache in Shakespeares Sonetten. Englische Studien, 51 (1917), 280-81.

3229. Wolff, Max J. Review of Rudolf Fischer, Shakespeares Sonette (Gruppierung, Kunstform) and Wilhelm Marschall, Aus Shakespeares poetischem Briefwechsel. Englische Studien, 63 (1928), 110-14.

3230. Wolff, M.J. Review of Shakespeares Sonette, tr. and ed. Karl Hauer. Englische Studien, 66 (1931), 115-16.

3231. Wolff, Max J. "Zu Shakespeares Sonetten." Englische Studien, 66 (1932), 468-69.

Discusses some Renaissance traditions that may have been influences for Shakespeare's "fair youth" and "dark lady."

3232. Wolpers, Theodor. "William Shakespeare: Die Sonette." Die Englische Lyrik: Von der Renaissance bis zur Gegenwart. Ed. Karl Heinz Goller. Dusseldorf: August Bagel, 1968, vol. 1, pp. 76-133.

Discusses and translates Sonnets 18, 29, 30, 60, 73, 116, 129, 146.

3233. Woodward, Frank. Francis Bacon's Cipher Signatures. London: Grafton, 1923.

Notes ciphers on the title page of the sonnets (1609) and elsewhere (pp. 78-79).

3234. Woodward, Parker. "Shake-speare Sonnets, 1609." Baconiana, 20 (1912), 17-23.

Bacon used the Sonnets as "a vehicle for a highly complex and difficult cipher which he hoped and expected would be solved in a future age . . . ."

3235. Worpenberg, Karl-Heinz. "Einfuhrung in das englische Sonett." Neueren Sprachen, 1966, 25-30.

This examination of Shakespeare's Sonnet 60 and Milton's Sonnet 19 ("On his Blindness") is accompanied by German translations.

3236. Woudhuysen, H.R. Review of F.J.M. Marrian, Shakespeare's Sonnet Friend. Notes and Queries, 224 (1979), 166-67.

3237. Wright, N.B. "Measuring Alliteration: A Study in Method." Computers in the Humanities. Ed. John Lawrence Mitchell. Minneapolis: University of Minnesota Press, 1974, pp. 82-93.

Discusses alliteration in Sonnets 18 and 30.

3238. Wuthenouw, Ralph-Rainer. Das fremde Kunstwerk: Aspekte der literarischen Ubersetzung. Gottingen: Vandenhoeck und Ruprecht, 1969.

First chapter deals with several German translations of Shakespeare's Sonnet 18 (pp. 11-28).

3239. Wyndham, George. "The Poems of Shakespeare." Essays in Romantic Literature. London: Macmillan, 1919, pp. 237-88.

The last third of the essay is devoted to the Sonnets (pp. 339-88) with much of his attention on imagery.

3240. Y., Y. "'Are Shakespeare's Sonnets Autobiographical?'" Bookman (London), 18 (1900), 13-15. Appears as "Shakespeare's Sonnets in French" in Bookman (New York), 12 (1900), 132-35.

A generally favorable review of Fernand Henry's French translation of the Sonnets in which Y.Y. takes critics to task for their penchant for autobiographical speculations.

3241. Yeatman, John Pym. "The Sonnets." The Gentle Shakspere: A Vindication. Birmingham: Moody Brothers, 1911, pp. 295-301.

Doubts the poems were by a single hand and believes they should not be read as a single work.

3242. Yoch, James Joseph, Jr. "Lust and Poetry in Shakespeare's Sonnets." Ph.D. Dissertation, Princeton, 1966. DA, 27 (1967), 2136A.

3243. Yoch, James J. Review of Shakespeare's Sonnets, ed. Stephen Booth. Shakespeare Studies, 12 (1979), pp. 289-94.

3244. Young, Alan R. Review of R.J.C. Wait, The Background to Shakespeare's Sonnets. Humanities Association Review, 24 (1973), 138-40.

3245. Young, H. McClure. The Sonnets of Shakespeare: A Psycho-Sexual Analysis. Columbia, Missouri: n.p., 1937.

Argues against the notion that the sonnets suggest any sexual abnormality.

3246. *Zemorah, Israel. "Broido's Hebrew Translation of Shakespeare's Sonnets." Moznayim (Tel Aviv), 47, i (1978), 55-57.

In Hebrew. A review of Ephrayim Broido's Sonnetoth Shakespeare.

3247. Zeydel, Edwin H. "Ludwig Tieck as a Translator of English." PMLA, 51 (1936), 221-42.

Gives Tieck's rendering, with comments, of Sonnet 18 and preliminary drafts of Sonnets 1 and 2 (pp. 234-38).

3248. Zillman, Lawrence John. The Art and Craft of Poetry: An Introduction. New York: Macmillan; London: Collier-Macmillan, 1966.

Talks briefly about the sonnet form in general (pp. 77-79); devotes a chapter to "The Poet and his Poem: A Reading of Six Sonnets from Five Centuries" (pp. 185-257), which includes Shakespeare's Sonnet 30, Milton's Sonnet 19 ("On His Blindness"), Keats's "On First Looking into Chapman's Homer," and Hopkin's "The Windhover."

3249. Zomnir, Oleksandr. "Renesansovyj homin: Shekspirovi sonety v perekladi Dmytra Palamarchuka." Dnipro: Literaturne-xudoznij Zurnal, 42, vi (1968), 150-56.

On Shakespeare's Sonnets in Ukrainian translation.

3250. Zuevs'kii, Oleg. "Elementi biografichnoi kontseptsii u Frankovikh perekladakh sonetiv Shekspira." Symbolae in Honorem Georgii Y. Shevelov. Ed. William E. Harkins, Olexa Horbatsch, and Jacob P. Hursky. Universitas Libera Ucrainensis Facultas Philosophica, Studia T. 7. Munchen: Logos, 1971, pp. 496-504.

Discusses the Ukrainian translation of Ivan Frankovich.

3251. *"Shakespeare's Sonnets." Rugby Magazine, 1 (1835), 146-60.

3252. "Shakespeare's Minor Poems." Fraser's Magazine, 52 (1855), 398-411.

Includes a discussion of the Sonnets (pp. 407-11).

3253. "The Sonnets of Shakespeare." Westminster Review, 68 (1857), 64-76.

After examining popular theories, the writer opts for William Herbert as Mr. W.H. He believes that while the plays show us Shakespeare the poet, the Sonnets show us Shakespeare the man. (Pagination refers to the American edition of the Westminster Review.)

3254. Review of Gerald Massey, Shakspeare's Sonnets, Never Before Interpreted. Notes and Queries, 3rd Series, 9 (1866), 382.

3255. "Royal Society of Literature.--June 25." Athenaeum, July 5, 1873, pp. 18-19.

A summary of C.M. Ingleby's paper, "On 'the Mr. W.H.' of the dedication signed 'T.T.' of Shakespeare's Sonnets, 1609," in which Ingleby concluded that "onlie begetter" meant Shakespeare.

3256. "Zur Sonetten-Frage: William Herbert's fruhe Verheirathung." Shakespeare Jahrbuch, 20 (1885), 326-27.

This note sheds some light on Sonnet 3 (ll. 9-10).

3257. "Recent Theories Regarding Shakspeare's Sonnets." Athenaeum, February 20, 1886, pp. 257-58.

Review of Shakespeare's Sonnets: The First Quarto, 1609. A Facsimile (Introduction by Thomas Tyler); The Songs, Poems, and Sonnets of William Shakespeare, ed. William Sharp. The reviewer finds little solid evidence to support Mary Fitton as the dark lady. He comments on the identity of W.H. as well.

3258. "The February Meeting of the New York Shakespeare Society." Literary World, 18 (1887), 107.

Contains an abstract of a paper by William J. Rolfe ("The Sonnets: some New Inferences from Old Facts"), which holds the Sonnets to be autobiographical.

3259. "Shakespeare's Sonnets." Knowledge (London), 10 (1887), 247-49.

The Sonnets reveal that Shakespeare had a knowledge of law, chemistry and astronomy, among other things.

3260. Review of H.L. Hosmer, Shakespeare and Bacon in the Sonnets. Literary World, 19 (1888), 76-77.

A not entirely unsympathetic review of this Baconian theory although the reviewer calls it "one of the most curious of the many curious books to which these perplexing poems have given rise."

3261. Review of Horace Davis, "Shakespeare's Sonnets." Literary World, 19 (1888), 108.
1772

3262. Review of Gerald Massey, The Secret Drama of the Sonnets. Poet-Lore, 1 (1889), 432-39.

3263. "Shakespeare's Sonnets and Mary Fitton." Academy, 36 (October 5, 1889), 220-21.

Reviews the theories about Pembroke and Mary Fitton expressed by Tyler and W.A. Harrison in earlier numbers of Academy.
2087, 2088, 3112

3264. Review of Shakespeare's Sonnets, ed. Thomas Tyler. Athenaeum, July 26, 1890, pp. 123-24.

3265. "New Shakspere Society.--(Friday, Dec. 11)." Academy 40 (December 19, 1891), 567-68.

Summarizes a paper given by Thomas Tyler, "The Latest Objections to the Herbert-Fitton Theory of the Sonnets." Pays particular attention to portraits of Mary Fitton.

3266. "Mr. Sidney Lee's Life of Shakespeare." Academy, 52 (July 10, 1897), 23.

The bulk of this review of "this definitive biography" (in DNB, vol. 51) deals with autobiographical elements in the sonnets.

3267. Review of Dictionary of National Biography, vol. LI, ed. Sidney Lee. Athenaeum, July 24, 1897, pp. 117-19.

Notes in Lee's articles in the DNB inconsistencies in statements about William Herbert in the "Shakespeare" and the "Herbert" articles.

3268. "The Dark Lady Unveiled." Academy, 52 (October 30, 1897), 341-42.

A review of Gossip from a Muniment Room, being Passages in the Lives of Anne and Mary Fytton, 1574 to 1618, ed. Lady Ann Emily (Garnier) Newdigate-Newdegate. London: David Nutt, 1897.

Touches on Mary's possible involvement with Shakespeare and her identity as the dark lady.

3269. "A German Mare's Nest." Academy, 53 (January 15, 1898), 79-80.

Reviews some of the recent work of Sarrazin and Isaac. The former finds a pun in Sonnet 143 that supports Southampton as the friend, while Isaac believes Essex to be the friend.

3270. Review of Thomas Tyler, The Herbert-Fitton Theory of Shakespeare's Sonnets. A Reply. Academy, 53 (April 30, 1898), 474.

3271. "Shakespeare." Literature (London), 4 (May 20, 1899), 516-17.

Review of Cuming Walters, The Mystery of Shakespeare's Sonnets.

3272. Review of Dictionary of National Biography, vol. LXIII, ed. Sidney Lee. Athenaeum, July 14, 1900, pp. 45-46.

The author includes a section on Lee's article about Shakespeare's Earl of Southampton, noting some apparent inaccuracies.

3273. Review of Parke Godwin, A New Study of the Sonnets of Shakespeare. Literature, 7 (1900), 392.

A brief but damning review of Godwin's dating and rearrangement.

3274. *"The Sonnets Again." Saturday Review, 89 (June 9, 1900), 717-18.

3275. "German Critics and Shakespeare's Sonnets." Academy, 65 (Nov. 7, 1903), 492.

Review of Max Wolff's translation of Shakespeare's Sonette and Theodor Eichhoff, Unser Shakespeare.

3276. Review of Arthur Acheson, Shakespeare and the Rival Poet. Athenaeum, January 30, 1904, pp. 139-40.

3277. Review of The Kings Shakespeare, Shakespeare's Sonnets with Notes and Introduction, ed. C.C. Stopes. New Shakespeareana, 3 (1904), 146-48.

3278. "Sonnets XXIII.-XXVI." Baconiana, 3rd Series, 6 (1908), 45-48.

Summarizes and comments on an article by R.D. in Westminster Gazette, which identifies the writer of these Sonnets with Ovid, Junior, a character in Jonson's Poetaster.

3279. *"Sonnet 116 Analysed." The Poet and the Philosopher, 1 (1913), 10-12.

3280. "Sonnets and Interpreters." TLS, April 18, 1918, p. 182.

Review of The Sonnets of Shakespeare, ed. R.M. Alden, and The Sonnets, ed. C. Knox Pooler.

3281. "The Sonnets." Bookman's Journal, 2 (1920), 381-82.

Although he does not utterly reject the notion that the Sonnets are directed to specific people, the writer feels it is more important to recognize the poems as being more universal in nature.

3282. "Shakespeare's Patron." TLS, February 9, 1922, p. 85.

A review of Charlotte Stopes, The Life of Henry, Third Earl of Southampton, Shakespeare's Patron.

3283. "Chaucer and the Rival Poet in Shakespeare's Sonnets." TLS, May 4, 1922, p. 294.

Review of Hubert Ord, Chaucer and the Rival Poet in Shakespeare's Sonnets.

3284. "Shakespeare Unlocks His Heart." TLS, December 14, 1922, p. 838.

Review of Arthur Acheson, Shakespeare's Sonnet Story: 1592-1598. Acheson is a proponent of the view that the Sonnets are closely autobiographical.

3285. Review of Colonel B.R. Ward, The Mystery of "Mr. W.H." TLS, April 12, 1923, pp. 249-50.

3286. Review of H.T.S. Forrest, The Five Authors of "Shake-speare's Sonnets." TLS, March 13, 1924, p. 162.

3287. "Shakespeare's Sonnets." TLS, December 11, 1924, p. 845.

Review of The Sonnets of Shakespeare, ed. T.G. Tucker; and J.A. Fort, The Two Dated Sonnets of Shakespeare.

3288. Review of J.A. Fort, The Two Dated Sonnets of Shakespeare. Archiv fur das Studium der neueren Sprachen und Literaturen, 148 (1925), 301.

3289. "The Order of Shakespeare's Sonnets." TLS, November 26, 1925, p. 797.

Review of Sir Denys Bray, The Original Order of Shakespeare's Sonnets.

3290. "A New Facsimile of 'Shakespeare's Sonnets' of 1609." TLS, December 3, 1925, p. 831.

Review of Shakespeare's Sonnets, A Facsimile with a note by A.T.B.

3291. Review of Rudolf Fischer, Shakespeares Sonette (Gruppierung, Kunstform). Archiv fur das Studium der neueren Sprachen und Literaturen, 150 (1926), 287-88.

3292. "The Sonnets of Shakespeare." Poetry Review, 17 (1926), 201-06.

Review of Shakespeare's Sonnets, a Facsimile; T.G. Tucker, The Sonnets of Shakespeare; and H.T.S. Forrest, The Five Authors of Shakespeare's Sonnets.

3293. Review of J.M. Robertson, The Problems of the Shakespeare Sonnets. Saturday Review, 142 (1926), 734-35.

3294. *"New Light on the Identity of W.H." Australasian, March 24, 1928, p. 6.

3295. Review of Randall Davies, Notes Upon Some of Shakespeare's Sonnets. TLS, June 14, 1928, p. 454.

3296. *"Shakespeare's Sonnets." Parents' Review, March 1929, pp. 163-75.

3297. Review of Bertram G. Theobald, Shakespeare's Sonnets Unmasked. TLS, March 27, 1930, p. 277.

Reviewer shows that Theobald's cipher technique, which purportedly "proves" Bacon wrote the Sonnets, is highly unreliable.

3298. Review of Gerald H. Rendall, Shakespeare Sonnets and Edward De Vere. English Review, April, 1930, pp. 520-21.

3299. "De Vere and the Sonnets." _TLS_, May 22, 1930, p. 430.

Review of Gerald H. Rendall, _Shakespeare Sonnets and Edward de Vere_.

3300. "Das Wunder Shakespeare." _Die Literatur_, 36 (1934), 671-72.

Review of _Shakespeares Sonette_, tr. Richard Flatter.

3301. "Oxford's Sonnets." _TLS_, March 28, 1935, p. 203.

Review of Gerald H. Rendall, _Personal Clues in Shakespeare Poems and Sonnets_, and G.W. Phillips, _Sunlight on Shakespeare's Sonnets_.

3302. Review of Ludwig W. Kahn, _Shakespeares Sonette in Deutschland_. _TLS_, June 13, 1935, p. 380.

3303. "The Problem of the Sonnets: Fresh Interpretations." _TLS_, May 14, 1938, p. 334.

A review article on _Shakespeare's Sonnets_, ed. Tucker Brooke; H. McClure Young, _The Sonnets of Shakespeare: A Psycho-sexual Analysis_; and _The Sonnets of William Shakespeare and Henry Wriothesly_, ed. Walter Thomson; and _The Phoenix and Turtle_, ed. Gerald Bullett.

3304. Review of Denys Bray, _Shakespeare's Sonnet-Sequence_. _TLS_, December 17, 1938, p. 806.

3305. "Dr. Hotson's Arguments." _TLS_, February 10, 1950, p. 88.

Review of Leslie Hotson, _Shakespeare's Sonnets Dated, and Other Essays_.

3306. "Shakespeare's Sonnets." _TLS_, December 29, 1950, p. 830.

Review of _Thorpe's Edition of Shakespeare's Sonnets 1609_, ed. C. Longworth de Chambrun.

3307. "A Study of the Sonnets." _TLS_, March 6, 1953, p. 151.

Review of Edward Hubler, _The Sense of Shakespeare's Sonnets_.

3308. "Shakespearian Critic." _TLS_, May 20, 1955, p. 268.

Review of G. Wilson Knight, _The Mutual Flame_.

3309. Review of Oscar Wilde, _The Portrait of Mr. W.H._, ed. Vyvyan Holland. _TLS_, November 21, 1958, p. 668.

3310. "The Necessity of Rejecting a Shakespeare Sonnet." _The Fifties_, 3 (1959), 20-21.

If Shakespeare submitted Sonnet 129 to a modern poetry editor, it would be rejected.

3311. "Behind the Sonnets. TLS, May 26, 1961, p. 326.

Review of J.B. Leishman, Themes and Variations in Shakespeare's Sonnets.

3312. "Oxford Historian Claims Solution of Sonnet Mystery." Shakespeare Newsletter, 13 (1963), 31.

Most of this report on A.L. Rowse's claims was written by Josephine Waters Bennett, who attended Rowse's public lecture.

3313. "The Sonnet Mystery--1." Shakespeare Newsletter, 13 (1963), 37.

Abstract of part 1 of a four-part article on A.L. Rowse's findings that appeared in The Times (London), Sept. 17, 1963, p. 13.

3314. "A.L. Rowse Addresses MLA in Chicago on Sonnets." Shakespeare Newsletter, 13 (1963), 47.

3315. "Shadow and Substance in Shakespeare." TLS, December 26, 1963, pp. 1062-63.

Review of A. L. Rowse, William Shakespeare: A Biography and John Dover Wilson, An Introduction to the Sonnets of Shakespeare for the Use of Historians and Others.

3316. "A.L. Rowse Continues to make Headlines." Shakespeare Newsletter, 14 (1964), 1.

3317. "Fair Youth and Dark Lady." TLS, September 10, 1964, p. 840.

Review of Hotson's Mr. W.H. in which Hotson's theories about the identities of the "fair youth" (whom he believes to be William Hatcliffe) and the "dark lady" are discussed.

3318. A Memorial of the Quarter-Centenary Year of William Shakespeare, 1564-1964, April 23. Callow End, England: Stanbrook Abbey Press, 1964.

3319. "Simplified Sonnets." TLS, March 12 , 1964, p. 216.

Review of Shakespeare's Sonnets, ed. A.L. Rowse, and Hilton Landry, Interpretations in Shakespeare's Sonnets.

3320. Review of Shakespeare's Sonnets, ed. A.L. Rowse. Quarterly Review, 302 (1964), 358.

3321. "Tidying Up." TLS, Nov. 7, 1968, p. 1248.

Review of Brents Stirling, The Shakespeare Sonnet Order in which we are told that Stirling has neither proved his case nor written a readable book.

3322. "The Harder the Better." TLS, November 24, 1972, p. 1420.

Review of Philip Martin, Shakespeare's Sonnets: Self, Love and Art. The reviewer believes the problem of the Sonnets is to be able to work through their ambiguities.

3323. "Dark Thoughts on the Dark Lady." TLS, March 30, 1973, p. 346.

Review of Leslie Fiedler, The Stranger in Shakespeare, and R.J.C. Wait, The Background to Shakespeare's Sonnets.

3324. "New Light on a Dark Lady." TLS, April 27, 1973, pp. 457-58.

Review of A.L. Rowse, Shakespeare the Man.

3325. "Dark Secrets." TLS, August 10, 1973, p. 919.

Review of A.L. Rowse's new edition of Shakespeare's Sonnets, in which the reviewer has some comments on Rowse's "discovery" of Emilia Lanier as the dark lady.

4
THE SONNET REVIVAL: EIGHTEENTH AND NINETEENTH CENTURIES

Anthologies

3326. Blunden, Edmund, and Bernard Mellor. Wayside Sonnets: 1750-1850. Hong Kong: Hong Kong University Press, 1971.

An anthology of English sonnets.

3327. Burpee, Lawrence J. A Century of Canadian Sonnets. Toronto: Musson Book Co., 1910.

This anthology does not include Archibald Lampman or Charles Roberts.

3328. Crandall, Charles H. Representative Sonnets by American Poets with an essay on the sonnet, its nature and history, including many notable sonnets of other literatures. Boston and New York: Houghton Mifflin, 1890.

3329. Griswold, Rufus Willmot. The Poets and Poetry of America. 1st ed. 1842; 11th ed., rev. Philadelphia: A. Hart, late Carey and Hart, 1852.

Includes sonnets by Washington Allston, Richard Henry Wilde, James Russell Lowell, William Burleigh, Henry Tuckerman, and Jones Very.

3330. Higginson, T.W., and E.H. Bigelow. American Sonnets. Boston and New York: Houghton Mifflin, 1890.

This anthology contains a brief introduction on the evolution of the American sonnet.

3331. Rowell, J.C. *The Sonnet in America*. Oakland, Cal.: Pacific Press, 1887.

Includes a list of sonnets by American authors found in magazines (pp. 19-24).

3332. Sharp, William. *Sonnets of This Century*. London: Walter Scott, 1886.

3333. Sharp, William. *Sonnets of the Nineteenth Century*. London: Walter Scott, 1900.

An enlarged and revised version of *Sonnets of This Century*.

3334. Sharp, William. *American Sonnets*. London: Walter Scott, [n.d.]

Contains a substantial introductory note on the sonnet in America.

3335. Waddington, Samuel. *English Sonnets by Living Writers*. London: George Bell and Sons, 1881. 2nd ed. enl., 1888.

General Criticism

3336. Agajanian, Shakeh Shahokram. "The Victorian Sonnet of Love and the Tradition: A Study in Aesthetic Morphology." Ph.D. Dissertation, New York University, 1963. *DA*, 27 (1966), 1777A.

Surveys both major and minor poets of the period.

3337. Attenborough, John Max. "The Sonnet from Milton to Wordsworth." *Gentleman's Magazine*, 292 (1902), 353-68.

3338. Aubin, Robert A. "Some Eighteenth Century Sonnets." *Modern Language Notes*, 49 (1934), 507-09.

On the appearance of some Spenserian sonnets in the eighteenth century.

3339. Ball, Patricia. Review of William T. Going, *Scanty Plot of Ground: Studies in the Victorian Sonnet*. *Browning Society Notes*, 7, ii (1977), 65-66.

3340. Bhattacharyya, Arunodoy. *The Sonnet and the Major English Romantic Poets*. Calcutta: Firma KLM Private Ltd., 1976.

3341. Bludau, Diethild E. *Das Sonett in der englischen Romantik. Ein Beitrag zum Formproblem in der Lyrik*. Munchen: Ludwig-Maximilians-Universitat, 1950.

Doctoral dissertation.

3342. Castorina, Giuseppe Gaetano. Le forme della malinconia: Ricerche sul sonetto in Inghilterra (1748-1800). Bologna: Patron, 1978.

In this book on the sonnet revival, Castorina has an appendix giving information (including rhyme schemes used) on each of the poets writing sonnets during this period.

3343. Clark, Bruce B. "The English Sonnet Sequence, 1850-1900: A Study of Fourteen Sequences." Ph.D. Dissertation, Utah, 1951.

Discusses sequences by Elizabeth Barrett Browning, David Gray, George Meredith, George Eliot, D.G. Rossetti, Algernon Swinburne, Christina Rossetti, Robert Bridges, Wilfrid Scawen Blunt, Eugene Lee-Hamilton.

3344. Clough, Arthur Hugh. "Sonnets in the Abstract." Rugby Magazine, 2 (1837), 270-74. Reprinted in Selected Prose Works of Arthur Hugh Clough. Ed. Buckner B. Trawick. University, Alabama: University of Alabama Press, 1964, pp. 48-52.

Major emphasis is on Wordsworth.

3345. Davidson, H. Carter. "The Sonnet in Seven Early American Magazines and Newspapers." American Literature, 4 (1932), 180-87.

Sterner's generalizations about American sonnets apparently omitted consideration of those sonnets published in periodicals. This article takes a look at some of those.
3368

3346. Evans, George Fullerton. "An Overlooked Sonnet." Modern Language Notes, 39 (1924), 184-85.

On the discovery of an anonymous sonnet published in a 1735 volume. At the time, this sonnet was believed to be one of only two published between Milton (1658) and Gray (1742). Both this sonnet and the other, presumed to be by William Walsh, were on the same subject--death.

3347. Evans, Oliver Houston. "The Sonnet in America." Ph.D. Dissertation, Purdue, 1972. DAI, 33 (1973), 5121A.

In his chapter on the sonnet in the 19th-century, Evans covers William Cullen Bryant, Jones Very, Ralph Waldo Emerson, Henry Wadsworth Longfellow, Walt Whitman and Frederick Goddard Tuckerman.

3348. Freeman, John, and Gregory Green. "A Literary Cul-de-Sac: The Sonnet and the Schoolroom Poets." American Transcendental Quarterly, No. 42 (1979), 105-22.

An examination of the way in which Longfellow, Bryant, Lowell, and Whittier used the sonnet.

3349. Gervais, Claude. "The Victorian Love-Sonnet Sequence." Ph.D. Dissertation, Toronto, 1970. DAI, 32 (1971), 964A-65A.

Discusses Elizabeth Barrett Browning, George Meredith, Dante Gabriel Rossetti, Christina Rossetti, and Robert Bridges.

3350. Going, William T. "The Term Sonnet Sequence." Modern Language Notes, 62 (1947), 400-02.

The term, first used by Rossetti to refer to The House of Life, became popular among other poets.

3351. Going, William T. Scanty Plot of Ground: Studies in the Victorian Sonnet. The Hague: Mouton, 1976.

3352. Golden, Arline Hersch. "Victorian Renascence: The Amatory Sequence in the Late Nineteenth Century." Ph.D. Dissertation, Indiana, 1970. DAI, 31 (1971), 6605A-06A.

Discusses Wilfrid Scawen Blunt, J.A. Symonds, D.G. Rossetti, George Meredith, and Elizabeth Barrett Browning.

3353. Golden, Arline. "Victorian Renascence: The Revival of the Amatory Sonnet Sequence, 1850-1900." Genre, 7 (1974), 133-47.

3354. Havens, Raymond D. The Influence of Milton on English Poetry. Cambridge, Mass.: Harvard University Press, 1922. rpt. New York: Russell and Russell, 1961.

Chapter 19 is entitled "Milton and the Sonnet with a history of the Sonnet in the Eighteenth and Early Nineteenth Centuries" (pp. 478-548). The book also includes a bibliography of all known sonnets published between 1700 and 1800 (pp. 685-97).

3355. Havens, Raymond D. "More Eighteenth-Century Sonnets." Modern Language Notes, 45 (1930), 77-84.

Updates his previous work.
3354

3356. Japp, Alexander H. "The English Sonnet and its History." Gentleman's Magazine, 275 (1893), 259-76.

A survey of contemporary work on the sonnet, considering such critics as Hall Caine, William Sharp, Theodore Watts-Dunton, etc.

3357. McCutcheon, R.P. "Notes on the Occurrence of the Sonnet and Blank Verse." Modern Language Notes, 40 (1925), 513-14.

Reprints a blank verse sonnet that appeared in 1692 and mentions several others that were published before 1725.

3358. McKillop, Alan D. "Some Details of the Sonnet Revival." Modern Language Notes, 39 (1924), 438-40.

Three notes on the revival of the sonnet in the middle third of the eighteenth century.

3359. Mitchell, Charles B. "The English Sonnet in the Seventeenth Century, Especially after Milton." Ph.D. Dissertation, Harvard, 1939.

3360. Morton, Edward Payson. "The English Sonnet (1658-1750)." Modern Language Notes, 20 (1905), 97-98.

Lists sonnets written and/or published during this period of minimal interest in the sonnet.

3361. Phelps, William Lyon. The Beginnings of the English Romantic Movement: A Study in Eighteenth Century Literature. Boston: Ginn, 1893.

Includes a comment on the virtual disappearance of the sonnet from Milton to Thomas Gray (1742). Phelps finds only "The sonnet on Death" by William Walsh (pp. 44-46). [Later scholars have found others.]

3346

3362. Reynolds, Paul Everett. "The English Sonnet Sequence, 1783-1845." Ph.D. Dissertation, Harvard University, 1938.

3363. Richardson, Patricia Lee. "Eighteenth Century English Sonnets." Ph.D. Dissertation, Auburn, 1971. DAI, 32 (1971), 3266A.

3364. Sanderlin, George W. "The Sonnet in English Literature, 1800-1850." Ph.D. Dissertation, Johns Hopkins, 1938.

3365. Sanderlin, George. "A Bibliography of English Sonnets 1800-1850." ELH, 8 (1941), 226-40.

This bibliography lists sonnets published in books between 1800-1850 and is a continuation of R.D. Havens's bibliography for the eighteenth century in The Influence of Milton on English Poetry.

3354, 3355

3366. Scott, Clive. "The Limits of the Sonnet: Towards a Proper Contemporary Approach." Revue de Litterature Comparee, 50 (1976), 237-50.

An examination of the sonnet form, including discussions of sonnets by Austin Dobson, and several other English and European poets.

3367. Steele, Mabel A.E. "The Authorship of 'The Poet' and Other Sonnets: Selections from a Nineteenth Century Manuscript Anthology." Keats-Shelley Journal, 5 (1956), 69-80.

Discusses the contents of a manuscript anthology entitled A Collection of English Sonnets by Robert Fletcher Housman, Esq. and dated 1835.

3368. Sterner, Lewis G. The Sonnet in American Literature. Philadelphia: University of Pennsylvania, 1930.

Surveys over two hundred American poets over a period of 150 years who wrote sonnets.

3369. Waddington, Samuel. Review of American Sonnets, ed. William Sharp. Academy, 35 (1889), 371-72.

A harsh indictment of the quality of American verse.

3370. Zasurskovo, Ia. N., ed. with A.F. Golovenchenko, N.P. Kozlova, and B.I. Kolesnikov. Zarubiezhnaia Literatura XIX Vek Romantizm: Khriestomatiia. Moskva: Prosvieschchenie, 1976.

Included in this anthology of European romantic poems translated into Russian are sonnets by Wordsworth, Keats, Byron, Shelley with an introduction.

3371. Review of Sonnets of This Century, ed. William Sharp. Athenaeum, April 3, 1886, pp. 452-53.

Matthew Arnold

3372. Anderson, Warren D. Matthew Arnold and the Classical Tradition. Ann Arbor: University of Michigan Press, 1965.

Dating of the last of the 3 "Rachel" sonnets (p. 62).

3373. Arnold, Matthew. The Poems of Matthew Arnold. Ed. Kenneth Allott. New York: Barnes and Noble; London: Longmans, 1965. New York: Norton, 1972.

3374. Baum, Paull F. Ten Studies in the Poetry of Matthew Arnold. Durham, N.C.: Duke University Press, 1958.

An essay on the sonnet "Shakespeare" (pp. 3-13).

3375. Culler, A. Dwight. Imaginative Reason: The Poetry of Matthew Arnold. New Haven, Conn.: Yale University Press, 1966.

Commentary on "Picture at Newstead" (pp. 30-31), "East London" (p. 269), "Immortality" (p. 242), four "undergraduate" sonnets--"To an Independent Preacher"; "To the Duke of Wellington"; "Written in Butler's Sermons"; "Written in Emerson's Essays" (pp. 46-49).

3376. D., A.E., and Henry Pettit. "Arnold on Shakespeare." Notes and Queries, 183 (1942), 52.
3385, 3386

3377. DeLaura, David J. "A Background for Arnold's 'Shakespeare'." Nineteenth-Century Literary Perspectives: Essays in Honor of Lionel Stevenson. Ed. Clyde deL. Ryals. Durham, N.C.: Duke University Press, 1974, pp. 129-48.

3378. Dudley, Fred A. "Arnold's 'Shakespeare'." Explicator, 4 (1946), Item 57.

3379. Fairclough, G. Thomas. "The Sestet of Arnold's 'Religious Isolation'." Notes and Queries, 207 (1962), 302-03.

3380. Fleissner, R.F. "Arnold's 'Shakespeare' Textually Revisited: Accidentals--or Cues?" Arnoldian, 8, ii (1981), 62-68.

After an examination of Arnold's manuscript, Fleissner concludes that the poet's "old-fashioned spelling and pointing" was not merely quaint but appropriate for his purposes.

3381. Forbes, George. "Arnold's 'Oracles'." Essays in Criticism, 23 (1973), 41-56.

Includes discussions of the "oracular" sonnets--"Quiet Work," "Religious Isolation," and "In Harmony with Nature."

3382. Going, William T. "Mathew Arnold's Sonnets." Papers in Language and Literature, 6 (1970), 387-406.

3383. Greenberg, Robert A. "Patterns of Imagery: Arnold's 'Shakespeare'." Studies in English Literature, 5 (1965), 723-33.

3384. Halliday, E.M., and Carlton F. Wells. "Arnold's 'Shakespeare'." Explicator, 6 (1947), Item 4.

3385. Hussey, Richard. "Arnold on Shakespeare." Notes and Queries, 182 (1942), 221, 348.
3376, 3386, 3389

3386. Jaggard, William. "Arnold on Shakespeare." Notes and Queries, 182 (1942), 276.
3385

3387. Johnson, Wendell Stacy. The Voices of Matthew Arnold: An Essay in Criticism. New Haven: Yale University Press, 1961.

Discusses several sonnets, including "Shakespeare" (pp. 20-24). Other references to some of his sonnets are scattered throughout.

3388. Leavis, F.R. Education and the University: A Sketch for an "English School." London: Chatto and Windus, 1943. New York: George W. Stewart, 1948.

In his explication of Arnold's sonnet "To Shakespeare," Leavis speaks of the "dead conventionality" of its phrasing.

3389. Morris, Joseph E. "Arnold on Shakespeare." Notes and Queries, 183 (1942), 264.

An understanding of Arnold's phrase, "victorious brow," helps bring his two sonnets, "Shakespeare" and "To a Friend," into harmony.
3385

3390. Philbrick, F.A. "Arnold's 'Shakespeare'." Explicator, 5 (1946), Item 24.

3391. Stange, G. Robert. Matthew Arnold: The Poet as Humanist. Princeton, N.J.: Princeton University Press, 1967.

Discusses "The World's Triumph" (p. 217); compares "Switzerland" to an Elizabethan sonnet sequence (pp. 221-22).

3392. Tinker, C.B., and H.F. Lowry. The Poetry of Matthew Arnold: A Commentary. London: Oxford University Press, 1940.

Contains a section on his sonnets (pp. 133-48).

3393. Truss, Tom J., Jr. "Arnold's 'Shakespeare'." Explicator, 19 (1961), Item 56.

3394. Van Aver, Albert. "Disharmony in Matthew Arnold's 'In Harmony with Nature'." Personalist, 48 (1967), 573-78.

The sonnet lacks "organic unity."

3395. Wilkins, Ernest H. "The Source of Arnold's Jacopone Sonnet." Modern Philology, 31 (1933), 200-02.

On the source and dating of "Austerity of Poetry."

3396. Wright, Herbert. "Matthew Arnold's 'East and West'." Modern Language Review, 13 (1918), 324-25.

Benjamin Bailey

3397. "Archdeacon Bailey." Athenaeum, March 13, 1886, p. 358.

Bailey, a friend of Keats, wrote several sonnets, one of which was written in continuation of Wordsworth's "Scorn not the Sonnet."

John Barlas

3398. *Barlas, John. Six Sonnets. Ed. with introduction by Ian Fletcher. London: Eric and Joan Stevens, 1981.

Wilfrid Scawen Blunt

3399. Blunt, Wilfrid Scawen. Poems. New York: A.A. Knopf, 1923.

Contains "The Love Sonnets of Proteus" and "Esther"--both sonnet sequences--and miscellaneous sonnets.

3400. Going, William T. "Wilfrid Scawen Blunt and the Tradition of the English Sonnet Sequence in the Nineteenth Century." Ph.D. Dissertation, Michigan, 1954. DA, 14 (1954), 674.

3401. Going, William T. "Wilfrid Scawen Blunt, Victorian Sonneteer." Victorian Poetry, 2 (1964), 67-85.

3402. Going, William T. "Blunt's Sonnets and Skittles: A Further Word." Victorian Poetry, 4 (1966), 136-41.

3403. Scott, Kenneth W. "Blunt's Sonnets and Another Poem to 'Skittles'." Victorian Poetry, 3 (1965), 141-43.

William Lisle Bowles

3404. Abrams, M.H. "Structure and Style in the Greater Romantic Lyric." From Sensibility to Romanticism: Essays Presented to Frederick A. Pottle. Ed. Frederick W. Hilles and Harold Bloom. New York: Oxford University Press, 1965, pp. 527-60.

Deals in part with the influence of Bowles's sonnets on the romantic lyric.

3405. Bowles, William Lisle. Fourteen Sonnets; Sonnets Written on Picturesque Spots; Verses to John Howard; The Grave of Howard; Verses on the Philanthropic Society; Elegy Written at the Hot Wells; Monody Written at Matlock; A Poetical Address to Edmund Burke; Elegiac Stanzas; Coombe Ellen. Ed. Donald H. Reiman. New York: Garland, 1978.

A facsimile reprint of editions published during 1789-1798, with an introduction by Reiman.

3406. ____________________. Sonnets and Other Poems, and The Spirit of Discovery. Ed. Donald H. Reiman. New York: Garland, 1978. Reprint of the 7th edition of Bowles's Sonnets and Other Poems (1800) and of the 4th edition of The Spirit of Discovery (1804).

Reiman's introduction, though largely biographical, contains some brief critical remarks about Bowles's sonnets.

3407. Doughty, Oswald. "Coleridge and a Poet's Poet: William Lisle Bowles." English Miscellany, 14 (1963), 95-114.

Discusses how Bowles's sonnets influenced Coleridge.

3408. Fayen, George S., Jr. "The Pencil and the Harp of William Lisle Bowles." Modern Language Quarterly, 21 (1960), 301-14.

Focuses particularly on his Fourteen Sonnets, Elegiac and Descriptive Written During a Tour (1789).

3409. Kellogg, Alfred Latimer. "William Lisle Bowles: The 'Sonnets' and Criticism of Pope. Ph.D. Dissertation, Yale, 1941. DAI, 32 (1972), 4569A-70A.

3410. Rietmann, Oskar. William Lisle Bowles (1762-1850): eine Begleitstudie zur Entstehung der englischen Romantik und zur Kulturgeschichte. Basel: Otto Fritz Knobel, Dornach, 1940.

Devotes part of his dissertation (pp. 21-53) to such matters as the publication of the sonnets, the experiences they describe, their form, etc.

3411. Wimsatt, W.K., Jr. The Verbal Icon: Studies in the Meaning of Poetry. Lexington: University of Kentucky Press, 1954.

"The Structure of Romantic Nature Imagery" (pp. 103-16) contains a discussion of Coleridge's sonnet "To the River Otter" (1796) and Bowles's "To the River Itchin" (1789).

Robert Bridges

3412. Guerard, Albert Joseph, Jr. Robert Bridges: A Study of Traditionalism in Poetry. Cambridge, Mass.: Harvard University Press, 1942.

Discusses the sonnet group called "The Growth of Love" (1876) in numerous places, particularly pp. 14-18.

3413. Young, F.E. Brett. Robert Bridges: A Critical Study. London: M. Secker, 1914; rpt. New York: Haskell House, 1970.

Discusses Bridges's The Growth of Love, a collection of sonnets (pp. 20-37).

Elizabeth Barrett Browning

3414. Boas, Louise Schutz. Elizabeth Barrett Browning. London: Longmans, Green, 1930.

The "Sonnets from the Portuguese" are discussed (pp. 126-35).

3415. Browning, Elizabeth Barrett. A Variorum Edition of Elizabeth Barrett Browning's Sonnets from the Portuguese. Ed. Miroslava Wein Dow. Troy, N.Y.: Whitston Publishing Co., 1980.

3416. ______________. Les Sonnets Portugais d'Elizabeth Barrett Browning traduits en sonnets francais avec notice, texte anglais, commentaire et notes par Fernand Henry. Paris: E. Guilmoto, 1905.

Henry's lengthy essay on the poet concludes with a few pages on the Sonnets (pp. lxi-lxiv).

3417. ______________. Sonnets from the Portuguese: A Facsimile Edition of the British Library Manuscript. Ed. William S. Peterson. Barre, Mass.: Imprint Society, 1977.

Contains an introduction.

3418. *______________. Sonnets from the Portuguese. Ed. Fanny Ratchford, and notes by Deoch Fulton. Centennial Variorum Edition. New York: P.C. Duschnes, 1950.

3419. Burdett, Osbert. The Brownings. London: Constable, 1928.

Contains a critical examination of a number of the Sonnets from the Portuguese (pp. 213-24).

3420. Clarke, Isabel C. Elizabeth Barrett Browning: A Portrait. London: Hutchinson, 1929. rev. 1935.

Discusses Sonnets from the Portuguese (pp. 160-64).

3421. Donaldson, Sandra M. "Elizabeth Barrett's Two Sonnets to George Sand." Studies in Browning and His Circle, 5, i (1977), 19-21.

3422. Dow, Miroslava Wein. "A Variorum Edition of Elizabeth Barrett Browning's 'Sonnets From the Portuguese'." Ph.D. Dissertation, Maryland, 1977. DAI, 38 (1978), 4177A-78A.
3415

3423. Edelman de Laurencio, Dalia. "Cromatismo, imagenes visionarias y simbolismo en Sonnets from the Portuguese." Revista de la Universidad de Costa Rica, No. 33 (1972), 65-72.

3424. Gay, Robert M. "E.B. Browning's Sonnets from the Portuguese." Explicator, 1 (1942), Item 24.

On Sonnet 22.

3425. Going, William T. "E.B. Browning's Sonnets from the Portuguese, XLIII." Explicator, 11 (1953), Item 58.

Reply to Heilman.

3426. Goldstein, Melvin. "Elizabeth Barrett Browning's Sonnets from the Portuguese in the Light of the Petrarchan Tradition." Ph.D. Dissertation, Wisconsin, 1958. DA, 19 (1958), 1371.

3427. Gosse, Edmund. "The Sonnets from the Portuguese." Critical Kit-Kats. New York: Dodd, Mead, 1896, pp. 1-17.

3428. Harrington, Elaine Ruth. "A Study of the Poetry of Elizabeth Barrett Browning." Ph.D. Dissertation, New York University, 1977. DAI, 38 (1978), 6142A.

3429. Hayter, Alethea. Mrs. Browning: A Poet's Work and its Setting. London: Faber and Faber, 1962.

Chapter 8 is devoted to "The Sonnets from the Portuguese" (pp. 102-08).

3430. Heilman, Robert B. "E.B. Browning's Sonnets from the Portuguese, XLIII." Explicator, 4 (1945), Item 3.

3431. Jackson, Rosemary. Review of Sonnets from the Portuguese: A Facsimile Edition of the British Library Manuscript by Elizabeth Barrett Browning, ed. William S. Peterson. Modern Language Review, 75 (1980), 636-37.

3432. Kay, Carol McGinnis. "An Analysis of Sonnet 6 in Sonnets from the Portuguese." Concerning Poetry, 4, i (1971), 17-21.

3433. Kenmare, Dallas. The Browning Love Story. London: P. Owen, 1957.

References to Sonnets from the Portuguese throughout.

3434. Lewes, George Henry. "A Box of Books." Blackwood's, 91 (1862), 434-51.

Comments on 3 of Elizabeth Barrett Browning's sonnets (pp. 449-51).

3435. Mackerness, E.D. Review of Sonnets from the Portuguese: A Facsimile Edition of the British Library Manuscript by Elizabeth Barrett Browning, ed. William S. Peterson. Notes and Queries, 224 (1979), 590-91.

3436. McCormick, James Patton. As a Flame Springs: The Romance of Robert and Elizabeth Browning. New York: Charles Scribner's Sons, 1940.

A couple of brief passages (pp. 73-75, 133-35) deal with Sonnets from the Portuguese.

3437. Mermin, Dorothy. "The Female Poet and the Embarrassed Reader: Elizabeth Barrett Browning's Sonnets from the Portuguese." ELH, 48 (1981), 351-67.

Elizabeth Barrett Browning must adopt both the conventional male role of speaker and the female role of beloved in her poems, the result of which is a clashing of incompatible roles.

3438. Moore, Virginia. Distinguished Women Writers. New York: E.P. Dutton, 1934.

Discusses E.B. Browning (pp. 177-87) and Sonnets from the Portuguese (pp. 184-87). Elsewhere she considers Christina Rossetti (pp. 45-58) and her sonnet sequence, Monna Innominata (pp. 53-54).

3439. Phillipson, John S. "'How Do I Love Thee?'--an Echo of St. Paul." Victorian Newsletter, No. 22 (1962), 22.

3440. Radley, Virginia L. Elizabeth Barrett Browning. Twayne's English Authors Series, 136. New York: Twayne, 1972.

Chapter 6: "Parnassus Attained: Sonnets from the Portuguese" (pp. 90-106).

3441. Saludok, Emma. "Stilkritische Untersuchungen der Sonette der Elizabeth Barrett-Browning im Verhaltnis zu Rainer Maria Rilkes Ubertragung." Ph.D. Dissertation, Marburg, 1933.

She pays special attention to Sonnets 5, 21 (pp. 6-30), and 39 (pp. 38-51).

3442. Sandstrom, Glenn. "'James Lee's Wife'--and Browning's." Victorian Poetry, 4 (1966), 259-70.

Includes discussion of Sonnets from the Portuguese.

3443. Taplin, Gardner B. The Life of Elizabeth Barrett Browning. New Haven: Yale University Press, 1957.

3444. Taplin, Gardner. Review of A Variorum Edition of Elizabeth Barrett Browning's Sonnets From the Portuguese, ed. Miroslava Wein Dow. Studies in Browning and his Circle, 8, ii (1980), 109-15.

3445. Thomson, Fred C. "All and Light: A Note on the Vocabularies of Elizabeth Barrett Browning and Matthew Arnold." Browning Society Notes, 8, ii (1978), 2-5.

Discusses word frequencies in Sonnets from the Portuguese and Arnold's Tristram and Iseult.

3446. Tucker, Cynthia Grant. "Studies in Sonnet Literature: Browning, Meredith, Baudelaire, Rilke, Weinheber." Ph.D. Dissertation, Iowa, 1967. DA, 28 (1968), 2659A-60A.

3447. Uhlmann, Wilfried. "Elizabeth Barrett Browning: 'Love'." Die Englische Lyrik: Von der Renaissance bis zur Gegenwart. Ed. Karl Heinz Goller. Dusseldorf: August Bagel, 1968, vol. 2, pp. 154-61.

Translation and discussion of the sonnet "We cannot live, except thus mutually."

3448. Whiting, Lilian. The Brownings: Their Life and Art. Boston: Little, Brown, 1911.

Discusses Sonnets from the Portuguese, (pp. 108-10, et passim).

3449. Zimmerman, Susan. "Sonnets from the Portuguese: A Negative and a Positive Context." Mary Wollstonecraft Newsletter, 2, i (1973), 7-20.

3450. "Origin of the 'Sonnets from the Portuguese'." Critic, 25 (1894), 398.

Quotes Edmund Gosse's account of how the Sonnets from the Portuguese came to be written and how the title was invented.

3451. Review of Les Sonnets Portugais d'Elizabeth Barrett Browning, tr. Fernand Henry. Athenaeum, April 15, 1905, pp. 457-58.

3452. Review of A Variorum Edition of Elizabeth Barrett Browning's "Sonnets from the Portguese," ed. Miroslava Wein Dow. Library, 6th Series, 2 (1980), 484-85.

Robert Browning

3453. DeVane, William C. A Browning Handbook, 2nd ed. New York: Appleton-Century-Crofts, 1955.

Several of his sonnets are discussed in the final chapter, "Uncollected Works" (pp. 554 ff.).

3454. Going, William T. "Browning and the Sonnet." Tennessee Studies in Literature, 17 (1972), 81-97.

3455. Griffin, William Hall, and Harry C. Minchin. The Life of Robert Browning: With Notices of his Writings, his Family, and his Friends. London: Methuen, 1910.

Appendix includes "Lady couldst thou know" and "Helen's Tower" with brief discussions of other sonnets (pp. 305-08).

3456. Hatcher, Harlan H. The Versification of Robert Browning. Columbus: Ohio State University Press, 1928. New York: Phaeton Press, 1968.

Discusses "The Sonnets" (pp. 132-33).

3457. Lentzner, Karl. "Robert Browning's Sonettdichtung." Anglia, 11 (1889), 500-17.

MacEachen calls this a "bold plagiarism" of Sagar's study.
3459, 3460

3458. Lloyd, Trevor. "Browning and Politics." Robert Browning. Ed. Isobel Armstrong. Writers and their Background. Athens: Ohio University Press, 1975, pp. 142-67.

Explains the context of his sonnet "Why I am a Liberal" (pp. 161-63).

3459. MacEachen, Dougald B. "Browning's Sonnets--One Word More." Browning Newsletter, No. 3 (Fall, 1969), 40-42.

3460. Sagar, Benjamin. "The Sonnets of Robert Browning." Papers of the Manchester Literary Club also issued as Manchester Quarterly, 13 (1887), 148-59.

After seeking to explain why Browning wrote only nine sonnets Sagar goes on to describe the sonnets by type.

William Cullen Bryant

3461. Giovannini, G., and Walter Gierasch. "Bryant's 'Inscription for the Entrance to a Wood'." Explicator, 4 (1946), Item 40.

3462. McLean, Albert. William Cullen Bryant. Twayne's United States Authors Series. New York: Twayne, 1964.

Discusses Bryant's work with the sonnet (pp. 114-18). Bryant was the first established poet in America to work successfully with this form.

Samuel Butler

3463. Butler, Samuel. The Note-Books of Samuel Butler. Ed. Henry F. Jones and A.T. Bartholomew. London: Jonathan Cape; New York: E.P. Dutton, 1912. 1926. Vol. 20 of The Shrewsbury Edition of the Works of Samuel Butler.

Contains his poems, which include a pair of sonnets entitled "Remorse," 3 others called "Karma," 3 called "The Life after Death," plus 2 others.

3464. Keynes, Geoffrey, and Brian Hill, ed. Letters between Samuel Butler and Miss E. M. A. Savage (1871-1885). London: Jonathan Cape, 1935.

Contains in an appendix three "Sonnets on Miss Savage," written after her death.

John Clare

3465. Barrell, John. The Idea of Landscape and the Sense of Place, 1730-1840: An Approach to the Poetry of John Clare. Cambridge and New York: Cambridge University Press, 1972.

Discusses sonnets and "the sense of place" (pp. 164-68).

3466. Gillin, Richard Lewis. "In That So Gentle Sky: A Study of John Clare's Sonnets." Ph.D. Dissertation, Bowling Green State, 1971. DAI, 32 (1972), 6374A-75A.

3467. Minor, Mark G. "The Poet in His Joy: A Critical Study of John Clare's Poetic Development." Ph.D. Dissertation, Ohio State, 1970. DAI, 31 (1971), 4784A.

Touches on the sonnets, love-songs, and poems of self-analysis in later chapters.

3468. Robinson, Eric, and Geoffrey Summerfield. "Unpublished Poems by John Clare." Malahat Review, No. 2 (1967), 106-20.

Includes two sonnets (p. 118) and two 14-line poems in rhymed couplets (p. 119).

3469. Todd, Janet M. In Adam's Garden: A Study of John Clare's Pre-Asylum Poetry. University of Florida Humanities Monograph, 39. Gainesville: University of Florida Press, 1973.

Discusses the "sonnet groups" that Clare wrote during the 1830's: "The Badger," "The Marten," "The Hedgehog," and "The Fox" (pp. 76-80).

3470. Todd, Janet M. "'Very Copys of Nature': John Clare's Descriptive Poetry." Philological Quarterly, 53 (1974), 84-99.

Discusses Clare's views on and use of the sonnet (pp. 95-99).

Hartley Coleridge

3471. Landow, George P. "Hartley Coleridge's Two Sonnets to Alfred Tennyson." Tennyson Research Bulletin, 2, i (1972), 37-38.

Samuel Taylor Coleridge

3472. Adair, Patricia M. The Waking Dream: A Study of Coleridge's Poetry. London: Edward Arnold, 1967. New York: Barnes and Noble, 1968.

Chapter 1--"The Early Poems"--has a number of comments on Coleridge's sonnets and on Coleridge's discussions on the subject.

3473. Erdman, David. "Coleridge as Nehemiah Higginbottom." Modern Language Notes, 73 (1958), 569-80.

About 3 burlesque sonnets published in Monthly Magazine (November, 1797) as "Sonnets, attempted in the Manner of 'Contemporary Writers'."

3474. Erdman, David V. "Newspaper Sonnets Put to the Concordance Test: Can They Be Attributed to Coleridge?" Bulletin of the New York Public Library, 61 (1957), 508-16, 611-20; 62 (1958), 46-49.

3475. Fairbanks, A. Harris. "'Dear Native Brook': Coleridge, Bowles, and Thomas Warton, the Younger." Wordsworth Circle, 6 (1975), 313-15.

On the relationship of Coleridge's sonnet "To the River Otter," Bowles's "To the River Itchin" and Warton's "To the River Lodon."

3476. Griggs, E.L. "Notes Concerning Certain Poems by Samuel Taylor Coleridge." Modern Language Notes, 69 (1954), 27-31.

Includes discussion of some very early published sonnets.

3477. Werkmeister, Lucyle. "Coleridge, Bowles, and 'Feelings of the Heart'." Anglia, 78 (1960), 55-73.

References to a number of sonnets by both poets.

3478. Werkmeister, Lucyle, and P.M. Zall. "Possible Additions to Coleridge's 'Sonnets on Eminent Characters'." Studies in Romanticism, 8 (1969), 121-27.

3479. Zall, Paul M. "Coleridge and 'Sonnets from Various Authors'." Cornell Library Journal, No. 2 (1967), 49-62.

Discusses the contents of this 16-page anthology of 28 sonnets collected by Coleridge in 1796.

G. J. DeWilde

3480. Taylor, John. "A Sonnet on Dryden." Notes and Queries, 9th Series, 4 (1899), 143.

A sonnet in the hand of G.J. De Wilde dated in 1869, was found on the last leaf of the History of Canon's Ashby by Sir Henry Dryden.

Thomas Edwards

3481. Rinaker, Clarissa. "Thomas Edwards and the Sonnet Revival." Modern Language Notes, 34 (1919), 272-77.

Edward's publication of thirteen sonnets in 1748 gives him a "preeminent place in the history of [the sonnet] revival."

Thomas Gray

3482. Bache, William B. "Gray's 'Sonnet: On the Death of Richard West'." CEA Critic, 31, ii (1968), 12.

3483. Cecil, Lord David. "The Poetry of Thomas Gray." Proceedings of the British Academy, 31 (1945), 43-60. Reprinted in Eighteenth-Century Literature. Ed. James L. Clifford. New York: Oxford University Press, 1959, pp. 233-50.

Discusses "Sonnet: On the Death of Richard West" (pp. 347-48).

3484. Foladare, Joseph. "Gray's 'Frail Memorial' to West." PMLA, 75 (1960), 61-65.

3485. Mell, Donald C., Jr. "Form as Meaning in Augustan Elegy: A Reading of Thomas Gray's 'Sonnet on the Death of Richard West'." Papers on Language and Literature, 4 (1968), 131-44.

3486. Moore, Judith K. "Thomas Gray's 'Sonnet on the Death of Richard West.' The Circumstances and the Diction." Tennessee Studies in Literature, 19 (1974), 107-13.

3487. Spacks, Patricia Meyer. "Statement and Artifice in Thomas Gray's Poetry." Studies in English Literature, 5 (1965), 519-32.

Discusses "Sonnet: On the Death of Richard West" (pp. 524-27).

3488. Spacks, Patricia Meyer. The Poetry of Vision: Five Eighteenth-Century Poets. Cambridge, Mass.: Harvard University Press, 1967.

In her chapter on "Thomas Gray: Action and Image," Spacks includes an explication of the "Sonnet on the Death of Richard West" (pp. 95-98).

3489. Tillotson, Geoffrey. "More About Poetic Diction." Augustan Studies. London: Athlone Press, 1961.

Brief comment on "Sonnet: On the Death of Richard West" (pp. 87-88).

Arthur Henry Hallam

3490. Kolb, Jack. "'They Were No Kings': An Unrecorded Sonnet by Hallam." Victorian Poetry, 15 (1977), 373-76.

Thomas Hardy

3491. Bailey, James O. The Poetry of Thomas Hardy: A Handbook and Commentary. Chapel Hill: University of North Carolina Press, 1970.

"She to Him" sonnets (pp. 58-59).

3492. Blackmur, R.P. "The Shorter Poems of Thomas Hardy." Southern Review (Baton Rouge), 6 (1940), 20-48.

Discusses the series of four Sonnets, "She to Him" (pp. 25-27).

3493. Prasad, Birjadish. The Poetry of Thomas Hardy. Salzburg Studies in English Literature, Romantic Reassessment, 57. 2 vols. Salzburg: Institut fur Englische Sprache und Literatur, Universitat Salzburg, 1977.

Briefly discusses "She to Him."

William Ernest Henley

3494. Cohen, Edward H. "An Early Sonnet-Portrait by W.E. Henley." Victorian Poetry, 14 (1976), 258-60.

Oliver Wendell Holmes

3495. Arms, George. The Fields Were Green: A New View of Bryant, Whittier, Holmes, Lowell, and Longfellow, with a Selection of Their Poems. Stanford, California: Stanford University Press, 1953.

The selection includes Holme's "Two Sonnets: Harvard" and an explication (pp. 113-14).

Gerard Manley Hopkins

3496. *Agrawala, D.C. "Hopkins on Shakespeare." Rajasthan University Studies in English, 1967-1968, pp. 57-66.

Special attention is paid to Hopkins's thoughts on Shakespeare's use of the sonnet form.

3497. Allison, Alexander W. "Hopkins' 'I Wake and Feel the Fell of Dark'." _Explicator_, 17 (1959), Item 54.

3498. Allsopp, Michael E. "'Felix Randall' and the Creative Spirit: A Centenary Study." _Hopkins Quarterly_, 7 (1980), 109-17.

3499. Arakelian, Paul G. "Evaluative Stylistics: A Non-Programmatic Study of 'The Windhover'." _Language and Style_, 9 (1976), 118-29.

Title appears as "Evaluative Stylistics . . ." in Table of Contents, and as "Evaluative Statistics . . ." above the article itself.

3500. Assad, Thomas J. "A Closer Look at Hopkins' '(Carrion Comfort)'." _Tulane Studies in English_, 9 (1959), 91-102.

3501. Assad, Thomas J. "Hopkins' 'The Windhover'." _Tulane Studies in English_, 11 (1961), 87-95.

3502. Assad, Thomas J. "Hopkins' 'Spelt from Sibyl's Leaves'." _Tulane Studies in English_, 22 (1977), 103-15.

3503. August, Eugene R. "Hopkins' Dangerous Fire." _Victorian Poetry_, 1 (1963), 72-74.

On "The Windhover."

3504. August, Eugene R. "The Growth of 'The Windhover'." _PMLA_, 82 (1967), 465-68.

3505. Ayers, Robert W. "Hopkins' 'The Windhover': A Further Simplification." _Modern Language Notes_, 71 (1956), 577-84.

3506. Bates, Ronald. "Hopkins' Embers Poems: A Liturgical Source." _Renascence_, 17 (1964), 32-37.

Relates "The Windhover" and "God's Grandeur" to the Ember Days ("periods in the Church year set apart for special prayer and fasting").

3507. Bates, Ronald. "'The Windhover'." _Victorian Poetry_, 2 (1964), 63-64.

3508. Bates, Ronald. "Downdolphinry." _University of Toronto Quarterly_, 36 (1967), 229-36.

On "The Windhover."

3509. Baxter, Ralph C. "Shakespeare's Dauphin and Hopkins' 'Windhover'." _Victorian Poetry_, 7 (1969), 71-75.

Henry V (III, vii) provides a source of imagery for "The Windhover."

3510. Bender, Todd K. "Hopkins' 'God's Grandeur'." Explicator, 21 (1963), Item 55.

3511. Bergonzi, Bernard. Gerard Manley Hopkins. New York: Macmillan, 1977.

On various sonnets (pp. 180-92) commencing from 1877.

3512. Beyette, Kent. "Grace and Time as Latent Structures in the Poetry of Gerard Manley Hopkins." Texas Studies in Literature and Language, 16 (1975), 705-21.

Examines a number of Hopkins's sonnets, but deals with "As kingfishers catch fire" at some length (pp. 709 ff.).

3513. Beyette, Thomas K. "Hopkins' Phenomenology of Art in 'The Shepherd's Brow'." Victorian Poetry, 11 (1973), 207-13.

3514. Black, Michael. "The Musical Analogy." English, 25 (1976), 111-34.

Part of the essay (pp. 114-24) deals with "Spelt from Sibyl's Leaves."

3515. Bodden, Horst, und Herbert Kaussen. "Structural Analyses of Modern English Poetry for Classroom Teaching. The Windhover by Gerard Manley Hopkins and Owl's Song by Ted Hughes." Der Fremdsprachliche Unterricht, 22 (Mai, 1972), 24-40.

3516. Boyle, Robert R., S.J. "A Footnote on 'The Windhover'." America, 82 (1949), 129-30.

3517. Boyle, Robert, S.J. Metaphor in Hopkins. Chapel Hill: University of North Carolina Press, 1960.

Chapter 2 deals with "God's Grandeur" (pp. 25-44); Chapter 4 with "The Windhover" (pp. 71-110); Chapter 7 with 2 other sonnets (69--"My own heart let me more have pity on," and "Harry Ploughman").

3518. Boyle, Robert, S.J. "Time and Grace in Hopkins' Imagination." Renascence, 29 (1976), 7-24.

Although the article focuses on stanza 6 of The Wreck of the Deutschland, Boyle makes some important observations about "The Windhover" (pp. 20-24).

3519. Bremer, R. "Hopkins' Use of the Word 'Combs' in 'To R.B'." English Studies, 51 (1970), 144-48.

3520. Bremer, R. "A New Interpretation of Hopkins' 'The Windhover'." Levende Talen, No. 266 (1970), 216-26.

3521. Bremer, Rudolf. Gerard Manley Hopkins: The Sonnets of 1865. Ph.D. Dissertation, Groningen, 1978.

After several introductory chapters, there follows a detailed analysis of nine sonnets.

3522. Brinlee, Robert W. "The Biblical Underthought of Hopkins' 'Terrible Sonnets'." Literature and Theology. Ed. Thomas F. Staley and Lester F. Zimmerman. University of Tulsa Department of English Monograph Series, 7. Tulsa, Oklahoma: University of Tulsa, 1969, pp. 12-22.

3523. Brophy, James. "The Noble Brute: Medieval Nuance in 'The Windhover'." Modern Language Notes, 76 (1961), 673-74.

3524. Campbell, Sister M. Mary Hugh, S.C.M.M. "The Silent Sonnet: Hopkins' 'Shepherd's Brow'." Renascence, 15 (1963), 133-42.

3525. Capellanus. "Windhover." America, 70 (1944), 531.

3526. Carson, J. Angela. "The Metaphor of Struggle in 'Carrion Comfort'." Philological Quarterly, 49 (1970), 547-57.

3527. Cervo, Nathan. "A Reading of 'Plough Down Sillion Shine'." Hopkins Quarterly, 5 (1978), 79-81.

On "The Windhover."

3528. Cervo, Nathan. "Catholic Humanism in 'The Windhover' and 'God's Grandeur'." Hopkins Quarterly, 8 (1981), 33-40.

3529. *Chamberlain, Robert L. "George MacDonald's 'A Manchester Poem' and Hopkins's 'God's Grandeur'." Person, 44 (1963), 518-27.

3530. Chard, Leslie F. "Once More Into The Windhover." English Language Notes, 2 (1965), 282-85.

3531. Chevigny, Bell Gale. "'Instress' and Devotion in the Poetry of Gerard Manley Hopkins." Victorian Studies, 9 (1965), 141-53.

Discusses "The Windhover," the "Terrible Sonnets," "Felix Randall," "The Candle Indoors."

3532. Clark, Robert Boykin, S.J. "Hopkins's 'The Shepherd's Brow'." Victorian Newsletter, No. 28 (1965), pp. 16-18.

3533. Cochran, George Leonard, O.P. "This Dappled World: The Poetic Vision of Gerard Manley Hopkins." Ph.D. Dissertation, Loyola (Chicago), 1976. DAI, 36 (1976), 7433A.

Contains an entire chapter on "Pied Beauty."

3534. Cohen, Selma Jeanne. "Hopkins' 'As Kingfisher's Catch Fire'." Modern Language Quarterly, 11 (1950), 197-204.

3535. Collins, Winston. "Tennyson and Hopkins." University of Toronto Quarterly, 38 (1968), 84-95.

This article, which deals with the question of man's meaning in a naturalistic universe, compares Tennyson's "Vastness" with Hopkins's "That Nature is a Heraclitean Fire," and "De Profundis" with "As kingfisher's catch fire" (pp. 84-88).

3536. Combs, John R. "The Trinity in Hopkins' 'God's Grandeur'." CEA Critic, 35, iv (1973), 27.

3537. Cornelia, Marie. "Images and Allusions in Hopkins' 'Carrion Comfort'." Renascence, 27 (1974), 51-55.

3538. Cotter, James Finn. "'Hornlight Wound to the West': The Inscape of the Passion in Hopkins' Poetry." Victorian Poetry, 16 (1978), 297-313.

Discusses symbolism of the passion in over a dozen of Hopkins's sonnets.

3539. Cotter, James Finn. Inscape: The Christology and Poetry of Gerard Manley Hopkins. Pittsburgh: University of Pittsburgh Press, 1972.

Chapter 8, "'Let him easter in us': Sonnets of 1877" (pp. 167-190) and the two following chapters deal primarily with sonnets.

3540. Couldrey, Oswald. "Hopkinsiana." TLS, September 24, 1954, p. 609.

On "The Windhover" in response to F.N. Lees (TLS, September 3, 1954, p. 557) and a TLS review of J. M. Guttierrez Mora (pp. 509-10).

3644, 3816

3541. Cullinan, W. "The Windhover." Unisa English Studies, No. 1 (March, 1964), 23-24.

3542. DeLaura, David J. "Hopkins and Carlyle: My Hero, My Chevalier." Hopkins Quarterly, 2 (1975), 67-76.

Compares a passage in Carlyle's Past and Present to "The Windhover."

3543. Digges, M. Laurentia. "Gerard Manley Hopkins: Sonnets of Desolation: An Analysis of Meaning." Ph.D. Dissertation, Catholic University of America, 1952.

3544. Doherty, Francis. "A Note on Spelt From Sibyl's Leaves." Essays in Criticism, 14 (1964), 428-32.

Reply to Andor Gomme's article earlier in this same volume of Essays in Criticism (pp. 327-31).

3592

3545. Donoghue, Denis. "The Bird as Symbol: Hopkins's Windhover." Studies, 44 (1955), 291-99.

3546. Downes, David A. Gerard Manley Hopkins, a Study of His Ignatian Spirit. New York: Bookman Associates, 1959.

Chapter 5, "The Desolate Self of the Terrible Sonnets" (pp. 115-48).

3547. Downey, Harris. "A Poem Not Understood." Virginia Quarterly Review, 11 (1935), 506-17.

Discusses "The Windhover."

3548. Doyle, Francis G. "A Note on Hopkins' Windhover." Studies, 45 (1956), 88-91.

3549. Driscoll, John P. "Hopkins' 'Spring,' line 2 and 'Spring and Fall: To a Young Child,' line 2." Explicator, 24 (1965), Item 26.

3550. Driskell, Leon V. "The Progressive Structure of 'The Windhover'." Renascence, 19 (1966), 30-36.

3551. Dunlap, Elizabeth D. "Sound and Sense in 'Pied Beauty'." Hopkins Quarterly, 3 (1976), 35-38.

3552. Durr, Robert A. "Hopkins' 'No Worst, There is None'." Explicator, 11 (1952), Item 11.

3553. Eagleton, Terry. "Nature and the Fall in Hopkins: A Reading of 'God's Grandeur'." Essays in Criticism, 23 (1973), 68-75.

3554. Ebbatson, J.R. "The Windhover and Richard Jefferies." English, 23 (1974), 26-29.

3555. Eble, Joseph. "Levels of Awareness: A Reading of Hopkins' 'Felix Randal'." Victorian Poetry, 13 (1975), 129-35.

3556. Editors. [Reply to Jack Stillinger.] Notes and Queries, 204 (1959), 338.
3762

3557. Eleanor, Mother Mary, S.H.C.J. "Hopkins' 'Windhover' and Southwell's Hawk." Renascence, 15 (1962), 21-22, 27.

3558. Elkins, Bill J. "Gerard Manley Hopkins' 'Carrion Comfort'." Cresset, 33 (November, 1969), 8-13.

3559. Elkins, Bill James. "Hopkins' 'Terrible Sonnets': A Study of the Poetic Progression." Ph.D. Dissertation, Ohio, 1967. DA, 27 (1967), 4219A.

3560. Empson, William. "Hopkinsiana." TLS, October 1, 1954, p. 625.

Concerned with the word "buckle" in "The Windhover."

3561. Empson, William, and W.A.M. Peters, S.J. "Hopkinsiana." TLS, October 29, 1954, p. 689.

Empson disagrees with F.N. Lees's reading of "The Windhover" described in earlier letters to TLS. Peters explains the origin of Hopkins's dedication of "The Windhover," "To Christ Our Lord."

3644

3562. Empson, William. "The Windhover." TLS, May 20, 1955, p. 269.

3563. *Enozawa, Kazuyoshi. "Hopkins no shi: 'Taka'." Eigo Kyoiku, 17 (1969), 38.

On "The Windhover."

3564. Erzgraber, Willi. "Gerard Manley Hopkins: 'That Nature is a Heraclitean Fire and the Comfort of the Resurrection." Die Englische Lyrik: Von der Renaissance bis zur Gegenwart. Ed. Karl Heinz Goller. Dusseldorf: August Bagel, 1968, vol. 2, pp. 246-65, 448-51.

Includes a German translation.

3565. Fausset, Hugh I'Anson. Poets and Pundits: Essays and Addresses. London: Jonathan Cape, 1947.

In one essay, "Gerard Hopkins: A Centenary Tribute," Fausset includes comments about several sonnets (pp. 96-103); in another essay, "The Conflict of Priest and Poet in Hopkins," he discusses "Spelt from Sibyl's Leaves" (pp. 104-13).

3566. Ferns, John. "'The Windhover': Alone and in Context." English Studies in Canada, 1 (1975), 317-25.

3567. Festa, Conrad. "The Cow, the Finch, and the Trout in 'Pied Beauty'." Hopkins Quarterly, 2 (1975), 93-96.

3568. Fike, Francis. "The Problem of Motivation in 'No Worst, There is None'." Hopkins Quarterly, 2 (1976), 175-78.

3569. Foltz, William D. "Hopkins' Greek Fire." Victorian Poetry, 18 (1980), 23-34.

"That Nature is a Heraclitean Fire and of the Comfort of the Resurrection" primarily exhibits Hopkins's continual devotion to early Greek philosophy.

3570. Fraser, Ronald. "'The Windhover' Again." Downside Review, 85 (1967), 71-73.

3571. Frazier, Charles R. Hopkins's 'Andromeda'." Language of Poems, 8 (November, 1979), 5-9.

3572. Frost, David L. "'The Windhover': A Commentary." Theology, 72 (1969), 10-13.

3573. Fuger, Wilhelm. "Gerard Manley Hopkins am Werk: Zum Entstehungsprozess von The Starlight Night." Neueren Sprachen, NF 16 (1967), 428-39.

3574. Fulweiler, Howard W. Letters from the Darkling Plain: Language and the Grounds of Knowledge in the Poetry of Arnold and Hopkins. University of Missouri Studies, 58. Columbia: University of Missouri Press, 1972.

Deals with the "terrible sonnets" (pp. 144-63).

3575. Fussell, Paul, Jr. "A Note on 'The Windhover'." Modern Language Notes, 64 (1949), 271.

3576. Gafford, Charlotte K. "Hopkins' 'God's Grandeur,' 3-4." Explicator, 29 (1970), Item 21.

3577. Gallet, R. "A Note on the Relationship Between 'The Windhover' and 'Hurrahing in Harvest'." Hopkins Quarterly, 5 (1978), 75-77.

3578. Gardner, Stephen L. "'The Caged Skylark'." Language of Poems, 1, ii (1972), 2-7.

3579. Gardner, W.H. Gerard Manley Hopkins (1844-1889): A Study of Poetic Idiosyncrasy in Relation to Poetic Tradition. 2 vols. London: Martin Secker and Warburg, 1944; rev. 1948. London: Oxford University Press, 1958.

In Vol. 1, Ch. 3, there is a major discussion on "Sonnet Morphology" (pp. 71-108) with comments about sonnets throughout.

3580. Gardner, W.H. "Hopkins and Newman." TLS, September 15, 1966, p. 868.

Responds to Vickers's article on "Carrion Comfort."
3787

3581. Gardner, W.H. "The Religious Problem in G.M. Hopkins." Scrutiny, 6 (1937), 32-42.

Discusses "The Windhover" and several of the later "terrible sonnets."

3582. Gardner, W.H. "The Windhover." TLS, June 24, 1955, p. 349.

3583. Gatlin, Barbara M. "A Reading of G.M. Hopkins' 'The Starlight Night'." Language of Poems, 5, i (1976), 17-21.

3584. Gavin, Sister Rosemarie Julie. "Hopkins' 'The Candle Indoors'." Explicator, 20 (1962), Item 50.

3585. Gibson, William M. "Hopkins' 'To R.B'." Explicator, 6 (1947), Item 12.

3586. Gidion, Jurgen. "Gerard Manley Hopkins: 'No Worst, there is None'." Die Englische Lyrik: Von der Renaissance bis zur Gegenwart. Ed. Karl Heinz Goller. Dusseldorf: August Bagel, 1968, vol. 2, pp. 266-75.

In his explication Gidion notes a connection between Hopkins's image of falling off a cliff with Gloucester's speech in Lear (IV.i.1-9).

3587. Giovannini, Giovanni. "A Literal Gloss of Hopkins' 'The Windhover'." Linguistic and Literary Studies in Honour of Helmut A. Hatzfeld. Ed. Alessandro S. Crisafulli. Washington: Catholic University of America Press, 1964, pp. 203-12.

3588. Giovannini, Margaret. "Hopkins' 'The Caged Skylark'." Explicator, 14 (1956), Item 35.

3589. Giovannini, Margaret. "Hopkins' 'God's Grandeur'." Explicator, 24 (1965), Item 36.

3590. Glavin, J.J. "'The Exercise of Saints': Hopkins, Milton, and Patience." Texas Studies in Literature and Language, 20 (1978), 139-52.

Considers the relation between Milton's sonnet "On His Blindness" (Sonnet 19) and Hopkins's "Patience, hard thing!"

3591. Goldsmith, Robert H. "The Selfless Self: Hopkins' Late Sonnets." Hopkins Quarterly, 3 (1976), 67-75.

3592. Gomme, Andor. "A Note on Two Hopkins Sonnets." Essays in Criticism, 14 (1964), 327-31.

On "Spelt from Sibyl's Leaves" and "Thou art Indeed Just, Lord."
3544

3593. Goodin, George. "Man and Nature in Hopkins' 'Ribblesdale'." Notes and Queries, 204 (1959), 453-54.

3594. Gorecki, John E. "A Reading of 'Harry Ploughman'." Language of Poems, 2, i (1973), 2-6.

3595. Grady, Thomas S. "Windhover's Meaning." America, 70 (1944), 465-66.

3596. Greene, Dorothy Mary. "An Explication of the 'Question and Answer' Sonnets of Gerard Manley Hopkins." Ph.D. Dissertation, St. Johns University, 1974. DAI, 35 (1975), 5344A.

3597. Greiner, Brother Francis, S.M. "Hopkins' 'The Windhover' Viewed as a Nature Poem." Renascence, 15 (1963), 68-75, 95.

3598. Grigson, Geoffrey. Gerard Manley Hopkins. Writers and Their Work, 59. London: Longmans, Green, 1955.

3599. Guardini, Romano. "Aesthetisch-theologische Gedanken zu Gerard Manley Hopkins' Sonett 'Der Sturmfalke'." Unterscheidung und Bewahrung: Festschrift fur Hermann Kunisch zum 60. Geburtstag. Ed. Klaus Lazarowicz und Wolfgang Kron. Berlin: de Gruyter, 1961, pp. 170-74.
3600

3600. Guardini, Romano. "Aesthetic-Theological Thoughts on 'The Windhover'." Hopkins: A Collection of Critical Essays. Ed. Geoffrey H. Hartman. Englewood Cliffs, N.J.: Prentice-Hall, 1966, pp. 76-79.

Translated from the German by Geoffrey Hartman and Christopher Levenson: "Aesthetisch-Theologische Gedanken zu Hopkins' Gedicht 'Der Sturmfalke'." Sprache--Dichtung--Deutung. Wurzburg: Werkbund Verlag, 1962.

3601. Guzie, Tad W., S.J. "Are Modern Poets Morbid?" Catholic World, 185 (1957), 27-32.

On "God's Grandeur."

3602. Gwynn, Frederick L. "Hopkins' 'The Windhover': A New Simplification." Modern Language Notes, 66 (1951), 366-70.

3603. Haas, Charles Eugene. "A Structural Analysis of Selected Sonnets of Gerard Manley Hopkins." Ph.D. Dissertation, Denver, 1964. DA, 25 (1965), 5443.

3604. Haas, Rudolf. "Gerard Manley Hopkins: 'Spring'." Die Englische Lyrik: Von der Renaissance bis zur Gegenwart. Ed. Karl Heinz Goller. Dusseldorf: August Bagel, 1968, vol. 2, pp. 237-45, 447-48.

Includes a German translation of the poem.

3605. Hafezi, F.V. "Hopkins's Method of Composition." Month, 246 (1980), 131-35, 165-69.

An examination of the revisions made by Hopkins as he composed several of his sonnets.

3606. Hallgarth, Susan A. "A Study of Hopkins' Use of Nature." Victorian Poetry, 5 (1967), 79-92.

Although the article is not about sonnets specifically, the writer comments frequently about them.

3607. Hardy, Barbara. Forms and Feelings in the Sonnets of Gerard Manley Hopkins. The Hopkins Society First Annual Lecture Given at University College, London, 12 February 1970. London: Hopkins Society, 1970.

3608. Harrison, Thomas P. "The Birds of Gerard Manley Hopkins." Studies in Philology, 54 (1957), 448-63.

Among the sonnets in which birds play an important part are "The Caged Skylark," "The Sea and the Skylark" and, of course, "The Windhover."

3609. Hartman, Geoffrey. The Unmediated Vision: An Interpretation of Wordsworth, Hopkins, Rilke and Valery. New Haven: Yale University Press, 1954.

On "The Windhover"(pp.48-67).

3610. Haskell, Ann Sullivan. "An Image of 'The Windhover'." Victorian Poetry, 6 (1968), 75-77.

3611. Haydock, James. "What The Windhover Says." Wisconsin Studies in Literature, 6 (1969), 27-38.

3612. Hentz, Ann L. "Language in Hopkins' 'Carrion Comfort'." Victorian Poetry, 9 (1971), 343-47.

3613. Heuser, Alan. The Shaping Vision of Gerard Manley Hopkins. London: Oxford University Press, 1958.

Comments on sonnets throughout.

3614. Hill, Archibald A. "An Analysis of The Windhover: An Experiment in Structural Method." PMLA, 70 (1955), 968-78. Reprinted as "An Analysis of The Windhover" in Englische Lyrik von Shakespeare bis Dylan Thomas. Ed. Willi Erzgraber. Darmstadt: Wissenschaftliche Buchgesellschaft, 1969, pp. 333-46. Also reprinted as "An Analysis of The Windhover: An Experiment in Method" in Constituent and Pattern in Poetry. Austin: University of Texas Press, 1976, pp. 28-38.

3615. Hill, Archibald A. "'The Windhover' Revisited: Linguistic Analysis of Poetry Reassessed." Texas Studies in Literature and Language, 7 (1966), 349-59.

3616. *Hirata, Tomiko. "G.M. Hopkins no 'Bokuyosha no Hitai mo' Ichi Kosatsu." [G.M. Hopkins's 'The shepherd's brow, fronting forked lightning, owns': A Consideration.] Shirayuri Joshi Daigaku Kenkyu Kiyo, No. 7 (December, 1972), 73-91.

3617. Holloway, Marcella M. "The Game-Motif in G.M. Hopkins' Sonnets." Hopkins Quarterly, 7 (1980), 101-08.

3618. Holloway, Sister Marcella M., C.S.J. "Hopkins' Sonnet 65 (No Worst, there is None)." Explicator, 14 (1956), Item 51.

3619. Hood, Sharon Ann. "Discordant Voices: Hopkins, Rossetti, and the Sonnet." Ph.D. Dissertation, Texas, 1980. DAI, 41 (1981), 4720A.

The similarities and differences between Hopkins and the pre-Raphaelites can be seen in the respective treatment of the sonnet by Hopkins and Rossetti.

3620. Hopkins, Gerard Manley. The Poems of Gerard Manley Hopkins. Ed. W.H. Gardner and N.H. MacKenzie. London: H. Milford, 1918. 4th ed. rev. and enl., London: Oxford University Press, 1967.

3621. Howard, John D. "Letter to the Editor." College English, 19 (1958), 312.

An objection to Peter Lisca's interpretation of "The Windhover."
3646

3622. Humiliata, Sister Mary. "Hopkins and the Prometheus Myth." PMLA, 70 (1955), 58-68.

On Sonnet 65 ("No worst, there is none").

3623. Hunter, Jim. Gerard Manley Hopkins. London: Evans, 1966.

Chapters 4-6 examine, respectively, "The 1877 Sonnets," "Poems 1878-1883" and "Last Poems" (pp. 64-105).

3624. Huntley, John F. "Hopkins' 'The Windhover' as a Prayer of Request." Renascence, 16 (1964), 154-62.

3625. Irwin, Robert. "Hopkins' 'God's Grandeur,' 3-4." Explicator, 31 (1973), Item 46.

3626. Jayantha, R.A. "The Dedication of 'The Windhover'." Literary Criterion, 10, i (1971), 21-27.

3627. Jayantha, R.A. "Does the 'Falcon' in 'The Windhover' Really Dive?" Literary Criterion, 11, ii (1974), 19-28.

3628. Johnson, Michael L. "Hopkins, Heraclitus, Cosmic Instress and of the Comfort of the Resurrection." Victorian Poetry, 10 (1972), 235-42.

3629. Johnson, W. Stacy. Gerard Manley Hopkins: The Poet as Victorian. Ithaca, N.Y.: Cornell University Press, 1968.

In addition to references to Sonnets throughout, there are two chapters devoted to "The Windhover" (pp. 77-97) and "That Nature Is a Heraclitean Fire" (pp. 125-63), respectively.

3630. Jordan, Frank, Jr. "Hopkins' 'The Caged Skylark'." Explicator, 28 (1970), Item 80.

3631. Joselyn, Sister M., O.S.B. "Herbert and Hopkins: Two Lyrics." Renascence, 10 (1958), 192-95.

On "Carrion Comfort."

3632. *Kasahara, Kei. "Hopkins' use of language in 'No worst'." Bulletin of the Hopkins Society of Japan, 2 (March, 1973), 38-43.

In Japanese

3633. Kelly, Bernard. The Mind and Poetry of Gerard Manley Hopkins, S.J. London: Pepler and Sewell, 1935. rpt. New York: Haskell House, 1971.

3634. Kelly, Hugh, S.J. "The Windhover--and Christ." Studies, 45 (1956), 188-93.

3635. King, Anne R. "Hopkins' 'Windhover' and Blake." English Studies, 37 (1956), 245-52.

3636. Kopper, Edward A., Jr. "Hopkins' 'The Windhover'." Explicator, 22 (1964), Item 54.

Discusses line 14.

3637. *Kopschlitz, Maria Helena Peixoto. "Algumas Notas em Torno dos 'Sonetos Terriveis' de Gerard Hopkins." VOZES, 70, ii (1976), 103-12.

3638. *Koriyama, Naoshi. "God's Grandeur--An Essay." Hopkins Research (Japan), No. 4 (1975), 34-37.

3639. *Kudo, Yoshimi. "Shi ni okeru Ambiguity ni tsuite-Hopkins no The Windhover wo Chushin ni." Eigo Seinen, 117 (1972), 666-70, 734-35.

Concerning the continuing ambiguity in Hopkins's poetry, with particular reference to "The Windhover."

3640. Kuhn, Joaquin. "The Completeness of 'Pied Beauty'." Studies in English Literature, 1500-1900, 18 (1978), 677-92.

3641. *Kuzumi, Kazushi. "Hopkins no The Candle Indoors ni tsuite." Ronshu (Ippan-kyoikubu-kai, Aoyama Gakuin Daigaku), 14 (February, 1974), 63-71.

Interpretation of "The Candle Indoors."

3642. Lahey, Gerald F., S.J. Gerard Manley Hopkins. London: Oxford University Press, 1930.

In his chapters called "The Craftsman" and "The Artist," (pp. 87-123), Lahey devotes considerable space to a discussion of the sonnets.

3643. Lees, F.N. "The Windhover." Scrutiny, 17 (1950), 32-37.

3644. Lees, F.N. "Hopkinsiana." TLS, September 3, 1954, p. 557; October 22, 1954, p. 673.

On "The Windhover"--the first in response to a review of J.M. Guttierrez Mora, Hopkinsiana (TLS, August 13, 1954, pp. 509-10), the second to a letter by Oswald Couldrey.
3540, 3816

3645. Leggio, James. "Hopkins and Alchemy." Renascence, 29 (1977), 115-30.

Most of the poems he discusses are the sonnets.

3646. Lisca, Peter. "The Return of 'The Windhover'." College English, 19 (1957), 124-26.

3647. Litzinger, Boyd. "The Pattern of Ascent in Hopkins." Victorian Poetry, 2 (1964), 43-47.

Two of the three poems he discusses are sonnets: "As Kingfishers Catch Fire," and "That Nature is a Heraclitean Fire."

3648. Litzinger, Boyd. "Once More, 'The Windhover'." Victorian Poetry, 5 (1967), 228-30.

3649. Litzinger, Boyd. "'To Seem the Stranger . . .'." Hopkins Quarterly, 1 (1974), 41-42.

3650. Loomis, Jeffrey B. "Chatter with a Just Lord: Hopkins' Final Sonnets of Quiescent Terror." Hopkins Quarterly, 7 (1980), 47-64.

3651. Ludwig, Hans-Werner. Barbarous in Beauty. Studien zum vers in Gerard Manley Hopkins' Sonetten. Munchen: Wilhelm Fink, 1972.

3652. Lynch, Joseph Anthony. "The Prosodic Practice of Gerard Manley Hopkins With Emphasis on the Sonnets." Ph.D. Dissertation, Catholic University of America, 1979. DAI, 40 (1980), 4607A-08A.

The study concentrates on rhythm.

3653. MacKenzie, Norman H. "Gerard Manley Hopkins' 'Spelt from Sibyl's Leaves'." Malahat Review, No. 26 (1973), 218-28.

Variorum readings and commentary.

3654. MacKenzie, Norman H. "The Making of a Hopkins Sonnet: 'Spelt from Sibyl's Leaves'." A Festschrift for Edgar Ronald Seary: Essays in English Language and Literature Presented by Colleagues and Former Students. Ed. A.A. MacDonald, P.A. O'Flaherty, and G.M. Story. St. Johns: Memorial University of Newfoundland, 1975, pp. 151-69.

3655. MacKenzie, Norman H. A Reader's Guide to Gerard Manley Hopkins. Ithaca, N.Y.: Cornell University Press, 1981.

Offers comments, in many cases detailed, on each of the poems in the Hopkins canon.

3656. Mann, James. "A Reading of 'That Nature is a Heraclitean Fire and of the Comfort of the Resurrection'." Language of Poetry, 2, i (1973), 7-15.

3657. Mariani, Paul L. "Hopkins' 'Felix Randall' as Sacramental Vision." Renascence, 19 (1967), 217-20.

3658. Mariani, Paul Louis. "Artistic and Spiritual Development in the Sonnets of Gerard Manley Hopkins, 1865-1889." Ph.D. Dissertation, City University of New York, 1968. DA, 28 (1968), 4639A-40A.

3659. Mariani, Paul L. "The Artistic and Tonal Integrity of Hopkins' 'The Shepherd's Brow'." Victorian Poetry, 6 (1968), 63-68.

3660. Mariani, Paul Louis. A Commentary on the Complete Poems of Gerard Manley Hopkins. Ithaca, N.Y.: Cornell University Press, 1970.

See in particular Appendix A, "Hopkins and the Sonnet" (pp. 318-29).

3661. Mariani, Paul L. "Hopkins' 'Andromeda' and the New Aestheticism." Victorian Poetry, 11 (1973), 39-54.

3662. Marsh, Derick. "Part, Pen, Pack: A Critical Reading of Two Poems by G.M. Hopkins." Balcony, No. 2 (1965), pp. 19-27.

A discussion of "God's Grandeur." See Norman Talbot for a reply.
3771

3663. Matchett, William H. "An Analysis of 'The Windhover'." PMLA, 72 (1957), 310-11.

3664. Mathison, John K. "The Poetic Theory of Gerard Manley Hopkins." Philological Quarterly, 26 (1947), 21-35.

Mathison uses the sonnet, "Tom's Garland," to illustrate what Hopkins meant when he used the term "explosive" (pp. 29-31).

3665. McChesney, Donald. A Hopkins Commentary: An Explanatory Commentary on the Main Poems, 1876-89. London: University of London Press, 1968.

3666. McDaniel, John N. "The 'Blight' in Hopkins! 'Spring and Fall': A Reinterpretation." Xavier University Studies, 9, iii (1970), 16-20.

3667. McLuhan, Herbert Marshall. "The Analogical Mirrors." Kenyon Review, 6 (1944), 322-32. Reprinted in Gerard Manley Hopkins by the Kenyon Critics. Norfolk, Conn.: New Directions Books, 1945, pp. 15-27; and in Hopkins: A Collection of Critical Essays. Ed. Geoffrey H. Hartman. Englewood Cliffs, N.J.: Prentice-Hall, 1966, pp. 80-88.

Deals primarily with "The Windhover."

3668. McNamara, Peter L. "Motivation and Meaning in the 'Terrible Sonnets'." Renascence, 16 (1964), 78-80, 94.

3669. McQueen, William A. "'The Windhover' and 'St. Alphonsus Rodriguez'." Victorian Newsletter, No. 23 (1963), 25-26.

3670. Mellown, Elgin W. "Hopkins, Hall Caine, and D.G. Rossetti." Notes and Queries, 204 (1959), 109-10.

Speaks of an occasion when Hall Caine rejected some sonnets that Hopkins submitted to him for publication.

3671. Mercer, W.C. "G.M. Hopkins and Richard Jefferies." Notes and Queries, 197 (1952), 217.

See E.E. Phare for an answer to this query about "The Windhover."
3703

3672. Miller Bruce E. "On 'The Windhover'." Victorian Poetry, 2 (1964), 115-19.

3673. Milward, Peter, S.J. A Commentary on the Sonnets of G.M. Hopkins. Tokyo: Hokuseido Press, 1969.

3674. *Milward, Peter, S.J. "Hopkins' Sonnets." The Meaning of English Masterpieces. Ed. Hideo Okamoto and Takao Suzuki. Tokyo: Kaibunsha, 1973.

3675. Milward, Peter. "On 'Sonnet on Spring' by G.M. Hopkins." A New Anthology of English Literature. Ed. Naoshi Koriyama. Tokyo: Hokyseido, 1969, pp. 276-80.

3676. Mizuta, Keiko. "That Nature is a Heraclitean Fire and of the Comfort of the Resurrection." Bulletin of the Hopkins Society of Japan, 2 (March, 1973), 33-37.

3677. Monsman, Gerald. "Hopkins and the 'here/Buckle!' of Creation." Hopkins Quarterly, 5 (1978), 23-31.

3678. Montag, George E. "Hopkins' 'God's Grandeur' and 'The Ooze of Oil Crushed'." Victorian Poetry, 1 (1963), 302-03.

3679. Montag, George E. "'The Windhover': Crucifixion and Redemption." Victorian Poetry, 3 (1965), 109-18.

3680. Moore, Michael D. "Newman and the Motif of Intellectual Pain in Hopkins' 'Terrible Sonnets'." Mosaic, 12, iv (1979), 29-46.

3681. Morgan, Edwin. "A Hopkins Phrase." TLS, May 27, 1949, p. 347.

Rejects Nicol's reading of "gash gold-vermilion."
3686

3682. *Muller-Schwefe, Gerhard. "Gerard Manley Hopkins: 'Spelt From Sibyl's Leaves'." Die moderne englische Lyrik: Interpretationen. Ed. Horst Oppel. Berlin: E. Schmidt, 1967, pp. 39-48.

3683. Murphy, Christina J. "Inverted Religious Imagery in Hopkins' 'Carrion Comfort'." University of Mississippi Studies in English, 13 (1972), 1-5.

3684. *Nagata, Yoshiko. "An Essay on Hopkins's Sonnets: In the Light of Duns Scotus." Fuji Joshi Daigaku, Tanki Daigaku Kiyo, 12 (December, 1974), 45-66.

3685. Nassar, Eugene Paul. "Hopkins, Figura, and Grace: God's Better Beauty." Renascence, 17 (1965), 128-30, 136.

Includes discussions of "To What Serves Mortal Beauty" and "Spelt from Sibyl's Leaves."

3686. Nicol, B. De Bear. "A Hopkins Phrase." TLS, May 13, 1949, p. 313.

Offers a new reading of "gash gold-vermilion" from "The Windhover." See Sansom and Morgan for replies.
3681, 3737

3687. Noel, Sister Mary. "Gathering to a Greatness: A Study of 'God's Grandeur'." English Journal, 53 (1964), 285-87.

3688. Nolan, Gerard L. "'The Windhover'." TLS, June 24, 1955, p. 349; August 5, 1955, p. 445.

3689. *Noorman-Boersma, A.A. "A Holy Sonnet and a Terrible Sonnet." Groningen, 1974, doctoraalscriptie.

3690. *Noppen, L.M. van. "The Last Rub: A Study of Gerard Manley Hopkins' 'The shepherd's brow'." Groningen, 1977, doctoraalscriptie.

3691. O'Brien, M.D., S.J. "Hurrahing in Harvest and some Central Motifs in G.M. Hopkins' Poetry." English Literature and Language (Sophia University, Japan), 10 (1973), 23-31.

3692. O'Brien, M.D., S.J. "'In Honour of St. Alphonsus Rodriguez,' and the Concept of Honour." Hopkins Research (Japan), No. 4 (1975), 11-16.

3693. *Omichi, Suekichi. "1877-nen ni okeru G.M. Hopkins no 14-gyo-shi." (On the 1877 Sonnets of G.M. Hopkins.) Takachiho Ronso 1970 (1971), pp. 1-33.

3694. Ong, Walter J., S.J. "Bird, Horse, and Chevalier in Hopkins' 'Windhover'." Hopkins Quarterly, 1 (1974), 61-75.

3695. *P., A.E. "Poetic Content of Hopkins's Sonnet." Daily Telegraph (London), January 11, 1971, p. 10.

3696. Pace, George B. "On the Octave Rhymes of The Windhover." English Language Notes, 2 (1965), 285-86.

3697. Page, Philip. "Unity and Subordination in 'Carrion Comfort'." Victorian Poetry, 14 (1976), 25-32.

3698. Payne, Michael. "Syntactical Analysis and 'The Windhover'." Renascence, 19 (1967), 88-92.

3699. Peirce, William P. "The Structural Unity of 'Spelt from Sibyl's Leaves'." Renascence, 23 (1971), 213-19.

3700. Pendexter, Hugh, III. "Hopkins' 'God's Grandeur,' 1-2." Explicator, 23 (1964), Item 2.

3701. Pepper, Stephen C. The Basis of Criticism In the Arts. Cambridge, Mass.: Harvard University Press, 1945.

Having developed "four definitional criteria" for criticism, Pepper applies his critical instruments to Shakespeare's Sonnet 30 and Hopkins's sonnet, "I wake and feel the fell of dark, not day." The final judgment is that Hopkins's sonnet is far inferior to Shakespeare's (pp. 115-41).

3702. Peters, W.A.M., S.J. Gerard Manley Hopkins: A Critical Essay Towards the Understanding of His Poetry. London: Oxford, 1948.

3703. Phare, Elsie Elizabeth. "Gerard Hopkins and Richard Jefferies." Notes and Queries, 200 (1955), 318.

On "The Windhover."

3704. Phare, Elsie Elizabeth. The Poetry of Gerard Manley Hopkins: A Survey and Commentary. Cambridge: University Press, 1933. rpt. New York: Russell and Russell, 1967.

3705. Pick, John. Gerard Manley Hopkins: Priest and Poet. New York: Oxford University Press, 1942. 1966.

Chapter 4, "Poems 1877-8" (pp. 52-72), discusses major sonnets. Chapter 8, "Last Poems 1884-9" (pp. 138-55), is on the "terrible sonnets."

3706. Pick, John. Gerard Manley Hopkins: "The Windhover." Merrill Casebooks. Columbus, Ohio: Charles E. Merrill, 1969.

3707. *Pick, John. "Hopkins and 'Ribblesdale'." Stonyhurst Magazine, 39 (1976), 337-43.

3708. Pick, John. "Approaches to Hopkins's 'The Windhover'." Durham University Journal, 71 (1978), 85-89.

3709. Pitchford, Lois W. "The Curtal Sonnets of Gerard Manley Hopkins." Modern Language Notes, 67 (1952), 165-69.

3710. Pouncey, Lorene. "An Analysis of Hopkins' 'Terrible' Sonnet, No. 65, 'No Worst'." Critical Survey, (1966), 242-45.

3711. Proffitt, Edward Louis Francis. "The Structure of Experience: Explications of the Mature Poems of G.M. Hopkins." Ph.D. Dissertation, Columbia, 1967. DA, 31 (1970), 1288A.

3712. Proffitt, Edward. "Hopkins, 'Dead Letters'." Hopkins Quarterly, 4 (1977), 16.

On "I wake and feel the fell of dark, not day."

3713. Proffitt, Edward. "Hopkins' 'ooze of oil / Crushed Once More'." Concerning Poetry, 10, ii (1977), 61-64.

3714. Proffitt, Edward. "Tone and Contrast in Hopkins' 'The Starlight Night'." Hopkins Quarterly, 5 (1978), 47-50.

3715. Rackin, Donald. "'God's Grandeur': Hopkins' Sermon to Wordsworth." Wordsworth Circle, 11 (1980), 66-73.

Hopkins's sonnet seems to be a response to Wordsworth's sonnet, "The world is too much with us."

3716. Rader, Louis. "Hopkins' Dark Sonnets: Another New Expression." Victorian Poetry, 5 (1967), 13-20.

3717. Rader, Louis. "Romantic Structure and Theme in 'The Windhover'." Hopkins Quarterly, 2 (1975), 79-92.

3718. Rader, Louis. "An Important Echo in Hopkins' 'The Windhover'." Hopkins Quarterly, 3 (1976), 77-79.

3719. R[aine], C[raig]. "Gerard Manley Hopkins: Harry Ploughman: Yokel-Beauty." TLS, September 21, 1973, p. 56.

3720. Reiman, Donald H. "Hopkins' 'Ooze of Oil' Rises Again." Victorian Poetry, 4 (1966), 39-42.

On "God's Grandeur."

3721. Richards, Bernard. "Hopkins' 'To Oxford (II)'." Explicator, 33 (1974), Item 24.

Refutes a reading given by Sulloway in Gerard Manley Hopkins and the Victorian Temper.
3766

3722. Richards, Bertrand F. "Meaning in Hopkins' 'Carrion Comfort'." Renascence, 27 (1974), 45-50.

3723. Richards, I.A. "Gerard Hopkins." Dial, 81 (1926), 195-203.

Discusses "The Windhover," "Spelt from Sibyl's Leaves," "Carrion Comfort," "No Worst There is None."

3724. Richards, Michael. "An Analysis of Gerard Manley Hopkins' 'The Candle Indoors'." Language of Poems, 5, i (1976), 2-5.

3725. Ritz, J.-G. "The Windhover." TLS, (May 6, 1955), p. 237.

3726. Ritz, Jean-Georges. "The Windhover de G.M. Hopkins." Etudes Anglaises, 9 (1956), 14-22.

3727. Ritz, Jean-Georges. Le Poete Gerard Manley Hopkins, S.J. (1844-1889): Sa Vie et Son Oeuvre. Paris: Didier, 1963.

In the second part of the book, he devotes a section (pp. 472-501) to "Les Sonnets."

3728. Rogers, Robert. "Hopkins' Carrion Comfort." Hopkins Quarterly, 7 (1980), 143-66.

A psychoanalytical approach to the sonnet.

3729. Rooney, William Joseph. "'Spelt from Sibyl's Leaves'--A Study in Contrasting Methods of Evaluation." Journal of Aesthetics and Art Criticism, 13 (1955), 507-19.

3730. Rose, Alan M. "Hopkins' 'Carrion Comfort': The Artful Disorder of Prayer." Victorian Poetry, 15 (1977), 207-17.

3731. Rosebury, B.J. "Hopkins: A Note on Scansion." Cambridge Quarterly, 8 (1979), 230-35.

Illustrates his thesis by discussing several of Hopkins's late sonnets.

3732. Rudanko, Juhani. "Gerard Manley Hopkins's 'The Windhover': An Explication." Neuphilologische Mitteilungen, 81 (1980), 174-86.

3733. Ruggles, Eleanor. Gerard Manley Hopkins, A Life. New York: Norton, 1944. Port Washington, N.Y.: Kennikat Press, 1969.

Discusses various sonnets throughout.

3734. *Russell, Gene. "The Teaching of Explication: A Reading of Hopkin's [sic] 'That Nature is a Heraclitean Fire and of the Comfort of the Resurrection'." Es (Univ. de Vallodolid), 1 (1971), 197-211.

3735. Russell, Jeremy F.J. A Critical Commentary on Gerard Manley Hopkins's "Poems." Macmillan Critical Commentaries. London: Macmillan, 1971.

3736. *Saito, Masako. "'The Windhover' and 'Over Sir John's Hill'." Hopkins Research (Japan), 3 (March, 1974), 53-56.

3737. Sansom, Clive. "A Hopkins Phrase." TLS, May 20, 1949, p. 329.

Rejects Nicol's reading of "gash gold-vermilion" in "The Windhover."
3686

3738. *Sato, Misao. "Hopkins and Critics on the 'Terrible Sonnets'." Shirayuri Joshi Daigaku Kenkyu Kiyo, 10 (February, 1974), 81-98.

3739. Schafer, Gerhard. "Das rhythmische Leitmotiv als strukturbildendes Element in zwei Sonetten G.M. Hopkins'." Festschrift fur Kurt Herbert Halbach zum 70. Geburtstag am 25 Juni 1972. Ed. Rose B. Schafer-Maulbetsch, Manfred G. Scholz, and Gunther Schweikle. Goppingen Arbeiten zur Germanistik, 70. Goppingen: Kummerle, 1972, pp. 453-66.

3740. Schlepper, Wolfgang. "Gerard Manley Hopkins: 'Spring'." Literatur in Wissenschaft und Unterricht, 4 (1971), 40-44.

3741. Schneider, Elisabeth W. The Dragon in the Gate: Studies in the Poetry of G.M. Hopkins. Perspectives in Criticism, 20. Berkeley and Los Angeles: University of California Press, 1968.

Chapter 7 deals with "Three Baroque Sonnets" ("The Windhover," "Spelt from Sibyl's Leaves," "That Nature is a Heraclitean Fire").

3742. Schneider, Elisabeth. "Hopkins' 'My Own Heart Let Me More Have Pity On'." Explicator, 5 (1947), Item 51; 7 (1949), Item 49.

3743. Schneider, Elisabeth W. "Hopkins' 'The Windhover'." Explicator, 18 (1960), Item 22. Reprinted in Gerard Manley Hopkins: Poems: A Casebook. Ed. Margaret Bottrall. London: Macmillan, 1975, pp. 183-85.

3744. Schoder, Raymond V., S.J. "Spelt from Sibyl's Leaves." Thought, 19 (1944), 633-48.

3745. Schoder, Raymond V., S.J. "What Does The Windhover Mean?" The Immortal Diamond: Studies in Gerard Manley Hopkins. Ed. Norman Weyand. New York: Sheed and Ward, 1949, pp. 275-306.

3746. *Schrage, F. "John Donne's 'Batter my heart, three person'd God' and Gerard Manley Hopkins's 'Thou art indeed just, Lord': A Comparison." Doctoraalscriptie, Groningen, 1974.

3747. Scott, Charles T. "Towards a Formal Poetics: Metrical Patterning in 'The Windhover'." Language and Style, 7 (1974), 91-107.

3748. Seland, John. "'God's Grandeur': An Explication. Hopkins Review, No. 8 (September, 1979), 5-8.

3749. *Seland, John, S.V.D. "The Starlight Night." Hopkins Research (Japan), No. 6 (1977), 10-13.

3750. Shea, F.X., S.J. "Another Look at 'The Windhover'." Victorian Poetry, 2 (1964), 219-39.

3751. Sherwood, H.C. "Hopkins' 'Spelt from Sibyl's Leaves'." Explicator, 15 (1956), Item 5.

3752. Shimane, Kunio. "The Sonnet of 'Endeavour': 'Thou art indeed just, Lord . . .'." Hopkins Quarterly, 7 (1980), 65-81.

Shimane discusses Hopkins's use of the sonnet form, confining himself to some of the major techniques and devices used in the "Thou art" sonnet.

3753. Silverstein, Henry. "On 'Tom's Garland'." Accent, 7 (1947), 67-81.

The circumstances surrounding the composition of "Tom's Garland" provides insight into Hopkins's diction in this unconventional sonnet.

3754. Slakey, Roger L. "The Grandeur in Hopkins' 'God's Grandeur'." Victorian Poetry, 7 (1969), 159-63.

3755. Smith, Julian. "Hopkins' 'Spring and Fall: To a Young Child'." Explicator, 27 (1969), Item 36.

Without the ninth line, the poem becomes a sonnet.

3756. Sprinker, Michael. A Counterpoint of Dissonance: The Aesthetics and Poetry of Gerard Manley Hopkins. Baltimore: Johns Hopkins University Press, 1980.

The text contains ample discussions of most of the principal sonnets.

3757. Stauffer, Ruth M. "Note on the Genesis of Hopkins' Sonnets of 1885." Renascence, 22 (1969), 43-48.

3758. Stempel, Daniel. "A Reading of 'The Windhover'." College English, 23 (1962), 305-07.

3759. Stephenson, A.A., S.J. "G.M. Hopkins and John Donne." Downside Review, 77 (1959), 300-20.

Examines the relationship between and relative merits of Donne's Holy Sonnets and Hopkins's poetry.

3760. Stevens, Sr. Mary Dominic, O.P. "Hopkins' 'That Nature Is a Heraclitean Fire'." Explicator, 22 (1963), Item 18.

3761. Stiles, G.W. "Nature's Bonfire--a brief examination of the imagery in Hopkins's 'That Nature is a Heraclitean Fire'." Unisa English Studies, No. 2 (June, 1967), 49-56.

3762. Stillinger, Jack. "Hopkins' 'Skate's Heel' in 'The Windhover'." Notes and Queries, 204 (1959), 215-16.

3763. *Stoenescu, Stefan. "Optiune si tentativa in creatia lui Gerard Manley Hopkins citeva observatii asupra evolutiei sensului in 'Binsey Poplars' si 'Felix Randal'." [Commitment and Tentativeness in G.M. Hopkins' Poetry: Some Remarks on the Development of Meaning in 'Binsey Poplars' and 'Felix Randal.'] Analele Universitatii Bucuresti: Limbi Germanice, 20 (1971), 135-44.

Romanian with English abstract.

3764. Stoneman, Patricia. "Hopkins: 'The Windhover: To Christ Our Lord'." Critical Survey, 6 (Summer, 1973), 81-85.

3765. Stonum, Gary L. "The Hermeneutics of 'Spelt from Sibyl's Leaves'." Hopkins Quarterly, 3 (1976), 117-29.

3766. Sulloway, Alison G. Gerard Manley Hopkins and the Victorian Temper. New York: Columbia University Press, 1972.

Sonnets discussed throughout.

3767. Sulloway, Alison G. "St. Ignatius Loyola and the Victorian Temper: Hopkins' Windhover as Symbol of 'Diabolic Gravity'." Hopkins Quarterly, 1 (1974), 43-51.

3768. Swinden, Patrick. "Gerard Manley Hopkins: 'The Starlight Night'." Critical Quarterly, 21, ii (1979), 57-60.

3769. *Takata, Hisatoshi. "Maguso Daka." Gaigo Bungaku, No. 8 (March, 1971), 48-50.

Japanese translation of "The Windhover" with some comments.

3770. *Takata, Hisatoshi. "The Windhover." Bulletin of the Hopkins Society of Japan, No. 1 (March, 1972), 13-15.

3771. *Talbot, Norman. "A Note on 'God's Grandeur'." Balcony, No. 3 (1965), p. 46.

Reply to Derick Marsh.
3662

3772. *Tamura, Kazuo. "G.M. Hopkins no Sonnet, 'To what serves Mortal Beauty?'." Soundings, No. 4 (1973), 21-35.

3773. Taylor, Michael. "Hopkins' 'God's Grandeur,' 3-4." Explicator, 25 (1967), Item 68.

3774. Templeman, William D. "Ruskin's Ploughshare and Hopkins' 'The Windhover'." English Studies, 43 (1962), 103-06.

Hopkins's use of the 'plow concept" may have been influenced by Ruskin--particularly by a passage from "Ad Valorem," an essay which appeared originally in Cornhill Magazine (November, 1860).

3775. Therese, Sister, S.N.D. "Hopkins' 'Spelt From Sibyl's Leaves'." Explicator, 17 (1959), Item 45.

3776. Thigpen, Sally. "A Reading of 'No Worst, There is None'." Language of Poems, 1, iii (1972), 9-13.

3777. Thomas, Alfred. "Hopkins's 'Felix Randal'; the man and the poem." TLS, March 19, 1971, pp. 331-32.

3778. Thomas, Alfred, S.J. "Hopkins's 'The Windhover'." Explicator, 33 (1974), Item 31.

3779. Thomas, Alfred, S.J. "Hawk and Buckle Hotel." TLS, November 29, 1974, p. 1344.

Points out that Hopkins wrote "The Windhover" only a few miles from The Hawk and Buckle Hotel, a name which was an important influence on the poem.

3780. Thomas, Alfred. "G.M. Hopkins: 'The Windhover'; Sources, 'Underthought,' and Significance." Modern Language Review, 70 (1975), 497-507.

3781. Thomas, J.D. "Hopkins' 'The Windhover'." Explicator, 20 (1961), Item 31.

3782. Thornton, R.K.R. Gerard Manley Hopkins: The Poems. London: Edward Arnold, 1973.

Brief references throughout to most of the major sonnets.

3783. Triggs, Tony D. "The Crucifixion of Harry Ploughman: A New Interpretation of Hopkins' Poem." Month, 236 (1975), 344-45.

3784. *Tsutsumi, Akiko. "'Churlsgrace' in 'Harry Ploughman'." Bulletin of the Hopkins Society of Japan, 2 (March, 1973), 24-29.

3785. Turpin, Elizabeth R. "Rhetoric and Rhythm in Twentieth-Century Sonnets by Hopkins, Auden, Frost, Cummings, Thomas, and Merrill Moore." Ph.D. Dissertation, Texas A & M, 1972. DAI, 33 (1973), 4368A.

3786. Tweedy, C.J. "A Note on Gerard Manley Hopkins: 'The Windhover'." Critical Quarterly, 19, ii (1977), 88-89.

3787. Vickers, Brian. "Hopkins and Newman." TLS, March 3, 1966, p. 178.

On "(Carrion Comfort)."

3788. Villarubia, Malcolm H., S.J. "Two Wills Unwound in the 'Terrible' Sonnets." Renascence, 27 (1975), 71-80.

3789. Walhout, Donald. Send My Roots Rain: A Study of Religious Experience in the Poetry of Gerard Manley Hopkins. Athens: Ohio University Press, 1981.

About nine sonnets get fairly heavy treatment in the text.

3790. Wallis, Bruce. "'The Windhover' and the Patristic Exegetical Tradition." University of Toronto Quarterly, 41 (1972), 246-55.

3791. Wallis, Bruce. "Hopkins' 'Dapple-Dawn-Drawn' Charioteer." Victorian Newsletter, No. 44 (1973), 26-28.

3792. Walliser, Stephan. That Nature is a Heraclitean Fire and of the Comfort of the Resurrection: A Case-Study in G.M. Hopkins' Poetry. Cooper Monographs on English and American Language and Literature, 26. Bern: Franke, 1977.

Chapter 3 deals with "The Development of Hopkins' Sonnet Form."

3793. Walsh, William. "G.M. Hopkins and a Sense of the Particular." The Use of Imagination: Educational Thought and the Literary Mind. London: Chatto and Windus, 1960, pp. 121-36.

The chapter includes comments about "Spring," "I wake and feel the fell of dark, not day," and "The Windhover."

3794. Ward, Dennis. "G.M. Hopkins: 'The Windhover: To Christ Our Lord'." Interpretations: Essays on Twelve English Poems. Ed. John Wain. London: Routledge and Kegan Paul, 1955, pp. 138-52. Reprinted in Gerard Manley Hopkins: Poems: A Casebook. Ed. Margaret Bottrall. London: Macmillan, 1975, pp. 168-82.

3795. Ward, Dennis. "Hopkins' 'Spelt From Sibyl's Leaves'." Month, 8, i (1952), 40-51.

3796. Warner, John M. "Belief and Imagination in 'The Windhover'." Hopkins Quarterly, 5 (1978), 127-37.

3797. Watson, Thomas L. "Hopkins' 'God's Grandeur'." Explicator, 22 (1964), Item 47.

3798. Weatherhead, A. Kingsley. "G.M. Hopkins: The Windhover." Notes and Queries, 201 (1956), 354.

3799. Weeks, Jerome C. "'An Ark for the Listener': The Musical Notations of Gerard Manley Hopkins on 'Spring' and 'In the Valley of the Elwy'." Language and Style, 13 (1980), 89-97.

3800. White, Gertrude M. "Hopkins' 'God's Grandeur': A Poetic Statement of Christian Doctrine." Victorian Poetry, 4 (1966), 284-87.

3801. White, Norman E. "'Hearse' in Hopkins' 'Spelt from Sibyl's Leaves'." English Studies, 49 (1968), 546-47.

3802. White, Norman. "Hopkins' 'Spelt from Sibyl's Leaves'." Victorian Newsletter, 36 (1969), 27-28.

3803. White, Norman. "Hopkins' 'Spelt from Sibyl's Leaves'." Explicator, 30 (1971), Item 24.

3804. White, Norman. "Hopkins' Sonnet 'Written in Blood'." English Studies, 53 (1972), 123-25.

3805. Whitlock, Baird W. "Gerard Hopkins' 'Windhover'." Notes and Queries, 201 (1956), 169-71.

3806. Wilds, Nancy. "'Carrion Comfort'." Language of Poems, 1, ii (1972), 7-11.

A linguistic analysis of the poem.

3807. Williams, Jacob. "A Reading of 'The Candle Indoors'." Language of Poems, 5 (1976), 6-9.

3808. Winter, J.L. "Notes on 'The Windhover'." Victorian Poetry, 4 (1966), 212-13

3809. Winters, Yvor. "The Poetry of Gerard Manley Hopkins." Hudson Review, 1 (1949), 455-76; 2 (1949), 59-93. Reprinted in The Function of Criticism. Denver: Alan Swallow, 1957, pp. 103-56.

On Hopkins's "The Windhover" and Donne's "Thou hast made me . . . ."

3810. Wolfe, Patricia A. "The Paradox of Self: A Study of Hopkins' Spiritual Conflict in the 'Terrible' Sonnets." Victorian Poetry, 6 (1968), 85-103. Partially reprinted in Gerard Manley Hopkins: Poems: A Casebook. Ed. Margaret Bottrall. London: Macmillan, 1975.

3811. Woodring, Carl R. "Once More, 'The Windhover'." Western Review, 15 (1950), 61-64.

3812. Wright, Brooks. "Hopkins' 'God's Grandeur'." Explicator, 10 (1951), Item 5.

3813. Yoder, Emily K. "Evil and Idolatry in 'The Windhover'." Hopkins Quarterly, 2 (1975), 33-46.

3814. Zelocchi, Rosanna. "'The Windhover' di G.M. Hopkins." Lingua e Stile, 2 (1967), 369-76.

Examines the identification of the falcon with Christ.

3815. "Poet and Priest: Gerard Hopkins: 1844-1889: The 'Dare-Gale' Skylark." TLS, June 10, 1944, p. 282, 284.

Includes comments on a number of the sonnets.

3816. "Pied Beauty in Spanish." TLS, August 13, 1954, pp. 509-10.

This review of J.M. Gutierrez Mora, Hopkinsiana deals in one section with the problem of translating "The Windhover."

3817. "Passionate Science." TLS, March 18, 1955, p. 165.

Summarizes and reacts to Geoffrey Grigson's reading of "The Windhover" in Gerard Manley Hopkins.
3598

3818. "Difficult Poetry." TLS, June 24, 1955, p. 349.

The writer faults recent criticism of "The Windhover" for asserting "that it has found the single key to a difficult point."

Leigh Hunt

3819. Raphael, Andre. "Sur Trois Sonnets Romantiques Anglais: Objectivite et subjectivite dans l'identification du style individuel." Travaux XXII. Explorations Linguistiques et Stylistiques. Saint-Etienne: Universite de Saint-Etienne, 1978, pp. 253-66.

A statistical analysis of the styles of three sonnets on the Nile by Hunt, Keats, and Shelley.

John Keats

3820. Bate, Walter Jackson. John Keats. Cambridge, Mass.: Harvard University Press, 1963.

In addition to numerous brief references to the poems, he writes about Keats's movement from the Petrarchan to the Shakespearean sonnet (pp. 297-300).

3821. Bate, Walter Jackson. The Stylistic Development of Keats. New York: Modern Language Association, 1945. New York: Humanities Press, 1958.

Contains sections on "The Early Sonnets" (pp. 8-19) and "The Later Sonnets" (pp. 118-25). Appendices B and C (pp. 191-96) also treat the sonnets.

3822. Baumgartner, Paul R. "Keats: Theme and Image in a Sonnet." Keats-Shelley Journal, 8 (1959), 11-14.

On "After dark vapours have oppress'd our plains."

3823. Beach, Joseph Warren. "Keats's Realms of Gold." PMLA, 49 (1934), 246-57.

Examines source material for "On First Looking into Chapman's Homer."

3824. Blackstone, Bernard. The Consecrated Urn. London: Longmans Green, 1959.

Discussion of the corpus of Keats's work, with some passages dealing with his sonnets.

3825. Bloom, Harold. The Visionary Company: A Reading of English Romantic Poetry. Garden City, N.Y.: Doubleday, 1961. rev. and enl., Ithaca, N.Y.: Cornell University Press, 1971.

Discusses Keats's sonnet, "Bright Star" (pp. 435-37).

3826. Briggs, H.E. "Swift and Keats." PMLA, 61 (1946), 1101-08.

Finds evidence of Swift's influence in the sonnet "To Homer" (1818) (pp. 1104-05).

3827. Brooks, E.L. "'The Poet' An Error in the Keats Canon?" Modern Language Notes, 67 (1952), 450-54.

3828. Burgess, Anthony. ABBA ABBA. London: Faber and Faber, 1977.

A novel about Keats in Italy in which the sonnet figures prominently. Followed by a sequence of sonnets by Burgess on biblical themes.

3829. Bushnell, Nelson S. "The Style of the Spenserian Stanza, Sonnets and Odes of Keats." Ph.D. Dissertation, Harvard, 1928.

3830. Chatterjee, Bhabatosh. John Keats: His Mind and Work. Calcutta: Orient Longman, 1971.

Much of his chapter on "The Early Phase" (pp. 183-232) is devoted to a discussion of Keats's sonnets.

3831. Connolly, Thomas E. "Keats' 'When I have Fears That I May Cease To Be'." Explicator, 13 (1954), Item 14.

3832. Cook, Thomas. "Keats's Sonnet, 'To Homer'." Keats-Shelley Journal, 11 (1962), 8-12.

3833. Creek, H.L. "Keats and Cortez." TLS, March 21, 1936, p. 244.

On Keats's "mistake" in "On First Looking into Chapman's Homer."

3834. D'Avanzo, Mario L. "Keats' 'If by Dull Rhymes'." Research Studies, 38 (1970), 29-35.

Shows a relationship between the Grecian mythical allusions of the poem and the sonnet form.

3835. Dickstein, Morris. Keats and His Poetry: A Study in Development. Chicago: University of Chicago Press, 1971.

Throughout the book are discussions of Keats's sonnets, including a lengthy passage on the "Lear" sonnet.

3836. Evans, B. Ifor. "Keats's Approach to the Chapman Sonnet." Essays and Studies by Members of the English Association, Vol. 16. Oxford: Clarendon Press, 1931, pp. 26-52.

3837. Evert, Walter H. Aesthetic and Myth in the Poetry of Keats. Princeton: Princeton University Press, 1965.

Discusses "On First Looking into Chapman's Homer" (pp. 43-45) and a number of other sonnets throughout.

3838. Finney, Claude Lee. The Evolution of Keats's Poetry. 2 vol. Cambridge, Mass.: Harvard University Press, 1936. rpt. New York: Russell and Russell, 1967.

Comments on most of the sonnets throughout.

3839. Ford, Newell F. The Prefigurative Imagination of John Keats. Stanford University Publications, Language and Literature, vol. 9, ii. Stanford, Cal.: Stanford University Press, 1951. rpt. Hamden, Conn.: Archon Books, 1966.

Discusses "Bright Star" (pp. 145-48 et passim).

3840. Garrod, H.W. Keats. Oxford: Clarendon Press, 1926.

The relationship between the sonnet and the ode is discussed on pp. 84 ff. In a separate closing essay, "Note on Keats's Use of the Sonnet" (pp. 138-57), Garrod goes more deeply into Keats's use of the form.

3841. Gentili, Vanna. "Anagrafe Metrica dei sonetti di Keats." Studi Inglesi, 5. Bari: Adriatica Editrice, 1978, pp. 441-74.

The study includes a chronological list of Keats's sonnets.

3842. Giovannini, G. "Keats's Elysium of Poets." Modern Language Notes, 63 (1948), 19-25.

Discusses Keats's use of source material as inspiration for his poetry, using "On First Looking into Chapman's Homer" as the principal illustration.

3843. Gittings, Robert. John Keats: The Living Year 21 September 1818 to 21 September 1819. London: Heinemann, 1954.

Chapter 3 deals with "Bright Star and the Beautiful Mrs. Jones" (pp. 25-36) and chapter 13 with "Sonnets and the First Ode" (pp. 124-30).

3844. Gittings, Robert. The Mask of Keats: A Study of Problems. Cambridge, Mass.: Harvard University Press, 1956.

Chapter 4 (pp. 54-68), "Bright Star," discusses some problems relating to that sonnet. Several other sonnets are also discussed in the book.

3845. Gittings, Robert. John Keats. Boston: Atlantic Monthly Press, Little Brown, 1968.

Frequent references to sonnets throughout, in particular, "On First Looking into Chapman's Homer" (pp. 81-83) and "Bright Star" (pp. 262-64).

3846. Griffith, Benjamin W. "Keats' 'On Seeing the Elgin Marbles'." Explicator, 31 (1973), Item 76.

3847. Grill, Neil G. "Keats's Odes and Two New Monthly Magazine Sonnets to an 'Antique Grecian Vase'." Keats-Shelley Memorial Bulletin, 26 (1975), 11-14.

3848. Haferkamp, Berta. "Die Entstehung von Shelleys, Keats' und Hunts Sonetten 'To the Nile'." Literatur-Kultur-Gesellschaft in England und Amerika: Aspekte und Forschungsbeitrage. Friederich Schubel zum 60. Geburtstag. Ed. Gerhard Muller-Schwefe und Konrad Tuzinski. Frankfurt: Moritz Diesterweg, 1966, pp. 337-48.

3849. Halpern, Martin. "Keats and the 'Spirit that Laughest'." Keats-Shelley Journal, 15 (1966), 69-86.

Touches on the sonnet "Why did I laugh tonight?" (pp. 78-80).

3850. Harris, Lynn H. "Keats's 'On First Looking into Chapman's Homer'." Explicator, 4 (1946), Item 35.

3851. Hawthorn, Jeremy. Identity and Relationship: A Contribution to Marxist Theory of Literary Criticism. London: Lawrence and Wishart, 1973.

Hawthorn discusses Keats's sonnet, "Bright Star," (pp. 171-73) in his chapter on "The Social and Temporal Context of Literary Response." He comments briefly on "On Sitting Down to Read King Lear Once Again" (pp. 108-09).

3852. Hewlett, Dorothy. A Life of John Keats. 2nd ed. rev. and enl., New York: Barnes and Noble, 1950. 1970. First edition was published under the title of Adonais, a Life of John Keats. London: Hurst and Blackett, 1937.

References to sonnets throughout.

3853. Keats, John. The Poetical Works of John Keats. Ed. H.W. Garrod. Oxford: Clarendon Press, 1939.

Includes discussion of the sonnets in the introduction. See particularly "Note on the Composition of Poems 1817."

3854. Keats, John. The Collected Sonnets of John Keats. with illustrations by John Buckland Wright. Ed. A.A.M. Stols. Maastricht: Halcyon Press, 1930.

3855. Knight, G. Wilson. The Starlit Dome: Studies in the Poetry of Vision. London: Oxford University Press, 1941.

He considers Keats's sonnet, "Bright Star," to be "probably Keats's greatest poem, and perhaps the most marvellous short poem in our language" (pp. 304-05).

3856. Larrabee, Stephen A. English Bards and Grecian Marbles: The Relationship between Sculpture and Poetry Especially in the Romantic Period. New York: Columbia University Press, 1943. Port Washington, N.Y.: Kennikat Press, 1964.

Discusses the two Elgin marble sonnets (pp. 211-14).

3857. Lord, John B. "Keats, Cortez and the Realms of Gold." Notes and Queries, 198 (1953), 390-91.

Gives a possible reason for Keats's celebrated error and for his use of the phrase "realms of gold" in "On First Looking into Chapman's Homer."

3858. Lowell, Amy. John Keats. 2 vol. Boston and New York: Houghton Mifflin, 1925.

An abundance of substantial passages on many of the sonnets.

3859. Mabbott, T.O. "Keats's 'On First Looking into Chapman's Homer'." Explicator, 5 (1946), Item 22.

3860. MacEachen, Dougald M. [Letter to the Editor.] College English, 18 (1956), 56.

Arguing against Wicker's thesis in an earlier article in College English, MacEachen maintains that Keats meant Balboa--although he said Cortez.
3898

3861. Mackay, David. "Keat's [sic] 'Bright Star' Sonnet." TLS, July 3, 1969, p. 731.

3862. Matsuura, Tohru. Keats and his Sonnets. Seijo English Monographs, 15. Tokyo: Seijo University, 1975.

3863. Maxwell, J.C. "Keats's Sonnet on the Tomb of Burns." Keats-Shelley Journal, 4 (1955), 77-80.

Includes the original text of the poem with commentary.

3864. Mayhead, Robin. John Keats. Cambridge: University Press, 1967.

Discusses "On the Grasshopper and the Cricket" (pp. 16-17), Sonnet 9 ("Keen, fitful gusts . . .") and "On First Looking into Chapman's Homer" (pp. 25-27)--three of only a handful from the 1817 volume that are "valuable" poems.

3865. *McGahan, E.C. "An Examination of the Structure of a Sonnet by Keats." Prace Historycznoliterackie (Uniwersytetu Jagiellonskiego), 24 (1973), 45-50.

3866. McNally, Paul. "Keats and the Rhetoric of Association: On Looking into the Chapman's Homer Sonnet." Journal of English and Germanic Philology, 79 (1980), 530-40.

An examination of the nature of Keats's metaphors in this sonnet.

3867. Murray, E.B. "Ambivalent Mortality in the Elgin Marbles Sonnet." Keats-Shelley Journal, 20 (1971), 22-36.

3868. Murry, John Middleton. Keats and Shakespeare. London: Oxford University Press, 1926.

Discusses "Why did I laugh to-night?" "On Fame," and "On a Dream" (pp. 122-29).

3869. Murry, J. Middleton. "The Birth of a Great Poem." Hibbert Journal, 27 (1928), 93-110. Reprinted as "The Realms of Gold" in Keats. 4th ed., rev. and enl., New York: Noonday Press, 1955, pp. 145-65.

An essay discussing "On First Looking into Chapman's Homer."

3870. Ormerod, David. "Nature's Eremite: Keats and the Liturgy of Passion." Keats-Shelley Journal, 16 (1967), 73-77.

Discusses the theme of the sonnet, "Bright star."

3871. Osler, Alan. "'On Seeing the Elgin Marbles'." Keats-Shelley Memorial Bulletin, 21 (1970), 32-34.

3872. Osler, Alan. "Keats and a Classical Grasshopper." Keats-Shelley Memorial Bulletin, 24 (1973), 25-26.

Keats's sonnet "On the Grasshopper and the Cricket" is indebted to Thomas Moore's translation of Anacreon's 34th ode, which addresses a grasshopper.

3873. Pfeiffer, Karl G. "A Possible New Source of Keats's Sonnet on Chapman's 'Homer'." Notes and Queries, 175 (1938), 203-04.

A poem by Jasper Mayne, a contemporary of Chapman, contains a similar theme and image.

3874. Rashbrook, R.F.. "Keats's Sonnet 'The House of Mourning'." Notes and Queries, 193 (1948), 498-99.

Dates the poem in 1820.

3875. Rashbrook, R.F.. "A Note on Keats's Poems." Notes and Queries, 195 (1950), 390-91.

Four brief notes, three of which concern three of his sonnets: 1) "Give me a golden pen"; 2) "Sonnet on the Elgin Marbles"; 3) "To J.R."

3876. Ricks, Christopher. Keats and Embarassment. Oxford: Clarendon Press, 1974.

Discusses "Bright Star" (pp. 111-14) making a connection between Fanny Brawne's breast and Keats's mother.

3877. Ridley, M.R. Keats's Craftsmanship: A Study in Poetic Development. Oxford: Clarendon Press, 1933. Lincoln: University of Nebraska Press, 1963.

He compares three sonnets with the Ode to Psyche to shed light on Keats's search for a stanza form (pp. 195-210).

3878. Riesner, Dieter. "John Keats, Benjamin Robert Haydon und die Parthenonskulpturen. Freundschaftsadresse und Kunstanschauung in den 'Elgin-Marbles-Sonetten'." Versdichtung der englischen Romantik: Interpretationen. Unter Mitarbeit zahlreicher Fachgelehrter. Hrsg. von Teut Andreas Riese und Dieter Riesner. Berlin: Erich Schmidt, 1968, pp. 334-67.

3879. Rollins, Hyder E. "Keats's Elgin Marbles Sonnets." Studies in Honor of A.H.R. Fairchild. Missouri University Studies, 21, i (1946), 163-66.

3880. Ross, Donald. "Structural Elements in Keats's Sonnets and Odes." Cahiers de Lexicologie, 31 (1977), 95-117.

3881. Ross, Donald, Jr. "The Use of Word-Class Distribution Data for Stylistics: Keats' Sonnets and Chicken Soup." Poetics, 6 (1977), 169-95.

3882. Ross, Donald, Jr. "Stylistics and the Testing of Literary Hypotheses." Poetics, 7 (1978), 389-416.

One section of the paper, "A Study of Sonnets," compares Keats's sonnets to the Elizabethan sonnets (pp. 401-05).

3883. Rossetti, William M. "Sonnet Queries." Notes and Queries, 4th Series, 8 (1871), 55.

On "To the Nile."

3884. Sen Gupta, D.P. "The Unconventional Sonnets of Keats." Studies in the Romantics. Ed. James Hogg. Salzburg Studies in English Literature, Romantic Reassessment, 81. Salzburg: Institut fur Anglistik und Amerikanistik, Universitat Salzburg, 1978, pp. 67-76.

Discusses "If by dull rhymes our English must be chained," "O thou whose face hath felt the Winter's wind," "To Sleep," and "On Fame."

3885. Severs, J. Burke. "Keats's Fairy Sonnet." Keats-Shelley Journal, 6 (1957), 109-13.

On "Had I a man's fair form . . . ."

3886. Slote, Bernice. "Of Chapman's Homer and Other Books." College English, 23 (1962), 256-60.

Slote comments on some of the books that Keats owned at the time of his death and how these books might help us understand his sonnet, "On First Looking into Chapman's Homer."

3887. Sperry, Stuart M. Keats the Poet. Princeton, N.J.: Princeton University Press, 1973.

In the first part of Chapter 3 ("The Early Verse") Sperry discusses some of the sonnets in the 1817 volume (pp. 72-80).

3888. Stallman, Robert Wooster. "Keats the Apollinian: The Time-and-Space Logic of His Poems as Paintings." University of Toronto Quarterly, 16 (1947), 143-56.

He sees "On First Looking into Chapman's Homer" as "the perfect occasion" for translating poetry into a painted perspective "removed from time" (pp. 153-54).

3889. Thomas, W.K. "Keats' 'To Sleep'." Explicator, 26 (1968), Item 55.

3890. Thorpe, Clarence DeWitt. The Mind of John Keats. New York: Oxford University Press, 1926. rpt. New York: Russell and Russell, 1964.

Discusses the two Elgin Marble sonnets in a chapter entitled "What is Beauty?" (pp. 129-31).

3891. Walcutt, Charles C. "Keats's 'On First Looking into Chapman's Homer'." Explicator, 5 (1947), Item 56.

3892. Ward, Aileen. "The Date of Keats's 'Bright Star' Sonnet." Studies in Philology, 52 (1955), 75-85.

July, 1819, is the date Ward chooses for "Bright Star."

3893. Ward, Aileen. "Nebuchadnezzar's Dream." Philological Quarterly, 34 (1955), 177-88.

3894. Ward, Aileen. John Keats--The Making of a Poet. New York: Viking Press, 1963.

Comments on many of the sonnets; see particularly remarks on "Bright Star" (pp. 297-300).

3895. Ware, Malcolm. "Keats' 'Stout Cortez': A Deliberate Error." English Language Notes, 4 (1966), 113-15.

"On First Looking into Chapman's Homer."

3896. Wasserman, Earl R. "Keats's Sonnet 'The Poet'." Modern Language Notes, 67 (1952), 454-56.

3897. Weller, Earle Vonard. "Keats and Mary Tighe." PMLA, 42 (1927), 963-85.

The earlier part of the article deals with how Mary Tighe's influence was evident in Keats's use of the sonnet.

3898. Wicker, C.V. "Cortez--not Balboa." College English, 17 (1956), 383-87.

In the sonnet, "On First Looking into Chapman's Homer," Keats did not mean to suggest that Cortez was the first white man to see the Pacific. He wanted to stress the thrill of an individual's first discovery--of either the Pacific or Homer.

3899. Williams, Melvin G. "To Be or to Have Been: The Use of Verbs in Three Sonnets by John Keats." CEA Critic, 32, iii (1969), 12.

The three sonnets are "On Seeing the Elgin Marbles," "On First Looking into Chapman's Homer," and "When I Have Fears."

3900. Wills, Garry. "Classicism in Keats's Chapman Sonnet." Essays in Criticism, 17 (1967), 456-60.

3901. Yost, George, Jr. "A Source and Interpretation of Keats's Minos." Journal of English and Germanic Philology, 57 (1958), 220-29.

Comments on the reference to Minos (l. 9) in the sonnet, "The Town, the churchyard, & the setting sun . . . ."

3902. Zillman, Lawrence J. "The Sonnets of John Keats: A Critical and Comparative Study in Versecraft." Ph.D. Dissertation, University of Washington, 1936.

3903. Zillman, Lawrence John. John Keats and the Sonnet Tradition: A Critical and Comparative Study. Los Angeles: Lymanhouse, 1939. New York: Octagon, 1966.

Archibald Lampman

3904. Connor, Carl Y. Archibald Lampman. Ottawa: Borealis Press, 1977.

During the latter half of this biography, Connor cites and discusses a number of Lampman's sonnets.

3905. Dudek, Louis. "The Significance of Lampman." Culture, 18 (1957), 277-90. Reprinted in Selected Essays and Criticism. Ottawa: Tecumseh Press, 1978, pp. 65-78. Reprinted also in Archibald Lampman. Ed. Michael Gnarowski. Critical Views on Canadian Writers, 3. Toronto: Ryerson, 1970, pp. 185-201.

3906. Dudek, Louis. "Lampman and the Death of the Sonnet." The Lampman Symposium. Ed. Lorraine McMullen. Ottawa: University of Ottawa Press, 1976, pp. 39-48. Reprinted in Louis Dudek, Selected Essays and Criticism. Ottawa: Tecumseh Press, 1978, pp. 349-61.

3907. Lampman, Archibald. Lampman's Sonnets 1884-1899. Ed. Margaret Coulby Whitridge. Ottawa: Borealis Press, 1976.

3908. Mackendrick, Louis K. "Sweet Patience and Her Guest, Reality: The Sonnets of Archibald Lampman." The Lampman Symposium. Ed. Lorraine McMullen. Ottawa: University of Ottawa Press, 1976, pp. 49-62.

3909. Untermeyer, Louis. "Archibald Lampman and the Sonnet." Poet Lore, 20 (1909), 432-37. Reprinted in Archibald Lampman. Ed. Michael Gnarowski. Critical Views on Canadian Writers, 3. Toronto: Ryerson, 1970, pp. 54-67.

Henry Wadsworth Longfellow

3910. [Arms, G.W.] "Longfellow's Divina Commedia, Sonnet I." Explicator, 2 (1943), Item 7.

3911. Arvin, Newton. Longfellow: His Life and Work. Boston: Little, Brown, 1962.

Discusses Longfellow's career as a sonneteer, which came, for the most part, late in his life (pp. 304-10).

3912. Durr, Robert A. "Longfellow's 'The Cross of Snow'." Explicator, 13 (1955), Item 32.

3913. Gilbert, Creighton. "On Longfellow's Translation of a Michael Angelo Sonnet." Philological Quarterly, 27 (1948), 57-62.

3914. Tenfelde, Nancy L. "Longfellow's 'Chaucer'." Explicator, 22 (1964), Item 55.

George Meredith

3915. Bailey, Elmer James. "A Note on Mr. Meredith's 'Modern Love'." Forum, 40 (1908), 245-54.

Some appreciative remarks.

3916. Bartlett, Phyllis. "A Manuscript of Meredith's 'Modern Love'." Yale University Library Gazette, 40 (1966), 185-87.

This hitherto unknown manuscript contains 35 of the sonnets in Modern Love and one that was never published.

3917. Bernstein, Carol L. Precarious Enchantment: A Reading of Meredith's Poetry. Washington, D.C.: Catholic University of America Press, 1979.

The author regards the triumph of Modern Love as a traditional sonnet sequence to be "commensurate with its achievements in a more 'radical' mode" (pp. 9-17).

3918. Chambers, E.K. "Meredith's 'Modern Love'." A Sheaf of Studies. London: Oxford University Press, 1942, pp. 71-83.

This essay was written in 1897.

3919. Coyle, Kathleen Mildred. "'Madhouse Cells': The Love Poem Sequences of Clough, Tennyson, Arnold, Meredith and Rossetti." Ph.D. Dissertation, Washington University, 1975. DAI, 36 (1976), 8071A-72A.

3920. Dohrenburg, Arlan Paul. "The Poetic Development of George Meredith from The Monthly Observer to 'Modern Love'." Ph.D. Dissertation, Northwestern, 1972. DAI, 33 (1973), 5719A.

3921. Faverty, Frederic E. "Browning's Debt to Meredith in James Lee's Wife." Essays in American and English Literature Presented to

Bruce Robert McElderry, Jr. Ed. Max F. Schulz with William D. Templeman and Charles R. Metzger. Athens: Ohio University Press, 1967, pp. 290-305.

Speaks specifically of Browning's debt to Modern Love.

3922. Friedman, Norman. "The Jangled Harp: Symbolic Structure in Modern Love." Modern Language Quarterly, 18 (1957), 9-26.

3923. Galland, Rene. George Meredith: Les Cinquante Premieres Annees. Paris: Les Presses Francaises, 1923.

Includes a discussion of Modern Love (pp. 137-49).

3924. Going, William T. "A Note on 'My Lady' of Modern Love." Modern Language Quarterly, 7 (1946), 311-14.

3925. Golden, Arline. "'The Game of Sentiment': Tradition and Innovation in Meredith's Modern Love." ELH, 40 (1973), 264-84.

Concentrates on elements of traditional sonnet sequences as they appear in Modern Love.

3926. Golden, Arline. "Hardy, Hopkins, and the Sonnet Sequence: The Influence of Modern Love." Archiv fur das Studium der neueren Sprachen und Literaturen, 212 (1975), 328-32.

"The neglected and incomplete sonnet sequences" of Hopkins and Hardy were influenced by Modern Love.

3927. Gretton, Mary Sturge. The Writings and Life of George Meredith. London: Oxford University Press, 1926.

In her discussion of Modern Love (pp. 54-67), Gretton objects to the characterization of the divisions of the poem as sonnets.

3928. Henderson, M. Sturge. George Meredith: Novelist, Poet, Reformer. London: Methuen, 1907.

Chapter 6 (pp.60-74) deals with Modern Love.

3929. Kelvin, Norman. A Troubled Eden: Nature and Society in the Works of George Meredith. Stanford, Cal. Stanford University Press, 1961.

Kelvin finds war imagery in Modern Love (pp. 25-35).

3930. Ketcham, Carl H. "Meredith's 'Modern Love, XXXI', 7-11." Explicator 17 (1958), Item 7.

3931. Koszul, A. "An Unpublished Sonnet by George Meredith." Nineteenth Century, 109 (1931), 1-3.

The sonnet was addressed to "P. A. Labouchere Esq."

3932. Kowalczyk, Richard L. "Moral Relativism and the Cult of Love in Meredith's Modern Love." Research Studies, 37 (1969), 38-53.

3933. Kwinn, David. "Meredith's Psychological Insight in Modern Love, XXIII." Victorian Poetry, 7 (1969), 151-53.

3934. Kwinn, David Carl. "'Nature and Song Allied': The Harmonious Outlook of George Meredith's Poetry." Ph.D. Dissertation, Cornell, 1971. DAI, 32 (1971), 1478A.

"Of Meredith's love poetry, 'Modern Love' is atypical because in it all harmony fails."

3935. Le Gallienne, Richard. George Meredith: Some Characteristics. London: E. Mathews, 1890. 5th ed. rev. London and New York: John Lane, 1900.

The author discusses Modern Love, which he calls "Meredith's one great achievement in poetic art" (pp. 112-33).

3936. Lewis, C. Day. The Poetic Image. New York: Oxford University Press, 1947.

Discusses some of Meredith's images in Modern Love, particularly in the last sonnet (pp. 82-85).

3937. Lindsay, Jack. George Meredith: His Life and Work. London: Bodley Head, 1956.

In a chapter entitled "Modern Love" Lindsay discusses the relationship between the married couple in the poem and George and Mary Meredith (pp. 82-87).

3938. Lucas, John. "Meredith as Poet." Meredith Now: Some Critical Essays. Ed. Ian Fletcher. London: Routledge and Kegan Paul; New York: Barnes and Noble, 1971, pp. 14-33.

A frequently negative appraisal of Modern Love but one nevertheless conscious of the work's complexity and value.

3939. McKay, Kenneth M. "Theme and the Myth of Lilith in Meredith's 'Modern Love'." Humanities Association Bulletin, 19, ii (1968), 13-16.

3940. Meredith, George. Selected Poems of George Meredith. Ed. Graham Hough. London: Oxford University Press, 1962.

The introduction is devoted largely to a discussion of Modern Love.

3941. ______________. Modern Love. Introd. by C. Day Lewis. London: Rupert Hart-Davis, 1948.

3942. Mermin, Dorothy M. "Poetry as Fiction: Meredith's Modern Love." ELH, 43 (1976), 100-19.

The poem "definitively marks Meredith's transition from poet to novelist."

3943. M[onroe], H[arriet]. "Meredith as Poet." Poetry, 32 (1928), 210-16.

Although the remarks on Modern Love are brief, it is the author's view that the sequence is "one of the finest poems of the nineteenth century."

3944. Perkus, Gerald Howard. "The Genesis and Art of George Meredith's Modern Love." Ph.D. Dissertation, Rochester, 1966. DA, 27 (1966), 1381A.

3945. *Perkus, Gerald H. "Struggling with the Devil: The Central Motif in Modern Love." Northeast Modern Language Association Newsletter, 1, ii (1969), 9-14.

3946. Perkus, Gerald H. "Meredith's Unhappy Love Life: Worthy of the Muse." Cithara, 9, ii (1970), 32-46.

Discusses the relationship between Modern Love and the events of Meredith's first marriage.

3947. Petter, Guy B. George Meredith and His German Critics. London: H.F. and G. Witherby, 1939.

In his chapter summarizing the work of Heinz Walz, "George Meredith's Early Works and Their Significance for His Personal Development," Petter discusses Modern Love in the context of other early works (pp. 172-75).

3948. Plunkett, P.M., S.J. "Meredith's 'Modern Love, I'." Explicator, 28 (1970), Item 42.

3949. Quiller-Couch, Sir Arthur. "The Poetry of George Meredith." Studies in Literature. New York: G.P. Putnam's Sons, 1918, pp. 168-88. Reprinted in Cambridge Lectures. London: J.M. Dent, 1943, pp. 259-73.

Very little of this lecture (p. 179) deals with Modern Love but what he does say is interesting because of its highly subjective and negative character.

3950. Reader, Willie D. "Stanza Form in Meredith's Modern Love." Victorian Newsletter, No. 38 (1970), 26-27.

3951. Reader, Willie D. "The Autobiographical Author as Fictional Character: Point of View in Meredith's Modern Love." Victorian Poetry, 10 (1972), 131-43.

3952. Robertson, Leo C. "Meredith the Poet." English Review, 44 (1927), 463-71.

A defense of Meredith as a poet with frequent illustrations from Modern Love.

3953. Sassoon, Siegfried. Meredith. New York: Viking, 1948.

Some remarks on the circumstances behind the composition of Modern Love and its critical reception (pp. 47-52).

3954. Simpson, Arthur L., Jr. "Meredith's Pessimistic Humanism: A New Reading of Modern Love." Modern Philology 67 (1970), 341-56.

3955. Smith, John Henry. "Similarities of Imagery and Diction Between The Ordeal of Richard Feverel and Modern Love. Ph.D. Dissertation, Colorado, 1961. DA, 22 (1962), 3209.

3956. Smith, John Henry. Hiding the Skeleton: Imagery in Feverel and Modern Love. Lincoln: Nebraska Wesleyan University Press, 1966.

The study attempts to show how Meredith drew images for The Ordeal of Richard Feverel and Modern Love from basically the same poetic material.

3957. Swinburne, Algernon Charles. "Mr. George Meredith's 'Modern Love'." Spectator, June 7, 1862, pp. 632-33. Reprinted in George Meredith: Some Early Appreciations. Ed. Maurice Buxton Forman. London: Chapman and Hall, 1909, pp. 99-103.

A response to an unfavorable review published earlier in the Spectator (May 24, 1862), pp. 580-81.

3958. Symons, Arthur. "George Meredith's Poetry." Westminster Review, 128 (1887), 693-97.

This essay contains a brief appraisal of Modern Love which he calls "the most 'modern' poem we have."

3959. Trevelyan, George Macaulay. The Poetry and Philosophy of George Meredith. London: Archibald Constable, 1906.

His discussion of Meredith's Modern Love (pp. 18-35) focuses on its variety. He also comments on Meredith's other sonnets (pp. 61-63).

3960. Tucker, Cynthia Grant. "Studies in Sonnet Literature: Browning, Meredith, Baudelaire, Rilke, Weinheber." Ph.D. Dissertation, Iowa, 1967. DA, 28 (1968), 2659A-60A.

3961. Tucker, Cynthia Grant. "Meredith's Broken Laurel: Modern Love and the Renaissance Sonnet Tradition." Victorian Poetry, 10 (1972), 351-65.

3962. Wilson, Phillip E. "Affective Coherence, a Principle of Abated Action, and Meredith's Modern Love." Modern Philology, 72 (1974), 151-71.

3963. Wright, Elizabeth Cox. "The Significance of the Image Patterns in Meredith's Modern Love." Victorian Newsletter, No. 13 (1958), 1-9.

3964. Wright, Walter F. Art and Substance in George Meredith: A Study in Narrative. Lincoln: University of Nebraska Press, 1953.

Discusses Modern Love as tragicomedy (pp. 164-68).

3965. Review of George Meredith, Modern Love, and Poems of the English Roadside, with Poems and Ballads. Athenaeum, May 31, 1862, pp. 719-20.

An unfavorable review, calling the poems obscure and diseased.

3966. "Mr. George Meredith's Poems." Saturday Review (London), 16 (1863), 562-63.

In this review of Modern Love, and Poems of the English Roadside the reviewer calls the sequence a "sickly little peccadillo."

Alice Meynell

3967. Archer, William. Poets of the Younger Generation. London: J. Lane, 1902. St. Clair Shores, Mich.: Scholarly Press, 1969.

Briefest of comments about Meynell's sonnets.

Thomas Percy

3968. Rinaker, Clarissa. "Percy as a Sonneteer." Modern Language Notes, 35 (1920), 56-58.

Though principally an antiquarian, Rev. Thomas Percy wrote several sonnets in the Spenserian form.

Edgar Allan Poe

3969. Bandy, W.T. "Poe's An Enigma (or Sonnet), 4." Explicator, 20 (1961), Item 35.

Christina Rossetti

3970. Cook, Wister Jean. "The Sonnets of Christina Rossetti: A Comparative Prosodic Analysis." Ph.D. Dissertation, Auburn, 1971. DAI, 32 (1972), 6419A-20A.

3971. Crump, R.W. "Eighteen Moments' Monuments: Christina Rossetti's Bouts-Rimes Sonnets in the Troxell Collection." Princeton University Library Chronicle, 33 (1972), 210-29. Reprinted in Essays on the Rossettis. Ed. Robert S. Fraser. Princeton, N.J.: Princeton University Library, 1972.

3972. Curran, Stuart. "The Lyric Voice of Christina Rossetti." Victorian Poetry, 9 (1971), 287-99.

Among the poems considered are the sonnets "Venus's Looking-Glass" and Sonnet 14 of Monna Innominata.

3973. Gosse, Edmund. "Christina Rossetti." Critical Kit-Kats. New York: Dodd, Mead, 1896, pp. 135-62.

In one portion of this essay (pp. 154-56) he praises her sonnets and holds them to be superior to those of her brother.

3974. Janowitz, K.E. "The Antipodes of Self: Three Poems by Christina Rossetti." Victorian Poetry, 11 (1973), 195-205.

The last of the three poems discussed is the sonnet "Acme" (pp. 203-05).

3975. Packer Lona Mosk. Christina Rossetti. Berkeley and Los Angeles: University of California Press, 1963.

This biography includes several long passages on Monna Innominata and other of her sonnets.

3976. Wenger, Helen H. "The Influence of the Bible in Christina Rossetti's Monna Innominata." Christian Scholar's Review, 3 (1973), 15-24.

3977. Wion, Ann Holt. "'Give Me the Lowest Place': The Poetry of Christina Rossetti." Ph.D. Dissertation, Cornell University, 1976. DAI, 37 (1976), 1574A-75A.

Includes a close reading of the sonnets in Monna Innominata.

Dante Gabriel Rossetti

3978. Adlard, John. "Rossetti's 'Willow-Wood': A Source?" Notes and Queries, 217 (1972), 253-54.

Discusses the origin of the title of these sonnets, which were published in 1869.

3979. Baker, Houston A., Jr. "The Poet's Progress: Rossetti's *The House of Life*." *Victorian Poetry*, 8 (1970), 1-14.

3980. Barth, J. Robert, S.J. "Mysticism in Rossetti's *House of Life*." *Barat Review*, 6, ii (1971), 41-48.

3981. Baum, Paull Franklin. *Dante Gabriel Rossetti: An Analytical List of Manuscripts in the Duke University Library, with Hitherto Upublished Verse and Prose*. Durham, N.C.: Duke University Press, 1931.

Includes fifteen previously unpublished sonnets (two in Italian).

3982. Benson, Arthur C. *Rossetti*. London: Macmillan, 1904.

His discussion of *The House of Life* and other sonnets (pp. 129-39) leads to the conclusion that the work has an "enervating effect upon the spirit," lacking in simplicity and naturalness.

3983. Bentley, D.M.R. "'The Song-Throe' by D.G. Rossetti." *Notes and Queries*, 222 (1977), 421-22.

This sonnet (LXI in *The House of Life*) employs a classical theme--"The Contest of Appollo and Marsyas."

3984. Bentley, D.M.R. "Rossetti's Pre-Raphaelite Manifesto: The 'Old and New Art' Sonnets." *English Language Notes*, 15 (1978), 197-203.

3985. Bentley, D.M.R. "Political Themes in the Work of Dante Gabriel Rossetti." *Victorian Poetry*, 17 (1979), 159-79.

Includes brief comments about several of his minor sonnets: "At the Sun-Rise in 1848," "After the French Liberation of Italy" (1859), "After the German Subjugation of France" (1871) and on the assassination of "Czar Alexander the Second."

3986. Bequette, M.K. "Dante Gabriel Rossetti: The Synthesis of Picture and Poem." *Hartford Studies in Literature*, 4 (1972), 216-27.

Discusses the relationship between two of the *Sonnets for Paintings* and the paintings for which they were intended: "A Venetian Pastoral" and "Proserpine."

3987. Bowra, C.M. "The House of Life." *The Romantic Imagination*. Cambridge, Mass.: Harvard University Press, 1949. New York: Oxford University Press, 1961, pp. 197-220. Reprinted in *Victorian Literature: Modern Essays in Criticism*. Ed. Austin Wright. New York: Oxford University Press, 1961, pp. 248-67.

3988. Boyd, Evelyn Mae. "Dante Gabriel Rossetti's 'The House of Life': a Study of its Italian Background." Ph.D. Dissertation, Columbia, 1954. *DA*, 14 (1954), 1217.

3989. Buttel, Helen. "Rossetti's 'Bridal Birth'." Explicator, 23 (1964), Item 22.

On Sonnet 2 from The House of Life.

3990. Charlesworth, Barbara. Dark Passages: The Decadent Consciousness in Victorian Literature. Madison: University of Wisconsin Press, 1965.

The story of Rossetti's search for "perfection of thought and feeling" united in perfection of form may be found in The House of Life (pp. 3-18).

3991. Christensen, Trilby Busch. "Theme and Image: The Structure of D.G. Rossetti's House of Life." Ph.D. Dissertation, Ohio, 1972. DAI, 33 (1973), 4403A-04A.

3992. Doughty, Oswald. Dante Gabriel Rossetti: A Victorian Romantic. New Haven: Yale University Press, 1949.

A number of the sonnets from The House of Life are discussed in Books 2, "Youth and Change" and 3, "Change and Fate."

3993. Eldredge, Harrison. "On an Error in a Sonnet of Rossetti's." Victorian Poetry, 5 (1967), 302-03.

Comments on an obscure passage (ll. 4-6) in Sonnet 34 ("The Dark Glass") of The House of Life.

3994. Forman, H. Buxton. Our Living Poets: An Essay in Criticism. London: Tinsley, 1871.

Claims supremacy for Rossetti's The House of Life over all other sonnet sequences including Shakespeare and Elizabeth Barrett Browning (pp. 207-13).

3995. Foster, Nancy K. "A Word for Rossetti." Poet Lore, 21 (1910), 322-29.

Observes of Rossetti that "in the 'House of Life' he attempts to realize in thought and feeling what all mystics try to realize--the immanence of the eternal in the temporal . . . ."

3996. Fredeman, William E. "Rossetti's 'In Memoriam': An Elegiac Reading of The House of Life." Bulletin of the John Rylands Library, 47 (1965), 298-341.

Includes an appendix with chronologies of composition and publication for the individual sonnets.

3997. Going, William T. "The Brothers Rossetti and Youth and Love." Papers on Language and Literature, 4 (1968), 334-35.

Offers some evidence in one of William Rossetti's sonnets to support the view that the title of Part I of The House of Life had originally been "Love and Change."

3998. Gordon, Kathryn Imelda. "Dante Gabriel Rossetti's House of Life: A Critical Edition." Ph.D. Dissertation, Boston, 1968. DA, 29 (1969), 2262A.

3999. Greene, Michael E. "The Severed Self: The Dramatic Impulse in The House of Life." Ball State University Forum, 14, iv (1973), 49-58.

4000. Harris, Ronald Luke. "Interior Action in Rossetti's 'The House of Life'." Ph.D. Dissertation, UCLA, 1970. DAI, 31 (1971), 5363A.

4001. Harris, Wendell V. "A Reading of Rossetti's Lyrics." Victorian Poetry, 7 (1969), 299-308.

Much of the essay deals with The House of Life.

4002. Hobbs, John Nelson. "The Poetry of Dante Gabriel Rossetti." Ph.D. Dissertation, Yale, 1968. DA, 29 (1968), 602A-03A.

Hobbs calls The House of Life "Rossetti's finest artistic achievement" with "the unity of a complex consciousness . . . built from the separate moments of the individual sonnets."

4003. Howard, Ronnalie Joanne Roper. "The Poetic Development of Dante Gabriel Rossetti, 1847-1872." Ph.D. Dissertation, Pennsylvania State, 1968. DA, 29 (1969), 3616A.

Only in the later poems, The House of Life in particular, does Rossetti emphasize the differences in love: erotic love destroys; spiritual love redeems.

4004. Howard, Ronnalie R. The Dark Glass: Vision and Technique in the Poetry of Dante Gabriel Rossetti. Athens: Ohio University Press, 1972.

Chapter 8, "The House of Life," focuses primarily on the structure of Rossetti's sonnets.

4005. Hume, Robert D. "Inorganic Structure in The House of Life." Papers on Language and Literature, 5 (1969), 282-95.

An examination of the poems in which there is no "biographical imperative."

4006. Ireland, Kenneth R. "A Kind of Pastoral: Rossetti's Versions of Giorgione." Victorian Poetry, 17 (1979), 303-15.

Discusses two versions of the sonnet "A Venetian Pastoral" inspired by a painting by Giorgione.

4007. Jarfe, Gunther. Kunstform und Verzweiflung: Studien zur Typologie der Sonettgestalt in Dante Gabriel Rossettis The House of Life. Europaische Hochschulschriften, 7. Bern: Lang, 1973.

4008. Jarvie, Paul, and Robert Rosenberg. "'Willowwood,' Unity and *The House of Life*." *Pre-Raphaelite Review*, 1,i (1977), 106-20.

4009. Johnston, Robert D. *Dante Gabriel Rossetti*. Twayne's English Authors Series, 87. New York: Twayne, 1969.

Two chapters are devoted to *The House of Life* and one to his final sonnets.

4010. Johnston, Robert DeSales. "Imagery in Rossetti's *House of Life*." Ph.D. Dissertation, Missouri, 1959. *DA*, 20 (1960), 2783-84.

4011. Kendall, J.L. "The Concept of the Infinite Moment in *The House of Life*." *Victorian Newsletter*, No. 28 (1965), 4-8.

4012. Lewis, Roger Carlisle. "The Poetic Integrity of D.G. Rossetti's Sonnet Sequence, *The House of Life*." Ph.D. Dissertation, Toronto, 1969. *DAI*, 31 (1971), 6016A.

4013. Lindberg, John. "Rossetti's Cumaean Oracle." *Victorian Newsletter*, No. 22 (1962), 20-21.

On Sonnet 101 ("The One Hope"), the last sonnet of *The House of Life*.

4014. Lottes, Wolfgang. "'Take Out the Picture and Frame the Sonnet': Rossetti's Sonnets and Verses for his Own Works of Art." *Anglia*, 96 (1978), 108-35.

4015. Megroz, R.L. *Dante Gabriel Rossetti: Painter Poet of Heaven in Earth*. London: Faber and Gwyer, 1928.

4016. Metzdorf, Robert F. "The Full Text of Rossetti's Sonnet on *Sordello*." *Harvard Library Bulletin*, 7 (1953), 239-43.

4017. Miyoshi, Masao. *The Divided Self: A Perspective on the Literature of the Victorians*. New York: New York University Press, 1969.

Discusses *The House of Life* (pp. 253-59).

4018. Nassaar, Christopher S. "Rossetti's *Astarte Syriaca:* A Neglected Sonnet." *Pre-Raphaelite Review*, 2 (1978), 63-65.

The poem, which refers to his painting of the same title, probes the powers of illusion of the siren.

4019. Pittman, Philip McMillan. "Mythologos: A Study in the Poetic Technique of Dante Gabriel Rossetti." Ph.D. Dissertation, Vanderbilt, 1967. *DA*, 28 (1968), 4140A-41A.

The House of Life, which is discussed in Chapters 4 and 5, is compared to Dante's *La Vita Nuova*.

4020. Pridgen, Rufus Allen. "Apocalyptic Imagery in Dante Gabriel Rossetti's *The House of Life*." Ph.D. Dissertation, Florida State, 1975. *DAI*, 36 (1976), 8079A.

4021. Prince, Jeffrey R. "D.G. Rossetti and the Pre-Raphaelite Conception of the Special Moment." Modern Language Quarterly, 37 (1976), 349-69.

It is in The House of Life that one is most likely to find "those poems which convey the conviction that moments of sensual experience actually have significant spiritual implications."

4022. Riede, David G. "Shelleyan Reflections in the Imagery of D.G. Rossetti." Victorian Poetry, 19 (1981), 167-84.

Rossetti, like Shelly, uses reflecting imagery (mirrors, etc.) in The House of Life and other poems indicating "a divided self seeking union with his own soul through a purified love."

4023. Robillard, Douglas J. "Rossetti's 'Willowwood' Sonnets and the Structure of The House of Life." Victorian Newsletter, No. 22 (1962), 5-9.

4024. Rossetti, Dante Gabriel. The House of Life: A Sonnet-Sequence. Ed. Paull Franklin Baum. Cambridge, Mass.: Harvard University Press, 1928.

Contains an extensive introduction.

4025. ______________________. Poems, Ballads and Sonnets: Selections from the Posthumous Poems and from His Translations: Hand and Soul. Ed. Paull Franklin Baum. Garden City, N.Y.: Doubleday, Doran, 1937.

Critical introduction contains a discussion of the sonnets and The House of Life.

4026. ______________________. The Works of Dante Gabriel Rossetti. Ed. William M. Rossetti. rev. ed. New York: A.L. Burt, 1911.

4027. Rossetti, William. Dante Gabriel Rossetti as Designer and Writer. London: Cassell, 1889.

A major section of this book by Rossetti's brother is a prose paraphrase of and commentary on The House of Life.

4028. Ryals, Clyde de L. "The Narrative Unity of The House of Life." Journal of English and Germanic Philology, 69 (1970), 241-57.

4029. Sehrt, Ernst Th. "Dante Gabriel Rossetti: 'Death-in-love'." Die Englische Lyrik: Von der Renaissance bis zur Gegenwart. Ed. Karl Heinz Goller. Dusseldorf: August Bagel, 1968, vol. 2, pp. 180-89.

Translation and discussion of the sonnet, "There came an image in Life's retinue."

4030. Sharp, William. Dante Gabriel Rossetti: A Record and a Study. London: Macmillan, 1882. rpt. New York: AMS Press, 1970.

Chapter 7, "The Sonnet--Sonnets for Pictures--Miscellaneous Sonnets," and Chapter 8, "The House of Life."

4031. Shine, Hill. "The Influence of Keats Upon Rossetti." Englische Studien, 61 (1926-27), 183-210.

The article includes comments on a number of sonnets by Keats and Rossetti.

4032. Sonstroem, David. Rossetti and the Fair Lady. Middletown, Conn.: Wesleyan University Press, 1970.

A major portion of the book deals with the treatment of the lady in The House of Life.

4033. Spector, Stephen J. "Love, Unity and Desire in the Poetry of Dante Gabriel Rossetti." ELH, 38 (1971), 432-58.

4034. Spector, Stephen J. "Rossetti's Self-Destroying 'Moment's Monument': 'Silent Noon'." Victorian Poetry, 14 (1976), 54-58.

On The House of Life, Sonnet 19.

4035. Stein, Richard L. "Dante Gabriel Rossetti: Painting and the Problem of Poetic Form." Studies in English Literature, 1500-1900, 10 (1970), 775-92.

Discusses Rossetti's use of the Petrarchan sonnet in showing how he conceived of a poem "as an arrangement of masses to be balanced as in a work of visual art."

4036. Stein, Richard L. The Ritual of Interpretation: The Fine Arts as Literature in Ruskin, Rossetti, and Pater. Cambridge, Mass.: Harvard University Press, 1975.

The essay on Rossetti discusses "Sonnets for Pictures" (pp. 130-43) and The House of Life (pp.187-203).

4037. Stuart, Donald C., III. "Bitter Fantasy: Narcissus in Dante Gabriel Rossetti's Lyrics." Victorians Institute Journal, 2 (1973), 27-40.

In a brief section Stuart explains how the myth of Narcissus is central to the "Willow-wood" sonnets in The House of Life.

4038. Suddard, S.J. Mary. "The House of Life." Keats, Shelley and Shakespeare: Studies and Essays in English Literature. Cambridge: University Press, 1912, pp. 261-78.

4039. Talon, Henri-A. D.G. Rossetti: The House of Life: quelques aspects de l'art et des themes. Archives des Lettres Modernes, 65. Paris: Lettres modernes, 1966.

Bound with this monograph under a separate title page is an essay, "D.G. Rossetti: The House of Life, quelques aspects du symbolisme" (pp. 57-83).

4040. Talon, Henri. "Dante Gabriel Rossetti: Peintre-Poete dans La Maison de Vie." Etudes Anglaises, 19 (1966), 1-14.

4041. Tietz, Eva. "Das Malerische in Rossettis Dichtung." Anglia, 51 (1927), 278-306.

The bulk of her article discusses poems from The House of Life.

4042. Tisdel, Frederick M. "Rossetti's House of Life." Modern Philology, 15 (1917), 257-76.

An attempt to give the chronology of the poems.

4043. Verkoren, L. "A Note on Two Sonnets on Keats." English Studies, 32 (1951), 220-21.

About "On Keats" ("A garden in a garden") by Christina Rossetti and "Five English Poets--IV. John Keats" ("The weltering London ways where children weep) by Dante Gabriel Rossetti.

4044. Vogel, Joseph F. Dante Gabriel Rossetti's Versecraft. University of Florida Humanities Monograph, 34. Gainesville: University of Florida Press, 1971.

In a section of the first chapter on "Meter," the author compares several groups of Rossetti's sonnets to those of Milton and Keats (pp. 9-29).

4045. Vogel, Joseph F. "Rossetti's 'Memorial Thresholds'." Explicator, 23 (1964), Item 29.

Sonnet 81 of The House of Life.

4046. Vogel, Joseph F. "Rossetti's 'The House of Life, LXXXVII'." Explicator, 21 (1963), Item 64.

4047. *Wagschal, Friedrich. "E.B. Brownings Sonnets from the Portuguese und D.G. Rossettis House of Life." Zeitschrift fur franzosischen und englischen Unterricht, 13 (1914), 207-17.

4048. Wallerstein, Ruth C. "Personal Experience in Rossetti's House of Life." PMLA, 42 (1927), 492-504.

4049. Weatherby, H.L. "Problems of Form and Content in the Poetry of D.G. Rossetti." Victorian Poetry, 2 (1964), 11-19.

In speaking of how Rossetti frequently failed to reconcile form with content, Weatherby uses two illustrations from The House of Life.

4050. Zakrzewska, Maja. "Untersuchungen zur Konstruktion und Komposition von Dante Gabriel Rossettis Sonnettenzyklus The House of Life." Ph.D. Dissertation, Freiburg, 1922.

4051. "The Poetical Writings of Mr. D.G. Rossetti." Westminster Review, 95 (1871), 26-42.

In this article reviewing two of Rossetti's collections, a number of sonnets receive comment, including "The Sun's Shame," which is compared to Shakespeare's Sonnet 66.

4052. "The Poetry of Rossetti." British Quarterly Review, 76 (1882), 109-27.

Focuses his review in the latter part of the article (pp. 118 ff.) on The House of Life.

William Michael Rossetti

4053. Arinshtein, Leonid M., and William E. Fredeman. "William Michael Rossetti's 'Democratic Sonnets'." Victorian Studies, 14 (1971), 241-74.

Includes fourteen previously unpublished Democratic Sonnets.

Charles Sedley

4054. Phelps, William Lyon. "Two Sonnets Hitherto Unnoticed." Modern Language Notes, 18 (1903), 173-74.

These two sonnets appear on pages 60 and 91 of Sedley's Poetical Works (1707).

Percy Bysshe Shelley

4055. Anderson, Erland. "'Upon the Wandering Winds . . .': A Note on the First Sonnet Discovered in the Byron and Shelley Notebooks in the Scrope Davies Find." English Language Notes, 17 (1979), 120-22.

On music metaphors in this lately discovered and rather difficult sonnet.

4056. Bache, William B. "Vanity and Art in 'Ozymandias'." CEA Critic, 31, v (1969), 20.

4057. Bequette, M.K. "Shelley and Smith: Two Sonnets on Ozymandias." Keats-Shelley Journal, 26 (1977), 29-31.

Compares Shelley's famous sonnet with one on the same subject by his friend, Horace Smith.

4058. Berry, Francis. "Shelley and the Future Tense." Poets' Grammar: Person, Time and Mood in Poetry. London: Routledge and Kegan Paul, 1958, pp. 143-56.

Berry notes that the Ode to the West Wind is not only an ode but also a sonnet sequence and a prayer.

4059. Bloom, Harold. The Visionary Company: A Reading of English Romantic Poetry. Garden City, N.Y.: Doubleday, 1961.

Includes discussion of Shelley's "Ode to the West Wind" (pp. 296-302) and Keats's sonnet "Bright Star" (pp. 435-37).

4060. Chernaik, Judith, and Timothy Burnett. "The Byron and Shelley Notebooks in the Scrope Davies Find." Review of English Studies, NS 29 (1978), 36-49.

Comments on two new poems--sonnets--in the Shelley notebook that were possibly written in response to Byron's Childe Harold (pp. 39-41).

4061. Haworth, Helen E. "'Ode to the West Wind' and the Sonnet Form." Keats-Shelley Journal, 20 (1971), 71-77.

4062. King-Hele, Desmond. Shelley: His Thought and Work. London: Macmillan, 1960.

Includes brief discussions of some sonnets, including "Ozymandias" (pp. 92-94) and "Sonnet to Byron" (pp. 321-22).

4063. Lengeler, Rainer. "Shelleys Sonett Ozymandias." Neueren Sprachen, 18 (1969), 532-39.

4064. Margolis, John D. "Shakespeare and Shelley's Sonnet 'England in 1819'." English Language Notes, 4 (1967), 276-77.

First line of the sonnet echoes two lines from Lear (III.ii.19-20).

4065. Parr, Johnstone. "Shelley's Ozymandias." Keats-Shelley Journal, 6 (1957), 31-35.

On Shelley's possible sources for the poem.

4066. Pollin, Burton R. "'Ozymandias' and the Dormouse." Dalhousie Review, 47 (1967), 361-67.

4067. Pottle, Frederick A. "The Meaning of Shelley's 'Glirastes'." Keats-Shelley Journal, 7 (1958), 6-7.

Glirastes, the name with which Shelley signed himself when "Ozymandias" was first published, "might plausibly be translated as 'the one who behaves like a dormouse'."

4068. Richmond, H.M. "Ozymandias and the Travelers." Keats-Shelley Journal, 11 (1962), 65-71.

Discusses a possible source--R. Pockocke, A Description of the East, and Some Other Countries (1743)--for Shelley's sonnet.

4069. Sen Gupta, D.P. "Some Sonnets of Shelley." Studies in the Romantics. Ed. James Hogg. Salzburg Studies in English Literature, Romantic Reassessment, 81. Salzburg: Institut fur Anglistik und Amerikanistik, Universitat Salzburg, 1978, pp. 54-66.

A look at eight sonnets including "Ozymandias" and "England in 1819."

4070. Short, Clarice. "Ozymandias and Nineveh." Notes and Queries, 201 (1956), 440-41.

A second "Ozymandias" was published shortly after Shelley's, which curiously foreshadows Rossetti's "Burden of Nineveh."

4071. Spanos, William V. "Shelley's 'Ozymandias' and the Problem of the Persona." CEA Critic, 30, iv (1968), 14-15.

4072. Steadman, John M. "Errors Concerning the Publication Date of Shelley's 'Ozymandias'." Notes and Queries, 201 (1956), 439-40.

4073. Thompson, D.W. "Ozymandias." Philological Quarterly, 16 (1937), 59-64.

Both Shelley and Horace Smith wrote sonnets about "Ozymandias" at about the same time that a head of Ramses II was put on exhibit in England. The article examines the connections.

4074. "Deux sonnets inedits de Shelley." La Quinzaine Litteraire, No. 313 (November 16-30, 1979), p. 17.

Contains two sonnets found among papers of Shelley and Byron with French translations of the two poems.

Charlotte Smith

4075. Gledhill, Peggy Willard. "The Sonnets of Charlotte Smith." Ph.D. Dissertation, Oregon, 1976. DAI, 37 (1977), 5848A-49A.

4076. Hunt, Bishop C., Jr. "Wordsworth and Charlotte Smith." Wordsworth Circle, 1 (1970), 85-103.

Charlotte Smith's Elegiac Sonnets (1784) were an important influence on Wordsworth's own later sonnets.

Algernon Charles Swinburne

4077. Bloom, Edward A., Charles H. Philbrick, and Elmer M. Blistein. The Order of Poetry. New York: Odyssey Press, 1961.

In the final chapter on "Versification" sonnets by Swinburne ("A Solitude") and Hopkins ("Hurrahing in Harvest") are discussed (pp. 126-34).

4078. Swinburne, Algernon Charles. The Complete Works of Algernon Charles Swinburne (Bonchurch Edition): Poetical Works. London: William Heinemann; New York: Gabriel Wells, 1925, vol. I, pp. 92-97.

The seven "Undergraduate Sonnets" are followed by two sonnets entitled "The Cup of God's Wrath."

4079. Wright, Brooks. "Swinburne's 'A Cameo'." Explicator, 12 (1953), Item 13.

John Addington Symonds

4080. Going, William T. "John Addington Symonds and the Victorian Sonnet Sequence." Victorian Poetry, 8 (1970), 25-38.

Symonds, who wrote around 340 sonnets, made several important contributions to the genre.

Alfred Lord Tennyson

4081. *Kabiljo-Sutic, Simha. "Tenison i njegov sonet 'Crna Gora'." Ed. Niksa Stipcevic. Uporedna istrazivanja. Belgrade: Inst. za knjizevnost i umetnost, 1976, vol. 1, pp. 501-45.

On "Montenegro". Summary in English.

4082. MacEachen, Dougald B. "Tennyson and the Sonnet." Victorian Newsletter, No. 14 (1958), 1-8.

4083. Moore, John Robert. "Sources of In Memoriam in Tennyson's Early Poems." Modern Language Notes, 31 (1916), 307-09.

The first nineteen lines of a group of discarded, irregular sonnets entitled "Love," published in Tennyson's 1830 volume, contain the central ideas of In Memoriam.

4084. Pyre, J.F.A. The Formation of Tennyson's Style. University of Wisconsin Studies in Language and Literature, 12. Madison: University of Wisconsin, 1921.

A brief paragraph on Tennyson's experiences with the sonnet (p. 38).

4085. Smith, R.B. "Sexual Ambivalence in Tennyson." CEA Critic, 27, ix (1965), 8-9. Reprinted in 28, i (1965), 12.

The sonnet being discussed, "Now sleeps the crimson petal," has no rhymes.

4086. Tennyson, Sir Charles. "Tennyson's 'Doubt and Prayer' Sonnet." Victorian Poetry, 6 (1968), 1-3.

Robert Tofte

4087. Coogan, R. "Tofte's Translations from Petrarch." Notes and Queries, 223 (1978), 508.

4088. Kahrl, George Morrow. "Robert Tofte's Annotations in The Blazon of Iealousie." Harvard Studies and Notes in Philology and Literature, 18 (1935), 47-67.

The annotations were to Tofte's translation of Lettura di M. Benedetto Varchi, sopra un Sonetto della Gelosia di Mons. Dalla Casa, which he called The Blazon of Iealousie.

Frederick Goddard Tuckerman

4089. Benet, William Rose. "Round About Parnassus." Saturday Review of Literature, 7 (February 7, 1931), 584.

This review of Witter Bynner's edition of the sonnets gives praise to Tuckerman's poems and encourages perusal of them.

4090. Cady, Edwin H. "Frederick Goddard Tuckerman." Essays on American Literature In Honor of Jay B. Hubbell. Ed. Clarence Gohdes. Durham, N.C.: Duke University Press, 1967, pp. 141-51.

This essay is a discussion of Tuckerman's sonnet sequence first published in Poems (1860).

4091. Eaton, Walter Prichard. "A Forgotten American Poet." Forum, 41 (1909), 62-70. Revised and reprinted in Penguin Persons and Peppermints. Boston: W.A. Wilde, 1922, pp. 51-64.

Comments on several sonnets in Tuckerman's sonnet sequences.

4092. England, Eugene. "Tuckerman's Sonnet I: 10: The first Post-Symbolist Poem." Southern Review, 12 (1976), 323-47.

Includes a discussion of Hallam's and Tennyson's influence on Tuckerman.

4093. Golden, Samuel A. Frederick Goddard Tuckerman: An American Sonneteer. University of Maine Studies, 2nd Series, 66. Orono, Maine: University Press, 1952.

4094. Golden, Samuel A. "Frederick Goddard Tuckerman: A Neglected Poet." New England Quarterly, 29 (1956), 381-93.

Summary and revision of material found in Frederick Goddard Tuckerman: An American Sonneteer.

4095. Golden, Samuel A. Frederick Goddard Tuckerman. Twayne's United States Authors Series, 104. New York: Twayne, 1966.

This biography focuses on Tuckerman's sonnets, which, Golden writes, "form a personal journal of a poet who sought to bring into order a life assailed by doubt and grief on one hand and fortified by certitude of its worth on the other."

4096. Howe, Irving. "An American Poet." New York Review of Books, March 25, 1965, pp. 17-19.

This review of The Complete Poems of Frederick Goddard Tuckerman, ed. N. Scott Momaday, calls special attention to his sonnets, which Howe refers to as "distinguished."

4097. Marcus, Mordecai. "The Poetry of Frederick Goddard Tuckerman: A Reconsideration." Discourse, 5 (1961-62), 69-82.

Commenting on a number of sonnets and Tuckerman's ode, "The Cricket," Marcus expresses some bewilderment about Tuckerman's undeserved neglect.

4098. Morrison, Theodore. Review of The Sonnets of Frederick Goddard Tuckerman, ed. Witter Bynner. Bookman (New York), 73 (1931), 205-06.

4099. Tuckerman, Frederick Goddard. The Sonnets of Frederick Goddard Tuckerman. Ed. Witter Bynner. New York: Alfred A. Knopf, 1931.

Contains the first printing of all the sonnet sequences plus a prefatory essay.

4100. ______________. The Complete Poems of Frederick Goddard Tuckerman. Ed. N. Scott Momaday with a critical foreword by Yvor Winters. New York: Oxford University Press, 1965.

4101. Walton, Eda Lou. "A Neglected Poet." Nation, 133 (1931), 234-35.

This review of Bynner's edition of the Sonnets praises Tuckerman and reprints two of his sonnets.

4102. Winters, Yvor. "A Discovery." Hudson Review, 3 (1950), 453-58.

Although this essay is predominantly a review of an edition of The Cricket (an ode), Winters speaks briefly about some sonnets (pp. 454-55).

4103. "A Contemporary of Lowell and Whittier." New York Times Book Review, May 24, 1931, p. 13.

A review of Witter Bynner's edition of the sonnets.

Charles Tennyson Turner

4104. Colloms, Brenda. Victorian Country Parsons. Lincoln: University of Nebraska Press, 1977.

One of the subjects of the book is "The Rev. Charles Tennyson Turner Parson and Sonneteer 1808-1879" (pp. 152-65). Although basically biographical, the essay quotes liberally from Turner's sonnets.

4105. Ebbatson, J.R. "The Lonely Garden: The Sonnets of Charles Tennyson Turner." Victorian Poetry, 15 (1977), 307-19.

4106. Hewlett, Henry G. "English Sonneteers: Mr. Charles Turner." Contemporary Review, 22 (1873), 633-42.

A review article of three of Charles Tennyson Turner's sonnet collections.

4107. Turner, Charles Tennyson. A Hundred Sonnets. Ed. John Betjeman and Sir Charles Tennyson. London: Rupert Hart-Davis, 1960.

Along with this selection from his 342 sonnets is an introduction which touches on Charles Tennyson Turner's published work--four volumes of sonnets.

Jones Very

4108. Dennis, Carl. "Correspondence in Very's Nature Poetry." New England Quarterly, 43 (1970), 250-73.

Some of the sonnets discussed are "Man in Harmony with Nature," "The True Light," "The Canary Bird," "The Tree" (both poems of that title), "The Columbine," and "The Lost."

4109. Robinson, David. "Four Early Poems of Jones Very." Harvard Library Bulletin, 28 (1980), 146-51.

A sonnet ("The Portrait") is among the four unpublished poems by Very printed in this article.

4110. Winters, Yvor. "Jones Very: A New England Mystic." American Review, 7 (1936), 159-78.

Comments on a number of Very's sonnets.

4111. Winters, Yvor. "Jones Very and R.W. Emerson: Aspects of New England Mysticism." Maule's Curse: Seven Studies in the History of American Obscurantism. Norfolk, Conn.: New Directions, 1938, pp. 125-46.

The essay, which discusses a number of Very's sonnets, seeks to save the poet from what Winters believes to be undeserved neglect.

Thomas Wade

4112. Forman, H. Buxton. "Thomas Wade: The Poet and His Surroundings." Literary Anecdotes of the Nineteenth Century: Contributions Towards a Literary History of the Period. Ed. W. Robertson Nicoll and Thomas J. Wise. London: Hodder and Stoughton, 1895, pp. 43-67.

This essay, which speaks of Wade as a sonneteer, is followed by a "Sonnet: To Certain Critics" (p. 68) and "Fifty Sonnets" (pp. 69-120).

Thomas Warton

4113. Baxter, Ralph C. "A Sonnet Wrongly Ascribed to Thomas Warton, Jr." Ball State University Forum, 11,iv (1970), 51-53.

4114. Kaiser, Rudolf. "Vier Sonette (Thomas Warton: To the River Lodon--W.L. Bowles: To the River Itchin--S.T. Coleridge: To the River Otter--W. Wordsworth: To the River Duddon XXI.)." Neueren Sprachen (1963), 252-62.

Oscar Wilde

4115. Fong, Bobby. "Oscar Wilde: Five Fugitive Poems." English Literature in Transition, 1880-1920, 22, i (1979), 7-16.

Deals with Wilde's early work, including the sonnets "Lotus Land" and "The Theatre at Argos."

William Wordsworth

4116. [Arms, G.W.] "The World is Too Much With Us." Explicator, 1 (1942), Item 4.

4117. Averill, James H. Wordsworth and the Poetry of Human Suffering. Ithaca, N.Y.: Cornell University Press, 1980.

Contains a rather long discussion of Wordsworth's "Sonnet, on Seeing Miss Helen Maria Williams Weep at a Tale of Distress" (pp. 33-38).

4118. B., W. "Wordsworth and Keats." Notes and Queries, 9th series, 10 (1902), 284.

Notes a similarity between Wordsworth's sonnet "Upon the Sight of a Beautiful Picture by Sir G. H. Beaumont, Bart." and Keats's "Ode on a Grecian Urn."

4119. Bagchi, P. "A Note on Wordsworth's Sonnet, 'I Heard (Alas! 'Twas Only in A Dream)'." Notes and Queries, 218 (1973), 44.

4120. Bayne, Thomas. "Wordsworth's 'Sonnet Composed upon Westminster Bridge; Sept. 3, 1802'." Notes and Queries, 7th series, 11 (1891), 53.

The date for this poem is corrected to July 30, 1802.

4121. Beach, Joseph Warren. A Romantic View of Poetry. Minneapolis: University of Minnesota Press, 1944. Gloucester, Mass.: Peter Smith, 1963.

In his fourth of the six lectures in this book, Beach begins by explaining how the sonnet "Composed upon Westminster Bridge" is an expression of Wordsworth's most private feelings (pp. 64-71).

4122. Beatty, Arthur. William Wordsworth: His Doctrine and Art in Their Historical Relations. Madison: University of Wisconsin Press, 1922.

Discusses the river in The River Duddon (pp. 220-22) as a symbol of the harmonizing powers of human life.

4123. Bhattacharyya, Arunodoy. "English Sonnets on Liberty and Patriotism in the Romantic Age." Essays Presented to Principal Amiya Kumar Sen. Bulletin of the Department of English (University of Calcutta), 13, ii (1977-78), 1-12.

Discusses sonnets on themes of patriotism by Wordsworth, Shelley, Byron and Keats.

4124. Boas, F.S. Wordsworth's Patriotic Poems and Their Significance Today. English Association Pamphlet, 30. Oxford: Clarendon Press, 1914.

Discusses the way Wordsworth uses the sonnet on subjects of public affairs.

4125. Bromley, James. "The Story of a Sonnet." Athenaeum, May 17, 1890, p. 641.

On the background of Wordsworth's sonnet entitled "Filial Piety," subtitled "On the Wayside between Preston and Liverpool."

4126. Campbell, Oscar James. "Wordsworth's Conception of the Esthetic Experience." Wordsworth and Coleridge Studies in Honor of George McLean Harper. Ed. Earl Leslie Griggs. Princeton, N.J.: Princeton University Press, 1939, pp. 26-46.

In the last several pages of the essay Campbell discusses The River Duddon and The Ecclesiastical Sonnets as examples of Wordsworth's mature aesthetic experience.

4127. Coe, Charles Norton. "A Source for Wordsworth's Sonnet 'At Rome'." Notes and Queries, 193 (1948), 430-31.

4128. Coe, Charles Norton. "A Source for Wordsworth's Sonnet, 'The Black Stones of Iona'." Modern Language Notes, 66 (1951), 102.

4129. Cohen, B. Bernard. "Haydon, Hunt, and Scott and Six Sonnets (1816) by Wordsworth." Philological Quarterly, 29 (1950), 434-37.

4130. Davis, Charles G. "The Structure of Wordsworth's Sonnet 'Composed upon Westminster Bridge'." English, 19 (1970), 18-21.

4131. Eason, Douglas Otis. "Wordsworth's Early Sonnets: 1802-1807." Ph.D. Dissertation, Vanderbilt, 1975. DAI, 36 (1976), 4504A-05A.

4132. Edwards, Thomas R. Imagination and Power: A Study of Poetry on Public Themes. New York: Oxford University Press, 1971.

In his section on "Wordsworth: The Bard as Patriot" (pp. 168-79), Edwards discusses a number of sonnets that deal with current political and military affairs--"October, 1803" and "Anticipation, October, 1803" at greatest length.

4133. Ellis, Patrick. "Wordsworth's 'Ode: Intimations of Immortality' and the Italian Sonnet." CEA Critic, 34,iii (1972), 26-29.

Detects a sonnet rhyme scheme in the "Ode."

4134. Evans, B. Ifor. "Unacknowledged Sonnet by Wordsworth." TLS, March 12, 1938, p. 172.

Concerns the discovery of a manuscript copy of Wordsworth's translation of a sonnet for Duppa's Life and Works of Michel Angelo Buonarroti.

4135. Fink, Z.S. "Wordsworth and the English Republican Tradition." Journal of English and Germanic Philology, 47 (1948), 107-26.

Discusses several "patriotic and admonitory" sonnets--"Milton! thou shouldst be living at this hour," "Great men have been among us . . . ," and "On the Extinction of the Venetian Republic" (pp. 117-19).

4136. Ford, C.L. "Wordsworth and Keats." Notes and Queries, 9th Series, 10 (1902), 398.

Lines from Wordsworth's sonnet, "Upon the Sight of a Beautiful Picture by Sir G. H. Beaumont, Bart.," are a repetition of a thought from "Peele Castle in a Storm."
4118

4137. Fox, Arnold B., and Martin Kallich. "Wordsworth's Sentimental Naturalism: Theme and Image in 'The World Is Too Much With Us'." Wordsworth Circle, 8 (1977), 327-32.

4138. Fussell, Paul, Jr. "Some Observations on Wordsworth's 'A Poet!--He hath put his heart to school'." Philological Quarterly, 37 (1958), 454-64.

4139. Garrison, Joseph M., Jr. "Knowledge and Beauty in Wordsworth's 'Composed Upon Westminster Bridge'." Research Studies, 40 (1972), 46-47.

4140. Gerber, Richard. "William Wordsworth: Sonnet XXXVI of the Miscellaneous Sonnets: Composed upon Westminster Bridge, Part II, September 3, 1802." Die Englische Lyrik: Von der Renaissance bis zur Gegenwart. Ed. Karl Heinz Goller. Dusseldorf: August Bagel, 1968, vol. 1, pp. 381-86.

4141. Gierasch, Walter. "Wordsworth's 'London, 1802'." Explicator, 2 (1944), Item 42.

4142. Grant, A.J. "A Line in Wordsworth." TLS, September 16, 1939, p. 539; September 30, 1939, p. 563.

Speculates on the meaning of "vagrant reed" in River Duddon Sonnets, XXIV. See response by Nowell Smith.
4179

4143. Groom, Bernard. The Unity of Wordsworth's Poetry. London: Macmillan; New York: St. Martin's, 1966.

Chapter 12 deals with "Three Series of Sonnets."

4144. Hall, B.G. "Wordsworth Emendations." TLS, May 21, 1931, p. 408.

Suggests that Wordsworth himself may have made an emendation in a line of the "Westminster Bridge" sonnet.

4145. Hartung, Charles V. "Wordsworth on Westminster Bridge: Paradox or Harmony?" College English, 13 (1952), 201-03.

Takes issue with a reading given by Cleanth Brooks in The Well Wrought Urn (pp. 5-7).

4146. Harvey, G.M. "The Design of Wordsworth's Sonnets." ARIEL, 6, iii (1975), 78-90.

The article covers "Composed upon Westminster Bridge," "I watch and long have watched with calm regret," and "The world is too much with us."

4147. Hayden, Donald E. After Conflict, Quiet: A Study of Wordsworth's Poetry in Relation to His Life and Letters. New York: Exposition Press, 1951.

Discusses theological implications in The River Duddon and Ecclesiastical Sonnets (pp. 169-72).

4148. Hill, Alan G. "On the Date and Significance of Wordsworth's Sonnet 'On the Extinction of the Venetian Republic'." Review of English Studies, 30 (1979), 441-45.

4149. Holland, Patrick. "The Two Contrasts of Wordsworth's 'Westminster Bridge' Sonnet." Wordsworth Circle, 8 (1977), 32-34.

4150. Hunt, Bishop C., Jr. "Wordsworth, Haydon, and the 'Wellington' Sonnet." Princeton University Library Chronicle, 36 (1975), 111-32.

"On a Portrait of the Duke of Wellington."

4151. Hutchinson, Thomas. "On the Structure of the Sonnets of Wordsworth." Transactions of the Wordsworth Society, No. 2 [1880-86], pp. 27-31.

Although his model was Milton, Wordsworth often varied rhyme schemes. In this study Hutchinson discusses the sonnets by class: itinerary, ecclesiastical, Duddon, political, etc.

4152. Hymes, Dell H. "Phonological Aspects of Style: Some English Sonnets." Style in Language. Ed. Thomas A. Sebeok. Cambridge: Technology Press of Massachusetts Institute of Technology; New York and London: John Wiley and Sons, 1960, pp. 109-31.

An analysis of sonnets, ten by Wordsworth and ten by Keats.

4153. Johnson, Lee M. Wordsworth and the Sonnet. Anglistica, 19. Copenhagen: Rosenkilde and Bagger, 1973.

This monograph examines each of Wordsworth's major sonnet groups-- Miscellaneous, River Duddon, Ecclesiastical.

4154. Johnson, Lee Milford. "Wordsworth and the Sonnet." Ph.D. Dissertation, Princeton, 1970. DAI, 31 (1971), 4167A.

4155. Kelley, Theresa M. "Proteus, Nature, and Romantic Mythography." Wordsworth Circle, 11 (1980), 78-79.

Comments on the relationship between Proteus and Triton in "The world is too much with us."

4156. Ketterer, David. "'Glimpses' in Wordsworth's 'The World is Too Much With Us'." Wordsworth Circle, 10 (1979), 122-23.

4157. Kroeber, Karl. "A New Reading of 'The World Is Too Much With Us'." Studies in Romanticism, 2 (1963), 183-88.

4158. La Borsiere, C.R. "Wordsworth's 'Go back to antique ages, if thine eyes', and "Paradise Lost," XII, 23-47." Notes and Queries, 220 (1975), 63.

The sonnet seems to follow Milton's account of the beginnings of future political dissension.

4159. Leavis, F.R. "Imagery and Movement: Notes in the Analysis of Poetry." Scrutiny, 13 (1945), 119-34.

Leavis uses several sonnets by Wordsworth to illustrate his thesis: "It is a beauteous evening, calm and free," "Surprised by joy--impatient as the Wind, and "Composed upon Westminster Bridge" (pp. 125-30).

4160. Mabbott, T.O. "A Sonnet by Wordsworth. Notes and Queries, 173 (1937), 455.

Reprints and discusses a sonnet purportedly by Wordsworth addressed to a picture by Luca Giordano.

4161. McNulty, John Bard. "Milton's Influence on Wordsworth's Early Sonnets." PMLA, 62 (1947), 745-51.

4162. McReynolds, Ronald Weldon. "A Handbook to Wordsworth's Sonnets." Ph.D. Dissertation, Texas, 1959. DA, 20 (1960), 2784.

4163. Molesworth, Charles. "Wordsworth's 'Westminster Bridge' Sonnet: The Republican Structure of Time and Perception." Clio, 6 (1977), 261-73.

4164. Perrin, Marius. "Avatar ou Etapes? La Religion de William Wordsworth d'apres les Ecclesiastical Sonnets." Mosaic, 12, ii (1979), 131-45.

4165. Poggemiller, Helmuth Carl. "Wordsworth's Concept of the Imagination in the Ecclesiastical Sonnets." Ph.D. Dissertation, Toledo, 1980. DAI, 41 (1980), 2618A.

4166. Pollin, Burton R. "Wordsworth's 'Misserrimus' Sonnet: Several Errors Corrected." Wordsworth Circle, 1 (1970), 22-24.

4167. Pollin, Burton R. "The World Is Too Much with Us": Two more Sources--Dryden and Godwin." Wordsworth Circle, 1 (1970), 50-52.

4168. Potts, Abbie Findlay. "Wordsworth's 'Ecclesiastical Sonnets': Date of Composition (Pt. iii, Nos. 16, 26, 27, 28, 29, 30 and 31.)" Notes and Queries, 12th series, 6 (1920), 81-83.

4169. Potts, Abbie Findlay. "The Ecclesiastical Sonnets of William Wordsworth: A Critical Edition." Ph.D. Dissertation, Cornell, 1922.

4170. Proffitt, Edward. "'This Pleasant Lea': Waning Vision in 'The World is Too Much with Us'." Wordsworth Circle, 11 (1980), 75-77.

4171. Rapin, Rene, and Lewis B. Horne. "Wordsworth's 'October, 1803'." Explicator, 24 (1965), Item 10.

Rapin writes on the bipartite structure of "When, looking on the present face of things," and Horne focuses on the last 4 lines.

4172. Rix, Herbert. "Notes on the Localities of the Duddon Sonnets." Transactions of the Wordsworth Society, No. 5 [1880-86], pp. 61-78.

In this walking tour of Wordsworth's River Duddon, Rix notes the scenic references in each of the sonnets.

4173. Robertson, Stuart. "Chaucer and Wordsworth." Modern Language Notes, 43 (1928), 104-05.

Explains a puzzling reference to Chaucer's Prioress's Tale that occurs in Wordsworth's sonnet "Edward VI" (Ecclesiastical Sonnets, Part II, No. 31).

4174. *Ryan, Frank L. "A Wordsworth Sonnet: One Phase of a Structural Linguistic Analysis." Studies in English Literature (Tokyo), 42 (1965), 65-69.

4175. Schluter, Kurt. "Wieder einmal 'Upon Westminster Bridge'." Literatur in Wissenschaft und Unterricht, 12 (1979), 202-05.

4176. Seronsy, Cecil C. "Daniel and Wordsworth." Studies in Philology, 56 (1959), 187-213.

Discusses Samuel Daniel's influence, mentioning some of Wordsworth's sonnets (particularly The River Duddon Sonnets) that owe something to Daniel's work.

4177. Sheats, Paul D. Review of Lee M. Johnson, Wordsworth and the Sonnet. Wordsworth Circle, 5 (1974), 145-48.

4178. Smith, G.C. Moore. "Wordsworth and George Herbert." Notes and Queries, 12th Series, 12 (1923), 30.

George Herbert is referred to in Wordsworth's sonnet "Seathwaite Chapel."

4179. Smith, Nowell. "A Line in Wordsworth." TLS, September 23, 1939, p. 551.

A response to Grant on River Duddon Sonnets, XXIV.
4142

4180. Steiner, Dorothea. The Essential Voice in the Later Wordsworth. Salzburg Studies in English Literature, Romantic Reassessment, 44. Salzburg: Institut fur Englische Sprache und Literatur, Universitat Salzburg, 1974, pp. 78-113.

Comments on River Duddon Sonnets.

4181. Sucksmith, Harvey Peter. "Ultimate Affirmation: A Critical Analysis of Wordsworth's Sonnet, 'Composed upon Westminster Bridge', and the Image of the City in The Prelude." Yearbook of English Studies, 6 (1976), 113-19.

4182. Swanson, Donald R. "Wordsworth's Sonnets." CEA Critic, 30, v (1968), 12-13.

Comments on the Miltonic influences in Wordsworth's sonnets and on the latter's broad use of the form.

4183. Taylor, Sir Henry. "Essay on Mr. Wordsworth's Sonnets." The Works of Sir Henry Taylor. London: C. Kegan Paul, 1878, vol. 5, pp. 53-122. First published in the Quarterly Review, 69 (1841), 1-51.

4184. Vann, W.H. "Two Borrowings of Wordsworth." Modern Language Notes, 32 (1917), 314-15.

One of the borrowings, the two opening lines of Wordsworth's sonnet "With how sad steps, O moon," is from Sidney's Astrophel and Stella, 21.

4185. Wain, John. "The Liberation of Wordsworth." Twentieth Century, 157 (1955), 66-78.

In the context of his discussion of F.W. Bateson's book, Wordsworth: A Re-Interpretation, Wain gives high praise to the sonnet "Mutability" (pp. 72-73).

4186. *Wicker, C.V. "On Wordsworth's Westminster Bridge Sonnet." Rocky Mountain Modern Language Association Bulletin, 9 (1955), 4.

4187. Wilcox, Stewart C. "The Sources of Wordsworth's 'After-Thought' Sonnet." Philological Quarterly, 32 (1953), 210-12.

On the mainly classical sources of the concluding sonnet of The River Duddon series.

4188. Wilcox, Stewart C. "Wordsworth's River Duddon Sonnets." PMLA, 69 (1954), 131-41.

4189. Wordsworth, William. Ecclesiastical Sonnets. Ed. Abbie F. Potts. New Haven, Conn.: Yale University Press, 1922.

4190. ____________. The Poetical Works of William Wordsworth. Miscellaneous Sonnets, Memorials of Various Tours, Poems Dedicated to National Independence and Liberty, The Egyptian Maid, The River Duddon Series, The White Doe and Other Narrative Poems, Ecclesiastical Sonnets. Ed. Ernest de Selincourt and Helen Darbishire. Oxford: Clarendon Press, 1946.

4191. Worth, George J. "A Troublesome Wordsworth Sonnet." Notes and Queries, 203 (1958), 466-68.

"On a Portrait of the Duke of Wellington upon the Field of Waterloo, by Haydon."

Contributor Index